ZAGAT®

Miami/So. Florida Restaurants
2012

LOCAL EDITOR
Bill Citara, Rochelle Koff, Jan Norris and Laura Reiley
STAFF EDITOR
Josh Rogers

Published and distributed by
Zagat Survey, LLC
4 Columbus Circle
New York, NY 10019
T: 212.977.6000
E: miami@zagat.com
www.zagat.com

ACKNOWLEDGMENTS

We thank contributing editor Victoria Pesce Elliott, Jimmy Barron, Sharon Kenny, Taylor Morgan, Steven Shukow and Scott Simmons, as well as the following members of our staff: Danielle Borovoy (assistant editor), Brian Albert, Sean Beachell, Maryanne Bertollo, Reni Chin, Larry Cohn, Bill Corsello, Nicole Diaz, Kelly Dobkin, Alison Flick, Jeff Freier, Curt Gathje, Michelle Golden, Matthew Hamm, Justin Hartung, Marc Henson, Anna Hyclak, Aynsley Karps, Rus Kehoe, Cynthia Kilian, Natalie Lebert, Mike Liao, Vivian Ma, Caitlin Miehl, James Mulcahy, Polina Paley, Amanda Spurlock, Chris Walsh, Jacqueline Wasilczyk, Yoji Yamaguchi, Sharon Yates, Anna Zappia and Kyle Zolner.

The reviews in this guide are based on public opinion surveys. The ratings reflect the average scores given by the survey participants who voted on each establishment. The text is based on quotes from, or paraphrasings of, the surveyors' comments. Phone numbers, addresses and other factual data were correct to the best of our knowledge when published in this guide.

Our guides are printed using environmentally preferable inks containing 20%, by weight, renewable resources on papers sourced from well-managed forests. Deluxe editions are covered with Skivertex Recover® Double containing a minimum of 30% post-consumer waste fiber.

SUSTAINABLE FORESTRY INITIATIVE | Certified Sourcing
www.sfiprogram.org
SFI-00993

ENVIROINK™

The inks used to print the body of this publication contain a minimum of 20%, by weight, renewable resources.

Contents

Ratings & Symbols

Zagat Top Spot	Name	Symbols	Cuisine	Zagat Ratings			
				FOOD	DECOR	SERVICE	COST

Area, Address & Contact

Ζ Tim & Nina's ● *Seafood*   ∇ 23 | 9 | 13 | $15

Miami Beach | 21120 Collins Ave. (10th St.) | 305-555-4550 | www.zagat.com

Review, surveyor comments in quotes

Reeling in fish fiends with its "all-around originality", this low-budget Miami Beach–front seafooder in a "wacky setting" (sand on the floor and a "talking stuffed marlin" by the door) features "fabulous" fare like conch-and-crab bruschetta; you may need to "shout your order" above the bar's roar, but the "cheerful mates" will likely be "too busy" to do much about it anyway.

Ratings   **Food, Decor** & **Service** are rated on a 30-point scale.

0 – 9   poor to fair

10 – 15   fair to good

16 – 19   good to very good

20 – 25   very good to excellent

26 – 30   extraordinary to perfection

∇   low response | less reliable

Cost   The price of dinner with a drink and tip; lunch is usually 25% to 30% less. For unrated **newcomers** or **write-ins,** the price range is as follows:

I $25 and below   E $41 to $65

M $26 to $40   VE $66 or above

Symbols   Ζ   highest ratings, popularity and importance

●   serves after 11 PM

Ƶ Ḿ   closed on Sunday or Monday

⊘   no credit cards accepted

About This Survey

Here are the results of our **2012 Miami/So. Florida Restaurants Survey,** covering 1,352 eateries in South Florida. Like all our guides, this one is based on input from avid local consumers – 6,671 all told. Our editors have synopsized this feedback, highlighting representative comments (in quotation marks within each review). To read full surveyor comments – and share your own opinions – visit **ZAGAT.com,** where you will also find the latest restaurant news, special events, deals, reservations, menus, photos and lots more, **all for free.**

ABOUT ZAGAT: In 1979, we started asking friends to rate and review restaurants purely for fun. The term "user-generated content" had yet to be coined. That hobby grew into Zagat Survey; 33 years later, we have over 375,000 surveyors and cover airlines, bars, dining, fast food, entertaining, golf, hotels, movies, music, resorts, shopping, spas, theater and tourist attractions in over 100 countries. Along the way, we evolved from being a print publisher to a digital content provider, e.g. **ZAGAT.com** and **Zagat To Go** mobile apps (for iPad, iPhone, Android, BlackBerry, Windows Phone 7 and Palm webOS). We also produce marketing tools for a wide range of blue-chip corporate clients. And you can find us on Twitter (twitter.com/zagat), Facebook, Foursquare and just about any other social media network.

UNDERLYING PREMISES: Three simple ideas underlie our ratings and reviews. First, we believe that the collective opinions of large numbers of consumers are more accurate than those of any single person. (Consider that our surveyors bring some 1.2 million annual meals' worth of experience to this survey, visiting restaurants regularly year-round, anonymously – and on their own dime.) Second, food quality is only part of the equation when choosing a restaurant, thus we ask our surveyors to rate food, decor and service separately and then report on cost. Third, since people need reliable information in an easy-to-digest, curated format, we strive to be concise and we offer our content on every platform – print, online and mobile.

THANKS: We're grateful to our local editors: Bill Citara, a food and wine writer; Rochelle Koff, a restaurant critic and editor at *The Miami Herald*; Jan Norris, publisher of the Florida food website jannorris.com; and Laura Reiley, the food critic at the *St. Petersburg Times.* Thank you, guys. We also sincerely thank the thousands of people who participated in this survey – this guide is really "theirs."

JOIN IN: To improve our guides, we solicit your comments – positive or negative; it's vital that we hear your opinions. Just contact us at **nina-tim@zagat.com.** We also invite you to join our surveys at **ZAGAT.com.** Do so and you'll receive a choice of rewards in exchange.

New York, NY
November 16, 2011

Nina and Tim Zagat

What's New

Are South Florida diners experiencing recession fatigue, or do sun and sand banish gloomy outlooks? Either way, surveyors report dining out more often this year: 3.4 meals per week vs. 3.2 in 2009, which is above the national average. And the area's average meal cost, $40.70, comes in behind only NYC ($43.36) and Vegas ($47.53). Moreover, 38% feel the dining scene improved in the past year.

MIAMI: Though surveyors split on celebrity chefs – 41% are more likely to dine at a restaurant associated with one, while 56% say there's no effect – big names figured in several Miami-area debuts. The Design District welcomed Michael Schwartz's **Harry's Pizzeria** and Michelle Bernstein's bakery/cafe **Crumb on Parchment.** NYC's Daniel Boulud checked in with **DB Bistro Moderne** Downtown, while Geoffrey Zakarian unveiled **Tudor House** in SoBe. Former *Top Chef* contestant Micah Edelstein is behind Downtown's **Nemesis.** Still, despite famous names, Norman Van Aken's **Norman's 180** shuttered and Allen Susser's **Chef Allen's** closed after 25 years. One vet holding steady: **Joe's Stone Crab,** again voted Miami's Most Popular. Top Food and Service honors went to Kevin Cory's 17-seat Japanese omakase **Naoe.**

BROWARD: In step with the 60% of surveyors who feel it's important that the food they eat be "green," arrivals such as **Market 17** and **Slow Food Truck** are emphasizing local, farm-fresh ingredients. The area also jumped on the small-plates bandwagon, with additions like **Dapur, M Bar** and **PL8 Kitchen.** Look out for changes at **Trina,** which plans to turn French as **East End Brasserie.**

PALM BEACH: As in Miami, Palm Beach saw an influx of big names. In Delray, Dennis Max surfaced with **Max's Harvest,** while Burt Rapoport launched **Deck 84.** NYC's **Philippe Chow** hit Boca, and Ft. Lauderdale's Dean Max colonized Singer Island with **3800 Ocean.** Other arrivals included Clay Conley's Eclectic hot spot **Buccan** (PB), the affordable **Blind Monk Wine Bar** (West Palm) and the green-leaning **DIG** (Delray).

NAPLES: Naples (new to our guide) had a low-key year, with entries such as **Agave,** a casual Southwestern grill. Looking ahead, the scene heats up: at press time, North Naples was about to welcome **L'Étoile,** a fine-dining French entry, and Fabrizio Aielli (**Sea Salt**) was readying the Italian **Barbatella** for a late 2011 debut.

MORE SURVEY STATS: Service is again the top dining-out complaint, cited by 74%, but that's down from 83% in 2007 . . . Food trucks are on a roll (e.g. **Dim Ssäm à Gogo, GastroPod, Latin Burger**), with 23% patronizing them at least occasionally . . . 69% will wait no more than 30 minutes at no-reserving places (15% simply avoid them).

Miami, FL   Bill Citara
Ft. Lauderdale, FL   Rochelle Koff
Palm Beach, FL   Jan Norris
Naples, FL   Laura Reiley
November 16, 2011

Key Newcomers

Our editors' picks among this year's arrivals. See full list at p. 296.

MIAMI/DADE COUNTY

Cecconi's | *Italian* | Miami Beach gets an elegant London import

City Hall | *Amer.* | Steven Haas' contempo comfort in Wynwood

DB Bistro Moderne | *French* | Daniel Boulud in Downtown Miami

1500 Degrees | *Amer./Steak* | Paula DaSilva at the Eden Roc

Harry's | *Pizza* | Michael Schwartz's gourmet pies in the Design District

Haven | *Eclectic* | Ultramodern lounge and small plates on Lincoln

Makoto | *Japanese* | Slick sushi at Bal Harbour via ex-Morimoto chef

Pubbelly | *Asian* | Pork-centric Miami Beach gastropub

2B Asian | *Asian* | SoBe style and Thai food on Calle Ocho

Yardbird | *Southern* | SoBe goes south for fried chicken 'n' bourbon

FT. LAUDERDALE/BROWARD COUNTY

Dapur | *Asian* | Hip Pan-Asian bistro on Federal Highway/U.S. 1

Market 17 | *Amer./Eclectic* | Ft. Lauderdale harvests local fare

Michele's | *Eclectic* | Classy supper club in Lauderdale

Saia | *SE Asian* | Upscale oceanfront dining at B Ocean Hotel

Sea | *Seafood* | Anthony Sindaco returns, in Lauderdale-by-the-Sea

PALM BEACH COUNTY

Buccan | *Eclectic* | Clay Conley magnetizes hip, young PB scenesters

Max's Harvest | *Amer.* | Dennis Max is back, with Delray farm-to-fork

Pangea | *Asian* | Asian fusion in Wellington from husband-wife team

Philippe Chow | *Chinese* | Boca's big-city Chinese by way of NYC

3800 Ocean | *Amer.* | Fancy fish and ocean views on Riviera Beach

BIG-NAME PROJECTS ON TAP:

Barceloneta | Catalan cuisine in Miami Beach by the Pubbelly partners

The Bazaar | Nuevo Spanish from José Andrés at SoBe's SLS Hotel

Dutch | Mod American from NY's Andrew Carmellini at W Hotel SoBe

Frank & Dino's | Deerfield Beach gets Dennis Max's Rat Packy Italian

J&G Grill | Jean-Georges Vongerichten colonizes St. Regis Bal Harbour

Kapow Noodle Bar | Upscale Boca noodle bar from the Dada team

Serendipity 3 | NY eatery cools SoBe with 'Frrrozen Hot Chocolate'

Spoonfed | Delray Beach comfort-fooder for locavores

S3 | YOLO crew adds steak, seafood, sushi to Hilton Ft. Lauderdale Beach

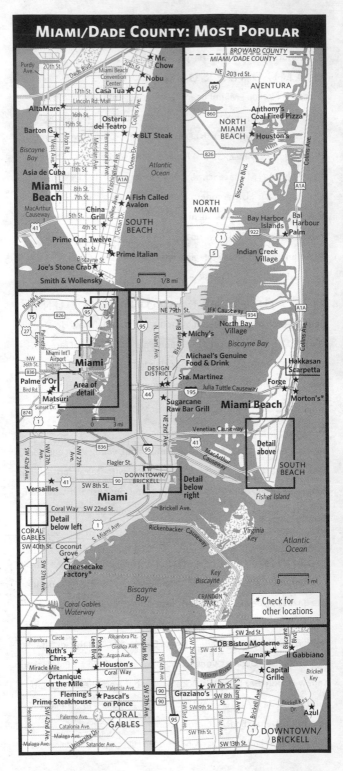

MIAMI/DADE COUNTY: MOST POPULAR

Miami Beach

- Mr. Chow
- Nobu
- Casa Tua
- OLA
- AltaMare
- Osteria del Teatro
- Barton G.
- BLT Steak
- Asia de Cuba
- A Fish Called Avalon
- China Grill
- Prime One Twelve
- Prime Italian
- Joe's Stone Crab
- Smith & Wollensky

Purdy Ave., 20th St., Dade Blvd., Miami Beach Convention Center, 17th St., Lincoln Rd. Mall, 16th St., 15th St., Collins Ave., Ocean Dr., 11th St., Meridian Ave., Pennsylvania Ave., Washington Ave., Alton Rd., West Ave., Biscayne Bay, Atlantic Ocean, A1A, 8th St., 7th St., 5th St., 4th St., Ocean Dr., SOUTH BEACH, MacArthur Causeway, 41, 1st St., Biscayne St.

0   1/8 mi

BROWCOUNTY MIAMI/DADE COUNTY
NE 203 rd St.
AVENTURA
95
860
NORTH MIAMI BEACH
- Anthony's Coal Fired Pizza*
- Houston's
826
NORTH MIAMI
Biscayne Blvd.
Collins Ave.
A1A
1
922
Indian Creek Village
5
Bay Harbor Islands
Bal Harbour
- Palm

Miami

- Palme d'Or
- Matsuri

Florida's Tpke., 826, 75, 95, 27, Palmetto Expwy., NW 36th St., Miami Int'l Airport, 836, Bird Rd., Sunset Dr., 874, 1, Area of detail

0   3 mi

NE 79th St.   JFK Causeway   934   A1A
North Bay Village
Biscayne Bay
- Michy's
N. Miami Ave.
95
N. Miami Ave.
Bisc. Blvd.
- Michael's Genuine Food & Drink
DESIGN DISTRICT
- Sra. Martinez
44   195   Julia Tuttle Causeway
- Hakkasan
- Scarpetta
- Forge
Miami Beach
- Morton's*
- Sugarcane Raw Bar Grill
NE 2nd Ave.
Venetian Causeway
41   MacArthur Causeway
Detail above
SOUTH BEACH

Miami

- Versailles
836   95   Flagler St.
NW 42nd Ave., NW 37th Ave., NW 27th Ave.
41   SW 8th St.
90   DOWNTOWN/ BRICKELL
Detail below right
Coral Way   SW 22nd St.
Brickell Ave.
CORAL GABLES
Detail below left
SW 40th St.   Coconut Grove
1   S. Miami Ave.
Rickenbacker Causeway
Virginia Key
- Cheesecake Factory*
SW 37th Ave.
Biscayne Bay
Key Biscayne
Atlantic Ocean
Coral Gables Waterway
CRANDON PARK
1 mi

*Check for other locations

CORAL GABLES

- Ruth's Chris
- Houston's
- Ortanique on the Mile
- Fleming's Prime Steakhouse
- Pascal's on Ponce

Alhambra Circle, Alhambra, Salzedo St., Ponce de Leon Blvd., Alhambra Plz., Giralda Ave., Aragon Ave., Douglas Rd., Miracle Mile, Coral Way, Valencia Ave., Hernando St., SW 42nd Ave., Palermo Ave., Catalonia Ave., Malaga Ave., Malaga Ave., University Dr., Satander Ave., SW 37th Ave.

DOWNTOWN/ BRICKELL

- DB Bistro Moderne
- Zuma
- Il Gabbiano
- Capital Grille
- Graziano's
- Azul
SW 2nd St., SW 3rd St., SW 4th St., Biscayne Blvd., Miami River, SW 7th St., SW 8th St., SW 9th St., 90, 95, SW 11th St., SW 13th St., Brickell Ave., Brickell Key Dr., Brickell Key, 1

Vote at ZAGAT.com

Miami/Dade County: Most Popular

1. Joe's Stone Crab | *Seafood*
2. Michael's Genuine | *American*
3. Prime One Twelve | *Sea./Steak*
4. Michy's | *American/French*
5. Il Gabbiano | *Italian*
6. Nobu Miami Beach | *Japanese*
7. Azul | *European*
8. Casa Tua | *Italian*
9. Barton G. | *American*
10. Sra. Martinez | *Spanish*
11. Hakkasan | *Chinese*
12. Houston's | *American*
13. BLT Steak | *Steak*
14. Ortanique | *Carib./New World*
15. Capital Grille | *Steak*
16. Palme d'Or | *French*
17. Zuma | *Japanese*
18. Palm | *Steak*
19. Versailles* | *Cuban*
20. Anthony's Coal Fired | *Pizza*
21. Morton's* | *Steak*
22. Scarpetta | *Italian*
23. Forge | *American*
24. DB Bistro Moderne | *French*
25. OLA | *Pan-Latin*
26. Smith & Wollensky* | *Steak*
27. Osteria del Teatro | *Italian*
28. Sugarcane | *Eclectic*
29. Pascal's on Ponce | *French*
30. Mr. Chow | *Chinese*
31. Cheesecake Factory | *American*
32. China Grill | *Asian*
33. A Fish Called Avalon | *Seafood*
34. AltaMare | *Med./Seafood*
35. Matsuri | *Japanese*
36. Ruth's Chris | *Steak*
37. Fleming's Prime Steak | *Steak*
38. Asia de Cuba | *Asian/Cuban*
39. Graziano's* | *Argent./Steak*
40. Prime Italian* | *Italian/Steak*

Many of the above restaurants are among the Miami/Dade area's most expensive, but if popularity were calibrated to price, a number of other restaurants would surely join their ranks. To illustrate this, we have added two pages of Best Buys starting on page 16.

Top Food

29 Naoe | *Japanese*

28 Palme d'Or | *French*
Zuma | *Japanese*
Palm | *Steak*

27 Il Gabbiano | *Italian*
OLA | *Pan-Latin*
Pascal's on Ponce | *French*
Michy's | *American/French*
Prime One Twelve | *Sea./Steak*
Nobu Miami Beach | *Japanese*
Azul | *European*
Matsuri | *Japanese*
Michael's Genuine | *American*
Hiro's Yakko-San | *Japanese*
Joe's Stone Crab | *Seafood*
Red Steak | *Steak*

26 Oishi Thai | *Japanese/Thai*
Frankie's Pizza | *Pizza*
La Dorada* | *Seafood/Spanish*
Francesco | *Peruvian*

DB Bistro Moderne | *French*
Osteria del Teatro | *Italian*
Tropical Chinese | *Chinese*
Romeo's Cafe | *Italian*
Capital Grille | *Steak*
Basilico | *Italian*
Yuga | *Asian*
Ortanique | *Carib./New World*
Sardinia | *Italian*
Hy-Vong | *Vietnamese*
Hakkasan | *Chinese*

25 Quinn's | *Seafood*
Chéen Huaye | *Mexican*
Timo | *Italian/Mediterranean*
Wish* | *American*
Ceviche 105 | *Peruvian*
Grimpa Steak | *Brazil./Steak*
Sra. Martinez | *Spanish*
Morton's | *Steak*
Asia Bay | *Japanese/Thai*

BY CUISINE

AMERICAN (NEW)
27 Michy's
Michael's Genuine
25 Wish
Meat Market
Whisk Gourmet

AMERICAN (TRAD.)
23 Burger & Beer Joint
Houston's
22 Grill on the Alley
21 Front Porch Cafe
Pelican RestCafé

ASIAN
26 Oishi (Thai)
Yuga (Pan-Asian)
Hy-Vong (Vietnamese)
25 Asia Bay (Japanese/Thai)
Red Koi (Thai)

CARIBBEAN/CUBAN
26 Ortanique
24 Enriqueta's Sandwich Shop
23 Puerto Sagua
La Casita
22 Asia de Cuba

CHINESE
26 Tropical Chinese
Hakkasan
24 Kon Chau
23 Tony Chan's Water Club
22 Mr. Chow

DELIS/SANDWICHES
25 Jimmy'z Kitchen
La Sandwicherie
Cheese Course
24 Enriqueta's Sandwich Shop
22 Perricone's

ECLECTIC
25 Jimmy'z Kitchen
Adriana
Sugarcane
24 Buena Vista Bistro
22 Icebox Café

FRENCH
28 Palme d'Or
27 Pascal's on Ponce
26 DB Bistro Moderne
23 Café Pastis
20 Paul Bakery

Excludes places with low votes, unless otherwise indicated

Vote at ZAGAT.com

FRENCH (BISTRO)

24 Le Bouchon du Grove
22 Le Provençal
21 La Goulue
   A la Folle Café
   George's/Grove

ITALIAN

27 Il Gabbiano
26 Osteria del Teatro
   Romeo's Cafe
   Basilico
   Sardinia

JAPANESE

29 Naoe
28 Zuma
27 Nobu Miami Beach
   Matsuri
   Hiro's Yakko-San

LATIN AMERICAN

27 OLA
26 Francesco
25 Ceviche 105
   Grimpa Steak
   Graziano's

MEDITERRANEAN

25 Timo
   Maroosh

PIZZA

26 Frankie's Pizza
25 Andiamo! Pizza
23 Bugatti Pasta
22 Anthony's Coal Fired
   Fratelli La Bufala

SEAFOOD

27 Joe's Stone Crab
25 Quinn's
   River Oyster Bar
24 Oceanaire
   AltaMare

SPANISH

26 La Dorada
25 Sra. Martinez
24 Casa Juancho
23 Por Fin
   Xixón Cafe

STEAKHOUSES

28 Palm
27 Prime One Twelve
   Red Steak
26 Capital Grille
25 Morton's

24 AltaMare
23 Por Fin
   660 @ The Angler's

BY SPECIAL FEATURE

BREAKFAST

23 Puerto Sagua
22 Islas Canarias
21 Versailles
   Front Porch Cafe
   A la Folie Café

BRUNCH

22 Icebox Café
   Perricone's
21 La Palma Ristorante
20 11th St. Diner
   Sergio's*

BUSINESS DINING

28 Palme d'Or
   Palm
27 Il Gabbiano
   Pascal's on Ponce
   Prime One Twelve

CHILD-FRIENDLY

23 Garcia's
   Carpaccio
21 Archie's Pizza
20 Dogma
19 CG Burgers

DOCK & DINE

28 Zuma
23 Garcia's
   Tony Chan's Water Club
22 Red Fish Grill
   Lido at The Standard

EXPENSE ACCOUNT

28 Palme d'Or
   Zuma
   Palm
27 Il Gabbiano
   Pascal's on Ponce

HOTEL DINING

- 28 Palme d'Or (Biltmore)
-    Zuma (Epic)
- 27 OLA (Sanctuary)
-    Nobu (Shore Club)
-    Azul (Mandarin Oriental)

LATE DINING

- 28 Zuma
- 27 Il Gabbiano
-    Prime One Twelve
-    Hiro's Yakko-San
- 26 La Dorada

MEET FOR A DRINK

- 28 Palme d'Or
- 27 Il Gabbiano
-    Michael's Genuine
- 25 Sra. Martinez
-    Bourbon Steak

NEWCOMERS (RATED)

- 26 DB Bistro Moderne
- 25 2B Asian Bistro
- 24 Gigi
-    1500 Degrees
-    Pubbelly

PEOPLE-WATCHING

- 28 Palme d'Or
-    Zuma
-    Palm
- 27 Prime One Twelve
-    Nobu Miami Beach

PRIVATE ROOMS

- 28 Palme d'Or
- 27 Prime One Twelve
- 26 La Dorada
-    Capital Grille
-    Ortanique

QUICK BITES

- 27 Michael's Genuine
- 25 La Sandwicherie
-    Cheese Course
- 24 Daily Bread Pinecrest
-    Joey's Italian Café

QUIET CONVERSATION

- 28 Palme d'Or
- 27 Pascal's on Ponce
- 26 Oishi Thai
-    La Dorada
-    Francesco

SINGLES SCENES

- 27 Prime One Twelve
- 25 Meat Market
-    Sugarcane
-    Fleming's Prime Steak
- 24 Gigi

TRENDY

- 28 Zuma
- 26 Ortanique
-    Sardinia
- 25 Ceviche 105
-    Sra. Martinez

WATERSIDE DINING

- 25 Morton's
- 24 Il Mulino New York
- 23 Red Light
- 22 Café Sambal
-    Area 31

WINNING WINE LISTS

- 28 Palme d'Or
-    Palm
- 27 Pascal's on Ponce
-    Michy's
-    Prime One Twelve

BY LOCATION

BAL/BAY HARBORS/ SUNNY ISLES/SURFSIDE

- 29 Naoe
- 28 Palm
- 25 Timo
-    Asia Bay
-    Adriana

BRICKELL AREA/ DOWNTOWN

- 28 Zuma
- 27 Il Gabbiano
-    Azul

- 26 DB Bistro Moderne
-    Capital Grille

COCONUT GROVE

- 24 Le Bouchon du Grove
- 22 Jaguar
- 21 George's
-    Las Culebrinas
- 20 Chart House

CORAL GABLES

- 28 Palme d'Or
- 27 Pascal's on Ponce

26 La Dorada
Francesco
Yuga

CORAL WAY

26 Romeo's Cafe
23 Xixón Cafe
22 El Carajo
20 Sergio's
Mykonos

DESIGN DISTRICT/ UPPER EAST SIDE

27 Michy's
Michael's Genuine
25 Sra. Martinez
Andiamo! Pizza
Mandolin

KENDALL

24 Shibui
23 Moon Thai
Bangkok/Kendall
22 Fuji Hana

KEY BISCAYNE

23 Cioppino
22 Sushi Siam
21 El Gran Inka
Archie's Pizza
Origin Asian Bistro

LITTLE HAVANA

26 Hy-Vong
25 2B Asian Bistro
24 Casa Juancho
22 Islas Canarias
21 Versailles

MIAMI BEACH

26 Sardinia
Hakkasan
25 Morton's
Scarpetta
Cafe Avanti

NORTH DADE

27 Hiro's Yakko-San
26 Oishi Thai
25 Chéen Huaye
Morton's
Bourbon Steak

PINECREST

25 Imlee
24 Daily Bread
Trattoria Luna
23 Captain's Tavern
Miss Saigon

SOUTH BEACH

27 OLA
Prime One Twelve
Nobu Miami Beach
Joe's Stone Crab
Red Steak

SOUTH MIAMI

27 Matsuri
25 Whisk Gourmet
24 Old Lisbon
23 Café Pastis
Lan

WEST DADE

26 Frankie's Pizza
Tropical Chinese
Basilico
25 Graziano's
24 Kon Chau

WYNNWOOD

25 Jimmy'z Kitchen
24 Gigi
Morgans
Enriqueta's Sandwich Shop
Joey's Italian Café

Top Decor

28	Villa By Barton G.		Red Fish Grill
	Setai	25	DB Bistro Moderne
27	Palme d'Or		Gotham Steak
	Hakkasan		Barton G.
	Crazy About You		Red Steak
	Azul		Wynwood Kitchen & Bar
	Zuma		Capital Grille
	Bourbon Steak		Area 31
	Tantra		Cecconi's Miami Beach
	Blue Door Fish		Wish
	Lido at The Standard		STK Miami
26	Il Gabbiano		Asia de Cuba
	Prelude By Barton G.		Atrio Restaurant
	Casa Tua	24	Sra. Martinez
	Forge		La Palma Ristorante
	Meat Market		Il Mulino New York
	Mr. Chow		Por Fin
	Cioppino		Maitardi
	Scarpetta		Truluck's
	La Cofradia		Fleming's Prime Steak

OUTDOORS

Cecconi's Miami Beach	Trio on the Bay
Fontana	Vic & Angelo's
News Cafe	Villa By Barton G.
Peacock Garden	Vita by Baoli
Perricone's	Wish

ROMANCE

Atrio Restaurant	Escopazzo
Azul	Palme d'Or
Bond St.	Pied à Terre
Casa Tua	Romeo's Cafe
Dining Room	Wish

ROOMS

Blue Door Fish	Makoto
Catch Grill & Bar	Mr. Chow
1500 Degrees	Setai
Gotham Steak	Soirée at Vice Lounge
Hakkasan	Zuma

VIEWS

Azul	Panorama/Sky Lounge
Café Sambal	Red Fish Grill
Garcia's	Red Light
Gibraltar	Smith & Wollensky
Il Gabbiano	Trio on the Bay

Top Service

28	Naoe

27	Palme d'Or
	Il Gabbiano

26	Romeo's Cafe
	Azul
	Christy's
	La Dorada

25	Grazie Italian
	Grimpa Steak
	Pascal's on Ponce
	Capital Grille
	Cafe Avanti
	Morton's
	Michy's
	Fleming's Prime Steak
	Palm
	Bourbon Steak
	DB Bistro Moderne
	Cioppino
	Caffe Vialetto

Il Mulino New York
OLA
Caffe Abbracci

24	Osteria del Teatro
	La Cofradia
	Villa By Barton G.
	Trattoria Luna
	Wish
	Oishi Thai
	Ruth's Chris
	Ortanique
	Oceanaire
	Red Steak*
	Tamarind*
	Su Shin
	Zuma
	Escopazzo
	Sra. Martinez
	Hakkasan
	Yuga

Best Buys

Everyone loves a bargain, and the Miami/Dade area offers plenty of them. All-you-can-eat options are mostly for lunch and/or brunch. For prix fixe menus, call ahead for availability.

ALL YOU CAN EAT ($30 AND UNDER)

26 | Olivos▽
25 | Copper Chimney▽
| Imlee
22 | Atrio Restaurant
| Café Sambal
| Perricone's
19 | Uvas

BURGERS/DOGS

23 | Burger & Beer Joint
22 | Shake Shack
| OneBurger
20 | Dogma Grill
14 | Scotty's Landing

CUBAN

24 | Enriqueta's Sandwich Shop
23 | Puerto Sagua
| La Casita
22 | Islas Canarias
21 | Las Vegas

DINERS

20 | Big Pink
| 11th St. Diner
| Original Pancake House
18 | News Cafe
17 | Gables Diner

EARLY-BIRD

26 | Osteria del Teatro
23 | Café Prima Pasta
21 | Tiramesu
20 | Quattro Gastronomia
17 | Here Comes the Sun

FOOD TRUCKS

CheescMe
Dim Ssäm à Gogo
GastroPod
Jefe's
Latin Burger
Miso Hungry
Ms. Cheezious
Nacho Mamas
Red Koi
Slow Food Truck (see Broward)

PRIX FIXE LUNCH

26 | La Dorada ($22)
| DB Bistro Moderne ($26)
| Ortanique ($22)
25 | Morton's ($29)
| Maroosh ($23)
24 | Truluck's ($25)
| Trattoria Luna ($15)
23 | Fogo de Chão ($27)
| Su Shin ($9)
| Two Chefs ($22)

PRIX FIXE DINNER

26 | Ortanique ($36)
25 | Maroosh ($28)
24 | 1500 Degrees ($35)
| Truluck's ($40)
23 | Fogo de Chão ($47)
| Two Chefs ($35)
22 | Prelude By Barton G. ($39)
21 | Peppy's in the Gables ($20)
| Mercadito ($30)
20 | Trattoria Sole ($29)

PUB GRUB

22 | Clarke's
18 | Gordon Biersch
17 | Fadó Irish Pub
| JohnMartin's
| Titanic Brewery

SEAFOOD SHACKS

23 | Garcia's
| Captain Jim Hanson's
20 | Bahamas Fish
17 | Monty's
14 | Scotty's Landing

TAKEOUT

25 | La Sandwicherie
| Andiamo! Pizza
24 | Shibui
23 | Lan
| Miss Saigon
| El Toro Taco
22 | Perricone's

BEST BUYS: BANG FOR THE BUCK

In order of Bang for the Buck rating.

1. Enriqueta's Sandwich Shop
2. Dogma Grill
3. Frankie's Pizza
4. Five Guys
5. La Sandwicherie
6. Daily Bread Pinecrest
7. Taco Rico
8. OneBurger
9. Shake Shack
10. Lime Fresh Mexican
11. Cheese Course
12. Bali Café
13. Big Cheese
14. El Toro Taco
15. Andiamo! Pizza
16. Pizza Rustica
17. Sergio's
18. Jimmy'z Kitchen
19. Original Pancake House
20. Shorty's Bar-B-Q
21. Anthony's Coal Fired
22. Islas Canarias
23. CG Burgers
24. 11th St. Diner
25. Rice House of Kabob
26. Archie's Pizza
27. Pasha's
28. Moon Thai
29. Heavy Burger
30. Mario The Baker
31. Bangkok/Kendall
32. Disco Fish
33. Café at Books
34. Kon Chau
35. Whisk Gourmet
36. Las Vegas
37. Puerto Sagua
38. Paul Bakery
39. Sakaya
40. Burger & Beer Joint

BEST BUYS: OTHER GOOD VALUES

A la Folie Café
Bahamas Fish
Bernie's L.A. Café
Berries
Big Pink
Blú la Pizzeria del Sole
Bulldog Barbecue
Captain Jim Hanson's
Clarke's
Crumb on Parchment
David's Cafe
Deli Lane
8 Oz. Burger Bar
El Atlakat
El Chalán
Flip Burger
Front Porch Cafe
Garcia's
Gigi
Guayacan Restaurant
Hy-Vong
Indomania
Irie Isle
Kabobji
Khoury's
La Casita
Lan
Lizawan
Lou's Beer Garden
Marhaba Mediterranean
Mike's Pizza & Rest.
Miss Saigon
Mr. Chef's
Mykonos
Naked Pizza
Off the Grille Bistro
100 Montaditos
Original Daily Bread
Oye Cuban Grill
Pancho Villa
Panya Thai
Paquito's
Pilar
Pincho Factory
Piola
Pita Hut
Salsa Fiesta
Spris
Tutto Pizza
Yuga

MIAMI/DADE COUNTY RESTAURANT DIRECTORY

Adriana *Peruvian/Seafood* 25 | 20 | 22 | $47

Surfside | 9477 Harding Ave. (bet. 94th & 95th Sts.) | 305-867-1220 |
www.adrianarestaurant.com

Expect "something different" at this bright, "upscale" Peruvian
where the menu's "quirky mix" encompasses seafood (including
"excellent" ceviche), *chifa* (Chinese-Peruvian fusion), Italian pasta
and "international" touches; locals aver "we need it" in the under-
served Surfside area, and folks from further afield also appreciate
what the "lovely, hard-working proprietors" have accomplished.

A Fish Called Avalon *Seafood* 23 | 21 | 21 | $55

South Beach | Avalon | 700 Ocean Dr. (7th St.) | Miami Beach |
305-532-1727 | www.afishcalledavalon.com

At the "heart of party-centric Ocean Drive" is this oasis of compar-
ative "fine dining" that pleases most with its "fabulous" fin fare,
"cute little bar" and live music nightly out on the "lovely veranda"
where patrons can scope a "passing parade" that includes "every
species of humankind"; still, a few hedgers say "decent but unre-
markable" – "for the price, I'd rather hang out with Wanda."

A la Folie Café *French* 21 | 16 | 17 | $25

South Beach | 1701 Purdy Ave. (Abe Resnick Blvd.) | Miami Beach |
305-672-9336
South Beach | 516 Española Way (Drexel Ave.) | Miami Beach |
305-538-4484 ☽
www.alafoliecafe.com

"The Left Bank has come to SoBe" at these inexpensive French bistros
where folks nosh on "yummy" crêpes and other "light fare" or just "sip
coffee"; the original on Española Way is "cozy" while Purdy Avenue
is deemed "dreary" inside but has "pleasant sidewalk seating" – at
both, the staff displays "just enough attitude to certify authenticity."

AltaMare *Mediterranean/Seafood* 24 | 20 | 23 | $54

South Beach | 1233 Lincoln Rd. (bet. Alton Ct. & Alton Rd.) |
Miami Beach | 305-532-3061 | www.altamarerestaurant.com

Claudio the owner is always on hand, "ensuring all are satisfied"
with the "beautifully executed" Med-accented seafood, meats and
"homemade" pasta emanating from the open kitchen of this SoBe
spot; if it's gotten more "pricey", it still pleases "locals" who "love the
new space" that's more "stylish" on a "mellow stretch" of Lincoln
Road that's "convenient for movies", theater and shopping.

Anacapri *Italian* 22 | 19 | 21 | $37

Coral Gables | 2530 Ponce de Leon Blvd. (bet. Andalusia & Valencia Aves.) |
305-443-8388
Pinecrest | 12669 S. Dixie Hwy. (SW 128th St.) | 305-232-8001
Airport Area | 5749 NW Seventh St. (57th Ct.) | Miami | 305-266-1355 ⊠
Anacapri To Go *Italian*
Cutler Bay | 20571 Old Cutler Rd. (SW 92nd Ave.) | 786-573-2277
www.anacaprifood.com

"Consistency" is the watchword at this trio of "casual" "neighborhood trattorias" known for their "classic" Italian menus, "afford-

able" wine lists and "prompt" service; the "chic" Coral Gables branch is a pre-theater "favorite", the Pinecrest original has a market operation "almost next door" and Seventh Street is convenient to the airport and shopping; P.S. the Cutler Bay take-out joint is closed Tuesdays.

NEW Andalus *Spanish* ∇ 20 | 19 | 17 | $40
Design District | 35 NE 40th St. (bet. 1st & Miami Aves.) | Miami | 305-400-4324 | www.andalusmiami.com
Offering "a taste of *la madre patria*" in the Design District, this new high-end Spaniard offers "authentic tapas" backed up by a "reasonable" wine list; an open kitchen, white banquettes and live flamenco guitar nightly add to the "easy ambiance."

Andiamo! Brick Oven Pizza *Pizza* 25 | 15 | 18 | $20
Upper East Side | 5600 Biscayne Blvd. (56th St.) | Miami | 305-762-5751 | www.andiamopizzamiami.com
Pie mavens hankering for a "thin, crispy crust" and "creative toppings" cruise into this Upper East Side pizzeria housed in a "cool" midcentury-modern "icon" (a "former tire shop" designed by a well-regarded Miami architect); "friendly" service, low tabs and a "lush", "well-shaded patio" have special appeal for "families", while sports fans head for the "barlike" side with a "large outdoor TV screen."

Angelique Euro Café Ⓜ *European* 18 | 20 | 21 | $33
Coral Gables | 117 Miracle Mile (Galiano St.) | 305-529-9922 | www.angeliqueeurocafe.com
This "sleek", "little" white-brick-walled spot on Miracle Mile in Coral Gables offers "shoppers" a chance to unwind with its "out-of-this-world" but "reasonably priced" wine list (including 40 by the glass) and "solid" menu of Spanish, Italian, French and Belgian fare; the "friendly owner makes you feel at home", though your home probably doesn't have live music most nights in high season.

Ⓩ Anthony's Coal Fired Pizza *Pizza* 22 | 16 | 20 | $23
Aventura | Aventura Plaza | 17901 Biscayne Blvd. (bet. NE 179th St. & Point East Dr.) | 305-830-2625
Pinecrest | 10205 S. Dixie Hwy. (bet. SW 102nd & 104th Sts.) | 305-740-5800
Miami Lakes | 15492 NW 77th Ct. (154th St.) | 305-558-3950
www.anthonyscoalfiredpizza.com
"Deliciously scorched" thin-crust pies with "high-end toppings" – plus "killer" wings and "awesome" salads for two – have made this burgeoning Florida-based chain "a hit" with "families" and other pizza partisans; its self-described "well-done" pies strike a few as simply "burned" and the "nothing-fancy", "fast-paced" settings can be "loud, loud, loud", but "prompt" service and "low costs" keep 'em "crowded."

Archie's Gourmet Pizza *Pizza* 21 | 15 | 16 | $21
Key Biscayne | Winn-Dixie Shopping Plaza | 600 Crandon Blvd. (Sunrise Dr.) | 305-365-5911
This "friendly" pizzeria in Key Biscayne is a "great place to take kids": the pies and salads are "satisfying", service is "fast" and the

price is right; however, it's not a place to linger on account of the "tiny" size and "basic" decor.

Area 31 *Seafood* 22 | 25 | 22 | $54

Downtown | Epic Hotel | 270 Biscayne Blvd. Way, 16th fl. (Brickell Ave.) | Miami | 305-424-5234 | www.area31restaurant.com

At this "swanky" seafooder atop Downtown's Epic Hotel, chef E. Michael Reidt prepares "delicious" "local and sustainable" fish, and the "gracious" staff is always willing to accommodate dietary restrictions (e.g. gluten-free, allergies); the interior is "light and airy" but the outside terrace, with its "fantastic" "views of the Miami skyline along the river", is "the place to be."

Asia Bay *Japanese/Thai* 25 | 21 | 22 | $40

Bay Harbor Islands | 1007 96th St. (E. Bay Harbor Dr.) | 305-861-2222 | www.asiabayrestaurants.com

See review in Ft. Lauderdale/Broward County Directory.

Asia de Cuba *Asian/Cuban* 22 | 25 | 20 | $64

South Beach | Mondrian South Beach | 1100 West Ave. (11th St.) | Miami Beach | 305-514-1940 | www.chinagrillmgt.com

Pretty young things share "delish" Asian-Cuban fusion fare with a "kick" in a "chic" "white-on-white" setting worthy of "Wonderland" at this "hot" SoBe "scene" in the Mondrian from the China Grill team; service can be "less than stellar" and tabs aren't cheap, but the "view of the beautiful lobby, sunset and people creates enough value" to make a trip down the rabbit hole "worth your while."

Atrio Restaurant *American* 22 | 25 | 23 | $63

Brickell Area | Conrad Miami Hotel | 1395 Brickell Ave., 25th fl. (SE 14th St.) | Miami | 305-503-6529 | www.conradmiami.com

"Drinks before dinner" on the outdoor terrace are de rigueur thanks to views that are even more "sweeping" than those from the "elegant" dining room at this New American aerie on the 25th floor of the Conrad Hotel; the "flavorful" fare and "attentive" service play second fiddle to the skyline, but the overall experience is "perfect for a date night", albeit an "expensive" one.

Aura ☻ *Eclectic* 19 | 18 | 19 | $46

South Beach | 613 Lincoln Rd. (Pennsylvania Ave.) | Miami Beach | 305-695-1100

There may be a "touristy" aura at this SoBe bistro, but supporters say it offers "solid" Eclectic fare and "reasonable" tabs "in the midst of overpriced" joints; dissenters shrug "just ok", but most would agree that it's "fun" to "watch the parade of people along Lincoln Road" from its outdoor seats.

☒ Azul ☒ *European* 27 | 27 | 26 | $76

Brickell Area | Mandarin Oriental Hotel | 500 Brickell Key Dr. (SE 8th St.) | Miami | 305-913-8358 | www.mandarinoriental.com

This "perennial favorite" in Brickell Key's Mandarin Oriental recently welcomed a new chef who switched its menu from Med to Modern European with American and Asian accents (not fully reflected in the rating); cuisine aside, its "attentive but unobtrusive" service, "serious" wine list and "sleek" setting with "spectacular bay views" help make it a "special occasion" "delight" – "even if prices are close to those for nearby condos."

Bahamas Fish Market *Cuban/Seafood*   20 | 11 | 18 | $22

West Miami | 13399 SW 40th St. (134th Ave.) | 305-225-4932
West Miami | 7200 SW Eighth St. (bet. 72nd & 73rd Aves.) | 305-264-1448

At this pair of "family"-friendly seafooders in West Miami, fin-atics can "choose fish right from the [on-site] market", get them grilled Cuban style and dine on the spot in "bare-bones" surroundings; for "crazy cheap" prices like this "don't expect any frills", and note that "it doesn't hurt to speak a little Spanish to improve the experience."

Balans *Eclectic*   19 | 18 | 18 | $31

Brickell Area | Mary Brickell Vill. | 901 S. Miami Ave. (SW 10th St.) | Miami | 305-534-9191 ◐
Upper East Side | 6789 Biscayne Blvd. (68th St.) | Miami | 305-534-9191
South Beach | 1022 Lincoln Rd. (bet. Lenox & Michigan Aves.) | Miami Beach | 305-534-9191 ◐
www.balans.co.uk

This London import has a "broad" Eclectic menu and "potent" cocktails that are "quite reasonably priced" for SoBe, making it one of the more "brunch-worthy spots" on Lincoln Road (and natch, there's "amazing people-watching"); even if "service is not their forte" it's always a "reliable" choice – likewise its newer outposts in Mary Brickell Village and on the Upper East Side.

Bali Café ⊄ *Indonesian*   25 | 17 | 22 | $22

Downtown | 109 NE Second Ave. (1st St.) | Miami | 305-358-5751

"If the food is this good in Bali I want to go" say enthusiasts who praise the "wonderfully authentic" Indonesian offerings at this "cozy little" Downtown storefront adorned with native artwork; the "friendly" staff makes patrons feel like "part of the family" so though it's cash-only, it's "worth a trip to the ATM"; P.S. sushi is also available.

Bangkok Bangkok *Thai*   19 | 16 | 20 | $28

Coral Gables | 157 Giralda Ave. (bet. Galiano St. & Ponce de Leon Blvd.) | 305-444-2397

For a "quick" lunch or "reasonably priced" dinner of "tasty" Thai food, this "friendly" joint on Coral Gables' Restaurant Row fits the bill; the "drab" decor is getting "a bit dated" but having the option "to sit on the floor to get the full experience" is "cool"; P.S. it's unrelated to Bangkok Bangkok in Kendall.

Bangkok Bangkok *Thai*   23 | 17 | 22 | $25

Kendall | Shops of Kendall | 12584 N. Kendall Dr. (127th Ave.) | 305-595-5839 | www.bangkokbangkok.net

Holding "steady" in the Shops of Kendall, this long-running Thai inspires confidence in fans: "whatever you order is going to be spectacular", and better yet, it's all "reasonably priced" – especially the lunch combos, most of which will get you change back from a $10 bill; a choice of seating at tables or on floor mats adds to the "authentic" aura; P.S. it's unrelated to Bangkok Bangkok in Coral Gables.

Z Barton G. The Restaurant *American*   22 | 25 | 23 | $74

South Beach | 1427 West Ave. (14th Ct.) | Miami Beach | 305-672-8881 | www.bartong.com

"If Willy Wonka owned a restaurant" it would be this "whimsical" SoBe fantasia known for its "over-the-top presentations" of New American comfort fare and "science-experiment" drinks; Veruca Salt types may whine that it's "overpriced" and "more flash than substance", but it still "wows" "out-of-towners", "teenagers" and plenty of "delighted" adults ("what a show!"); P.S. the Food and Decor scores may not reflect post-Survey changes including a refreshed menu (though many favorites remain), redone dining room and newly added terrace bar and upstairs private-dining space.

Barú Urbano *Eclectic*   ▽ 15 | 19 | 17 | $27

Brickell Area | 1001 S. Miami Ave. (SE 10th St.) | Miami | 305-381-5901 | www.barurbano.com

"Beautiful" people out for some "late-night fun" head to this Brickell Area "restaurant/lounge" with a clublike "vibe" and "hottie bartenders"; the Eclectic eats take a back seat, but they work for "a quick bite before hitting the town"; P.S. a Doral offshoot is set to open in fall 2011.

Basilico *Italian*   26 | 18 | 23 | $34

Airport Area | 5879 NW 36th St. (57th Ave.) | Miami | 305-871-3585 Ⓢ
Doral | 10405 NW 41st St. (bet. 102nd & 107th Aves.) | Miami | 305-406-3737
www.basilicomiami.com

"One of those hidden treasures that you just want to share with everyone" say diners who are "always happy" with the "outstanding" Northern Italian cuisine and excellent "value" at the tiny strip-mall original near the airport; the newer Doral sibling is a bit bigger and has the "same delicious food" and good service thanks to the watchful eye of the "wonderful" manager and owners.

Bella Luna *Italian*   23 | 18 | 21 | $38

Aventura | Aventura Mall | 19575 Biscayne Blvd. (NE 195th St.) | 305-792-9330

"Aventuristas" declare "the only decent answer to the question 'where do you want to grab a bite after shopping?'" is this "quality" Italian with "fresh ingredients", a "nice ambiance" and "professional" service – "not what one expects to find in a mall"; "moderate" prices are another reason to "put your Macy's bag to rest and fill up."

NEW Bernie's L.A. Café *Pan-Latin*   ▽ 26 | 13 | 20 | $20

South Beach | 1570 Alton Rd. (bet. 15th & 16th Sts.) | Miami Beach | 305-535-8003 | www.bernieslacafe.com

Bernard Matz, "the brains behind Café at Books & Books", brings a "creative flair" and a "healthy skew" to the "fresh, delicious" Pan-Latin vittles at this addition to SoBe's Alton Road dining scene; it's a "no-frills, no-fuss" place in "tiny" "cafeteria" digs, but "delivery is a great option" and either way, it's such a "good value."

Berries *Eclectic*   20 | 16 | 18 | $25

Coconut Grove | 2884 SW 27th Ave. (Coconut Ave.) | 305-448-2111 | www.berriesinthegrove.com

"Can you say variety?" – this "cute", "very Grove-y" Eclectic near the rail station has it in spades, from "tasty", "inexpensive" smoothies, soups, salads and sandwiches to pasta, pizza and more, with many "healthy options mixed in"; "casual dress seems to imply casual service", but it's hard to get worked up about anything sitting out on the "lovely" patio "under the canopy of trees."

Big Cheese *Pizza*   21 | 13 | 20 | $18

South Miami | 8080 SW 67th Ave. (S. Dixie Hwy.) | 305-662-6855 | www.bigcheesemiami.com

"Big families, big groups and big hungry college kids" equal "long lines" at this "home-grown" South Miami pizza-and-pasta "mainstay" known for its "heaping portions" of "cheesy garlicky goodness" – in fact, "everything about this place is big except the check"; U. of Miami fans also appreciate the "memorabilia festooning" the joint ("go 'Canes!").

Big Pink ◐ *Diner*   20 | 15 | 17 | $24

South Beach | 157 Collins Ave. (2nd St.) | Miami Beach | 305-532-4700 | www.bigpinkrestaurant.com

"Early-morning hangovers" and "late-night munchies" are both cured at this "funky" "'50s flashback" in SoBe boasting a "huge" menu of "satisfying" diner grub in "bikini-body-attacking" portion sizes; although aesthetes find the atmosphere "one grade above a dump" and service can be "erratic" ("why is it always my waiter's first day?") "kids, grandparents, models and cops" all seem to "love" it.

Bin No. 18 *Italian*   23 | 17 | 20 | $33

Downtown | 1800 Biscayne Plaza | 275 NE 18th St. (Biscayne Blvd.) | Miami | 786-235-7575 | www.bin18miami.com

As a quick stop-off "before or after the Arsht Center" or a place to linger with "good friends or a date", chef-owner Alfredo Patino's Downtown enoteca satisfies with "terrific" beers, wines and "tons of interesting" Italian small plates, charcuterie and cheeses served in an "urban" atmosphere; at prices like these, consider the "knowledgable" staff and free parking a "bonus."

Bizcaya *American/Mediterranean*   ∇ 24 | 26 | 25 | $67

Coconut Grove | Ritz-Carlton Coconut Grove | 3300 SW 27th Ave. (bet. Bayshore Dr. & Tigertail Ave.) | 305-644-4675 | www.ritzcarlton.com

This "beautiful" restaurant adorned with stately marble floors and columns in the Ritz-Carlton Coconut Grove is still flying mostly under the radar with surveyors; a revamped American-Med menu, "excellent" brunch, "quiet" (some say "stuffy") atmosphere and a staff that "pays attention" can make for "very enjoyable" dining, and while it's "pricey", "hey . . . it's the Ritz."

	FOOD	DECOR	SERVICE	COST

NEW Blade/Vida *American/Japanese* — — — E

Miami Beach | Fontainebleau Miami Beach | 4441 Collins Ave.
(W. 44th St.) | 877-326-7412 | www.fontainebleau.com

An unlikely but complementary pair – Blade, a modern sushi and
sake bar open for lunch and dinner, and Vida, an American brasserie
serving updated comfort classics all day – shares a sleek space with
an open kitchen off the lobby in the Fontainebleau Miami Beach;
both can cut a bit of a hole in your wallet depending on what you order.

Z BLT Steak *Steak* 25 23 23 $71

South Beach | The Betsy Hotel | 1440 Ocean Dr. (bet. 14th & 15th Sts.) |
Miami Beach | 305-673-0044 | www.bltsteak.com

"A bit more hip" than old-school meat palaces, this Betsy Hotel outpost of a "quality brand" steakhouse chain excels with its "perfectly
charred" chops, "inventive" sides and "terrific" wine list – that's ic-
ing on the cake for fans who admit "they had me at the popovers";
tabs are "steep" and some "don't love the lobbyish atmosphere",
but most deem it a "refined" escape from the SoBe "riffraff."

NEW Blue Door Fish ❶ *Seafood* 23 27 23 $78

South Beach | Delano Hotel | 1685 Collins Ave. (17th St.) | Miami Beach |
305-674-6400 | www.chinagrillmgt.com

Claude Troisgros recently rebooted this spot in South Beach's "opulent" Delano Hotel, switching from a Brazilian-French menu to focus
on seafood, from "timeless classics" to more "innovative" preparations; what hasn't changed is the "sexy", "stunning" interior and
"verdant" patio studded with a "beautiful staff" catering to an
equally "beautiful" crowd; P.S. bring "big bucks."

Blue Sea ❶ *Japanese* ▽ 24 27 24 $79

South Beach | Delano Hotel | 1685 Collins Ave. (17th St.) | Miami Beach |
305-674-6400 | www.delano-hotel.com

"Sushi lovers" declare this SoBe "scene" a "must" for "interesting rolls"
and other "innovative" albeit "expensive" Japanese creations featuring fish "so fresh you want to slap the waiter" (but you won't
since service is "a delight"); you'll "sit next to complete strangers"
at two communal tables in the Delano Hotel's lobby, but "keep the
sake coming" and they might become your new "best friends."

Blú la Pizzeria del Sole *Pizza* 21 17 20 $25

South Miami | 7201 SW 59th Ave. (Sunset Dr.) | 305-666-9285

"Just the place for a family night out", this "small" South Miami pizzeria (a sibling of Trattoria Sole) offers "crispy" thin-crust pies with
"real brick-oven flavor" and a small menu of Italian standards and
"delish salads"; "people-watching" from the "charming" sidewalk
tables adds more "bang for the buck."

Bombay Darbar *Indian* ▽ 23 16 20 $29

Coconut Grove | 3195 Commodore Plaza (Main Hwy.) | 305-444-7272 |
www.bombaydarbarrestaurant.com

Judging by the "fab curries" and other "authentic" subcontinental fare,
"there's some serious cooking going on in the tiny kitchen" of this In-

dian "in the heart of the Grove"; moderate prices and a staff that "really cares" make it a "delight" that's, mercifully, still under the radar.

Bond St. Lounge *Japanese*   25 | 20 | 19 | $56

South Beach | Townhouse Hotel | 150 20th St. (Collins Ave.) | Miami Beach | 305-398-1806 | www.townhousehotel.com

"Tucked away" in the basement of SoBe's Townhouse Hotel, this "secret" "nook" turns out "terrific" sushi that "rivals" its NYC counterpart in taste (and price); the "dark, romantic", "lounge"-like environs are well "suited for dates", though "uncomfortable seating" and service that "needs improvement" mar the mood for a few.

Z Bonefish Grill *Seafood*   22 | 19 | 21 | $36

Kendall | 12520 SW 120th St. (125th Pl.) | 786-293-5713
Westernmost Dade | 14218 SW Eighth St. (bet. 142nd & 143rd Aves.) | Miami | 305-487-6430
www.bonefishgrill.com
See review in Ft. Lauderdale/Broward County Directory.

Bongos Cuban Café *Cuban*   16 | 22 | 17 | $38

Downtown | 601 Biscayne Blvd. (bet. 6th & 7th Sts.) | Miami | 786-777-2100 **M**
South Beach | 820 Ocean Dr. (bet. 8th & 9th Sts.) | Miami Beach | 305-532-9577
www.bongoscubancafe.com

"Bring on the mojitos" because it's all about the "nightlife" at Gloria Estefan's "electric" "Latin party" Downtown near American Airlines Arena (with outposts in Miami Beach and Hollywood's Seminole Hard Rock); detractors find the Cuban food "overpriced" and cite "a lot of style, not much substance", but as a place to "get that Miami vibe" and dance (on weekends) it excels.

Bourbon Steak *Steak*   25 | 27 | 25 | $83

Aventura | Turnberry Isle Hotel & Resort | 19999 W. Country Club Dr. (Aventura Blvd.) | 786-279-6600 | www.michaelmina.net

From its "gorgeous", "spacious" setup designed by Tony Chi to its "decadent" chops, "delish" burgers and "addictive" fries, Michael Mina's steakhouse in Aventura's Turnberry Isle Hotel strikes fans as "ahead of the herd" in many respects; a "passionate" staff (a "rare find in Miami") mixes "well-balanced drinks" and helps diners navigate an "extensive" wine list that's loaded with "treasures" – and they'll gladly accept your "gold card" at meal's end.

Brazaviva Churrascaria **Z M** *Brazilian*   ∇ 20 | 18 | 21 | $43

Doral | 7910 NW 25th St. (79th Ave.) | Miami | 305-513-6373 | www.brazaviva.com
See review in Ft. Lauderdale/Broward County Directory.

Buena Vista Bistro ● *Eclectic/French*   24 | 17 | 21 | $33

Upper East Side | 4582 NE Second Ave. (bet. 45th & 46th Sts.) | Miami | 305-456-5909 | www.buenavistabistro.com
Housed in a "cute storefront" in an "unassuming" area on the Upper East Side, this "neighborhood find" pleases "locals" who sa-

lute its "divine" French bistro fare with Eclectic leanings; a "nice wine selection", "modest" prices and a "bohemian setting" indoors and out add to the allure; P.S. "bonus": their sister deli almost "next door" offers breakfast.

Bugatti, The Art of Pasta *Italian*   23 | 18 | 21 | $35

Coral Gables | 2504 Ponce de Leon Blvd. (Andalusia Ave.) | 305-441-2545 | www.bugattirestaurant.com

This Coral Gables "fixture" has been cranking out "very fine" "homemade pasta" for over 25 years and more recently expanded the menu to other Italian staples; a "relaxed", "contemporary atmosphere" and generally "personable" staff are pluses, but regulars advise "arrive early since reservations are not accepted"; P.S. the "first Wednesday of each month is white lasagna night" – "a must."

Bulldog Barbecue *BBQ*   18 | 13 | 17 | $24

North Miami | 15400 Biscayne Blvd. (156th St.) | 305-940-9655 | www.bulldog-bbq.com

Former *Top Chef* contender Howie Kleinberg pleases fans with "creative", "well-prepared" takes on the classics served by a "friendly" (if sometimes "slow") crew at this "gourmet barbecue" joint in a North Miami strip mall; he also draws a few ribs from critics ("wannabe" 'cue), but the fact that the "casual" digs are "always crowded" says a lot; P.S. it recently beefed up with the addition of its Bulldog Burger annex.

Burger & Beer Joint ● *Burgers*   23 | 17 | 20 | $26

Brickell Area | 900 S. Miami Ave. (SE 9th St.) | Miami | 305-523-2244

Miami Beach | 1766 Bay Rd. (bet. Abe Resnick Blvd. & 18th St.) | 305-672-3287

www.burgernbeerjoint.com

"Freakin' big", "juicy" burgers named for hit tunes – e.g. Mustang Sally, Stairway to Heaven – pair perfectly with the "99 bottles of beer" and "adult milkshakes" on offer at these Brickell Area–Miami Beach bar scenes with strong "townie" followings; friendly "inked" staffers and "loud music" add to the "casual cool" atmosphere and help distract from prices that are "on the expensive side" for the genre.

Café at Books & Books *American*   21 | 18 | 19 | $23

Coral Gables | 265 Aragon Ave. (bet. Ponce de Leon Blvd. & Salzedo St.) | 305-448-9599

South Beach | 927 Lincoln Rd. (bet. Jefferson & N. Michigan Aves.) | Miami Beach | 305-695-8898

www.booksandbooks.com

"A glass of wine, a tuna sandwich, an author and thou" is paradise regained – especially in the "relaxing" garden – for "literary" types at this Coral Gables New American cafe housed in a "fantastic neighborhood bookshop"; the South Beach branch is distinguished by "Lincoln Road people-watching" plus "more food options" and "attentive" service.

Café Avanti *Italian*

FOOD	DECOR	SERVICE	COST
25	20	25	$42

Miami Beach | 732 41st St. (bet. Chase & Prairie Aves.) | 305-538-4400 | www.cafeavanti.com

"Superior" traditional Italian fare and an owner who "is always there" with a "warm and cordial welcome" are the main selling points at this "venerable" "mid-Beach" "neighborhood" spot; "some excellent values on the wine list" and "plenty of free street parking" also endear it to locals.

NEW Cafe L'Attico ● *American/Italian*

FOOD	DECOR	SERVICE	COST
-	-	-	E

Miami Beach | 17100 Collins Ave. (NE 17th St.) | 305-944-2215

At this new Miami Beach trattoria, there's a little something for everyone on the all-purpose menu of Italian and American standards, including grilled pizzas, pastas, steak and salads; big comfy booths line the dark-wood interior while plenty of windows provide views to a pretty brick-paved patio.

Café Pastis ⊠ *French*

FOOD	DECOR	SERVICE	COST
23	16	21	$36

South Miami | 7310 S. Red Rd. (bet. 73rd & 74th Sts.) | 305-665-3322 | www.cafepastis.com

Between this midpriced cafe's "authentic" Gallic fare, waiters with "accents" and "cute" country bistro trappings, "you'd think you were in France", not a South Miami strip mall; two bits of *bon conseil*: "make reservations" because it's popular, and "eat outside" unless you want to "get to know your neighbors" in the "cramped" dining room.

Café Prima Pasta ● *Italian*

FOOD	DECOR	SERVICE	COST
23	20	22	$41

Miami Beach | 414 71st St. (Abbott Ave.) | 305-867-0106 | www.primapasta.com

This "family-owned" "favorite" in Miami Beach "specializes in pasta" with "wonderful" "homemade sauce", though there's plenty of other Northern Italiana on the menu too; "locals" appreciate its "late-night" hours and the fact that it's "one of the only affordable family options in the area" (it's even cheaper before 6 PM).

Café Ragazzi ● *Italian*

FOOD	DECOR	SERVICE	COST
23	18	21	$55

Surfside | 9500 Harding Ave. (95th St.) | 305-866-4495 | www.caferagazzi.com

The "straightforward Italian classics" are "fantastic" at this "long-standing" Surfsider that's something of a "Latin celebrity" hang; sure, it's often "noisy" and pretty "expensive", but they "make you feel like family" and ease occasional waits with complimentary wine.

Café Sambal *Asian*

FOOD	DECOR	SERVICE	COST
22	22	23	$51

Brickell Area | Mandarin Oriental Hotel | 500 Brickell Key Dr. (SE 8th St.) | Miami | 305-913-8288 | www.mandarinoriental.com

"Life is great" sigh surveyors soaking up "breathtaking views" of Biscayne Bay from the huge outdoor terrace at this "classy but casual" lounge at the Mandarin Oriental on Brickell Key; a "cordial" staff proffers Pan-Asian bites and sushi that are perfectly "fine" if "pricey" for what they are – still, it's a "relaxing" respite "from the South Beach crowds."

	FOOD	DECOR	SERVICE	COST

Caffe Abbracci ● *Italian*   25 | 21 | 25 | $54

Coral Gables | 318 Aragon Ave. (bet. 42nd Ave. & Salzedo St.) | 305-441-0700 | www.caffeabbracci.com

This "high-end" Coral Gables "institution" is a "place to be seen" while enjoying "exceptional" pastas and other "wonderful" Lombardian cuisine in a "busy", often "noisy" setting oveseen by owner Nino Pernetti, whose "well-trained staff" makes just about everyone "feel at home"; decor that's "old-fashioned" to some is "dated" to others but that's a quibble given its "year after year" "consistency."

Caffe Da Vinci *Italian*   17 | 19 | 19 | $42

Bay Harbor Islands | 1009 Kane Concourse (E. Bay Harbor Dr.) | 305-861-8166 | www.caffedavinci.com

After a hiatus, this Bay Harbor Islands Italian is back, with a renovated dining room and new late-night lounge offering small plates designed by the longtime executive chef, who took over ownership; locals are still "getting used to" the fresh look, and if some find the overall package "nothing spectactular", it's still a "comfortable" place for a "pleasant" meal.

Caffé Milano ● *Italian*   ▽ 17 | 18 | 17 | $60

South Beach | 850 Ocean Dr. (bet. 8th & 9th Sts.) | Miami Beach | 305-532-0707

Expect "authentic Italian ambiance" at this South Beach stalwart serving a dependable menu of staples from The Boot; some find it "pricey", but it offers a "real Ocean Drive experience" so "grab a sidewalk table and watch the parade."

Caffe Portofino *Italian*   ▽ 24 | 18 | 24 | $44

Pinecrest | 13615 S. Dixie Hwy. (Howard Dr.) | 305-252-2869 | www.cportofino.com

Pinecresters say it's "nice to have this cozy nook in the 'hood", what with its "excellent" Italian cuisine and "wide wine selection" at midrange prices; an "attentive" staff and convenient location across from a megamall are further assets.

Caffe Vialetto *Italian*   25 | 19 | 25 | $50

Coral Gables | 4019 Le Jeune Rd. (Bird Rd.) | 305-446-5659 | www.caffevialetto.com

"Wish we'd discovered it sooner" say fans who only recently unearthed this "hidden gem" in a Coral Gables strip mall lauded for its "excellent" Italian fare with "creative" Latin-Caribbean touches; the "small", "dimly lit" room is somewhat "lacking" in atmosphere, but "charming hosts" and middling tabs make amends.

Calamari *Italian*   18 | 20 | 20 | $33

Coconut Grove | 3540 Main Hwy. (Franklin Ave.) | 305-441-0219 | www.calamarirestaurant.com

The seafood-centric Italian fare at this "casual" Coconut Grover from Tommy Billante (Villagio et al.) strikes some as "consistently good", others as "basically average", but it's "enjoyable" enough when sitting on the "beautiful" patio with "big umbrellas, shade trees and a fountain"; "informal but polite" service, moderate prices and a "small gourmet shop" on-site are added draws.

Z Canyon Ranch Grill *Health Food*   19 | 21 | 19 | $48

Miami Beach | Canyon Ranch Hotel & Spa | 6801 Collins Ave. (bet. 67th & 69th Sts.) | 305-514-7474 | www.canyonranch.com
Figure-conscious types are drawn to this oceanfront eatery at Miami Beach's Canyon Ranch Hotel & Spa where the "well-executed", "health-oriented" menu features low-calorie fare made with "wonderful ingredients"; some find it "pricey" for "minuscule" portions, but the staff is "very accommodating to special needs" (e.g. gluten-free) and the "serene" setting and "beautiful" water views act as additional restoratives.

Z Capital Grille *Steak*   26 | 25 | 25 | $67

Brickell Area | 444 Brickell Ave. (SE 5th St.) | Miami | 305-374-4500 | www.thecapitalgrille.com
"Where the elite meet to eat meat" sums up these chophouses that admirers deem a "cut above other national steak chains" – not just for their "perfect sear" but also for their "impeccable" service that ensures "everyone is treated like a VIP"; a "solid wine list", including many by the glass, and "clubby", "dark-wood" environs make for a "relaxing" time, so go ahead and "break the bank."

Captain Jim Hanson's   23 | 7 | 19 | $27
Seafood *Seafood*

North Miami | 12950 W. Dixie Hwy. (bet. NE 129th & 130th Sts.) | 305-892-2812
For "just-caught fish", "bargain stone crabs" and "fabulous" seafood salads on the "cheap", locals "in the know" flock to this "one-of-a-kind" North Miami market/eatery; it's something of a "dive" with "no pretensions", but fans shrug off the "plastic plates" and proclaim it's "just what it should be."

Captain's Tavern *Seafood*   23 | 14 | 21 | $37

Pinecrest | 9625 S. Dixie Hwy. (SW 98th St.) | 305-666-5979 | www.captainstavernmiami.com
"Ahoy, matey!" – the "lines form early" at this "Old Miami" fish house in Pinecrest with a rep for "outstandingly fresh" seafood at a "reasonable" cost; the maritime decor seemingly "hasn't changed in 100 years", but wallet-watchers flip for the "wonderful" wines at "wine-store" prices and "deals" like Tuesday night's two-for-one Maine lobsters (though it's "difficult to get a table" then).

NEW Carillon Lounge *American*   - | - | - | M

Miami Beach | Canyon Ranch Hotel & Spa | 6801 Collins Ave. (bet. 67th & 69th Sts.) | 305-514-7000 | www.canyonranch.com
Named for the original hotel on the site – a Miami Beach hot spot in the 1950s – this new lobby bar/lounge in the Canyon Ranch Hotel & Spa offers tranquil ocean views and a limited menu of wholesome New American snacks and light bites; the drinks also have a spa-like bent: cocktails made with fresh ingredients and bio-dynamic and sustainable wines.

	FOOD	DECOR	SERVICE	COST

Carpaccio *Italian*
23 | 20 | 21 | $47

Bal Harbour | Bal Harbour Shops | 9700 Collins Ave. (96th St.) | 305-867-7777 | www.carpaccioatbalharbour.com

"Terrific" Italian cuisine at relatively "moderate prices" served in a "timely" fashion is one big reason why this ristorante in the "high-end shopping mecca" Bal Harbour Shops is "always packed"; but for some surveyers, the "main event" is the "scenery" on the outdoor patio, which includes "glamorous young women" guided by "aging lotharios" and the "Lamborghinis and Maseratis" from which they alight.

Casa Juancho *Spanish*
24 | 22 | 21 | $47

Little Havana | 2436 SW Eighth St. (bet. 24th & 25th Aves.) | Miami | 305-642-2452 | www.casajuancho.com

"Outstanding paella", tapas and other "traditional" Spanish fare in-cluding "hard-to-find" items like "real *fabada*" (bean stew) are matched by "quality" wines at this "upscale" "hacienda" in Little Havana run by an "attentive" staff; a "roving" band of musicians adds to the "fun", "lively" experience.

Casa Larios *Cuban*
19 | 17 | 19 | $26

South Miami | 5859 SW 73rd St. (58th Ct.) | 305-662-5656
West Miami | 7705 W. Flagler St. (SW 79th Ave.) | 305-266-5494
www.casalariosonline.com

These all-day South and West Miami cafes are especially popu-lar as "breakfast hangouts" and for "quick lunches", dishing up "large portions" of "inexpensive" Cuban "comfort food" ("I wake at night salivating over the *vaca frita*") in simple tiled environs; "walk-up windows" make grabbing takeout or a "*cafecito* pick-me-up" easy; P.S. there are "traditional" live bands on the weekend at 73rd Street.

Casa Paco *Cuban/Spanish*
21 | 16 | 19 | $30

South Miami | 8868 Bird Rd. (88th Pl.) | 305-554-7633 | www.casapacomiami.com

This "been-around-forever" South Miamian has garnered a strong "local following" for its "authentic" Spanish and Cuban food "just like mama used to make"; loyalists also appreciate the "great-value" prices and that everything comes "without the Eighth Street theater."

❷ Casa Tua *Italian*
24 | 26 | 23 | $87

South Beach | Casa Tua | 1700 James Ave. (17th St.) | Miami Beach | 305-673-1010 | www.casatualifestyle.com

"There's no sign" outside this "hidden", "villa"-like Northern Italian in a SoBe boutique inn, which just adds to its "romantic" allure, es-pecially in the flower-strewn courtyard with "votives hanging from the trees" and "beautiful people" at the tables; most find the food equally "fabulous", so "if money is no object" and you can ignore the occasional dose of "attitude", it "does not disappoint" – just "make reservations early."

FOOD · DECOR · SERVICE · COST

NEW Catch Grill & Bar *Seafood*   – | – | – | E

Biscayne | Marriott Biscayne Bay | 1633 N. Bayshore Dr. (NE 16th St.) | Miami | 305-536-6414 | www.catchonthebaymiami.com

This arrival in the Marriott Biscayne Bay specializes in "fresh" seafood (with land-based options including a build-your-own-burger bar) in a modern, ocean-themed setting awash with undulating wood panels and beds of water-worn rocks; sitting outside on the large patio overlooking the marina is so "delightful" it's easy to forget the expensive tabs.

NEW Cecconi's Miami Beach *Italian*   22 | 25 | 19 | $74

Miami Beach | SoHo Beach House | 4385 Cullins Ave. (W. 43rd St.) | 786-507-7902 | www.cecconismiamibeach.com

The Venetian offerings from chef Sergio Sigala (ex Casa Tua) at this "chic" London import in Miami Beach's SoHo Beach House may be "delicious", but they pale in comparison to the "gorgeous garden" setting with a retractable awning and buttonwood trees strung with lights; "service is not quite up to par" and tabs are "Brink's"-level, but there are values at the bar serving cicchetti and "excellent" cocktails.

Ceviche 105 *Peruvian*   25 | 19 | 22 | $32
(aka Cvi-Che 105)

Downtown | 105 NE 3rd Ave. (Biscayne Blvd.) | Miami | 305-577-3454 | www.ceviche105.com

Take note: the "true flavors of Peru come alive" in the "beyond fresh" ceviche, tiraditos and other "authentic", moderately priced fare at this Downtown Miami "hot spot" with a "friendly" staff; "cement floors" and other "minimalist" touches appeal to the "young", "raucous" crowd sipping drinks, but they "echo" – so "bring a bullhorn" if you want to converse.

NEW Cevichery *Pan-Latin/Peruvian*   – | – | – | M

South Beach | 448 Española Way (Drexel Ave.) | Miami Beach | 305-532-6620 | www.cevichery.com

The semi-industrial, exposed-brick environs at this hip, moderately priced Pan-Latin arrival in SoBe are almost as raw as its ceviche and tiraditos; after dinner, the DJ cranks the volume and the pisco sours flow as it morphs into a nightspot.

NEW CG Burgers *Burgers*   19 | 13 | 15 | $18

Bal Harbour | 1732 N. Federal Hwy. (bet. NE 17th Ct. & 17th St.) | 954-618-6450
Kendall | Palms Town & Country | 8525 Mills Dr. (SW 117th Ave.) | 786-439-2560
www.cgburgers.com

See review in Palm Beach County Directory.

Chart House *American/Seafood*   20 | 22 | 20 | $48

Coconut Grove | 51 Chart House Dr. (S. Bayshore Dr.) | 305-856-9741 | www.chart-house.com

The "varied menus" at these "reliable", "well-run" outposts of the American seafood-focused chain do right by most diners, whether they're in the mood for a "fish dinner", "famous prime rib" or filling up at "over-the-top" salad bars; the Coconut Grove locale offers "beautiful views" of Biscayne Bay, but it may be more fun watching "drunken boaters bang into the pier" at Ft. Lauderdale's slickly renovated Intracoastal outlet (formerly Charley's Crab).

Chéen Huaye *Mexican*   25 | 18 | 23 | $29

North Miami | 15400 Biscayne Blvd. (NE 151st St.) | 305-956-2808 | www.cheenhuaye.com

Its name means 'only here', an apt description of the "seriously authentic" Yucatán-style cuisine "served with appropriate pride by the owners themselves" at this North Miami Mexican in a "nondescript strip mall"; it's "quiet enough for a first date" and delivers "great bang for the buck" too; P.S. it's adding a market selling its own bottled sauces and salsa plus Mexican imports.

☑ Cheesecake Factory ● *American*   20 | 19 | 19 | $30

Aventura | Aventura Mall | 19501 Biscayne Blvd. (NE 195th St.) | 305-792-9696
Coconut Grove | CocoWalk | 3015 Grand Ave. (Virginia St.) | 305-447-9898
Kendall | Dadeland Mall | 7497 N. Kendall Dr. (S. Dixie Hwy.) | 305-665-5400
www.thecheesecakefactory.com

"Always reliable" and "always mobbed", this "chain satisfies "all ages" with its "Bible"-length menu of American "comfort food" ("if you can't find something to eat, you're not hungry") in "steroidal" portions that beg the question "who has room for cheesecake?"; just expect "no surprises" and "plan on waiting" and putting up with "noise" and "chaos" in return for a "reasonable" bill.

Cheese Course *Eclectic*   25 | 17 | 18 | $20

Downtown | 3451 NE First Ave. (Midtown Blvd.) | Miami | 786-220-6681 | www.thecheesecourse.com

See review in Ft. Lauderdale/Broward County Directory.

CheeseMe *American*   - | - | - | I

Location varies; see website | Miami | 305-323-1883 | www.cheeseme.com

This mobile American fromagerie, often found in or around Jefferson Avenue, is all about the glory of molten cheese sandwiches; you can choose a house combo or customize your own creation, choosing from a half-dozen breads, just as many cheeses and 'insertions' ranging from braised short ribs to three-onion marmalade.

Chef Adrianne's ☒ *Eclectic*   ▽ 25 | 20 | 24 | $51

Kendall | 11510 SW 147 Ave. (Hammocks Blvd.) | 305-408-8386 | www.chefadriannes.com

SoFla suburbia is soon forgotten amid the rustic wine barrels and earth tones recalling a Napa Valley wine bar at this cozy Kendall enoteca with a pricey Eclectic menu that mostly pleases the few who know it; chef-owner Adrianne Calvo presides over the small space, which serves lunch and dinner and hosts 'dark dining' events.

	FOOD	DECOR	SERVICE	COST

China Grill ❂ *Asian*

| 22 | 23 | 20 | $56 |

South Beach | 404 Washington Ave. (4th St.) | Miami Beach |
305-534-2211 | www.chinagrillmgt.com

"Exotic" Pan-Asian dishes served "family-style" by "hot servers" in
a "cavernous", "high-energy" space is what you can expect at this
"expensive" SoBe "mainstay"; if it's "not quite the scene" it was in its
"pioneer" days, someone better tell the "crowds" that still pack it
nightly; P.S. the Ft. Lauderdale link boosts the eye candy with "fantastic views of mega yachts."

NEW Cholo's Ceviche & Grill *Peruvian*

| - | - | - | I |

North Miami Beach | 1127 NE 163rd St. (bet. 11th & 12th Aves.) |
305-947-3338

Peruvian expats in North Miami Beach exit this new strip-mall storefront looking as cheerful as the bright, colorful paintings inside
thanks to the authentic cuisine at ultralow prices; adventurous eaters recommend the palate-puckering 'leche de tigre' shots: fish,
shrimp or octopus in tangy-spicy chile marinades.

Chow Down Grill *Chinese*

| - | - | - | I |

Surfside | 9517 Harding Ave. (95th St.) | 305-397-8494
NEW **South Beach** | 920 Alton Rd. (9th St.) | Miami Beach |
305-674-1674 ❂
www.chowdowngrill.com

Hip Chinese bites – ranging from dumplings (like a reworked crab
rangoon that's filled with spinach and mascarpone cheese) to entrees that let diners mix and match proteins, sauces and veggies –
and super-low prices make for loyal regulars at this sliver of a
space in Surfside, an area not known for its great dining options;
P.S. its brand-new South Beach spin-off is a bit bigger but has a
similarly small menu.

Christy's ✉ *Steak*

| 24 | 22 | 26 | $55 |

Coral Gables | 3101 Ponce de Leon Blvd. (Malaga Ave.) | 305-446-1400 |
www.christysrestaurant.com

This "venerable" steakhouse in Coral Gables continues to
"please" patrons with its "considerate" service and "fine" chops,
which may be "expensive" but include sides and what many call
"the best Caesar salad in town"; its dark-wood looks add to the
"old-school awesomeness", but longtime loyalists consider the
addition of a piano bar with live music Thursday–Saturday evenings
"a positive step."

NEW Cinco Cantina &
Tequila Bar *Mexican*

| - | - | - | M |

Coral Gables | Village of Merrick Park | 4251 Salzedo St. (San Lorenzo Ave.) |
786-439-1730 | www.cincomiami.com

Amid the designer finery of Coral Gables' Village of Merrick
Park, shopaholics can knock back a few margaritas and tequilas at
this warehouse-sized Mexican newcomer whose lengthy midpriced menu lists all the expected faves, some with sophisticated flourishes; the decor has plenty of flourishes too, e.g. giant

| | FOOD | DECOR | SERVICE | COST |

starburst chandeliers, a mural of a smiling bandito and low-rider bikes scattered about.

Cioppino *Italian* — 23 | 26 | 25 | $66

Key Biscayne | Ritz-Carlton Key Biscayne | 455 Grand Bay Dr. (Crandon Blvd.) | 305-365-4500 | www.ritzcarlton.com

At this "sublime refuge" in the Ritz-Carlton Key Biscayne, "exceptional" service and a "terrific" wine list accompany "delicious" Italian offerings; the Sunday brunch buffet is pricey ($82 for adults, half-price for children) but popular with families, while "romantic" couples prefer the "lovely" water and sky views, especially during the monthly Moonrise Dinner events, which feature tabletop telescopes for stargazing.

NEW City Hall *American* — - | - | - | M

Wynwood | 2004 Biscayne Blvd. (20th St.) | Miami | 305-764-3130 | www.cityhalltherestaurant.com

If only the real city hall were run as smoothly as this new Wynwood brasserie from Steven Haas (founder of Miami Spice), where former Emeril's chef Tom Azar plates up tricked-out New American comfort food at moderate prices; the stylish, deco-esque dining room features a mezzanine that overlooks all the action below, plus colorful murals and rows of cozy booths that offer prime Biscayne Boulevard views.

Clarke's ● *American/Irish* — 22 | 18 | 22 | $31

South Beach | 840 First St. (bet. Alton Rd. & Washington Ave.) | Miami Beach | 305-538-9885 | www.clarkesmiamibeach.com

Of course there's "great beer (duh)" at this "upscale Irish pub" in SoBe, but there's also a surprisingly "fantastic wine list" and "better food than you'd expect", including an "enjoyable burger" and some "American classics" beyond the "basic" tavern fare; "moderate prices" and a "convivial" atmosphere seal the deal for "locals and tourists alike."

NEW Copper Chimney ● *Indian* — ▽ 25 | 17 | 24 | $34

Sunny Isles Beach | RK Plaza | 18090 Collins Ave. (182nd St.) | 305-974-0075 | www.copper-chimney.com

What a "pleasant surprise" say surveyors who rate the "flavorful, well-prepared" Northern Indian cuisine at this new midpriced Sunny Isles spot on par with its counterparts in "London"; also currying favor are the upscale orange-and-gold-hued digs with a full bar and "warm owners" who make diners "feel at home."

NEW Crazy About You ● *Eclectic* — 21 | 27 | 22 | $35

Brickell Area | The Mark Bldg. | 1155 Brickell Bay Dr. (bet. SE 11th & 12th Sts.) | Miami | 305-377-4442 | www.crazyaboutyourestaurant.com

Miamians are going 'crazy' for the "stunning" bay views from the terrace at this "super-classy" "waterside" cousin of Dolores But You Can Call Me Lolita; adding to its appeal are "interesting" Eclectic eats and "affordable" tabs, though its location in a Brickell condo is "not the easiest to find."

FOOD | DECOR | SERVICE | COST

NEW Crumb on Parchment ⊠ *American*   –|–|–|I

Design District | 3930 NE Second Ave. (40th St.) | Miami | 305-572-9444

"Food goddess" Michelle Bernstein (Michy's, Sra. Martinez) has done it again with her latest venture, a "casual" American cafe in the Design District serving "creative and delicious" soups, salads, sammies and baked goods at affordable prices; occupying the airy atrium space of a retail building, it features serve-yourself coffee, free WiFi for laptoppers and lots of natural light.

NEW Daddy's Soul Food *Soul Food*   –|–|–|M

South Beach | 637 Washington Avenue (bet. 6th & 7th Sts.) | Miami Beach | 305-532-9885 | www.daddysmiami.com

South Beach may not be the first neighborhood people think of for soul food, but this new go-to joint is changing that with its fried-chicken, collard greens and cornbread served in a down-home setting right in the middle of the action; given the rents in this zip code, it's no wonder prices might seem high for the genre, but that doesn't keep folks from gathering in the popular bar.

Daily Bread Pinecrest *Mideastern*   24|11|21|$16

Pinecrest | 12131 S. Dixie Hwy. (SW 121st St.) | 305-253-6115 | www.dailybread2.com

This Pinecrest Middle Eastern is "excellent for what it is": a counter-serve operation attached to a grocery selling imported staples; the food is "incredibly tasty", "fresh" and "cheap", and it's run by "nice folks" who recently expanded the retail section and seating area and bumped up the menu's offerings.

Da Leo Trattoria ● *Italian*   18|16|19|$42

South Beach | 819 Lincoln Rd. (bet. Jefferson & Meridian Aves.) | Miami Beach | 305-674-0350 | www.daleotrattoria.com

"Reliable" Italian fare in "plentiful portions", "unobtrusive" service and relatively modest prices combine at this stalwart with a "convenient location" in the "midst of bustling Lincoln Road"; but its main selling point is "pleasant" outdoor seating where diners can "gape at the SoBe crowds."

NEW Damn Good Burger *Burgers*   –|–|–|I

Downtown | 20 Biscayne Blvd. (E. Flagler St.) | Miami | 305-718-6565 | www.dgbmiami.com

No question what this splashy Downtown entry is all about: all-natural Angus beef patties that can be customized with anything from avocado to sweet-chili mayo (dogs, sammies, wings and fries are customizable too); the sleek interior – with its hardwood floor, towering ceiling and giant floor-to-ceiling windows framed by vivid red curtains – feels more white tablecloth than blue collar, but the modest tabs please every budget.

David's Cafe ● *Cuban*   19|13|17|$21

South Beach | 1058 Collins Ave. (bet. 10th & 11th Sts.) | Miami Beach | 305-534-8736

(continued)

(continued)

David's Cafe

South Beach | 1654 Meridian Ave. (Lincoln Ln.) | Miami Beach |
305-672-8707
www.davidscafe.com

Locals gravitate to this pair of 24/7 SoBe cafes for zippy "cafe con leche" and "hearty", "true-to-the-culture" Cuban fare at "bargain prices", especially at the "self-service lunch buffet"; there's a "warm family feel" by day, while club-goers in need of "alcohol-soaking-up meals" show up in the wee hours.

❶❸❹ DB Bistro Moderne *French*   26 | 25 | 25 | $76

Downtown | JW Marriott Marquis Miami | 255 Biscayne Blvd. Way
(bet. SE 2nd & 3rd Aves.) | Miami | 305-421-8800 | www.danielnyc.com

Proof positive that NYC's Daniel Boulud is a "genuine food god" is the "perfectly prepared" French fare at this "chic" yearling in Downtown Miami's JW Marriott Marquis; service is "attentive" and the "airy" Yabu Pushelberg–designed trifecta of dining room, lounge and outdoor terrace is "beautiful", so if you "can handle the tab", "what's not to like?"; P.S. "burger fanatics" shouldn't miss the $32 sirloin, foie gras and truffle burger.

Deli Lane Café & Tavern *Deli*   17 | 13 | 16 | $22

Brickell Area | 1401 Brickell Ave. (SE 14th St.) | Miami | 305-377-8811
South Miami | 7230 SW 59th Ave. (72nd St.) | 305-665-0606
www.delilane.com

"Breakfast staples", sandwiches and "good strong cups of coffee" are the "basics" on tap at this "campus-area standard" in South Miami (with a smaller branch in Brickell); the place "needs to be re-done" and service is just "adequate", but fans are happy to scarf down "cheap" eats at the "mostly outdoor" tables.

Democratic Republic of Beer ● *Eclectic*   – | – | – | M

Downtown | 255 NE 14th St. (Biscayne Blvd.) | Miami | 305-372-4161 |
www.drbmiami.com

"All those beers, not enough time" murmur hipster hops-hounds who wish they could sample all 500 international brews at this pint-sized suds house where the "hot chicks behind the bar" are "generally knowledgeable" if not outright "geeks"; the surprisingly ambitious Eclectic food's "good too" (and affordable), while late-night hours and proximity to the Arsht Center make it a logical "after show hang."

❶❸❹ De Rodriguez   21 | 20 | 18 | $53
Cuba on Ocean *Cuban/Nuevo Latino*

South Beach | Hilton Bentley Miami/South Beach | 101 Ocean Dr.
(1st St.) | Miami Beach | 305-672-6624 | www.drodriguezcuba.com

After a stutter start in late 2010 as De Rodriguez Ocean (a high-end seafood concept), this entry in SoBe's Hilton Bentley switched to mostly "upscale Cuban" when Nuevo Latin maestro Douglas Rodriguez moved his Astor Hotel operation here, resulting in the combined name; it now offers the best of both menus, including "amazing" ceviche plus items from a 25-ft.-long raw bar, and if the "friendly but disorganized" staff is still ironing out the kinks, there's "pretty" poolside seating for distraction.

NEW Dim Ssäm à Gogo *Asian*  - | - | - | I
Location varies; see website | Miami | 305-576-8096 |
www.sakayakitchen.com
A kind of roving ambassador for its brick-and-mortar parent, Downtown Miami's popular Sakaya Kitchen, this truck emblazoned with the motto 'munch and move on!' takes Asian dim sum to a whole new level; Kurobuta pork belly buns and 'KFC' (Korean Fried Chicken) wings are just a few of the items available for just a few bucks.

NEW Dining Room ◑ *Eclectic* - | - | - | E
South Beach | 413 Washington Ave. (bet. 4th & 5th Sts.) | Miami Beach | 305-397-8444 | www.diningroommiami.com
With its single chandelier, flickering candlelight and framed family photos, this handsome South Beach nook really does feel as intimate as someone's dining room – if that someone had seating for two dozen guests and executive chef Horacio Rivadero (also of OLA) turning out a pricey Eclectic menu of small plates made with sustainable, locally sourced ingredients; there's a small patio for alfresco meals.

Disco Fish *Seafood/Spanish* 19 | 10 | 16 | $18
West Miami | 1540 SW 67th Ave. (16th St.) | 305-266-7323
There's "nothing fancy" at this drop-ceilinged "mom-n-pop seafood stop" in West Miami, just "fresh" fish prepared à la España; there's "not much English spoken" either, but the "reasonable prices" are right, especially for the "lunch specials."

Dogma Grill *Hot Dogs* 20 | 9 | 17 | $12
Upper East Side | 7030 Biscayne Blvd. (bet. NE 70th & 71st Sts.) | Miami | 305-759-3433 | www.dogmagrill.com
"Classic and innovative" wieners (and burgers and "corndogs too!") with "all the extras" "hit the spot" at this "quick", cheap take-out window on the Upper East Side; frankenfans fret about the patio seating a few feet from a busy intersection, saying you practically have to "eat on the street", but they admit "the flavors are worth putting up with" any inconveniences.

Dolores But You Can Call Me Lolita ◑ *Eclectic* 19 | 23 | 20 | $37
Brickell Area | 1000 S. Miami Ave. (SW 10th St.) | Miami | 305-403-3103 | www.doloreslolita.com
The "strange name" reflects the dual nature of this Brickell "winner" set in a 1923-vintage firehouse: Dolores, upstairs, serves "creative" Eclectic plates at "down-to-earth" prices in "beautiful", mod environs including a "romantic" rooftop terrace; Lolita, her loungey sis downstairs, has a more limited menu and dancing to DJs Thursdays–Saturdays to help "burn off the calories"; up or down, it's always packed with a "young", "dressed-to-kill" crowd.

	FOOD	DECOR	SERVICE	COST

Doraku *Japanese* | 23 | 20 | 19 | $40
South Beach | 1104 Lincoln Rd. (Lenox Ave.) | Miami Beach |
305-695-8383 | www.sushidoraku.com

Even if this "hip" sushi joint with "inventive rolls" "doesn't cost an
arm and a leg like other SoBe places", the kicking DJ "music tells you
where you are": at "the heart of 'the Road'" (Lincoln, that is); insiders advise "take advantage" of the "amazing happy hour" deals (5–
7 PM daily) that extend beyond drink specials to some food items.

Dynamo Café *Eclectic* | - | - | - | I
South Beach | Wolfsonian Museum | 1001 Washington Ave. (10th St.) |
Miami Beach | 305-535-1457 | www.wolfsonian.org

"Hidden away" inside FIU's Wolfsonian, this inexpensive Eclectic
cafe makes a fine museum "pit stop" even if it's "not worth a special
visit"; the "Vienna, 1930" decor includes an antique library shelving
system with volumes of banned books, making it "as close to culture
as you're going to get in South Beach"; P.S. closed Wednesdays.

NEW Eden ● *Eclectic* | ∇ 21 | 21 | 22 | $51
South Beach | 210 23rd St. (Collins Ave.) | Miami Beach | 305-397-8760 |
www.edensouthbeach.com

Chef Christopher Lee (ex NYC's Aureole) has created an Eclectic as-
semblage of "imaginative", pricey dishes marked by "fabulous presentations" for his new SoBe bistro in the former Talula space; the
setting includes a wine bar and comfy banquettes overlooking a
"beautiful", "verdant" garden that lives up to the restaurant's name.

NEW Egg & Dart *Greek/Mediterranean* | - | - | - | E
Design District | 4029 N. Miami Ave. (41st St.) | Miami | 786-431-1022 |
www.egganddartmiami.com

This sleek, chic Greek has a cool urban vibe and high-style decor –
concrete floors, white walls and furnishings – that befits the Design
District's aesthetics; proprietors Costa Grillas and Niko Theodorou
both come from restaurant families, with Theodorou's mom adding
her tweaks to rustic Hellenic staples that come at citified prices.

8 Oz. Burger Bar ● *Burgers* | 20 | 15 | 16 | $23
South Beach | 1080 Alton Rd. (11th St.) | Miami Beach | 305-397-8246 |
www.8ozburgerbarmiami.com

Govind Armstrong's late-night SoBe patty place pleases fans with its
"first-class designer burgers" customizable with "every gourmet top-
ping imaginable" ("try the foie gras"); ok, it's kind of "divey", the
"better-looking-than-you" staff can be "slow" and most "wish it were
cheaper", but with "plenty of TVs" and a "low-key" feel it's a decent
"sports bar" and the craft-beer "selection itself is reason to visit."

El Carajo International | 22 | 18 | 21 | $29
Tapas & Wines *Spanish*
Coral Way | 2465 SW 17th Ave. (bet. S. Dixie Hwy. & 24th Terr.) | Miami |
305-856-2424 | www.elcarajointernationaltapasandwines.com

"Walking through the minimart is part of the fun" at this "relatively
inexpensive" Spanish tapas bar/wine shop housed in a working gas

station in Coral Way; the food is "authentic", the "impressive" wines are sold at a "discount" and, despite the venue, the decor is quaint enough that you could be in a "Madrid taperia."

El Chalán *Peruvian*   23 | 9 | 16 | $25

South Beach | 1580 Washington Ave. (bet. 15th & 16th Sts.) | Miami Beach | 305-532-8880
Westchester | 7971 Bird Rd. (79th Ave.) | Miami | 305-266-0212
Take a "flavorful foray" into Peruvian cuisine via the "wide variety" of "down-home" staples available at these "inexpensive" SoBe and Westchester holes-in-the-wall; no, they're "not the prettiest" places around, but takeout is available and the staffers are "pleasant" (though "if you don't speak Spanish, good luck").

11th St. Diner ● *Diner*   20 | 16 | 19 | $22

South Beach | 1065 Washington Ave. (11th St.) | Miami Beach | 305-534-6373 | www.eleventhstreetdiner.com
This "classic" midcentury "railroad-style dining car" staffed by an "efficient" crew has long been a "favorite" for all-day breakfasts and other "basic" chow at "prices that are great for South Beach"; a few shrug "nothing special", but clubgoers say it's "fabulous" late at night "after partying" – and the party can continue "as they serve alcohol"; P.S. it's open 24/7 except in summer when it closes around midnight.

El Gran Inka *Peruvian*   21 | 19 | 19 | $37

Brickell Area | The Plaza | 947 Brickell Ave. (SE 10th St.) | Miami | 786-220-7930
Key Biscayne | Winn-Dixie Shopping Plaza | 606 Crandon Blvd. (Sunrise Dr.) | 305-365-7883
Aventura | 3155 NE 163rd St. (Interama Blvd.) | 305-940-4910
www.graninka.com
This mini-chain is a "solid option" for a "large variety of ceviche" and other Peruvian favorites that are "always on the mark"; libations include "pisco sours", "reasonably priced" wines and for "fans of Inca Kola" they even have "diet!"; P.S. the Aventura and Brickell branches get extra shout-outs for "nice decor."

El Mago de las Fritas 🗷 *Cuban*   - | - | - | I

Little Havana | 5828 SW 8th St. (bet. 58th Ct. & 59th Ave.) | Miami | 305-266-8486 | www.elmagodelasfritas.com
The magician ('*el mago*') of *fritas* – Cuban burgers made of ground beef/chorizo and topped with potato sticks – has been at it for a quarter century at this Little Havana joint where everyone from locals to President Obama has bellied up to the fake-wood counter; prices are as no-frills as the setting.

El Novillo *Nicaraguan/Steak*   22 | 20 | 23 | $33

Coral Terrace | Ludlum Shopping Ctr. | 6830 Bird Rd. (68th Ave.) | Miami | 305-284-8417
Miami Lakes | 15450 New Barn Rd. (67th Ave.) | 305-819-2755
www.elnovillorestaurant.com
"If you have a crowd to feed", these "meat-dominated" Nicaraguan haciendas in Coral Terrace and Miami Lakes are "the place for

FOOD | DECOR | SERVICE | COST

churrasco" and other "filling", "savory" fare; "service with a smile" and "reasonable" tabs ('executive' lunch specials start at $8) are additional seling points.

El Rancho Grande *Mexican*

19 | 17 | 19 | $27

Miami Beach | 314 72nd St. (bet. Abbott & Collins Aves.) | 305-864-7404
South Beach | 1626 Pennsylvania Ave. (Lincoln Rd.) | Miami Beach | 305-673-0480 ☽
Kendall | 12881 N. Kendall Dr. (SW 127th Ave.) | 305-382-9598
www.elranchograndemexicanrestaurant.com

"Hefty portions" of "tasty", "reliable" Mexican fare are served by "actually friendly people" at this Miami-area trio; add to the equation "strong" margs plus "beer in oversized glasses" and it equals a "fun" time that won't subtract many pesos from your wallet.

El Toro Taco ⓜ *Mexican*

23 | 11 | 18 | $18

Homestead | 1 S. Krome Ave. (W. Mowry Dr.) | 305-245-8182
It's "worth a drive to Homestead" for "mouthwatering" Mexican that "doesn't get more authentic" than at this "unpretentious" little spot; not only is it "cheap" but the "hard-working" family that has run it for "sooo many years" is extremely "caring", and it shows; P.S. it's BYO.

ⓩ Enriqueta's Sandwich Shop ⓩ *Cuban/Sandwiches*

24 | 8 | 19 | $12

Wynwood | 186 NE 29th St. (2nd Ave.) | Miami | 305-573-4681
"Business is always booming" at this decades-old Wynwood breakfast/lunchroom thanks to Cuban sandwiches considered "among Miami's best" plus other cheap eats that "beat fast food any day" (indeed, it's voted Miami's No. 1 Bang for the Buck); the "packed parking lot" and "nothing-fancy" digs don't deter the "masses", in part because there's a grab-and-go window.

Eos *Mediterranean*

21 | 22 | 18 | $58

Brickell Area | The Viceroy Hotel | 485 Brickell Ave., 15th Fl. (SE 5th St.) | Miami | 305-503-4400 | www.viceroymiami.com
On the 15th floor of the "fabulously over-the-top" Viceroy Hotel in Brickell, "high-end" Mediterranean plates "with a twist" are offered in a "date"-worthy (some say "gaudy") setting; despite the pre-Survey departure of the original team (NYC's power duo Michael Psilakis and Donatella Arpaia) and service kinks, admirers still see "much potential" here.

Escopazzo ☽ⓜ *Italian*

25 | 19 | 24 | $62

South Beach | 1311 Washington Ave. (bet. 13th & 14th Sts.) | Miami Beach | 305-674-9450 | www.escopazzo.com
SoBe "insiders", "locavores" and "gourmets" know that this "nondescript storefront" on "busy" Washington Avenue houses a "hidden jewel", where chef-owner Giancarla Bodoni "does wonders" with the "fresh, organic ingredients" that go into "one-of-a-kind" Italian creations; her "love and creativity justify high prices", so consider the "über-friendly" service, "quiet", "low-key" vibe and large wine selection pure gravy.

	FOOD	DECOR	SERVICE	COST

Essensia *American* ▽ 21 | 26 | 19 | $69

Miami Beach | The Palms Hotel & Spa | 3025 Collins Ave.
(Indian Creek Dr.) | 305-534-0505 | www.thepalmshotel.com
"Peace of mind" is served up along with "imaginative", health-
conscious New Americana fare (organic, low-cal) and wine (biody-
namic, sustainable) at this restaurant with a "gorgeous setting" in
Miami Beach's Palms Hotel & Spa; expensive tabs don't mar the "romantic" mood, especially on the "wonderful" expansive terrace.

NEW Fadó Irish Pub & 17 | 21 | 19 | $27
Restaurant ● *Pub Food*

Brickell Area | Mary Brickell Vill. | 900 S. Miami Ave. (bet. SW 9th &
10th Sts.) | Miami | 786-924-0972 | www.fadoirishpub.com
They pull a fine pint ("best Guinness stateside") at this "upscale"
Gaelic pub chain link in Brickell that "feels like the real thing" in
each of its themed sections: old-timey tavern, grand Victorian hall,
etc.; the standard pub grub is "solid" and if some find "only a hint
of Irishness" on the plate, it's hard to knock the moderate tabs;
P.S. entertainment includes TV sports, Tuesday quiz nights and
DJs/bands Thursdays–Saturdays.

NEW 1500 Degrees *American/Steak* 24 | 22 | 20 | $71

Miami Beach | Eden Roc Renaissance | 4525 Collins Ave. (W. 41st St.) |
305-674-5594 | www.1500degreesmiami.com
Set in Miami Beach's storied Eden Roc Hotel, this "classy" newcomer is named for the temperature at which chef Paula DaSilva
(*Hell's Kitchen* finalist and 3030 Ocean alum) cooks "juicy", "melt-
in-your-mouth" steaks, a "specialty" on the "creative" New American
menu; it's expensive and service is "erratic", but diners appreciate
being able to "speak without shouting" in the "pretty" dining room
or on the "breezy" patio.

5300 Chop House *Steak* 24 | 23 | 22 | $64

Doral | The Blue | 5300 NW 87th Ave. (53rd St.) | Miami | 305-597-8600
Golfers and carnivores alike give a "thumbs-up" to the "excellent"
steaks and "fish cooked to perfection" at this chophouse that par-
tially overlooks the PGA championship course at Hyatt's Blue resort
in Doral; "attentive" service, a modern wood-and-marble setting
and a bar/lounge area help soften the expensive tabs.

Filling Station ⊠ *Burgers* ▽ 17 | 13 | 17 | $18

Downtown | 95 SE 2nd St. (bet. 1st & 2nd Aves.) | Miami |
786-425-1990 | www.thefillingstationmiami.com
After a long hiatus, this "friendly" "local burger joint" and bar reap-
peared Downtown in new bi-level digs, and fans ask with "plenty of
TVs", "beer" and "tater tots", "what's not to love?"; still, dissenters
say the concept's "cute" (the 'sedanwiches' have names like
Hamborghini and Porschebello) but the chow's "average."

Z Five Guys *Burgers* 20 | 10 | 16 | $13
Coral Gables | 1540 S. Dixie Hwy. (Yumuri St.) | 305-740-5972
(continued)

(continued)

Five Guys

Miami Beach | Shops at Midtown Miami | 3401 N. Miami Ave. (NE 36th St.) | 305-571-8345
South Beach | 1500 Washington Ave. (15th St.) | Miami Beach | 305-538-3807
Kendall | Kendall Vill. | 10471 SW 88th St. (107th Ave.) | Miami | 305-270-4990
Kendall | London Sq. | 13440 SW 120th St. (135th Ct.) | Miami | 786-573-9623
Pinecrest | 9457 S. Dixie Hwy. (Rte. 826) | 305-669-2115
www.fiveguys.com

"Delicious" "greasy" burgers "cooked to order" with "lots of free toppings", "sinful" fries "fresh cut from whole potatoes" and "complimentary peanuts" while you wait are the simple pleasures at these "bare-bones" "fast-food" chain links; some may ask "what's the fuss?", but they've got "Obama" cred and are "cheap" to boot.

NEW 5 Napkin Burger ● *Burgers*   — | — | — | M

South Beach | 455 Lincoln Rd. (Drexel Ave.) | Miami Beach | 305-538-2277 | www.5napkinburger.com

You may need more than five napkins to wipe up after exploring the burgers-n-more menu at this yupscale SoBe outpost of the NYC-bred chain; alongside the signature 10-oz. patty are sushi, matzo ball soup, fish tacos and more, all served in a setting with comfy red-and-black leather booths, subway-tile walls, industrial-chic lighting and walls of windows affording good Lincoln Road people-watching.

Flanigan's Seafood Bar & Grill ● *American*   19 | 15 | 19 | $24

Coconut Grove | 2721 Bird Rd. (SW 27th Ave.) | 305-446-1114 | www.flanigans.net

"Fall-off-the-bone" babyback ribs are the specialty at this chain link in Coconut Grove that's "been in business forever", no doubt thanks to its "mountainous portions" of "inexpensive" American standards; it's "rugrat"-friendly, has "blaring TVs" at "game time" and serves as a come-down spot for late-night partyers, so "earplugs" are a good idea.

Fleming's Prime Steakhouse & Wine Bar *Steak*   25 | 24 | 25 | $59

Coral Gables | 2525 Ponce de Leon Blvd. (Andalusia Ave.) | 305-569-7995 | www.flemingssteakhouse.com

Funny, it "doesn't *feel* like a chain steakhouse" muse patrons of these franchise links in Coral Gables and Naples – maybe it's the "succulent" steaks, or the "extensive wine selection" or the "comfortable, clubby" environs with "excellent" service; penny-pinchers say the "bar, burger and happy-hour menus" are the best bargains.

NEW Flip Burger Bar Ⓜ *Burgers*   ▽ 25 | 18 | 23 | $20

North Miami | 1699 NE 123rd St. (Biscayne Blvd.) | 305-891-0055 | www.flip-burgerbar.com

North Miamians enamored of the "outstanding" "juicy" patties and "toasted goodness" of the brioche buns at this "friendly" plain-Jane joint claim it's a "real competitor to the South Beach burger scene"; it scores extra points for a 50-plus beer list, low tabs and free parking.

Fogo de Chão *Brazilian/Steak*   23 | 21 | 23 | $60

South Beach | 836 First St. (bet. Alton Rd. & Meridian Aves.) | Miami Beach | 305-672-0011 | www.fogodechao.com

"Carnivores rejoice" over "mucho meat" (and "salad lovers" are equally "excited" by the "huge, diverse" buffet-table offerings) at this handsome SoBe link of the Brazilian rodizio chain; the staff is "always smiling and available" to help folks "gorge", so for "big eaters, it's well worth the price."

Fontana *Italian*   ▽ 26 | 27 | 25 | $65

Coral Gables | Biltmore Hotel | 1200 Anastasia Ave. (Columbus Blvd.) | 305-445-1926 | www.biltmorehotel.com

Coral Gables' historic Biltmore "shows that it's more than just a great hotel" via this Italian offering "impeccable" cuisine served "without pretentiousness" in "beautiful" surroundings; lovebirds say the "gorgeous" courtyard with its central fountain is a "world"-class "romantic" setting, so all in all it's "worth every dime" for a "special night out."

Forge Restaurant & Wine Bar *American*   24 | 26 | 24 | $78

Miami Beach | 432 41st St. (Sheridan Ave.) | 305-538-8533 | www.theforge.com

The recent "reinvention" of this Miami Beach "landmark" included an "over-the-top", "Alice in Wonderland"–esque "makeover" of its many "special rooms" and an updated New American menu bearing the "magic touch" of chef Dewey LoSasso; yet it also "stayed true to its roots" as a playground for "celebrities" and other "monied" types and still boasts a "museumlike wine cellar", so while a few holdouts miss "the old place", boosters find it "better than ever" – "bravo!"

NEW Forno 52 Ⓜ *Pizza*   – | – | – | M

Palmetto Bay | 17225 S. Dixie Hwy. (SW 95th Ave.) | 305-259-7676 | www.forno52.com

Don't plan to order a slice, extra cheese or crazy toppings at this minimalist-modern Palmetto Bay pizza parlor, the brick-and-mortar incarnation of a former truck; its Verace Pizza Napoletana certification means strict adherence to simple, traditional deliciousness: expect dough fermented for 30 hours, mozzarella made daily, hand-crushed San Marzano tomatoes and fresh herbs, all fired in an approved wood-burning oven.

☑ Francesco Ⓢ *Peruvian*   26 | 17 | 23 | $55

Coral Gables | 325 Alcazar Ave. (bet. Salzedo St. & SW 42nd Ave.) | 305-446-1600 | www.francescorestaurantmiami.com

According to fans, the "best ceviche in Miami" is to be found at this "first-rate" Peruvian in Coral Gables dishing up "expensive" but "consistently amazing" seafood and other dishes, some "authentic", others with Italian touches; the small space gets "tightly packed" and the "decor could use a refresh", but the "owner is always on-site and it shows" in the overall "welcoming" vibe.

	FOOD	DECOR	SERVICE	COST

ⓩ Frankie's Pizza Ⓜ 🖙 *Pizza* | 26 | 7 | 20 | $14 |

Westchester | 9118 Bird Rd. (92nd Ave.) | Miami | 305-221-0221 | www.frankiespizzaonline.com

Since the 1950s, the Pasquarella family has been slinging square (read: "not your standard") pies at this cheap, cash-only pizza joint in Westchester, and folks who've "been going since they were little runts" insist "that should tell you" it's "worth" it; there's a "few picnic tables" in back, but it's "primarily a take-out" spot – indeed, they ship 'half-baked' pies anywhere in the country.

Fratelli La Bufala ● *Italian* | 22 | 15 | 17 | $33 |

South Beach | 437 Washington Ave. (bet. 4th & 5th Sts.) | Miami Beach | 305-532-0700 | www.fratellilabufala.com

This SoBe outpost of a "truly Neapolitan" pizza-and-pasta chain turns out "chewy, deliciously airy" pies topped with "amazing" mozzarella di bufala (buffalo cheese and meat figure in many other dishes also); "too bad the place is so fast-food casual" and has rather "pedestrian service", but "nominal" tabs erase most complaints.

Fratelli Lyon *Italian* | 22 | 21 | 20 | $49 |

Design District | Driade | 4141 NE Second Ave. (bet. 41st & 42nd Sts.) | Miami | 305-572-2901 | www.fratellilyon.com

Style and substance unite at this Design District Italian in the Driade furniture showroom, where a "hip crowd" enjoys "light", "sophisticated" cuisine in a "bright and open" space with "cool" "industrial-modern" decor; tabs that are "pretty pricey" to some strike others as "fair", but either way you may be tempted to "take home all the tableware."

Fritz & Franz Bierhaus *German* | 17 | 19 | 19 | $27 |

Coral Gables | 60 Merrick Way (bet. Aragon & Giralda Aves.) | 305-774-1883 | www.bierhaus.cc

A "German biergarten with palm trees?" – folks sitting at the "long wooden tables" at this "fun" Gables place raise their "steins" to "something rare in South Florida"; it's more sports bar than food hall, but it's the only game in town for those with a "hankering for sauerbraten", "schnitzel" *und* so forth for not many marks; P.S. the Ft. Lauderdale location opened post-Survey.

Front Porch Cafe ● *American* | 21 | 17 | 18 | $26 |

South Beach | Z Ocean Hotel | 1458 Ocean Dr. (15th St.) | Miami Beach | 305-531-8300 | www.frontporchoceandrive.com

The waits aren't as long now that this "friendly" "all-day" breakfast place has resettled in a "bigger", "sleeker" porch-equipped space a block up the street in SoBe's Z Ocean Hotel (though some diners "miss the ocean view" from the former locale); the "lumberjack"-sized portions of "diner-type" American comfort fare remain "consistently" "reliable" and, better yet, "reasonably priced."

Fuji Hana *Japanese/Thai* | 22 | 15 | 19 | $30 |

Aventura | Loehmann's Plaza | 2775 NE 187th St. (Biscayne Blvd.) | 305-932-8080

(continued)

Fuji Hana

Kendall | 11768 N. Kendall Dr. (117th Ave.) | 305-275-9003 |
www.fujihanakendall.com

"Hidden" in Aventura and Kendall malls, this duo offers a "huge"
"non-fusiony" menu of Thai and Japanese standards, including
"fresh", "simple" sushi rolls; "attentive" service and "affordability"
win out over "decor that could use an upgrade"; P.S. the outdoor
area at 187th Street is "dog-friendly."

Gables Diner *Diner*

| 17 | 13 | 17 | $25 |

Coral Gables | 2320 Galiano St. (Aragon Ave.) | 305-567-0330 |
www.gablesdiner.com

Coral Gables' "blue and white collars rub shoulders" at this joint that
perhaps looks a tad "worn" but dishes up "big portions" of "solid
American comfort food" from a menu with "lots of choices"; still, some
say it falls "a bit short of what it would like to be – a NY-style diner" –
as it's "a little on the expensive side" and lacks "late-night" hours.

Garcia's *Seafood*

| 23 | 16 | 19 | $33 |

Miami River | 398 NW North River Dr. (4th St.) | Miami | 305-375-0765

"Authentic with a capital A", this "old-school" "Miami experience" is
always "full of local" yokels "kicking back with cold beer" and some of
the "freshest seafood" around; there are "no frills", but tabs are moderate and its Miami River location means the "slow-moving riverboat
traffic" can be enjoyed from the patio; P.S. there's an on-site market.

GastroPod ⊠⇗ *Eclectic*

| - | - | - | I |

Location varies; see website | Miami | no phone |
www.gastropodmiami.com

Considered the first of the new generation of Miami food trucks, this
gleaming silver 1962 Airstream from chef Jeremiah 'Bullfrog' is a
distinctive presence at area food-truck rallies (it roves all over
Miami so check online for daily whereabouts); a résumé that includes a stint at Spain's famed El Bulli informs an Eclectic menu of
creative dishes like short-rib sliders, red-curry duck tacos and
bacon-infused cream soda; P.S. cash only.

George's in the Grove *French/Mediterranean*

| 22 | 19 | 21 | $40 |

Coconut Grove | 3145 Commodore Plaza (Main Hwy.) | 305-444-7878 |
www.georgesinthegrove.com

George Farge may have moved on from his "groovy Grove" namesake, but the "lively, loud" festivities remain in full swing, abetted by
"complimentary" champagne and "disco lights" flashing whenever a
"sparkler"-topped birthday cake is presented; flash aside, the
kitchen takes its "tasty" French bistro fare "seriously", the staff is
"attentive" and the whole package is "reasonably priced."

George's on Sunset *French/Mediterranean*

| 20 | 20 | 20 | $41 |

South Miami | 1549 Sunset Dr. (56th Ave.) | 305-284-9989 |
www.georgesrestaurants.com

"King" George (Farge) reigns over this "festive" bistro with a "hot"
bar in South Miami, greeting each subject with "a complimentary

glass" of bubbly to kick off meals featuring "authentic", if rather "pricey", French fare; a note to the "happening" throng that jams the "close quarters": "be sure to mention" whatever you might be celebrating to the "warm" staff so you can be feted with "loud music and a light show."

George's Restaurant & Lounge ● *Italian* ∇ 23 | 19 | 19 | $46

Miami Beach | 300 72nd St. (Harding Ave.) | 305-864-5586 | www.georgesmiamibeach.com

A "mostly high-end" crowd patronizes this "friendly neighborhood" trattoria on a Miami Beach corner serving "steady" Italian favorites; bean-counters appreciate that being just "10 minutes outside of SoBe" means "prices drop" – and there's "easy parking" to boot.

Gibraltar *American* ∇ 20 | 27 | 18 | $61

Coconut Grove | Grove Isle Hotel & Spa | 4 Grove Isle Dr. (off S. Bayshore Dr.) | 305-857-5007 | www.groveisle.com

"Amazing views" of Biscayne Bay from an "unbeatable" waterside location are the rock upon which all else is based at this upscale New American in the Grove Isle Hotel; the patio, "nestled in tropical gardens", is equally "romantic", but critics crab it's "overpriced" given less-than-stellar service and comparatively "average" fare.

NEW Gigi ● *Asian* 24 | 18 | 19 | $33

Wynwood | 3470 N. Miami Ave. (NW 35th St.) | Miami | 305-573-1520 | www.giginow.com

The "local hipsterati" refuel on "heavenly" buns, noodles and other snacks at this "modern", "dinerlike" Asian fusion arrival in Wynwood "after partying" next door at Bardot or elsewhere, giving it a "major heartbeat" (and "noise level") "into the wee" hours; don't fret about the "no-reservations" policy because "tables turn quickly", including spots on the "ample patio" or at the counter with views of the open kitchen's "ballet"; P.S. beer and wine only.

Globe Cafe & Bar ●☒ *Eclectic* ∇ 17 | 17 | 18 | $34

Coral Gables | 377 Alhambra Circle (SW 42nd Ave.) | 305-445-3555 | www.theglobecafe.com

"They pour a good drink" at this "quaint, little" European-looking boîte in Coral Gables with a "big happy hour" that draws "young" "local businesspeople" and "singles" (it also sizzles with live jazz on Saturday nights); even though the midpriced Eclectic eats are secondary to the bar scene and entertainment, for a "late-night" bite, it works.

Gordon Biersch ● *American* 18 | 18 | 19 | $28

Brickell Area | 1201 Brickell Ave. (12th St.) | Miami | 786-425-1130 | www.gordonbiersch.com

As an "after-work" hang, this chain microbrewery/"sports bar" is a no-brainer thanks to its Brickell location, "great brews" and "excellent happy hour", and it also works for a "quick" "business lunch", with "attentive" service and an American menu that suits "different budgets"; still, those who find the eats "dull" may need the spark that "live music" provides (Thursdays and Fridays).

	FOOD	DECOR	SERVICE	COST

Gotham Steak *Steak*
23 | 25 | 23 | $82

Miami Beach | Fontainebleau Miami Beach | 4441 Collins Ave. (W. 44th St.) | 305-674-4780 | www.fontainebleau.com

A "beautiful setting" featuring a dramatic showcase kitchen and bi-level glassed-in wine tower overseen by a "great steward" is a clue that this "chichi" meatery from Alfred Portale (NYC's Gotham Bar & Grill) in the Fontainebleau Miami Beach is "not your typical steakhouse"; another is the menu's "interesting" tweaks on traditional favorites, though what is fairly common for the genre are the "mortgage payment" prices.

Gourmet Diner *French*
∇ 18 | 9 | 19 | $35
(aka Hanna's Gourmet Diner)

North Miami Beach | 13951 Biscayne Blvd. (140th St.) | 305-947-2255

This old-fashioned chrome diner has been on Biscayne Boulevard seemingly "forever", offering "quite a large menu" of decidedly non-greasy-spoonish yet still "hearty" French bistro fare; service gets mixed marks and dissenters find the eats "ho-hum", but the price is right and daily specials make meals "even more reasonably priced."

Grand Lux Cafe *Eclectic*
19 | 20 | 20 | $31

Aventura | Aventura Mall | 19575 Biscayne Blvd. (NE 195th St.) | 305-932-9113 | www.grandluxcafe.com

These "fancy-schmancy" spin-offs of Cheesecake Factory follow the same basic playbook as their parent: a "varied menu" of "reliable" midpriced Eclectic fare in "oversized portions" bound to please the entire "family"; the "airplane hangar"–sized setups are also similarly "deafening", but the staff is "accommodating" and the showy, "upscale" decor looks "straight out of a Cecil B. DeMille movie."

Graziano's Restaurant *Argentinean/Steak*
25 | 21 | 23 | $47

Brickell Area | 177 SW Seventh St. (bet. 1st & 2nd Aves.) | Miami | 305-860-1426
Coral Gables | 394 Giralda Ave. (42nd Ave.) | 305-774-3599
Hialeah | 5993 W. 16th Ave. (60th St.) | 305-819-7461
Westchester | 9227 SW 40th St. (92nd Ave.) | Miami | 305-225-0008
www.parrilla.com

The "flavor of Argentina comes alive" via "mouthwatering" cuts of meat "as good as they get outside of Buenos Aires" at these "classy" Miami-area *parillas* (grills) whose "quality is worth the price"; they're also appreciated for "amiable" staffers who ably suggest "on-the-money wine pairings" from an "impressive" list of vintages.

Grazie Italian Cuisine *Italian*
25 | 21 | 25 | $57

South Beach | 701 Washington Ave. (7th St.) | Miami Beach | 305-673-1312 | www.grazieitaliancuisine.com

In the midst of South Beach, this "down-to-earth" oasis is refreshingly "not full of tourists" and boasts "delicious", honest Italian fare complemented by wines with relatively "small markups"; "impeccable" service from a "knowledgeable" staff plus an owner who "greets everyone as a dear friend" is also exceptional for the area.

FOOD | DECOR | SERVICE | COST

Green Street Cafe *French/Mediterranean* 19 | 17 | 18 | $29

Coconut Grove | 3110 Commodore Plaza (Main Hwy.) | 305-444-0244 | www.greenstreetcafe.net

"Is there some local ordinance requiring everyone to hang out here?" wonder surveyors who note that this "long-standing Grove hot spot" is always "packed" – chalk it up to "good" (a few say "so-so"), "reasonably priced" French-Med fare enhanced by "people-watching at its finest" from "sidewalk" seating; there's always a "long wait Sunday mornings" for breakfast, but the staff generally "keeps up with the bustling scene."

NEW **Green Table** Ⓩ *American/Vegetarian* - | - | - | I

Coral Gables | 4702 S. Le Jeune Rd. (Greco Ave.) | 786-362-5255 | www.greentablemiami.com

All the current buzzwords – organic, local, sustainable – apply to the "light", "healthy", affordable New American bites, including a large selection of vegetarian dishes, at this little slip of an arrival in Coral Gables; the spare interior is dressed with reclaimed wood and a few vintage tables, and if you want to do takeout the helpful staff suggests picnicking at Merrie Christmas Park, a mile further south on Le Jeune.

Grillfish *Seafood* 20 | 18 | 20 | $50

South Beach | 1444 Collins Ave. (Española Way) | Miami Beach | 305-538-9908 | www.grillfish.com

In the SoBe "sea of fast-buck restaurants", this "non-touristy" seafood "stalwart" swims against the current, offering "solid" fare at "reasonable" rates; a "humble", "accommodating" staff patrols the "old-world" dining room and slings drinks from a "grand bar."

Grill on the Alley *American* 22 | 23 | 23 | $54

Aventura | Aventura Mall | 19501 Biscayne Blvd. (NE 195th St.) | 305-466-7195 | www.thegrill.com

The "delicious" steaks, chops, fish and other "workmanlike" Americana are definitely "not mall food", despite this chain link's location in Aventura's shopping mecca; your wallet may "feel the pain", but the "beautiful" art deco interior and "divine people-/car-watching" from the patio is "worth the money."

Grimpa Steakhouse *Brazilian/Steak* 25 | 23 | 25 | $58

Brickell Area | Mary Brickell Vill. | 901 S. Miami Ave. (SW 10th St.) | Miami | 305-371-5444 | www.grimpa.com

"Gluttony at its best" is how carnivores assess the "endless" helpings of "superb-quality meat" that arrive via "courteous, professional" skewer-handlers at this Brazilian churrascaria in Mary Brickell Village; a "huge salad bar" further helps justify the rather "expensive" tab, just bring "willpower" to "avoid overeating."

Guayacan Restaurant *Nicaraguan* ▽ 21 | 11 | 21 | $26

Little Havana | 1933 SW Eighth St. (19th Ave.) | Miami | 305-649-2015

"If you need to satisfy that Nica fix", check out the "delicious and filling" fare at this "authentic", longtime piece of Little Managua in

FOOD | DECOR | SERVICE | COST

Little Havana; the shabby digs are "nothing to look at" but that doesn't detract from the "great value."

Guru ● *Indian*   ∇ 22 | 14 | 18 | $33

South Beach | 232 12th St. (bet. Collins & Washington Aves.) | Miami Beach | 305-534-3996 | www.gurufood.com

An "extensive" menu of "finely presented" Northern Indian fare comes midpriced at this "tiny" pumpkin-hued South Beacher, where a "helpful" staff provides gurulike guidance; portions are "generous", so "exercise some control" or you'll feel "like a stuffed naan yourself."

Hakan Turkish Grill ● *Turkish*   ∇ 20 | 11 | 19 | $32

South Beach | 1040 Alton Rd. (bet. 10th & 11th Sts.) | Miami Beach | 305-534-9557 | www.hakanturkishgrill.com

Hakan Aksu is the "friendliest owner in town" gush acolytes of the "honest" Turkish "delights" at this "unassuming" storefront hiding one of the "few good values" in SoBe; note that belly dancers wiggle on weekends and the place can be "overrun by noisy fans" during televised soccer matches.

Z Hakkasan *Chinese*   26 | 27 | 24 | $78

Miami Beach | Fontainebleau Miami Beach | 4441 Collins Ave. (W. 44th St.) | 786-276-1388 | www.fontainebleau.com

"Wow, so *this* is Chinese food" declare converts whose "eyes are opened" by the "incredible" modern Cantonese fare at the Miami Beach outpost of the London original hidden in the "sprawling" Fontainebleau; assets include "superior" dim sum (most welcome in a city with a "significant shortage"), generally "knowledgeable" service and "chic" environs that are surprisingly "intimate" given the "big" space – just expect to pay "crazy money" to enjoy it all.

NEW Harrison's Sports Grill *Pub Food*   - | - | - | I

West Miami | 1674 S. Red Rd. (16th St.) | 305-262-5517

The playbook for this rookie sports bar in West Miami reads like this: offer pizzas, pub grub and cold beer in a setting outfitted with lots of green and orange, angry-looking ibises (to please U. of Miami fans), a few pool tables and TVs aplenty for watching 'Canes games; add affordable prices and it could prove a winning strategy.

NEW Harry's Pizzeria ⓢ *Pizza*   - | - | - | M

Design District | 3918 N. Miami Ave. (bet. NE 39th & 40th Sts.) | Miami | 786-275-4963 | www.harryspizzeria.com

Local celeb chef Michael Schwartz (Michael's Genuine) recently debuted this Design District pizzeria, where dough made in-house daily is topped with everything from braised fennel to slow-roasted pork before hitting the wood-fired oven; the midpriced menu also includes other Italian bites (meatballs, polenta fries, biscotti), and the rustic-contemporary space features modern artwork and streetside floor-to-ceiling windows.

Havana Harry's *Cuban*   19 | 16 | 18 | $27

Coral Gables | 4612 Le Jeune Rd. (Ponce de Leon Blvd.) | 305-661-2622
(continued)

(continued)

Havana Harry's

Kendall | 9525 Kendall Dr. (bet. SW 94th & 97th Aves.) | 305-595-1116
www.hharrys.com

"Despite the gringo name" this "friendly" Coral Gables mainstay is "like going to *abuela*'s" for "humongous" portions of "simple" Cuban "comfort food" ("the *vaca frita* rocks!"); the atmosphere is "pleasant" enough, but also like grandma's house, the decor could probably stand some "improvement"; P.S. there's a newer sibling in Kendall.

NEW Haven Gastro-Lounge ❶ *Eclectic* — | — | — | E

South Beach | 1237 Lincoln Rd. (Alton Ct.) | Miami Beach |
305-987-8885 | www.havenlounge.com

Tech-centric scenesters may feel as if they've been downloaded into *Tron* thanks to decor elements like a 100-ft. video wall, a ceiling studded with starlike lights and a white-onyx bar that changes color at this pricey new SoBe Eclectic lounge helmed by chef Todd Erickson (ex Zuma), presenting a roster of organic-focused small plates, sushi and liquid-nitrogen smoking cocktails; at midnight it turns into a full-on nightclub – kiddies need not apply.

NEW Heavy Burger *Burgers* 22 | 14 | 20 | $22

Aventura | 19004 NE 29th Ave. (190th St.) | 305-932-7553 |
www.heavyburger.com

"Awesome" "oversized" burgers with names like Maiden and Motley plus "hand-cut" fries and other monstrous sides are "made with TLC" at this budget-friendly, hard rock–themed "hangout" in Aventura; hecklers with axes to grind say it "looks like a nightclub basement", but maybe that's the point, and besides, loads of TVs make it a "great place to watch games."

Here Comes the Sun ⓈVegetarian 17 | 5 | 16 | $18

North Miami | 2188 NE 123rd St. (bet. N. Bayshore Dr. & Sans Souci Blvd.) |
305-893-5711

"Groovy" proclaim vegetarians and other devotees of the "dependable" "health-conscious" eats (the "famous" 'sun sauce' is "ridiculously good") at this hippie-era eatery and natural-foods market in North Miami; given "inattentive" service and "tired" (to put it mildly) digs, romeos advise "don't take a first date there or it will be your last."

Hillstone *American* — | — | — | M

Coral Gables | 201 Miracle Mile (Ponce de Leon Blvd.) | 305-529-0141 |
www.hillstone.com

Like its close chain cousin, Houston's, this slightly more spiffed-up brand in Coral Gables trades on its rep for delivering quality American comfort food at relatively attractive prices; its big, handsome setting features banquettes, a large bar and a sushi station.

Hiro Japanese ❶ *Japanese* 21 | 13 | 18 | $35

North Miami Beach | 3007 NE 163rd St. (Biscayne Blvd.) |
305-948-3687 | www.hiro163.com

"Young" clubgoers "love the late-night hours" at this North Miami Beach "sober-up" spot sporting a "sizable menu" of "reliable" sushi and other Japanese fare (plus a "full bar" for those who want to keep raging); the neon lights are garish to some (and just serve to illuminate the tatty digs) and service can be a bit "slapdash", but "reasonable" prices keep it "busy."

☑ Hiro's Yakko-San ● *Japanese* | 27 | - | 21 | $31 |

North Miami Beach | Intracoastal Mall | 3881 NE 163rd St. (Sunny Isles Blvd.) | 305-947-0064 | www.yakko-san.com

"Feel like Andrew Zimmern" sampling the "unusual" "izakaya-style" small plates and "inspired" sushi at this "adventurous" strip-center Japanese; a recent move to a "larger" North Miami Beach space outdates the Decor rating (folks say the modern setting, sporting a large sushi bar, is more "fancy" than the old address), but longtime fans are pleased it added lunch while retaining the same dependable service and "low" prices – especially during the late-night happy hour, 11 PM–close.

Hosteria Romana ● *Italian* | 21 | 19 | 19 | $45 |

South Beach | 429 Española Way (bet. Drexel & Washington Aves.) | Miami Beach | 305-532-4299 | www.hosteriaromana.com

Take a "Roman" holiday at this "boisterous" SoBe trattoria serving up "pasta like mama" made and other "solid", "reasonably priced" favorites; but the real "fun" is watching the "gorgeous" "singing waiters" do their thing.

House of India *Indian* | 19 | 15 | 17 | $25 |

Coral Gables | 22 Merrick Way (S. Douglas Rd.) | 305-444-2348 | www.houseofindiamiami.com

This Coral Gables subcontinental "staple" has "withstood the test of time" thanks to its "delicious", "reasonably priced" menu; the decor may be long in the tooth ("the 1980s are calling"), but the "awesome" lunch buffet is "particularly well handled" and a "bargain" at $11.95.

☑ Houston's *American* | 23 | 21 | 22 | $39 |

North Miami Beach | 17355 Biscayne Blvd. (NE 172nd St.) | 305-947-2000 | www.hillstone.com

Even folks who "usually avoid chains" can't help but admit that these "corporate" spots "never disappoint" with their "consistently excellent" American classics at prices that, while "not cheap, won't break the bank"; also working in their favor: "comfortable", rather masculine "upscale-casual" settings and a level of "attentiveness rarely found in these parts"; P.S. Pompano Beach boasts "beautiful" Intracoastal views.

Hy-Vong ☒ *Vietnamese* | 26 | 8 | 15 | $30 |

Little Havana | 3458 SW 8th St. (bet. 34th & 35th Aves.) | Miami | 305-446-3674 | www.hyvong.com

"Amazing" Vietnamese fare including "perfect" "pork rolling cakes" have made this "cramped" Little Havana "hole-in-the-wall" a "cult" favorite for over 30 years; "modest prices" add appeal, but you must be "strong and patient" to brave the constant "line spilling into the street" (no reserving) and "snail's pace" service once seated – or else just grab a prepared meal to go.

	FOOD	DECOR	SERVICE	COST

Icebox Café *Bakery/Eclectic*
22 | 14 | 17 | $29

South Beach | 1657 Michigan Ave. (Lincoln Rd.) | Miami Beach | 305-538-8448 | www.iceboxcafe.com

The Eclectic menu is "always inventive" at this all-day bakery/cafe in South Beach, but whatever you order – breakfast, sandwiches, steak, pasta – "please! save room for dessert" because the cakes and such are "out of this world"; even if it's "lacking atmosphere" and service is "casual", it's a "cool" place to "chill" at a "nice price."

☑ Il Gabbiano ●☑ *Italian*
27 | 26 | 27 | $81

Downtown | One Miami Tower | 335 S. Biscayne Blvd. (SE 3rd St.) | Miami | 305-373-0063 | www.ilgabbianomia.com

From the antipasti to the after-dinner limoncello (both gratis), this Downtown sibling of Il Mulino in NYC (and Sunny Isles Beach) exhibits "true Italian class"; expect an "inspired menu", "extensive" wine list, "stellar" service and "elegant" digs that extend to a "beautiful" outdoor terrace where diners can "gaze at Biscayne Bay or into their companion's eyes" – welcome distractions from tabs that reflect the "top-notch" quality.

Il Grissino *Italian*
▽ 22 | 21 | 22 | $49

Coral Gables | 127 Giralda Ave. (bet. Ponce de Leon Blvd. & SW 37th Ave.) | 305-461-3391

This "hidden gem" in Coral Gables is a "safe bet" for "upscale Italian fare" and brick-oven "thin-crust pizza" (diners can also "order dishes that are not on the menu"); the staff is "accommodating" too, which leaves fans thinking it deserves a bigger following.

Il Mulino New York *Italian*
24 | 24 | 25 | $80

Sunny Isles Beach | Acqualina Hotel | 17875 Collins Ave. (bet. 178th & 183rd Sts.) | 305-466-9191 | www.ilmulino.com

"Superb" Northern Italian cuisine pairs with "wonderful wines" in an "opulent" space dressed in red carpet, dark woods and earth tones at this standout in the "posh" oceanfront Acqualina Hotel in Sunny Isles Beach; you "couldn't ask for better service", but even so, a few tough customers gripe it's "not the same" as the NYC original – "except the prices"; P.S. "try the homemade grappa."

Imlee *Indian*
25 | 17 | 21 | $33

Pinecrest | South Park Ctr. | 12663 S. Dixie Hwy. (bet. 124th & 128th Sts.) | 786-293-2223 | www.imleeindianbistro.com

"Everything is fantastic" – "even the rice is out of this world" – at this "gourmet Indian" in Pinecrest, which is why it's often as "overcrowded as Bombay"; other assets include a fairly "intimate setting with tasteful decor" for a strip mall, an "accommodating" staff and the bargain lunch buffet ($14.95 weekdays, $17.95 weekends).

Indomania *Indonesian*
▽ 25 | 18 | 25 | $37

Miami Beach | 131 26th St. (Collins Ave.) | 305-535-6332 | www.indomaniarestaurant.com

At this Indonesian "find" "tucked away" in Miami Beach, the Dutch owners are "always there with a smile" and ready with "excellent" service; it's especially "fun for groups" who order the *rijsttafel,* an "amazing array" of "salty, sweet, spicy and crunchy" tastes on a platter that's "bigger than the tables in this teeny place."

Irie Isle *Jamaican*

| - | - | - | I |

North Miami Beach | 168 NE 167th St. (2nd Ave.) | 305-354-7678
With reggae pumping in the background, this rock-steady Jamaican joint in a North Miami Beach strip mall has been slinging ultracheap jerk chicken, meat patties and other island favorites for a couple of decades now; the modest storefront is mostly takeout, which appeals to the passing traffic on busy 167th Street.

Islas Canarias *Cuban*

| 22 | 13 | 18 | $21 |

Little Havana | 285 NW 27th Ave. (3rd St.) | Miami | 305-649-0440
Sweetwater | 13697 SW 26th St. (137th Ave.) | Miami | 305-559-6666
www.islascanariasrestaurant.net
There's "nothing fancy" at this "popular" Little Havana–Sweetwater duo, just "big portions" of "well-executed" "Cuban classics"; most don't mind the "lack of atmosphere" given the "family"-friendly vibe, "affordable" tabs and "consistency" over the years.

Jaguar Restaurant *Pan-Latin*

| 22 | 20 | 21 | $36 |

Coconut Grove | 3067 Grand Ave. (McFarlane Rd.) | 305-444-0216 | www.jaguarspot.com
This tropical Pan-Latin eatery "in the middle of the Grove" hosts a "cool as cool can be" "scene" but also boasts a "caring" staff and "versatile", "miraculously inexpensive" menu; "addictive" ceviche sampler spoons are a favorite, and if some find the rest "average", after a "must-have" pitcher of red sangria at the long bar everything looks "delicious."

NEW Jamon Jamon Jamon *Spanish*

| - | - | - | E |

Miami River | Neo Lofts | 10 SW South River Dr. (5th Ave.) | Miami | 305-324-1111 | www.jamonjamonjamon.com
As the name suggests, patrons can pig out on several varieties of cured hams at this pricey Spanish yearling in a small basementlike space in the Neo Lofts building on the Miami River; it also has a huge tapas menu, paella stirred in a giant vat with a boat oar and a big selection of Iberian wines.

NEW Jefe's 🖉 *Burgers/Mexican*

| - | - | - | I |

Location varies; see website | Miami | 305-600-9636 | www.jefesoriginal.com
"*Vatos* making tacos" is the apt slogan for this orange truck dispensing classic Ensenada-style fish tacos (soft tortilla, crispy beer-battered fish, cabbage, pico de gallo, lime) as well as pork versions, taquitos and all-American burgers; it's cash-only but the chow's cheap – see the website for its whereabouts.

Jimmy'z Kitchen *Eclectic/Sandwiches*

| 25 | 14 | 19 | $21 |

NEW **Wynwood** | Cynergi | 2700 N. Miami Ave. (28th St.) | Miami | 305-573-1505

(continued)

(continued)

Jimmy'z Kitchen

South Beach | 1542 Alton Rd. (15th St.) | Miami Beach | 305-534-8216
www.jimmyzkitchen.com

Chef-owner Jimmy Carey has developed a "following" for his "value"-driven Eclectic "gourmet" sandwiches, salads and a few Puerto Rican dishes; the small SoBe original in an "unprepossessing" location is an area "office favorite for delivery", while the newer Wynwood site is more "spacious", attractive and boasts an "expanded menu"; P.S. look for "spectacular" *mofongo* (fried plantains) Fridays–Sundays in SoBe, daily in Wynwood.

☑ Joe's Stone Crab *Seafood* 27 | 20 | 23 | $68

South Beach | 11 Washington Ave. (bet. 1st St. & S. Pointe Dr.) | Miami Beach | 305-673-0365 | www.joesstonecrab.com

"Rob a bank, sell the house, [do] whatever it takes" to afford the "succulent" stone crabs that again make this "legendary" SoBe eatery Miami's Most Popular – though "the irony is that everything else on the menu is reasonably priced" and standouts like fried chicken and Key lime pie are equally "to die for"; "looong waits" and "rushed" service from "track-star" waiters racing through the "gigantic" space are the norm, but you can "avoid the madness" by heading to the recently "upgraded" take-out cafe; P.S. closed mid-May to mid-October.

Joey's Italian Café ☒ *Italian* 24 | 20 | 21 | $40

Wynwood | 2506 NW Second Ave. (bet. 25th & 26th Sts.) | Miami | 305-438-0488 | www.joeyswynwood.com

Emerging as an anchor restaurant in "fun", up-and-coming Wynwood, this "cute", modern-looking cafe offers a "young crowd" of art-lovers "light and tasty" Italian fare like "terrific pizzas and salads" at "good prices"; service is "attentive" and sitting outside on the "terrace is lovely" – just be sure to "make reservations" if you want to go "during the Second Saturday" gallery walk.

JohnMartin's ● *American/Irish* 17 | 18 | 19 | $31

Coral Gables | 253 Miracle Mile (bet. Ponce de Leon Blvd. & Salzedo St.) | 305-445-3777 | www.johnmartins.com

"Cheers!" to the "friendly" lads and lasses who sling the "decent" midpriced Irish and American grub at this "nothing fancy" Coral Gables pub that "hasn't changed in decades"; "live music" Fridays–Sundays and an "outstanding selection" of ale make it a "fun" place where folks can easily "plop down, relax and make a dozen new friends."

NEW Joint Bar & Grill ● *American* - | - | - | M

Pinecrest | Dadeland Plaza | 9559 S. Dixie Hwy. (Palmetto Expwy.) | 305-603-9929 | www.thejointbarandgrill.com

At this slick but simple New American gastropub in Pinecrest run by a father-and-son team, traditional bar food gets kicked up a notch (think truffle fries, guava cream cheese pizza and Thai-style donuts) and bumped up a price point too; a couple dozen

FOOD DECOR SERVICE COST

artisan beers on tap please suds savants, and there's live music/DJs Thursdays–Saturdays.

Julio's *Vegetarian*

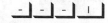

North Miami Beach | 1602 NE Miami Gardens Dr. (bet. 15th Ave. & 18th Rd.) | 305-947-4744 | www.juliosnaturalfoodsmiami.com

Vegetarians and health nuts descend on this wallet-friendly North Miami Beach cafe for fresh, organic breakfasts, salads, soups and sandwiches plus steamed rice and quinoa entrees; the utilitarian digs don't encourage lingering, so many just order a smoothie to go from the enormous juice menu.

Jumbo's ●⇗ *Diner*

Liberty City | 7501 NW Seventh Ave. (75th St.) | Miami | 305-751-1127 | www.jumbosrestaurant.com

It's "worth the drive" to "nowhere" (Liberty City) in Westernmost Dade to sit at the counter of this old-school diner that's been operating 24/7 since 1955; mixed in with the greasy-spoon standards are a few Southern and Bahamian specialties (the "best fried shrimp" gets a nod), but everything on the cash-only menu is affordable.

Kabobji *Mideastern*

∇ 22 | 11 | 22 | $27

NEW **North Bay Village** | 1624 79th Street Cswy. (Hispanola Ave.) | 305-397-8039

Aventura | 3055 NE 163rd St. (Sunny Isles Blvd.) | 305-354-8484 www.eatkabobji.com

Meat on a stick (slathered with a "wonderful secret marinade") is the succulent specialty of this "charming", "friendly" Middle Eastern duo in Aventura and North Bay Village with moderate prices; both locations have basic setups, but the original on 163rd Street has plans to expand its seating area.

Kampai *Japanese/Thai*

22 | 15 | 19 | $34

Aventura | Waterways Shopping Ctr. | 3575 NE 207th St. (34th Ave.) | 305-931-6410

South Miami | 8745 Sunset Dr. (SW 87th Ave.) | 305-596-1551 www.kampaisunset.com

These Japanese-Thai twins in Aventura and South Miami have stood "the test of time" thanks to their "reliable" eats, including "expertly crafted" sushi, at a "reasonable cost"; also appreciated are the "quiet" environs and "eager-to-please" staffers who bring "hot towels" the moment diners are seated.

NEW Kane Steakhouse ● *Steak*

South Beach | 431 Washington Ave. (5th St.) | Miami Beach | 305-704-2900 | www.kanesteakhouse.com

This thoroughly modern meatery recently arrived in the trendy SoFi (South of Fifth Street) section of SoBe searing all the usual cuts of high-priced designer beef (Waygu et al.) alongside a roster of swanky sides (hash browns crisped in duck fat, lobster mac 'n' cheese); no gloomy men's club here, though, not with an airy room of cream-colored leather booths and walls of pecky cypress and stacked rock.

	FOOD	DECOR	SERVICE	COST

Khoury's *Lebanese* | 21 | 12 | 19 | $32

South Miami | 5887 SW 73rd St. (S. Dixie Hwy.) | 305-662-7707
"Generous portions" of "quality" Lebanese fare please thrifty patrons of this "small" but "welcoming" South Miami cafe; if some note "parking limitations", checkmarks in the pro column include hookahs and a full bar stocked with Lebanese wine and beer plus regional liquors like Arak.

Kon Chau *Chinese* | 24 | 6 | 19 | $20

Westchester | 8376 Bird Rd. (SW 84th Ave.) | Miami | 305-553-7799
"Be adventurous" and overlook the "worn" dining room of this "friendly" Westchester strip-maller, because its "incredible", "dirt-cheap" Cantonese cuisine is "Chinese food the way the Chinese eat it"; bonus: the "extensive dim sum" offerings are "cooked to order."

La Casita *Cuban* | 23 | 15 | 21 | $25

Coral Gables | 3805 SW Eighth St. (Galiano St.) | 305-448-8224
"Terrific prices" are the thing at this Coral Gables storefront known for Cuban cooking rife with "flavor" and "zest" served in "large" portions; "friendly" service and occasional "live music" are more reasons to leave your own casita and stop by.

La Casona *Cuban* | - | - | - | I

West Sunset | 9606 Sunset Dr. (SW 97th Ave.) | Miami | 305-270-1017 | www.lacasonarestaurantmiami.com
An "abundance" of traditional Cuban dishes (including the namesake sandwich) are accompanied by a small selection of beer and wine at this basic, family-friendly eatery in West Sunset; there are no reservations taken but cheap tabs more than compensate.

La Cofradia ⊠ *Peruvian* | 25 | 26 | 24 | $57

Coral Gables | 160 Andalusia Ave. (Ponce de Leon Blvd.) | 305-914-1300 | www.lacofradia.com
It's "top-notch all the way" at this "stylish", loftlike enclave in Coral Gables touted for its "spectacular" nouvelle Peruvian cooking with international influences; yes, it's "expensive" given the "small portions", but no one cares after a few pisco sours.

⊠ La Dorada ◐⊠ *Seafood/Spanish* | 26 | 21 | 26 | $77

Coral Gables | 177 Giralda Ave. (Ponce de Leon Blvd.) | 305-446-2002 | www.ladoradamiami.com
This Coral Gables Spaniard offers "elegant, wonderfully simple preparations" of seafood "flown in daily from the Mediterranean" – via "first-class airfare", judging by the cost; wallet-watchers say the "awesome" prix fixe lunch is a "great value", while "friendly service", a "good wine selection" and live music on weekends are further pluses.

La Goulue *French* | 21 | 20 | 19 | $53

Bal Harbour | Bal Harbour Shops | 9700 Collins Ave. (96th St.) | 305-865-2181 | www.lagouluebalharbour.com
"Blink your eyes and you're in Paris" at this "stage-set perfect" simulacrum of a Parisian bistro in the Bal Harbour Shops serving "well-executed" traditional French cuisine; it's a "quieter alternative to

Carpaccio" across the way and the staff is "friendly", but what's with the "quiche-at-filet-mignon prices"?

La Locanda ● *Italian*
24 | 18 | 23 | $43

South Beach | 419 Washington Ave. (bet. 4th & 5th Sts.) | Miami Beach | 305-538-6277 | www.lalocandasobe.com

"Local" South Beachers beat a path to this "cute little" late-night trattoria known for its "delish" pastas and brick-oven pizzas; the staffers are "warm but slow" (not the worst combination in a handsome Italian waiter), and there's a "narrow" strip of sidewalk seating for those who don't mind "cars driving by continuously."

La Loggia ☒ *Italian*
21 | 17 | 20 | $32

Downtown | 68 W. Flagler St. (1st Ave.) | Miami | 305-373-4800 | www.laloggia.org

A "who's who of the legal community" packs the Romanesque environs of this "popular" weekday-only lunch spot across from the courthouse, judging the Italian fare "solid" and the moderate prices "awesome"; it's also a decent bet after court is adjourned, with "good happy-hour specials" offered 4–7 PM and relatively quiet evenings; P.S. the kitchen closes at 9 PM.

Lan *Asian*
23 | 11 | 22 | $25

South Miami | Dadeland Station | 8332 S. Dixie Hwy. (bet. N. Kendall Dr. & 67th Ave.) | 305-661-8141 | www.lanpanasian.com

"Lost amid its big-box neighbors" in South Miami, this "tiny" powerhouse "surprises" with an exceptionally "wide variety" of Pan-Asian choices that rewards "adventurous" eaters; decorwise, it's "utilitarian" and "too bright" by a few thousand watts, but not many folks mind since the lunch specials are "a steal – even in this economy."

La Palma Ristorante ● *Italian*
21 | 24 | 21 | $47

Coral Gables | 116 Alhambra Circle (Galiano St.) | 305-445-8777 | www.lapalmaristorante.com

"So pretty" and "so romantic", this pricey, "old-world" Coral Gables Tuscan features a flower-filled, Med-style courtyard; "management is always around to make sure things are right" for everyone from "VIPs" to "tourists", and insiders say Sunday brunch is "outstanding."

Lario's on the Beach *Cuban*
20 | 20 | 18 | $42

South Beach | 820 Ocean Dr. (bet. 8th & 9th Sts.) | Miami Beach | 305-532-9577 | www.bongoscubancafe.com

Seekers of Gloria-fied (Estefan, that is) Cuban fare and "too-die-for mojitos" get "a lot for their money" at this tropical eatery with a "great Ocean Drive location"; "local celebrity" sightings and weekend DJs make it "fun" even if some think "you can do better in SoBe"; P.S. no reservations, except for large groups.

La Riviera *French/Mediterranean*
- | - | - | E

Airport Area | Sofitel Miami | 5800 Blue Lagoon Dr. (57th Ave.) | Miami | 305-264-4888 | www.larivieramiami.com

Near the airport and just minutes from Downtown Coral Gables, this pricey respite in the Sofitel Hotel offers a limited French-Med menu;

FOOD | DECOR | SERVICE | COST

La Sandwicherie ● *French/Sandwiches*   25 | 9 | 18 | $15

NEW **Brickell Area** | 34 SW Eighth St. (Miami Ave.) | Miami | 305-374-9852

South Beach | 229 14th St. (bet. Collins & Washington Aves.) | Miami Beach | 305-532-8934

www.lasandwicherie.com

"All that and a bag of chips!" chirp champions of the "fantastic", "authentically French" sandwiches and "fresh smoothies" at this "iconic" "hut" in SoBe that's open "virtually around the clock and is almost always busy"; when something's this "cheap" and "amazing" few are put off by small annoyances like the staff's "French attitude" or that there's "only a handful of stools" on the sidewalk; P.S. the new Brickell branch opened post-Survey.

NEW **La Scalina** *Italian*   - | - | - | E

Downtown | 315 S. Biscayne Blvd. (SE 3rd St.) | Miami | 305-789-9933 | www.scalinamiami.com

This elegant Downtown Italian newcomer displays its cheeses, pastas and wines like jewelry for diners to ooh and aah over, offset by spectacular views of Biscayne Bay; chef Enrico Giraldo (for more than 20 years top toque at the Big Apple's Scalinatella) rolls out a classic menu that includes vitello tonnato, penne arrabbiata and zuppa di pesce, all at rather steep prices.

Las Culebrinas *Cuban/Spanish*   21 | 15 | 18 | $31

Coconut Grove | 2890 SW 27th Ave. (Coconut Ave.) | 305-448-4090

Pinecrest | 12257 S. Dixie Hwy. (124th St.) | 305-969-3995

Airport Area | 4700 W. Flagler St. (47th Ave.) | Miami | 305-445-2337

Hialeah | 4590 W. 12th Ave. (46th St.) | 305-823-5828

Both Spanish and Cuban cuisines share space on the menu at this "friendly" foursome known for its "flavorful", "monster"-size portions; "reasonable" rates make it a fine choice for a "casual dinner with family and friends", just "don't forget to finish it off with flan" – it's "phenomenal."

Las Vacas Gordas ● *Argentinean/Steak*   24 | 16 | 15 | $42

Miami Beach | 933 Normandy Dr. (Bay Dr.) | 305-867-1717 | www.lasvacasgordas.com

There's "plenty of value" in the "big portions" of "quality" meat (and on the "reasonable wine list") served at this modern-looking Argentinean steakhouse in Miami Beach; but the un-moo-ved feel there's "room to improve", starting with the "snooty" staff and music so "loud" that conversation is impossible.

Las Vegas *Cuban*   21 | 14 | 20 | $23

Miami Beach | 6970 Collins Ave. (69th St.) | 305-864-1509

See review in Ft. Lauderdale/Broward County Directory.

	FOOD	DECOR	SERVICE	COST

Latin Burger *Burgers/Mexican* | - | - | - | I |

Location varies; see website | Miami | 305-787-4911 | www.latinburger.com

Roving around Miami, this striking black-and-hot-pink food truck (co-owned by Food Network personality Ingrid Hoffman) specializes in low-cost, hand-held items popular in both the U.S. and Mexico – e.g. the hamburger and the taco; the former blends chorizo, chuck and sirloin with *queso Oaxaca* and 'avocadolicious' sauce, while the latter comes in three versions: chicken tomatillo, chicken mole or pulled pork.

Le Bouchon du Grove *French* | 24 | 19 | 20 | $41 |

Coconut Grove | 3430 Main Hwy. (Grand Ave.) | 305-448-6060 | www.lebouchondugrove.com

This small French bistro in Coconut Grove has "lasted a Miami eternity" (since 1994), and "delighted" patrons tout its "fantastic" cooking, "diverse" wine list and moderate prices; it "couldn't be cuter" or more "romantic", what with all the Gallic posters, "signs and memorabilia" on the walls.

Le Croisic ☒ *French* | ∇ 22 | 15 | 18 | $61 |

Key Biscayne | Arcade Shopping Ctr. | 180 Crandon Blvd. (bet. Harbor & Sonesta Drs.) | 305-361-5888

It's "worth the search" for this "little gem" hidden behind a Key Biscayne strip mall offering a "vast menu" of French fare (plus some Lebanese items at lunch); however, naysayers fret it's "expensive" for the location and note that "service isn't up to par."

Le Provençal *French* | 22 | 18 | 22 | $43 |

Coral Gables | 266 Miracle Mile (Ponce de Leon Blvd.) | 305-448-8984 | www.leprovencalrestaurant.com

This "family-owned", "been-around-forever" Coral Gables bistro is now fully settled in at its new "convenient" Miracle Mile address, and diners are happy to report the "authentic Provençal" cuisine (including "homemade pâté") is as "thoroughly satisfying" as ever; similarly, the prix fixe lunch remains a "bargain" – just "be ready for a nap afterwards."

Lido at The Standard *Mediterranean* | 22 | 27 | 17 | $42 |

South Beach | The Standard | 40 Island Ave. (Venetian Way) | Miami Beach | 305-673-1717 | www.standardhotel.com

"Fabulous" folk sip "great drinks", "soak up the sun" and take in the "incredible" water views from the "romantic" bayside deck at this "pricey" "chill"-out spot in the Standard; in keeping with the hotel's spa services, the "imaginative" Med bites are on the "healthy side", and the staff is "laid-back but not lax", which is "pretty good" for SoBe.

Lime Fresh | 19 | 14 | 17 | $16 |
Mexican Grill *Californian/Mexican*

NEW **Downtown** | 7 W. Flagler St. (Miami Ave.) | Miami | 305-789-0252

Wynwood | The Shops at Midtown Miami | 3201 N. Miami Ave. (32nd St.) | Miami | 305-576-5463

(continued)

(continued)

Lime Fresh Mexican Grill

North Miami Beach | Biscayne Commons | 14831 Biscayne Blvd.
(bet. NE 146th & 151st Sts.) | 305-949-8800
South Beach | 1439 Alton Rd. (bet. 14th & 15th Sts.) | Miami Beach |
305-532-5463
Kendall | 9005 SW 72nd Pl. (Dadeland Blvd.) | 305-670-1022
www.limefreshmexicangrill.com

Limeys "love, love, love" the "fresh", "healthy" Mexican eats with a
"Californian influence" served at these "fast-casual" outlets of a
"quickly expanding" local chain; cynics fault the "crowds, "loud music" and "inauthentic" cooking, but given the low pricing, most agree
"you can't go wrong" here.

Little Havana *Cuban*   22 | 16 | 19 | $29

North Miami | 12727 Biscayne Blvd. (NE 127th St.) | 305-899-9069 |
www.littlehavanarestaurant.com

"Tummies smile" at the thought of the "hearty" Cuban chow on
offer at these "well-priced" North Miami and Deerfield Beach
fueling stations; the "fast-food restaurant" settings are "spacious"
and the staffers "friendly", making meals here "fine" choices for
the "whole family."

Little Saigon ●⇄ *Vietnamese*   ∇ 19 | 9 | 19 | $33

North Miami Beach | 16752 N. Miami Ave. (bet. NW 167th & 168th Sts.) |
305-653-3377

There's "good eating" in store at this late-night Vietnamese "sleeper"
in North Miami Beach, where noodleheads advise "don't miss the
pho!"; the basic decor is offset by "reasonable prices", but keep in
mind that "no credit cards are accepted."

NEW Lizarran *Spanish*   - | - | - | E

Coral Gables | 65 Alhambra Pl. (37th Ave.) | 786-558-8539 |
www.lizarran-ca.com

This new Coral Gables outpost of a Madrid-based chain has a novel
billing system: all tapas are skewered pintxos-style by a toothpick,
and the tab is determined by counting up all the toothpicks at the
end (and they do pile up); the menu extends to larger entrees like
paella, meat and fish, while drink choices include beer, wine and
kalimotxo (the house red mixed with Coke).

NEW Local Craft Food & Drink *American*   - | - | - | M

Coral Gables | 150 Giralda Ave. (bet. Galiano St. & Ponce de Leon Blvd.) |
305-648-5687 | www.thelocal150.com

Early adopters of this Gables gastropub rave that the "quality and
care" that goes into the New American comfort fare make it a "foodie
haven" (think buffalo sweetbreads and squid-ink meatballs); the
small, exposed-brick space features a handsome wood bar dispensing
"exceptional beer", and plans are in the works to add outdoor seating.

Los Ranchos *Nicaraguan/Steak*   21 | 18 | 19 | $31

Biscayne | Bayside Mktpl. | 401 Biscayne Blvd. (bet. NE 4th & 5th Sts.) |
Miami | 305-375-8188

(continued)

Los Ranchos

Kendall | The Falls Shopping Ctr. | 8888 SW 136th St. (S. Dixie Hwy.) | 305-238-6867
Sweetwater | Holiday Plaza | 125 SW 107th Ave. (W. Flagler St.) | Miami | 305-552-6767
www.beststeakinmiami.com

"Churrasco so tender you can cut it with a fork" is the menu highlight at this "reliable" Nicaraguan steakhouse trio, though the "rich" *tres leches* is a close second; additional draws include "great value", "attentive" service and live music on weekends.

Lost & Found Saloon ● *Southwestern*   ∇ 17 | 15 | 15 | $22

Design District | 185 NW 36th St. (2nd Ave.) | Miami | 305-576-1008 | www.thelostandfoundsaloon-miami.com

Wagon-wheel chandeliers and six-ft.-tall steel cacti set the way-out-West mood at this Design District Southwesterner where the vittles are just "ok", but the microbrew list and low pricing are fine as is; still, since there's no piano player or hard liquor at this "hidden" late-night "hangout", some wonder "why call it a saloon?"

NEW LouLou Le Petit Bistro ☒ *French*   - | - | - | M

Miami River | 638 S. Miami Ave. (bet. SE 7th & 8th Sts.) | Miami | 305-379-1404 | www.loulou-miami.com

Owner Jacques Ardisson recently jettisoned his Indochine concept at this Miami River space for a "welcome" new French bistro menu; a "young, fun" crew enlivens the hybrid diner-bistro setting done up with ornate chandeliers, tufted banquettes and long tiled bar with red leather high chairs.

Lou's Beer Garden ● *American*   ∇ 21 | 17 | 19 | $27

Miami Beach | New Hotel | 7337 Harding Ave. (bet. 73rd & 74th Sts.) | 305-704-7879 | www.lousbeergarden.com

"Don't blink" – it's "easy to miss" this "hideaway" behind Miami Beach's New Hotel, where "friendly" staffers proffer a "solid" but "limited" menu of fancy American pub grub; "terrific" microbrews on tap and a tropical open-air setting near the pool keep things "fun" here; P.S. it's open nightly till 2 AM.

NEW LuLu in the Grove ● *Eclectic*   ∇ 16 | 18 | 16 | $31

Coconut Grove | 3105 Commodore Plaza (Main Hwy.) | 305-447-5858 | www.luluinthegrove.com

"Tourists" and "well-heeled" Coco Grovers dig into an assortment of Eclectic small plates at this "upscale", industrial-chic newcomer across the street from sibling Green Street Cafe; a few call it a bit of a "disappointment", but fans like its sidewalk seating, strong drinks and late-night hours.

Macaluso's ☒ *Italian*   25 | 19 | 20 | $61

South Beach | 1747 Alton Rd. (bet. Abe Resnick Blvd. & 17th St.) | Miami Beach | 305-604-1811 | www.macalusosmiami.com

Of South Florida's "zillion Italian restaurants", this "little" SoBe "gem" stands out thanks to "exquisite", "carefully prepared" favorites that taste "better than grandma used to make"; they still don't take reservations or make substitutions but at least have "eased back a bit" on the "take-it-or-leave-it" attitude; P.S. there's a cheaper, more casual lunchroom and prepared-foods market next door.

Magnum 🅈 Ⓜ *American* ▽ 23 | 21 | 24 | $42
Upper East Side | 709 NE 79th St. (Biscayne Blvd.) | Miami | 305-757-3368
A "diverse crowd" of golden throats have a "campy good time" belting out "showtunes" and "Sinatra" at this "très gay" piano bar on Miami's Upper East Side; the New American cuisine is surprisingly "excellent", the service "wonderful" (credit "consummate host" Jeffrey) and the joint exudes a "1940s" "NY feel."

Mahogany Grille Ⓜ *Soul Food* - | - | - | M
Miami Gardens | 2190 183rd St. NW (22nd Ave.) | 305-626-8100
The "upscale" Southern fixin's really "rock" – indeed, the "fried chicken and cornbread are on a whole other level" – at this "quality" soul food provider in Miami Gardens; moderate prices, a staff that "really cares" and live weekend music are further pluses that can be enjoyed in the brightly lit dining room or a moody lounge.

Maiko ● *Japanese* - | - | - | M
South Beach | 1255 Washington Ave. (bet. 12th & 13th Sts.) | Miami Beach | 305-531-6369 | www.maikosushi.com
"No-nonsense sushi" and a "good selection" of other Japanese favorites (plus some Thai items) are yours at this "little" SoBe joint that provides the goods "without a big scene"; there's "not much atmosphere", but the staff is "pleasant" and the tabs "affordable."

Maitardi Ⓜ *Italian* 21 | 24 | 20 | $42
Design District | 163 NE 39th St. (bet. 1st & 2nd Aves.) | Miami | 305-572-1400 | www.maitardimiami.com
The "magnificent" patio is set under an "impressive canopy of white oaks" at this "beautiful" Design District meeting place, where a "varied menu" of Northern Italiana and brick-oven pizzas works for "carnivores", "vegans" and "picky children" alike; a "reasonable wine list", "attentive" service and DJs/live music most evenings ice the cake.

NEW Makoto *Japanese* ▽ 25 | 26 | 25 | $60
Bal Harbour | Bal Harbour Shops | 9700 Collins Ave. (96th St.) | 305-864-8600 | www.makoto-restaurant.com
PA powerhouse Stephen Starr extends his reach to Miami with this "top-class" Japanese sushi and robata arrival in chichi Bal Harbour helmed by chef Makoto Okuwa, a Morimoto protégé; its "sleek", "sedate" setting with a sexy outdoor patio is "so cool you'll forget you're in a mall", but be aware: prices are as posh as the eats.

Mandolin 🅈 *Greek* 25 | 22 | 21 | $39
Design District | 4312 NE Second Ave. (bet. 43rd & 44th Sts.) | Miami | 305-576-6066 | www.mandolinmiami.com
"Excellent" mezes and other "traditional" Hellenic and Turkish dishes transport diners to the Aegean at this Design District "find"

FOOD | DECOR | SERVICE | COST

set in a 1930s-era house equipped with a "beautiful backyard garden"; moderate tabs and "friendly" service make "reservations" a must here.

Mango's Tropical Cafe ● *Eclectic* 13 | 18 | 16 | $38

South Beach | 900 Ocean Dr. (9th St.) | Miami Beach | 305-673-4422 | www.mangostropicalcafe.com

"Party" down with the "wild crowd" knocking back "stiff drinks" and ogling the "beautiful" male and female dancers "gyrating in skimpy outfits" on the central stage of this huge bi-level après beach place in SoBe; even those who call it a "silly tourist trap" admit it can be "fun" if you "skip" the "nonserious" Eclectic bites; P.S. it's 21-plus after 6 PM with a cover charge starting at 8 PM; no beachwear.

Marhaba Mediterranean Cuisine *Lebanese* ∇ 25 | 23 | 23 | $22

South Miami | The Shops at Sunset Pl. | 5701 Sunset Dr. (SW 57th Ave.) | 305-740-5880 | www.marhabainmiami.com

Lovers of Lebanese cuisine swear the "delicious" offerings at this South Miamian are "as good as it gets" in these parts – and "cheap" to boot; after "shopping" nearby, it's nice to "relax" outside with a hookah and a cup of "aromatic" Turkish coffee, facilitated by a "courteous" crew.

Mario The Baker *Italian/Pizza* 20 | 11 | 18 | $20

Downtown | 250 NE 25th St. (Biscayne Blvd.) | Miami | 305-438-0228
Downtown | 43 W. Flagler St. (NW Miami Ct.) | Miami | 786-316-0166
Coral Gables | Red Bird | 5755 SW 40th St. (bet. 58th Ave. & Red Rd.) | 305-665-0941
Bay Harbor Islands | 1067 95th St. (Bay Harbor Terr.) | 305-868-5225
Aventura | 18679 W. Dixie Hwy. (186th St.) | 305-466-1777
North Miami | 13695 W. Dixie Hwy. (NE 137th St.) | 305-891-7641
Westchester | 8565 SW 24th St. (87th Ave.) | Miami | 305-261-6155
www.mariothebakerpizza.com

"Red-gravy" basics and "NY-style" pizzas satisfy everyone from "senior citizens" to the "post-Little-League-game" set at these separately owned "pick-up-or-eat-in" Italians; they're "friendly" enough "without any hoo-ha", but in return you get "a lot for the money" – plus justifiably "famous" garlic rolls.

Maroosh Ⓜ *Mediterranean/Mideastern* 25 | 22 | 24 | $35

Coral Gables | 223 Valencia Ave. (bet. Ponce de Leon Blvd. & Salzedo St.) | 305-476-9800 | www.maroosh.com

Diners "can't go wrong" with the "tasty" kebabs, kibbeh and other "authentic" offerings tendered at this Coral Gables Med-Mideasterner featuring belly dancers on the weekends and moderate prices all week long; the "calm", "better-than-average setting" is enhanced by "welcoming", "unobtrusive" service.

☒ Matsuri Ⓜ *Japanese* 27 | 20 | 21 | $36

South Miami | 5759 Bird Rd. (bet. Red Rd. & SW 58th Ave.) | 305-663-1615

"Luscious" fish so "fresh" it "tastes like it swam into the restaurant" is the big lure at this longtime South Miami strip-mall mecca for

| | FOOD | DECOR | SERVICE | COST |

"true sushi aficionados", but it also dishes up "good cooked items" (brush up on your kanji and "ask for the Japanese-language menu" for more "unique" offerings); the "austere" setting isn't always warmed by service that can swing from "attentive" to "abrupt" – but "who cares with prices like this?"

Maya Tapas & Grill ❶ *Eclectic*   ▽ 17 | 16 | 19 | $33

South Beach | 530 Ocean Dr. (bet. 5th & 6th Sts.) | Miami Beach | 305-532-4747
South Beach | 809 Lincoln Rd. (Meridian Ave.) | Miami Beach | 305-538-0058
www.mayatapasandgrill.com

"People-watching" on the bustling Lincoln Road/Ocean Drive corridors is the name of the game at this South Beach Eclectic duo; though the varied menu divides voters ("interesting" vs. "somewhat disappointing"), at least it's affordable, especially for locals who enjoy a 10% discount.

Meat Market ❶ *Steak*   25 | 26 | 22 | $70

South Beach | 915 Lincoln Rd. (bet. Jefferson & Michigan Aves.) | Miami Beach | 305-532-0088 | www.meatmarketmiami.com

This "sexy", "very Miami twist on the standard steakhouse" provides delightful "sensory overload" via its "gorgeous" clientele, "spectacular", "sleek" SoBe setting and "pricey" but "pitch-perfect" "hunks of red meat" delivered by a "professional" staff; a "big wine list" and "busy bar scene" keep the vibe throbbing late into the night.

Melting Pot *Fondue*   19 | 18 | 20 | $42

North Miami Beach | 15700 Biscayne Blvd. (157th St.) | 305-947-2228
West Sunset | 11520 Sunset Dr. (SW 117th Ave.) | Miami | 305-279-8816
www.meltingpot.com

"Romantic" hearts flutter at these "wayback machines to the '70s" where "cooking your own" food in "rich" fondue appeals to everyone from date-nighters to "groups" to "kids"; sure, the tabs are "pricey" and you may "smell like a Bunsen burner" afterward, but there's no doubt that this "unique" experience is a "memorable" one.

Mercadito ❶ *Mexican*   21 | 23 | 19 | $41

Downtown | 3252 NE First Ave. (bet. 36th & 38th Sts.) | Miami | 786-369-0430 | www.mercaditorestaurants.com

"Spice and everything nice" go into the "authentic" tacos, "homemade guacamole" and other Mexican delectables on offer at this pricey "NY transplant" in Downtown Miami; the "stylish" space – outfitted with white banquettes, blond wood and pop art – attracts a "hip" following, while an "excellent selection of tequilas" seals the deal.

Mesazul *Nuevo Latino/Steak*   - | - | - | VE

Doral | Doral Golf Resort & Spa | 4400 NW 87th Ave. (41st St.) | Miami | 305-591-6616 | www.doralresort.com

Part of the Doral Golf Resort's $16 million face-lift was spent creating this contemporary Latin take on a traditional American steakhouse with a sleek design including a semicircular glassed-in wine display, a private dining area and sweeping views of the Blue Monster; the expensive tabs are par for the course.

Miami's Chophouse *Steak*
19 | 22 | 21 | $66

Downtown | Metropolitan One | 300 S. Biscayne Blvd. (SE 2nd Ave.) | Miami | 305-938-9000 | www.chophousemiami.com

"Steak-aholics" returning to this modern Downtown meatery will find that it recently assumed new ownership, getting a new chef and menu in the process (and thus putting the Food score in question); what hasn't changed: stellar drinks from the "cool bar" and the "views" of Brickell Key from the covered outdoor terrace.

ⓩ Michael's Genuine
Food & Drink *American*
27 | 20 | 23 | $56

Design District | Atlas Plaza | 130 NE 40th St. (bet. 1st & 2nd Aves.) | Miami | 305-573-5550 | www.michaelsgenuine.com

The name of this "trendy" Design District "hot spot" is "a statement of intent that they deliver on" via chef-owner Michael Schwartz's "ambitious" yet "down-to-earth" small, medium and large plates of locally sourced New American "comfort" food, backed by "inspired" treats from "genius" pastry chef Hedy Goldsmith and a "well-considered" wine list; staffers can seem "a touch snooty" at times but their "efficiency", plus a "lovely" outdoor courtyard and "decent" prices, compensates.

ⓩ Michy's Ⓜ *American/French*
27 | 19 | 25 | $63

Upper East Side | 6927 Biscayne Blvd. (69th St.) | Miami | 305-759-2001 | www.michysmiami.com

Chef Michelle Bernstein is "at the top of her game" at this "pricey" Upper East Side "showcase" for "novel takes" on French–New American comfort food; though opinion diverges on the decor – "funky" vs. "Aunt Mildred's living room" – most applaud the staff's "attention to detail"; P.S. those with "commitment issues" can order multiple entrees in half portions.

Mike's Italian New York Style
Pizza & Restaurant *Pizza*
- | - | - | I

Kendall | 13712 84th St. SW (137th Ave.) | 305-382-6200 | www.mikespizza.info

For 20 years, this family-friendly pizza parlor has been baking its signature NY-style pies for budget-minded Kendallites; it's a typical checkered-plastic-tablecloth joint, but satisfies most palates by adding a wide variety of Italian standards to the mix.

Mint Leaf Indian Brasserie *Indian*
21 | 17 | 17 | $37

NEW **Brickell Area** | 1063 SE First Ave. (11th St.) | Miami | 305-358-5050

Coral Gables | 276 Alhambra Circle (bet. Ponce de Leon Blvd. & Salzedo St.) | 305-443-3739
www.mintleafib.com

Given the "wonderfully flavored", "not Americanized" subcontinental cooking and the flat-screens broadcasting "Bollywood spectacles", this contemporary-looking Coral Gables Indian sure "tries to please"; service is "inconsistent" ("pleasant" vs. "a hassle"), but moderate tabs keep regulars regular; P.S. the new Brickell branch opened post-Survey.

NEW Miso Hungry ⌀ Asian
- | - | - | I

Location varies; see website | Miami | 305-322-7132 | www.misohungrymobile.com

The brainchild of local culinary-school grads, this cash-only food truck with a punny name and cutesy graphics vends a variety of affordable Asian bites; the 'Miso Box', its take on the bento box, features fried rice and veggies with a choice of Indonesian-style beef, Chinese-style chicken, curry chicken or sautéed tofu; P.S. check online for the schedule.

Miss Saigon Bistro Vietnamese
23 | 17 | 22 | $30

Coral Gables | 148 Giralda Ave. (bet. Galiano St. & Ponce de Leon Blvd.) | 305-446-8006
South Beach | 710 Washington Ave. (6th St.) | Miami Beach | 305-531-4200
Pinecrest | 9503 S. Dixie Hwy. (bet. Datran Blvd. & SW 95th St.) | 305-661-2911
www.misssaigonbistro.com

"Lovingly prepared" Vietnamese cuisine is purveyed at this "tasty" mini-chain that feels "like a family business" thanks to its "charming owner"; "fair prices" encourage sampling multiple dishes, though insiders put themselves in the hands of the "helpful" staffers – you "can't go wrong with their choices."

NEW Miss Yip Chinese Cafe Chinese
16 | 17 | 16 | $31

Downtown | 900 Biscayne Blvd. (bet. NE 9th & 10th Sts.) | Miami | 305-358-0088 | www.missyipchinesecafe.com

After changing ownership, this "hip", "affordable" Chinese eatery moved from SoBe to "kitschy" Downtown digs that evoke a "1940s NY chop suey joint", but critics yip it's "more style than substance", citing "middle-of-the-road" fare (including a "limited" dim sum menu) and slow service; P.S. there are plans to open additional branches.

NEW Mister Collins American
- | - | - | E

Bal Harbour | One Bal Harbour Resort | 10295 Collins Ave. (96th St.) | 305-455-5460 | www.mistercollins.com

You needn't call this fresh-faced New American entry 'Mister' – despite the posh Bal Harbour address and relatively expensive tabs, its down-to-earth American menu suggests a first-name basis via easy eats like burgers, soft pretzels and shrimp cocktail, not to mention a selection of craft beers; minimalist white walls and dark wood put the focus squarely on the panoramic ocean views.

Molina's Cuban
∇ 25 | 15 | 22 | $23

Hialeah | 4100 E. Eighth Ave. (41st St.) | 305-687-0008

For a true taste of Havana in Hialeah, expats head to this "casual but nice" *cocina* serving "cooked to perfection" Cuban fare; limited English may present difficulties for some, but the "reasonable prices" are universally understood.

| | FOOD | DECOR | SERVICE | COST |

Monty's *Seafood*
| | 17 | 19 | 17 | $33 |

South Beach | Miami Beach Marina | 300 Alton Rd. (3rd St.) |
Miami Beach | 305-672-1148 | www.montyssobe.com

Monty's Raw Bar *Seafood*

Coconut Grove | Monty's Marina | 2550 S. Bayshore Dr. (Aviation Ave.) |
305-856-3992

"Happy hour is jammin'" with live tunes and "fruity drinks" at these
SoBe/Coco Grove tiki "dives"; besides "popular raw bars", the "fried
somethings-or-other" on the seafood menu are "serviceable"
enough for not much bank, but most folks are there primarily for the
"remarkable" water views and "lowbrow" bar scenes.

Moon Thai & Japanese *Japanese/Thai*
| | 23 | 16 | 20 | $24 |

Coral Gables | 1118 S. Dixie Hwy. (Augusto St.) | 305-668-9890
Kendall | Kendall Plaza | 16311 N. Kendall Dr. (SW 162nd Ave.) |
305-388-5901
www.moonthai.com

There's "something for everyone" on the "excellent", "price-is-
right" menu of this Thai-Japanese mini-chain that's particularly
touted for its "well-made" sushi; "speedy" service makes it an especially good "pre-movie theater" bet at Coral Springs, and helps U
Miami students in Coral Gables get back to their books quickly.

Morgans *American*
| | 24 | 19 | 20 | $35 |

NEW **Miami Beach** | 1787 Purdy Ave. (18th St.) |
305-397-8753
Wynwood | 28 NE 29th St. (bet. Miami & 2nd Aves.) | Miami |
305-573-9678
www.themorgansrestaurant.com

An "unexpected gem" in a "desolate" patch of Wynwood, this midpriced American gives "honest" home cooking a "wonderful" contemporary spin; housed in an "old mansion", the interior has an
"IKEA" feel, while the outside area feels as "laid-back" as a "friend's
front porch" – and there's lots of "free parking" to boot; P.S. the
Miami Beach location opened post-Survey.

Morton's The Steakhouse *Steak*
| | 25 | 23 | 25 | $70 |

Brickell Area | 1200 Brickell Ave. (SW 13th St.) | Miami |
305-400-9990
Coral Gables | 2333 Ponce de Leon Blvd. (bet. Aragon Ave. & Miracle Mile) |
305-442-1662
Miami Beach | The Crown at Miami Beach | 4041 Collins Ave.
(bet. 40th & 41st Sts.) | 786-454-4022
North Miami Beach | 17399 Biscayne Blvd. (NE 173rd St.) |
305-945-3131
www.mortons.com

"Melt-in-your-mouth" beef "prepared as ordered" is the rule at this
"high-end steakhouse" chain with "impeccable" service and "clubby"
"dignified surroundings"; "credit cards cringe" at the mere mention
of its name, but it's worth a "splurge" for "special occasions" (or
check out the "value-laden bar menu"); P.S. the tableside raw-meat
presentation and lecture is "fun once, but pass on it otherwise."

	FOOD	DECOR	SERVICE	COST

NEW Mr. Chef's Fine Chinese Cuisine & Bar *Chinese*

▽ 24 | 18 | 19 | $26

Aventura | 18800 NE 29th Ave. (188th St.) | 786-787-9030 |
www.aventurachef.com

"Wonderful" Chinese fare including dim sum and some "dishes that you can't find anywhere else in Miami" draws followers to this "friendly" Aventura newcomer where the pricing's equally friendly; the contemporary space is "nicely decorated" with tasteful artwork and includes a dark-wood bar and a small outdoor patio.

Mr. Chow *Chinese*

22 | 26 | 20 | $84

South Beach | W South Beach | 2201 Collins Ave. (bet. 22nd & 23rd Sts.) | Miami Beach | 305-695-1695 | www.mrchow.com

"Glitterati" are rendered "speechless" by the "gorgeous" decor (highlighted by a 123-ft. gold-leaf-and-Swarovski-crystal chandelier) at this "chic" resto-lounge in SoBe's W Hotel; Michael Chow's "designer", "expense account"–worthy Chinese chow also wins kudos, and service gets an 'A', though surveyors are split over whether that stands for "attentive" or "arrogant."

Mr. Yum *Asian*

- | - | - | M

Little Havana | 1945 SW 8th St. (19th Ave.) | Miami | 786-360-2371 | www.mryummiami.com

Something of an anomaly when it first opened in Little Havana's Cuban enclave, this compact Japanese-Thai now has fans saying 'yum' for its traditional sushi and Siamese preparations, as well as such Calle Ocho nods as the Havana Roll (fried whitefish, avocado, cucumber, masago and spicy mayo); the chic, sleek minimalist setting and moderate pricing make it a cool date-on-a-budget place.

NEW Ms. Cheezious 🖾⇆ *American*

- | - | - | I

Location varies; see website | Miami | 305-989-4019 | www.mscheezious.com

Using cheesecake to sell its grilled-cheese sandwiches, this good-humored food truck is easy to spot given the stylized blond bombshell in a polka-dot bikini painted on its side; the cash-only, build-your-own menu offers eight different cheeses and a half-dozen add-ons (from bacon to spiced apples) along with a daily selection of breads.

Mykonos *Greek*

20 | 12 | 18 | $26

Coral Way | 1201 SW 22nd St. (12th Ave.) | Miami | 305-856-3140

"Out of the way but worth a trip", this "no-frills" Hellenic in Coral Way dishes out "decent" classics at "low, low" prices; it's been around for "so many years" that the "dated" digs are going "the way of the Greek ruins", but "super-value" pricing keeps fans loyal; P.S. order the *galaktoboureko* for dessert.

NEW Nacho Mamas *Mexican*

- | - | - | I

Location varies; see website | Miami | 862-246-6262 | www.nachomamasgrill.com

The 'mamas' behind this vividly painted food truck are financial planner Ted Baturin and real-estate developer Nick Diamond, who have launched a second career via this mobile Mexican; mucho na-chos (cheese, chicken, chorizo, steak and shrimp) share space with other cheap eats like tacos, burritos and quesadillas; P.S. unlike many trucks, it takes Visa and MasterCard.

NEW Naked Pizza ● *Pizza*   ▽ 18 | 12 | 18 | $13

South Beach | 1260 Washington Ave. (13th St.) | Miami Beach | 305-809-8595 | www.nakedpizza.biz

"Healthy pizza seems like an oxymoron" but this new South Beach link of a New Orleans–based chain "pulls it off" with 10-grain pizza dough and "fresh", all-natural toppings; its sleek, Apple Store look features a media wall displaying menus and other info, which aids the "prompt" take-out service (it's also possible to eat in at a small stand-up counter).

Z Naoe Ⓜ *Japanese*   29 | 23 | 28 | VE

Sunny Isles Beach | 175 Sunny Isles Blvd. (Collins Ave.) | 305-947-6263 | www.naoemiami.com

"I can't believe this exists in Miami" since it would be "outstanding even in Japan" gush fans of this "teeny" 17-seat Sunny Isles Beach star, rated the city's tops for Food and Service; Kevin Cory's "creative" omakase meals include a bento box "revelation" and "impossibly good" sushi, all presented with "warm", "personal" care by "charming" manager Wendy Maharlika; it's not cheap (price varies according to the day's offerings and how many courses you opt for), but it's so "worth it" – just book "well in advance" (two seatings, Wednesday-Sunday); P.S. it plans to relocate to Brickell Key in early 2012.

NEW Nemesis Urban Bistro Ⓜ *Eclectic*   – | – | – | E

Downtown | 1035 N. Miami Ave. (NW 11th St.) | Miami | 305-415-9911 | www.nemesisbistro.com

Former *Top Chef* contestant Micah Edelstein jets all over the culinary map at this pricey new Downtown Eclectic, serving everything from 'Tuscan sushi' (prosciutto, mascarpone, Gorgonzola and figs) to American bison with dark-chocolate sauce; the dining room decor is equally diverse, juxtaposing church-pew seating, batik prints and a flamboyant necktie sculpture with exposed ductwork and umbrellas suspended from the ceiling.

New Chinatown *Chinese*   20 | 15 | 19 | $29

South Miami | 5958 S. Dixie Hwy. (SW 73rd St.) | 305-662-5650

South Miamians jonesing for "well-prepared" Chinese "classics" at moderate tabs head to this "relaxing" neighborhood spot that's "been around since the Ming Dynasty"; other pluses include a "well-thought-out wine list", flat-screens for "enjoying ballgames" and the fact that there's "never a wait."

News Cafe ● *Diner*   18 | 17 | 17 | $28

South Beach | 800 Ocean Dr. (8th St.) | Miami Beach | 305-538-6397 | www.newscafe.com

News flash: this "original" South Beach "icon" is still the place to "see and be seen" 24/7, whether "lingering" over a "cheap" breakfast or recovering "after a hard night on the town"; since most of the diner's space is outdoors, its easy to eyeball the Ocean Drive action "up close."

Nexxt Cafe *Eclectic* 18 | 13 | 13 | $30
South Beach | 700 Lincoln Rd. (Euclid Ave.) | Miami Beach | 305-532-6643 | www.nexxtcafe.com
A "crazy big menu" of midpriced Eclectic eats plated in "enormous" portions makes for a feeding frenzy at this off-brand "Cheesecake Factory knock-off" in SoBe; detractors *no comprendo* the "painfully slow" service and "sitting-on-top-of-the-table-next-to-you" dimensions, but find it easy to understand the attractive views of "Lincoln Road passersby."

Nikki Beach *Eclectic* 16 | 24 | 17 | $52
South Beach | Penrod's | 1 Ocean Dr. (1st St.) | Miami Beach | 305-538-1111 | www.nikkibeach.com
"Sand at your feet", "great drinks" in hand and "hot bodies" in view make this "on-the-beach" open-air "lounge" a model par excellence of "South Beach decadence" – with prices to match; there's a light menu of Eclectic fare ("they serve food?") not helped by "slow" service, but the main thing is the "people-watching" and dancing on weekend nights.

Z Nobu Miami Beach *Japanese* 27 | 22 | 22 | $83
South Beach | Shore Club | 1901 Collins Ave. (19th St.) | Miami Beach | 305-695-3232 | www.noburestaurants.com
"Beautiful fish and beautiful people" dazzle at this "über-hip" "pregame warm-up for SoBe's clubs", part of Nobu Matsuhisa's far-flung fusion empire renowned for its "incredible" Japanese-Peruvian cuisine crowned by "sushi to die for" (indeed, the bill alone "may kill you"); the space is "beyond minimalist compared to the rest of the Shore Club's glitz" and critics contend service is "not up to par with the prices", but "have a sake, chill" and "keep your eyes open – you'll be surprised who you might see."

Novecento *Argentinean* 19 | 19 | 19 | $39
Brickell Area | 1414 Brickell Ave. (SE 14th St.) | Miami | 305-403-0900 ☽
Key Biscayne | 620 Crandon Blvd. (bet. Enid & Sunrise Drs.) | 305-362-0900
www.novecento.com
It's a "young, pretty" "after-work" crowd that flocks to these "energetic" Argentinean "watering holes" that make good lifting-off points "before hitting the clubs"; "quality" food offerings include "great steak" and prices modest enough to leave ample booze money in patrons' pockets.

Oasis *Mediterranean* ▽ 21 | 17 | 20 | $26
Miami Beach | 976 Arthur Godfrey Rd. (Alton Rd.) | 305-674-9005
The Mediterranean plates are always "fresh and healthy" at this casual "neighborhood spot" in Miami Beach; wallet-friendly tabs and "friendly" staffers lure "families with children", while a list of craft beers and wine appeals to over-21 types.

Oceanaire Seafood Room *Seafood*   24 | 24 | 24 | $61

Brickell Area | Mary Brickell Vill. | 900 S. Miami Ave. (bet. SW 9th & 10th Sts.) | Miami | 305-372-8862 | www.theoceanaire.com

"Teak woodwork" and "wavy architectural" details lend a luxury "ocean liner" feel to this upscale chain seafooder moored in Mary Brickell Village; it may be "expensive", but "exceptionally fresh" fish, a "great" raw bar and "consistently good" service are the payoffs.

Off the Grille Bistro *Eclectic*   ∇ 26 | 16 | 25 | $16

Kendall | 12578 N. Kendall Dr. (bet. SW 125th & 127th Aves.) | 305-274-2300

NEW **Airport Area** | Mall of the Americas | 7795 W. Flagler St. (Miami Dairy Rd.) | Miami | 305-403-3083
www.otggrill.com

"Creative" Caribbean, Med and Asian accents dress up the "generously" sized Eclectic wraps, salads and entrees at this "finger-licking good" quick bite in Kendall and at the Mall of the Americas; there's "limited seating", but frugal folk like the low tabs and enthuse that "BYO cuts down the price" even more.

Oggi Caffe *Italian*   25 | 20 | 23 | $40

North Bay Village | 1666 79th Street Cswy. (Hispanola Ave.) | 305-866-1238

North Bay Villagers who have been patronizing this "cozy" "neighborhood gem" for years feel as if the staffers are "old friends"; since its "homemade" pasta is the "gold standard" of the genre (and "reasonably" priced to boot), it's no wonder the place is "so perfect for families that it's often overrun with them."

☑ Oishi Thai *Japanese/Thai*   26 | 22 | 24 | $44

North Miami | 14841 Biscayne Blvd. (146th St.) | 305-947-4338 | www.oishithai.com

"Delicious" sushi and other "fabulous" Japanese fare shares billing with "exotic" Thai creations at this North Miami strip-maller, "admirably run" by a onetime Nobu chef; a "cool" modern Asian look, servers who "do everything they can to make for an enjoyable meal" and an optimal "quality/price ratio" further boost its appeal.

☑ OLA *Pan-Latin*   27 | 22 | 25 | $66

South Beach | Sanctuary Hotel | 1745 James Ave. (bet. 17th & 18th Sts.) | Miami Beach | 305-695-9125 | www.olamiami.com

"Ceviche is king" at this "quiet" Pan-Latin respite from the "craziness of SoBe", offering a culinary "trip from Mexico to Argentina" courtesy of chef Douglas Rodriguez; set in the boutique Sanctuary Hotel well "off the main drag", it has a "trendy" yet "comfortable" vibe, a "thoughtful" wine list parsed by a "knowledgeable" crew and a "delightful" terrace.

Old San Juan Ⓜ *Puerto Rican*   ∇ 22 | 15 | 22 | $33

West Miami | 1200 SW 57th Ave. (12th St.) | 305-263-9911 | www.oldsanjuanmiami.com

Maybe this Puerto Rican eatery in West Miami is "not fancy", but it's certainly "one of a kind" owing to "quality" staples like mofongo, a fried plantain–based dish; the "calories add up fast" so "bring a calculator" – though you won't need to figure the tab on the super-value weekday lunch specials.

Olivos *Pan-Latin*
▽ 26 | 24 | 24 | $35

Doral | 10455 NW 41st St. (bet. 102nd & 107th Aves.) | Miami | 305-718-9968 | www.olivosrestaurant.com

Those in the know say "you can't go wrong" at this "upscale" Doral sleeper featuring "well-prepared and well-presented" nouveau Pan-Latin dishes – especially the must-try morcilla (blood sausage) spring rolls; "good" service and an extensive Argentinean wine list add further charms to the rustic-elegant room.

OneBurger *Burgers*
22 | 12 | 15 | $15

Coral Gables | 367 Alhambra Circle (SW 42nd Ave.) | 305-529-5555 | www.oneburger.com

One can grab a "great" "nontraditional burger" of any variety (e.g. Kobe beef, turkey, fish, veggie) for a "good price" at this "tiny" Coral Gables joint, yet ultimately "it's still fast food" so seating is "limited" and the service "just ok"; fans who say "it would be perfect if they just had beer" head for its next-door sibling, Globe Cafe & Bar.

NEW 100 Montaditos *Sandwiches/Spanish*
– | – | – | I
(aka Cerveceria 100 Montaditos)

Downtown | Shops at Midtown | 3252 NE First Ave. (NW 34th St.) | Miami | 305-921-4373 | www.100montaditos.com

SoBe is the first U.S. beachhead made by this Spain-based fast-food conquistador with branches throughout Europe; the tiny sandwiches it's known for are super cheap (starting at $1) and available in samplers of varying numbers – just check off your order, take it to the counter and nosh in the utilitarian digs.

Original Daily Bread
▽ 26 | 15 | 20 | $16
Marketplace *Mideastern*

Coconut Grove | 2400 SW 27th St. (S. Dixie Hwy.) | 305-856-0363 | www.dailybreadmarketplace.com

Aisles of Middle Eastern groceries provide an appropriately authentic backdrop for an "informal" meal of "delish" Arabian cuisine at this family-owned Coconut Grove cafe-in-a-market; hummus and pita made in-house are standouts on the inexpensive menu.

Original Pancake House *American*
20 | 11 | 16 | $18

Aventura | 21215 Biscayne Blvd. (NE 213th St.) | 305-933-1966
Kendall | Total Sunset Plaza | 11510 SW 72nd St. (115th Ct.) | 305-274-9215
Doral | 9901 NW 41st St. (bet. 97th & 102nd Aves.) | Miami | 786-507-0564
www.originalpancakehouse.com

"Anything a person could want for breakfast" turns up on the menu of this all-American chain known for its "hearty portions" and "affordable" tabs; service is "merely functional" (they "do their best" given the "crowds") and the "utilitarian" decor could use a "pick-me-up", but overall "your taste buds will be happy."

FOOD | DECOR | SERVICE | COST

Origin Asian Bistro *Asian*

21 | 15 | 21 | $30

Key Biscayne | 200 Crandon Blvd. (bet. Harbor & Sonesta Drs.) | 305-365-1260
South Miami | 5850 Sunset Dr. (SW 58th Ct.) | 305-668-8205
www.originbistro.com

What's the solution for diners who "have no clue what type of Asian cuisine they want"? – this Pan-Asian duo in Key Biscayne and South Miami that rolls out a "diverse" menu ranging from sushi and Malaysian food to Thai- and Vietnamese-influenced dishes; "friendly" service and "reasonable" tabs are further pluses.

🅉 Ortanique on the Mile *Caribbean/New World*

26 | 23 | 24 | $57

Coral Gables | 278 Miracle Mile (Salzedo St.) | 305-446-7710 | www.cindyhutsoncuisine.com

The real "'miracle' on the Mile" in Coral Gables is chef Cindy Hutson's "delightfully different" Caribbean–New World "standout", where she constantly "experiments" with the "freshest local ingredients", including each day's catch; it can be "pretty pricey" but it's "very worth it", especially when you factor in the "responsive" service and "must-have mojitos" that make the "tropical", island"-esque setting feel even more "relaxed."

Osteria del Teatro 🅉 *Italian*

26 | 18 | 24 | $66

South Beach | 1443 Washington Ave. (Española Way) | Miami Beach | 305-538-7850 | www.osteriadelteatromiami.com

"Incredible" Northern Italian cuisine takes *paesani* "back to the old country" at this "legendary" "white-tablecloth" "oasis of relaxation" "in crazy SoBe"; prices are "high" and quarters that some find "cozy" strike others as "uncomfortable, unless you're a sardine", but "sublime" wines and an "alert" staff that "anticipates your every move" help make it "a must."

Otentic *French*

- | - | - | M

South Beach | 710 Washington Ave. (7th St.) | Miami Beach | 305-531-1464 | www.otentic-restaurant.com

This "authentic", 26-seat French bistro in SoBe may be "small", but the "tastes are big" in its crêpes, ratatouille and other Provençal soul food; the basic setup isn't much to look at, but there are "values" to be had.

Outback Steakhouse *Steak*

18 | 15 | 19 | $31

North Miami Beach | 3161 NE 163rd St. (bet. Biscayne & Interama Blvds.) | 305-944-4329
Kendall | Town & Country Ctr. | 11800 Sherry Ln. (bet. Mills Dr. & SW 117th Ave.) | 305-596-6771
Miami Lakes | 15490 NW 77th Ct. (154th St.) | 305-558-6868
Sweetwater | Flagler Park Plaza | 8255 W. Flagler St. (NW 82nd Ave.) | Miami | 305-262-9766
Westchester | Briar Bay Shopping Ctr. | 13145 SW 89th Pl. (Howard Dr.) | Miami | 305-254-4456
www.outback.com

"Defying the expensive-steakhouse convention", this "trusted" Aussie-themed chain delivers "steak for the masses" at "affordable"

FOOD DECOR SERVICE COST

prices and is an "easy place to take the kids"; yes, the menu may be "predictable" and the "always busy" joints "loud – just like their TV ads" – but the "friendly" staff is willing to "hop around like kangaroos" in order to please.

🆕 Oye Cuban Grill Cuban   ▽ 20 | 17 | 17 | $18

Pinecrest | 11327 S. Dixie Hwy. (Kilian Pkwy.) | 786-249-4001 | www.oyecubangrill.com

With "decent prices" and servers who "aim to please", this somewhat "Americanized Cuban" concept newly arrived in Pinecrest includes some "healthier items" on the menu along with "create-your-own" sandwich combos; also unusual for the genre is the minimalist modern setting outfitted with sleek chrome-and-clear-plastic chairs, drum-pendant lights and brick-clad columns.

Ƶ Palm, The Steak   28 | 20 | 25 | $73

Bay Harbor Islands | 9650 E. Bay Harbor Dr. (96th St.) | 305-868-7256 | www.thepalm.com

"Top-quality meat cooked right", "great sides" and "strong drinks" are what you can expect "every time" at this Bay Harbor Islands outpost of the "quintessential NY steakhouse" chain; caricatures line the walls and "local bigwigs" fill the seats of the "clubby" environs, which are overseen by "old-school waiters" and host an "amiable bar scene", but it doesn't come cheap: "my credit card won't allow me near the place."

Ƶ Palme d'Or 🅂🅼 French   28 | 27 | 27 | $92

Coral Gables | Biltmore Hotel | 1200 Anastasia Ave. (Columbus Blvd.) | 305-913-3201 | www.biltmorehotel.com

"The prize of Coral Gables, if not all of Miami/Dade", is this "superb" New French stunner where chef Philippe Ruiz "consistently outdoes himself" crafting "delectable" small plates matched by a "well-considered" wine list and "seamless" service in a "luxurious", "refined" setting; "not cheap" understates things, especially if you go all out and "stay the night" at the "beautiful" Biltmore for the "ultimate romantic evening."

🆕 Pancho Villa Mexican   - | - | - | I

North Miami | 16605 NE Fourth Ave. (167th St.) | 786-955-6927
North Miami | 899 NE 125th St. (9th Ave.) | 305-891-1991
www.panchovillamexican.com

Baja-style Mexican fast food is the name of el game at these brightly painted North Miami newcomers; there are no frills, but all the usual suspects – tacos, burritos, tostadas, quesadillas – are available for a quick bite at rock-bottom tabs.

Panorama Restaurant & Sky Lounge American/Peruvian   - | - | - | E

Coconut Grove | Sonesta Bayfront Hotel | 2889 McFarlane Rd., 8th fl. (bet. Grand Ave. & S. Bayshore Dr.) | 305-447-8256 | www.sonesta.com

At this eighth-floor aerie in Coconut Grove's Sonesta Bayfront Hotel, it's all about the sweeping views of Biscayne Bay seen through floor-to-ceiling windows in the elegant dining room or on the large outdoor terrace; the Peruvian offerings (along with some American favorites) are expensive, but the payoff is that swooningly romantic panorama.

Panya Thai *Thai*   ▽ 25 | 19 | 25 | $27
North Miami Beach | 520 NE 167th St. (bet. 5th & 6th Aves.) | 305-945-8566

"Not for the pad Thai crowd", this North Miami Beach Siamese thrills heat-seekers with "vibrant, spicy" cooking (further proof of its authenticity: there's no sushi on the menu); a strip-mall setting is a drawback to some, but fans say this place "really delivers" the goods at a moderate price.

Papichi *Italian*   20 | 16 | 19 | $31
Pinecrest | 9619 S. Dixie Hwy. (Datran Blvd.) | 305-668-1848 | www.papichirestaurant.com

"Pasta, pizza and chicken" (paillard, picatta, parmigiana, caprese, Marsala) rule the roost at this Brazilian-influenced Italian in Pinecrest that's a "consistent" "neighborhood" pleaser; some cluck that the quarters are a bit "too small and noisy", but it works for "casual" family dining for not much scratch.

Paquito's *Mexican*   22 | 18 | 21 | $28
North Miami Beach | RK 162nd Biscayne Plaza | 16265 Biscayne Blvd. (Sunny Isles Blvd.) | 305-947-5027 | www.paquitosmiami.com

"Real Mexican food" is "hidden in the corner of a strip mall" at this North Miami Beach cantina, where a "large Latin crowd" chows down on "huge portions" of "cheap", "authentic" chow; compadres congregate in the "friendly" bar for "excellent margaritas" and take in the weekend mariachi music.

Z Pascal's on Ponce Ⓢ *French*   27 | 20 | 25 | $66
Coral Gables | 2611 Ponce de Leon Blvd. (Valencia Ave.) | 305-444-2024 | www.pascalmiami.com

"Creativity abounds" in the "*magnifique*" New French fare at chef-owner Pascal Oudin's "unassuming" storefront bistro "just off the Mile" in Coral Gables; the space is about as "small" as the bills are "big", but "first-rate" service and "soufflés so light that you won't gain a pound" help explain why most find it "always a treat."

Pasha's *Mediterranean*   19 | 14 | 17 | $20
Brickell Area | 1414 Brickell Ave. (SE 14th St.) | Miami | 305-416-5116
Brickell Area | Four Seasons Hotel | 1441 Brickell Ave. (SE 14th Terr.) | Miami | 305-381-3938
Downtown | 1120 NW 14th St. (Highland Rd.) | Miami | 305-243-7693 Ⓢ
Coral Gables | 130 Miracle Mile (bet. Galiano St. & Ponce de Leon Blvd.) | 305-764-3040
Design District | 3801 N. Miami Ave. (I-195) | Miami | 305-572-1150 Ⓢ
Aventura | Aventura Mall | 19501 Biscayne Blvd. (NE 195th St.) | 305-917-4007
South Beach | 900 Lincoln Rd. (Jefferson Ave.) | Miami Beach | 305-673-3919 ◗
www.pashas.com

For a "quick", "healthy" bite, these mostly counter-service Med "fast-food" joints are just what the doctor ordered (and are officially endorsed by the South Beach Diet folks); surveyors agree that they're "well run", but split on the price: "great value" vs. "costly kebabs."

Paul Bakery *Bakery/Sandwiches*   20 | 16 | 14 | $21

Aventura | Aventura Mall | 19575 Biscayne Blvd. (NE 195th St.) | 305-682-8012

South Beach | 450 Lincoln Rd. (bet. Drexel & Washington Aves.) | Miami Beach | 305-531-1200

www.paulusa.com

"Almost Paris" is the vibe at these French bakery/cafe combos whose "light bites" include "fresh sandwiches", "wonderful bread" and "lip-smacking desserts" served in a cafeteria-style, counter-serve format; sure, it's possible to "spend more time in line than eating", but "amazingly" low tabs keep it popular; P.S. Lincoln Road boasts prime "people-watching" frontage.

NEW Peacock Garden Café *Eclectic*   - | - | - | M

Coconut Grove | 2889 McFarlane Rd. (bet. Grand Ave. & S. Bayshore Dr.) | 305-774-3332 | www.peacockspot.com

Eduardo "Lalo" Durazo (owner of Jaguar and Talavera) "has done it again" at this new midpriced Eclectic grill that's "utterly hidden" in the oldest part of the Grove but certainly "worth" hunting down; it gets bonus points for one of the "most beautiful gardens imaginable" outfitted with wrought-iron tables and landscaped with "exuberant tropical foliage."

Pelican RestCafé ● *American/Italian*   21 | 18 | 20 | $48

South Beach | Pelican Hotel | 826 Ocean Dr. (bet. 8th & 9th Sts.) | Miami Beach | 305-673-1000 | www.pelicanhotel.com

The extensive American and Italian offerings are "better than many other places on Ocean Drive" at this "small", morning-to-late-night cafe in the Diesel-owned Pelican Hotel; the "expensive" tabs are justified by an "accommodating" staff and a "comfortable"-as-a-favorite-pair-of-jeans veranda that's a perfect perch to "watch the parade" go by.

Peppy's in the Gables *Italian*   21 | 14 | 22 | $32

Coral Gables | 216 Palermo Ave. (Ponce de Leon Blvd.) | 305-448-1240

"Delicious" Northern Italiana that "tastes homemade" is the draw at this "wonderful little gem" in Coral Gables, where candlelight lends an "intimate" vibe; aesthetes shrug it's a bit "run-down", but there's nothing wrong with the "reasonable" tabs (i.e. the "great wine prices" and that $20 four-course dinner deal).

Perricone's Marketplace & Cafe *Italian*   22 | 21 | 22 | $35

Brickell Area | 15 SE 10th St. (S. Miami Ave.) | Miami | 305-374-9449 | www.perricones.com

Just about "every Brickellite" from "business types to "first dates" makes "repeat visits" to this "charming" oasis – a rustic "old Vermont barn" plunked down in the middle of Miami – for its "excellent" country Italian cooking; efficient" but "unobtrusive" service, a "beautiful" garden with "lots of foliage" and live jazz Wednesday–

Sunday nights add to the overall "pleasure"; P.S. there's also an on-site gourmet market.

Petit Rouge ☒ French
▽ 26 | 18 | 24 | $47

North Miami | 12409 Biscayne Blvd. (NE 124th St.) | 305-892-7676 | www.petitrougebistro.com

"So civilized" and "so delicious", this "outstanding" North Miami French bistro offers a menu that's limited in scope but "consistent" and made from "quality" ingredients; the "professional" staff lends a "civilized" air to the "tiny" space, which remains a "hidden secret."

P.F. Chang's China Bistro *Chinese*
20 | 20 | 19 | $34

Brickell Area | Mary Brickell Vill. | 901 S. Miami Ave. (SW 10th St.) | Miami | 305-358-0732

North Miami Beach | 17455 Biscayne Blvd. (bet. NE 172nd St. & Point East Dr.) | 305-957-1966

Pinecrest | The Falls Shopping Ctr. | 8888 SW 136th St. (S. Dixie Hwy.) | 305-234-2338

🆕 **Doral** | Dolphin Mall | 11361 NW 12th St. (111th Ave.) | Miami | 305-591-5603
www.pfchangs.com

This "chain that doesn't feel like a chain" is a "reliable" "crowd-pleaser", dispensing "tasty" Chinese food with "a twist"; though some critics cite a "formulaic" approach, "interminable waits" at prime times and "zoo"-like crowds, at least the zookeepers are "attentive" and the price of admission "reasonable"; P.S. celiacs "love" the extensive gluten-free offerings.

🆕 Pied à Terre *Mediterranean*
‑ | ‑ | ‑ | VE

South Beach | Cadet Hotel | 1701 James Ave., 2nd fl. (17th St.) | Miami Beach | 305-531-4533 | www.piedaterrerestaurant.com

A limited menu of well-prepared Mediterranean dishes is served at this elegant new home away from home hidden away on the second floor of the historic, 1940s-era Cadet Hotel; though decidedly pricey, it's a quiet, romantic respite from the SoBe scene.

Pilar *American/Seafood*
23 | 20 | 22 | $38

Aventura | 20475 Biscayne Blvd. (NE 203rd St.) | 305-937-2777 | www.pilarrestaurant.com

Clearly, the chef-owner of this Aventura eatery plainly "loves his job" as evidenced by the "excellent" New American seafood offered at a "decent price"; "superb" service and "serene" atmospherics make for an "elegant" dining experience "despite the location in a strip mall anchored by a Chuck E. Cheese's."

🆕 Pincho Factory ❂ *Eclectic*
‑ | ‑ | ‑ | I

Westchester | 9860 Bird Rd. (SW 99th Ave.) | Miami | 305-631-2038 | www.pinchofactory.com

The Eclectic menu at this Westchester fueling station is almost as narrow as its dining room: grilled skewered meats in a choice of pita, salad or rice bowl with a limited range of toppings (a burger and hot dog round out the offerings); its cheap tabs are in keeping with the tightly packed tables and minimalist look.

	FOOD	DECOR	SERVICE	COST

Piola ◐ *Pizza*   22 | 17 | 19 | $26

Brickell Area | 1250 S. Miami Ave. (SW 13th St.) | Miami |
305-374-0031
South Beach | 1625 Alton Rd. (bet. Lincoln Rd. & 16th St.) |
Miami Beach | 305-674-1660
www.piola.it

"Cravable" thin-crust pizzas and "quality" pasta are the lures at
these SoFla outposts of an international Italian chain; "electronic
music", potent drinks like the signature *sgroppino al limone* (lemon
ice cream with vodka) and "popular happy hours" make them "fun
hangouts" for "trendy" types.

Pita Hut *Israeli*   ▽ 20 | 10 | 15 | $18

Miami Beach | 530 Arthur Godfrey Rd. (bet. Prairie & Royal Palm Aves.) |
305-531-6090 | www.pita-hut.com

This Miami Beach "favorite" specializes in Israeli staples like "outstanding falafel and shawarma" but ups the ante with kosher
sushi; it's "reliable" and "cheap", though patrons must endure
mixed service ("friendly" vs. "surly") so "grab-and-go isn't as
easy as it could be" and "unassuming", utilitarian digs.

Pit Bar-B-Q *BBQ*   ▽ 21 | 8 | 13 | $21

Westernmost Dade | 16400 SW Eighth St. (Krome Ave.) | Miami |
305-226-2272 | www.thepitbarbq.com

'Cue connoisseurs maintain it's "worth the long drive on the
Tamiami Trail" to this landmark smokehouse that's been dishing up
"authentic", "down-home" barbecue in Westernmost Dade since
1965; beyond live salsa music on Sundays, amenitywise it's strictly
ceiling fans and plastic tableware and visitors are advised to bring
along "mosquito repellent."

Pizza Rustica ◐ *Pizza*   19 | 10 | 15 | $15

NEW **Brickell Area** | 500 Brickell Ave. (bet. 5th & 6th Sts.) | Miami |
786-787-8422
South Beach | 1447 Washington Ave. (Española Way) | Miami Beach |
305-538-6009
South Beach | 667 Lincoln Rd. (bet. Euclid & Meridian Aves.) |
Miami Beach | 305-672-2334
South Beach | 863 Washington Ave. (bet. 8th & 9th Sts.) |
Miami Beach | 305-674-8244
South Miami | 6800 SW 57th Ave. (Ponce de Leon Blvd.) |
305-740-6464
NEW **Doral** | 9769 NW 41st St. (97th Ave.) | Miami |
305-499-9757
NEW **West Miami** | West Miami University Shoppes |
1671 SW 107th Ave. (SW 16th St.) | 786-458-8100
www.pizza-rustica.com

"Huge square slices" sporting thick "chewy crusts" and loaded with
"quality toppings" are the trademarks of these separately owned,
counter-serve pizzerias; there's "no atmosphere" and some purists
are turned off by the "reheated"-from-the-display-case system, but
overall they do the trick "after a night of partying"; P.S. the popular
SoBe branches feature "great people-watching."

Por Fin *Mediterranean/Spanish*
23 | 24 | 22 | $53

Coral Gables | 2500 Ponce de Leon Blvd. (Andalusia Ave.) | 305-441-0107 | www.porfinrestaurant.com

The "bold", "sophisticated" dishes at this pricey Coral Gables Spanish-Med remain "true to their roots" in Catalonia while exhibiting "many modern touches"; furthering the seaside "vacation" feel is the space's "classic Mediterranean look", "professional" staff and relaxing drinks at the "great little bar upstairs."

Prelude By Barton G. Ⓜ *American*
22 | 26 | 22 | $57

Downtown | Adrienne Arsht Ctr. | 1300 Biscayne Blvd. (NE 14th St.) | Miami | 305-357-7900 | www.preludebybartong.com

"Flashy", "knockout" scenery steals the spotlight from the perfectly "pleasant" contemporary American cuisine on the menu at this Arsht Center eatery that's a "convenient" staging ground for ticket-holders who note that "quick" service makes for a "seamless" theatergoing experience; dinner service begins with a $39 three-course prix fixe, but à la carte is available after 8 PM (reservations are highly suggested).

Prime Italian ● *Italian/Steak*
24 | 22 | 22 | $77

South Beach | Hilton Bentley Miami/South Beach | 101 Ocean Dr. (1st St.) | Miami Beach | 305-695-8484 | www.mylesrestaurantgroup.com

"Gigantic portions" of high-end Italian steakhouse fare (e.g. "delicious" Kobe meatballs and short-rib risotto) make it all too easy to "eat yourself into oblivion" at this modern-deco spot in SoBe's Hilton Bentley; an "engaged" staff attends to the roaring "scene", but "since nothing is free, expect to be charged for people-watching"; P.S. it's an excellent plan B if you can't access its "sister across the street", Prime One Twelve.

⛝ Prime One Twelve ● *Seafood/Steak*
27 | 23 | 22 | $87

South Beach | 112 Ocean Dr. (1st St.) | Miami Beach | 305-532-8112 | www.prime112.com

"Super sexy" yet "serious", this South Beach surf 'n' turfer dishes up "monstrous" portions of "amazing" food, but it's just as well known for hosting the "scene of scenes", with "Bentleys, Ferraris and Lambos" pulling up out front and "wannabes" "rubbing elbows" ("literally; they pack 'em in") with "movie stars", "sports legends" and "models" inside; downsides include "noise", "long waits", variable service and "black-card" tabs, but hey, "you'll have a story to tell."

Provence Grill *French*
∇ 24 | 17 | 25 | $42

South Beach | 1223 Lincoln Rd. (bet. Alton Rd. & West Ave.) | Miami Beach | 305-531-1600 | www.provencegrill.com

A "little bit of France" turns up in South Beach at this "classy" but "affordable" bistro at the western edge of Lincoln Road (i.e. "not on the mall"); a "polished" staff working in sync with "smooth kitchen service" does justice to the "finely prepared" Franco fare, and there's a bonus parking lot.

FOOD | DECOR | SERVICE | COST

NEW Pubbelly ● Ⓜ *Asian*

24 | 22 | 22 | $38

Miami Beach | 1418 20th St. (bet. Bay Rd. & Purdy Ave.) | 305-532-7555 | www.pubbelly.com

"Porktastic!" squeal fans of this pig-centric Miami Beach gastropub that pairs "rich", "creative" Asian fusion fare with a strong selection of craft brews and wine; the "'in' crowd" that throngs the rustic "hole-in-the-wall" digs declares it a "great spot to start, end or make an evening" thanks to its small- and large-plate options, moderate prices and "down-to-earth service.

NEW Pubbelly Sushi *Asian*

- | - | - | M

Miami Beach | 1424 20th St. (Purdy Ave.) | 305-531-9282 | www.pubbellysushi.com

Miami Beach's Sunset Harbor is home to this new Asian fusion sushi specialist, the second entry in the burgeoning Pubbelly empire (at press time Barceloneta, a Spaniard, was about to debut nearby); the industrial space lined with concrete floors, exposed air ducts and Japanese anime murals exudes an upscale-casual vibe that matches the midrange tabs and hip list of sake, wine and microbrews.

Puerto Sagua ● *Cuban*

23 | 10 | 18 | $21

South Beach | 700 Collins Ave. (7th St.) | Miami Beach | 305-673-1115

"Nothing has changed" at this Cuban diner "landmark" in South Beach since "before the revolution" (or at least since it opened in 1962); "waiters in little red jackets" are still ferrying "rock-solid" comfort food around the "greasy spoon"–style digs "without any fuss", and best of all the bills are still low.

Quattro Gastronomia Italiana *Italian*

20 | 22 | 18 | $64

South Beach | 1014 Lincoln Rd. (bet. Lenox & Michigan Aves.) | Miami Beach | 305-531-4833 | www.quattromiami.com

A "stylish", "air-kissing" clientele tucks into "solid" Northern Italian food and "great drinks" at this "beautiful" SoBe venue; critics complain that the staff is "not pro", but admit that the experience is "better than it needs to be" given its primary purpose: watching the "show unfolding" on Lincoln Road.

Quinn's Restaurant *Seafood*

25 | 23 | 23 | $59

South Beach | Park Central Hotel | 640 Ocean Dr. (bet. 6th & 7th Sts.) | Miami Beach | 305-673-6400 | www.quinnsmiami.com

"Yes, Virginia, there is fine dining on Ocean Drive" at this spendy, "grown-ups"-only "touch of class" in the Park Central Hotel, where chef-owner Gerry Quinn prepares "superb" seafood (his Bam! Bam! shrimp is a "must-have"); an "accommodating" staff and "beautiful" nightly guitar music play supporting roles to the grand *Casablanca*-esque decor and the "runway" show out front.

Racks Italian Kitchen *Italian*

20 | 18 | 18 | $37

North Miami Beach | Intracoastal Mall | 3933 NE 163rd St. (Biscayne Blvd.) | 305-917-7225 | www.grrestaurant.com

"Waitresses dressed in skimpy outfits" lead some to label this North Miami Beach trattoria the "Italian Hooters", but beyond the bustiers, it

FOOD DECOR SERVICE COST

offers "amazing" pizzas and "well-done" primi and secondi at moderate prices, not to mention "beautiful water views"; P.S. Wednesday's $5 hamburger night is a "winner."

Randazzo's Little Italy *Italian*   20 | 20 | 19 | $41
Coral Gables | 385 Miracle Mile (SW 42nd Ave.) | 305-448-7002 | www.randazzoslittleitaly.com

Festooned with "memorabilia" from co-owner Marc Randazzo's "days as a Chicago prizefighter", this bi-level Coral Gables Italian serves "stick-to-your-ribs" dishes in "gargantuan" portions (think "softball-size meatballs"); featherweights fuss that "big isn't always better", but fans call it a "hoot."

Ra Sushi *Japanese*   19 | 21 | 18 | $34
South Miami | 5829 SW 72nd St. (bet. 58th Ave. & 58th Ct.) | 305-341-0092 | www.rasushi.com
See review in Palm Beach County Directory.

Red Fish Grill Ⓜ *Seafood*   22 | 26 | 22 | $46
Coral Gables | Matheson Hammock Pk. | 9610 Old Cutler Rd. (96th St.) | 305-668-8788 | www.redfishgrill.net

"Tucked away down a dirt road" in Coral Gables is this "historic building" in Matheson Hammock Park flaunting "scenic" bay views from its "beautiful outdoor terrace" that are catnip for "romantic" types; a few say the piscatorial offerings are a bit "ordinary" (though perfectly "fresh") and the tabs a tad "pricey", but ultimately the "ambiance" alone is "worth it"; P.S. "bathrooms are shared with beachgoers."

🆕 Red Koi Food Truck ♥ *Japanese/Thai*   - | - | - | I
Location varies; see website | Miami | no phone | www.redkoilounge.com

Coral Gables' Red Koi Lounge recently added this baby fish to the crowded food truck pond, but it stands out with an eye-catching black-and-red paint job and a cash-only high-tech menu displayed on twin plasma screens; if you're coy about eating sushi off the side of a van, there are veggie spring rolls, Bangkok shrimp tacos, pad Thai and other Siamese treats for cheap.

Red Koi Thai &   25 | 20 | 23 | $31
Sushi Lounge *Japanese/Thai*
Coral Gables | 317 Miracle Mile (Le Jeune Rd.) | 305-446-2690 | www.redkoilounge.com

"One of the largest sushi selections" in Coral Gables is yours at this "fun" Japanese-Thai where the cooking is "inventive" and the drinks "yummy"; a near-"perfect" staff oversees the sleek minimalist dining room and sidewalk patio (with "coveted" Miracle Mile frontage), while a candelit lounge upstairs hosts "crazy" Thursday night karaoke.

Red Light *American*   23 | 12 | 13 | $37
Upper East Side | Motel Blu | 7700 Biscayne Blvd. (76th St.) | Miami | 305-757-7773 | www.redlightmiami.com

"Bohemian gourmets" gravitate to this "funky" Upper East Sider attached to a "retro motel", where "awesome chef" Kris Wessel turns out "creative" contemporary Americana with Big Easy spins ("those shrimp!") at "good prices"; the dinerlike digs prompt debate ("enjoyably seedy" vs. a "dive", though there is riverside alfresco seating) and service takes lots of flak ("useless", "slooow"), but for most, the "food makes it all worthwhile"; P.S. closed seasonally from July to mid-August.

⛴ Red, The Steakhouse *Steak*

27 | 25 | 24 | $83

South Beach | 119 Washington Ave. (1st St.) | Miami Beach | 305-534-3688 | www.redthesteakhouse.com

As the name implies, this "classy" South Beach steakhouse is a true "red meat/red wine lover's paradise" with its "juicy", "velvety" Angus beef and "extensive wine collection" displayed behind a glass wall – though the "extravagant" price tags require a lot of green; an "attentive" staff, a "cool ambiance" and a "stylish" "contemporary" look complete the "first-rate" experience.

Revales *Italian*

– | – | – | E

Upper East Side | 8601 Biscayne Blvd. (bet. NE 86th & 87th Sts.) | Miami | 305-758-1010 | www.revalesitalianrestaurant.com

At this "nice neighborhood" catchall, Upper East Siders are as likely to start their day with American breakfast staples as they are to stop by for a quick lunch of panini or enjoy an evening of more expensive "old-fashioned" Italian classics; the bright, airy dining room is dressed simply in sunny gold and earth colors and features a small bar.

Rice House of Kabob *Persian*

22 | 12 | 17 | $20

NEW **Brickell Area** | 50 SW 10th St. (bet. 1st & Miami Aves.) | Miami | 305-755-9588

NEW **North Miami** | 14480 Biscayne Blvd. (NE 146th St.) | 305-944-4899

South Beach | 1318 Alton Rd. (bet. 13th & 14th Sts.) | Miami Beach | 305-531-0332

Kendall | 13742 SW 56th St. (137th Ave.) | 305-387-6815

Doral | 1450 NW 87th Ave. (15th St.) | Miami | 305-418-9464

www.ricehouseofkabob.com

"Tasty morsels" of meat, chicken and fish "grilled to perfection" and other Persian "delectables" are the draw at this "fast-food" kebabery with multiple outposts in the greater Miami area; the counter-serve setups have "no atmosphere", but the "efficient" staff is "quick" and the "value" high.

NEW Rickenbacker Fish Company *Seafood*

∇ 20 | 20 | 19 | $38

Key Biscayne | 3301 Rickenbacker Cswy. (Arthur Lamb Jr. Rd.) | 305-361-0040 | www.rickenbackerfishcompany.com

"Spectacular" views of Biscayne Bay and the Miami skyline from the tip of Virginia Key make this new "upscale" seafood spot a "fun place to eat on the Causeway"; dock-and-diners appreciate the "moderate prices" and nautical trappings, while the outdoor tiki bar is staffed by a "showman" bartender who "takes pride" crafting "great drinks."

	FOOD	DECOR	SERVICE	COST

River Oyster Bar *Seafood* | 25 | 20 | 22 | $49 |

Miami River | 650 S. Miami Ave. (SW 7th St.) | Miami | 305-530-1915 | www.therivermiami.com

This "sophisticated" bar and grill near the Miami River "hits all the right notes" for Downtown's "after-work" crowd via an "impressive array" of bivalves and "fresh fish prepared with style", paired with a "wonderful wine list"; its "sleek interior" works equally well as a "pickup bar" for "handsome" professionals or a place to "dine alone" – either way, expect "attentive" service and "fair prices."

Rock Fish Grill Ⓜ *American/Seafood*   ▽ 24 | 18 | 21 | $24 |

Kendall | Kendall Gates Shopping Ctr. | 12042 N. Kendall Dr. (SW 122nd Ave.) | 305-271-1251 | www.rockfishmiami.com

Near Florida's Turnpike in West Kendall, this "super-affordable" "hidden gem" turns out "tasty" fish dinners along with familiar American standards; it also channels the Hard Rock Cafe with walls plastered with rock 'n' roll memorabilia from the friendly owners' collection; P.S. sample staffer T-shirt: "if the music's too loud, you're too old!"

Romeo's Cafe Ⓢ Ⓜ *Italian*   26 | 19 | 26 | $88 |

Coral Way | 2257 SW 22nd St. (22nd Ave.) | Miami | 305-859-2228 | www.romeoscafe.com

The "personal touch" is an art form at this "tiny", "romantic" Northern Italian in Coral Way where "friendly" chef-owner Romeo Majano stops by each table to discuss "your tastes", then whips up "one amazing dish after the other" customized "just for you"; it's "on the pricey side" (four-course dinner for $60, six for $90; no à la carte) but that befits a "unique", "special-occasion" place; reservations required.

Rosalia's *Italian*   17 | 15 | 18 | $37 |

Aventura | Aventura Mall | 19501 Biscayne Blvd. (NE 195th St.) | 305-792-2006 | www.aventuramall.com

"Quick service", modest costs and a wide "variety" of "basic" (some say "bland") Italiana – panini, pizzas, pasta and more – make this small bistro a solid alternative to busier spots in the Aventura Mall; thanks to a "nice" wine-by-the-glass list on the outside patio, weary shoppers may "not even realize they're in a mall."

Rosa Mexicano *Mexican*   22 | 23 | 21 | $41 |

Brickell Area | Mary Brickell Vill. | 900 S. Miami Ave. (bet. SW 9th & 10th Sts.) | Miami | 786-425-1001

NEW **South Beach** | 1111 Lincoln Rd. (Alton Rd.) | Miami Beach | 305-695-1005 ☻

www.rosamexicano.com

"Not your run-of-the-mill taco joints", these transplants of a NYC-based chain serve "creative" "gourmet Mexican" fare like "delicious" guacamole "made tableside", washed down with lethal pomegranate margaritas; both the Brickell and SoBe outlets boast "fun, festive" settings enhanced by "engaged" front-of-the-house crews.

	FOOD	DECOR	SERVICE	COST

Rosinella *Italian*   20 | 13 | 19 | $33

Brickell Area | 1040 S. Miami Ave. (bet. 10th & 11th Sts.) | Miami | 305-372-5756
South Beach | 525 Lincoln Rd. (bet. Drexel & Pennsylvania Aves.) | Miami Beach | 305-672-8777 ◗
www.rosinella.net

These "reliable" "neighborhood joints" in Brickell and SoBe are prized for their "scrumptious" homemade pasta ("you don't have to say 'al dente'" here) and other "simple" Italian staples; "fairly priced wines" add to the "value", and if they look too "ordinary", just "close your eyes and think of Trastevere."

NEW Route 9 Ⓜ *Floribbean/Mediterranean*   ▽ 20 | 16 | 21 | $39

Coral Gables | 1915 Ponce de Leon Blvd. (bet. Majorca & Navarre Aves.) | 305-569-9009 | www.route9miami.com

A "nice new addition" to Coral Gables, this simple but "stylish" bistro is run by a "young CIA-grad couple" who aim to please with midpriced Floribbean-Med cooking; fans say they may "need to step up the effort" a bit, though, to become more than just a "neighborhood" spot.

NEW Roxy ◗ *Pub Food*   - | - | - | I

North Miami | 12600 Biscayne Blvd. (bet. NE 126th & 127th Sts.) | 305-899-7699 | www.roxymiami.com

Waitresses in midriff-baring shirts aren't the only part of the decor that's exposed at this late-night pub in North Miami (the brick and ductwork are too); the cheap American eats include a variety of burgers and a large selection of wings plus a full slate of adult beverages.

NEW Royal, The *American*   - | - | - | E

South Beach | Raleigh Hotel | 1775 Collins Ave. (17th St.) | Miami Beach | 305-534-6300 | www.raleighhotel.com

This fresh face at the celeb-dormitory Raleigh Hotel is a "welcoming" all-day "oasis", starting with its "wonderful breakfasts by the beautiful pool" and concluding with "romantic" dinners beneath "illuminated" foliage; the contemporary American dishes are shot through with Italian influences and made from locally sourced ingredients, accounting for the high prices.

Royal Bavarian   ▽ 21 | 18 | 23 | $33
Schnitzel Haus Ⓜ *German*

Upper East Side | 1085 NE 79th St. (10th Ave.) | Miami | 305-754-8002 | www.schnitzelhausmiami.com

Nein, this ain't no ersatz Bavarian food hall – devotees tout its "real-deal" schnitzel, spaetzle and potato pancakes, served by "authentic Germans" to boot; though the "heavy" dishes are "not an easy sell" on Miami's Upper East Side, "almost-cheap" prices, a "charming" outdoor biergarten and "good dark beer" compensate.

Ruth's Chris Steak House *Steak*   25 | 23 | 24 | $65

Coral Gables | 2320 Salzedo St. (Aragon Ave.) | 305-461-8360 | www.ruthschris.com

That "sizzling" noise is the sound of "delicious" steaks slathered in butter approaching your table at these "special-occasion" steak-

	FOOD	DECOR	SERVICE	COST

houses imported from New Orleans; service is close to "impeccable" and the wine list "extensive", but "high prices" leave some wishing that they would "throw in a side for free."

Sakaya Kitchen *Korean* | 22 | 14 | 16 | $22 |

Downtown | Midtown Shops | 3401 N. Miami Ave. (entrance on Buena Vista Ave., bet. 34th & 36th Sts.) | Miami | 305-576-8096 | www.sakayakitchen.com

"Some of the best Korean food in town" turns up at this "no-frills" Downtown counter-service joint offering "seriously flavorful" fare from the Peninsula; "quick" service and prices that "don't take a toll on the wallet" are further pluses, and it also has a drolly named food truck: Dim Ssäm à Gogo.

Sake Room ☒ *Japanese* | – | – | – | M |

Downtown | 1800 Biscayne Plaza | 275 NE 18th St. (Biscayne Blvd.) | Miami | 305-755-0122 | www.sakeroom.com

A Downtown crowd slides into this stylish sliver of a space – decked out with paper lanterns and modern Zen furnishings – for its artfully presented Japanese dishes, sushi and reverse-engineered fusion items (tiraditos, ceviche); prices are relatively moderate and, as the name suggests, it's brimming with sake.

Sakura *Japanese* | ∇ 24 | 16 | 24 | $30 |

Coral Gables | 440 S. Dixie Hwy. (SW 42nd Ave.) | 305-665-7020 | www.sakuragables.com

This "established neighborhood" Japanese in Coral Gables has been around forever thanks to "excellent sushi" made from the "freshest" fish; the "small", "simple" setting could stand a "makeover", but the moderate prices and hands-on owners who "go above and beyond to please" are fine as is.

Salmon & Salmon *Peruvian* | ∇ 25 | 8 | 23 | $32 |

Little Havana | 2907 NW Seventh St. (bet. 29th & 30th Aves.) | Miami | 305-649-5924

For 30 years, this Peruvian enclave in Little Havana has been serving "outstanding quality" ceviche and other traditional dishes to a loyal following; the only "issue" is that the stuccoed, wood-paneled room has "limited seating", so "get there early or risk waiting."

Salsa Fiesta *Mexican* | – | – | – | I |

Wynwood | 2929 Biscayne Blvd. (bet. NE 29th & 30th Sts.) | Miami | 305-400-8245 | www.salsafiestagrill.com

Made-to-order salsas prepare the taste buds for the "fresh" gourmet tacos and burritos served at this upscale-"casual" fast-food Mexican in Wynwood, where patrons order from the "pleasant" counter crew, then await their food in the "colorful" industrial dining area; the newer Pembroke Pines branch is a step toward a planned empire.

S&S Restaurant ⊅ *Diner* | ∇ 23 | 16 | 23 | $16 |

Downtown | 1757 NE Second Ave. (17th St.) | Miami | 305-373-4291

"Friendly waitresses" have been smiling at patrons seated around the U-shaped counter at this "authentic" corner diner in Downtown

Miami "since the Depression"; a "tiny remnant of yesteryear", it serves "old-fashioned comfort food" that's "typical" but "oh-so-good" and comes "value"-priced (though you must pay cash); hours are 6 AM–6 PM weekdays and 6 AM–2 PM weekends.

Sardinia ◐ *Italian* — 26 | 20 | 23 | $56

Miami Beach | 1801 Purdy Ave. (18th St.) | 305-531-2228 | www.sardinia-ristorante.com

There's always a "good crowd" of "locals" and a convivial "buzz" at this "romantic" and "expensive" Sardinian spot in a "quiet" "out-of-the-way" corner of Miami Beach; the "personable" staff aids novices attempting to navigate the "unusual", "super-delicious" cuisine choices that include items baked in a wood-burning oven, and oenophiles are excited by "hard-to-find" Sardinian wines.

Sawa ◐ *Mediterranean/Mideastern* — ▽ 21 | 21 | 18 | $39

Coral Gables | Village of Merrick Park | 360 San Lorenzo Ave. (SW 42nd Ave.) | 305-447-6555 | www.sawarestaurant.com

Choices abound at this "fun" midpriced Coral Gables multitasker that boasts a "more interesting menu than usual for a Florida restaurant" – mainly Med and Middle Eastern dishes, but also a full slate of sushi and a smattering of other international specialties (plus a rather robust 'doggy menu' – it's a pooch-friendly establishment); patrons can also pick the setting: a sexy bar, elegant dining room, outdoor patio or hookah lounge.

Scarpetta *Italian* — 25 | 26 | 23 | $79

Miami Beach | Fontainebleau Miami Beach | 4441 Collins Ave. (W. 44th St.) | 305-674-4660 | www.fontainebleau.com

"Spaghetti with oomph", the "best polenta this side of heaven" and other "outstanding" Italian fare make diners "happy to have Scott Conant's talents in Miami" at this Fontainebleau spin-off of the NYC original; yes it's "pricey", but "you get what you pay for", including "thoughtful, efficient" service and a "captivating" setting complete with "fantastic" water views and *Top Model*-like patrons.

Scotty's Landing *American* — 14 | 18 | 15 | $22

Coconut Grove | 3381 Pan American Dr. (S. Bayshore Dr.) | 305 854-2626

"If they had better food, you could never get into" this "open-air" waterfront "dive bar" in Coconut Grove that flaunts "beautiful Biscayne Bay" views; despite "sometimes-slow service", the "beer is cold", the "simple" American menu is "ok" if you stick to basics like burgers or fish sandwiches, and there's always a "breeze."

☒ Seasons 52 *American* — 23 | 24 | 23 | $42

NEW **Coral Gables** | 321 Miracle Mile (Salzedo St.) | 305-442-8552 | www.seasons52.com

See review in Ft. Lauderdale/Broward County Directory.

Sergio's ◐ *Cuban* — 20 | 14 | 18 | $19

Coral Way | 3252 SW 22nd St. (32nd Ave.) | Miami | 305-529-0047
Kendall | 13550 SW 120th St. (137th Ave.) | 305-278-2024

(continued)
Sergio's
Westchester | 9330 SW 40th St. (bet. 93rd & 94th Aves.) | Miami | 305-552-9626
www.sergios.com

"Packed" at breakfast and late-night, this cafe chainlet offers "tremendous value" via "big portions" of "quality" Cuban and Latin "standards"; the staffers are "pleasant" (despite an occasional language barrier) and accommodating to "families", but those unimpressed by the "hole-in-the-wall" ambiance say delivery is the "best feature."

☑ Setai, Retaurant at The *Asian* | 23 | 28 | 23 | $86 |
South Beach | The Setai | 2001 Collins Ave. (21st St.) | Miami Beach | 305-520-6000 | www.setai.com

"Zen elegance" dazzles the eye at this "stunning" Setai Hotel dining room in SoBe – and the "sumptuous" Pan-Asian dishes "measure up" to the "exotic" decor; a "superb" staff and "fabulous Sunday brunch" with live jazz are further draws, but brace yourself for "astonishingly expensive" tabs.

Shake Shack *Burgers* | 22 | 15 | 17 | $17 |
South Beach | 1111 Lincoln Rd. (Lenox Ave.) | Miami Beach | 305-434-7787 | www.shakeshack.com

"Warning: this place is addicting" report those "waiting in line" for the "dang good burgers" and Key lime pie concretes at this "funky" SoBe outpost of the famed NYC original; it's "serve and seat yourself" and a few feel "let down" by "brilliant branding" but only "so-so" food, yet overall the majority has joined the "cult" of Danny Meyer; P.S. "bring Lipitor."

Shibui ● *Japanese* | 24 | 19 | 23 | $32 |
Kendall | 10141 SW 72nd St. (102nd Ave.) | 305-274-5578 | www.shibuimiami.com

"Sushi snobs" flip over the "excellent", fairly priced raw fish sliced at this "friendly" Kendall Japanese that "never has an off day" – "no wonder it's been there" for 30 years; reservations are recommended, and the "strip-mall" digs are easier to abide if you "lose your shoes and head to the upstairs seating area."

Shorty's Bar-B-Q *BBQ* | 22 | 14 | 19 | $21 |
South Miami | 9200 S. Dixie Hwy. (Dadeland Blvd.) | 305-670-7732
Doral | 2255 NW 87th Ave. (bet. 21st Terr. & 25th St.) | Miami | 305-471-5554
Westchester | 11575 SW 40th St. (117th Ave.) | Miami | 305-227-3196
www.shortys.com

"Roll up your sleeves" and "get down and dirty" gnawing on the "fall-off-the-bone" BBQ and "buttery corn" at this homegrown chain of rib joints (the 1951 South Miami original is a "local landmark"); "cheap" tabs and "friendly" staffers work well against the "Western bunkhouse" decor that unfortunately includes "uncomfortable" picnic-table seating.

	FOOD	DECOR	SERVICE	COST

Shula's Steak House *Steak*   `23` `21` `22` `$65`

Miami Beach | Alexander Hotel | 5225 Collins Ave.
(north of Beach View Park) | 305-341-6565
Miami Lakes | 6842 Main St. (Ludlam Rd.) | 305-820-8047
Miami Lakes | Don Shula's Golf Club | 7601 NW Miami Lakes Dr.
(east of Palmetto Expwy.) | 305-820-8102 Ⓢ Ⓜ
www.donshula.com

This steakhouse chain from the former Dolphins coach "exudes testosterone" via "big honking steaks", "monster lobsters" and "bold red wines" – the menu is even printed on a pigskin; "excellent" service and clubby settings partly account for the "bring-your-banker" pricing, but disgruntled types ask "didn't Don make enough in football?"

Siam Palace *Thai*   ▽ `23` `19` `20` `$30`

South Miami | 9999 Sunset Dr. (SW 102nd Ave.) | 305-279-6906 |
www.siampalacemiami.com

In a town with "many Thai restaurants", this midpriced South Miami Siamese stands out as "one of the better" of the genre with its "flavorful curries" and "terrific pad Thai"; sashimi fans "love the fact" that it recently added sushi and other Japanese items to the mix.

660 @ The Angler's Ⓜ *American/Med.*   `23` `21` `19` `$58`

South Beach | The Angler's | 660 Washington Ave. (6th St.) |
Miami Beach | 786-594-5811 | www.theanglersresort.com

Well-heeled "grown-ups" are drawn to this "quiet" respite "off the beaten track" in SoBe's historic 1930s-era Angler's Hotel where a "creative chef" who's "willing to experiment" turns out a "solid" American-Med menu with eclectic influences; a "great bar" and lounge gives way to a "small, romantic" dining room, though regulars advise "sit outdoors if you can."

Smith & Wollensky ❶ *Steak*   `23` `24` `24` `$69`

South Beach | 1 Washington Ave. (S. Pointe Park.) | Miami Beach |
305-673-2800 | www.smithandwollensky.com

"Succulent" dry-aged hunks of meat, "killer wines" and "potent cocktails" slide down easy at this "expense-account" South Beach outpost of the NYC-based steakhouse chain, tended by "old-school" waiters in full-on "pampering" mode; "everything tastes better" on the patio with its "fabulous view" of "towering cruise ships" passing through the Government Cut channel "so close you can almost touch them."

NEW Soi Asian Bistro *Japanese/Thai*   `-` `-` `-` `M`

Downtown | 134 NE 2nd Ave. (bet. 1st & 2nd Sts.) | Miami |
305-523-3643

"Downtowners are lucky" to have this new arrival offering midpriced Japanese and Thai dishes that "pack a lot of flavor"; the tiny space ramps up the arty minimalism of its older sibling, Mr. Yum, with stark white walls offset by wasabi-green banquettes, plus hundreds of hanging paper bags lit from above and one giant piece of pop art.

NEW Soirée at Vice Lounge ◐ *Eclectic* — — — VE

South Beach | 330 Lincoln Rd. (Washington Ave.) | Miami Beach |
305-438-7835 | www.viceloungemiami.com

Tarted up like a Victorian brothel (think ornate gilt mirrors, red
flocked wallpaper and baroque chandeliers), this florid arrival in the
former O Asian/Rumi space is all about the scene, the booze and
the kickin' DJ; when bright young things break away from stronger
vices, food is also available: a premium-priced limited menu of
contemporary Eclectic eats.

Soya & Pomodoro 🗷 *Italian* ▽ 23 21 23 $24

Downtown | 120 NE First St. (bet. 1st & 2nd Aves.) | Miami |
305-381-9511

"Fresh" pasta and other Italiana is made with "love" at this "friendly"
"little" Downtowner that follows through with a very "romantic" vibe;
fans applaud the grand "architecture" of its quirky setting (an old
bank) as well as the live music: Cuban on Thursdays, jazz on Fridays.

Soyka *American* 20 21 20 $35

Upper East Side | 5556 NE Fourth Ct. (Biscayne Blvd.) | Miami |
305-759-3117 | www.soykarestaurant.com

"Fine dining on the cheap" is the ethos behind the "creatively prepared" New Americana at this "casual", "welcoming" Upper East Side
trailblazer; housed in a "way-cool" warehouse space, the main dining
area is open and airy, while the "little garden is gorgeous in winter."

NEW Spartico *Italian/Pizza* — — — M

Coconut Grove | Mayfair Hotel & Spa | 3000 Florida Ave. (Virginia Ave.) |
305-779-5135 | www.sparticorestaurant.com

A stone-faced wood-burning oven from Milan anchors this casual
spot in Coconut Grove's Mayfair Hotel, and likewise its crispy thin-
crust pies anchor a limited menu that also includes a few pastas and
Italian entrees; rustic decor, bar and patio areas and a parking lot
add value to the already moderate tabs.

Spiga *Italian* 24 20 23 $55

South Beach | 1228 Collins Ave. (bet. 12th & 13th Sts.) | Miami Beach |
305-534-0079 | www.spigarestaurant.com

"Grown-ups" gravitate to this "calm" "oasis" in "frenetic South
Beach" for "terrific", "straightforward" Northern Italian cuisine
served by a team that "makes you feel like you just landed in your
own private jet" (with a briefcase of money, naturally); "romance"
blooms in the villa's "lovely" front garden while the "intimate" interior is more staid.

Spris ◐ *Pizza* 22 15 19 $26

Coral Gables | 2305 Ponce de Leon Blvd. (Giralda Ave.) | 305-444-3388 |
www.spriscoralgables.com

South Beach | 731 Lincoln Rd. (bet. Euclid & Meridian Aves.) |
Miami Beach | 305-673-2020 | www.spris.cc

These "Italian comfort-food" purveyors in SoBe and Coral Gables
turn out an "excellent product": "crisp", "thin-crust" pizzas accompanied by "fresh salads" (the entrees are just "so-so"), served by

"cute" waiters for "reasonable" sums; Lincoln Road's large outdoor area is particularly great for "primo people-watching."

☑ Sra. Martinez Ⓜ *Spanish* 25 | 24 | 24 | $55

Design District | 4000 NE Second Ave. (bet. 40th & 41st Sts.) | Miami | 305-573-5474 | www.sramartinez.com

"Another winner for Michelle Bernstein", aka Señora Martinez, this "cool" Spaniard draws a "young, hip Design District crowd" with its "fabulous array" of "exciting" tapas ("good for sharing"), served by a "proficient" staff in a "cavernous" former post office dressed up with "smart", "colorful" decor; "tabs grow quickly", but "amazing cocktails" emanating from a "gem of a bar upstairs" ease the pain.

STK Miami ❶ *American/Steak* 22 | 25 | 21 | $74

Miami Beach | Gansevoort South Beach Hotel | 2377 Collins Ave. (24th St.) | 305-604-6988 | www.togrp.com

Sure, the beef's "delicious" (shout out to chef Ralph Pagano of *Hell's Kitchen* fame), but this slick "scene" in Miami Beach's Gansevoort Hotel is also tons "more fun than your average steakhouse"; "delicious cocktails", "awesome DJs" blasting "upbeat" "'80s music" and "energetic" staffers set a party vibe in the "beautiful" multi-tiered space – just note that the tab is "not as pretty."

Sugarcane Raw Bar Grill ❶ *Eclectic* 25 | 24 | 20 | $50

Downtown | 3250 NE First Ave. (32nd St.) | Miami | 786-369-0353 | www.sugarcanerawbargrill.com

A "happening scene" unfolds at this Downtown SushiSamba sibling where the "excellent" menu of Eclectic small plates offers "something for everyone" (raw bar, robata grill, sushi, etc.), and the airy "Key West/Havana" decor transports the "attractive" crowd to an "island paradise"; just know that bills can climb and the "360-degree" indoor-outdoor bar can be a "real meat market."

Sushi House ❶Ⓜ *Asian/Japanese* ▽ 22 | 19 | 19 | $46

North Miami Beach | Avanti Shopping Ctr. | 15911 Biscayne Blvd. (Sunny Isles Blvd.) | 305-947-6002 | www.sushihousenmb.com

"High-tech", white-on-white decor sets the scene for the "creative", impeccably "fresh" sushi and modern Pan-Asian dishes proffered at this North Miami Beach lounge; some say it's "overpriced", but most are happy to have a late-night raw-fish option in these parts.

Sushi Maki *Japanese* 21 | 16 | 19 | $27

Brickell Area | 1000 S. Miami Ave. (SW 10th St.) | Miami | 305-415-9779
Coral Gables | 2334 Ponce de Leon Blvd. (Aragon Ave.) | 305-443-1884
Kendall | 11531 N. Kendall Dr. (bet. 113th Place Circle W. & 117th Ave.) | 305-595-2332
Palmetto Bay | King's Bay Shopping Ctr. | 14491 S. Dixie Hwy. (Mitchell Dr.) | 305-232-6636
South Miami | 5812 Sunset Dr. (SW 58th Ave.) | 305-667-7677 ❶
www.sushimakirestaurants.com

To satisfy "basic" raw-fish cravings on the "cheap", fans head to this "friendly" mini-chain for "giant", "decent"-tasting rolls (you may "need a fork and knife" to deal with them properly); "eye-rolling pur-

FOOD   DECOR   SERVICE   COST

ists" dismiss it as "supermarket sushi" and find the atmosphere "undistinguised", but admit the lunch specials sure are "awesome."

Su Shin Izakaya ⊠ *Japanese*   23 | 16 | 24 | $30

Coral Gables | 159 Aragon Ave. (bet. Coral Way & Giralda Ave.) | 305-445-2584 | www.izakayarestaurant.com

This semi-"secret" Coral Gables joint is "where the Japanese in Miami go" for "high-quality" sushi and more "unusual" delicacies, washed down with "great" sake; the "basic" digs are trumped by "affordable" tabs and a "warm welcome" from an owner who's a "blast."

Sushi Rock Cafe ● *Japanese*   21 | 15 | 20 | $33

South Beach | 1351 Collins Ave. (bet. 13th & 14th Sts.) | Miami Beach | 305-532-2133 | www.sushirockcafe.com

South Beach scenesters roll into this "reliable" rock music–themed sushi spot for "fresh" preparations of raw fish and "reasonably priced sake"; throw in a staff with "positive energy" and late-night hours, and no wonder it's "usually busy."

SushiSamba dromo ● *Japanese/S American*   23 | 22 | 18 | $49

South Beach | 600 Lincoln Rd. (Pennsylvania Ave.) | Miami Beach | 305-673-5337 | www.sushisamba.com

"Deafening but delicious" sums up this SoBe "trendsetter" that cranks "hip" Latin American "house music" as a soundtrack for "exotic", "spicy" Japanese-Brazilian-Peruvian combos including "nouveau sushi" emanating from the central sushi-bar-in-the-round, the focal point of the undulant modern lounge space; "great drinks" and "primo" "people-watching" on Lincoln Road help the "fab" crowd forget any service kinks and the "expensive" tabs.

Sushi Siam *Japanese/Thai*   22 | 16 | 19 | $36

Brickell Area | 931 Brickell Ave. (bet. 8th & 10th Sts.) | Miami | 786-220-7677
Key Biscayne | 632 Crandon Blvd. (bet. Enid & Sunrise Drs.) | 305-361-7768
Aventura | 19575 Biscayne Blvd. (NE 192nd St.) | 305-932-8955
South Beach | 647-649 Lincoln Rd. (Pennsylvania Ave.) | Miami Beach | 305-672-7112
South Miami | 5582 NE Fourth Ct. (54th St.) | 305-751-7818

Sushi Rock *Japanese/Thai*

Pinecrest | 11293 S. Dixie Hwy. (Killian Pkwy.) | 305-259-0022
www.sushisiam.com

"Fresh", "solid" sushi is the draw at this "reliable" Miami-area chainlet, though the secondary Siamese side of the menu is "good too"; the decor may be "nothing special" (though there are "people-watching" opportunities galore in SoBe), but midrange pricing and a "family-friendly" atmosphere make it a popular option; P.S. the Pinecrest outlet has a rock 'n' roll theme.

NEW Sustain Restaurant + Bar *American*   21 | 22 | 22 | $44

Downtown | 3252 NE 1st Ave. (bet. N. Miami Ave. & SE 2nd Ave.) | Miami | 305-424-9079 | www.sustainmiami.com

Locavores applaud this "welcome addition" to Downtown's "new Restaurant Row" offering items like a "50-mile salad" and other

FOOD DECOR SERVICE COST

American fare featuring "good ingredients" sourced "from local providers"; its green-minded "mission" extends to the "smart-looking" dining room adorned with "recycled" elements, and if a few hedgers like the concept better than the food, "reasonable prices" and a "friendly" staff help sustain interest.

NEW Symcha's *American* | ▽ 25 | 25 | 25 | $61

South Beach | 22 Washington Ave. (1st St.) | Miami Beach | 305-604-0000 | www.symchas.com

"Beautiful people" look even better ensconced in the rustic-elegant digs of this handsome SoBe newcomer fitted out with lots of wood and stone; the owner and chef "try hard to please" and succeed with the "fabulous" New American cooking, but some say it's a "bit pricey" if it's "striving to be a neighborhood place."

Taco Rico Tex-Mex *Tex-Mex* | 22 | 8 | 17 | $15

Coral Gables | 473 S. Dixie Hwy. (Le Jeune Rd.) | 305-663-3200
South Beach | 1608 Alton Rd. (16th St.) | Miami Beach | 305-535-5757
Pinecrest | 12275 S. Dixie Hwy. (SW 124th St.) | 786-573-4940
www.tacoricomiami.com

"Great greasy tacos" and other "sinfully" "delicious" grub are the lures at these "casual" Tex-Mex spots; they're "nothing fancy", but the counter staff is "nice" and the "price is right", so who cares if the experience is like eating at a "sit-down food truck."

NEW Tagliatelle Miami *Italian/Seafood* | - | - | - | E

South Beach | 124 Collins Ave. (1st St.) | Miami Beach | 305-397-8019 | www.tagliatelle-miami.com

Diners are "pleasantly surprised" by this new Italian seafooder in South Beach set "just beyond the Ocean Drive craziness"; diners can almost feel the breeze off the Mediterranean wafting past the white stucco walls and volcanic stone tables or outside in the sidewalk seating area – and the American dollar goes just about as far here as it does over there.

Talavera *Mexican* | 24 | 23 | 23 | $38

Coral Gables | 2299 Ponce de Leon Blvd. (Giralda Ave.) | 305-444-2955 | www.talaveraspot.com

"Knock-your-socks-off" contemporary Mexicana and regional specialties are yours at this "upscale" south-of-the-border venue in Coral Gables; the staff is "always available but not overbearing" and the "pretty" surroundings include a bar operated by an "outstanding mixologist" – all that for "surprisingly affordable" dough.

Tamarind Ⓜ *Thai* | 24 | 16 | 24 | $35

Miami Beach | 946 Normandy Dr. (71st St.) | 305-861-6222 | www.tamarindthai.us

"Every dish is delicious" at this "terrific", moderately priced Thai in Miami Beach whose white setting is enlivened by silkscreened prints made by chef-partner (and cookbook author) Vatcharin Bhumichitr; it's also one of the few "relaxing places" in the area, and since it's "never full", it's usually possible to "just walk in."

	FOOD	DECOR	SERVICE	COST

Tantra ❶ *Eclectic*
21 | 27 | 18 | $71

South Beach | 1445 Pennsylvania Ave. (bet. Española Way & 15th St.) | Miami Beach | 305-672-4765 | www.tantra-restaurant.com

"Glamorous partyers" populate this "sexy aphrodisiac" of an eatery in South Beach where the "unique" Eclectic menu is just a prop for the eye-popping "scenery" that includes Far East bordello decor, "celebrities" and the servers' "way-too-short miniskirts"; some speculate that the "real grass on the floor" is there to provide a soft landing if "you pass out from the drinks" – or when you get the final "credit-card-melting" bill.

Tapas & Tintos ❶ *Mediterranean/Spanish*
20 | 19 | 18 | $34

NEW **Wynwood** | 3535 NE 2nd Ave. (35th Terr.) | Miami | 305-392-0506
South Beach | 448 Española Way (bet. Drexel & Washington Aves.) | Miami Beach | 305-538-8272
www.tapasytintos.com

"Friends" meet up at this "funky" SoBe spot to share "authentic" Spanish and Mediterranean tapas, throw down glasses of sangria and "dance" along to the nightly live music; moderate tabs and a "picturesque" setting help disguise occasional service lapses; P.S. the Wynwood branch opened post-Survey.

Tap Tap Haitian *Haitian*
22 | 20 | 19 | $29

South Beach | 819 Fifth St. (bet. Jefferson & Meridian Aves.) | Miami Beach | 305-672-2898 | www.taptaprestaurant.com

"Out-of-towners", "families" and off-islanders tap into this South Beach "treasure" for "delectable" Haitian fare that's hard to find anywhere else; the drinks (including the signature mojito) are "sweet and strong", but it's the "colorful" murals and "inviting vibe" from the "down-to-earth" staff that make for repeat visits.

Tarpon Bend *Seafood*
20 | 19 | 19 | $32

Coral Gables | 65 Miracle Mile (bet. Douglas Rd. & Galiano St.) | 305-444-3210 | www.tarponbend.com

A bit "better than your average sports bar", these midpriced seafooders in Coral Gables and Ft. Lauderdale excel at "simple grilled fish" and "actually know how to cook a burger to order"; still, they're probably better known as "lively" singles bars with "fantastic happy hour" scenes that can get "noisy."

Taverna Opa *Greek*
19 | 16 | 18 | $36

Doral | Dolphin Mall | 11401 NW 12th St. (111th Ave.) | Miami | 305-513-8388 | www.tavernaoparestaurant.com
See review in Ft. Lauderdale/Broward County Directory.

Thai House South Beach ❶ *Thai*
∇ 19 | 13 | 17 | $32

South Beach | 1137 Washington Ave. (11th St.) | Miami Beach | 305-531-4841 | www.thaihousesobe.com

This "reliable" South Beach Siamese snags hungry diners looking for "large portions" of "solid" Thai cuisine; picky eaters complain that the food and decor are "plain-Jane" and the service "distracted", but "reasonable" costs (especially the under-$10 lunch specials) keep reeling them in.

	FOOD	DECOR	SERVICE	COST

Thai House II *Thai*   24 | 20 | 22 | $33

North Miami Beach | 2250 NE 163rd St. (bet. Biscayne Blvd. & W. Dixie Hwy.) | 305-940-6075 | www.thaihouse2.com

This "local favorite" in a North Miami Beach strip mall has "been around forever" thanks to moderate pricing and a "wide variety" of "authentic" Thai dishes and equally "excellent sushi"; the "friendly" owners take pride in a dining room "filled with artifacts from Thailand" that "still looks fresh" after all these years.

NEW 3 Chefs *Chinese*   - | - | - | M

Downtown | 1800 Biscayne Blvd. (NE 19th St.) | Miami | 305-373-2688 | www.3chefs-mia.com

Debuting near the Arsht Center, this Chinese boasts a midpriced menu almost as long as the Great Wall, offering more than 150 items, including Vietnamese specialties (there's also a 'secret' Chinese-language menu); though it does lots of takeout, those who dine in will find a cozy setting accented by gold vinyl chairs at faux-black-marble tables.

Timo *Italian/Mediterranean*   25 | 19 | 23 | $56

Sunny Isles Beach | 17624 Collins Ave. (bet. 175th Terr. & 178th St.) | 305-936-1008 | www.timorestaurant.com

It's always "worth the schlep" to Sunny Isles Beach to check out the "new surprises" on Tim Andriola's "creative", "frequently changing" Italian-Med menu, and "you gotta try" the wood-fired pizzas with "thin, crisp crusts" too; "reasonable prices" and "friendly" servers are more reasons why it's considered a "keeper" despite its sometimes "noisy" setting in a "nondescript shopping mall."

Tiramesu ● *Italian*   21 | 16 | 19 | $38

South Beach | 721 Lincoln Rd. (Meridian Ave.) | Miami Beach | 305-532-4538 | www.tiramesu.com

"Neither stuffy nor sceney", this Italian "survivor" smack dab in the "middle of one of the world's great sidewalk shows" draws in patrons with "nice bowls of pasta"; "accommodating" service and "reasonable" tabs also buck the SoBe norm, especially the "great beat-the-clock specials" from 5:30 to 7 PM.

Titanic Brewery *American*   17 | 16 | 19 | $23

Coral Gables | 5813 Ponce de Leon Blvd. (San Amaro Dr.) | 305-667-2537 | www.titanicbrewery.com

U Miami undergrads haunt this "friendly" Coral Gables microbrewery that's known for brewing its "quality" suds on-site; sure, it's "nothing fancy", but regulars say the affordable American pub grub "doesn't disappoint", and there's occasional live music as a bonus.

T-Mex Cantina ● *Tex-Mex*   ▽ 17 | 11 | 16 | $19

South Beach | 235 14th St. (bet. Collins & Washington Aves.) | Miami Beach | 305-538-3009 | www.t-mex.net

"Down and dirty" burritos and other "fresh" Tex-Mex "fast food" does the job at these late-night SoBe-Lauderdale "hole-in-the-wall" cantinas that "don't skimp on quantity"; the "cheap" tabs get even cheaper during Tuesdays' two-for-one taco deal.

	FOOD	DECOR	SERVICE	COST

Toni's Sushi Bar ● *Japanese* | 25 | 18 | 23 | $58 |

South Beach | 1208 Washington Ave. (12th St.) | Miami Beach |
305-673-9368 | www.tonisushi.com

"Fresh fish" and the "flawless technique" of chefs who are "really
from Japan" combine for some of "Florida's best sushi" at this pricey
SoBe old-timer; its "traditional" look and "sunken tables" may not
have the "cool factor" of other Miami spots, but many prefer perks
like "intriguing sake" and a "tourist-free environment."

Tony Chan's Water Club *Chinese* | 23 | 20 | 21 | $43 |

Downtown | Grand Doubletree Hotel | 1717 N. Bayshore Dr
(bet. NE 15th St. & 17th Terr.) | Miami | 305-374-8888 |
www.tonychans.com

Sinophiles applaud the "terrific, high-end" Chinese cooking at this
sprawling venue set in the Doubletree Downtown that's known for
some of the "best Peking duck south of Mott Street" (sushi is also
available); ask the "pleasant" staff for a table "overlooking the bay" or
one facing the cooks through the kitchen's floor-to-ceiling windows.

Town Kitchen & Bar *Eclectic* | 19 | 19 | 17 | $33 |

South Miami | Plaza 57 Bldg. | 7301 SW 57th Ct. (bet. 73rd & 74th Sts.) |
305-740-8118 | www.townkitchenbar.com

South Miamians are jazzed to have a "big-city vibe" in their "subur-
ban enclave" via this "perfect combination" of eatery and "meeting
place" that boasts a "lively bar scene" yet is "comfortable for the
whole family"; the "well-rounded" Eclectic menu may skew "run-of-
the-mill", but the "trendy" rustic-industrial digs are as easy on the
eyes as the tabs are easy on the wallet.

Trattoria Luna *Italian* | 24 | 20 | 24 | $38 |

Pinecrest | Dadeland Plaza | 9477 S. Dixie Hwy. (Palmetto Expwy.) |
305-669-9448 | www.trattorialuna.com

This "quality trattoria" in a Pinecrest strip mall may appear "small"
and "ordinary", but the food is "superb" and fairly priced; even better, service is on par with the cuisine thanks to a "friendly owner who
knows every regular by name" and a staff that "makes a big fuss at
birthdays and anniversaries."

Trattoria Sole *Italian* | 20 | 19 | 20 | $40 |

South Miami | 5894 Sunset Dr. (S. Dixie Hwy.) | 305-666-9392 |
www.blurestaurantsgroup.com

Paesani point to the "authentic" Italian cuisine backed up by an "excellent wine" list as the primary assets of this "dependable"
South Miami trattoria, a sibling of Blú la Pizzeria del Sole; alright,
it's a bit "pricey for what you get", but the "wonderful" staff and
"relaxed" ambiance compensate.

NEW Trio on the Bay M *American* | – | – | – | M |

North Bay Village | 1601 79th St. Cswy. (bet. Adventure &
Hispanola Aves.) | 305-866-1234 | www.trioonthebay.com

"Unbeatable water views" mean you can "watch the sun set over
Biscayne Bay" whether outdoors on the 10,000-sq.-ft. patio or in-

side the even bigger resto-lounge portion of this "gorgeous" New American in Miami's North Bay Village; early buzz has it that the small plates are "terrific", the staff is "genuinely nice", prices are "more than reasonable" and there's "ample parking" to boot.

Tropical Chinese *Chinese*   26 | 17 | 21 | $33

Westchester | Tropical Park Plaza | 7991 SW 40th St. (Bird Rd.) | Miami | 305-262-7576 | www.tropicalchinesemiami.com

"Amazing dim sum" cart service at lunch is a big draw at this venerable Westchester Chinese, where the "fast" trolley-pushers are "stern" but "effective"; the rest of the "authentic", Hong Kong–style cuisine is similarly "high quality" (the "Peking duck is a worthy experience in itself") and prices are moderate, so few mind the "lacking" decor.

NEW Truluck's *Seafood/Steak*   24 | 24 | 24 | $61

Brickell Area | Suntrust Bldg. | 777 Brickell Ave. (SE 7th St.) | Miami | 305-579-0035 | www.trulucks.com

See review in Palm Beach County Directory.

NEW Tudor House *American*   - | - | - | E

South Beach | Dream South Beach | 1111 Collins Ave. (11th St.) | Miami Beach | 305-534-8455 | www.tudorhousemiami.com

This stylish yet casual South Beach American via celeb chef/Food Network star Geoffrey Zakarian offers a spendy modern menu featuring everything from organic fried chicken with gingered slaw to English pea soup with lime marshmallows; the decor blends modern and vintage items including cocktail bars made from repurposed check-in desks, a nod to its setting in the Dream Hotel lobby.

Tutto Pasta 🆘 *Italian*   22 | 14 | 20 | $31

Brickell Area | 1751 SW Third Ave. (bet. 17th & 18th Rds.) | Miami | 305-857-0709 | www.tuttopasta.com

Shhh, Brickellites "don't want more people to know about" this "dependable" little "neighborhood" pasta-maker and its affordable specials (half-price wine on Mondays and Tuesdays, Maine lobster dinner on Wednesdays); the "accommodating" staff and low corkage fee are other secrets that locals want to keep.

Tutto Pizza Beer House *Pizza*   ▽ 24 | 14 | 21 | $24

Brickell Area | 1763 SW Third Ave. (bet. 17th & 18th Rds.) | Miami | 305-858-0909 | www.tuttopizzamiami.com

"Excellent" thin-crust pizzas with "unusual" toppings are yours at this affordable, no-frills Brickell pizzeria where "easy parking" right in front can get you "in and out in 30 minutes"; it recently moved to "new digs" a bit further down the block from its papa, Tutto Pasta.

NEW 2B Asian Bistro *Asian*   25 | 21 | 23 | $37

Little Havana | 1444 SW Eighth St. (bet. 14th & 15th Aves.) | Miami | 786-235-7600

Calle Ocho is a "quirky location for a Thai place" – not to mention one with "hip", "modern" SoBe-style decor – but the "imaginative" midpriced menu, including "exceptional" "designer" sushi, means "you'll want 2B coming back for more"; as at his earlier venture, Mr. Yum, the "colorful" owner ("and his hair") make dining here "an event."

Two Chefs ⊠ *American* | 23 | 18 | 22 | $49
South Miami | 8287 S. Dixie Hwy. (SW 67th Ave.) | 305-663-2100 | www.twochefsrestaurant.com

South Miamians tout this "quiet" "gem" tucked away in a shopping center as a "comfortable" nexus to "unwind with family and friends" over "wonderful" home-cooked New Americana; repeat visitors talk up the "fairly" priced, "super wine list" and insist the chocolate soufflé is a "must-have"; P.S. its cooking classes are "a lot of fun."

Uvas *French/Mediterranean* | 19 | 14 | 19 | $30
(fka Uva 69)
Upper East Side | 6900 Biscayne Blvd. (NE 69th St.) | Miami | 305-754-9022 | www.uvasrestaurant.com

Other than a name tweak under new ownership (fka Uva 69), everything remains the same at this "small" Upper East Sider where "friends meet" up for glasses of vino and "casual" bites of "interesting" French-Med cooking; "reasonable" prices are another perk for neighborhood denizens, and there's "live music" every other weekend.

Van Dyke Cafe ● *Eclectic* | 16 | 17 | 16 | $31
South Beach | 846 Lincoln Rd. (Jefferson Ave.) | Miami Beach | 305-534-3600 | www.thevandykecafe.com

This all-day/late-night SoBe sibling of News Cafe serves a "broad" Eclectic menu that aims to "please everyone" but ends up being just "passable" (like the "impersonal service"); a huge patio offers a great vantage point for watching the "best of South Beach pass by", while the upstairs jazz lounge is a nice alternative to the typical "house music played all along Lincoln Road."

⊠ Versailles ● *Cuban* | 21 | 14 | 19 | $26
Little Havana | 3555 SW Eighth St. (35th Ave.) | Miami | 305-444-0240

Now in its 40th year, this "venerable" Calle Ocho "institution" is Miami's "quintessential Cuban experience" given its "large portions" of "classic" island eats at moderate tabs; it's a hybrid affair – a "bakery/dining room/lunch counter/walk-up window" that "takes up half a block" – and functions as a "community hub" for homesick expats, so naturally it "helps if you *habla Español*."

NEW Vic & Angelo's *Italian* | 21 | 21 | 20 | $43
South Beach | 150 Ocean Dr. (2nd St.) | Miami Beach | 305-531-0911 | www.vicandangelos.com

See review in Palm Beach County Directory.

⊠ Villa By Barton G. ● *Continental* | 24 | 28 | 24 | $116
South Beach | The Villa by Barton G. | 1116 Ocean Dr. (bet. 11th & 12th Sts.) | Miami Beach | 305-576-8003 | www.thevillabybartong.com

Set in the "former Versace mansion", this SoBe Continental in Barton Weiss' swank boutique hotel flaunts a "gaudy opulence"

FOOD | DECOR | SERVICE | COST

that's "worth the price of admission alone" (though even "Russian oligarchs" might blush at the cost); happily, the "formal" service and "unforgettable" contemporary cooking are a near match for the "spectacular" beauty of the place (it's voted Miami's No. 1 spot for Decor); P.S. reservations required.

Villagio *Italian*
21 | 21 | 20 | $35

Coral Gables | Village of Merrick Park | 358 San Lorenzo Ave. (bet. Ponce de Leon Blvd. & SW 42nd St.) | 305-447-8144
Kendall | Dadeland Mall | 7491 N. Kendall Dr. (S. Dixie Hwy.) | 305-669-4599

Always "bustling with shoppers", these "contemporary"-looking mall-based Italians are "classy" alternatives to food-court fare offering "delicious" food plated in "generous portions"; devotees appreciate the "fairly priced" wines and moderate tabs, while the "cordial", kid-friendly service is a bonus.

Vita by Baoli ● *Mediterranean*
- | - | - | E

South Beach | 1906 Collins Ave. (bet. 19th & 20th Sts.) | Miami Beach | 305-674-8822 | www.baoli-group.com

In SoBe, this resto-lounge matches Med plates with selections from a 200-label wine library housed in a floor-to-ceiling rack; decked out with oversized banquettes and crystal chandeliers, the modern dining room is "absolutely beautiful" (ditto the lush Tuscan garden patio), and thanks to "great music" and "lots of shots between courses", it's a "fun night out."

Whisk Gourmet *American*
25 | 19 | 22 | $27

South Miami | 7382 SW 56th Ave. (Sunset Dr.) | 786-268-8350 | www.whiskgourmet.com

"Delectable" American "gourmet comfort food with Southern flair" makes this affordable caterer-cum-cafe "very popular", especially now that it's moved to roomier digs in South Miami; the new space is "modern yet homey" and the staff's "happy", leaving "limited parking" as the sole "flaw."

White Lion Cafe ⊠Ⓜ *American*
▽ 18 | 19 | 20 | $23

Homestead | 146 NW Seventh St. (bet. 1st & 2nd Aves.) | 305-248-1076 | www.whitelioncafe.com

"Home-cooked" American staples taste like they're straight from "momma's stove" at this "quaint" Homestead cottage that's a "throwback to another era" – and that extends to the "good-value" tabs; added draws include a "pretty patio" and a live weekend guitarist.

NEW Wine Depot &
20 | 20 | 20 | $41

Bistro 555 *Mediterranean/Wine Bar*

South Beach | 555 Jefferson Ave. (6th St.) | Miami Beach | 305-672-6161 | www.winedepotmiami.com

This new addition to the SoBe scene has a "unique concept", uniting a retail shop, bistro and bar under one vino-centric umbrella; the wines are "reasonably priced" (though "subject to a minimal corkage fee" in the dining room) and pair well with the Med bites served in the warehouse-chic interior or outside on the "breezy" patio.

Wish ☒ *American*   25 | 25 | 24 | $74

South Beach | The Hotel | 801 Collins Ave. (8th St.) | Miami Beach | 305-674-9474 | www.wishrestaurant.com

Wishes do come true at this "sublime" New American in The Hotel on Collins Avenue serving a "superb" menu ferried by a "wonderful" team; the "lush" tropical garden outside draws "romantic" types, though the "luminescent fountain", "killer" cocktails and "glowing" ice cubes are reminders that it's still South Beach; P.S. drinks on the rooftop Spire Bar are a must.

W Wine Bistro ☒ *Eclectic/Wine Bar*   ∇ 16 | 19 | 19 | $45

Design District | 3622 NE Second Ave. (36th St.) | Miami | 305-576-7775 | www.winebistromiami.com

For an "after-work" glass of vino (or two or three), this "hidden" Design District bar-cum-wine merchant fits the bill; the pricey Eclectic bistro menu is fairly limited, so regulars stick to "snacks" like the "heavenly" complimentary chocolate-covered almonds.

NEW Wynwood Kitchen & Bar ☒ *Eclectic*   17 | 25 | 18 | $37

Wynwood | 2550 NW Second Ave. (bet. 25th & 26th Sts.) | Miami | 305-722-8959 | www.wynwoodkitchenandbar.com

A "real work of art" in Wynwood, this "cool" indoor-outdoor restaurant/bar is festooned with "colorful" murals by Shepard Fairey and other artists; the Eclectic bites with Latin and North American accents may play second fiddle to the decor, but it's still a "good date place for young people on a budget" or a "fun" stop for gallery browsers.

Xixón Cafe ☒ *Spanish*   23 | 19 | 19 | $37

Coral Way | 2101 SW 22nd St. (21st Ave.) | Miami | 305-854-9350 | www.xixoncafe.com

All areas – dining rooms, wine cellar, patio, market and deli – are usually "bustling" at this "modern"-looking Coral Way Spaniard dispensing "delicious tapas" and other "authentic" Asturian offerings at wallet-friendly prices; "fantastic" vino and a "big plus, parking", make up for the "English"-challenged service.

NEW Yardbird *Southern*   - | - | - | M

South Beach | 1600 Lenox Ave. (16th St.) | Miami Beach | 305-538-5220 | www.runchickenrun.com

Putting the 'South' in South Beach, this newfangled Southern comfort-fooder from exec chef Jeff McInnis (ex Gigi) vends down-home dishes with contemporary twists for not a lot of scratch; the rather large nest is feathered with rustic elements like butcher-block tables and tractor-seat stools and includes a well-stocked bourbon bar.

Yard House ◗ *American*   19 | 19 | 19 | $31

Coral Gables | Village of Merrick Park | 320 San Lorenzo Ave. (bet. Ponce de Leon Blvd. & SW 42nd St.) | 305-447-9273 | www.yardhouse.com

See review in Palm Beach County Directory.

	FOOD	DECOR	SERVICE	COST

Yuca *Nuevo Latino*
20 | 21 | 19 | $52

South Beach | 501 Lincoln Rd. (Drexel Ave.) | Miami Beach |
305-532-9822 | www.yuca.com

Now with a new neighbor, the Frank Gehry–designed New World
Symphony, this "perennial favorite" on Lincoln Road remains a
"solid" stop for "upscale" Nuevo Latino dishes washed down with
"huge cocktails"; the budget-minded find it "overpriced", but agree
it's hard to beat for "people-watching" and weekly "Latin music."

Yuga 🅢 *Asian*
26 | 16 | 24 | $33

Coral Gables | 357 Alcazar Ave. (bet. Salzedo St. & SW 42nd Ave.) |
305-442-8600 | www.yugarestaurant.com

"Intensely tasty", "fresh and fabulous" Pan-Asian cuisine at "reasonable prices" is the name of the game at this "neighborhood gem"
"on a quiet side street" in Coral Gables; add a "simple" but "spacious" setting where there's "never a wait" and "extremely friendly
service" to know why loyalists proclaim it "too good to share."

🆉 Zuma ◑ *Japanese*
28 | 27 | 24 | $83

Downtown | Epic Hotel | 270 Biscayne Blvd. (Brickell Ave.) | Miami |
305-577-0277 | www.zumarestaurant.com

"Book way ahead" to secure a seat at Downtown's new "it" spot in the
Epic Hotel because this European import (and "international sensa-
tion") is drawing throngs with its "Zen mastery" of modern izakaya-
inspired Japanese fare plus sushi, robata grill items and more; "fabulous views" can be had from the terrace overlooking the Miami River,
or you can just watch the "beautiful people" burning many "ben-
jamins" in the "stunning" dining room and "vibrant" sake bar/lounge.

Zuperpollo ◑ *S American*
18 | 12 | 18 | $26

Coral Way | 1247 SW 22nd St. (bet. 12th & 13th Aves.) | Miami |
305-856-9494

As the name suggests, the "simple" cooking is poultry-focused –
who "knew there were so many different ways to serve chicken"? –
at this Coral Way South American, though there's beef and fish on
the menu too; no one minds that it "looks like a dump from the outside" since service is "friendly" and the tabs "zupercheap."

KEY WEST & THE KEYS RESTAURANT DIRECTORY

MOST POPULAR
1. Louie's Backyard | *Amer./Carib.*
2. Blue Heaven | *Floribbean*
3. Michaels | *American*
4. Cafe Marquesa | *American*
5. A&B Lobster House | *Seafood*

TOP FOOD
28 Din. Rm./Little Palm | *Fr./Latin*
Cafe Marquesa | *American*
27 Pisces | *American/Seafood*
Pierre's | *Eclectic*
Seven Fish | *Seafood*

TOP DECOR
28 Din. Rm. at Little Palm
Pierre's
Morada Bay Beach Café
27 Hot Tin Roof
Upper Deck at Louie's*

TOP SERVICE
29 Din. Rm. at Little Palm
26 Pierre's
Upper Deck at Louie's
Cafe Marquesa
Pisces

Z A&B Lobster House *Seafood*   23 | 21 | 22 | $48

Key West | 700 Front St. (Simonton St.) | 305-294-5880 |
www.aandblobsterhouse.com

Where does the frustrated angler go "after a less-than-successful fishing trip"? – this Key West "fixture" known for "reliably tasty" fish and crustaceans that "couldn't be fresher"; its location "overlooking the harbor" is a "nice spot to view the boats" but dinner's "not cheap" (wallet-watchers prefer the lower-cost sibling, Alonzo's Oyster Bar, located below); P.S. there's an on-site cigar bar.

Abbondanza *Italian*   20 | 18 | 21 | $29

Key West | 1208 Simonton St. (Louisa St.) | 305-292-1199 |
www.abbondanzakeywest.com

The name of this "comfortable red-sauce" joint in Key West spells it out: expect "huge" "family-style" portions of decent fare; the overwhelmed and unimpressed posit that "size doesn't matter" (i.e. "a lot of food doesn't make it great") but large groups and those with kids call it an "amazing value"; P.S. reservations not taken.

Alabama Jacks *Seafood*   20 | 20 | 20 | $22

Key Largo | 58000 Card Sound Rd. (west of the toll bridge) |
305-248-8741

"Yeehaw!" folks "from all walks of life" – "bikers", "rednecks", "seniors", "celebrities" – "let their hair down" at this "ultimate roadhouse" in the "middle of nowhere" in Key Largo that's gotta be "the funnest place in all of South Florida" with its "cold beer" (and twist-cap wine), "scenic" water views and "down-home music" with clogging and line dancing some weekends; oh yeah, they also serve cheap "fresh" seafood, including what's "maybe the best conch fritter anywhere."

Ambrosia *Japanese*   26 | 21 | 21 | $44

Key West | Santa Maria Suites Resort | 1401 Simonton St. (South St.) |
305-293-0304 | www.keywestambrosia.com

The "superb" sushi is "pure ambrosia" and the cooked Japanese fare "delights too" at this "elegant" boîte in the Santa Maria Suites Resort with a "cool factor" that feels more "South Beach" than Key West; prices are moderate for what it is, service is "attentive" and the "extensive sake" menu will "make your head spin."

---

* Indicates a tie with restaurant above

Antonia's *Italian*
27 | 23 | 25 | $55

Key West | 615 Duval St. (bet. Angela & Southard Sts.) | 305-294-6565 | www.antoniaskeywest.com

"Amid the craziness of Duval Street stands this classy yet casual bastion" of "top-shelf" Italian cuisine – a veritable city-state of "pasta perfection" in the heart of "the Conch Republic"; the "first-rate" experience doesn't come cheap, but toss in an "impressive" wine list, a "welcoming" staff and a "relaxing" vibe in the upscale-cottagelike setting, and it's "worth the money."

Azur *Mediterranean*
25 | 21 | 23 | $47

Key West | 425 Grinnell St. (bet. Eaton & Fleming Sts.) | 305-292-2987 | www.azurkeywest.com

"Away from the Key West craziness" is this "quiet respite for the locals" in Old Town with a "creative" Mediterranean menu that's "delicious" "not just at dinner but, amazingly, at breakfast and lunch too"; "warm, friendly" service buoys a "lovely ambiance" that's best savored on the "beautiful" patio.

Bad Boy Burrito Ⓧ⏁ *Mexican*
∇ 24 | 10 | 15 | $13

Key West | 1220½ Simonton St. (bet. Front & Greene Sts.) | 305-292-2697 | www.badboyburrito.com

"Massive" burritos using "only the freshest ingredients" in "every imaginable combination" plus smoothies and coffee are the draw at this cheap, cash-only Mexican "hole-in-the-wall"; since seating is almost nonexistent, get everything to go in biodegradable packaging and "head to the nearby beach for the best picnic in KW."

Bagatelle *Caribbean/Seafood*
21 | 22 | 20 | $50

Key West | 115 Duval St. (bet. Front & Greene Sts.) | 305-296-6609 | www.bagatellekeywest.com

This "lovely" historic 1884 conch house in Key West sets the stage for "tasty" Caribbean fare, including a "nice assortment" of local fish; it's "on the expensive side" and can be "slow" at times, but it's a pleasure to dine outside on the upper- or lower-level wraparound porches and watch the "tourists ramble down" Duval Street.

Banana Cafe *French*
23 | 19 | 22 | $32

Key West | 1215 Duval St. (Louisa St.) | 305-294-7227 | www.bananacafekw.com

"Amazing sweet and savory crêpes plus masterful egg dishes" are a "pleasant" way to "begin the day in Uptown Key West" at this "relaxed" French bistro with a "small" patio on the "quieter end of Duval Street"; dinner is a slightly "more serious" affair, but the staff, "especially the owner", is always "personable" and the prices are modest.

Barracuda Grill *Eclectic*
21 | 16 | 20 | $40

Marathon | 4290 Overseas Hwy. (43rd St.) | 305-743-3314

Ok, "it doesn't look it" but this little storefront in Marathon is capable of whipping up a "varied, unexpected and delicious" Eclectic bill of fare with an "emphasis on local seafood"; the no-reservations policy can lead to a "long wait on weekends", but the "personable" staff, moderate tabs and "air-conditioning" make it worthwhile.

Bentley's *Seafood* | 23 | 19 | 23 | $40 |

Islamorada | 82779 Overseas Hwy. (mi. marker 82.7) | 305-664-9094 | www.keysdining.com

This tropical neon-green building in Islamorada beckons passing motorists on the Overseas Highway to pull over for "fish as fresh as it gets", including raw-bar selections, plus standard American favorites served in "serene surroundings"; happy hour (4-7 PM) is a godsend "if on a budget" as are the early-bird specials (4-6 PM).

Blackfin Bistro *Eclectic* | ∇ 22 | 19 | 23 | $41 |

Key West | 918 Duval St. (bet. Olivia St. & Truman Ave.) | 305-509-7408 | www.blackfinbistro.com

A "peaceful" balm for those tired of "crazy Key West", this "upscale but informal" "up-and-comer" on the quieter end of Duval near the Hemingway House offers a midpriced Eclectic menu that hits "high notes" with its appetizers, "excellent" burgers and "fresh" fish; a "friendly" staff, "beautiful" tree-shaded back patio and, gasp, "free parking!" add to the appeal.

⭐ Blue Heaven *Floribbean* | 25 | 22 | 22 | $35 |

Key West | 729 Thomas St. (Petronia St.) | 305-296-8666 | www.blueheavenkw.com

For a "peek at Hemingway's Key West", folks wait in "interminable" lines at this Bahama Village "landmark" offering "delicious" midpriced Floribbean fare "that screams fresh" and "exceptionally strong Bloody Marys" that explain its "can't-beat"-brunch rep; an "eclectic mishmash" of artwork, tables and chairs adorns the "funkiest-of-the-funky" setting: a "backyard" with "chickens and roosters" "running around underfoot", dodging the "happy" "laid-back" staff; P.S. there's live music nightly in season.

B.O.'s Fish Wagon *Seafood* | 24 | 16 | 17 | $17 |

Key West | 801 Caroline St. (William St.) | 305-294-9272 | www.bosfishwagon.com

It "looks like a hurricane just dumped a pile of flotsam on a street corner" in Key West but the "pieced-together plywood" at this "hole-in-the-wall (wait, there are no walls)" hides a casual seafooder serving up "awesome" fish sandwiches and "incredible" conch fritters so cheap that it ranks as the Keys' No. 1 Bang for the Buck; it's a cash-only counter operation so "service is nonexistent", but that's part of its "laid-back" "charm."

Braza Leña *Brazilian* | ∇ 24 | 23 | 22 | $51 |

Key West | 421 Caroline St. (bet. Duval & Whitehead Sts.) | 305-432-9440 | **Islamorada** | 83413 Overseas Hwy. (mi. marker 83.5) | 305-664-4940 Ⓜ www.brazalena.com

"Lots and lots of meat" is the name of the game at these "fun" Brazilian all-you-can-eateries in Key West (check out the Peter Lik photos lining its walls) and Islamorada known for their "outstanding selection of beef, pork and seafood"; included in the "hefty price" are "amazing salad bars" with "lots to choose from", and though wine costs extra the lists are lengthy.

Cafe, The ⊠ *Vegetarian* ▽ 26 | 18 | 21 | $25

Key West | 509 Southard St. (bet. Bahama & Duval Sts.) | 305-296-5515

A "great option for vegetarians" (and pescatarians thanks to a few fish choices) is this "innovative" little eatery "right near the center" of town in Key West; the staff is "attentive", but despite rotating local artwork, "don't expect much atmosphere" at prices like these.

Z Cafe Marquesa *American* 28 | 24 | 26 | $63

Key West | Marquesa Hotel | 600 Fleming St. (Simonton St.) | 305-292-1244 | www.marquesa.com

In Key West, "nothing else touches" this "small", "romantic" bistro attached to the Marquesa Hotel for its "impressive" and "imaginative" New American cuisine (its "big-city prices" are up near the top too); while some deem it "a little too formal" for the area, most say it strikes a balance of "hip and old-world elegance" – add to that mix "great cocktails" and "flawless", "well-paced" service, and the experience is "unforgettable."

Café Solé *Caribbean/French* 24 | 20 | 22 | $49

Key West | 1029 Southard St. (Frances St.) | 305-294-0230 | www.cafesole.com

The "friendly folks" who run this "funky" little bistro turn out "fabulous" French-Caribbean fare, including "not-to-be-missed hog snapper" (heck, "even the lima beans are to die for"); it's not cheap, but the fact that it's "off the beaten path" in Key West and "has one of the best wine lists on the island" makes it quite the "romantic hideout", especially on the covered terrace.

Calypso's Seafood Grille ⊭ *Seafood* ▽ 23 | 14 | 17 | $28

Key Largo | Ocean Bay Marina | 1 Seagate Blvd. (Ocean Bay Dr.) | 305-451-0600 | www.calypsoskeylargo.com

Fans of the "delicious she-crab soup" and other "fresh" fin fare "can't make their way through the Keys without stopping" at this dockside shack in Key Largo; beach bums who "don't expect much ambiance" beyond "Styrofoam bowls", "plastic silverware" and the ocean breeze find it suitably "laid-back"; P.S. cash only; closed Tuesdays except the last Tuesday of each month for a paella dinner.

Camille's *American* 22 | 18 | 19 | $29

Key West | 1202 Simonton St. (Catherine St.) | 305-296-4811 | www.camilleskeywest.com

"Wonderful" breakfasts and lunches "draw a crowd" to this "dependable" all-day American eatery with a "diner atmosphere" that's long been a "favorite" in Key West; its "child-friendliness", "reasonable prices" and "experienced" staff are pluses; P.S. it serves dinner too.

Chanticleer South Ⓜ *French* - | - | - | E

Islamorada | 81671 Old Hwy. (Johnston Rd.) | 305-664-0640

Admirers of this Islamorada French restaurant laud "master chef" Jean-Charles Berruet's "perfection" when it comes to his

Gallic classics as well as what he does with a few "local specialties" like hogfish; it's "pricey", but the "outstanding dining experience" is *trés* "romantic" despite the fact that the dining room has "no view and it's not on the beach"; P.S. it's closed seasonally Memorial Day–Thanksgiving.

Chico's Cantina *Mexican* | - | - | - | M |

Key West | 5230 Overseas Hwy. (Cross St.) | 305-296-4714 |
www.chicoscantina.com

This "family-run" Key West cantina "endures" thanks to a "seafood-centric menu that surprises with excellent fresh fish" plus the "usual Mex" staples; "reasonable" rates and a "casual" atmosphere appeal to "locals" and off-islanders alike.

Commodore Waterfront Restaurant *Seafood/Steak* | ▽ 23 | 26 | 25 | $55 |

Key West | A & B Marina | 700 Front St. (Simonton St.) | 305-294-9191 |
www.commodorekeywest.com

When Key West sojourners want a "departure from beer shacks and shrimp-peeling" they climb the economic rungs to reach the "staid elegance" of this waterfront dining room; its surf 'n' turf menu is supported by an equally "great" staff, but the "wonderful view" of Old Town Harbor and its "many yachts" ranks high enough to suit even the admiralty.

Conch Republic Seafood Co. *Seafood* | 17 | 19 | 19 | $33 |

Key West | 631 Greene St. (bet. Elizabeth & Simonton Sts.) |
305-294-4403 | www.conchrepublicseafood.com

Best for "first-time visitors" craving "atmosphere over food", this midpriced, "fun" "open-air" seafooder provides "fabulous people-and boat-watching" out in the marina; "stick to the basics" and the fish can be pretty "tasty" too and the staff is usually "on point", but it's really all about bellying up to the 80-ft. bar and the "entertainment" that live bands afford.

Croissants de France *Bakery/French* | 24 | 17 | 19 | $20 |

Key West | 816 Duval St. (bet. Olivia & Petronia Sts.) | 305-294-2624 |
www.croissantsdefrance.com

"Buttery, flaky, mmm good" croissants and equally tasty pastries and bread are tops at this open-air spot with "fast and efficient" service (sit-down or take-out) so folks can get right back to doing the Duval Street "crawl"; it also doubles as a "first-rate bistro" that's perfect for "breakfast and lunch", though loyalists shake their heads wondering why it's "empty for dinner" since it has the "same impeccable food."

DiGiorgio's Cafe Largo *Italian* | - | - | - | M |

Key Largo | 99530 Overseas Hwy. (Ocean Bay Dr.) | 305-451-4885 |
www.digiorgioscafelargo.com

Locals "tired of fish" can at least get it bathed in red sauce at this "friendly" family-run Italian in Key Largo; the look is a bit "outdated" (e.g. checkered tablecloths) but midpriced staples like clams casino, eggplant parm and tiramisu do the job.

	FOOD	DECOR	SERVICE	COST

⊿ Dining Room at
Little Palm Island Resort *French/Pan-Latin*

28 | 28 | 29 | $89

Little Torch Key | Little Palm Island Resort | 28500 Overseas Hwy.
(mi. marker 28.5) | 305-872-2551 | www.littlepalmisland.com

It's a "short boat ride to paradise", aka this restaurant in a private island resort off Little Torch Key that surveyors rate No. 1 for Food, Decor and Service in the Keys; expect "amazing" "gourmet" French and Pan-Latin cuisine served by an "attentive" staff in an elegant dining room or on a torchlit, "secluded romantic" beach that's straight "out of a tropical movie set" – you'll need a "full wallet", but the only drawback is a "yearning to stay longer."

Duffy's Steak &
Lobster House *Seafood/Steak*

18 | 17 | 19 | $36

Key West | 1007 Simonton St. (Truman Ave.) | 305-296-4900 | www.duffyskeywest.com

The pleasures of this Key West surf 'n' turfer are simple ones: "good" lobster and prime rib for relatively "cheap" tabs; add to that a "nice" staff and a "comfy", "informal" setting, and it's a solid dinner option.

El Meson de Pepe *Cuban*

18 | 18 | 18 | $29

Key West | 410 Wall St. (Front St.) | 305-295-2620 | www.elmesondepepe.com

Offering a bit of "Cuba in the Keys", this "popular" KW eatery with "great a/c" slings "solid" standards for the "right price"; but tourists say it's all about the "unbeatable location overlooking Mallory Square" and its famous sunset celebration, made more festive by "strong mojitos" and "incredible" live salsa that you can dance to "inside or outside."

El Siboney *Cuban*

25 | 11 | 20 | $21

Key West | 900 Catherine St. (Margaret St.) | 305-296-4184 | www.elsiboneyrestaurant.com

A "generous meal can be had for pennies" at this "backstreet secret" in Key West beloved by "locals" for its "freakin' awesome" "home-cooked" Cuban fare; it's "loud" and "no frills" but most are pleased as punch after the "friendly" staff brings over the "fabulous sangria."

Finnegan's Wake Irish Pub ◑ *Pub Food*

19 | 19 | 19 | $24

Key West | 320 Grinnell St. (bet. Eaton & James Sts.) | 305-293-0222 | www.keywestirish.com

Beer drinkers raise their pints to the "wide selection" of "international" brews at this "classic Irish pub" a bit "off the beaten path" in Key West, but the "decent" Irish eats and other bar grub also deserve a toast; the staff "works hard to make visits enjoyable", and most do have "fun" – especially when live bands play; P.S. it's open till the wee hours.

Grand Café Key West ◑ *Eclectic*

▽ 22 | 23 | 20 | $48

Key West | 314 Duval St. (bet. Caroline & Eaton Sts.) | 305-292-4740 | www.grandcafekeywest.com

The "fine" Eclectic fare at this Key West bistro set in a "charming" Victorian house tastes even better on the front porch – and since the

| | FOOD | DECOR | SERVICE | COST |

porch is "elevated" it offers even better than usual "people-watching" on Duval Street (i.e. diners are "part of the action, but not *too much* a part of it"); P.S. the Red Barn Theatre across the way makes it an "excellent" "pre-theater" choice.

Green Turtle Inn Ⓜ *Seafood*   22 | 18 | 20 | $39

Islamorada | 81219 Overseas Hwy. (Parker Dr.) | 305-664-2006 | www.greenturtleinn.com

First opened in 1947 but recently "remodeled and freshened", this "classic" seafood "way station" on the Overseas Highway in Islamorada is a "must-stop" for a "solid" breakfast, lunch or dinner; the staff remains as "personable" as ever, prices are moderate and there are "vintage Keys pictures and artifacts" scattered around, although it now has more of an upscale "sports bar" look.

Half Shell Raw Bar *Seafood*   23 | 18 | 20 | $27

Key West | 231 Margaret St. (Caroline St.) | 305-294-7496 | www.halfshellrawbar.com

Well shucks, folks just "love" this "laid-back" local "institution" – an "open-air" "fish house"/"bar scene" set in a former shrimp-packing facility in Key West Bight Marina; the "picnic table" setup is "divey but fun", and the "fresher than fresh oysters" and ice-cold beer are always an exceptional "deal."

Hot Tin Roof *Pan-Latin*   25 | 27 | 25 | $58

Key West | Ocean Key Resort | 0 Duval St. (Front St.) | 305-295-7057 | www.oceankey.com

This "charming" dining room in the Ocean Key Resort off Mallory Square recently switched chefs and shifted away from Eclectic-Caribbean fare to focus on Pan-Latin cooking, adding small plates in the process (thus outdating its Food rating); the staff is as "delightful" as ever and the "floaty white curtains" and "spectacular" views of the "sunset" keep the "romantic" vibe afloat – if you're willing to shell out.

Island Grill *Seafood*   24 | 21 | 21 | $36

Islamorada | 85501 Overseas Hwy. (after Snake Creek Bridge) | 305-664-8400 | www.keysislandgrill.com

The "yummm" "tuna nachos" are "worth the trip" to Islamorada by themselves say surveyors smitten by this "reasonably priced" seafooder with a "casual" "Keys" vibe and decor; most folks gravitate to the outdoor deck that's a "phenomenal" spot to watch the "sunset" and lots of "fun" when the live music gets going each evening; P.S. they'll even "cook your catch."

Jimmy Buffett's   13 | 19 | 16 | $30
Margaritaville Cafe *American*

Key West | 500 Duval St. (bet. Fleming & Southard Sts.) | 305-292-1435 | www.margaritaville.com

A "mecca" for Parrot Heads, this Key West American provides "huge" margaritas, the requisite "cheeseburger in paradise" and a chance to hit the "gift shop" so you can "say you ate there"; most everyone else slams the "institutional" grub, but hey, at least you can "happily get drunk"; P.S. it's "loud" when there's live music Tuesdays–Sundays.

Jimmy Johnson's Big Chill *Eclectic*   18 | 20 | 17 | $35

Key Largo | Fisherman's Cove | 104000 Overseas Hwy. (Ave. A) | 305-453-9066 | www.jjsbigchill.com

The "view of the bay" from the outdoor deck "will take your breath away" at this sprawling Key Largo complex that includes dining areas, a sports bar and a waterfront swimming pool; the Eclectic eats are "basic" but won't shave off much from your roll of dough, and if service is a "little below average", it's still a "favorite place" for fans of the owner, former Dolphins/Hurricanes coach and current TV sports analyst Jimmy Johnson.

Kaiyo Grill *American/Asian*   - | - | - | M

Islamorada | 81701 Old Hwy. (mi. marker 82) | 305-664-5556 | www.kaiyokeys.com

Asia, America, the Gulf – they really "know how to bring the flavors together" in the "creative" dishes at this Islamorada grill set in a vibrantly painted clapboard house; "friendly" service, moderate tabs and a full sushi menu are added draws, plus they'll "prepare your catch."

Kelly's Caribbean   21 | 23 | 21 | $35
Bar, Grill & Brewery *American/Caribbean*

Key West | 301 Whitehead St. (Caroline St.) | 305-293-8484 | www.kellyskeywest.com

"Tucked away" just a "short walk from" Mallory Square is "one of the most beautiful patios in Key West" with a "buzzing bar scene", "reliable" midpriced Caribbean and American eats and a "friendly" ground crew; co-owned by actress Kelly McGillis (*Top Gun*), the facility is the birthplace of Pan American Airways so visitors can "absorb the old aviation history" on display while also absorbing "great" margaritas and "tasty" beer from the on-site brewery.

Keys Fisheries *Seafood*   26 | 14 | 16 | $22

Marathon | 3502 Gulfview Ave. (Louisa St.) | 305-743-4353 | www.keysfisheries.com

This "reliably wonderful", inexpensive open-air fish house/market in Marathon is "as real as it gets", making it worth a "stop every drive down" through the Keys – especially for its "rightly famous" "lobster Reuben"; the staff "knows how to move the crowd" so get in "line", "order at the window" and wait for them to "holler" so you can plunk yourself down at a picnic table and take in the water "views."

La Trattoria *Italian*   22 | 19 | 22 | $46

NEW **Key West** | 3593 S. Roosevelt Blvd. (Atlantic Blvd.) | 305-295-6789
Key West | 524 Duval St. (Applerouth Ln.) | 305-296-1075
www.latrattoria.us

Regulars know they can "sit back and relax" in the staff's "capable hands" at this "always reliable" trattoria on Duval Street that serves "very solid" Italian cuisine and what's "possibly the best martini in Key West"; some folks like to "hang at or dine at" the convivial bar and, if there's any money left over, head to Virgilio's Martini Bar behind the restaurant for live music after dinner; P.S. the new Roosevelt Boulevard branch opened post-Survey.

⚡ Louie's Backyard *American/Caribbean* 26 | 27 | 24 | $61

Key West | 700 Waddell Ave. (Vernon St.) | 305-294-1061 | www.louiesbackyard.com

This venerable Key West beacon, voted the archipelago's Most Popular, simply "has it all": a "fabulous" Caribbean-American menu, a "breathtaking waterfront view" complete with its own kind of "music" ("the crash of waves") and an "outstanding" staff ("I wanted to adopt my waiter"); such a "romantic" experience is "priced accordingly" but "clearly worth it" – just "make reservations" as "it's not a large restaurant"; P.S. the separate Upper Deck wine bar is "pretty cool too" (open 5–10 PM, Tuesdays–Saturdays).

Mangia Mangia *Italian* 20 | 17 | 18 | $34

Key West | 900 Southard St. (Margaret St.) | 305-294-2469 | www.mangia-mangia.com

"Badda bing!" – Key West "tourists on a budget" flood this family-owned Italian joint for "large portions" of "homemade pasta" deemed a "cut above ordinary"; it's "bare-bones" but "comfortable", especially on the "casual" patio, and the "nice" folks who run the place add to its appeal; P.S. no reservations.

Mangoes *Seafood* 18 | 17 | 18 | $36

Key West | 700 Duval St. (Angela St.) | 305-292-4606 | www.mangoskeywest.com

The "perfect location" for "people-watching" – a large outdoor patio on a prime corner – makes this "busy" hang a "Duval Street favorite"; the midpriced fish-focused fare is "decent" and the "enjoyable atmosphere" is pure Key West thanks to the "fun" staff and a "bar to match."

Marker 88 *Seafood* 21 | 21 | 19 | $46

Islamorada | 88000 Overseas Hwy. (Plantation Blvd.) | 305-852-9315 | www.marker88.info

"Keep your eye on the mile markers" or you might miss this "classic" Islamorada seafooder that pleases most with its "consistently very good" fare; the "rustic" interior is "nothing special", but the "beautiful sunsets" and "wonderful views" of the water outside are worth the "pricey" tabs.

Martin's *European* ▽ 22 | 22 | 21 | $51

Key West | 917 Duval St. (Truman Ave.) | 305-295-0111 | www.martinskeywest.com

"Venison!", "schnitzel!" – "who would have thought" you'd find "classically prepared European cuisine" in Key West? – but this pleasant upscale "surprise" "pulls it off", providing a "nice change from all the seafood" in the area; sure, the kitchen puts a few Caribbean spins on the menu, and the "great" backyard patio is typically tropical, but the modern Berlin "fine-dining" aesthetic and "hip bar scene" are decidedly non-Keysy.

	FOOD	DECOR	SERVICE	COST

☑ Michaels *American* | 26 | 21 | 24 | $58 |

Key West | 532 Margaret St. (bet. Fleming & Southard Sts.) |
305-295-1300 | www.michaelskeywest.com

Chef Michael Wilson presides over this "special treat" in Key West,
turning out "excellent" American dishes, including "incredible steaks";
diners choose from three settings: the more "formal" "elegant" dining
room, the "delightful" "romantic" patio or the "classy" outdoor bar
serving fondue and a martini-heavy list of "specialty cocktails";
P.S. thrifty folks opt for the 'Light Side' menu, served 5:30–7:30 PM.

☑ Morada Bay | 22 | 28 | 21 | $36 |
Beach Café *American/Caribbean*

Islamorada | 81600 Overseas Hwy. (Palm Ave.) | 305-664-0604 |
www.moradabay-restaurant.com

"What a divine spot" sigh champions of this plein-air cafe in
Islamorada where most of the tables are literally "on the beach under
umbrellas"; the American-Caribbean fare is "delicious" enough, the
tabs are friendly and the service is "polite", but the reason this place is
"always jumping" are those "picturesque" views and the sand beneath
your toes (the monthly Full Moon party, featuring bonfires on the
beach and various performers, is also a draw); P.S. no reservations.

Mo's ☒ *Caribbean* | 23 | 15 | 23 | $32 |

Key West | 1116 White St. (Eliza St.) | 305-296-8955

The Caribbean "soul food" is "big on flavor" (and "frankly, under-
priced for the quality") at this "small", "crowded" island-style eatery
in Key West; it's "nothing fancy" but it's a "favorite" of "locals" and
others who appreciate the "relaxing" atmosphere engendered by
the "friendly owners and staff."

Nine One Five Bistro & | 25 | 23 | 24 | $50 |
Wine Bar *American/Mediterranean*

Key West | 915 Duval St. (Truman Ave.) | 305-296-0669 |
www.915duval.com

The "interesting" small and large Med–New American plates could
be "habit forming" (and an expensive habit at that) admit admirers
of this "reliably excellent" Uptown Key West "find"; it also hooks repeat visitors with its "sexy setting" in a beautiful "old conch house"
whose wraparound porch provides stellar "street-scene" entertainment; P.S. the upstairs wine bar is open until 2 AM.

Outback Steakhouse *Steak* | 18 | 15 | 19 | $31 |

Key West | Searstown Shopping Plaza | 3230 N. Roosevelt Blvd.
(F Moller Rd.) | 305-292-0667 | www.outback.com
See review in Miami/Dade County Directory.

Pepe's Cafe & Steakhouse *Seafood/Steak* | 24 | 21 | 24 | $33 |

Key West | 806 Caroline St. (bet. Margaret & William Sts.) | 305-294-7192 |
www.pepescafe.net

Its motto – 'a fairly good place, for quite a long while' – is an under-
statement say loyalists who laud the "fantastic breakfasts" and
"outstanding" surf 'n' turf options at this Key West "landmark"

that feels like "stepping back in time" 100 years, which is how long it's been operating; maybe it's a little "better for breakfast than dinner" but it "should never change", and that includes the gentle tabs and the host who "remembers" diners and makes the place "*Cheers* South."

⊠ Pierre's *Eclectic*

27 | 28 | 26 | $63

Islamorada | 81600 Overseas Hwy. (Palm Ave.) | 305-664-3225 | www.pierres-restaurant.com

Watching a "beautiful sunset" from the wraparound balconies at this "elegant" "plantation-style" manse on the beach in Islamorada feels like being "in a postcard"; happily, the "wonderful" Eclectic dishes and "top-notch" staff are a match for the "romantic" setting; P.S. its next-door sibling, Morada Bay Beach Café, is comparatively cheap.

Pilot House *Seafood*

▽ 19 | 17 | 17 | $36

Key Largo | 13 Seagate Blvd. (N. Channel Dr.) | 305-451-3142 | www.pilothousemarina.com

Since 1950, this nautically themed fish house in a Key Largo marina complex has been a locals' hangout, and at no time is that more apparent than the 4-7 PM daily happy hour; tourists have also been known to have "fun" at the bar and especially dig its 'world-famous glass bottom' (basically, a few windows cut in the floor so you can watch the occasional fish/crab/mermaid swim by).

⊠ Pisces *American/Seafood*

27 | 24 | 26 | $68

Key West | 1007 Simonton St. (Truman Ave.) | 305-294-7100 | www.pisceskeywest.com

"Away from the hustle" is this "quiet and refined" spot whose "wonderful" fish-focused New American cuisine presents "one of the few" options for "fine dining in Key West"; it's a "great date place" made all the more "romantic" by an "impeccable" staff and "excellent" wine list (going Dutch helps with the bill, if not the romance); P.S. signed Warhol lithographs lining the walls are "an extra treat."

Prime Steakhouse *Steak*

25 | 22 | 24 | $71

Key West | 951 Caroline St. (Grinnell St.) | 305-296-4000 | www.primekeywest.com

"Best beef on the Island" boast boosters of this "classic old-school" steakhouse with a "dark, men's club" look that, refreshingly, "doesn't feel" very Key West; high prices mean it's best for "special occasions", but when those roll around the professional staff helps make the experience "worth every penny."

Rusty Anchor ⊠ *Seafood*

▽ 21 | 11 | 18 | $31

Stock Island | 5510 Third Ave. (5th St.) | 305-296-2893

It's "rusty", "crusty" and "dark", but the "locals" who pack this shabby seafooder on Stock Island are focused on the "fresh and tasty" fish and stone crabs available "at a fraction of the price" that fancier places charge; a "huge saltwater fish tank" and other marine paraphernalia mean it's not entirely devoid of decor - either way it's "worth the effort to locate."

	FOOD	DECOR	SERVICE	COST

Salute! On The Beach *Italian/Seafood*   22 | 21 | 22 | $38

Key West | 1000 Atlantic Blvd. (bet. Reynolds & White Sts.) |
305-292-1117 | www.saluteonthebeach.com

"Another winner by the Blue Heaven" saints, this "casual", "friendly"
Key Wester directly on the sand doles out "creative" fish-based
Italiana at "moderate" prices to a "bathing-suit-clad" crowd; lunch
is especially "satisfactory" because there's an "excellent view of the
action on Higgs Beach."

Santiago's Bodega *Eclectic*   27 | 20 | 22 | $43

Key West | 207 Petronia St. (Emma St.) | 305-296-7691 |
www.santiagosbodega.com

Though it's just a short "trek into Bahama Village", this "charming"
Key West tapas place "feels as far from the cruise-ship Duval Street
crashers as you can get"; the Eclectic small plates' "little flavor ex-
plosions" pair perfectly with "tasty" house sangria, and since they
recently expanded the cute, "tiny" space it's "easier to get in."

Sarabeth's ⓜ *American*   24 | 20 | 24 | $36

Key West | 530 Simonton St. (bet. Fleming & Southard Sts.) |
305-293-8181 | www.sarabethskeywest.com

The scent of "scrumptious on-premise baking" leads noses to this Key
West outpost of the NYC original, set in a cute little Old Town house
with a "lovely" garden patio, and whose "warm", "hospitable" staff
serves up American favorites at moderate prices; the "amazing breakfast" (featuring "awesome French toast") is its trademark, but those in
the know say "don't give the lunch and dinner short shrift";
P.S. closed Tuesdays; also closed Mondays Easter–Christmas.

Schooner Wharf *Seafood*   14 | 16 | 17 | $23

Key West | 202 William St. (Greene St.) | 305-292-3302 |
www.schoonerwharf.com

Beach boys seeking "good libations" and cheap seafood often wash
up at this "extremely Key West casual" "outdoor dive" and "locals'
hangout" hard on the harbor; with not one but two happy hours (7
AM–noon, 5–7 PM) and a full bill of live entertainment from lunchtime on, it's a fun place to "grow old disgracefully."

ⓩ Seven Fish *Seafood*   27 | 17 | 23 | $48

Key West | 632 Olivia St. (bet. Elizabeth & Simonton Sts.) |
305-296-2777 | www.7fish.com

Sea-foodies "cram" "dorsal fin to hip" into this "tiny" corner bistro
"off the main drag" in Key West for "fantastic" "locally caught" fish
"cooked to perfection" on a menu that's full of "surprises"; if the
"decor falls short" of the "pricey" tabs, it's still worth "making reservations before you book your airline ticket"; P.S. closed Tuesdays.

Shor American Seafood Grill *Seafood*   - | - | - | E

Key West | Hyatt Key West Resort & Marina | 601 Front St.
(Simonton St.) | 305-809-4000 | www.shorgrill.com

"Fresh" fish (and "tender" steak) are a "pleasant surprise" at this
upscale seafooder in the Hyatt Resort & Marina; it's on the pricey

side for the area and the space has a modern look, but the "famous sunsets" over the harbor are 100% pure Key West.

Sloppy Joe's Bar *American*   13 | 18 | 15 | $23

Key West | 201 Duval St. (Greene St.) | 305-294-5717 | www.sloppyjoes.com

This "famous" former "Hemingway" haunt is "Key West at its laid-back best" say the "mix of locals and tourists" who come here "ready to party" (others cry it's a complete "victim of cruiseshipification"); the "run-of-the-mill bar food" is heavy stuff, but folks can "dance off the calories" to the almost continual live music.

Snapper's Waterfront   20 | 20 | 20 | $37
Restaurant *Seafood*

Key Largo | 139 Seaside Ave. (Ocean View Blvd.) | 305-852-5956 | www.snapperskeylargo.com

"Simple" seafood served by a "pleasant" crew and backed by "beautiful" water views lures a "T-shirt-shorts-and-flip-flops"–clad crowd to this "casual" Key Largo spot; live music Fridays–Sundays, indoor/outdoor bars and "tarpons" to feed mean you "get a lot for your dollar."

Spanish Gardens Café 🗷🅜 *Spanish*   – | – | – | M

Islamorada | Galleria Plaza | 80925 Overseas Hwy. (Parker Dr.) | 305-664-3999 | www.spanishgardenscafe.com

A small local following supports this sleeper in Islamorada's Galleria Plaza whose simple cafe/market setup belies the authenticity of its Spanish cuisine; midpriced pintxos and tapas are on tap at dinner, and lunch's sandwich and salad offerings are an even bigger bargain.

Square One *American*   ▽ 21 | 23 | 24 | $48

Key West | Duval Sq. | 1075 Duval St. (bet. Truman Ave. & Virginia St.) | 305-296-4300 | www.squareonerestaurant.com

Loyalists are drawn to this "pleasant" Duval Square stalwart in part because they "love" the friendly owner-host who really "knows how to take care of his guests"; the expensive New American cuisine is "well prepared" and accompanied by live piano music nightly in the "classic and elegant" space.

Strip House *Steak*   ▽ 24 | 24 | 21 | $64

Key West | Reach Resort | 1435 Simonton St. (South St.) | 305-294-3330 | www.striphouse.com

Don Draper wouldn't look out of place tearing into a "high-quality" steak or "wonderful" piece of fish at this posh chain chophouse in Key West's Reach Resort outfitted with retro-looking banquettes, flocked scarlet wallpaper and naughty vintage pin-ups; it's Madison Avenue "expensive but worth it", especially given the "romantic" ocean views from the floor-to-ceiling windows.

Tasters Grille & Market *Eclectic*   – | – | – | M

Tavernier | Tavernier Towne Ctr. | 91252 Overseas Hwy. (mi. marker 91.2) | 305-853-1177 | www.tropicaltasters.food.officelive.com

Value abounds at this Eclectic cafe ensconced in the Tavernier Towne Shopping Center with a limited but "creative" midpriced menu at lunch (panini, salads, ceviche) and dinner (small and large plates plus pizza) and retail-priced wine from its market side, which also stocks cheese and specialty foods; bonus: a "nice" outdoor deck was recently added.

Thai Cuisine *Thai*

— | — | — | M

Key West | 513 Greene St. (Ann St.) | 305-294-9424 |
www.keywestthaicuisine.com

"Just plain old good Thai food" at recession-friendly prices is the raison d'être of this Eastward-leaning Key Wester that also sports a sushi bar; takeout/delivery is a favored option because the digs are as utilitarian as the name.

Thai Island *Thai*

— | — | — | I

Key West | 711 Eisenhower Dr. (Palm Ave.) | 305-296-9198 |
www.thaiislandrestaurant.com

If "affordable" Thai/sushi combinations are a dime a dozen in South Florida, this particular joint stands out for its use of locally harvested Thai herbs and spices in its "authentic and delicious" dishes; ok, so it's "not much too look at", but there's plenty of parking (a real luxury in Key West) and an outdoor patio with a view of Garrison Bight Marina.

Turtle Kraals *BBQ/Seafood*

18 | 19 | 18 | $30

Key West | Land's End Marina | 231 Margaret St. (Caroline St.) |
305-294-2640 | www.turtlekraals.com

This "quasi-tropical" Key West mainstay housed in a former turtle cannery in Land's End Marina is "touristy" but still makes a "passable" stop on any "waterfront bar crawl" for "cheap drinks overlooking the water" during the daily happy hour (4–6:30 PM); "excellent oysters" are the standout on the seafood- and barbecue-heavy menu, though some say "Friday turtle races are the best" part.

Two Friends Patio ● *American*

18 | 16 | 19 | $29

Key West | 512 Front St. (bet. Ann & Duval Sts.) | 305-296-3124 |
www.twofriendskeywest.com

A breezy "Key West–casual atmosphere" prevails at this mostly open-air spot a "short walk from Mallory Square" that, as the name suggests, feels like sitting on "a friend's patio"; "decent", "reasonably priced" American breakfast, lunch and dinner fare is surpassed by "fun" rounds of "energetic karaoke" every evening fueled by "liquid courage."

Z Upper Deck at Louie's ⊠Ⓜ *Eclectic/Wine Bar*

25 | 27 | 26 | $44

Key West | 700 Waddell Ave. (Vernon St.) | 305-294-1061 |
www.louiesbackyard.com

"Count the setting sun as part of the decor" and this "waterfront" wine bar in Key West is a real winner; a "wonderful" Eclectic assortment of small plates pairs nicely with "well-priced" wines by the glass and "impeccable" service, and though "tabs can creep up", at least patrons "don't need reservations" as they would downstairs at its sibling, Louie's Backyard; it closes seasonally for the month of September.

Ziggie & Mad Dog's *Seafood/Steak* | 25 | 22 | 25 | $52 |

Islamorada | 83000 Overseas Hwy. (mi. marker 83) | 305-664-3391 | www.ziggieandmaddogs.com

The chops are "NY steakhouse serious" and you "can't go wrong" with the "fresh" seafood either at this relatively "upscale" (i.e. "expensive"), decidedly "un-Keysy" "oasis" in Islamorada; the service remains dependable, but regulars already "miss" "enjoying" the "colorful crowd" with the former owner, late "football great" Jim 'Mad Dog' Mandich.

FT. LAUDERDALE/
BROWARD COUNTY

Broward County: Most Popular

1. Blue Moon Fish | *Seafood*
2. Casa D'Angelo | *Italian*
3. Greek Islands Taverna | *Greek*
4. Anthony's Coal Fired | *Pizza*
5. Bonefish Grill* | *Seafood*
6. Capital Grille | *Steak*
7. Cafe Maxx | *American/Eclectic*
8. Eduardo de San Angel | *Mexican*
9. 3030 Ocean | *American/Seafood*
10. Anthony's Runway | *Italian*
11. Cafe Martorano | *Italian*
12. Canyon | *Southwestern*
13. Seasons 52 | *American*
14. 15th Street Fisheries | *Seafood*
15. Houston's | *American*
16. Sage | *French*
17. Five Guys | *Burgers*
18. Johnny V | *Floribbean*
19. Il Mulino | *Italian*
20. Cheesecake Factory | *American*
21. Cafe Vico | *Italian*
22. Ruth's Chris | *Steak*
23. Casablanca Cafe | *American/Mediterranean*
24. Thai Spice | *Thai*
25. Acquolina Ristorante | *Italian*
26. P.F. Chang's* | *Chinese*

Many of the above restaurants are among the Broward area's most expensive, but if popularity were calibrated to price, a number of other restaurants would surely join their ranks. To illustrate this, we have added two lists comprising 80 Best Buys on page 127.

* Indicates a tie with restaurant above

Top Food

28 La Brochette | *Mediterranean*
Café Sharaku | *Asian*

27 Canyon | *Southwestern*
Casa D'Angelo | *Italian*
Eduardo de San Angel | *Mex.*
Valentino's Cucina | *Italian*
Kitchenetta Trattoria | *Italian*
Cafe Maxx | *American/Eclectic*

26 Thai Spice | *Thai*
Sette Bello | *Italian*
Market 17 | *American/Eclectic*
Rainbow Palace | *Chinese*
3030 Ocean | *Amer./Seafood*
Toa Toa Chinese | *Chinese*
Bistro Mezzaluna | *Amer./Ital.*
Capital Grille | *Steak*
Il Mercato Café | *Eclectic*

25 Cafe Vico | *Italian*
LaSpada's Hoagies | *Deli*
Silver Pond | *Chinese*

Mustard Seed | *Eclectic*
Bluefin Sushi | *Japanese/Thai*
Cafe Seville | *Spanish*
Morton's | *Steak*
Asia Bay | *Japanese/Thai*
Greek Islands Taverna | *Greek*
By Word of Mouth | *American*
Ruth's Chris | *Steak*
Tom Jenkins' Bar-B-Q | *BBQ*
Hi-Life Café | *American*
Cheese Course | *Eclectic*
D'Angelo Pizza | *Italian/Pizza*
Chima Brazilian | *Brazil./Steak*

24 Vienna Café | *European*
Calypso | *Caribbean/Seafood*
Sunfish Grill | *Amer./Seafood*
Martorano's | *Italian*
Council Oak Steaks | *Steak*
Blue Moon Fish | *Seafood*
Sukhothai | *Thai*

BY CUISINE

AMERICAN

27 Canyon
Cafe Maxx
26 Market 17
3030 Ocean
25 By Word of Mouth

AMERICAN (TRAD.)

25 Hi-Life Café
23 Houston's
22 Station House
Lucille's
21 Jaxson's

ASIAN

28 Café Sharaku (Fusion)
24 Saigon (Vietnamese)
Coco Asian (Japanese)
23 Moon (Japanese/Thai)
Eddie Hills (Japanese)

CARIBBEAN/CUBAN

24 Calypso
Sugar Reef
22 Little Havana
21 Las Vegas
Padrino's

CHINESE

26 Rainbow Palace
Toa Toa Chinese
25 Silver Pond
22 Christine Lee's
21 Christina Wan's

ECLECTIC

27 Cafe Maxx
26 Market 17
Il Mercato Café
25 Mustard Seed
Cheese Course

FRENCH

22 Le Bistro
Sage
Café La Bonne Crepe
20 Paul Bakery

ITALIAN

27 Casa D'Angelo
Valentino's Cucina
Kitchenetta Trattoria
26 Sette Bello
Bistro Mezzaluna

Excludes places with low votes, unless otherwise indicated

Vote at ZAGAT.com

MED/GREEK

28	La Brochette
25	Greek Islands Taverna
21	Casablanca Cafe
20	My Big Fat Greek Rest.
19	Taverna Opa

SEAFOOD

26	3030 Ocean
24	Calypso
	Sunfish Grill
	Council Oak Steaks
	Blue Moon Fish

STEAKHOUSES

26	Capital Grille
25	Morton's
	Ruth's Chris
	Chima Brazilian
24	Council Oak Steaks

THAI

26	Thai Spice
25	Bluefin Sushi
	Asia Bay
24	Sukhothai
23	Galanga

BY SPECIAL FEATURE

BREAKFAST

25	Mustard Seed
23	Shula's
22	Café La Bonne Crepe
	Bin 595
20	Original Pancake House

BRUNCH

24	Blue Moon Fish
	Steak 954
	Sugar Reef
22	Sage
	YOLO

BUSINESS DINING

27	Casa D'Angelo
	Eduardo de San Angel
	Cafe Maxx
26	Market 17
	Rainbow Palace

CHILD-FRIENDLY

25	LaSpada's Hoagies
	Greek Islands Taverna
22	Anthony's Coal Fired
	Rustic Inn
21	Jaxson's

DOCK & DINE

24	Blue Moon Fish
	Grille 66
23	Serafina
	Da Campo Osteria
	Coconuts

EARLY-BIRD

21	Ambry German
	Christina Wan's
20	Mama Mia
19	Old Florida Sea.
16	Mai-Kai

NEWCOMERS (RATED)

26	Market 17
21	Rare Las Olas∇
20	GG's Waterfront∇
	Tokyo Blue*
19	Dos Caminos∇

PEOPLE-WATCHING

25	D'Angelo
24	Martorano's
	Council Oak Steaks
	Anthony's Runway
22	China Grill

QUICK BITES

25	LaSpada's Hoagies
	Tom Jenkins' Bar-B-Q
	Cheese Course
24	Saigon Cuisine
23	Caffé Europa

QUIET CONVERSATION

28	Café Sharaku
27	Eduardo de San Angel
	Valentino's Cucina
26	Market 17
	Rainbow Palace

SINGLES SCENES

26	Market 17
24	Johnny V
23	Houston's
21	SoLita
20	Rocco's Tacos

TRENDY

27	Canyon
26	Market 17
	Capital Grille
25	D'Angelo
21	YOLO

BY LOCATION

FT. LAUDERDALE

28 Café Sharaku
27 Canyon
   Casa D'Angelo
   Eduardo de San Angel
   Valention's Cucina

GREATER FT. LAUDERDALE

25 LaSpada's Hoagies
   By Word of Mouth
   D'Angelo Pizza
24 Blue Moon Fish
23 Galanga

NE BROWARD

27 Cafe Maxx
24 Calypso
   Casa Maya Grill
   Gianni's
   Papa Hughie's

NW BROWARD

25 LaSpada's Hoagies
   Bluefin Sushi

   Cheese Course
24 Blue Moon Fish
   Saigon Cuisine

SE BROWARD

28 Il Mercato Café
25 Cheese Course
24 Martorano's
   Council Oak Steaks
   Sugar Reef

SW BROWARD

28 La Brochette
23 Capriccio
22 Anthony's Coal Fired
21 Las Vegas
   Brio Tuscan Grille

WEST/W. CENTRAL BROWARD

26 Toa Toa Chinese
25 LaSpada's Hoagies
   Silver Pond
   Mustard Seed
   Cheese Course

Top Decor

26 Steak 954	Casablanca Cafe
25 Market 17	D'Angelo Pizza
Mai-Kai	China Grill
Capital Grille	22 Tarantella
24 Grille 66	Chart House
Chima Brazilian	Canyon
Truluck's	Brio Tuscan Grille
Hollywood Prime	Bongos Cuban
Rainbow Palace	Timpano Chophouse
Bin 595	Vienna Café*
Seasons 52	SoLita
23 YOLO	Da Campo Osteria
Sublime	Eduardo de San Angel
Council Oak Steaks	Thai Spice
Blue Moon Fish	Casa D'Angelo
Caffé Europa	Latitudes
Morton's	21 Grateful Palate
III Forks	Houston's
3030 Ocean	Shula's
Ruth's Chris	Galanga

OUTDOORS

Asia Bay	Latitudes
Blue Moon Fish	Oceans 234
Caffé Europa	Steak 954
Coconuts	Sugar Reef
GG's Waterfront	Via Luna
JB's on the Beach	Wild E. Asian Bistro

ROMANCE

Cafe Seville	Il Mercato Café
Café Sharaku	La Brochette
Casablanca Cafe	La Dolce Vita
Casa D'Angelo	Saia
Eduardo de San Angel	Saint Tropez
Grille 66	Serafina

ROOMS

Capital Grille	Rare Las Olas
Casablanca Cafe	Steak 954
Chima Brazilian	Sublime
Council Oak Steaks	Tatiana Cabaret
Mai-Kai	III Forks
Market 17	Via Luna

VIEWS

Aizia	15th Street Fisheries
Aruba Beach	GG's Waterfront
Blue Moon Fish	Le Tub
China Grill	North Ocean Grill
Coconuts	Pelican Landing
Da Campo Osteria	Pier Top

Top Service

26 La Brochette
Rainbow Palace
Eduardo de San Angel

25 Valentino's Cucina
Capital Grille
Market 17
Cafe Vico
Café Sharaku
Council Oak Steaks*
Il Mercato Café*
Morton's
Cafe Seville
Chima Brazilian*
Thai Spice
Sette Bello

24 Cafe Maxx
Casa D'Angelo
Ruth's Chris
La Veranda
3030 Ocean

Vienna Café
Grille 66
Bistro Mezzaluna
Casa Maya Grill*
Hollywood Prime
Hi-Life Café
Truluck's

23 Seasons 52
D'Angelo Pizza
Steak 954
Canyon
Brooks
Sukhothai
Lola's
Ambry German
Capriccio
Sunfish Grill
Blue Moon Fish
By Word of Mouth
Serafina

Best Buys

In order of Bang for the Buck rating.

1. LaSpada's Hoagies
2. Five Guys
3. Jaxson's
4. Lime Fresh Mexican
5. Casa Maya Grill
6. Cheese Course
7. Pizza Rustica
8. Lucille's
9. Original Pancake House
10. Shorty's Bar-B-Q
11. Anthony's Coal Fired
12. CG Burgers
13. Moon Thai
14. Mario the Baker
15. Big Al's Steaks
16. Toa Toa Chinese
17. Las Vegas
18. El Tamarindo
19. Tom Jenkins' Bar-B-Q
20. Paul Bakery
21. Floridian
22. Basilic Vietnamese
23. Southport Raw Bar
24. Saigon Cuisine
25. Christina Wan's
26. Stir Crazy
27. Piola
28. Tarantella
29. D'Angelo Pizza
30. Sukhothai
31. TooJay's Deli
32. Coconuts
33. Le Tub
34. Noodles Panini
35. Fritz & Franz
36. Padrino's
37. Kelly's Landing
38. Café La Bonne Crepe
39. Whale's Rib
40. Cheesecake Factory

OTHER GOOD VALUES

Blue Ginger
Bonefish Grill
Café Emunah
Café Jamm
Cafe Seville
Cafe Vico
Fin & Claw
Gianni's
Giovanni's
Gold Coast Grill
Havana's Cuban Cuisine
Hi-Life Café
Houston's
Il Mulino
Indian Chillies
Jasmine Thai
Kingshead Pub
La Dolce Vita
Le Bistro
Little Havana
Madras Café
Marumi Sushi
Mason Jar
My Big Fat Greek Rest.
Myung Ga Tofu & BBQ
Old Florida Sea.
On the Menu
Pasha
P.F. Chang's
Rock n Roll Ribs
Saxsay
Seasons 52
Shuck N Dive
Star Bistro
Tarpon Bend
Tokyo Sushi
Udipi
Village Grille
Village Tavern
Viva Chile

FT. LAUDERDALE/
BROWARD COUNTY
RESTAURANT
DIRECTORY

	FOOD	DECOR	SERVICE	COST

Acquolina Ristorante Italiano *Italian*

22	21	22	$45

Hallandale | 124 S. Federal Hwy. (SE 2nd St.) | 954-454-2410
Weston | 2320 Weston Rd. (Royal Palm Blvd.) | 954-389-1880
www.acquolinaweston.com

This Weston-Hallandale duo is "wonderful for families" and groups who find "good value" in the "huge" family-style portions – even the "individual sizes are enough for two" – of "delicious" "NYC-style" Italian fare; both locations are "classy" and "convivial", but Weston's alfresco lakeside seating is "a plus" ("when it's not a million degrees").

Aizia *Asian*

▽ 19	25	18	$56

Hallandale | Diplomat Landing | 3660 S. Ocean Dr.
(E. Hallandale Beach Blvd.) | 954-602-8393 |
www.aiziahollywood.com

"Pretty fish, pretty people, pretty trendy" sums up this pricey resto-lounge sporting a sweet Intracoastal view from Hallandale's Diplomat Landing; the wide-ranging Asian menu has "something for everyone", but with its sexy look, clubby soundtrack and VIP rooms with bottle service, it's primarily a venue for twentysomethings.

A La Turca *Turkish*

23	18	20	$31

Hollywood | 2027 Hollywood Blvd. (N. 21st Ave.) | 954-925-5900 | www.myalaturca.com

The "authentic" Turkish fare at this "friendly" "family-run" store-front in Hollywood appeals to "carnivores and vegetarians" alike and stirs up "memories of the eastern Mediterranean"; two-for-one "happy-hour mezes" (daily, from 4–7 PM) are a "delicious" way to start a meal, and the "homemade baklava" is a "perfect end."

Ambry German & American Restaurant 🗷 *American/German*

21	19	23	$34

Ft. Lauderdale | 3016 E. Commercial Blvd. (Bayview Dr.) | 954-771-7342

At this "dark and cozy" "time warp" in Ft. Lauderdale run by a "cheerful" family, a "large German contingent dines frequently", but they're not the only ones who enjoy the "genuine" Teutonic fare that includes a "wide variety of schnitzels" washed down by imported lager; a salad bar is included with all entrees, making dinner a "reasonable" deal, and there's a typical steakhouse menu for the less adventurous.

🗷 Anthony's Coal Fired Pizza *Pizza*

22	16	20	$23

Ft. Lauderdale | 2203 S. Federal Hwy. (SE 22nd St.) | 954-462-5555
Pompano Beach | 1203 S. Federal Hwy. (SE 12th St.) | 954-942-5550
Coral Springs | Magnolia Shops | 9521 Westview Dr. (University Dr.) | 954-340-2625
Cooper City | Home Depot Shopping Ctr. | 11037 Pines Blvd. (Hiatus Rd.) | 954-443-6610
Weston | Weston Commons | 4527 Weston Rd. (Griffin Rd.) | 954-358-2625
Plantation | 512 N. Pine Island Rd. (bet. Broward & Cleary Blvds.) | 954-474-3311
www.anthonyscoalfiredpizza.com
See review in Miami/Dade County Directory.

FOOD | DECOR | SERVICE | COST

☑ Anthony's Runway 84 Ⓜ *Italian*   24 | 20 | 22 | $49

Ft. Lauderdale | 330 State Rd. 84 (bet. SW 3rd & 4th Aves.) |
954-467-8484 | www.runway-84.com

This "boisterous" "red-sauce" Italian joint in Ft. Lauderdale has
long proven a popular layover when heading "to or from the airport" thanks to "huge", "stick-to-your-ribs" feasts that are strictly
"first class"; the "charming" (some surveyors say "cheesy") ambiance mixes airplane-themed decor with a crowd that feels
straight out of "a Martin Scorsese movie", but it's always "packed",
so prepare to wait.

Argentango Grill *Argentinean*   18 | 15 | 17 | $36

Hollywood | 1822 Young Circle (Harrison St.) | 954-920-9233 |
www.argentangogrillhollywood.com

The parking might be "tough" but the steaks are "tender" at this
"busy" Argentinean grill in Hollywood, where the meaty dishes
come in "shareable" portions at "modest" rates; still, a few find
the food "inconsistent" (the Food score is down three points this
year), the service "uneven" and decor "dated", lamenting it's
"not what it used to be."

Aruba Beach Cafe *American/Caribbean*   17 | 19 | 17 | $30

Lauderdale-by-the-Sea | 1 E. Commercial Blvd. (Andrews Ave.) |
954-776-0001 | www.arubabeachcafe.com

"Grab a piña colada" from one of several bars and "watch the waves"
at this "tropical" party "smack dab on the beach" in Lauderdale-by-
the-Sea; despite reports of only "passable" American-Caribbean
eats and seafood and "spotty" service, locals still "take visitors for
lunch" on account of the "sea breezes", "people-watching" and
"reasonable" rates; P.S. there's live guitar nightly and steel drum-
ming daytime on weekends, plus a "great" brunch on Sunday.

Asia Bay *Japanese/Thai*   25 | 21 | 22 | $40

Ft. Lauderdale | 1111 E. Las Olas Blvd. (bet. SE 10th Terr. & 12th Ave.) |
954-848-9900 | www.asiabayrestaurants.com

"Both sides of the menu are winners" at this "sleek" Ft. Lauderdale
dual concept offering "authentic" Thai fare and a "large"
Japanese selection that includes cooked dishes plus over 60
choices of sushi and sashimi; diners deem the moderate bills a "fair
price for such wonderful food", especially if you "sit outside overlooking" the Tarpon River; P.S. the original Miami location is smaller
but just as "terrific."

Basilic Vietnamese Grill *Vietnamese*   22 | 17 | 21 | $25

Lauderdale-by-the-Sea | 218 E. Commercial Blvd. (bet. Bougainvilla &
Seagrape Drs.) | 954-771-5798

This "cool spot" in Lauderdale-by-the-Sea is "not your typical
Chinatown Vietnamese" – its "elevated" menu ("delightful" banh
mi, "fresh summer rolls") is "lighter", which appeals to those
baring midriffs at the nearby beach; a "knowledgeable" staff and
"great values" help fill the void that some feel staring at the
"sparse" "modern" decor.

	FOOD	DECOR	SERVICE	COST

Big Al's Steaks *Cheesesteaks*   19 | 9 | 16 | $18

Coconut Creek | 5607 Regency Lakes Blvd. (Rte. 441) | 954-480-8550 | www.bigalssteaks.com

See review in Palm Beach Directory.

Big City Tavern ☻ *American*   19 | 19 | 19 | $36

Ft. Lauderdale | 609 E. Las Olas Blvd. (Federal Hwy.) | 954-727-0307 | www.bigtimerestaurants.com

"Tourists and locals" rub elbows at this "upscale-casual" "hot spot" on "cutesy wootsy Las Olas Boulevard" offering a "something-for-everyone" American menu at a "reasonable" price; some tipplers aver the "drinks are better than the food" and it does host a "happening bar scene", which "makes the dining room noisy at peak times" (so sit outside and "watch the people stroll by").

Billy's Stone Crab   23 | 17 | 21 | $54
Restaurant & Market *Seafood*

Hollywood | 400 N. Ocean Dr. (Arizona St.) | 954-923-2300 | www.crabs.com

"Darn fine claws" (in season) grab the attention of crustacean connoisseurs who liken this "classic" Hollywood seafooder to "Joe's without the wait"; it's "pricey", but the dockside "water views" and service "with a smile" "can't be beat", and for quickie crabs the attached market "cracks 'em and packs 'em" to go; P.S. closed seasonally September through mid-October.

Bimini Boatyard Bar & Grill *American*   17 | 21 | 18 | $35

Ft. Lauderdale | 1555 SE 17th St. (bet. Eisenhower Blvd. & 15th Ave.) | 954-525-7400 | www.biminiboatyard.com

This sprawling canalside complex in Ft. Lauderdale is "still a favorite after more than 20 years" and appeals to "all ages", from "grandkids" who "gawk at the yachts" to "older singles" on the "hunt" who slur "it's a nice place to get sloshed"; besides the "must-order" Bimini bread, the midpriced American eats "need a bit more bam", but the setting is "beautiful" and "comfortable" – "what more do you want on a lazy day?"

Bin 595 *American*   22 | 24 | 22 | $49

Plantation | Renaissance Ft. Lauderdale Cruise Port Hotel | 1230 S. Pine Island Rd. (State Rd. 84) | 954-308-4595 | www.bin595.com

Guests of the Renaissance Hotel and well-healed locals appreciate the "small but excellent" New American menu at this "quiet", "elegant" dining room in Plantation aswirl with curvy ceiling coffers, crescent-shaped booths and striped columns; it's "a bit out of the way", but that also means it's always "easy to get into."

Bistro 555 *Italian*   ▽ 24 | 21 | 21 | $35

Davie | Sheridan Shoppes | 15651 Sheridan St. (I-75) | 954-358-0808

"Film buffs" give the thumbs-up to this "quaint" Italian ristorante in Davie's Sheridan Shoppes, citing "surprisingly good" food, "attentive" service and moderate prices as reasons why it's the "best place to eat after a movie" at the nearby Cinemark megaplex; a convenient location right off I-75 also gives oenophiles easy access to its "reasonable corkage fees."

Z Bistro Mezzaluna *American/Italian* 26 | 21 | 24 | $57

Ft. Lauderdale | 741 SE 17th St. (S. Federal Hwy.) | 954-522-6620 | www.bistromezzaluna.com

"Locals love" this "hidden gem" in a Ft. Lauderdale strip mall, a "favorite" for "delicious" Italian–New American fare in a "high-energy" setting chock-full of area "power brokers"; "terrific service" takes the sting off "pricey" tabs, as does the "fantastic happy hour", with deals 5–7 PM daily.

Bluefin Sushi *Japanese/Thai* 25 | 18 | 22 | $38

Parkland | Parkland Town Ctr. | 6694 Parkside Dr. (bet. Holmberg Rd. & NW 70th Pl.) | 954-755-0120 | www.bluefinparkland.com
See review in Palm Beach Directory.

NEW Blue Ginger *Japanese* - | - | - | M

Pembroke Pines | 15791 Sheridan St. (bet. Dykes Rd. & I-75) | 954-680-9998

Whatever floats your boat is up for grabs at this new Japanese in Pembroke Pines, where a fleet of sushi and sashimi float on little wooden rafts along a 'river' that runs the course of the sushi bar; a hip, modern setting plus a bevy of decadent desserts including tempura cheesecake and Thai donuts cap the unique experience.

Z Blue Moon Fish Co. *Seafood* 24 | 23 | 23 | $49

Lauderdale-by-the-Sea | 4405 W. Tradewinds Ave. (Commercial Blvd.) | 954-267-9888
Coral Springs | 10317 Royal Palm Blvd. (Coral Springs Dr.) | 954-755-0002 **M**
www.bluemoonfishco.com

"Thoughtfully chosen and prepared" seafood and "gorgeous" views of the Intracoastal's "yacht parade" make this "upscale" Lauderdale-by-the-Sea fish house Broward's Most Popular eatery, whether "for a romantic dinner or just to show friends why you moved to South Florida"; there's "attentive" service plus "ambiance to spare" on the outdoor deck, though "steep" prices convince many to opt for the "doubly wonderful" two-for-one lunch "bargains"; P.S. Coral Springs is separately owned, sans view and cheaper.

Bluepoint Ocean Grill ● *Seafood* ∇ 18 | 23 | 17 | $50

Hollywood | Seminole Paradise at Hard Rock Hotel & Casino | 5730 Seminole Way (Rte. 441) | 954-327-8911 | www.seminolehardrockhollywood.com

Highrollers say the staff is "well informed" and the small surf 'n' turf menu "satisfies" "kids as well as adults" at this eatery located in the Paradise Shopping area in the Seminole Hard Rock Casino complex; pretty lakeside views from the patio are a plus, yet some are "underwhelmed" given the price.

Z Bonefish Grill *Seafood* 22 | 19 | 21 | $36

Ft. Lauderdale | 6282 N. Federal Hwy. (NE 62nd St.) | 954-492-3266
(continued)

(continued)

Bonefish Grill

Coral Springs | 1455 N. University Dr. (Shadow Wood Blvd.) | 954-509-0405
Davie | Weston Commons | 4545 Weston Rd. (Griffin Rd.) | 954-389-9273
Plantation | 10197 W. Sunrise Blvd. (Nob Hill Rd.) | 954-472-3592
www.bonefishgrill.com

"Just-out-of-the-water fish in many forms" "draws droves" to these "delightful", "easygoing" seafooders ("hard to believe it's a chain"); "longish waits, even with a reservation" and "noise, noise, noise" are balanced by "prompt and courteous" service and "competitive prices"; P.S. the "Bang Bang shrimp is bang-on."

NEW Bongos Cuban Café *Cuban*   16 | 22 | 17 | $38

Hollywood | Seminole Paradise at Hard Rock Hotel & Casino | 5733 Seminole Way (Rte. 442) | 954-791-3040 | www.bongoscubancafe.com

See review in Miami/Dade County Directory.

Bongusto! Ristorante ⑤ *Italian*   ▽ 24 | 22 | 27 | $52

Ft. Lauderdale | 5640 N. Federal Hwy. (NE 56th St.) | 954-771-9635 | www.bongustoitalian.com

This Ft. Lauderdale mainstay pleases fans with "traditional" Italian spreads that are "excellent" but expensive; the staid dining room and pro staff are a "throwback in time" – but to a "very nice time."

Brazaviva Churrascaria *Brazilian*   ▽ 20 | 18 | 21 | $43

Sunrise | 14301 W. Sunrise Blvd. (144th Ave.) | 954-514-5851 | www.brazaviva.com

"Friendly" waiters "keep coming" by the tables with skewer after skewer of "tasty meats" at this Brazilian churrascaria in Sunrise; the prix fixe meal includes a run on the salad bar, but it's still "pricey" so the budget-minded suggest going "for lunch", which is almost half the cost; P.S. the separately owned Doral offshoot opened post-Survey.

Brio Tuscan Grille *Italian*   21 | 22 | 21 | $36

Hallandale | Village at Gulfstream Park | 600 Silks Run (bet. E. Hallandale Beach Blvd. & S. Federal Hwy.) | 954-362-1600
Pembroke Pines | The Shops at Pembroke Gardens | 14576 SW Fifth St. (Pines Blvd.) | 954-431-1341
www.brioitalian.com

Mall mavens "fortify" themselves for "shopping" at these "upscale chain" spots with "reliable" Italian fare that "doesn't cost an arm and a leg"; "solicitous" staffers patrol the "huge, bustling" Tuscan villa-esque spaces and outdoor patios, which are smaller and less "noisy."

Brooks Ⓜ *Continental*   21 | 20 | 23 | $50

Deerfield Beach | 500 S. Federal Hwy. (¼ mi. south of Hillsboro Blvd.) | 954-427-9302 | www.brooks-restaurant.com

Entering its fourth decade, Deerfield Beach's citadel of "old-style elegance" harks back to "a time without gimmicks" when mature "grown-ups" celebrated "special occasions" with a "quality" dinner (Continental, natch) at a "good value"; modernists seem to think it "needs refurbishing", but it's still ideal for private "events" thanks to its multiple rooms and "impeccable" service; P.S. closed Mondays and Tuesdays (in summer, closed Mondays–Thursdays).

By Word of Mouth 🗷 *American*   25 | 16 | 23 | $48

Oakland Park | 3200 NE 12th Ave. (E. Oakland Park Blvd.) | 954-564-3663 | www.bywordofmouthfoods.com

Word has been spreading for years about this "tiny", "hard-to-find" eatery in Oakland Park and its "delightful" New American cuisine, "divine" fresh-baked desserts and "unusual" ordering concept: "no menus", just a "display case" with the "offerings of the day" explained by a "warm" staff; it's "light on decor" but "who needs fancy when all you want to do is eat", and besides, it offers takeout.

Café Emunah *Kosher/Seafood*   ▽ 25 | 18 | 23 | $34

Ft. Lauderdale | 3558 N. Ocean Blvd. (bet. 35th & 36th Sts.) | 954-561-6411 | www.myemunah.com

"This is kosher?" ask devotees of the "inventive", "pure" and "nourishing fare" at this novel concept: a sushi and tea bar adhering to Jewish dietary restrictions; the "healing, happy and hip" vibe is enhanced by WiFi, modern Zen (or rather, Kabbalah) decor and a small library of books on that mystical strain of Judaism; P.S. closed Fridays; Saturday hours are from one hour after sunset till 1 AM.

NEW Café Jamm Ⓜ *American*   - | - | - | M

Ft. Lauderdale | 2364 N. Federal Hwy. (E. Oakland Park Blvd.) | 954-835-5305 | www.cafejamm.com

Fans of Hollywood's erstwhile Sushi Blues will be happy to see two sisters who grew up in the restaurant now running their own new venue, this small storefront in Ft. Lauderdale with a midpriced American menu ranging from homey dishes (with a few of their mom's recipes sprinkled in) to Asian-influenced specials; the casual dining room is sleek with muted colors and decor, and there's also sidewalk seating.

Café La Bonne Crepe *French*   22 | 17 | 20 | $30

Ft. Lauderdale | 815 E. Las Olas Blvd. (bet. SE 8th & 9th Aves.) | 954-761-1515 | www.labonnecrepe.com

Most "fun for breakfast", this "authentic crêperie" turns out "savory and sweet" Franco-flapjacks so "addictive" that some junkies may "need a fix" for lunch or dinner, when other French bistro staples are also offered; the prices are right, so if the interior feels "cramped", head to the "sidewalk tables" and watch "Las Olas parade" by.

🖅 Cafe Martorano *Italian*   24 | 19 | 19 | $64

Ft. Lauderdale | 3343 E. Oakland Park Blvd. (N. Ocean Blvd.) | 954-561-2554 | www.cafemartorano.com

🖅 Martorano's Ⓜ *Italian*
(aka Cafe Martorano)

Hollywood | Seminole Paradise at Hard Rock Hotel & Casino | 5751 Seminole Way (bet. Griffin & Stirling Rds.) | 954-584-4450 | www.martoranoshollywood.com

There "ain't no place like" this Ft. Lauderdalian, chef-owner Steve Martorano's kooky love letter to his "South Philly" Italian upbringing, with its "disco ball", "earsplitting" dance music and *"Rocky"* movies blaring from "wall-to-wall TVs", but despite the "gimmicks" the "fantastic food" is "really the star"; even with "sticker shock" prices and an "arrogant" staff, many endure "looong waits" (no reservations) for what they call "the best meatballs in town"; P.S. Seminole Hard Rock has similar "bada bing" "without the wait."

☑ Cafe Maxx *American/Eclectic*   27 | 19 | 24 | $57

Pompano Beach | 2601 E. Atlantic Blvd. (NE 26th Ave.) | 954-782-0606 | www.cafemaxx.com

Chef Oliver Saucy's "innovative" Eclectic–New American cuisine is "always prepared with a special touch" and complemented by co-owner Darrel Broek's "inspired" wine list and "pleasantly low-key" service at this "one-of-a-kind" "treasure" in Pompano Beach; it's "not cheap" and some gripe that the strip-mall setting "doesn't do [the experience] justice", but longtime loyalists plead "don't move – it's part of the charm."

Cafe Seville ☒ *Spanish*   25 | 19 | 25 | $50

Ft. Lauderdale | 2768 E. Oakland Park Blvd. (Bayview Dr.) | 954-565-1148 | www.cafeseville.com

For a "true taste of Spain", Ft. Lauderdale "locals" head to this "small" strip-mall spot for "phenomenal tapas", "outstanding" paella and fish dishes and an Iberian-California wine list; the rustic setting "could use sprucing", but the "terrific" treatment from the "amiable" owners and "longtime" staff justifies the prices, while live guitar on weekend nights is another perk.

☑ Café Sharaku Ⓜ *Asian*   28 | 15 | 25 | $44

Ft. Lauderdale | 2736 N. Federal Hwy. (bet. E. Oakland Park Blvd. & NE 26th St.) | 954-563-2888 | www.cafesharaku.com

"Don't tell anyone!" say fans who worry they might "betray their own interests" by raving about the "sophisticated", "beautifully presented" Asian fusion cuisine at this "tiny" (18-seat) not-quite-so-"hidden gem" in Ft. Lauderdale; there's "not much" decor but it's "quiet", and chef-owner Iwao Kaita and his servers "work so well together to pace" meals that it's lovely to linger for a "romantic" repast; P.S. the prix fixe dinner is an "excellent buy."

☑ Cafe Vico *Italian*   25 | 21 | 25 | $43

Ft. Lauderdale | IHOP Plaza | 1125 N. Federal Hwy. (E. Sunrise Blvd.) | 954-565-9681 | www.cafevicorestaurant.com

At this "romantic" Ft. Lauderdale ristorante, owner Marco Vico Rodrigues greets each guest "like a long-lost relative", and that "caring" attitude continues with service that's "attentive without hovering"; the "authentic" Northern Italian cuisine is equally "excellent" and a relative "bargain", ditto the "value-filled wine list."

Caffè Europa *Italian*   23 | 23 | 22 | $55

Ft. Lauderdale | 910 E. Las Olas Blvd. (bet. SE 9th & 10th Aves.) | 954-763-6600 | www.caffeeuropalasolas.com

The "beautiful" "flower-filled" environs "sparkle" at this "old name with a new look" on Las Olas known for "superior" Italian cuisine, a

FOOD | DECOR | SERVICE | COST

"nurturing" staff and "expensive" tabs; but a "society crowd" dressed to the nines says the real specialty is "ambiance", whether that means stately "Chopin nocturnes" played by a "wonderful" pianist or involves draining the dregs at the "swinging" wine bar.

Calypso ⊠ *Caribbean/Seafood* 24 | 14 | 20 | $32

Pompano Beach | 460 S. Cypress Rd. (5th St.) | 954-942-1633 | www.calypsorestaurant.com

"All that's missing is the sand and the sea" say fans swept away by the midpriced, "down-home" Caribbean eats like "fresh" fish and "can't-miss jerk wings" at this "island hideaway" in an "unassuming" Pompano Beach strip mall; there's "no glitz" and it "tends to be crowded" as it's only open weekdays, but the "friendly", "hands-on owners" really "care."

Cantina Laredo *Mexican* 20 | 20 | 19 | $33

Hallandale | Village at Gulfstream Park | 501 Silks Run (bet. E. Hallandale Beach Blvd. & S. Federal Hwy.) | 954-457-7662 | www.cantinalaredo.com

See review in Palm Beach Directory.

☑ Canyon *Southwestern* 27 | 22 | 23 | $52

Ft. Lauderdale | 1818 E. Sunrise Blvd. (N. Federal Hwy.) | 954-765-1950 | www.canyonfl.com

It's "quite a scene" at this "popular" Ft. Lauderdale bistro offering an "imaginative", "pricey" menu of Southwestern and American "fusion" fare with occasional Asian touches; "enormous portions", prickly pear margaritas that "wow" and "helpful" servers are the reward "once you are finally seated" after often long "waits", the result of a "small" space and a no-reserving policy that can be "a real drag."

☑ Capital Grille *Steak* 26 | 25 | 25 | $67

Ft. Lauderdale | 2430 E. Sunrise Blvd. (Bayview Dr.) | 954-446-2000 | www.thecapitalgrille.com

See review in Miami/Dade County Directory.

Capriccio ❶ *Italian* 23 | 20 | 23 | $40

Pembroke Pines | 2424 N. University Dr. (Sheridan St.) | 954-432-7001 | www.capriccios.net

Pembroke Pines "sweethearts" swear nothing says "romance" like a "violinist who takes requests at your table", but if that's not music to everyone's ears there's also a "piano player" nightly at this "relaxed", "old-fashioned" white-tablecloth ristorante where even the "friendly" owner joins in "singing your favorite Italian" songs; the "delicious" fare, including "excellent" "fish specials", is "reasonably priced", as is the wine list – there's also a large central bar.

Cap's Place Island *Seafood* 17 | 19 | 18 | $44

Lighthouse Point | 2765 NE 28th Ct. (take ferry from dock) | 954-941-0418 | www.capsplace.com

"Take a boat ride back in time" to this "historic" "old Florida landmark" "with a story to tell" (it involves "rum running" and "Al Capone") on a "little island" off Lighthouse Point; some may call it an "overpriced tourist" trap and say it "won't win any culinary awards", but the "fresh fish" holds up, the "hearts of palm salad is justifiably legend-ary" and the "rustic" setting (you can see the "marsh through the floorboards") is "wonderful fun."

Casablanca Cafe *American/Mediterranean*   21 | 23 | 21 | $40
Ft. Lauderdale | 3049 Alhambra St. (Seabreeze Blvd.) | 954-764-3500 | www.casablancacafeonline.com
A "lovely setting" in a "beautiful old" Mediterranean Revival home and "unbeatable" ocean views push this "romantic" beachside Ft. Lauderdalian into "special-occasion" territory – though relatively modest tabs mean it could be part of a regular dining rotation; an "eclectic crowd" praises "tasty" Med-American plates and "incred-ible drinks" bolstered by classy touches like "old-style" service and a pianist nightly.

Z Casa D'Angelo *Italian*   27 | 22 | 24 | $61
Ft. Lauderdale | Sunrise Square Plaza | 1201 N. Federal Hwy. (bet. E. Sunrise Blvd. & NE 13th St.) | 954-564-1234 | www.casa-d-angelo.com
Chef-owner Angelo Elia's "outstanding" Northern Italian fare, in-cluding a "wide variety of homemade pasta", takes diners on a "de-lightful" "journey to Italy" without leaving Ft. Lauderdale (or Boca, thanks to the younger sib); it's "expensive" (i.e. an excuse to "wear your Valentino") and tables are "a tad too cozy" in the "bustling" space, but "warm" service and a "wine room that has to be seen to be believed" help explain why it's "beloved" by many – reservations are highly recommended.

Casa Maya Grill *Mexican*   24 | 19 | 24 | $22
Deerfield Beach | Cove Shopping Ctr. | 301 SE 15th Terr. (E. Hillsboro Blvd.) | 954-570-6101 | www.casamayagrill.com
For the "best mole north of Mexico" and similarly "outstanding" fare, spice-hunters head to this "authentic" Yucatán specialist in Deerfield Beach; add a "welcoming" atmosphere, warm hues and Mayan artwork plus "cheap" prices and surveyors definitely "get their money's worth."

NEW CG Burgers *Burgers*   19 | 13 | 15 | $18
Coral Springs | 4320 N. State Rd. 7 (Turtle Creek Dr.) | 954-510-4801 | www.cgburgers.com
See review in Palm Beach Directory.

NEW Chart House *Seafood*   20 | 22 | 20 | $48
Ft. Lauderdale | 3000 NE 32nd Ave. (Ocean Blvd.) | 954-561-4800 | www.chart-house.com
See review in Miami/Dade County Directory.

Checkers Old Munchen *German*   22 | 15 | 19 | $29
Pompano Beach | 2209 E. Atlantic Blvd. (bet. 22nd & 23rd Aves.) | 954-785-7565
Diners enter this "old-fashioned" Bavarian food hall in Pompano Beach "speaking English and leave two hours later wearing

	FOOD	DECOR	SERVICE	COST

brunch is also a big win, but you'll need to cash in a lot of chips because it's "not cheap."

Da Campo Osteria *Italian*

| 23 | 22 | 22 | $56 |

Ft. Lauderdale | Il Lugano Hotel | 3333 NE 32nd Ave. (34th St.) | 954-226-5002 | www.dacampofl.com

"Tucked away" in the Il Lugano Hotel in Ft. Lauderdale is this somewhat "hidden" Todd English outpost turning out "memorable meals" of "top-notch" Northern Italian cuisine in casual, modern surroundings; the staff is "helpful", even "entertaining" when they "create fresh mozzarella tableside" – and some say that experience alone is "worth its weight in cheese."

D'Angelo Pizza *Italian/Pizza*

| 25 | 23 | 23 | $33 |

Oakland Park | 4215 N. Federal Hwy. (bet. 38th & 43rd Sts.) | 954-561-7300 | www.pizzadangelo.com

Call it "Casa D'Angelo lite" say smitten surveyors (referring to its pricier, more traditional siblings) about this Oakland Park wine bar/bistro offering a range of "perfect" pizzas and other "wonderful" noshes including Italian-style small plates, bruschetta, cheeses, cured meats and panini; the "crisp contemporary" space and "hip" atmosphere add to the allure, along with an "attentive" staff.

NEW Dapur *Asian*

| - | - | - | M |

Ft. Lauderdale | 1620 N. Federal Hwy. (NE 16th Ct.) | 954-306-2663 | www.dapurkitchen.com

This hip Pan-Asian, newly arrived in Ft. Lauderdale, tramps all over the East spending serious time in Japan while also making stops in Indonesia, Korea, Malaysia, Thailand and Vietnam with its mid-priced small and large plates; locavores will love that the owner (who founded Galanga) uses herbs, spices and roots from the organic garden behind the restaurant – and tipplers will appreciate that the vibrantly plum-colored contemporary space also includes a separate lounge featuring a large bar.

NEW Dos Caminos *Mexican*

| ∇ 19 | 15 | 16 | $41 |

Sheraton Ft. Lauderdale Beach Hotel | 1140 Seabreeze Blvd. (N. Ocean Blvd.) | 954-727-7090 | www.doscaminos.com

Ft. Lauderdale is "lucky" to host Florida's first outpost of this NYC-based chain say fans of its "creative" Mexican fare; inside the Sheraton Beach Hotel patrons will find more than 100 types of tequila and a Day of the Dead motif that features painted skulls soundtracked by "deafeningly loud" music; P.S. breakfast and dinner only.

East City Grill ☒ *American*

| 19 | 20 | 21 | $42 |

Weston | Weston Town Ctr. | 1800 Bell Tower Ln. (Bonaventure Blvd.) | 954-659-3339 | www.eastcitygrill.com

This contemporary bistro in Weston Town Center is "still turning out" "imaginative" New American fare that satisfies the "western 'burbs"; it's "pricey" so most folks opt for the "lovely" outdoor patio overlooking the water to "get their money's worth."

	FOOD	DECOR	SERVICE	COST

Eddie Hills Sushi & Thai *Japanese/Thai* | 23 | 10 | 17 | $27 |

Hallandale | 134 N. Federal Hwy. (NE 2nd St.) | 954-454-0023 |
www.eddiehills.com

Well "kiss my grits!" exclaim surprised surveyors when they discover "authentic" Thai dishes and "fresh" "sushi in a diner", of all places, at this Hallandale greasy spoon/chopstick combo (it serves typical coffee shop items at breakfast); there are no frills, but it's "family-friendly" and "always busy" with folks who "don't want to pay an arm and a leg" to dine out.

☑ Eduardo de San Angel ⌧ *Mexican* | 27 | 22 | 26 | $59 |

Ft. Lauderdale | 2822 E. Commercial Blvd. (bet. Bayview Dr. & NE 28th Ave.) | 954-772-4731 | www.eduardodesanangel.com

This Ft. Lauderdale "favorite" is "not your typical" "neighborhood taco place" – rather, "under the artful eye" of chef-owner Eduardo Pria, it's a "scintillating" tribute to "refined" "haute Mexicano" that some find "even better than high-end Mexico City restaurants"; a "quiet" ambiance and staffers who "provide the fascinating history of each dish" make it "enjoyable" despite the slight "dent in your wallet."

Elle's *Eclectic*   ▽ | 21 | 24 | 21 | $36 |

Miramar | 12312 Miramar Pkwy. (off S. Flamingo Rd.) | 954-437-0071 | www.ellesrestaurant.com

What a "lovely surprise" to find this "modern" "slice of Brickell Avenue" in Miramar say sophisticates who appreciate its "innovative" Eclectic mix of small and large plates; "reasonable prices" extend to the wines, which are also available from the owner's next-door market.

El Tamarindo *Salvadoran* | 22 | 14 | 22 | $24 |

Ft. Lauderdale | 233 State Rd. 84 (SW 3rd Ave.) | 954-467-5114

El Tamarindo Coal Fired Pizza *Pizza/Salvadoran*

Hallandale | 712 Atlantic Shores Blvd. (N. Federal Hwy.) | 954-456-4447

A "reliable" stop near the Ft. Lauderdale/Hollywood International Airport is this "friendly" "diner-like place turning out "reasonably" priced Salvadoran dishes with "skill and authenticity"; its Hallandale offspring is similar, except "delicious" thin (i.e. Italian) is its specialty, along with "other unexpected items" (i.e. Italian is its specialty.

Ferdo's Grill ⌧ *Mideastern*   ▽ | 20 | 14 | 21 | $29 |

Ft. Lauderdale | 4300 N. Federal Hwy. (NE 43rd St.) | 954-492-5552 | www.ferdosgrill.net

The "authentic" midpriced Middle Eastern fare, including some Syrian specialties, comes in portions so "generous" that "most everyone" seems to leave this basic Ft. Lauderdale joint "with a take-out box"; "lunch deals" make it a popular midday repast, while "fun" belly dancing attracts a crowd on Saturday nights.

☑ 15th Street Fisheries *Seafood* | 19 | 19 | 19 | $43 |

Ft. Lauderdale | Lauderdale Marina | 1900 SE 15th St. (Cordova Rd.) | 954-763-2777 | www.15streetfisheries.com

"Kids (ok, grown-ups too) love to feed the tarpons from the dock" and "breathe in the salty air" at this "touristy" "old-time Florida" seafooder in the Lauderdale Marina with "scenic" Intracoastal views and "fresh", "basic" fare; others say it's "living on its history" and "needs a face-lift", and complain that "the best fish here are the ones you feed"; P.S. those who find it "overpriced" should descend to the dockside level where "the real value is."

Fin & Claw *Austrian/Seafood*   ▽ 20 | 15 | 18 | $41

Lighthouse Point | 2476 N. Federal Hwy. (Copans Rd.) | 954-782-1060
"Fresh local seafood" prepared with an Austrian flair is the unique draw at this "longtime favorite" in Lighthouse Point; the "warm" owners, Willie and Donna Schlager, make folks feel at home in the simple but "pleasant" storefront setting.

☑ Five Guys *Burgers*   20 | 10 | 16 | $13

Ft. Lauderdale | Harbor Shops | 1818 Cordova Rd. (N. Ocean Blvd.) | 954-358-5862
Margate | 7268 W. Atlantic Blvd. (Rock Island Rd.) | 954-975-4818
Tamarac | Midway Plaza | 5701 N. University Dr. (NW 57th St.) | 954-580-0378
www.fiveguys.com
See review in Miami/Dade County Directory.

Floridian, The ☽ *Diner*   18 | 12 | 17 | $20

Ft. Lauderdale | 1410 E. Las Olas Blvd. (SE 15th Ave.) | 954-463-4041
Whether it's "the crack of dawn or after a night out", this "worthy legend" on Las Olas Boulevard "pushes out prodigious quantities" of "hearty diner" eats on the cheap 24/7; the digs are "seedy yet strangely homey", the "waitresses are right out of central casting" and it's always packed with "colorful" patrons, so "go with the Flo'" and watch the show; P.S. bring cash or American Express.

NEW Fritz & Franz Bierhaus *German*   17 | 19 | 19 | $27

Ft. Lauderdale | 2861 E. Commercial Blvd. (Bayview Dr.) | 954-530-6147 | www.bierhaus.cc
See review in Miami/Dade County Directory.

Fulvio's 1900 *Italian*   22 | 20 | 22 | $50

Hollywood | 1900 Harrison St. (19th Ave.) | 954-927-1900 | www.fulvios1900.com
There's "a long history of quality" at this "upscale" Downtown Hollywood "classic" known for its unvarying commitment to "authentic homemade" Italian cuisine and "wonderful" service; diners diverge on cost ("good value" vs. "overpriced"), but wine enthusiasts are jazzed about the "extensive" vino list, of which about 25 labels can be sampled by the glass thanks to an enomatic dispenser behind the bar.

Galanga *Japanese/Thai*   23 | 21 | 22 | $40

Wilton Manors | 2389 Wilton Dr. (NE 9th Ave.) | 954-202-0000 | www.galangarestaurant.com
A local "straight-gay alliance" unites to sing the praises of the "contemporary" Thai-Japanese dishes with "fusion flair" at this "trendy" Wilton Manors Asian that also boasts an "excellent" sushi bar

suited to purists; it may be "pricey" but everything's "served with style by a seasoned and good-looking" crew, plus there's a garden patio for those who just want to "drink and mingle."

NEW GG's Waterfront Bar & Grill *Seafood* ▽ 20 | 20 | 22 | $38

Hollywood | 606 N. Ocean Dr. (Hollywood Blvd.) | 954-929-7030
Patrons soak up "memorable sunsets" at this Hollywood seafooder in the refurbished Giorgio's Grill space, with a new 50-seat outdoor lounge plus alfresco tables along 80 ft. of dock, both offering "fantastic" Intracoastal views; new owners, who offer sunset specials that are "tasty" and "plentiful", have dropped the Mediterranean motif in favor of dark wood, ivory hues and black-and-white photos of local scenes.

Gianni's *Italian* 24 | 17 | 23 | $38

Pompano Beach | 1601 E. Atlantic Blvd. (NE 16th Ave.) | 954-942-1733 | www.giannisofpompano.com
Aromas of 'the stinking rose' greet "garlic lovers" from out "in the parking lot" of this "Brooklyn Italian" old-timer in Pompano Beach whose "big portions" are "priced right"; a "pleasant" staff navigates the "cramped and noisy" environs with aplomb, which is good because it's "always packed: off season, during the week, you name it" (consequently, "reservations are a must").

Giovanni's *Italian/Peruvian* - | - | - | M

Pembroke Pines | Pines Professional Campus | 17864 NW Second St. (Pines Blvd.) | 954-441-3474 | www.giovannicafe.com
Pembroke Pine locals praise this "reliable" Italian-Peruvian spot hidden in a medical complex for its "filling" fare at relatively gentle prices; despite some outré design choices (giant gold angels and glittery faux-bronze accents) folks find the atmosphere "inviting" on account of the "great" staff.

Gold Coast Grill *American* 21 | 20 | 21 | $35

Coral Springs | The Walk at University | 2752 N. University Dr. (bet. NW 25th Ct. & 28th St.) | 954-255-3474 | www.goldcoastseafoodgrill.com
The kitchen's "grilling acumen" is apparent in the "crowd-pleasing" preparations of "fresh" fish and steak at this American strip-mall spot in Coral Springs; neighborhood denizens call it an "enjoyable" time thanks to a "warm and knowledgeable" staff and a fun bar.

Grand Lux Cafe *Eclectic* 19 | 20 | 20 | $31

Sunrise | Colonnade Outlets | 1780 Sawgrass Mills Circle (Sunrise Blvd.) | 954-838-9711 | www.grandluxcafe.com
See review in Miami/Dade County Directory.

Grateful Palate ⊠ *Eclectic* 24 | 21 | 22 | $52

Ft. Lauderdale | 817 SE 17th St. (Miami Rd.) | 954-467-1998 | www.thegratefulpalate.net
Long known as a caterer to the "yacht crowd", this provisioner has moved in a new direction – creating a sophisticated fine-dining des-

FOOD | DECOR | SERVICE | COST

tination in their Ft. Lauderdale storefront (the catering facility has moved to another location); the Eclectic menu is a "delightful change from the usual fare" and a sommelier is on hand to help navigate the "wonderful" wine list, making "cost the only possible complaint."

☑ Greek Islands Taverna *Greek*   25 | 15 | 21 | $37

Ft. Lauderdale | 3300 N. Ocean Blvd. (Oakland Park Blvd.) | 954-565-5505 | www.greekislandstaverna.com

"*Opa!*" exclaim fans of this "crowded", "convivial" Greek in Ft. Lauderdale offering "authentic" Hellenic fare, including "insanely good" lamb chops, at "unusually affordable prices"; "decor is not part of the deal" and there's no reserving, but "don't be discouraged" by "lines out the door" (or "down the street") because the operation "moves like clockwork" – which also means that service, though "courteous", can feel "rushed."

Grille 66 *Seafood/Steak*   24 | 24 | 24 | $66

Ft. Lauderdale | Hyatt Regency Pier 66 | 2301 SE 17th St. (23rd Ave.) | 954-728-3500 | www.grille66andbar.com

"Everything is right" at this "quality" surf 'n' turfer in Ft. Lauderdale's Hyatt Pier 66 complex – from the "professional" staffers to the "stylish" space and 800-bottle wine list; the "beautiful setting", with views of the Intracoastal and marina, makes the expense "worth it", and harbor rats suggest "wandering among the million-dollar yachts" "before or after dinner" to complete the experience.

Havana's Cuban Cuisine *Cuban*   - | - | - | I

Cooper City | Timberlake Plaza | 8600 Griffin Rd. (S. Pine Island Rd.) | 954-530-1400 | www.havanasrestaurants.com

Cooper City citizens are still discovering this "pleasantly surprising" yearling serving up "inexpensive Cuban favorites" (and a few Mexican and Argentinean dishes) in an "unassuming" strip-mall location; the simple "modern" decor may be extra appealing "if the standard Little Havana cramped restaurant bothers you"; P.S. a Sunrise branch is planned for fall 2011.

Helen Huang's
Mandarin House *Chinese/Vegetarian*   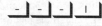 - | - | - | I

Hollywood | 2031 Hollywood Blvd. (Dixie Hwy.) | 954-923-1688 | www.helensmandarinhouse.com

"All of your Chinese favorites are here and then some" at this affordable, veggie-friendly "old faithful" in Hollywood; it's "open on most holidays", the staff is "friendly" and Helen herself "usually comes around to say hello", so even though the decor won't win any awards, the "constant flow of people" "says it all."

Hi-Life Café Ⓜ *American*   25 | 18 | 24 | $47

Ft. Lauderdale | Plaza 3000 | 3000 N. Federal Hwy. (bet. E. Oakland Park Blvd. & NE 26th St.) | 954-563-1395 | www.hilifecafe.com

Former *Top Chef* contender Carlos Fernandez "should have won" say fans of the chef's "inventive" Southern-accented American "comfort food" that keeps this "small" Ft. Lauderdale "gem" hopping;

high tabs are made additionally worthwhile by the "charming" space and a "caring" staff that makes patrons feel as if they "are 'coming home' to dinner."

Hollywood Prime 🏠 M *Steak* | 24 | 24 | 24 | $76 |

Hollywood | Westin Diplomat Resort | 3555 S. Ocean Dr. (E. Hallandale Beach Blvd.) | 954-602-6000 | www.hollywoodprime.com

"Expertly prepared steaks" and sides, "beautiful" traditional steakhouse decor and "impeccable" service all add up to an "excellent" experience at this beef palace in Hollywood's Westin Diplomat; patrons also value that it's "quiet" enough to actually hold a "conversation" but even then, it's still "way too expensive" for some.

Z Houston's *American* | 23 | 21 | 22 | $39 |

Pompano Beach | 2821 E. Atlantic Blvd. (NE 28th Ave.) | 954-783-9499 | www.hillstone.com

See review in Miami/Dade County Directory.

H2O *Italian/Mediterranean* | 18 | 20 | 16 | $37 |

Ft. Lauderdale | 101 S. Ft. Lauderdale Beach Blvd. (Cortez St.) | 954-414-1024 | www.h2ocafe.net

This casual all-day cafe's "superb location" on Ft. Lauderdale's "strip" accounts for the "lovely" ocean and beach views and steady "stream of amazing people and vehicles" to ogle from the spacious front patio; it's sometimes "touristy", but the midpriced Italian-Med offerings are "decent" enough to make it a locals' stop too.

Ichiban *Japanese* | 19 | 17 | 19 | $32 |

Davie | Shoppes of Arrowhead | 2411 S. University Dr. (Nova Dr.) | 954-370-0767 | www.ichibanatdavie.com

"High-quality" sushi and other "solid" Japanese offerings are gently priced at this "authentic" kitchen in an unassuming Davie strip mall; true Japanophiles opt for the traditional tatami seating area, which is also fun for kids (there's even a separate children's menu).

Ilios *Mediterranean/Spanish* | - | - | - | E |

Ft. Lauderdale | Hilton Ft. Lauderdale Beach Resort | 505 N. Ft. Lauderdale Beach Blvd., 6th fl. (bet. Las Olas & Sunrise Blvds.) | 954-414-2630 | www.hilton.com

You'd never know it, but an "edgy, club-type" restaurant and lounge is perched on the sixth floor of the "upscale" Hilton on Ft. Lauderdale Beach serving a "limited" menu of Med-Spanish tapas and pricier large plates; patrons who seek it out have their pick of an "intimate" dining room, sleek bar area or an open-air deck "overlooking the pool and ocean."

Z Il Mercato Café & Wine Shop M *Eclectic* | 26 | 16 | 25 | $36 |

Hallandale | 1454 E. Hallandale Beach Blvd. (NE 14th Ave.) | 954-457-3700 | www.ilmercatocafe.com

"What a wonderful find" say fans of this "quiet" "little neighborhood" bistro "hidden" next to a "Publix" in Hallandale; it's run by

FOOD | DECOR | SERVICE | COST

a "hardworking husband-and-wife team" – "she's in back" "lovingly" preparing the Eclectic choices that seem to "please every taste", "he's out front" greeting diners and making "wine suggestions" – and you can dine here without losing "your retirement fund" (they're all about "fair prices").

⚡ Il Mulino *Italian*
22 | 17 | 21 | $40

Ft. Lauderdale | 1800 E. Sunrise Blvd. (N. Federal Hwy.) | 954-524-1800 | www.ilmulinofl.com

Reasons why this Ft. Lauderdale Italian "standby" is "always packed to the gills": "outstanding garlic rolls" and "big portions" of "rich" red-sauce dishes at prices that "won't wound your wallet" served in a "cozy, unpretentious atmosphere"; patrons may have to "hunt for a parking space", but a "quick", "efficient" staff and proximity to Gateway Cinema picks up the slack, making it an "easy bite before or after a movie."

Il Toscano *Italian*
20 | 21 | 20 | $37

Weston | Waterway Shoppes | 2282 Weston Rd. (Royal Palm Blvd.) | 954-385-5883 | www.iltoscanoweston.net

"Consistent" "quality" is the hallmark of the Tuscan cuisine at this moderately priced Weston ristorante at the Waterway Shoppes; it can get "noisy" at times inside the more formal dining room, so those in the know head to the quieter outdoor patio with a lakeside view.

India House *Indian*
21 | 12 | 17 | $27

Plantation | Quality Inn | 1711 N. University Dr. (Sunrise Blvd.) | 954-565-5701 | www.indiahouserestaurant.com

For an "authentic" subcontinental dining experience in Plantation, head to the lobby of the Quality Inn (no, really) for the real deal in terms of cuisine ("they're not afraid to use heat" in the dishes), "Indian TV" at the bar, heck, even "Indian newspapers"; the lunch buffet is especially popular given the extensive choices and bargain prices ($8.95 weekdays, $10.95 weekends).

Indian Chillies *Chinese/Indian*
- | - | - | I

Pembroke Pines | 2092 N. University Dr. (bet. Sheridan & Taft Sts.) | 954-392-0999 | www.indianchillies.com

This tiny Pembroke Pines storefront specializes in chaat (Indian street fare) and Hakka (an Indo-Chinese fusion cuisine), but also serves more traditional staples; there may not be much in the way of decor, but the novel fare and the call of the $7.99 weekday lunch buffet is impossible to ignore.

Ireland's 🅱🅼 *Seafood/Steak*
∇ 26 | 23 | 26 | $62

Weston | Hyatt Regency Bonaventure Conference Center & Spa | 250 Racquet Club Rd. (bet. E. Mall & W. Mall Rds.) | 954-349-5656 | www.bonaventure.hyatt.com

"Weston's best-kept secret" is this upscale surf 'n' turfer in the Hyatt Regency Bonaventure say "repeat guests" who appreciate that the "amazing" staff "remembers" them and what they like to order; the "fabulous" steaks are "not cheap" but they're "worth it."

	FOOD	DECOR	SERVICE	COST

J. Alexander's *American* | 20 | 20 | 21 | $35 |

Ft. Lauderdale | 2415 N. Federal Hwy. (26th St.) | 954-563-9077
Plantation | 8550 W. Broward Blvd. (S. Pine Island Rd.) | 954-916-8837
www.jalexanders.com
See review in Palm Beach Directory.

Jasmine Thai *Thai* | 22 | 14 | 18 | $28 |

Margate | Cocogate Plaza | 5103 Coconut Creek Pkwy. (State Rd. 7) |
954-979-5530 | www.jasminethai-sushi.com
This Margate strip-maller is many locals' "go-to" spot for solid,
"well-priced" Thai food and sushi, especially during lunch when the
specials (entree, rice and spring roll) don't break $10; although the
restaurant "has not kept up appearances over the years", "warm"
service makes most feel welcome.

**Jaxson's Ice Cream Parlor &
Country Store** *Ice Cream* | 21 | 19 | 19 | $18 |

Dania Beach | 128 S. Federal Hwy. (Stirling Rd.) | Dania | 954-923-4445 |
www.jaxsonsicecream.com
"Kids" (and "secretly" adults) "love going" to this "old-time ice-cream
parlor"/country store/roadside "attraction" in Dania Beach to furi-
ously lick "phenomenal", "frighteningly huge" scoops before meltage
occurs; there's also a menu of red-blooded "American goodness" (hot
dogs, etc.), but the "long lines" form for the cold comfort fare and to
ogle the "treasure trove of memorabilia" festooning the walls.

JB's on the Beach *Seafood/Steak* | 18 | 20 | 19 | $37 |

Deerfield Beach | 300 N. Ocean Blvd. (E. Hillsboro Blvd.) | 954-571-5220 |
www.jbsonthebeach.com
You "can't beat the Atlantic Ocean for a front yard" say supporters
of this "fun" and "friendly" Deerfield Beach spot hard by the pier
that's "almost touching the sand"; the midpriced seafood and meat
offerings are merely "solid" but improve noticeably when paired
with "delicious tropical drinks", "boisterous" live music at night and
those "fabulous" views.

J. Mark's *American* | 19 | 18 | 20 | $34 |

Ft. Lauderdale | Sunrise Square Plaza | 1245 N. Federal Hwy.
(NE 13th St.) | 954-390-0770
Pompano Beach | 1490 NE 23rd St. (N. Federal Hwy.) | 954-782-7000
www.jmarksrestaurant.com
These convivial Pompano Beach–Ft. Lauderdale "meeting places"
are based on a "simple" conceit: provide a "diverse menu" of "well-
prepared" American standards at "moderate prices" in an "informal" setting, and the "crowds" will come; both locations have "attentive" crews and live music on weekend nights, while Ft. Lauderale
has a larger "gay" scene and a more "spacious" patio.

Z Johnny V *Floribbean* | 24 | 19 | 21 | $57 |

Ft. Lauderdale | 625 E. Las Olas Blvd. (Federal Hwy.) | 954-761-7920 |
www.johnnyvlasolas.com
"Exciting" Floribbean cuisine from "one of South Florida's most
imaginative" chef-owners, Johnny Vincencz, is incentive enough

for the "young and wealthy" to throng this "cool contemporary bistro" in the middle of Ft. Lauderdale's "Shoppers' Row" (aka Las Olas); "knowledgeable wine stewards" help parse the 700-label list, while outdoor tables provide "first-class people-watching" opportunities.

Kelly's Landing *New England/Seafood* | 21 | 13 | 21 | $28 |

Ft. Lauderdale | 1305 SE 17th St. (Cordova Rd.) | 954-760-7009 | www.kellyslandingseafood.com

"Displaced Bostonians" and other "homesick" members of the New England Diaspora are hooked on this "casual, no-frills" Ft. Lauderdale seafood shack, which has been serving classics like fried haddock, boiled lobster and clam chowder at "decent prices" since 1987; during baseball season Red Sox Nation is in full force, but even "Yankees fans" admit it's "good."

Kiko *Japanese/Thai*   ▽ | 26 | 26 | 25 | $35 |

Plantation | Fountains Shoppes of Distinction | 801 S. University Dr. (SW 78th Ave.) | 954-473-0077 | www.kikorestaurant.com

Plantation denizens are so delighted by this "refined" Japanese-Thai spot that they claim it's not just a "great neighborhood" place, it's a "destination restaurant"; "super-fresh" fish from the sleek sushi bar is the primary draw, though the cooked dishes are also "fabulous" – add in gentle prices and a full sake bar and it may be worth a trip to West Broward.

Kingshead Pub, Restaurant &   ▽ | 21 | 15 | 19 | $22 |
British Market ◑ *Pub Food*

Sunrise | 2692 N. University Dr. (NW 26th St.) | 954-572-5933 | www.kingsheadpubsunrise.com

British expats and Anglophiles say there's a "surprisingly good kitchen" turning out all the proper stuff (e.g. "great fish 'n' chips") at this Tudor-style pub in Sunrise; a wide range of ales, stouts, ciders and lager complements footie (and American football) on the telly; P.S. its adjacent market sells take-home dishes and imported goods.

Ƶ Kitchenetta Trattoria | 27 | 18 | 22 | $41 |
Tipica Italiana Ⓜ *Italian*

Ft. Lauderdale | 2850 N. Federal Hwy. (bet. E. Oakland Park Blvd. & NE 26th St.) | 954-567-3333 | www.kitchenetta.com

"Monster portions" of "delicious" housemade Italian fare – including wood-fired brick-oven flatbreads that are "meals in themselves" – garner "raves" (and an improved Food score) for this reasonably priced Ft. Lauderdale trattoria/enoteca; a "friendly" staff and open kitchen add to its "casual" appeal, but the "concrete" "industrial"-style space can be "deafening" on "busy nights", so conversationalists often "opt for an outdoor table."

Kuluck *Persian* | - | - | - | M |

Tamarac | Midway Plaza | 5879 N. University Dr. (Commercial Blvd.) | 954-720-6980 | www.kuluck.com

Persian restaurants are few and far between in SoFla, so those with a taste for "authentic" Iranian fare head to this midpriced Tamarac outpost for "decent" dishes at "reasonable" prices; nightclubby decor, an outdoor hookah lounge and exotic belly dancing on the weekends help "distance" it from its "strip-mall surroundings"

La Barraca Ⓜ *Spanish*   20 | 17 | 18 | $39

Hollywood | 115 S. 20th Ave. (Hollywood Blvd.) | 954-925-0050 | www.labarracatapas.com

For fans, there's a "richness of flavor and culture" in the "authentic" tapas, paella and sangria and "fun" flamenco shows (Thursdays–Saturdays) at this rustic, "festive" Hollywood Iberian; however, a few foes find fault with the same things, calling the food "bland" and the dancing "kitschy" – either way, the prices are decent.

ⓩ La Brochette Bistro Ⓜ *Mediterranean*   28 | 19 | 26 | $54

Cooper City | Embassy Lakes Plaza | 2635 N. Hiatus Rd. (Sheridan St.) | 954-435-9090 | www.labrochettebistro.com

"Who would expect to find" Broward County's top spot for Food and Service "tucked away" in a Cooper City strip mall "a couple doors down from Winn-Dixie"? ask fans who marvel at the "gastronomical delights" on chef-owner Aboud Kobaitri's moderately expensive, seafood-focused Med menu; the "intimate" "European" environs are conducive to "romantic" meals, and diners are "well cared for" by the "sweet, old-fashioned" staffers; P.S. it plans to add a wine bar.

La Creperie Ⓜ *French*   ▽ 24 | 19 | 22 | $33

Lauderhill | Sun Village Plaza | 4589 N. University Dr. (NW 44th St.) | 954-741-9035 | www.lacreperieinternational.com

The "charming couple" that runs this "quaint", "cozy" bistro in Lauderhill "never rushes" patrons and yet can be "quick" if needed; they're no slouches in the food *département* either, what with the "excellent" Franco fare highlighted by a "long list of crêpes" and capped with what some empirically claim is "the best Napoleon in the world."

🆕 La Dolce Vita *Italian*   - | - | - | M

Ft. Lauderdale | 3331 NE 33rd St. (bet. E. Oakland Park & N. Ocean Blvds.) | 954-565-5707 | www.ladolcevitaflorida.com

Ah, it's a sweet life indeed at this midpriced Ft. Lauderdale Italian that recently premiered in digs decorated with stills from the famed Fellini film; homemade pasta is the scene-stealer, but starters, some entrees and intriguing desserts each play strong supporting roles and are complemented by a wine list that, like the owners, is all Italian.

ⓩ LaSpada's Original Hoagies *Deli/Sandwiches*   25 | 8 | 22 | $12

🆕 **Ft. Lauderdale** | 1495 SE 17th St. (Cordova Rd.) | 954-522-3483
Lauderdale-by-the-Sea | 4346 Seagrape Dr. (Commercial Blvd.) | 954-776-7893
Coral Springs | 7893 W. Sample Rd. (bet. Riverside & Woodside Drs.) | 954-345-8833
Davie | Shoppes of Arrowhead | 2645 S. University Dr. (Nova Dr.) | 954-476-1099
www.laspadashoagies.com

Broward's No. 1 Bang for the Buck is this no-frills chain slapping together "quality" cold cuts for the "best hoagies around" (they should be "bronzed"); there's "always a line" but you'll be "entertained" almost "Benihana"-style by the "experienced" counter folks' "rapid"-fire "comedy" show (the "meat goes flying between the slicer and sandwich-maker" etc.); P.S. there's also an outpost in Boca Raton.

Las Vegas *Cuban*   21 | 14 | 20 | $23

Ft. Lauderdale | 2807 E. Oakland Park Blvd. (Bayview Dr.) | 954-564-1370

Hollywood | 1212 N. State Rd. 7 (bet. Arthur & Garfield Sts.) | 954-961-1001

Pembroke Pines | Westfork Plaza | 15941 Pines Blvd. (136th Ave.) | 954-443-7440

Pembroke Pines | 9905 Pines Blvd. (101st Ave.) | 954-431-6883

Plantation | 7015 W. Broward Blvd. (NW 70th Ave.) | 954-584-4400

"Sizable", "value-priced" portions of "homestyle" Cuban eats make fans wonder how this South Florida chainlet "makes any money"; the "family-owned" operations, headed by Antonio Vilariño, are also "friendly", making them "reliable" places to take the "kids."

Latitudes *Floribbean*   18 | 22 | 18 | $38

Hollywood | Hollywood Beach Marriott | 2501 N. Ocean Dr. (Carolina St.) | 954-924-2202 | www.latitudesonthebeach.com

Seemingly inches from the sand is this "relaxing" midpriced Floribbean bistro "hidden" in the Hollywood Beach Marriott; the menu is "satisfying" if "basic" and the service is "spotty", but folks "love the atmosphere" because you can see the "ocean" and "beachgoers in their bikinis" from both the retro old Florida dining room and terrace.

La Veranda *Italian*   24 | 21 | 24 | $39

Pompano Beach | 2121 E. Atlantic Blvd. (N. Federal Hwy.) | 954-943-7390

For over three decades this "consistent" Pompano Beacher has been faithfully dishing up "abundant" portions of "delicious" "old-fashioned" Italian cuisine at moderate prices; its "romantic" courtyard looks "right out of Tuscany" while the "warm and friendly" staff add to the feel that "mama is in the kitchen."

Le Bistro Ⓜ *French*   22 | 18 | 21 | $44

Lighthouse Point | Main Street Plaza | 4626 N. Federal Hwy. (bet. NE 44th & 48th Sts.) | 954-946-9240 | www.lebistrorestaurant.com

Francophiles call this "intimate" nook "nestled in a nondescript strip mall" in Lighthouse Point a "real find" on account of its "high"-priced but "honest" French fare prepared "with care and love" by the chef-owner, Andy Trousdale; his wife and co-owner, Elin, sets a "welcoming" tone, and a "well-rounded" wine list rounds out the perks; P.S. cooking classes are also offered.

❷ Lemongrass Asian Bistro *Asian*   22 | 18 | 20 | $34

Ft. Lauderdale | 3811 N. Federal Hwy. (bet. 38th & 39th Sts.) | 954-564-4422 | www.lemongrassasianbistro.com

See review in Palm Beach Directory.

	FOOD	DECOR	SERVICE	COST

Le Tub ● *Burgers* `21` `15` `11` `$23`

Hollywood | 1100 N. Ocean Dr. (N. Ocean Blvd.) | 954-921-9425 | www.theletub.com

In a "crummy old" former "gas station" in Hollywood festooned with "driftwood", "old tubs and toilets" you'll find what some (e.g. Oprah) say are "the best burgers ever": "artery-clogging beasts" worth ditching your "diet" for; a bit of advice: "have patience" ("throw back a few brews" and soak up the Intracoastal view) because these "bad boys take time to cook", and expect occasionally "rude service"; P.S. "they finally accept credit cards!"

Lime Fresh Mexican `19` `14` `17` `$16`
Grill *Californian/Mexican*

Coconut Creek | Promenade at Coconut Creek | 4425 Lyons Rd. (Wiles Rd.) | 954-586-2999
Pembroke Pines | The Shops at Pembroke Gardens | 601 SW 145th Terr. (Pines Blvd.) | 954-436-4700
www.limefreshmexicangrill.com
See review in Miami/Dade County Directory.

Little Havana *Cuban* `22` `16` `19` `$29`

Deerfield Beach | 721 S. Federal Hwy. (SE 7th Ct.) | 954-427-6000 | www.littlehavanarestaurant.com
See review in Miami/Dade County Directory.

Lola's Ⓜ *American* `24` `20` `23` `$47`

Hollywood | 2032 Harrison St. (bet. S. Dixie Hwy. & 20th Ave.) | 954-927-9851 | www.lolasonharrison.com

Chef-owner (and "really cool guy") Michael Wagner gets "creative" with everything from "great burgers to fine dinners" at his New American "gem" located in Downtown Hollywood; the professional staff sets a "relaxed" tone in the "modern" space, which is enhanced by an "extensive" beer list, "reasonably priced" wines and "amazing" cocktails; P.S. it now has gluten-free, vegetarian and vegan offerings.

Lucille's American Café *American* `22` `17` `22` `$21`

Weston | 2250 Weston Rd. (Commerce Pkwy.) | 954-384-9007 | www.lucillescafe.com

You'll "need a nap" or a good long "walk" after chowing down on the American "home-cooking" classics at this "family-oriented", "retro" diner in Weston; the "friendly" waiters leave mini muffins with the mini bills, leaving fans wishing for just one thing: "too bad they don't serve breakfast."

Madras Café *Indian* `22` `10` `16` `$27`

Pompano Beach | Palm Plaza | 1434 S. Powerline Rd. (W. McNab Rd.) | 954-977-5434 | www.madrascafe.net

"Try everything" advise admirers of the "flavorful" fare at this "authentic" subcontinental in Pompano Beach where "'spicy' is really spicy"; its "bare" strip-mall digs and "slow" service is a turnoff for some, though thrifty types can't stay away from the "reasonably priced" lunch buffet.

	FOOD	DECOR	SERVICE	COST

Maguires Hill 16 *Pub Food*
▽ 16 | 18 | 19 | $23

Ft. Lauderdale | 535 N. Andrews Ave. (NE 6th St.) | 954-764-4453 |
www.maguireshill16.com

It's St. Paddy's Day all year long at this "real Irish pub" in Ft. Lauderdale
with a cozy, dark-wood interior, known for its "reasonably good"
Irish grub, Guinness on tap and occasional live Irish music; so "have
a pint, throw some darts, suck up the vibe" and don't forget to check
out the new outdoor patio.

Ƶ Mai-Kai *Chinese*
16 | 25 | 20 | $49

Ft. Lauderdale | 3599 N. Federal Hwy. (NE 37th St.) | 954-563-3272 |
www.maikai.com

"Tiki fans" can take a trip back to the 1950s when their "grandparents
made believe they were in the South Pacific" at this "kitschy"
"Polynesian theme park" "landmark" in Ft. Lauderdale; the "expensive" Chinese eats are mostly "forgettable" but no matter – it's all
about watching the "fun" floor show.

Mama Mia Restaurant ● *Italian*
20 | 15 | 18 | $31

Hollywood | 1818 Young Circle (Harrison St.) | 954-923-0555 |
www.miagrill.com

"Big portions" of "homestyle" Italian standards are "enough for the
next meal too", making this "quality" "red-sauce joint" on Hollywood's
Young Circle a "great value for the money"; tougher customers cite
a "lack of decor" and "inconsistent" service although they admit the
food, if not "overly imaginative, is utterly reliable."

Mario's Catalina *Cuban/Spanish*
- | - | - | M

Ft. Lauderdale | 1611 N. Federal Hwy. (NE 16th Ct.) | 954-563-4141 |
www.catalinarestaurant.net

Patrons may feel like they're dining in an art gallery with all the oil
paintings displayed at this Ft. Lauderdale spot serving "high-end",
yet moderately priced, Cuban-Spanish dishes; the "quintessential
host", chef-owner Mario Flores, greets regulars and newcomers like
old friends, while white tablecloths, soft lighting and gilt mirrors
provide old-world charm with a little romance tossed in.

Mario The Baker *Italian/Pizza*
20 | 11 | 18 | $20

🆕 **Weston** | 1691 Bonaventure Blvd. (bet. Creek Ford Dr. &
Royal Palm Blvd.) | 954-384-8505 |
www.mariothebakerpizza.com

Sunrise | 2220 N. University Dr. (bet. Sunrise Blvd. & Sunset Strip) |
954-742-3333 | www.mariothebakerofsunrisefl.com

See review in Miami/Dade County Directory.

Ƶ🆕 Market 17 *American/Eclectic*
26 | 25 | 25 | $58

Ft. Lauderdale | 1850 SE 17th St. (Eisenhower Blvd.) | 954-835-5507 |
www.market17.net

"Innovative" New American–Eclectic fare made with a "deft"
touch and "farm-fresh" ingredients is earning kudos for this sophisticated "new kid on the block" in Ft. Lauderdale; "superlative" service, "elegant" environs and a "wonderful wine and cocktail list" also
help justify the "expensive" tabs; P.S. a small private room hosts

"memorable" "dining-in-the-dark" tasting meals "packed with sensory", if not visual, "delights."

Marumi Sushi ● *Japanese*   - | - | - | M

Plantation | 8271 W. Sunrise Blvd. (bet. N. Pine Island Rd. & University Dr.) | 954-318-4455

"Life is good" declare raw-fish devotees who have wandered into this tiny storefront sleeper in Plantation and discovered its "extremely authentic Japanese cuisine" at cut-rate prices; it's open late (till 1:30 AM), so there's no rush: just "sit at the [sushi] bar, talk to the chefs" and sample something from its "fantastic selection" of sake.

Mason Jar *American*   - | - | - | M

Hollywood | 2980 N. Federal Hwy. (bet. E. Oakland Park Blvd. & NE 26th St.) | 954-568-4100 | www.themasonjarcafe.com

The "chicken pot pie is just like mom used to make" gush fans of this small Ft. Lauderdale spot specializing in "homestyle" American comfort food; all in all, it's a "charming" experience, from the beverages served in cute mason jars to the "good values."

Mazza Mediterranean   - | - | - | M
Cuisine *Greek/Lebanese*

Pembroke Pines | 15749 Pines Blvd. (bet. NE 155th Ave. & Westfork Plaza Way) | 954-436-9997 | www.mazzarestaurant.net

Little known but well loved, this simple Greek-Lebanese effort in Pembroke Pines has a "never-go-wrong" menu on which "everything is awesome"; "good values" abound, the staff is "friendly" and belly dancing on the weekends is an added attraction.

NEW M Bar *Eclectic*   - | - | - | E

Ft. Lauderdale | 1301 E. Las Olas Blvd. (SE 13th Ave.) | 954-766-4946 | www.mbarlasolas.com

Manhattan's trendy Meatpacking District inspired the contemporary decor at this pricey Ft. Lauderdale tapas bar that recently debuted on Las Olas offering a long list of international, but not necessarily Spanish, small plates; craft beers, a DJ on weekends and a promising bar scene are among its other attractions.

Melting Pot *Fondue*   19 | 18 | 20 | $42

Ft. Lauderdale | 1135 N. Federal Hwy. (E. Sunrise Blvd.) | 954-568-1581

Coral Springs | 10374 W. Sample Rd. (bet. Coral Springs & NW 101st Ave.) | 954-755-6368

Cooper City | Countryside Shops | 5834 S. Flamingo Rd. (bet. Stirling Rd. & SW 55th St.) | 954-880-0808

www.meltingpot.com

See review in Miami/Dade County Directory.

NEW Michele's Dining   - | - | - | VE
Lounge ⊠ *Eclectic*

Ft. Lauderdale | 2761 E. Oakland Park Blvd. (Bayview Dr.) | 954-533-1919 | www.michelesdl.com

Most evenings live music fills the air, taking patrons "back to the '50s when supper clubs were all the rage" at this contemporary

	FOOD	DECOR	SERVICE	COST

Eclectic boîte newly arrived in a Ft. Lauderdale strip mall; an "attentive" staff patrols the classy dining room and lounge areas, featuring dark wood and gold accents; P.S. a late-night bar menu allows thrifty types to bypass high tabs.

Mickey Byrne's Irish Pub & Restaurant *Pub Food*

	-	-	-	I

Hollywood | 1921 Hollywood Blvd. (bet. N. 19th & 20th Aves.) | 954-921-2317 | www.mickeybyrnes.com

This "slightly Irish sports bar" named for a Tipperary hurling legend (an ancient Gaelic stick-and-ball game) is known for its "traditional" Irish comfort foods at affordable prices, pints of imported ales and cozy atmosphere, making it a prime Hollywood destination on St. Paddy's Day.

Moon Thai & Japanese *Japanese/Thai*

23	16	20	$24

Coral Springs | 9637 Westview Dr. (bet. N. University Dr. & NW 98th Ln.) | 954-752-4899
Weston | 2818 Weston Rd. (S. Commerce Pkwy.) | 954-384-7275
www.moonthai.com
See review in Miami/Dade County Directory.

Morton's The Steakhouse *Steak*

25	23	25	$70

Ft. Lauderdale | 500 E. Broward Blvd. (bet. SE 3rd Ave. & S. Federal Hwy.) | 954-467-9720 | www.mortons.com
See review in Miami/Dade County Directory.

Mustard Seed 🗷 *Eclectic*

25	15	22	$39

Plantation | 256 S. University Dr. (W. Broward Blvd.) | 954-533-9326 | www.mustardseedbistro.com

An "all-around enjoyable" time is in store at Tim and Lara Boyd's "little jewel" of a bistro in a Plantation strip center, turning out an "innovative" Eclectic menu; the "cute, shabby-chic" digs are "family-friendly" and so are the prices at breakfast and lunch (dinner's pricier).

My Big Fat Greek Restaurant *Greek*

20	15	19	$31

Dania Beach | 3445 Griffin Rd. (SW 34th Terr.) | Dania | 954-961-5030 | www.mbfgr.com

From the waiters' "wildly enthusiastic" Greek dancing to shouts of "*opa!*", live bouzouki music and belly dancers on the weekend, this waterfront Dania Beach venue "entertains while you eat"; besides the "real" saganaki flambé ("yes, it's actually set on fire tableside"), there are "no surprises" on the menu but it's a "lotta food for a little price."

Myung Ga Tofu & BBQ *Korean*

∇ 29	17	26	$25

Weston | Shoppes of Weston | 1944 Weston Rd. (N. Corporate Lakes Blvd.) | 954-349-7337

Those "in the know" always leave this Weston mall spot "stuffed" full of "excellent" Korean barbecue like "mouthwateringly good" ribs and the like; some want to keep the welcoming" atmosphere and "good values" to themselves, saying they're "glad not everyone knows how awesome it is."

FOOD | DECOR | SERVICE | COST

Noodles Panini *Italian* | 23 | 15 | 19 | $28

Ft. Lauderdale | 821 E. Las Olas Blvd. (bet. SE 8th & 9th Aves.) | 954-462-1514 | www.noodlespaninirestaurant.com

This "cute" "tiny venue with tiny tables" has an equally small menu, but it "knows what it's good at": Americanized Italian "staples" like panini, red-sauce pasta and "major meatballs"; it's a "popular" midday repast for lunching ladies who "sit outside" so they can "enjoy the passing Las Olas parade."

North Ocean Grill *Seafood/Steak* | - | - | - | M

Ft. Lauderdale | Pelican Beach Resort | 2000 N. Ocean Blvd. (NE 21st St.) | 954-568-9431 | www.pelicanbeach.com

Folks who "love watching the ocean and feeling the breeze" on the veranda of this surf 'n' turf spot in Ft. Lauderdale's Pelican Beach Resort feel like they could be in the West Indies; beyond the sunset, its child-friendliness (kids' menu, crayons, etc.) recommends it.

Oceans 234 *Seafood* | 19 | 21 | 17 | $42

Deerfield Beach | 234 N. Ocean Blvd. (NE 2nd St.) | 954-428-2539 | www.oceans234.com

"Lulled by sea breezes" and "gorgeous sunsets", patio perchers are willing to overlook sometimes "spotty" service and declare this "popular" Deerfield Beach spot a "wonderfully relaxing" respite; further pluses are "creative", "fresh" seafood preparations including sushi and "strong" drinks from the crackerjack bar – "young gals in bikinis" cavorting nearby with their hunky male counterparts "don't hurt the experience" either.

Old Florida Seafood House Ⓜ *Seafood* | 19 | 11 | 19 | $34

Wilton Manors | 1414 NE 26th St. (bet. N. Dixie Hwy. & 16th Ave.) | 954-566-1044 | www.oldflaseafood.com

"Just what it says it is", this "tried-and-true" "charmer" in Wilton Manors has been pumping out "traditional" seafood classics for over three decades; a well-seasoned staff that "knows the trade" takes good care of the "senior set" that swarms here for the "famous" early-bird specials, but some younger critics complain the "throwback" digs "need a face-lift."

Old Heidelberg ● *German* | 21 | 19 | 21 | $33

Ft. Lauderdale | 900 State Rd. 84 (SW 9th Ave.) | 954-463-6747 | www.oldheidelbergdeli.com

"Stick-to-your-ribs" Bavarian specialties like "*schweinhaxe*" (roast ham hock) offer a "nice change of pace" to seafood-weary Ft. Lauderdalians who dig the "oompah atmosphere" of this "old favorite"; "real German beer (sigh)", weekend music and "homemade sausage" and other victuals sold at the attached delicatessen are further pluses.

101 Ocean ● *American* | 21 | 21 | 19 | $42

Lauderdale-by-the-Sea | 101 E. Commercial Blvd. (El Mar Dr.) | 954-776-8101 | www.101oceanlbts.com

Beach bums flock to this "laid-back" "hangout" near Anglin's Fishing Pier in Lauderdale-by-the-Sea that's equal parts "open-air

| | FOOD | DECOR | SERVICE | COST |

and morning cocktails help make it "worth the price"; P.S. "book well in advance."

Piola ❂ *Pizza* | 22 | 17 | 19 | $26 |

Hallandale | 1703 E. Hallandale Beach Blvd. (Layne Blvd.) | 954-457-9394 | www.piola.it
See review in Miami/Dade County Directory.

Pizza Rustica ❂ *Pizza* | 19 | 10 | 15 | $15 |

Ft. Lauderdale | 3327 E. Oakland Park Blvd. (Ocean Blvd.) | 954-567-2992
Hollywood | 1928 Hollywood Blvd. (bet. S. 19th & 20th Aves.) | 954-923-3878
www.pizza-rustica.com
See review in Miami/Dade County Directory.

NEW Pl8 Kitchen *American/Eclectic* | - | - | - | M |

Ft. Lauderdale | 210 SW Second St. (bet. 2nd & 3rd Aves.) | 954-524-1818 | www.pl8kitchen.com
Himmarshee Bar & Grille's owner recently reimagined his Downtown Ft. Lauderdale mainstay, transforming its identity via a new name and new look and switching to a more casual Eclectic-American menu in a small-plates format, with dishes like mini bratwurst sliders and duck-fat-roasted potatoes; with the addition of communal and high-top tables, the feel is now less industrial and more comfy; P.S. tabs are midrange, but pl8s can add up if you're not careful.

Primavera *Italian* | 20 | 17 | 20 | $43 |

Oakland Park | Primavera Plaza | 830 E. Oakland Park Blvd. (NE 8th Terr.) | 954-564-6363 | www.primaveraflorida.com
"Long trusted" as a provider of "traditional" Northern Italian cuisine, this "understated" stalwart in an Oakland Park strip mall is a "restful" retreat with tasteful decor featuring wine racks and a coffered ceiling; chef-owner Giacomo Dresseno oversees a "welcoming" crew and prices his dishes "right" so that most "keep coming back."

Z Rainbow Palace *Chinese* | 26 | 24 | 26 | $58 |

Ft. Lauderdale | 2787 E. Oakland Park Blvd. (Bayview Dr.) | 954-565-5652 | www.rainbowpalace.com
Tuxedoed waiters who supply "superb" service set a "decidedly upscale" tone at this "gourmet" Chinese powerhouse in Ft. Lauderdale; the "amazing" meals and "lovely" "subdued" setting are "expensive" but "worth the extra money."

NEW Rare Las Olas *Steak* | ▽ 21 | 25 | 21 | $59 |

Ft. Lauderdale | 401 E. Las Olas Blvd. (Financial Plaza) | 954-527-3365 | www.centraarchy.com
Big and beefy describes the pricey menu at this see-and-be-seen steakhouse (a sibling of New York Prime in Boca) that recently set up shop on Ft. Lauderdale's posh Las Olas Boulevard, where locals say it was much "needed"; the "modern" interior is dramatic, with a black-and-white color palette, 10-ft. crystal chandelier, sweeping ceilings and an upstairs loft.

	FOOD	DECOR	SERVICE	COST

Ra Sushi *Japanese* — 19 | 21 | 18 | $34

Pembroke Pines | 201 SW 145th Terr. (142nd Ave.) | 954-342-5454 | www.rasushi.com

See review in Palm Beach Directory.

NEW Rocco's Tacos ● *Mexican* — 20 | 20 | 19 | $32

Ft. Lauderdale | 1313 E. Las Olas Blvd. (bet. SE 13th & 15th Aves.) | 954-524-9550 | www.roccostacos.com

See review in Palm Beach Directory.

Rock n Roll Ribs *BBQ* — ∇ 24 | 21 | 19 | $23

Coral Springs | 4651 State Rd. 7 (bet. Alexandra Blvd. & Wiles Rd.) | 954-345-7429 | www.rocknrollribs.org

If you like your barbecue with a side of heavy metal, stop by this Coral Springs spot co-owned by Nicko McBrain, drummer for the legendary band Iron Maiden; music fans can savor the "delicious" ribs while watching concert videos in a storefront setting decorated with guitars, a drum set and "terrific memorabilia"; P.S. takeout is suggested for those "overpowered" by the "loud" tunes.

Runyon's *Continental* — 22 | 19 | 22 | $52

Coral Springs | 9810 W. Sample Rd. (bet. Coral Hills Dr. & NW 99th Way) | 954-752-2333 | www.runyonsofcoralsprings.com

"Solid and steady" describes this "old-school" Continental holdover in Coral Springs whose beef is a "cut above your average steakhouse" and whose experienced staff "has been there for years"; all the "regulars" at the "busy" piano bar area up front are a clue that it's "much nicer" than the rear dining room, "which looks like an old basement"; high prices mean it's best for a "special occasion."

Rustic Inn Crabhouse *Seafood* — 22 | 14 | 19 | $38

Ft. Lauderdale | 4331 Anglers Ave. (bet. Griffin Rd. & SW 42nd St.) | 954-584-1637 | www.rusticinn.com

"Don't wear your Sunday best" – just "grab a bib and mallet and get crackin'" when you come to this circa-1955 "classic" seafooder situated on a "picturesque canal" near the airport; the "garlicky, oily crabs" are a "delicious" mess and a lot of "fun" to shell in the rustic environs amid the "noise and chaos", especially with a "bucket of ice-cold beer."

Ruth's Chris Steak House *Steak* — 25 | 23 | 24 | $65

Ft. Lauderdale | 2525 N. Federal Hwy. (bet. Oakland Park & Sunrise Blvds.) | 954-565-2338 | www.ruthschris.com

See review in Miami/Dade County Directory.

Z Sage French American Café *French* — 22 | 20 | 20 | $39

Ft. Lauderdale | Regions Shopping Plaza | 2378 N. Federal Hwy. (NE 21st St.) | 954-565-2299 | www.sagecafe.net

Z Sage Oyster Bar *French*

Hollywood | 2000 Harrison St. (20th Ave.) | 954-391-9466 | www.sageoysterbar.com

"C'est magnifique!" cry Francophiles sampling the "country cooking" (particularly the standout duck, crêpes and onion soup) offered for

	FOOD	DECOR	SERVICE	COST

"everyday prices" at these "classic"-looking bistros in Ft. Lauderdale and Hollywood; an "incredible" wine list and a "pleasant", "attentive" staff round out their strengths.

NEW Saia *SE Asian*

| | - | - | - | E |

Ft. Lauderdale | B Ocean Fort Lauderdale |
999 N. Ft. Lauderdale Beach Blvd. (bet. N. Ocean & Sunrise Blvds.) |
954-302-5252 | www.saiasushi.com

Tourists and locals breathe a saia relief at the vacation vibe suffusing this upscale oceanfront Southeast Asian–and-sushi spot inside the newly renovated B Ocean Hotel in Ft. Lauderdale; there are prime beach views from the contemporary Zen dining room, and how better to work off the decadent desserts than with an after-dinner stroll under the stars?

Saigon Cuisine *Vietnamese*

| | 24 | 16 | 18 | $25 |

Margate | 1394 N. State Rd. 7 (Coconut Creek Pkwy.) | 954-975-2426 |
www.saigoncuisineflorida.com

"All your favorites and then some" appear on the "big menu" that flits from banh mi to pho to regional Vietnamese specialties at this "excellent-value" eatery in Margate; "don't be put off by the decor", what little of it there is anyway, instead enjoy the fact that the "nice" owners personally "see to your satisfaction"; P.S. closed Thursdays.

Saint Tropez *French*

| | ▽ 22 | 21 | 22 | $39 |

Ft. Lauderdale | 1010 E. Las Olas Blvd. (SE 10th Terr.) | 954-767-1073 |
www.sainttropezbistro.com

The "owner, chef and waiters are actually French" and that goes a long way toward creating an "authentic" French bistro experience at this "chic-casual" nook on Las Olas; "generous portions" of "all the classics" can be had at modest prices, accompanied by a "great wine-by-the-glass list."

Saito's Japanese Steakhouse *Japanese/Steak*

| | 19 | 16 | 18 | $35 |

Coconut Creek | Promenade at Coconut Creek | 4443 Lyons Rd. (Wiles Rd.) | 954-582-9888 | www.saitosteakhouse.com
See review in Palm Beach Directory.

NEW Salsa Fiesta *Mexican*

| | - | - | - | I |

Pembroke Pines | Cobblestone Plaza | 14914 Pines Blvd. (I-75) |
954-432-0005 | www.salsafiestagrill.com
See review in Miami/Dade County Directory.

Saxsay *Peruvian*

| | - | - | - | I |

Sunrise | 9160 W. Commercial Blvd. (bet. 91st & 94th Aves.) |
954-746-5099

"Good" Peruvian food is "hard to find in Broward County", but seekers have found a gem in this pea-sized spot in Sunrise; it's fun to "watch" the "delicious" dishes being "prepared in the open kitchen", and even better scarfing them down and paying mere pennies for the pleasure.

FOOD | DECOR | SERVICE | COST

NEW Sea 🅱 Seafood | - | - | - | M

Lauderdale-by-the-Sea | 235 Commercial Blvd. (W. Tradewinds Ave.) | 954-533-2580 | www.searestaurant.com

Chef Anthony Sindaco (formerly at Sunfish Grill) is back on the restaurant scene after a three-year absence with this new sardine-sized seafooder in a Lauderdale-by-the-Sea storefront; à la carte is available, but most wallet-watchers are zeroing in on the modestly priced three-course prix fixe menu – either way, expect to find a few of the chef's classics like tuna Bolognese, black-and-white crème brûlée and bread pudding.

Z Seasons 52 American | 23 | 24 | 23 | $42

Ft. Lauderdale | Galleria Mall | 2428 E. Sunrise Blvd. (NE 24th Ave.) | 954-537-1052 | www.seasons52.com

"Guilt-free" food (all items are under 475 calories) that "actually tastes exciting" – like "out-of-this-world" flatbreads and "cute" desserts in shot glasses – is the "unique concept" behind this "health-oriented but not health-nutty" New American chain; "warm decor", "well-trained" servers, "interesting" wines and "active" bar scenes with nightly live piano further explain why it's so "popular."

Serafina Italian | 23 | 21 | 23 | $54

Ft. Lauderdale | 926 NE 20th Ave. (Sunrise Blvd.) | 954-463-2566 | www.serabythewater.com

Surveyors feel "transported" to "Sicily" by the "authentic" Southern Italian cooking at this tastefully rustic and romantic "hideaway" in Ft. Lauderdale; it's pricey, but the staff is "outstanding" and dining out on the "lovely" terrace overlooking the Middle River is a "real treat."

Z Sette Bello Italian | 26 | 21 | 25 | $52

Ft. Lauderdale | 6241 N. Federal Hwy. (NE 62nd St.) | 954-351-0505 | www.settebellofla.com

At this "authentic" "family-owned" Italian in Ft. Lauderdale, diners feel "welcomed" by a chef-owner who "oversees everything", both in the kitchen (preparing "tasty" pastas and other "reasonably priced" fare) and out ("appearing at tables" to "ask about the food"); the "attention to detail" extends to the "small" room's "pretty" decor and "nice" wine list, with "knowledgeable" staffers ready to "suggest good pairings."

Shorty's Bar-B-Q BBQ | 22 | 14 | 19 | $21

Deerfield Beach | 120 S. Powerline Rd. (W. Hillsboro Blvd.) | 954-596-2448

Davie | 5989 S. University Dr. (Stirling Rd.) | 954-680-9900 | www.shortys.com

See review in Miami/Dade County Directory.

Shuck N Dive Cajun/Creole | ∇ 19 | 16 | 21 | $25

Ft. Lauderdale | 650 N. Federal Hwy. (bet. NE 6th & 7th Sts.) | 954-462-0088

"Not exactly N'Awlins" but still one of the few local spots serving Cajun-Creole cuisine, this inexpensive "joint" in Ft. Lauderdale dishes up crawfish, gumbo and fried green tomatoes in a laid-back setting with an outdoor patio; it doubles as a "terrific sports bar" popular, of course, with fans of the LSU Tigers and New Orleans Saints.

Shula's on the Beach *Steak*
23 | 21 | 22 | $65

Ft. Lauderdale | Westin Beach Resort | 321 N. Ft. Lauderdale Beach Blvd. (N. Ocean Blvd.) | 954-355-4000 | www.donshula.com
See review in Miami/Dade County Directory.

Siam Cuisine *Thai*
∇ 19 | 15 | 19 | $33

Wilton Manors | 2010 Wilton Dr. (NE 20th St.) | 954-564-3411 | www.siamcuisinefl.com
This perennial Wilton Manors "favorite" remains a wallet-friendly answer to Thai and sushi cravings with its "consistent" "quality" fare; "friendly" service and tasteful wood paneling make it a tad more "inviting" than similar efforts, though takeout is a popular option.

☑ Silver Pond ◑ *Chinese*
25 | 10 | 16 | $30

Lauderdale Lakes | 4285 N. State Rd. 7 (NW 44th St.) | 954-486-8885
"Better than Chinatown in NY" say fans of the "authentic" Hong Kong–style eats at this Lauderdale Lakes strip-maller whose "delicious" "bargains" rise above "crazy waits" and service that can be "downright rude"; interior decorator types do best if they "don't look around", and the menu can be "hard to figure out" ("I could hardly recognize a single dish"), but Silver surfers advise "bring your sense of adventure" and "join the hordes"; P.S. closed July and August.

NEW Slow Food Truck *American*
- | - | - | I

Location varies; see website | Ft. Lauderdale | 954-234-2327 | www.slowfoodtruck.com
Follow the tweets to this Ft. Lauderdale–based wheeled wonder – which turns up everywhere from the Keys to West Palm Beach – to grab items like their popular short-rib sandwich as well as salads, burgers and other casual Americana made from local ingredients; P.S. on Monday nights, this slowpoke usually idles at the food-truck rally in Hollywood's ArtsPark.

SoLita Las Olas *Italian*
21 | 22 | 20 | $49

Ft. Lauderdale | 1032 E. Las Olas Blvd. (SE 11th Ave.) | 954-357-2616 | www.solitaitalian.com
Surveyors give "good" marks to the spendy Italian dishes at this resto-lounge on "busy Las Olas", but with "dramatic" details like "black wallpaper", "crystal fixtures" and a "beautiful bar" plus a crowd of "eye candy" that seems to get "younger as the night progresses", it's really all about the "nightlife"; the new branch in Delray Beach is already a similarly "happening" "hot spot."

Southport Raw Bar ◑ *Seafood*
20 | 12 | 20 | $23

Ft. Lauderdale | 1536 Cordova Rd. (bet. SE 15th & 16th Sts.) | 954-525-2526 | www.southportrawbar.com
For four decades, this "affordable" Ft. Lauderdale "dive" has been a "favorite" of "happy" folks who like nothing better than to "throw a

few back" while grazing a "delicious" raw bar; everything is "really fresh (including the servers)", and if you look beyond the "grim" interior there's a "great patio overlooking the Intracoastal."

NEW Star Bistro ⓩ *American/Mediterranean*   – – – E

Cooper City | 8616 Griffin Rd. (S. Pine Island Rd.) | 954-252-5545 | www.starbistrorestaurant.com

Easily missed in a Cooper City strip mall, this tiny family-run entry from a Serbian-born chef-owner serves pricey American dishes with Asian and Med influences; while the place is modestly decorated, it's bright and comfortable with huge booths lining the walls.

Station House *Seafood/Steak*   22 12 19 $47

Deerfield Beach | 1544 SE Third Ct. (15th Ave.) | 954-420-9314 | www.stationrestaurants.com

See review in Palm Beach Directory.

ⓩ Steak 954 *Steak*   24 26 23 $76

Ft. Lauderdale | W Ft. Lauderdale | 401 N. Ft. Lauderdale Beach Blvd. (Bayshore Dr.) | 954-414-8333 | www.steak954.com

"A hot spot even for a W Hotel", this "chic" chophouse from Stephen Starr (Buddakan in Philly and NYC, etc.) dazzles the eyes with its "fascinating" 15-ft. jellyfish tank and "gorgeous" beach and ocean views, helping it grab the top Decor rating in Broward; taste buds are also treated to some "inventive twists on traditional steakhouse standards" delivered by an "attentive" crew making it "worth every [one] of the many dollars."

Stir Crazy *Asian*   19 17 18 $25

Pembroke Pines | The Shops at Pembroke Gardens | 14571 SW Fifth St. (Pines Blvd.) | 954-919-4900 | www.stircrazy.com

Picky patrons "love" the "create-your-own-stir-fry" concept and enjoy "watching the chefs" cook it up at these Pan-Asian chain spots that are not only a "huge hit" with children, but also provide a "fun way to get them to eat their veggies"; casual digs and "inexpensive" tabs please all comers.

Sublime Ⓜ *Vegan/Vegetarian*   21 23 23 $38

Ft. Lauderdale | 1431 N. Federal Hwy. (bet. 13th St. & 14th Ct.) | 954-615-1431 | www.sublimerestaurant.com

This "vegan's dream come true" in Ft. Lauderdale puts out "well-spiced" albeit "faux" meat and other vegetable-based dishes that satisfy even "certified carnivores"; it may be a bit "overpriced" for such "small portions", but the service is "excellent" and the "upscale" digs – featuring cascading waterfalls, skylights and vivid Peter Max artwork – are "as pretty as any place in town."

Sugar Reef *Caribbean*   24 20 21 $41

Hollywood | 600 N. Surf Rd. (bet. Fillmore & New York Sts.) | 954-922-1119 | www.sugarreefgrill.com

Chef Patrick Farnault's French culinary background informs the "exquisite" and "sophisticated" Caribbean preparations served at this "funky" islandesque "oasis" on the Hollywood Beach Boardwalk; the

	FOOD	DECOR	SERVICE	COST

hefty tabs are in keeping with the "fine" cuisine and "romantic" views of the "surf" "framed by palm trees."

Sukhothai Thai
24	18	23	$31

Ft. Lauderdale | Gateway Shopping Ctr. | 1930 E. Sunrise Blvd. (Federal Hwy.) | 954-764-0148 | www.sukhothaiflorida.com
The "sensuous Thai sauces", like the "silky, spicy" red curry, at this Ft. Lauderdale strip-mall "gem" "transport" diners to its "namesake ancient city" "without the hassle of airport security pat-downs" (and for a fraction of the fare); the "quiet" space feels "welcoming" on account of the "friendly" woman who owns it.

Sunfish Grill 🗷 Ⓜ American/Seafood
24	21	23	$58

Ft. Lauderdale | 2775 E. Oakland Park Blvd. (bet. Bayview Dr. & NE 27th Ave.) | 954-564-6464 | www.sunfishgrill.com
"Incredible" fish dishes have their day in the sun at this "wonderful" New American bistro in Ft. Lauderdale helmed by chef-owner Erika Di Battista; a "nice wine list" and "elegant" touches like "candles and wispy curtains" set a "romantic" vibe, while the capable staffers who "seem to anticipate" needs make it a lock for "special occasions" – with prices to match.

Su Shin Thai Japanese/Thai
▽ 22	15	19	$38

Lauderhill | 4595 N. University Dr. (NW 44th St.) | 954-741-2569 | www.sushinthai.net
Insiders hip to this longtime Lauderhill Japanese "hole-in-the-wall" say "it's all about the harusame salad" (crispy rice noodles mixed with cabbage and spicy sauce) and, of course, "fresh" "awesome" sushi at "moderate" prices; a separate Thai menu doesn't rate a mention, though patrons are happy to speak up for the "attentive" staff.

Tarantella Ristorante Italian
21	22	22	$30

Weston | Weston Town Ctr. | 1755 Bell Tower Ln. (Town Center Circle) | 954-349-3004 | www.tarantellas.net
"Every community needs" one of these – a "warm", "reliable" neighborhood Italian place – and Weston's version can be found at the Town Center development, where an "enjoyable" menu of modestly priced favorites, including pizzas from the showpiece brick oven, is served by a "wonderful" staff; Sicilian furniture and hand-painted tiles make for an "atmospheric" dining experience.

Tarpon Bend Seafood
20	19	19	$32

Ft. Lauderdale | 200 SW Second St. (SE 2nd Ave.) | 954-523-3233 | www.tarponbend.com
See review in Miami/Dade County Directory.

Tatiana Cabaret
Restaurant ● Continental/Russian
-	-	-	E

Hallandale | 1710 E. Hallandale Beach Blvd. (bet. Layne Blvd. & 16th Ave.) | 954-454-1222 | www.fltatianarestaurant.com
This "glitzy" Russian Hallandale "party place" (and twin of a Brighton Beach, Brooklyn, supper club) is "extravagant in so many ways", from the gold-leaf ceilings and Murano glass chandeliers right down to

its foundation; pricey? – yes, but it's a "good value" considering that the cost of that the Continental-Russian fare "includes a [cabaret] show and music for dancing" (Fridays–Sundays at least).

Taverna Opa ❶ *Greek* | 19 | 16 | 18 | $36 |

Hollywood | 410 N. Ocean Dr. (bet. Arizona & Taylor Sts.) | 954-929-4010 | www.tavernaoparestaurant.com

Brace yourself for "earsplitting" decibels at these "shabby" SoFla "*opa!*"-fests where the evening can include "singing waiters", "dancing on the tables" and "throwing napkins"; ok, they also supply "solid" Hellenic eats for "reasonable" sums, but the "college" kids, "bachelorette parties" and young at heart are there mainly to "party."

☑ Thai Spice *Thai* | 26 | 22 | 25 | $38 |

Ft. Lauderdale | 1514 E. Commercial Blvd. (bet. NE 13th Ave. & 15th Terr.) | 954-771-4535 | www.thaispicefla.com

With a "litany" of daily specials recited by a "smiling" staff plus an "extensive" printed menu, there's "way more than pad Thai" at this "excellent" Siamese in a Ft. Lauderdale strip mall; "fresh orchids" adorning "beautifully presented" plates and an "upscale" setting with "spectacular" "tropical fish tanks" set the scene for "romance", while "fair" prices seal the deal; P.S. it's expanding, adding a bar/lounge.

☑ 3030 Ocean *American/Seafood* | 26 | 23 | 24 | $57 |

Ft. Lauderdale | Harbor Beach Marriott Resort & Spa | 3030 Holiday Dr. (Seabreeze Blvd.) | 954-765-3030 | www.3030ocean.com

"Ultrafresh" fish prepared with "imagination" by the "personable" Dean James Max is the lure at this "upscale" Ft. Lauderdale New American; it's in the "hectic" lobby of an "oceanfront" Marriott so there could be "noisy conventioneers" or "a family in their bathing suits" nearby, but "get over it" and "ask for a window" with "beautiful" water views or a "quiet table at the rear" away from the "lively" bar.

III Forks *Steak* | 20 | 23 | 21 | $62 |

Hallandale | Village at Gulfstream Park | 501 Silks Run (bet. E. Hallandale Beach Blvd. & S. Federal Hwy.) | 954-457-3920 | www.iiiforks.com

See review in Palm Beach Directory.

Timpano Chophouse *Italian/Steak* | 23 | 22 | 21 | $47 |

Ft. Lauderdale | 450 E. Las Olas Blvd. (SE 3rd Ave.) | 954-462-9119 | www.timpanochophouse.net

It's easy to picture Frankie and Dino sliding into one of the plush leather booths at this swanky "'50s"-style Italian steakhouse in Ft. Lauderdale whose "quality" chops may be eclipsed by "outrageously delicious" skillet-roasted mussels; the "downtown crowd" who holds court here appreciates business-lunch "deals" during working hours and "martinis" and standards at the piano bar after punching out.

T-Mex Cantina ❶ *Tex-Mex* | ∇ 17 | 11 | 16 | $19 |

Ft. Lauderdale | 204 SW Second St. (2nd Ave.) | 954-463-2003 | www.t-mex.net

See review in Miami/Dade County Directory.

	FOOD	DECOR	SERVICE	COST

ⓩ Toa Toa Chinese Restaurant & Authentic Dim Sum *Chinese*

26 | 11 | 20 | $23

Sunrise | Pine Plaza | 4145 NW 88th Ave. (Pine Island Rd.) | 954-746-8833 | www.toatoachineserestaurant.com

Dim sum connoisseurs don't need foofaraw like carts when the bite-sized delectables are "as good or better than" their counterparts in "San Francisco, Hong Kong and New York" – and fans say they are at this inexpensive and "unassuming" purveyor in Sunrise; picture menus and a helpful staff can aid diners navigating the full slate of "authentic" Chinese fare; P.S. closed Wednesdays.

NEW Tokyo Blue ●M *Asian*

20 | 18 | 18 | $56

Ft. Lauderdale | Ocean Manor Resort | 4040 Galt Ocean Dr. (N. Ocean Blvd.) | 954-566-2122 | www.tokyoblueonthebeach.com

This high-end "meat market" inside the slightly "shabby" Ocean Manor Resort in Ft. Lauderdale attracts "hip", "young" tourists and locals looking for more nightlife than the typical neighborhood sushi joint provides, and they find it mingling at the high-tech bar, which changes colors all night; service hiccups suggest the staff is "still working out the kinks", but the "decent" rolls and Pan-Asian fare taste a bit sweeter at the outside tables overlooking the sea.

Tokyo Sushi *Japanese*

∇ 23 | 8 | 17 | $29

Ft. Lauderdale | 1499 SE 17th St. (15th Ave.) | 954-767-9922 | www.iluvtokyosushi.net

"Fresh fish" and can't-go-wrong tabs make a pretty pair at this no-frills "go-to" spot for "yummy" sushi and other Japanese specialties in Ft. Lauderdale; an "accommodating" staff and lunch-box specials are added enticements.

Tom Jenkins' Bar-B-Q 🖂M *BBQ*

25 | 10 | 13 | $20

Ft. Lauderdale | 1236 S. Federal Hwy. (Davie Blvd.) | 954-522-5046 | www.tomjenkinsbbq.com

"Outstanding ribs" and other "top-notch" meat come "with all the fixin's" at this Ft. Lauderdale barbecue "role model"; it's counter-serve and "mostly carryout" because those who decide to eat at the "communal" "picnic tables" usually end up getting "smoked too."

Tommy's Italian Restaurant *Italian*

∇ 23 | 18 | 23 | $32

Davie | 4777 S. University Dr. (Griffin Rd.) | 954-680-0113

For the kiddies, families on a budget can order half-priced half-portions of most dishes at this "family-owned" Davie Italian, known for its thin-crust pies and "homestyle" pastas and entrees; the staff "treats guests like old friends", and indeed, customers are likely to bump into their neighbors here.

TooJay's Original Gourmet Deli *Deli*

18 | 12 | 17 | $23

Coral Springs | The Walk at University | 2880 N. University Dr. (bet. NW 28th St. & 31st Ct.) | 954-346-0006
Plantation | The Fountains | 801 S. University Dr. (bet. Broward Blvd. & Peters Rd.) | 954-423-1993
www.toojays.com

See review in Palm Beach Directory.

	FOOD	DECOR	SERVICE	COST

Trata *Greek* — — — M

Ft. Lauderdale | 1103 E. Las Olas Blvd. (bet. NE 11th & 12th Aves.) |
954-712-8933 | www.tratagreektaverna.com

You'll find yourself "back in Greece" while sampling a variety of "well-prepared", "reasonably priced" dishes at this "fine" Ft. Lauderdale taverna with cozy dining inside or people-watching outside on the covered patio; while it's not a partying place, you may hear an occasional '*opa!*' at the bar.

Trattoria Bella Cibo *Italian* — — — M

Margate | 5801 Margate Blvd. (NW 58th Ave.) | 954-969-1100 |
www.trattoriabellacibo.com

This "casual" Margate Boulevard trattoria can be counted on for "truly tasty" "classic" Italian cuisine at moderate prices – Wednesday's all-you-can-eat lunch buffet is about as "low" as they go ($5.99); other perks are the breezy covered patio and occasional live entertainment in the evenings.

Truluck's *Seafood* 24 24 24 $61

Ft. Lauderdale | The Galleria | 2584 E. Sunrise Blvd. (NE 26th Ave.) |
954-396-5656 | www.trulucks.com

See review in Palm Beach Directory.

Tumi *Peruvian* ∇ 20 15 20 $31

Margate | Caroline Springs Plaza | 7926 W. Sample Rd. (Riverside Dr.) |
954-510-8000 | www.tumirestaurant.com

"Consistently on-the-money" Peruvian specialties "at reasonable prices" draw green-sauce-loving surveyors to this "quiet" strip-mall eatery in Margate's Caroline Springs Plaza; service is "attentive", which also makes it "great before" a show at the Broward Stage Door Theatre a few doors down.

Tuscan Grill ℳ *Italian* 20 18 19 $52

Ft. Lauderdale | 1105 E. Las Olas Blvd. (bet. SE 10th Terr. & 12th Ave.) |
954-766-8700

"Deliciously straightforward" Northern Italian fare served by a "nice" crew makes for a "relaxing" meal at this rustic Las Olas "local"; entertainment includes a "fabulous" piano player and watching folks "move their boats around" in the canal below from either the upstairs bar or "outside on the patio."

NEW Two Georges at the Cove *Seafood* 15 17 17 $29

Deerfield Beach | 1754 SE Third Ct. (17th Ave.) | 954-421-9272 |
www.twogeorgesrestaurant.com

See review in Palm Beach Directory.

Udipi *Indian/Vegetarian* ∇ 23 8 18 $22

Sunrise | 2100 N. University Dr. (Sunrise Blvd.) | 954-748-5660

"Roti makes me smile" chirp vegetarians who crowd into this "friendly" Sunrise South Indian offering "not [just] your typical curries"; despite virtually "no decor", the popular lunch buffet ($8.50 weekdays, $10.95 weekends) draws those who love an "incredible bargain"; P.S. no alcohol.

⊠ Valentino's Cucina

27 | 16 | 25 | $71

Italiana ⊠Ⓜ *Italian*

Ft. Lauderdale | 1145 S. Federal Hwy. (SE 11th Ct.) | 954-523-5767 |
www.valentinoscucinaitaliana.com

The "innovative" fare at this "pricey" Ft. Lauderdale Italian is so
"blow-you-away" good that some find themselves "creating excuses
to call things 'special occasions'" just to go back again; service is
"excellent", and those who find its strip-mall locale a tad "dumpy"
and the "small" interior "uninteresting" can look forward to a move
down the street to new, larger digs in early 2012.

Via Luna *Italian*

▽ 21 | 22 | 23 | $62

Ft. Lauderdale | Ritz-Carlton Ft. Lauderdale |
1 N. Ft. Lauderdale Beach Blvd. (Castillo St.) | 954-302-6460

This "lovely" Italian ristorante in the Ritz-Carlton Hotel in Ft.
Lauderdale boasts sweeping "ocean views" from the airy, cream-
and-earth-toned dining room, plus a professional staff that's "always looking to please" – all at upscale prices, naturally; "a relaxing
lunch on the terrace" is one way to go, but tipplers may feel the pull
of the handsome wine room, with a list of over 5,000 bottles and
many rare scotches.

Vienna Café & Wine Bar *European*

24 | 22 | 24 | $40

Davie | Pine Island Plaza | 9100 W. State Rd. 84 (Pine Ridge Dr.) |
954-423-1961 | www.viennacafeandwinebar.com

"Are we in Europe or Davie?" ask first-time nibblers of the "excellent" schnitzel, Danish meatballs, strudel and other "terrific"
European specialties at this "Tyrolean" "surprise in a nondescript
shopping center"; "fair prices", a "warm" staff, and a "fine wine list"
suggest why the "small" space is always so "crowded."

Vigneto's Italian Grill *Italian*

21 | 17 | 22 | $32

Weston | Indian Trace Square Shopping Ctr. | 1342 SW 160th Ave.
(Indian Trace) | 954-660-0470
Plantation | 1663 S. University Dr. (bet. Peters Rd. & Rte. 84) |
954-915-0806
www.vignetos.com

"All the Italian standards" are "well done" and "superbly abundant" at these "neighborhood" favorites in Plantation and
Weston; the digs may be "getting a little dated" and the "wine
list isn't very strong" but "corkage is a reasonable $12" so just
"bring your own."

Village Grille *American*

20 | 16 | 20 | $33

Lauderdale-by-the-Sea | 4404 El Mar Dr. (Commercial Blvd.) |
954-776-5092 | www.villagegrille.com

A "home away from home" for Lauderdale-by-the-Sea locals,
this all-day eatery turns out all manner of "tasty" American
dishes plus rolls from a newly added sushi bar; an alternative to
the "loud" "crowded" interior is the patio where you can "watch
the world and the ocean go by" and listen to live music on Friday
nights, weather permitting.

	FOOD	DECOR	SERVICE	COST

Village Tavern *American*

| 19 | 19 | 19 | $31 |

Pembroke Pines | Shops at Pembroke Pines | 14555 SW Second St. (3rd St.) | 954-874-1001 | www.villagetavern.com

Budget-minded "couples, families and large groups" brave "daunting noise levels" at these "always mobbed" "reliable" chain spots in Pembroke Pines and Boynton Beach to get their mitts on a "wide range" of "everyday" American eats; the "comfortable" environs are staffed by an "attentive" crew who help parse the "great selection" of wine (by-the-glass choices are half-off on Wednesdays).

Villagio *Italian*

| 21 | 21 | 20 | $35 |

Sunrise | Colonnade Outlets | 1760 Sawgrass Mills Circle (Sunrise Blvd.) | 954-846-2176

See review in Miami/Dade County Directory.

Viva Chile *Chilean*

| - | - | - | I |

Davie | 6013 Stirling Rd. (bet. 58th & 61st Aves.) | 954-581-8138

Providing an alternative to SoFla's usual Latin staples, this "excellent" Davie spot focuses on authentic Chilean fare, including empanadas and *pastel de choclo* (a traditional corn pie); it's tiny and under the radar, but the housemade bread, "nice" staffers and Saturday night music keep those in the know coming back for more.

Whale Raw Bar & Fish House *New England*

| 17 | 14 | 18 | $26 |

Parkland | 7619 N. State Rd. 7 (bet. Marina & W. Hillsboro Blvds.) | 954-345-9190 | www.thewhalerawbar.com

Those hunting for a "casual meal" "centered around fish" say this "publike" Parkland place is a decent catch for fare that's a "throwback to the old days"; although some surveyors harpoon the "dark and crowded" interior and call the New England–style grub "disappointing", economical weekly "specials" indicate why there's "usually a wait."

Whale's Rib *Seafood*

| 20 | 13 | 20 | $27 |

Deerfield Beach | 2031 NE Second St. (Ocean Blvd.) | 954-421-8880

"Abundantly portioned seafood practically swims onto your plate" at this "bustling" Deerfield Beach "sardine can" servicing the area's "T-shirt-and-shorts-clad" "beach bums" who "chow down" on everything from "lobster bisque" to "decadent whale fries" (potato chips made in-house); locals "love to take out-of-towners here for the quintessential South Florida experience", a guaranteed "noisy", "divey", "friendly" time.

Wild East Asian Bistro *Asian*

| 17 | 20 | 17 | $35 |

Ft. Lauderdale | 1200 E. Las Olas Blvd. (SE 12th Ave.) | 954-828-1888 | www.wildeastbistro.com

"Let your palate journey" all over Asia via the "far-ranging", midpriced offerings (Chinese, Korean, Thai, sushi, etc.) at this "friendly" spot on lively Las Olas; the modern, vaguely Asian interior is easy on the eyes, and "it's always fun to sit canal-side" on the outdoor deck.

	FOOD	DECOR	SERVICE	COST

Woodlands Ⓜ *Indian/Vegetarian* ▽ 26 | 15 | 22 | $21

Lauderhill | Blvd. | 4816 N. University Dr. (NW 47th St.) | 954-749-3221 | www.woodlandsus.com

"Delicious", "fresh" South Indian food comes at wallet-friendly prices at this "always excellent" Lauderhiller that serves up a "big selection" of vegetarian delicacies "prepared with the utmost attention"; those who line up for the popular "lunch buffet" don't seem to "miss the meat" or mind the no-frills character of the casual setting (though new ownership plans to spruce the place up).

NEW Yard House ◑ *American* 19 | 19 | 19 | $31

Hallandale | Village at Gulfstream Park | 601 Silks Run (SE 9th St.) | 954-454-9950 | www.yardhouse.com

See review in Palm Beach Directory.

YOLO *American* 21 | 23 | 20 | $45

Ft. Lauderdale | 333 E. Las Olas Blvd. (SE 3rd Ave.) | 954-523-1000 | www.yolorestaurant.com

"California cool" suffuses this "vibrant" resto-lounge on Las Olas in the "yummy" American menu, "hot, hot, hot" servers and a "gorgeous", "happening" scene perfect for "socializing" and "beautiful-people-watching"; some feel only "pickup artists" and the "young" profit from the "loud dance music" and "bar scene", but hey, as its acronymic name suggests, "you only live once."

PALM BEACH/
PALM BEACH COUNTY

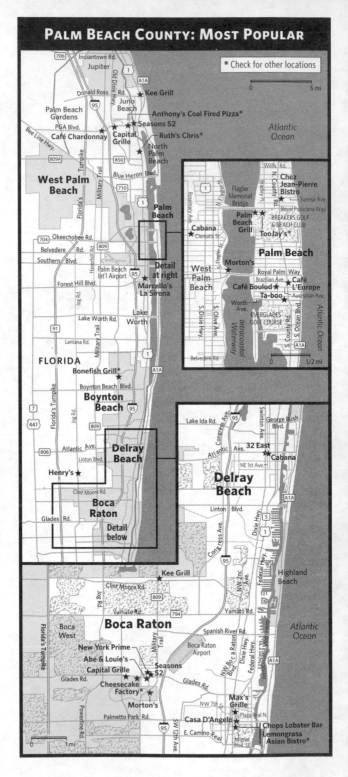

PALM BEACH COUNTY: MOST POPULAR

* Check for other locations

0   5 mi

Atlantic Ocean

Indiantown Rd.
Jupiter
★ Kee Grill
Donald Ross Rd.
Juno Beach
★★ Anthony's Coal Fired Pizza*
Palm Beach Gardens
PGA Blvd.
★ Seasons 52
★ Café Chardonnay
★ Capital Grille
★ Ruth's Chris*
North Palm Beach
Blue Heron Blvd.

West Palm Beach

Palm Beach

Okeechobee Rd.
Belvedere Rd.
Southern Blvd.
Palm Beach Int'l Airport
★ Marcello's La Sirena

Detail at right

Cabana ★
Clematis St.

FLORIDA

Lake Worth

Bonefish Grill* ★
Boynton Beach Blvd.

Boynton Beach

Atlantic Ave.
Linton Blvd.

Delray Beach

Henry's ★

Clint Moore Rd.

Boca Raton

Glades Rd.

Detail below

Kee Grill ★
Clint Moore Rd.
Yamato Rd.

Boca Raton

Boca West

New York Prime ★
Abe & Louie's ★
Capital Grille ★★
Seasons 52 ★
Cheesecake Factory* ★
Morton's ★
Palmetto Park Rd.
Casa D'Angelo ★

0   1 mi

Detail at right

Wells Rd.
Chez Jean-Pierre Bistro ★
Flagler Memorial Bridge
Royal Poinciana Way
Palm Beach Grill ★★
BREAKERS GOLF & BEACH CLUB
TooJay's* ★

Palm Beach

Morton's ★
Royal Palm Way

West Palm Beach

Café Boulud ★
Ta-boo ★
Café L'Europe ★
Worth Ave.
EVERGLADES GOLF COURSE

Belvedere Rd.

0   1/2 mi

Atlantic Ocean

Detail below

Lake Ida Rd.
George Bush Blvd.
Atlantic Ave.
32 East ★
Cabana ★
NE 1st Ave.

Delray Beach

Linton Blvd.

Highland Beach

Atlantic Ocean

Max's Grille ★
Plaza Real N.
Chops Lobster Bar ★
Lemongrass Asian Bistro* ★
Mizner Blvd. SE.

Palm Beach County: Most Popular

1. Café Boulud | *French*
2. Abe & Louie's | *Steak*
3. Kee Grill | *Seafood/Steak*
4. Seasons 52 | *American*
5. Bonefish Grill | *Seafood*
6. Chops Lobster Bar | *Seafood/Steak*
7. 32 East | *American*
8. Café Chardonnay | *American*
9. Capital Grille | *Steak*
10. Café L'Europe | *Continental*
11. Anthony's Coal Fired | *Pizza*
12. Max's Grille | *American*
13. Casa D'Angelo | *Italian*
14. Chez Jean-Pierre | *French*
15. New York Prime | *Steak*
16. Palm Beach Grill | *American*
17. Henry's | *American*
18. Cabana | *Nuevo Latino*
19. Cheesecake Factory | *American*
20. Lemongrass Bistro | *Asian*
21. Ta-boo | *American/Continental*
22. Ruth's Chris | *Steak*
23. Marcello's La Sirena | *Italian*
24. TooJay's Deli* | *Deli*
25. Morton's | *Steak*

Many of the above restaurants are among the Palm Beach area's most expensive, but if popularity were calibrated to price, a number of other restaurants would surely join their ranks. To illustrate this, we have added two lists comprising 60 Best Buys on page 180.

* Indicates a tie with restaurant above

Top Food

28 Marcello's La Sirena | *Italian*
Chez Jean-Pierre | *French*

27 11 Maple St. | *American*
Captain Charlie's | *Seafood*
Café L'Europe | *Continental*
Casa D'Angelo | *Italian*

26 Abe & Louie's | *Steak*
Trattoria Romana | *Italian*
Café Boulud | *French*
Chops Lobster Bar | *Sea./Steak*
Little Moir's | *Seafood*
Capital Grille | *Steak*
Flagler Steak | *Steak*

25 LaSpada's Hoagies | *Deli*
Bluefin Sushi | *Japanese/Thai*
Four Seasons | *Seafood*
Morton's | *Steak*
New York Prime | *Steak*
Café Chardonnay | *American*
Palm Beach Grill | *American*
32 East | *American*
Ruth's Chris | *Steak*

Cut 432 | *Steak*
Kathy's Gazebo | *Continental*
Cheese Course | *Eclectic*
Tramonti | *Italian*
Asian Fin | *Asian*
Il Girasole | *Italian*
Buccan | *Eclectic*

24 Talay Thai | *Thai*
Arturo's | *Italian*
Echo | *Asian*
Cafe Cellini | *Continental*
La Cigale | *Mediterranean*
Cafe Sapori | *Italian*
Truluck's | *Seafood*
Buonasera | *Italian*
Caruso's | *Italian*
Vagabondi* | *Italian*
Kee Grill | *Seafood/Steak*
Brass Ring Pub | *Pub Food*
Rhythm Café | *American*
Lazy Loggerhead | *Seafood*
Renato's | *Italian*

BY CUISINE

AMERICAN

27 11 Maple St.
25 Café Chardonnay
Palm Beach Grill
32 East
24 Rhythm Café

ASIAN

25 Bluefin (Japanese/Thai)
Asian Fin (Fusion)
24 Echo (Pan-Asian)
23 Uncle Tai's (Chinese)
Sushi Jo's (Japanese)

CARIBBEAN/CUBAN

21 Havana
Padrino's
19 Don Ramon's
Cuban Cafe

CONTINENTAL

27 Café L'Europe
25 Kathy's Gazebo
24 Cafe Cellini
23 Ta-boo
21 Bistro

FRENCH

28 Chez Jean-Pierre
26 Café Boulud
23 Café des Artistes
Pistache French Bistro
─ Paris in Town

ITALIAN

28 Marcello's La Sirena
27 Casa D'Angelo
26 Trattoria Romana
25 Tramonti
Il Girasole

PIZZA

22 Anthony's Coal Fired
Renzo's Café
21 Cucina Dell' Arte
Mellow Mushroom
Vic & Angelo's

SEAFOOD

27 Captain Charlie's
26 Chops Lobster Bar
Little Moir's
25 Four Seasons
24 Truluck's

Excludes places with low votes, unless otherwise indicated

Vote at ZAGAT.com

STEAKHOUSES

26 Abe & Louie's
Chops Lobster Bar

Capital Grille
Flagler Steak
25 Morton's

BY SPECIAL FEATURE

BRUNCH

26 Abe & Louie's
Café Boulud
23 Ta-boo
22 Sundy House
20 Caffe Luna Rosa

BUSINESS DINING

27 Café L'Europe
26 Abe & Louie's
Café Boulud
Chops Lobster Bar
Capital Grille

CHILD-FRIENDLY

26 Little Moir's
24 Lazy Loggerhead
23 Houston's
22 Anthony's Coal Fired
Sloan's Ice Cream

DOCK & DINE

23 Seasons 52
22 River House
Jetty's
21 Prime Catch
19 Deck 84

EARLY-BIRD

27 Captain Charlie's
25 Tramonti
24 Kee Grill
23 Okeechobee Steak
Uncle Tai's

HOTEL DINING

26 Café Boulud (Brazilian Court)
Flagler Steak (Breakers)
25 Four Seasons
24 Michelle Bernstein/Omphoy
23 Sushi Jo's (Ritz-Carlton)

NEWCOMERS (RATED)

26 Umi FishBar & Grill▽
25 Buccan
23 Russell's Blue Water Grill
3800 Ocean▽
22 Piñon Grill

PEOPLE-WATCHING

27 Café L'Europe
26 Chops Lobster Bar
25 New York Prime
Palm Beach Grill
32 East

QUICK BITES

24 Brass Ring Pub
23 Café des Artistes
Pistache French Bistro
Sushi Jo's
21 Havana

SINGLES SCENE

25 32 East
Buccan
24 Rhythm Café
23 Pistache French Bistro
Russell's Blue Water Grill

BY LOCATION

CENTRAL COUNTY

28 Marcello's La Sirena
Chez Jean-Pierre
27 Café L'Europe
26 Café Boulud
Flagler Steak

NORTH CENTRAL COUNTY

26 Capital Grille
Café Chardonnay
Ruth's Chris
Asian Fin
24 Talay Thai

NORTH COUNTY

27 Captain Charlie's
26 Little Moir's
24 Buonasera
Kee Grill
Lazy Loggerhead

SOUTH COUNTY

27 Casa D'Angelo
26 Abe & Louie's
Trattoria Romana
Chops Lobster Bar
Capital Grille

Top Decor

27	Guanabanas		Leopard Lounge

27 Guanabanas
  Sundy House
  Café L'Europe

26 Four Seasons
  Piñon Grill
  Michelle Bernstein/Omphoy
  Café Boulud

25 Chops Lobster Bar
  Capital Grille
  Renato's
  Flagler Steak

24 Truluck's
  Abe & Louie's
  Seasons 52

23 Echo
  Buccan
  Morton's
  III Forks
  River House
  Ruth's Chris

Leopard Lounge
22 Pistache French Bistro
  Jetty's
  Arturo's
  Ta-boo
  Racks Downtown
  Brio Tuscan Grille
  La Cigale
  Chez Jean-Pierre
  Bice
  Sailfish Marina*
  Café Chardonnay
  Joseph's Wine Bar
  New York Prime
  SoLita
  Deck 84
  Caruso's
  Casa D'Angelo
  Palm Beach Grill
  11 Maple St.

OUTDOORS

Bice
Café Boulud
Café des Artistes
Caffe Luna Rosa
Deck 84

Four Seasons
Guanabanas
Jetty's
Max's Harvest
Sundy House

ROMANCE

Arturo's
Bice
Café Boulud
Café Chardonnay
Café L'Europe

Casa D'Angelo
Four Seasons
La Cigale
Renato's
Sundy House

ROOMS

Arturo's
Café Boulud
Café L'Europe
Four Seasons
La Cigale

Leopard Lounge
Renato's
Sundy House
Temple Orange
3800 Ocean

VIEWS

Café Boulud
Deck 84
Four Seasons
Guanabanas
Jetty's
Michelle Bernstein/Omphoy

River House
Sailfish Marina
Seasons 52
Sundy House
Temple Orange
3800 Ocean

Top Service

27	Café L'Europe

26	Chez Jean-Pierre
	Four Seasons
	Flagler Steak
	Chops Lobster Bar
	Marcello's La Sirena
	Café Boulud

25	Capital Grille
	Cafe Cellini
	Abe & Louie's
	Morton's
	11 Maple St.
	Kathy's Gazebo

24	Rhythm Café
	Casa D'Angelo
	Joseph's Wine Bar
	Ruth's Chris
	Arturo's
	La Cigale
	Vagabondi

Cafe Sapori
Truluck's
Renato's

23	Palm Beach Grill
	Seasons 52
	Café Chardonnay
	Captain Charlie's
	Piñon Grill
	32 East
	River House
	Tin Muffin Café
	Il Girasole
	Pistache French Bistro

22	Michelle Bernstein/Omphoy
	Sundy House
	Houston's
	Echo
	Trattoria Romana
	Grille on Congress
	New York Prime

Best Buys

In order of Bang for the Buck rating.

1. Sloan's Ice Cream
2. LaSpada's Hoagies
3. Five Guys
4. Lazy Loggerhead
5. Tin Muffin Café
6. Cheese Course
7. Mellow Mushroom
8. Pizza Rustica
9. Brass Ring Pub
10. Howley's
11. Original Pancake House
12. Anthony's Coal Fired
13. CG Burgers
14. Hamburger Heaven
15. Dune Deck Café
16. Big Al's Steaks
17. Grease Burger Bar
18. Park Avenue BBQ Grille
19. Blue Anchor
20. Ben's Kosher
21. Stir Crazy
22. Mississippi Sweets BBQ
23. TooJay's Deli
24. Flakowitz
25. Uncle Joe's
26. Don Ramon's
27. Carmine's Pizza
28. Padrino's
29. Havana
30. Figs
31. Brewzzi
32. Cheesecake Factory
33. Bar Louie
34. Grand Lux Cafe
35. Guanabanas
36. Sláinte Irish Pub
37. Hurricane Café
38. Cuban Cafe
39. China Dumpling
40. Rocco's Tacos

OTHER GOOD VALUES

Cafe Cellini
China Beach Bistro
Chuck Burger
City Diner
English Tap
Gratify American
John G's
Kevin's Dock
Mondo's
Paddy Mac's
Palm Beach Grill
Pita Grille
Royal Café
Russo's Subs
Sara's Kitchen
Scuola Pizza Vecchia
Smokehouse Grille & Wingery
Snappers
Stresa
This Is It Café

PALM BEACH/ PALM BEACH COUNTY RESTAURANT DIRECTORY

FOOD | DECOR | SERVICE | COST

☑ Abe & Louie's *Steak*

26 | 24 | 25 | $66

Boca Raton | 2200 W. Glades Rd. (NW Sheraton Way) | 561-447-0024 | www.abeandlouies.com

The bone-in filet is "as good as it gets" ("you could cut it with a fork"), the "sides are a great match" and the wine list is "impressive" at this Boston-bred beef palace in Boca favored for "power lunches" and "special occasions"; the "clubby" environs are "comfy" and "well managed" by "experienced" pros – "when you have a reservation for 8 PM, you sit down at 8 PM" – so while it costs "big bucks", most feel it delivers big-time.

Absinthe *American*

18 | 20 | 17 | $45

Boca Raton | Boca Raton Marriott | 5150 Town Center Circle (Military Trail) | 561-620-3754 | www.marriott.com

Those who find "promise" at this all-day eatery in the Boca Raton Marriott deem the atmosphere "pleasant" (outside is "exceptional") and the "small" contemporary American menu "enjoyable" if expensive; critics counter the service is "average" and the menu is "limited", adding up to an experience that's "nothing special."

Alladin Mediterranean Grill *Mediterranean*

∇ 18 | 11 | 18 | $26

Palm Beach Gardens | Northlake Commons Plaza | 3896 Northlake Blvd. (off I-95) | 561-622-1660 | www.aladdinmediterranean.com

Tucked into a corner of a Palm Beach Gardens shopping complex is this "great local find" for "authentic" Mediterranean eats, particularly "fabulous" lamb dishes and pastries; the setup isn't much more than cafe tables, food cases and a take-out counter, but it's packed at lunchtime for its "value" specials and there's a crowd on weekend nights lured by belly dancers and hookahs.

Andros ☒Ⓜ *Greek/Mediterranean*

21 | 16 | 21 | $33

Lake Worth | 7012 Charleston Shores Blvd. (Hagen Ranch Rd.) | 561-965-7377 | www.androsrestaurant.com

A "charming", "hands-on" owner greets "loyal customers" at this "busy" Lake Worth strip-maller serving "enjoyable" Greek-Med eats with a few "innovative" twists; "low prices" (including a popular five-course early-bird special) "keep the locals coming back" and also ensure that "there's often a wait even with reservations."

☑ Anthony's Coal Fired Pizza *Pizza*

22 | 16 | 20 | $23

Stuart | Stuart Ctr. | 2343 SE Federal Hwy. (Hwy. 714) | 772-287-7741
Palm Beach Gardens | Marshall's Plaza | 2680 PGA Blvd. (Prosperity Farms Rd.) | 561-804-7777
Boca Raton | 21065 Powerline Rd. (bet. Glades Rd. & W. Palmetto Park Rd.) | 561-218-6600
Delray Beach | 115 NE Sixth Ave. (bet. 1st & 2nd Sts.) | 561-278-7911
Wellington | Shops of Isla Verde | 1000 State Rd. 7 (Victoria Groves Blvd.) | 561-615-1255
www.anthonyscoalfiredpizza.com
See review in Miami/Dade County Directory.

FOOD | DECOR | SERVICE | COST

Arturo's Ristorante *Italian*
24 | 22 | 24 | $59

Boca Raton | 6750 N. Federal Hwy. (Berkeley St.) | 561-997-7373 |
www.arturosrestaurant.com

"Waiters with white gloves and tails set the stage" for "special occasions" at this "elegant" "old-world" Italian in Boca Raton with a "fabulous" antipasto cart, "wonderful" desserts and a "well-stocked
wine cellar"; "dreamy" live piano is favored by the "older" crowd ("I
can almost hear Rudy Vallee crooning away"), but even "younger"
folks "should try this place to see what fine dining is all about."

Asian Fin ⊠ *Asian*
25 | 21 | 21 | $38

Palm Beach Gardens | Donald Ross Vill. | 4650 Donald Ross Rd.
(bet. Central Blvd. & Military Trail) | 561-694-1900 |
www.asianfin.net

At this midpriced Pan-Asian affair tucked into a Palm Beach Gardens
shopping center, fence-sitters "find it hard to make a decision" since
the menu offers so many "different kinds of food", from "amazing"
sushi to "surprising takes" on cooked Japanese fare and "excellent"
Asian fusion (e.g. red-miso bouillabaisse); though "small", the interior is dark and "attractive" with a "hip" bar pouring an "extensive"
array of sake, plus there's sidewalk seating.

Banana Boat *Seafood*
15 | 18 | 17 | $29

Boynton Beach | 739 E. Ocean Ave. (SE 6th St.) | 561-732-9400 |
www.bananaboatboynton.com

"If you just landed from Ohio and want to feel like you're in Florida",
this "nautically themed" Boynton Beach dock-and-dine "landmark"
is a "fun place to enjoy a drink" – and drink in "wonderful" views of
the Intracoastal; despite "so-so" service and "mediocre" seafood
and burgers, moderate tabs attract "families" for lunch while singles
belly up to the "active bar" at night (and boogie to live reggae on
Wednesdays and Fridays–Sundays).

Bar Louie ◑ *American*
17 | 17 | 17 | $26

Boynton Beach | 1500 Gateway Blvd. (N. Congress Ave.) |
561-853-0090 | www.barlouieamerica.com

A "young, noisy" crowd loudly declares this Boynton Beach sports
bar (with a branch in Ft. Myers) a "fun spot to meet friends" for
"cheap" drinks, "decent" American grub and game-watching; others
find the whole experience just "ok" and say "Tuesday is the only day
to go" (for the $1 burger specials).

Ben's Kosher Restaurant &
Caterers *Deli/Jewish*
20 | 15 | 17 | $24

Boca Raton | The Reserve | 9942 Clint Moore Rd. (Rte. 7) | 561-470-9963 |
www.bensdeli.net

Those hankering "for a New York deli fix" look no further than this
"good-value" kosher feedbag in West Boca, a spin-off of the
Manhattan original, legendary for "Jewish soul food" staples like
"mile-high pastrami", "delicious pickles" and "chicken-noodle soup
like bubbe used to make"; noshers face "long lines" and a staff with
"chutzpah", but what could be more "authentic"?

FOOD | DECOR | SERVICE | COST

Bice Ristorante *Italian* — 22 | 22 | 22 | $61

Palm Beach | 313½ Worth Ave. (bet. Cocoanut Row & Hibiscus Ave.) | 561-835-1600 | www.bicegroup.com

"Ladies who lunch" at this Palm Beach outpost of an "upscale" Italian mini-chain enthuse that dining "alfresco in the courtyard" feels "like an instant trip to Europe" despite it being "packed with northerners" (Americans, that is); the "consistent" "high quality" of the cuisine paired with exceptional "people-watching" opportunities and "attentive" service accounts for the "pricey" tabs.

Big Al's Steaks *Cheesesteaks* — 19 | 9 | 16 | $18

NEW **Palm Beach Gardens** | Legacy Pl. | 11290 Legacy Ave. (Old Dixie Hwy.) | 561-275-7260

NEW **Boynton Beach** | Boynton Town Ctr. | 1000 N. Congress Ave. (Savannah Lakes Dr.) | 561-424-0089

Delray Beach | 450 E. Atlantic Ave. (S. Federal Hwy.) | 561-819-1888 ●
www.bigalssteaks.com

The "quality" cheesesteaks at these "cheap" SoFla counter-service sibs are "heartburn heaven" to some, and even if they "won't make you forget Philly, they may delay the flight for a while"; there's "no ambiance" to speak of, but they make "handy bar-hopping" pit stops and hey, "they even have Tastykakes!"

Bimini Twist *Seafood/Steak* — 21 | 21 | 20 | $37

West Palm Beach | 8480 Okeechobee Blvd. (Sansbury Way) | 561-784-2660 | www.mybiminitwist.com

"Fresh" fish star at this "casual" "island-style" surf 'n' turfer in West Palm Beach, a lower-priced cousin of Kee Grill; it can be a "madhouse", especially 5–6 PM when early birds hunting "bargains" roost amid the palm trees in the "tropical" setting.

Bistro, The *Continental* — 21 | 19 | 21 | $54

Jupiter | Driftwood Plaza | 2133 U.S. 1 (Olympus Circle) | 561-744-5054 | www.thebistrojupiter.com

Savvy locals seeking "comfort", "quiet" and "good values" find all three at this "friendly" "neighborhood place" hiding in a Jupiter shopping plaza known for the "consistency" of its Continental cuisine; since it "doubles as a wine merchant", its selection of vintages has "breadth", samples from which are best enjoyed on the "pretty" patio overlooking a fountain and waterfall.

Bizaare Avenue Cafe ● *Eclectic* — 19 | 18 | 18 | $35

Lake Worth | 921 Lake Ave. (S. H St.) | 561-588-4488 | www.bizaareavecafe.com

It's "like eating in a consignment shop" at this "funky, fun" cafe-lounge combination in Lake Worth because "everything in the place is for sale": the "cushy couches" and other "mismatched" furniture, the "original art" and random "tchotchkes" – even the dishware used to serve the Eclectic array of tapas, sandwiches, entrees and wine; the dinner-only bistro upstairs "costs more", but takes reservations.

FOOD | DECOR | SERVICE | COST

NEW Blind Monk Wine Bar ◐ *Wine Bar* ▽ 18 | 26 | 24 | $27

West Palm Beach | 410 Evernia St. (bet. N. Dixie Hwy. & Quadrille Blvd.) |
561-833-3605 | www.theblindmonk.com

With its "wide variety of wines by the glass", "cool vibe" and "old
movies" flickering on the wall, this affordable wine bar in West Palm
Beach is a "great place for a date" say the young professionals who
"hang out" there, upping their viticulture knowledge with frequent
tastings and classes; beyond vino, there's also a "wonderful" beer
list and "snacks" (mainly "cheese and charcuterie").

Blue Anchor ◐ *Pub Food* 17 | 17 | 20 | $24

Delray Beach | 804 E. Atlantic Ave. (Palm Sq.) | 561-272-7272 |
www.theblueanchor.com

"Limeys confirm" this "friendly" English pub in Delray Beach is "authentic in every respect", from the exterior facade that was
shipped cross-pond to the "basic" grub (fish 'n' chips, liver and on-
ions); "dark" environs provide a great "escape from the froufrou set"
on Atlantic Avenue, with beer on tap, soccer on TV and "rockin'
tunes" Thursdays–Sundays.

Bluefin Sushi *Japanese/Thai* 25 | 18 | 22 | $38

Boca Raton | VPC Ctr. | 861 Yamato Rd. (Congress Ave.) | 561-981-8986 |
www.bluefinthaisushi.com

"First-rate sushi at a reasonable price" (try the "dynamite" lobster
bomb roll) accounts for the "popularity" of this "attractive", "modern" Japanese in Boca also turning out "excellent", "inventive" Thai
dishes elevated by "pleasant" service; the Parkland offshoot is further flung, but allies assess it's well "worth the search."

☑ Bonefish Grill *Seafood* 22 | 19 | 21 | $36

Lake Worth | 9897 Lake Worth Rd. (Woods Walk Blvd.) |
561-965-2663
Stuart | Stuart Ctr. | 2283 SE Federal Hwy. (Monterey Rd.) |
772-288-4388
Palm Beach Gardens | 11658 U.S. 1 (PGA Blvd.) | 561-799-2965
Boca Raton | Shops at Boca Grove | 21065 Powerline Rd.
(bet. Glades Rd. & W. Palmetto Park Rd.) | 561-483-4949
Boynton Beach | 1880 N. Congress Ave. (Gateway Blvd.) |
561-732-1310
www.bonefishgrill.com
See review in Ft. Lauderdale/Broward County Directory.

Brass Ring Pub ◐ *Pub Food* 24 | 10 | 19 | $18

North Palm Beach | 200 U.S. 1 (Northlake Blvd.) | 561-848-4748
Royal Palm Beach | 10998 Okeechobee Blvd. (bet. Sparrow Dr. &
Wildcat Way) | 561-296-4563
www.brassringpub.net

"Don't be put off by the appearance" of this North Palm Beach "dive"
because everyone "from Harley dudes to family groups" settles into
the "old wooden booths" for "affordable" grub, including "one of the
best burgers anywhere" and a "never-ending supply of frosty
glasses" of brew; the Royal Palm Beach location is easier on the
eyes, has arcade games and hosts "fun" trivia nights.

	FOOD	DECOR	SERVICE	COST

Brewzzi *American/Italian*　　17　17　18　$27

West Palm Beach | CityPlace | 700 S. Rosemary Ave. (Okeechobee Blvd.) | 561-366-9753
Boca Raton | Glades Plaza | 2222 Glades Rd. (NW Executive Center Dr.) | 561-392-2739
www.brewzzi.com

"Dependable" American comfort food plus pizzas and pasta comes in "monstrous" portions at these brewpubs in Boca and West Palm are "popular" with "families" on a "budget" looking to "please everyone"; others shrug "eh", that's precisely the problem: the fare is "ordinary" and the service is "so-so" – in short, "nothing really stands out."

Brio Tuscan Grille *Italian*　　21　22　21　$36

Palm Beach Gardens | The Gardens | 3101 PGA Blvd. (U.S. 1) | 561-622-0491 | www.brioitalian.com
See review in Ft. Lauderdale/Broward County Directory.

NEW Buccan *Eclectic*　　25　23　21　$52

Palm Beach | 350 S. County Rd. (Australian Ave.) | 561-833-3450 | www.buccanpalmbeach.com

"An instant hit", this "utterly hip" Eclectic helmed by Clay Conley (ex Miami's Azul) is "exactly what Palm Beach needed", drawing a "beautiful" "young crowd" that makes it a "zoo on weekend nights"; the mix of "imaginative" small bites (think hot dog panini, bacon-wrapped Florida peaches), wood-fired pizzas and entrees can add up, but that doesn't faze many since it's "not easy to snag a prime-time table" or happy-hour berth at the bar.

Buonasera *Italian*　　24　20　22　$61

Jupiter | Driftwood Plaza | 2145 U.S. 1 (Olympus Circle) | 561-744-0543 | www.buonaserajupiter.com

The "strip-mall" location "doesn't do justice to the quality" of the "excellent" "classic Italian" cuisine and "extensive wine list" on offer at this Jupiter ristorante (sister to Paradiso in Lake Worth), nor does it suggest such a "professional" degree of "hospitality" – or such "expensive" tabs; otherwise, there are "no surprises" here.

Z Cabana *Nuevo Latino*　　22　20　21　$39

West Palm Beach | 533 Clematis St. (Rosemary Ave.) | 561-833-4773
Delray Beach | 105 E. Atlantic Ave. (1st Ave.) | 561-274-9090
www.cabanarestaurant.com

For "305 flavors without the drive", Latin lovers in Delray and West Palm head to these "festive", "fun spots" for "perfectly spiced" Nuevo fare, "real mojitos" and "top-notch sangria", all at "reasonable" prices; "alfresco people-watching" and a strong "singles scene" are standouts at the more popular Delray locale.

Cabo Flats ☾ *Mexican*　　16　18　16　$31

Palm Beach Gardens | Downtown at the Gdns. | 11701 Lake Victoria Gardens Ave. (PGA Blvd.) | 561-624-0024 | www.caboflats.com

This brightly painted Palm Beach Gardens cantina hosts a "vibrant" "young crowd" that digs the "bar scene", even if many find

FOOD | DECOR | SERVICE | COST

the Mexican fare "mediocre", the service "distracted" and the bills "overpriced"; whether it's "jumping" or just plain "too loud" is up for debate, although most agree it's so "crowded" it turns dining into a "contact sport."

☑ Café Boulud *French*
26 | 26 | 26 | $75

Palm Beach | Brazilian Court Hotel | 301 Australian Ave. (Hibiscus Ave.) | 561-655-6060 | www.danielnyc.com

"Beautiful people" "break out their diamonds and gold" at this "un-Florida" "class act" in the Brazilian Court Hotel that's voted Palm Beach's Most Popular thanks to "sophisticated" French fare that "does Daniel [Boulud] proud", backed by "excellent" wines and a staff operating at "the peak of hospitality" in the "casually elegant" interior or on the "lush" terrace; sure it's "pricey", but the $20 prix fixe lunch and $25 weekend brunch are "bargains"; P.S. there was a post-Survey chef change.

Cafe Cellini *Continental*
24 | 20 | 25 | $52

Palm Beach | Palm Beach President | 2505 S. Ocean Blvd. (north of Lake Worth Bridge) | 561-588-1871 | www.cafecellini.com

A mostly "older" crowd of "well-heeled Palm Beachers" prefers the "refined atmosphere" that makes "conversation possible" at this "reliable" bastion of "fine dining" "hidden in an apartment building" on South Ocean Boulevard; "exceptional" Continental cuisine backed by "lovely" service make the prices seem quite "fair."

Café Centro *Italian*
19 | 17 | 20 | $44

West Palm Beach | 2409 N. Dixie Hwy. (Northwood Rd.) | 561-514-4070 | www.mycafecentro.com

An important "anchor establishment" in West Palm Beach's "gentrifying" Northwood neighborhood, this trattoria supplies homesteaders with a "varied menu" that includes "authentic" Northern Italiana like seafood and pizza; there's sidewalk seating, but many insist the "formal" bar room with live piano is the "place to be"; P.S. free valet parking increases the "value per dollar."

☑ Café Chardonnay *American*
25 | 22 | 23 | $59

Palm Beach Gardens | Garden Square Shoppes | 4533 PGA Blvd. (Military Trail) | 561-627-2662 | www.cafechardonnay.com

This "classy" American in a "nondescript" Palm Beach Gardens strip mall "must be doing something right" because after 25 years it's still many folks' "first choice" for a "night on the town"; the "innovative" food is served by "skilled" staffers, the "quiet", "charming" space is conducive to "conversations" and there's a "wonderful wine list" to boot, key ingredients for those celebrating "special occasions."

Café des Artistes *French*
23 | 21 | 21 | $55

Jupiter | 318 U.S. 1 (E. Indiantown Rd.) | 561-747-0998 | www.cafedesartistesjupiter.com

Oui, you'll find "French food the way it should be" – it even comes with "typically Parisian" service – at this "cozy" bistro in Jupiter; several say it's "overpriced", but the outdoor patio does offer "million-dollar" views of Jupiter Yacht Club's marina; P.S. closed July and August.

	FOOD	DECOR	SERVICE	COST

☒ Café L'Europe Ⓜ *Continental* — 27 | 27 | 27 | $78

Palm Beach | 331 S. County Rd. (Brazilian Ave.) | 561-655-4020 |
www.cafeleurope.com

"Bump elbows with the country's wealthiest people" at this "fine-dining icon" that's "still hitting all the right notes" after three decades with its "scrumptious" Continental cuisine, 2,000-bottle wine list and "superb" staff – rated tops in Palm Beach – that treats diners "like royalty"; add in an "old-world" setting filled with fresh flowers and "lovely" music via a "magical pianist", and even if tabs are "astronomical", it's "worth it."

Cafe Sapori *Italian* — 24 | 19 | 24 | $58

West Palm Beach | 205 Southern Blvd. (Washington Rd.) |
561-805-7313 | www.cafesapori.com

An "enormous menu" of "wonderful" Italian favorites with a smattering of Japanese and Spanish dishes "thrown in" lures "PB cognoscenti across the bridge" to this West Palm Beach sophisticate; the "classic" "white linen" setting gets a jolt from "unusual contemporary art" and a "noisy" crowd (shushers say the patio is "quieter").

Caffe Luna Rosa *Italian* — 20 | 18 | 18 | $38

Delray Beach | 34 S. Ocean Blvd. (bet. E. Atlantic Ave. & Miramar Dr.) |
561-274-9404 | www.caffelunarosa.com

Given its "enviable location" "across from the beach", this "small but stylish" bistro in Delray is a "hot spot all day long" – from its "absolutely wonderful" Americana at breakfast to dinnertime, when the midpriced menu becomes fully Italian and the vibe "romantic"; those who aren't over the moon cite "iffy" service and "crowds" as turnoffs, but the "beautiful" view from the outdoor tables "trumps all."

Caliente Kitchen *Mexican* — ▽ 22 | 23 | 20 | $25

NEW **Boynton Beach** | 1500 Gateway Blvd. (N. Congress Ave.) |
561-244-7335

Delray Beach | 8 E. Atlantic Ave. (Swinton Ave.) | 561-450-6940
www.calientekitchen.net

The "hot atmosphere" can get *muy caliente* indeed at this cheap, "fun" Mexican in Delray mixing "huge margaritas" made from "any tequila you can think of", nightly DJs and a youthful crowd; oh yeah, the "food is very good too" and looks even more "tempting" in the stylish space with reclaimed barn lumber, distressed metal and graffiti; P.S. the Boynton branch is new.

Cantina Laredo *Mexican* — 20 | 20 | 19 | $33

Palm Beach Gardens | Midtown Plaza | 4635 PGA Blvd. (Military Trail) |
561-622-1223 | www.cantinalaredo.com

"Not your typical taco" joint, this "upscale" Mexican chain, with outposts in Hallandale, Palm Beach Gardens and Ft. Myers, woos fans with "solid" modern fare including "excellent" tableside guac and gluten-free items; "upbeat contemporary" settings with "busy bar scenes" (thanks, tequila!) and a "friendly, young" staff make it an ideal "meeting spot for friends" that "won't break the bank."

☑ Capital Grille *Steak* 26 | 25 | 25 | $67

Palm Beach Gardens | Legacy Pl. | 11365 Legacy Ave. (PGA Blvd.) |
561-630-4994
Boca Raton | Town Ctr. | 6000 Glades Rd. (St. Andrews Blvd.) |
561-368-1077
www.thecapitalgrille.com
See review in Miami/Dade County Directory.

Capri Ristorante Italiano ☑ *Italian* ▽ 23 | 21 | 24 | $44

Boca Raton | 39 SE First Ave. (S. Federal Hwy.) | 561-391-8044 |
www.capriristorante.com
To Boca locals, this casual ristorante that recently blew in from Chicago already feels like a "neighborhood" spot say patrons who appreciate the "quality" and price point of its "lovely Italian meals"; a
three-course early-bird menu for $19.95 and live music Thursdays–
Saturdays are added perks.

Captain Charlie's Reef Grill *Seafood* 27 | 14 | 23 | $36

Juno Beach | Beach Plaza | 12846 U.S. 1 (bet. Juno Isles Blvd. &
Olympus Dr.) | 561-624-9924
"Don't be put off by the dumpy strip-mall exterior" or no-reservation
policy – this "wildly popular" Juno Beach seafooder is a "classic not
to be missed" on account of its "strikingly fresh fish" in "creative"
preparations; "professional" service and a "large" list of wines "at ridiculously low prices" offset the "spartan surroundings and noise";
P.S. try its takeout-oriented sib 3 Doors Up in the same strip.

Carmine's Coal Fired Pizza *Italian/Pizza* 19 | 17 | 18 | $27

Jupiter | Abacoa | 4575 Military Trail (Indian Creek Pkwy.) |
561-340-3930 | www.carminescfp.com
This "decent" Italian eatery/pizzeria adjoining CG Burgers in Jupiter
works for quick lunches or "family dinners"; it's "noisy" – on account of
the back bar's TVs – but reasonably priced, and takeout is an option.

Caruso's *Italian* 24 | 22 | 21 | $56

Boca Raton | Royal Palm Plaza | 187 SE Mizner Blvd. (S. Federal Hwy.) |
561-367-7488 | www.carusoristorante.net
SoFla certainly has "no lack of Italian" choices, but even so, the "superb" regional specialties stand out at this "authentic" purveyor in
Boca; it's "expensive" and the "tables are on top of each other", but an
"attentive" staff, "beautiful" outdoor seating by a fountain and the
"cutest little bar" in the adjacent space make it "worth" visit.

☑ Casa D'Angelo *Italian* 27 | 22 | 24 | $61

Boca Raton | 171 E. Palmetto Park Rd. (bet. Mizner Blvd. &
N. Federal Hwy.) | 561-996-1234 | www.casa-d-angelo.com
See review in Ft. Lauderdale/Broward County Directory.

Cay Da ☑ *Vietnamese* 21 | 11 | 20 | $30

Boca Raton | Colony Plaza | 7400 N. Federal Hwy. (NE 74th St.) |
561-998-0278 | www.caydavietnameseatboca.com
"Flavorful" Vietnamese food, including some "unusual", "authentic"
dishes, is priced to move at this "small" "hidden gem" in a North

Boca shopping center; be forewarned, however, that although the owners are "eager to please", service can be "slow" "when busy" because it's mostly the "husband-and-wife team that do it all."

CG Burgers *Burgers*
19 | 13 | 15 | $18

NEW **Palm Beach Gardens** | 2000 PGA Blvd. (N. Ocean Blvd.) | 561-275-2185

Jupiter | Abacoa | 4575 Military Trail (Indian Creek Pkwy.) | 561-340-3940
www.cgburgers.com

Abutting its counterpart pizza joint Carmine's is this "self-serve burger bar" in Jupiter that's applauded for its "quality of meat and produce" and "outstanding" fresh-cut fries; some say the "hole-in-the-wall" look is "not inviting", but gosh, the "inexpensive" tabs sure are; P.S. most other branches of the mini-empire opened post-Survey.

Charley's Crab *Seafood*
20 | 19 | 19 | $52

Palm Beach | 456 S. Ocean Blvd. (Hammon Ave.) | 561-659-1500 | www.muer.com

Amid the "neighboring superhomes" on South Ocean Boulevard, this "real Palm Beach tradition" has been luring "tourists" and locals for "fresh and tasty" seafood dishes for over 30 years; while the "heavy food and dark space" are "not for the young at heart" (or faint of wallet), for admirers it remains an old "standby."

☑ Cheesecake Factory *American*
20 | 19 | 19 | $30

West Palm Beach | CityPlace | 701 S. Rosemary Ave. (Okeechobee Blvd.) | 561-802-3838 ☽

Palm Beach Gardens | Downtown at the Gdns. | 11702 Lake Victoria Gardens Ave. (PGA Blvd.) | 561-776-3711

Boca Raton | 5530 Glades Rd. (Butts Rd.) | 561-393-0344 ☽
www.thecheesecakefactory.com

See review in Miami/Dade County Directory.

Cheese Course *Eclectic*
25 | 17 | 18 | $20

Boca Raton | Mizner Park | 305 Plaza Real (NE 3rd St.) | 561-395-4354 | www.thecheesecourse.com

See review in Ft. Lauderdale/Broward County Directory.

☑ Chez Jean-Pierre Bistro ☒ *French*
28 | 22 | 26 | $74

Palm Beach | 132 N. County Rd. (bet. Sunrise & Sunset Aves.) | 561-833-1171 | www.chezjean-pierre.com

"*Mais oui*" exclaims the "very Palm Beach" crowd that flocks to this "family-run" "country kitchen" for chef Jean-Pierre Leverrier's "consistently awesome" French fare including "outstanding Dover sole" and profiteroles with "chocolate sauce worth drowning in"; the "elegant" space is lined with "unique" modern art and warmed by "attentive" service, and while it helps to have "money to burn", most say it "always delivers"; P.S. closed July through mid-August.

NEW China Beach Bistro ☒ *Chinese*
- | - | - | M

West Palm Beach | 407 Northwood Rd. (Dixie Hwy.) | 561-833-4242 | www.chinabeachbistrowpb.com

Modern dim sum and classic Chinese dishes are made by New York chefs at this Northwood newcomer in West Palm Beach (a sibling of

FOOD DECOR SERVICE COST

Café Centro across the street), where patrons can dine alfresco on the patio or in the dining room under a tin ceiling and chandeliers; a full bar and affable service with moderate prices, especially at happy hour, keep folks smiling.

China Dumpling *Chinese*

20 | 13 | 18 | $27

Boynton Beach | 1899 N. Congress Ave. (Gateway Blvd.) | 561-737-2782 | www.chinadumplings.com

In "Chinese-challenged" South Florida, this "authentic" effort in the Boynton Beach area is "as close as you can get to NYC's Chinatown", say fans of its modestly priced, wide-ranging menu prepared in an open kitchen; though it's certainly nothing fancy, a "helpful" staff is on hand for recommendations, and the weekend dim sum with its "terrific variety of dumplings" is a particular "draw."

⚡ Chops Lobster Bar *Seafood/Steak*

26 | 25 | 26 | $71

Boca Raton | Royal Palm Pl. | 101 Plaza Real S. (1st St.) | 561-395-2675 | www.chopslobsterbar.com

From "excellent steaks" and "fabulous" "flash-fried lobster" to "top-notch" service, this "happening" Boca branch of an Atlanta-based surf 'n' turfer "rarely misses"; the full menu is offered in both the "clubby" steakhouse side and in the replica of NYC's famed Oyster Bar complete with vaulted, tiled ceiling, and there's a lively "bar scene" with live music most nights; of course, some balk at "billfold-fracturing" tabs, but most feel it's "worth it."

NEW Chuck Burger Joint *Burgers*

- | - | - | I

Palm Beach Gardens | 4665 PGA Blvd. (Military Trail) | 561-629-5191

Tight wallets welcome this casual Palm Beach Gardens arrival set in retro-inspired surroundings; the menu puts a wholesome spin on fast-food favorites with hormone- and antibiotic-free beefburgers, crinkle-cut fries, handmade frozen custard and craft beers; P.S. there's an 'off-the-menu menu' for online fans that lists special, limited-availability items.

City Cellar
Wine Bar & Grill *Mediterranean*

20 | 20 | 20 | $39

West Palm Beach | CityPlace | 700 S. Rosemary Ave. (Okeechobee Blvd.) | 561-366-0071 | www.bigtimerestaurants.com

A "wonderful wine" library encased in a glass tower and a "convenient" location in West Palm Beach's CityPlace make this "chic" enoteca a no-brainer for performing-arts patrons gearing up for or winding down from shows at the Kravis Center; "consistent" mid-priced Med eats, "terrific" happy hours and good service make it a "repeat place" for many.

City Diner *American*

∇ 20 | 14 | 23 | $22

West Palm Beach | 3400 S. Dixie Hwy. (El Vedado) | 561-659-6776

Fancy types in their Lilly Pulitzer gear rub elbows with working Joes in jeans and T-shirts at breakfast and lunch (and dinner most evenings) at this "better-than-your-average diner" in West Palm Beach whose "home cooking" feels like a "return to the old days"; so does everything else, including anachronistic prices, "Superman-in-the-phone-booth-fast" service and "kitschy" decor that features "old license plates" and a working jukebox.

City Oyster & Sushi Bar *Seafood*   22 | 19 | 20 | $45

Delray Beach | 213 E. Atlantic Ave. (2nd Ave.) | 561-272-0220 | www.cityoysterdelray.com

"Great drinks" from an "extremely active bar" fuel a "strong undercurrent of energy" at this "yuppie hangout" in Downtown Delray that "caters to the young crowd"; insiders advise you to "stick to" the "standout" raw bar and "simple" seafood preparations and head outside to watch the "crowd go by" if the interior seems "excessively loud."

Conchy Joe's Seafood *Seafood*   19 | 18 | 18 | $34

Jensen Beach | 3945 NE Indian River Dr. (Jensen Beach Blvd.) | 772-334-1130 | www.conchyjoes.com

This "funky, fun" Jensen Beach "biker bar" on the Intracoastal exudes oodles of "bohemiam charm" – from its "order-pad-in-hand diner-style" service to its "shack"-like setting that "feels like the Keys"; the "fresh" seafood dishes, including its signature conch chowder are affordable, but take a backseat to the strong drinks and live reggae Thursdays–Sundays.

Cool'A Fishbar *Seafood*   22 | 18 | 20 | $34

Palm Beach Gardens | Legacy Pl. | 11340 Legacy Ave. (PGA Blvd.) | 561-622-2227

"Bargain prices for Palm Beach Gardens" and "quick service that gets you out fast" are key selling points of this "modern" "tropical"-looking seafooder (and sibling of Kee Grill); what makes it a "dining experience instead of just eating" is "low lighting" and "nice presentations", including the "must-have" potatoes au gratin; P.S. no reservations.

Cottage, The ● *Eclectic*   ▽ 20 | 20 | 15 | $30

Lake Worth | 522 Lucerne Ave. (bet. N. L & M Sts.) | 561-586-0080 | www.thecottagelw.com

A "lovely" patio plus "imaginative" fare and a "nice wine list" make this Eclectic small-plates purveyor in Downtown Lake Worth a "great place to hang out"; although service can be "so slow it's almost in reverse", it always "seems packed" – maybe it's the easygoing tabs or the nightly entertainment, which runs the gamut from live jazz to DJs, karaoke and drag shows.

Couco Pazzo *Italian*   22 | 15 | 21 | $43

Lake Worth | 915-917 Lake Ave. (S. Dixie Hwy.) | 561-585-0320 | www.coucopazzo.com

This Lake Worther is a "favorite" of the "post-retirement crowd" who appreciate its "solid" Italian standards, "good value" and "professional", "efficient" service; perhaps the setting "needs serious updating", but at least it's "not too noisy" and always "easy to get a table."

	FOOD	DECOR	SERVICE	COST

Cuban Cafe *Cuban*

19 | 13 | 19 | $27

Boca Raton | Plumtree Ctr. | 3350 NW Boca Raton Blvd. (bet. 40th St. & Glades Rd.) | 561-750-8860
Delray Beach | Shoppes at Delray | 14400 S. Military Trail (W. Atlantic Ave.) | 561-450-8470
www.cubancafe.com

"When you just can't get down to Miami", these Cubans in Boca and Delray make perfectly acceptable Little Havana stand-ins with their "authentic" fare in "plentiful" portions; the decor is "nonexistent", but the staff makes sure the experience is "warm" and "pleasant" and the prices are "modest."

Cucina Dell' Arte ● *Italian*

21 | 19 | 22 | $49

Palm Beach | 257 Royal Poinciana Way (bet. Bradley Pl. & N. County Rd.) | 561-655-0770 | www.cucinadellarte.com

One of the more "alive places on the island", this "popular" Palm Beach trattoria is often "packed" with "hip", "young" moneyed things due to its "vibrant" after-dark bar scene when it morphs into a club; earlier in the evening and at breakfast and lunch, it may be easier to enjoy its perks – like "solid" Italian entrees and pizza plus an "attentive" staff that "tries to please."

Cut 432 ● *Steak*

25 | 21 | 22 | $63

Delray Beach | 432 E. Atlantic Ave. (bet. NE 4th & 5th Aves.) | 561-272-9898 | www.cut432.com

A "mature glittering crowd looking to mingle" hits up this boutique chophouse on Atlantic Avenue matching its "South Beach"–style "scene" with "fabulous" aged steaks in a "cool modern" setting; yes, it's "expensive", although the "exceptional" happy-hour menu with discounted drinks and snacks offers some relief.

Dada ● *American/Eclectic*

20 | 20 | 20 | $37

Delray Beach | 52 N. Swinton Ave. (bet. E. Atlantic Ave. & 1st St.) | 561-330-3232 | www.dadaofdelray.com

"Truly unique", this Delray Beacher is set in an "old house" adorned with "offbeat" artwork, tables outside "under huge trees" and a revolving slate of live entertainment; some servers may have "weird piercings and serious tats", but they're perfectly "polite and attentive", although compared with the "funky" setting, many surveyors find the "fairly priced" Eclectic-American menu rather "ordinary."

Darbster Ⓜ *Vegan*

- | - | - | M

Lake Worth | 8020 N. Dixie Hwy. (Arlington Rd.) | 561-586-2622 | www.darbster.com

This Lake Worth entry fills a niche for vegans with its well-priced offerings like falafel and tempeh Reubens plus beer and wine, and raw foodists rejoice over items like Beet Rawvioli since uncooked choices are "limited in South Florida"; the space is airy and modern with a patio overlooking the ocean that's even open to pooches (the restaurant is named after the owners' dog); P.S. closed Mondays and Tuesdays.

	FOOD	DECOR	SERVICE	COST

Dave's Last Resort & Raw Bar ◐ *Pub Food* `17` `14` `16` `$25`

Lake Worth | 632 Lake Ave. (bet. S. K & L Sts.) | 561-588-5208 |
www.daveslastresort.com

"Tipsy" sorts tout this "local institution" in Lake Worth, a "noisy, busy" watering hole serving up cheap, "reliable" pub grub with its suds; the staff is "cheerful" but "not in a hurry", so get "comfortable" and "watch sports" on one of its 15 indoor TVs or pick a sidewalk table for some stellar "people-watching."

NEW Deck 84 *American* `19` `22` `19` `$36`

Delray Beach | 840 E. Atlantic Ave. (Marine Way) | 561-665-8484 |
www.deck84.com

Eye candy abounds at this latest entry in Delray from Burt Rapoport (Henry's), from the "beautiful" Intracoastal views to the "young, noisy" crowd and the "hunks and hotties" serving up midpriced American bites; views on the food are mixed ("amazing" vs. "mediocre") although the DIY Bloody Mary bar at weekend brunch is a hit with many.

NEW DIG *American* `-` `-` `-` `M`

Delray Beach | 5199 W. Atlantic Ave. (S. Military Trail) | 561-638-0500 |
www.digdelray.com

This brand-new American in west Delray is 'doing it green' by adhering to strict sustainability standards, from its organic offerings to its dedication to recycling all food waste; expect a well-priced menu featuring Berkshire pork, Florida-raised beef plus vegetarian, vegan and gluten-free options, as well as a salad bar, smoothie bar and organic wine and beer; the recycled decor is on the plain side, although some windows overlook – what else? – an urban garden.

NEW Dirty Martini ◐ *Eclectic* `-` `-` `-` `M`

Palm Beach Gardens | Downtown at the Gdns. |
11701 Lake Victoria Gardens Ave. (Gardens Pkwy.) |
561-799-1115 | www.dirtymartinipalmbeach.com

More watering hole than restaurant, this sprawling space in Downtown at the Gardens pulses with a beat that grows as the hours wane and the neon gets brighter; its patio bar is the see-and-be-seen spot for downing specialty martinis and noshing on an Eclectic array of sharing plates that won't break the bank.

Dockside Sea Grille *Seafood* `19` `15` `18` `$35`

Lake Park | 766 Northlake Blvd. (Flagler Blvd.) | 561-842-2180 |
www.docksideseagrille.com

"Ample" portions of "decent" "fresh" seafood at everyday prices attract easygoing types to this "divey" "hideaway" perched on a little canal inlet in Lake Park; service can be "so-so", and the "casual" setting could use a "spruce up", but the outdoor seating supplies "one of the best water views around."

Don Ramon's *Cuban* `19` `14` `17` `$25`

West Palm Beach | 300 Clematis St. (S. Dixie Hwy.) | 561-832-5418
West Palm Beach | 502 S. Military Trail (Sunny Lane Ave.) | 561-687-0161

(continued)

Don Ramon's

West Palm Beach | 7101 S. Dixie Hwy. (Forest Hill Blvd.) | 561-547-8704 |
www.donramonrestaurant.com
Wellington | 11924 W. Forest Hill Blvd. (Southshore Blvd.) | 561-795-1932
"Down-home" Cubano cooking comes in "large" helpings at prices
that "won't break the bank" at this "casual" chainlet; the settings are
modest and service is "just ok", but most folks leave with "a smile
and a full belly"; P.S. South Dixie Highway is separately owned.

Dune Deck Café ⊭ *American*   20 | 17 | 19 | $23

Lantana | 100 N. Ocean Blvd. (Ocean Ave.) | 561-582-0472 |
www.dunedeckcafe.com
"What could be better than breakfast on the beach?" ask fans of this
open-air, oceanfront American cafe in Lantana serving "tasty", "reasonably priced" daytime eats in "bathing suit–casual" environs;
there's often a "wait" on weekends, although the staff "works their
butts off" to keep tables turning; P.S. cash only; no dinner.

Echo 🅼 *Asian*   24 | 23 | 22 | $56

Palm Beach | 230 Sunrise Ave. (bet. Bradley Pl. & N. County Rd.) |
561-802-4222 | www.echopalmbeach.com
"Hip, young" trust-funders seeking a break from the "stodgy Palm
Beach" scene head to this "chic" venue managed by the Breakers resort featuring a "lively" bar; "inventive" Pan-Asian dishes and "amazing sushi" are "beautifully plated" and ferried by a staff that's "spot-
on", although such a "first-class" experience certainly "ain't cheap."

11 Maple Street 🅼 *American*   27 | 22 | 25 | $66

Jensen Beach | 3224 NE Maple Ave. (Jensen Beach Blvd.) |
772-334-7714 | www.11maplestreet.net
This "out-of-the-way" New American in "funky" Jensen Beach is a
place to "escape the hustle" while enjoying chef-owner Mike Perrin's
"inventive" seafood-strong menu, featuring mostly small plates presented like "works of art" and "costing about the same"; set in a
"quaint" "Old Florida house", it has a "lovely" vibe and "friendly" staffers who are "knowledgeable" about the food and substantial wine list.

NEW English Tap & Beer Garden 🌙 *Pub Food*   - | - | - | M

Boca Raton | The Shops at Boca Ctr. | 5050 Town Center Circle
(Military Trail) | 561-544-8000 | www.theenglishtap.com
After shuttering Wild Olives in Boca Center, celeb chef Todd English
moved next door to launch this new concept: a spiffed-up pub serving dolled-up American and British fare at everyday prices; the
menu includes almost 100 beers available in the spacious, clubby
interior or outside at the wraparound bar.

Entre Nous 🅷 *American*   23 | 17 | 21 | $45

North Palm Beach | 123 U.S. 1 (Northlake Blvd.) | 561-863-5883 |
www.entrenousbistro.com
"Talented" chef Jason Laudenslager is behind this North Palm Beach
"jewel" matching "excellent", "imaginative" American dishes with

FOOD | DECOR | SERVICE | COST

selections from a "surprisingly good" wine list; a few find it "inconsistent" and "expensive", but most are won over by the "comfortable" digs, "knowledgeable" staff and "outstanding" early-bird "deals."

E.R. Bradley's Saloon ● American   16 | 18 | 16 | $30

West Palm Beach | 104 Clematis St. (Flagler Dr.) | 561-833-3520 | www.erbradleys.com

"The scene is better than the chow" at this open-air watering hole near the Intracoastal in West Palm Beach where the pubby American eats draw mixed marks ("decent" vs. "you only eat to absorb the alcohol") and service can be "amateurish"; still, it draws quite the "rowdy" crowd late at night, when the "drinks flow freely" and "ladies routinely dance on the bar"; P.S. by contrast, lunch and Sunday brunch are more tame.

Evo Italian   - | - | - | E

Tequesta | County Line Plaza | 626 U.S. 1 (County Line Rd.) | 561-745-2444 | www.evoitalian.com

Its Tequesta locale may keep this Italian flying under the radar, but diners who've discovered it find an ever-changing menu of creative dishes, including family recipes, fresh-picked salad greens and unique homemade pastas; a bold-colored setting and fine white linens belie its strip-mall location, and oenophiles should note there's a value-based wine list – but bring a wallet anyway because the bills can be lofty.

Figs Italian   21 | 18 | 20 | $30

Palm Beach Gardens | Macy's at the Palm Beach Gardens Mall | 3107 PGA Blvd. (bet. Fairchild Gardens & Kew Gardens Aves.) | 561-775-2384 | www.toddenglish.com

"Tucked inside" the Palm Beach Gardens Macy's, this "casual", mid-priced Italian from celeb chef Todd English provides the perfect "break from shopping" with "gourmet" pizzas, salads and "nice" glasses of wine; since it remains something of a "secret", it's "easy to get a table" and the staff's attention, even if a minority finds it "disappointing compared to the Boston locations."

Fiorentina Italian   ▽ 19 | 13 | 15 | $39

Lake Worth | 707 Lake Ave. (bet. S. J & K Sts.) | 561-588-9707 | www.fiorentinarestaurant.com

Still somewhat new on the Lake Worth dining scene, this Downtown yearling lures "locals" with simple, "well-prepared" Italian fare like grilled pizza and pastas plus a warm setting with exposed brick and red accents; prices are "not too expensive" either, although a few find that service glitches take it "down a notch."

☒ Five Guys Burgers   20 | 10 | 16 | $13

Palm Beach Gardens | Legacy Pl. | 11320 Legacy Ave. (Fairchild Gardens Ave.) | 561-625-3888
Boca Raton | Glades Plaza | 2240 NW 19th St. (Rennaissance Way) | 561-368-8384
Boynton Beach | Boynton Town Ctr. | 1000 N. Congress Ave. (Savannah Lakes Dr.) | 561-369-4460

FOOD | DECOR | SERVICE | COST

(continued)

Five Guys

Wellington | The Pointe at Wellington Green | 10200 W. Forest Hill Blvd. (Rte. 441) | 561-790-7500
www.fiveguys.com
See review in Miami/Dade County Directory.

Flagler Grill *Floribbean*

∇ 24 | 22 | 25 | $58

Stuart | 47 SW Flagler Ave. (bet. S. Colorado & SW St. Lucie Aves.) | 772-221-9517 | www.flaglergrill.com
If you find yourself shopping or gallery-hopping in historic Downtown Stuart, a "nice meal" can be had at this quaint little American grill; however, given the high tabs some wish for more consistent quality, griping that sometimes it's "very good and other times [it's] not so special."

Flagler Steakhouse *Steak*

26 | 25 | 26 | $73

Palm Beach | The Breakers | 2 S. County Rd. (bet. Royal Palm & Royal Poinciana Ways) | 561-653-6355 | www.thebreakers.com
A bastion of "old Palm Beach dining", this "exceptional" steakhouse at The Breakers provides "impeccable" fare and "superb" service in an "elegant" "country-club" atmosphere with "lovely" views of the golf course; no surprise, it all "comes at a price", although lunch is comparitively "inexpensive."

Flakowitz Bagel Inn *Deli*

18 | 9 | 15 | $20

Boca Raton | 1999 N. Federal Hwy. (NE 20th St.) | 561-368-0666

Flakowitz of Boynton *Deli*

Boynton Beach | Hagen Ranch Commons | 7410 W. Boynton Beach Blvd. (Hagen Ranch Rd.) | 561-742-4144 | www.flakowitzofboynton.com
You feel "like you've died and gone to Brooklyn" at these "old-line" deli/bakeries in Boca and Boynton Beach putting out "huge" sandwiches, "good" bagels and tons of other Jewish staples "you grew up with"; just "be prepared for a large helping of NY attitude" from the "ornery" staff, along with "long lines" (it's "senior central") and digs that are "no-frills" at best.

❷ Four Seasons – The Restaurant *Seafood*

25 | 26 | 26 | $77

Palm Beach | Four Seasons Resort | 2800 S. Ocean Blvd. (Lake Ave.) | 561-533-3750 | www.fourseasons.com
"It's the Four Seasons – that's all you need to know" aver fans who declare this "delightful" grande dame in Palm Beach is "hotel dining done right", from Darryl Moiles' "sensational seafood" to the "pampering" treatment; the "pretty" room is enhanced by water views, but be aware that "special evenings" like this "don't come cheap."

Gol! The Taste of Brazil *Brazilian*

16 | 18 | 17 | $52

Delray Beach | 411 E. Atlantic Ave. (4th Ave.) | 561-272-6565 | www.golthetasteofbrazil.com
Feeling anemic? – "increasing your iron" level is no problem at this Brazilian rodizio in Delray Beach because the "attentive" staff keeps the skewered meats in "heavy rotation" in dining areas that range

FOOD | DECOR | SERVICE | COST

from open and airy to comfy and cozy; detractors declare it's "too much" to pay for such "typical" fare, but savvy savers say "you can get away real cheap" if you only select the "enormous salad bar."

NEW Gourmet Burger Co. *Burgers* — | — | — | I

Jupiter | North Bay Plaza | 251 U.S. 1 (E. Indiantown Rd.) | 561-746-6200
There's "lots of different toppings" to choose from at this burgerama in Jupiter, where diners customize patties with homemade sauces, plus there are several unusual sides (e.g. lobster mac 'n' cheese); it's a bit pricier than others in its category, but the setting is fancier than usual too, with warm woods, pendant lighting and a full bar.

Grand Lux Cafe *Eclectic* 19 | 20 | 20 | $31

Boca Raton | Town Ctr. | 6000 Glades Rd. (St. Andrews Blvd.) | 561-392-2141 | www.grandluxcafe.com
See review in Miami/Dade County Directory.

Gratify American Gastropub *American* — | — | — | M

West Palm Beach | 125 Datura St. (bet. Flagler Dr. & Narcissus Ave.) | 561-833-5300 | www.gratifypub.com
Creative American small plates are paired with a limited selection of craft beers and cocktails at this moderately priced waterfront gastropub in Downtown West Palm Beach sporting a stark modern interior with hard granite, concrete and wood (it gets "noisy"); a "fun" crowd gathers at the big bar on weekends when it shifts into meat-market mode, but those looking to escape the throng can find relative peace – and views – on the outdoor patio.

Grease Burger Bar ● *Burgers* 20 | 17 | 16 | $23

West Palm Beach | 213 Clematis St. (Olive Ave.) | 561-651-1075 | www.greasewpb.com
It takes two hands to manage the "juicy" 10-oz. patties at this "attractive", and attractively priced, burger bar in West Palm Beach (from the folks behind Rocco's Tacos) also boasting a "vast" selection of suds; a "friendly" crew, games on the TVs and a working fireplace add to the "fun" vibe, even if unimpressed eaters say it's "not worth going out of your way for."

Green Gourmet *Health Food* — | — | — | M

Delray Beach | The Shoppes at Addison Pl. | 16950 Jog Rd. (bet. Clint Moore Rd. & Linton Blvd.) | 561-455-2466 | www.thegreengourmetdelray.com
Right across from the Morikami Museum is this modest cafe from chef Joey Giannuzzi (ex Henry's) offering "healthy" organic sandwiches, salads and wraps, plus beer and wine; there's also a juice bar, prepared food for takeout and an organic greenmarket outside on Sundays in season.

Grille on Congress ⊠ *American* 19 | 18 | 22 | $38

Boca Raton | 5101 Congress Ave. (Yamato Rd.) | 561-912-9800 | www.thegrilleoncongress.com
Fans say the "no-surprises" American "comfort food" "never disappoints" at this "reliable", "reasonable" "neighborhood joint in tony

Boca", where meals kick off with fresh biscuits "hot out of the oven"; the staff is "welcoming" and the "dark", "casual" interior works equally well for "business lunches" or "weeknight" "family" dinners, but it gets "packed" so make a reservation.

NEW Grimaldi's Pizza *Pizza*
`- | - | - | M`

Palm Beach Gardens | Downtown at the Gdns. | 11701 Lake Victoria Gardens Ave. (Hwy. 1A) | 561-625-4665 | www.grimaldis.com

Photos of the Big Apple remind 'za-eaters of the NYC roots anchoring this pizzeria chain recently arrived in SoFla; the coal-fired, thin-crusted goodness can be customized with any number of $2 toppings, and since a small pie is big enough to share, many add a big-bowl salad and a generous glass of wine and still find the bill easy to stomach.

Guanabanas *Floribbean*
`18 | 27 | 19 | $34`

Jupiter | 960 Ocean Dr. (U.S. 1) | 561-747-8878 | www.guanabanas.com

A "tropical paradise", this "delightful" "island" fantasy in Jupiter overlooks the water and features "lush vegetation" and "tiki"-style furnishings that make you "feel as though you're in the Bahamas"; compared with the setting (voted PB's best in the Decor department), some find the fish-centric Floribbean fare "nothing to write home about", although it's "fun for drinks"; P.S. there can be "interminable" waits (no reservations).

Gulfstream Bistro & Market *Seafood*
`▽ 18 | 12 | 20 | $34`

West Palm Beach | 3815 S. Dixie Hwy. (Conniston Rd.) | 561-366-1346 | www.gulfstreambistro.com

Surveyors "stuff" themselves "relatively inexpensively" on "ample" portions of "simply prepared" fish hauled in by this plain-Jane seafood restaurant and market in West Palm Beach; a "nice" staff is an added perk, and look for "fantastic lunch specials", as well as crab boils and lobster bakes on the deck some weekends.

Hamburger Heaven 🗷 *Burgers*
`21 | 11 | 19 | $20`

Palm Beach | 314 S. County Rd. (bet. Brazilian Ave. & Royal Palm Way) | 561-655-5277

The "grande dame" of Palm Beach "burger joints", this "cute" "classic diner" from 1945 is known for its "great" patties, "thick" shakes and "wonderful" layer cakes served up by a staff that "calls you 'hon'"; it's cheap to boot, but you can't put a price on seeing the local gentry "with their big hats and suits" slumming it at the counter.

Harry & the Natives 🅼 *American*
`▽ 19 | 19 | 18 | $23`

Hobe Sound | 11910 S. Federal Hwy. (SE Bridge Rd.) | 772-546-3061 | www.harryandthenatives.com

"Find the old Florida" at this open-air hangout in Hobe Sound pumping out inexpensive American grub ("stick with simple" stuff like the burgers and fish); it also doubles as a "tourist attraction" with its gift shop, kitschy signs and gags festooning the place and live music nightly in season.

FOOD | DECOR | SERVICE | COST

Havana ◑ *Cuban* | 21 | 14 | 19 | $27

West Palm Beach | 6801 S. Dixie Hwy. (Forest Hill Blvd.) | 561-547-9799 | www.havanacubanfood.com

"It tastes like Miami" at this West Palm Beach Cuban turning out "excellent-value", "authentic" fare like grilled sandwiches and roast pork in "family-friendly" digs; an "unflappable" staff keeps it going 24/7 with a "walk-up window" deemed a "godsend to bar patrons" and other late-night snackers.

☒ Henry's *American* | 21 | 19 | 21 | $42

Delray Beach | Addison Pl. | 16850 Jog Rd. (bet. Clint Moore Rd. & Linton Blvd.) | 561-638-1949 | www.henrysofbocaraton.com

"A little of everything" shows up on the menu of this "popular" Delray American (a Deck 84 sibling) where most find the "expertly prepared" "comfort food" and "dependable" service well suited to an "easy lunch or dinner"; "the early-bird special is a good deal", so prepare yourself for "packed", "noisy" conditions and a crowd that can make a 60-year-old feel like "the youngest person in the room."

Hog Snappers Shack & Sushi *Eclectic/Seafood* | ▽ 26 | 17 | 22 | $34

Tequesta | Village Sq. | 279 U.S. 1 (Tesquesta Dr.) | 561-972-4723

"Excellent" sushi, "inventive" seafood and "reasonable" pricing are the hooks at this "locals' secret", a "tiny" Eclectic spot in a Tequesta strip mall whose dining room is centered around a snaking tiki-style bar; there's good news for those distressed by "cramped" seating and perpetual "waits": at press time, it's finishing up an expansion that will add half a dozen more tables.

Hot Pie Pizza *Pizza* | ▽ 26 | 22 | 21 | $24

West Palm Beach | 123 S. Olive Ave. (bet. Clematis & Datura Sts.) | 561-655-2511 | www.hotpiepizza.com

"Perfection!" proclaim partisans of the "authentic NYC" flatbreads coming out of the coal-fired oven at this brick-walled-and-wooden-boothed pizza parlor and pub from John Ries (of the erstwhile Fire Rock); the rest of the "small" menu is "good too", but the best bet is some 'za and a $2 "frosted beer mug."

☒ Houston's *American* | 23 | 21 | 22 | $39

Boca Raton | 1900 NW Executive Center Circle (Glades Rd.) | 561-998 0550 | www.hillstone.com

See review in Miami/Dade County Directory.

Howley's ◑ *Diner* | 18 | 17 | 20 | $20

West Palm Beach | 4700 S. Dixie Hwy. (Russlyn Dr.) | 561-833-5691

"Classic '50s decor meets modern hipster swagger" at this "one-of-a-kind" West Palm Beach diner where a "cool" clientele chows down on "edgy" "comfort food" served "with a side of sass" from the tattooed staff (they wouldn't have it any other way); "decent" prices, a full bar and one of the "best jukeboxes in town" keep it rocking into the wee hours.

FOOD | DECOR | SERVICE | COST

Hurricane Café *American*

20 | 13 | 19 | $27

Juno Beach | 14050 U.S. 1 (Donald Ross Rd.) | 561-630-2012 | www.hurricanecafe.com

A "neighborhood spot" that "seldom disappoints", this Juno Beach "hole-in-the-wall" is known for its "nothing-fancy" "down-home" American cooking, including "one of the best breakfasts" around; affordable tabs, "fast" service and a dog-friendly patio are additional pluses.

Il Bellagio *Italian*

20 | 20 | 19 | $39

West Palm Beach | CityPlace | 700 S. Rosemary Ave. (Okeechobee Blvd.) | 561-659-6160 | www.ilbellagiocityplace.com

"Any closer to the CityPlace fountains and you'll be swimming" attest patrons of this West Palm trattoria whose "lovely" location with a terrace overlooking the water makes it a "tourist" magnet; "generous" helpings of "well-prepared" Italian fare at "reasonable" rates served by a "pleasant" staff also make it a good "pre-Kravis standby", even if a few find the fare on the "bland" side.

Il Girasole *Italian*

25 | 17 | 23 | $49

Delray Beach | Tropics Sq. | 1911 S. Federal Hwy. (Linton Blvd.) | 561-272-3566

This "been-around-forever" Italian is a Delray "institution" that's "always satisfying" thanks to its "classic", "expertly prepared" Tuscan dishes and "old-world" service that "makes you feel at home"; it's not inexpensive and perhaps the decor could use some freshening up, but its "older" clientele doesn't seem to mind.

NEW Indus *Indian*

- | - | - | M

West Palm Beach | Forum Pl. | 1649 Forum Pl. (Congress Ave.) | 561-249-0123 | www.indusdine.com

Indian restaurants are "few and far between" in West Palm Beach, so this "good-quality" entry is a "welcome" culinary addition; just ignore its location in a bleak strip center next to the abandoned Palm Beach Mall and focus on the "pleasant" interior with comfy semi-lune booths and moderate tabs; P.S. there's also a popular lunch buffet and live entertainment on weekends.

Ironwood Grille *American*

∇ 18 | 21 | 18 | $54

Palm Beach Gardens | PGA National Resort | 400 Ave. of the Champions (PGA Blvd.) | 561-627-2000 | www.ironwoodgrille.com

This American grill in the lobby of the PGA National Resort in Palm Beach Gardens is "convenient" for a pre-tee or post-18th meal; but other than the agreeable "country club atmosphere", some duffers deem the experience "overpriced" and under-par.

Jade 🖼Ⓜ *American*

∇ 23 | 15 | 20 | $45

West Palm Beach | 422 Northwood Rd. (N. Dixie Hwy.) | 561-366-1185 | www.jadekitchen.com

A "gem (no pun intended)" in West Palm Beach's "up-and-coming" Northwood neighborhood, this pricey comer "breaks the mold of standard American fare" with its "constantly" changing, "innovative" nouveau dishes; the "modern" warehousey setting is warmed by an "open kitchen" and kind treatment that "makes you feel like [part of the] family" that owns the place.

J. Alexander's *American* | 20 | 20 | 21 | $35 |

Palm Beach Gardens | Midtown Plaza | 4625 PGA Blvd. (Military Trail) | 561-694-2711
Boca Raton | University Commons | 1400 Glades Rd. (NW 10th Ave.) | 561-347-9875
www.jalexanders.com

Surveyors say you "can't go wrong" at this "convivial", "bustling" chain turning out "well-prepared" "casual American fare" in "modern-plushy surroundings"; a few diners find the formula feels like "everything has been vetted by a focus group", although everyone appreciates the "considerate" service and prices that "won't break the bank."

Jetty's *Seafood* | 22 | 22 | 20 | $43 |

Jupiter | 1075 Ocean Dr. (Donald Ross Rd.) | 561-743-8166
This "popular" seafooder on the Jupiter Inlet presents its "excellent", "fresh" fin fare against a "phenomenal" backdrop of "fabulous" views of the lighthouse; add in a "friendly" atmosphere and a "smashingly good" early-bird that takes a bite out of the cost and it's little wonder there are always "lines out front."

Jimmy's Bistro *American/Italian* | ∇ 26 | 18 | 24 | $47 |

Delray Beach | 9 S. Swinton Ave. (Atlantic Ave.) | 561-865-5774
"One of Delray's best-kept secrets", this "off-the-beaten-path" New American–Italian from chef-owner Jimmy Mills turns out an array of "inspiring" "modern" dishes that change daily (insiders say "get there before your favorites on the chalkboard menu are 86ed"); tabs are relatively reasonable and the space is "tiny", so "make a reservation."

NEW John G's ⊉ *American* | – | – | – | I |

Manalapan | Plaza del Mar | 264 S. Ocean Blvd. (E. Ocean Ave.) | 561-585-9860 | www.johngs.com
This American landmark left its longtime Lake Worth berth and headed a couple of miles south, recently reopening in Manalapan's Plaza del Mar; the new space boasts brighter, updated decor, ample room and free parking, but familiar faces greet diners and inexpensive menu items like fish 'n' chips and French toast remain the same; P.S. cash only.

Josephine's Italian Restaurant *Italian* | 20 | 18 | 18 | $45 |

Boca Raton | 5751 N. Federal Hwy. (bet. Kingsbridge & Newcastle Sts.) | 561-988-0668 | www.josephinesofboca.com
"It feels like eating in someone's elegant dining room" insist well-cared-for "regulars" of this midpriced Boca Italian putting out "good, basic" Northern fare like osso buco and Dover sole in a flower-filled setting; less-frequent diners find the service and setting "cold" and food "ordinary", although the "bargain" prix fixe dinners ($26.95) are a "great deal."

FOOD | DECOR | SERVICE | COST

Joseph's Wine Bar & Café *Mediterranean* `23` `22` `24` `$51`

Delray Beach | Pineapple Grove | 200 NE Second Ave. (2nd St.) |
561-272-6100 | www.josephswinebar.com

"Lovely, personal service" enhances the "excellent" Lebanese-inspired Mediterranean cuisine at this "family-run" bistro and wine bar in Delray Beach boasting an "outstanding" array of vintages; it's on the pricey side, but pays off with a "charming", "intimate" setting that makes the overall experience a "pleasure."

Kathy's Gazebo Restaurant Ⓢ *Continental* `25` `21` `25` `$65`

Boca Raton | 4199 N. Federal Hwy. (Spanish River Blvd.) | 561-395-6033 |
www.kathysgazebo.com

Surveyors "still get dressed up" to dine at this "island of refinement" in Boca, "one of the few classics left" specializing in "delicately prepared" Continental cuisine (the Dover sole is "not to be missed"); even if some find the dining room "staid" and "stuffy", most "cherish" the "exceptional" service enough to pay the premium prices.

Ⓩ Kee Grill *Seafood/Steak* `24` `21` `22` `$47`

Juno Beach | 14020 U.S. 1 (Donald Ross Rd.) | 561-776-1167
Boca Raton | 17940 N. Military Trail (Clint Moore Rd.) | 561-995-5044

"Consistent quality and value" are the hallmarks of this Boca–Juno Beach duo offering "finely prepared fish dishes" along with land-based options and "wonderful sides" like creamed spinach ("heaven in a ramekin"); the "tropical island" digs get "jammed" by an "older crowd" so "don't linger" because the staff, though "friendly", will "take the water glass out of your hand", leading insiders to recommend the "terrific" early-bird hour's more "relaxed pace."

Kevin's Dockside Deli *Deli* `-` `-` `-` `I`

Palm Beach Gardens | Harborside Plaza | 2401 PGA Blvd.
(Prosperity Farms Rd.) | 561-694-7945

When transplanted NYers are looking for a good pastrami on rye, they find it here on the marina in Palm Beach Gardens at this authentic delicatessen; credit cards are now accepted by new owners doing the same old foods in the nautical-themed dining room where you are served after ordering at the counter (or move outside to the deck); P.S. call in your order for pickup on weekends: the line is lengthy.

La Cigale *Mediterranean* `24` `22` `24` `$56`

Delray Beach | 253 SE Fifth Ave. (bet. 2nd & 3rd Sts.) | 561-265-0600 |
www.lacigaledelray.com

Loyalists laud this Delray bistro for its "wonderful" French-inflected Mediterranean fare set down in an "elegant", "beautifully designed" dining room punctuated by a striking modern mural; a "welcoming" staff adds to the "inviting" vibe, just "bring a full wallet."

La Luna *Italian* `17` `13` `17` `$36`

Boca Raton | Polo Shoppes | 5030 Champion Blvd. (N. Military Trail) |
561-997-1165 | www.lalunabistro.com

This "red-sauce" "standby" in Boca is "popular" with penny-pinchers thanks to its "oversized" portions, sunset specials and "bargain" two-for-one dinner entrees in summer; but despite the "reasonable" bills, critics are not over the moon about the "run-of-the-mill" eats or "tired" decor.

La Rosa Nautica *Peruvian/Seafood*   - | - | - | M

Boca Raton | 515 NE 20th St. (N. Federal Hwy.) | 561-296-1413

The "definition of a neighborhood gem", this humble storefront in a Boca strip mall turns out "wonderful" ceviche and other seafood-focused Peruvian specialties; handmade plywood booths, wood paneling and plain tile floors add up to a more pleasant setting than it might sound – and knowledgeable staffers and moderate prices further recommend a try.

☑ LaSpada's Original Hoagies *Deli/Sandwiches*   25 | 8 | 22 | $12

Boca Raton | Commons at Town Ctr. | 2240 NW 19th St. (Rennaissance Way) | 561-393-1434 | www.laspadashoagies.com

See review in Ft. Lauderdale/Broward County Directory.

La Tre *Vietnamese*   ▽ 22 | 10 | 18 | $38

Boca Raton | 249 E. Palmetto Park Rd. (Mizner Blvd.) | 561-392-4568

The decor "leaves a lot to be desired", but intrepid eaters still praise this Boca Raton Vietnamese – one of the few in the area – where the owner "guides you through the menu" of traditional and fusion dishes; on the downside are bills that can feel "expensive for a strip mall."

La Villetta *Italian*   ▽ 22 | 18 | 20 | $54

Boca Raton | Christopher Ctr. | 4351 N. Federal Hwy. (bet. 43rd & 44th Sts.) | 561-362-8403 | www.lavillettaboca.com

"Popular" with Boca locals, this strip-center stalwart puts out "reliable" Italian dishes like its signature whole fish baked in sea salt; a "friendly" staff plus tasteful linens and soft lighting help folks "relax" about the somewhat "expensive" tabs.

Lazy Loggerhead Café *Seafood*   24 | 13 | 22 | $18

Jupiter | Carlin Park | 401 Ocean Dr. (E. Indiantown Rd.) | 561-747-1134

Dunes obscure the water views, but folks in their swimsuits still throng this Jupiter "shack" "steps from the ocean" for its "great breakfasts" and lunches of "fresh" seafood and sandwiches (closed for dinner); the staff's a "delight" and prices are "reasonable", but "get there at a decent time" or prepare to wait.

Legal Sea Foods *Seafood*   21 | 18 | 20 | $40

Boca Raton | Town Ctr. | 6000 Glades Rd. (St. Andrews Blvd.) | 561-447-2112 | www.legalseafoods.com

This Boca outpost of the "famed Boston seafood purveyor" courts customers with "delish", "dependable" New England favorites, including a "to-die-for" clam "chowdah"; bills may be "a bit pricey", but it comes through with a "courteous" staff and a comfortable (if "generic") setting that features a full bar, fish tanks and a patio – "you could do worse at the mall."

	FOOD	DECOR	SERVICE	COST

Leila *Mideastern* — 22 | 18 | 21 | $41

West Palm Beach | 120 S. Dixie Hwy. (Datura St.) | 561-659-7373 |
www.leilawpb.com

"Authentic" meze and other "well-seasoned" Middle Eastern favorites call to mind "a street cafe in Istanbul" at this "upscale" West Palm Beacher draped with silk and mirrors; added appeals include a "pleasant" patio, hookah pipes and belly dancing on weekends.

☑ Lemongrass Asian Bistro *Asian* — 22 | 18 | 20 | $34

Boca Raton | Royal Palm Pl. | 101 Plaza Real S. (1st St.) | 561-544-8181
Boynton Beach | Renaissance Commons | 1800 N. Congress Ave. (Renaissance Dr.) | 561-733-1344
Delray Beach | 420 E. Atlantic Ave. (Federal Hwy.) | 561-278-5050
www.lemongrassasianbistro.com

When you're "in the mood for Asian", this mini-chain is a "sure bet" with its "wide variety" of midpriced offerings that run the gamut from "creative" sushi rolls to pad Thai, with "enough new tastes to keep you coming back"; the "industrial" interiors can get "loud", so many find the "quieter" outside areas more "desirable."

Leopard Lounge *American/Eclectic* — 18 | 23 | 21 | $56

Palm Beach | Chesterfield Hotel | 363 Cocoanut Row (Australian Ave.) |
561-659-5800 | www.chesterfieldpb.com

"What a hoot!" (er, "roar") proclaim those entering this "time warp" in the Chesterfield Hotel that "never changes its fabulous spots" – the ones covering the chairs, tablecloths, curtains, even the leopard-print-vested waiters; the pricey Eclectic–New American menu is "reliable" but "secondary" to the "main sport": watching the "Palm Beach socialites" do lunch or dance the night away.

Limoncello *Italian* — 20 | 16 | 18 | $47

North Palm Beach | 11603 U.S. 1 (PGA Blvd.) | 561-622-7200 |
www.limoncellorestaurant.com

"Don't be fooled by the cheesy sign" and "nondescript" decor because this North Palm Beach Italian is "not your [typical] neighborhood joint" – its "basic" menu shows a "little flair" in its homemade pastas and such; just ask the "professional" staff for some of the signature housemade limoncello to ease the pain when the bill arrives.

Linda Bean's Perfect Maine *Seafood* — 17 | 12 | 14 | $26

Delray Beach | 200 E. Atlantic Ave. (2nd Ave.) | 561-276-2502 |
www.lindabeansmainelobster.com

It's "not perfect and it's not Maine", but for a taste of New England in Delray Beach, this "self-service" chain spot (from an L.L. Bean heiress) fills the bill with its "limited" seafood menu centered around a "tasty" lobster roll; gourmands gripe that they're "underwhelmed" by the "overpriced" sandwich, and say the "fast-food" setting needs "more attention to decor."

Little Moir's Food Shack ☒ *Seafood* — 26 | 15 | 21 | $36

Jupiter | Jupiter Sq. | 103 U.S. 1 (E. Indiantown Rd.) |
561-741-3626

(continued)

FOOD · DECOR · SERVICE · COST

(continued)

Little Moir's Leftovers Café 🗷 *Seafood*

Jupiter | Abacoa Bermudiana | 451 University Blvd. (Military Trail) | 561-627-6030
www.littlemoirsfoodshack.com

Fish fanciers "queue up" at these "funky", "colorful" seafood "shacks" in different Jupiter malls for "a wide array" of "killer" Florida catch at "reasonable" prices; the original looks a bit "run-down" while the bigger Abacoa locale has a slightly "more grown-up atmosphere", but both have a "laid-back" charm enhanced by an "eclectic collection of craft beer" and "friendly" service.

Living Room ◑ *American*

▽ 15 | 21 | 15 | $35

Boynton Beach | 1709 N. Congress Ave. (Gateway Blvd.) | 561-742-4399

For an "enjoyable", "inexpensive evening out" thrifty types drift to this "cute" Boynton Beach bistro/lounge that looks like a "furniture consignment store" with lots of "comfy" couches and "quality" live music; unfortunately, both the modern American comfort eats and service "fall short", so it may be best just for drinks (good craft beers and a wine list full of 'finds').

NEW Luigi's *Italian*

- | - | - | M

West Palm Beach | 118 Clematis St. (Flagler Dr.) | 561-833-4456 | www.luigiswpb.com

The usual suspects – pastas, panini and brick-oven pizzas – are in the lineup at this family-oriented Italian newcomer in West Palm Beach whose large portions make it "reasonable" for lunch and dinner; sidewalk seating and large windows in the open dining room allow solid views of the fountain across Clematis Street in Centennial Park.

Maison Carlos 🗷 *French/Italian*

▽ 26 | 18 | 26 | $46

West Palm Beach | 3010 S. Dixie Hwy. (Monceaux Rd.) | 561-659-6524 | www.maisoncarlos.com

Surveyors "hate to tell you how good" this West Palm strip-maller really is "because then everyone will know"; too late, the secret's out about "outstanding" French-Italian food and a "smart, efficient" staff, even if some say the tiny storefront's minimalist-rustic whimsy doesn't quite measure up to the "high" prices; P.S. closed seasonally mid-August to mid-September.

☑ Marcello's La Sirena 🗷 *Italian*

28 | 19 | 26 | $66

West Palm Beach | 6316 S. Dixie Hwy. (bet. Franklin & Nathan Hale Rds.) | 561-585-3128 | www.lasirenaonline.com

There are "no surprises" at this 25-year-old West Palm Beach "icon", just "unforgettable" Italian "soul food" – which rates as the No. 1 meal in the county – accompanied by a wine list full of "character" and "professional" service, making it perfect for "special occasions"; its "old-style, white-tablecloth" setting can get "crowded", but tables are in better supply if you "eat later than the senior set"; P.S. closed in summer.

	FOOD	DECOR	SERVICE	COST

☑ Max's Grille *American* `22` `20` `20` `$41`

Boca Raton | Mizner Park | 404 Plaza Real (N. Federal Hwy.) |
561-368-0080 | www.maxsgrille.com

"Haven't seen enough Lamborghinis lately" – grab a patio table and
watch the Mizner Park "street scene" unfold at this "pioneer" "gathering place for Boca's glitterati" where "hair flipping and posing are
an art"; happily, the "delicious" New American bites and drinks hold
their own – and at "fair prices" to boot – meaning it's "always bustling", especially at the "swinging bar."

NEW Max's Harvest *American* `-` `-` `-` `M`

Delray Beach | Pineapple Grove | 169 NE Second Ave. (bet. 1st &
2nd Sts.) | 561-381-9970 | www.maxsharvest.com

Restaurateur Dennis Max resurfaces in Delray's Pineapple Grove
with a modern American menu tuned to local and heritage foods
with smart wine pairings; reservations are prudent for dinner in season, regardless of where you want to sit in the four-part space: lush
back patio and bar, front sidewalk tables or a pair of inner rooms,
one with views of an open kitchen.

McCormick & Schmick's *Seafood* `20` `20` `21` `$46`

West Palm Beach | CityPlace | 651 Okeechobee Blvd.
(bet. Quadrille & S. Sapodilla Blvds.) | 561-655-6363 |
www.mccormickandschmicks.com

"Standards are high throughout" this chain seafood operation in
West Palm Beach, starting with the "refreshingly professional" servers
who help patrons chart a course through the "huge", "daily changing"
variety of fish in preparations that range from "traditional" to "adventurous"; most don't mind the "modest" decor or slight dents in
their wallets because the place is so "dependable"; P.S. there's also
a branch in Naples.

Mellow Mushroom *Pizza* `21` `18` `20` `$20`

Delray Beach | 25 SE Sixth Ave. (E. Atlantic Ave.) | 561-330-3040 |
www.mellowmushroom.com

"Never leave the crust behind" advise avid fans of the "doughy"
goodness ringing the "awesome" pies at this cheap chain pizza spot
in Delray Beach "right off pricey Atlantic Avenue"; despite the "psy-
chedelic" theme, it's appropriate for "families", with an affable staff
and an "amazing beer list" for the parents.

Melting Pot *Fondue* `19` `18` `20` `$42`

Palm Beach Gardens | 11811 U.S. 1 (PGA Blvd.) | 561-624-0020 🛇
Boca Raton | 5455 N. Federal Hwy. (bet. NE 51st & Newcastle Sts.) |
561-997-7472
www.meltingpot.com

See review in Miami/Dade County Directory.

Michael R. McCarty's *American* `18` `18` `18` `$45`

Palm Beach | Royal Poinciana Plaza | 50 Cocoanut Row
(Royal Poinciana Way) | 561-659-1899 | www.michaelrmccartys.com

All of "old Palm Beach" seems to wind up at this "reliable" American
"institution" whenever they want a "casual, solid meal that won't

break the bank" (not that they're worried about their balances); the tropical British colonial look is a "nice" touch, but many say the "best part" is the "happening" bar scene.

Michelle Bernstein
at the Omphoy *Mediterranean*
(fka MB at the Omphoy)

24 | 26 | 22 | $66

Palm Beach | Omphoy Resort | 2842 S. Ocean Blvd. (Lake Ave.) | 561-540-6440 | www.omphoy.com

Michelle Bernstein lends her name and "adventurous" culinary spirit to this "swank" spot in Palm Beach's Omphoy Resort featuring a "spectacular" seafood-focused Med menu with "Latin twists"; factor in the "attentive" staff and "gorgeous" room (with "the ocean as one wall") and it's "worth every penny", but note that while there are "wonderful" water views by day, "at night it's quite dark and somber."

Mississippi Sweets BBQ *BBQ*

22 | 11 | 19 | $24

Lake Worth | 9859 Lake Worth Rd. (Rte. 441) | 561-642-4748
Boca Raton | 2399 N. Federal Hwy. (NE 24th St) | 561-394-6779
www.mississippisweetsbbq.net

'Cue heads who "never wait in line" for anything make an exception at these "small" Boca and Lake Worth "holes-in-the-wall" and queue up for "fall-off-the-bone ribs", "terrific" sweet potato fries and other "down-home cooking"; the staff is "pleasant" and the bills are "affordable", but you should get "takeout if you're looking for ambiance."

Mondo's *American/Mediterranean*

18 | 13 | 18 | $31

North Palm Beach | 713 U.S. 1 (Lighthouse Dr.) | 561-844-3396 | www.mondosnpb.com

"Families" favor this "comfortable" North Palm Beach restaurant for "comfort food of all types" – from New American to Mediterranean – at a "steal"; detractors decry "too many TVs", although defenders appreciate the "sports-bar" vibe and also like the "great happy hour"; P.S. it recently added a patio.

Morton's The Steakhouse *Steak*

25 | 23 | 25 | $70

West Palm Beach | Phillips Point Office Bldg. | 777 S. Flagler Dr. (Lakeview Ave.) | 561-835-9664
Boca Raton | Boca Ctr. | 5050 Town Center Circle (S. Military Trail) | 561-392-7724
www.mortons.com

See review in Miami/Dade County Directory.

⚡ New York Prime *Steak*

25 | 22 | 22 | $70

Boca Raton | 2350 NW Executive Center Dr. (Glades Rd.) | 561-998-3881 | www.newyorkprime.com

At this "classic", "masculine"-looking steakhouse chain link in Boca, the "magnificent" cuts of red meat are "cooked to perfection", but they don't come cheap and service can be "brusque" "if you're not a regular"; luckily, there's added value in the "glitzy" scene featuring 'prime' people-watching ("young ladies with their 'uncles'" and a "lively crowd at the bar").

	FOOD	DECOR	SERVICE	COST

Nick & Johnnie's *American*
16 | 16 | 20 | $40

Palm Beach | 207 Royal Poinciana Way (N. County Rd.) | 561-655-3319 | www.nickandjohnniespb.com

This "adorable sidewalk cafe" in the same strip as sibling Cucina Dell' Arte is a "nice shift" from "more formal options" in Palm Beach with its "friendly", "young" staff, "casual" setup and moderately priced American menu; the atmosphere is equally well suited to a "business lunch", "early drinks" or just passing the time "people-watching" outside.

Office, The *American*
20 | 21 | 20 | $37

Delray Beach | 201 E. Atlantic Ave. (2nd Ave.) | 561-276-3600 | www.theofficedelray.com

More *Mad Men* than *The Office,* this "happening" Delray gastropub (across from big bro Vic & Angelo's) flaunts "eye candy" galore, from its retro leather-and-cowhide chairs and other "swanky" accents to the "ogle"-worthy guys and gals clinking "creative cocktails" and craft beers at the long bar; the New American comfort eats (homemade tater tots, "amazing" burgers) are "genuinely good" and available at reasonable rates.

Okeechobee Steakhouse *Steak*
23 | 15 | 21 | $49

West Palm Beach | 2854 Okeechobee Blvd. (Palm Beach Lakes Blvd.) | 561-683-5151 | www.okeesteakhouse.com

A "dazzling platter" of "raw steaks" – just "point to one and you're done" – is the menu at this circa-1947 "institution" for the consumption of red meat in West Palm Beach; it looks a bit "tired and worn out", but the the mood's still pleasant and there's a "super selection of liquid refreshments", so at least "go on your birthday and get a free steak" (though "the bill will run up anyway").

Old Calypso *American/Creole*
19 | 20 | 19 | $40

Delray Beach | 900 E. Atlantic Ave. (Venetian Dr.) | 561-279-2300 | www.oldcalypso.com

"Wonderful views" of the Intracoastal take center stage at this Delray Beach spot on the waterway serving a "diverse", "decent" American menu with an "emphasis on fish" and Creole specialties; the "likable" staff, "quiet", "Caribbean" vibe and "sumptuous drinks" from the bar create a "relaxing" experience that's worth the midrange tabs.

Original Pancake House *American*
20 | 11 | 16 | $18

Palm Beach Gardens | 4364 Northlake Blvd. (Military Trail) | 561-721-2213
Boca Raton | Del Mar Vill. | 8903 Glades Rd. (Lyons Rd.) | 561-395-2303
Delray Beach | 1840 S. Federal Hwy. (Linton Blvd.) | 561-276-0769
Royal Palm Beach | 105 S. State Rd. 7 (Southern Blvd.) | 561-296-0878
www.originalpancakehouse.com
See review in Miami/Dade County Directory.

FOOD | DECOR | SERVICE | COST

Outback Steakhouse *Steak*

18 | 15 | 19 | $31

Lake Worth | 6266 Lantana Rd. (Jog Rd.) | 561-963-7010
Stuart | 3101 SE Federal Hwy. (Indian St.) | 772-286-2622
Palm Beach Gardens | 10933 N. Military Trail (PGA Blvd.) | 561-625-0793
Jupiter | 103 U.S. 1 (E. Indiantown Rd.) | 561-743-6283
Boca Raton | Boca Green Shopping Ctr. | 19595 State Rd. 7
(bet. Kimberly & New England Blvds.) | 561-479-2526
Boca Raton | 6030 SW 18th St. (bet. Military Trail &
Via de Sunrisa del Sur) | 561-338-6283
Delray Beach | 1300 Linton Blvd. (Wallace Dr.) | 561-272-7201
Royal Palm Beach | 11101 Southern Blvd. (Royal Palm Beach Blvd.) |
561-795-6663
www.outback.com
See review in Miami/Dade County Directory.

NEW Ovenella Pizza, Pasta e Vino *Italian/Pizza*

- | - | - | M

Boca Raton | 499 S. Federal Hwy. (SE 5th St.) | 561-395-1455 |
www.ovenella.com
This chic Italian entry near Mizner Park in Boca serves up ample-
portioned Italian favorites plus pizzas for a fair price; potent classic
and modern cocktails are also poured at the long bar in the swinging
space that's lined with mirrored walls and leatherette booths and
features an open kitchen.

Paddy Mac's *Pub Food*

∇ 19 | 15 | 20 | $32

Palm Beach Gardens | Garden Square Shoppes | 10971 N. Military Trail
(PGA Blvd.) | 561-691-4366 | www.paddymacspub.com
A "real Irish pub in South Florida" is as rare as a four-leaf clover, and
this Palm Beach Gardens specimen boasts "tastier" grub "than one
might expect" – and at a solid "value"; besides, what's not to like
when the "nice" staff puts a stout in your hand while "excellent" live
music plays on the weekend?

Padrino's *Cuban*

21 | 14 | 19 | $27

Boca Raton | Mission Bay Plaza | 20455 State Rd. 7 (Glades Rd.) |
561-451-1070 | www.padrinos.com
These SoFla "old faithfuls" have *"comida Cubana"* "down to a sci-
ence" and if much of it is merely "solid", a few standouts are even
"better than your madre's"; the friendly staff makes patrons feel
"wanted" and rewards them with an "enjoyable" lunch buffet that's
priced "right" ($8.99).

Z Palm Beach Grill *American*

25 | 22 | 23 | $53

Palm Beach | Royal Poinciana Plaza | 340 Royal Poinciana Way
(Cocoanut Row) | 561-835-1077 | www.hillstone.com
Like Harvard and Yale, this "energetic" restaurant/"Ivy-League
mixer" in Palm Beach can be "tough to get into", so unless you "know
someone" make reservations "well in advance" for a shot at scarfing
"perfectly executed" American comfort eats (it's basically a
"Houston's upgrade" from the same restaurant group); service is
"good despite the crowds", and though prices look tuition-bill high,
it's possible to "eat for less" if you're smart.

	FOOD	DECOR	SERVICE	COST

Palm Beach Steak House *Steak* | 21 | 17 | 22 | $51 |

Palm Beach | 191 Bradley Pl. (bet. Oleander & Seminole Aves.) |
561-671-4333 | www.thepalmbeachsteakhouse.com

When the chef-owner starts singing along "while the belly dancer
shows her stuff" on Thursday's 'Greek Night', it's a clue that this
"pleasant", "old-style" spot is a "quirky" "alternative to the big steak
joints"; prices are "reasonable for Palm Beach", especially the "terrific" $35 early-bird special, which includes a glass of wine.

NEW Pangea Bistro ⊠ *Asian* | - | - | - | E |

Wellington | 10140 W. Forest Hill Blvd. (Rte. 441) | 561-793-9394 |
www.pangeabistro.net

An amuse bouche sent by the ever-present chef often precedes the
rest of the exotic Asian-fusion offerings at this new Wellington hideaway near the mall; it's not cheap, but wallet-watchers can relax
thanks to the tropical setting with wicker seats and tables and a sleek
bar dispensing don't-miss housemade sangria and other libations.

Paradiso *Italian* | ▽ 25 | 22 | 23 | $64 |

Lake Worth | 625 Lucerne Ave. (bet. S. K & L Sts.) | 561-547-2500 |
www.paradisolakeworth.com

"Exquisite", "beautifully prepared" Italian cuisine is expertly ferried
through the "serene" muraled dining room of this Lake Worth mainstay by a formal staff; though some find the "costly" tabs "out of
line" with its location in SoFla, fans feel it "would pass muster in
NYC or Roma."

NEW Paris in Town Bistro *French* | - | - | - | M |

Palm Beach Gardens | Downtown at the Gdns. |
11701 Lake Victoria Gardens Ave. (PGA Blvd.) | 561-622-1616 |
www.parisintownbistro.com

No need for a plane ticket, this midpriced French newcomer in
Downtown at the Gardens gives diners a taste of the Left Bank with
classics like croque monsieur and steak au poivre; the look is cafe
society with a wine-friendly bar, booths and tables under mirrors
and photos of Parisian scenes that mimic the decor here.

Park Avenue BBQ Grille *BBQ* | 21 | 12 | 19 | $23 |

Lake Worth | 2401 N. Dixie Hwy. (Cornell Dr.) | 561-586-7427
West Palm Beach | 2215 Palm Beach Lakes Blvd. (Village Blvd.) |
561-689-7427
Stuart | 769 NW Federal Hwy. (Wright Rd.) | 772-692-0111
North Palm Beach | 525 U.S. 1 (Anchorage Dr.) | 561-842-7427
Tequesta | 236 U.S. 1 (bet. Glynn Mayo Hwy. & Tequesta Dr.) |
561-747-7427
Boca Raton | 1198 N. Dixie Hwy. (Glades Rd.) | 561-416-7427
Boynton Beach | 4796 N. Congress Ave. (Hypoluxo Rd.) | 561-357-7427
Port St. Lucie | 220 NW Peacock Blvd. (St. Lucie W. Blvd.) | 772-873-0977
Wellington | 13897 Wellington Trace (Greenview Shores Blvd.) |
561-795-7427
www.pabbqgrille.com

"Rib lovers delight" in the "moist, tender" 'cue – "not too sweet, with
a gentle smoke taste" – on offer at this homegrown PB County-

based chainlet that's "easy" to "take the kids" to on account of the "fast" service (just "count on washing up when you get home"); "bargain" prices are another selling point, especially the all-you-can-eat deals on certain days.

Pelican Café ☒ *American/Italian*   21 | 19 | 19 | $43

Lake Park | 612 U.S. 1 (Park Ave.) | 561-842-7272 | www.thepelicancafe.com

This "enjoyable neighborhood" cafe in Lake Park is beloved for breakfast and brunch and "good", moderately priced Italian-American dishes at dinner; the staff makes folks "feel welcome" in the "cute" "Cape Codish" space whose "small" separate areas "keep the din in check"; P.S. outdoor tables overlook Kelsey Park.

Pelican Restaurant *American*   - | - | - | M

Lake Worth | 610 Lake Ave. (bet. S. K & L Sts.) | 561-582-4992

Breakfast is the thing at this daytime American "hole-in-the-wall" in Lake Worth also putting out a handful of Indian items; the shotgun setup – stools along the counter, tables along the wall – is well served by the friendly staff; P.S. it's closed for dinner except Fridays when it serves an all-Indian menu.

P.F. Chang's China Bistro *Chinese*   20 | 20 | 19 | $34

West Palm Beach | The Gardens | 3101 PGA Blvd. (U.S. 1) | Palm Beach Gardens | 561-691-1610

Boca Raton | University Commons | 1400 Glades Rd. (NW 10th Ave.) | 561-393-3722

www.pfchangs.com

See review in Miami/Dade County Directory.

NEW Philippe Chow *Chinese*   - | - | - | E

Boca Raton | 200 E. Palmetto Park Rd. (SE Mizner Blvd.) | 561-393-4666 | www.philippechow.com

Chic New York Chinese arrives in east Boca via this outpost of the big-city original flaunting semi-reduced prices; a large full bar frames the main dining room where a chef performs handmade-noodle demos nightly, and there's also an outside patio.

NEW Piñon Grill *American*   22 | 26 | 23 | $45

Boca Raton | Town Ctr. | 6000 Glades Rd. (St. Andrews Blvd.) | 561-391-7770 | www.pinongrill.com

A "welcome addition" to the Boca scene, this "invigorating", upscale entry in the Town Center mall offers a "well-rounded menu" of "innovative" American eats delivered by a staff that "seeks to please"; the dining room is trimmed with "fantastic" Southwest-inspired decor, and it's "worth a visit just to see" the "stunning bar" where the "beautiful people gather"; P.S. free parking or valet available.

Pistache French Bistro *French*   23 | 22 | 23 | $46

West Palm Beach | 101 N. Clematis St. (Flagler Dr.) | 561-833-5090 | www.pistachewpb.com

"Magnifique" coo connoisseurs of the "authentic" fare at this "boisterous" West Palm bistro dressed up in art nouveau and "overlook-

ing the park" by the Downtown waterfront; the staff is made up of "friendly, hip Floridians", and if you "dive into a carafe de vin", your wallet won't feel a thing.

Pita Grille *Mediterranean/Mideastern*   ∇ 23 | 13 | 19 | $30

North Palm Beach | 12100 U.S. 1 (bet. Juno Rd. & Pleasant Dr.) | 561-630-0115

Find a bit of "Beirut" in North Palm Beach at this "pleasant" but no-frills sit-down/take-out joint on U.S. 1 offering "excellent" Mediterranean and Middle Eastern eats like kebabs for dinner and dips, salads and sandwiches for its popular, good-"value" lunch; if the staffers are sometimes "slow", they do create a "pleasant" atmosphere.

Pizza Girls *Pizza*   ∇ 20 | 9 | 17 | $14

West Palm Beach | 114 S. Clematis St. (bet. Flagler Dr. & Narcissus Ave.) | 561-833-4004 | www.pizzagirls.com

"Huge slices" of "not too thin, not too thick, but always crispy" pizza please partisans at this affordable counter-serve in West Palm Beach; but the basic space is "not a place to sit for dinner", so grab a pie and "take it to the new waterfront [park] across the street."

Pizza Rustica ● *Pizza*   19 | 10 | 15 | $15

Delray Beach | 1155 E. Atlantic Ave. (Ocean Blvd.) | 561-279-8766 | www.pizza-rustica.com

See review in Miami/Dade County Directory.

Pizzeria Oceano ⊅ *Pizza*   - | - | - | M

Lantana | 201 E. Ocean Ave. (S. Oak St.) | 561-429-5550 | www.pizzeriaoceano.com

"Awesome pizza" made with organic ingredients – plus a small selection of calzones and apps – means insatiable pie-holes "can't stop eating" at this pea-size parlor on Ocean Avenue in Lantana; just know that a cash-only, no-takeout and no-substitutions policy is part of the package.

Player's Club Restaurant *Seafood/Steak*   ∇ 17 | 21 | 18 | $52

Wellington | 13410 Southshore Blvd. (Greenview Shores Blvd.) | 561-795-0080 | www.playersclubrestaurant.com

This "ritzy" Wellington surf 'n' turfer is a "clubhouse" for the horsey set and other Palm Beach "society types" featuring an "expensive" menu backed by stiff drinks; some say the real attractions are the "lovely" digs overlooking the polo grounds and the active bar scene with a piano player or DJ often in the house.

Portobello *Italian*   23 | 19 | 21 | $52

Jupiter | Jupiter Bay Plaza | 351 U.S. 1 (E. Indiantown Rd.) | 561-748-3224 | www.portobellojupiter.com

This "old-world Italian" ristorante in a "not-very-noticeable" storefront in Jupiter is known for its "high-quality" classics and "divine" specials (which are often "much more expensive" than the standard menu items); the staffers are "helpful" and the atmosphere's "lively", although some say "it's so noisy, you can't hear yourself eat."

FOOD | DECOR | SERVICE | COST

Prime Catch *Seafood*
21 | 21 | 20 | $42

Boynton Beach | 700 E. Woolbright Rd. (S. Federal Hwy.) | 561-737-8822 | www.primecatchboynton.com

"Sit outside and soak in" the "scenic" views of the Intracoastal ("heaven on a breezy day") at this "popular" Boynton Beach seafooder featuring a "broad" selection of "fresh" fish "done your way"; prices are moderate, but if some say it's "good but nothing exceptional", it still draws frequent "crowds", so "make a reservation."

Racks Downtown
Eatery + Tavern *American*
21 | 22 | 20 | $43

Boca Raton | Mizner Park | 402 Plaza Real (N. Federal Hwy.) | 561-395-1662 | www.grrestaurant.com

"Hot", "young" things are getting in on the "action" at Gary Rack's "breath of fresh air" in Boca that sports "hip" decor, a "killer bar" and patio seating ensconced in a Mizner Park piazza; the "friendly" crew that takes your order is also easy on the eyes, while the wide-ranging American menu presents "good value for the money", even if it can be "uneven."

Ra Sushi *Japanese*
19 | 21 | 18 | $34

Palm Beach Gardens | Downtown at the Gdns. | 11701 Lake Victoria Gardens Ave. (PGA Blvd.) | 561-340-2112 | www.rasushi.com

A "hip" take on sushi, this "popular" Japanese chain reels in a "young crowd" with "unusual" rolls and teriyaki served in "modern", "club"-like digs with a DJ spinning most weekends; detractors decry "inauthentic" fare and "hit-or-miss" service, but they're missing the point: "killer drinks" and an "unbeatable happy hour."

Relish *Burgers*
∇ 21 | 11 | 20 | $21

West Palm Beach | Old Northwood | 401 Northwood Rd. (N. Dixie Hwy.) | 561-629-5377 | www.relishburger.com

"It's all in the toppings" at this casual West Palm Beach burger joint in the Northwood Village neighborhood, where "gourmet" patties (beef, buffalo, mahi mahi, etc.) can be punched up with about 20 "creative" housemade relishes like tzatziki or scotch-bonnet mango; the counter staff is solid, the price is right and the "interesting" shakes and craft-beer offerings go great with the backyard patio feel.

Renato's *Italian*
24 | 25 | 24 | $68

Palm Beach | 87 Via Mizner (Worth Ave.) | 561-655-9752 | www.renatospalmbeach.com

Whether for a "first date" or "60th anniversary", this "elegant Italian" ristorante in Palm Beach is "romantic perfection" thanks in part to its "lovely" courtyard dining and "fine" fare; the "steep" prices are warranted by the "amazing" staff that takes "care of every desire."

Renzo's of Boca *Italian*
22 | 16 | 19 | $43

Boca Raton | 5999 N. Federal Hwy. (bet. Dixie Hwy. & NE 7th Ave.) | 561-994-3495

(continued)

Renzo's Café & Pizzeria *Italian*

Boca Raton | 6900 N. Federal Hwy. (Appleby St.) | 561-997-8466
www.renzosofboca.com

The lengthy "classic" Italian menu at this Boca mainstay covers the "standards" as well as some Sicilian specialties, and though "it ain't cheap" the "quality justifies the price"; it's "cozy" even if there's "no decor" to speak of, and the "courteous" staff led by a "personable, hands-on" owner inspires many "loyal followers"; P.S. the cafe branch is a simpler pizzeria affair.

Rhythm Café *American* 24 | 20 | 24 | $40

West Palm Beach | 3800 S. Dixie Hwy. (Southern Blvd.) | 561-833-3406 |
www.rhythmcafe.cc

With its "whimsical" retro decor, this "quirky, little" American fits right in with the "antique shops" dotting its "funky" stretch of West Palm; the "innovative" "something-for-everyone" menu featuring small and large plates is brought by an "excellent" staff that helps take the sting off tabs deemed a "little pricey."

Riggins Crabhouse *Seafood* 20 | 11 | 19 | $38

Lantana | 607 Ridge Rd. (I-95, exit 61) | 561-586-3000 |
www.rigginscrabhouse.com

Bringing "Bawlmer" to Lantana is this "authentic" Maryland-style crabhouse supplying "steamed-in-Old-Bay" blues and other fresh catch; it's a "glorified" "shack", but the staff "never rushes you" and modest tabs mean you never have to shell out much.

River House *Seafood/Steak* 22 | 23 | 23 | $55

Palm Beach Gardens | Harborside Plaza | 2373 PGA Blvd.
(Prosperity Farms Rd.) | 561-694-1188 | www.riverhouserestaurant.com

A "special-occasion mainstay", this "old-fashioned steakhouse on the water" provides "classic" surf 'n' turf, a "great salad bar" and "attentive" service; it's priced high, but "always a pleasure" with a "relaxing" tiki bar for a pre- or post-meal drink; P.S. no reservations except Fridays and Saturdays upstairs.

Rocco's Tacos ◐ *Mexican* 20 | 20 | 19 | $32

West Palm Beach | 224 Clematis St. (bet. Narcissus & Olive Aves.) |
561-650-1001

Boca Raton | 5250 Town Center Circle (Military Trail) | 561-416-2131
www.roccostacos.com

"What a blast!" shouts the "hip", "young" crowds hanging at these "buzzing", "upscale" Mexican "hot spots" offering "above-average" eats backed by a "fabulous" selection of tequila; an "enthusiastic" staff matches the "energetic" vibe and "booming" music; P.S. get ready for "free tequila shots" when Rocco is in the house.

Royal Café in Jupiter ⊄ *Diner* ▽ 20 | 9 | 22 | $18

Jupiter | Calle Vieja Shopping Ctr. | 75 E. Indiantown Rd. (Old Dixie Hwy.) |
561-747-7426

There's "no pretense" at this family-owned Jupiter cafe, just "solid" American chow at "reasonable" rates; service is "fast, cour-

FOOD | DECOR | SERVICE | COST

teous and pleasant", and prices are decent too; P.S. breakfast and lunch only.

NEW Russell's Blue Water Grill *Seafood* | 23 | 21 | 22 | $52 |
Palm Beach Gardens | 2450 PGA Blvd. (Prosperity Farms Rd.) | 561-318-6344 | www.russellsbluewatergrill.com
Early word says this Palm Beach Gardens eatery shows "great promise" with its "excellent", "creative" seafood and New American dishes; a "seasoned" staff and "upscale" dining room with an open kitchen and live piano on weekends make it an "easy" if "somewhat pricey" place to relax.

Russo's Subs *Sandwiches* | - | - | - | I |
West Palm Beach | 1477 S. Military Trail (14th Rd. S.) | 561-964-1014 🗷
West Palm Beach | 415 S. Dixie Hwy. (bet. Fern & Gardenia Sts.) | 561-659-4333
Lake Park | 1246 Northlake Blvd. (Old Dixie Hwy.) | 561-845-7722 🗷
www.russossubs.com
Sub rolls that taste like they "just came out of grandma's oven" are loaded up with "more than enough meat" at these West Palm and Lake Park houses of heros; there's "no decor", but they remain a "local favorite" (expats can have the signature sammies shipped elsewhere) and you "can't beat the value."

Ruth's Chris Steak House *Steak* | 25 | 23 | 24 | $65 |
West Palm Beach | CityPlace | 651 Okeechobee Blvd. (bet. Quadrille & S. Sapodilla Blvds.) | 561-514-3544
North Palm Beach | 661 U.S. 1 (Lighthouse Dr.) | 561-863-0660
Boca Raton | 225 NE Mizner Blvd. (2nd St.) | 561-392-6746
www.ruthschris.com
See review in Miami/Dade County Directory.

Safire 🅜 *Asian* | ▽ 26 | 17 | 23 | $30 |
Lake Worth | 817 Lake Ave. (N. J St.) | 561-588-7768 | www.safirelakeworth.com
A "best-kept secret" in Lake Worth, this modestly priced Asian fusion serves up "delicious" fare that's heavy on the Thai influence; there's a "warm family atmosphere" in the "tiny" bistro space, although insiders insist the patio and takeout are both equally good options.

Saigon Tokyo *Japanese/Vietnamese* | ▽ 22 | 11 | 22 | $22 |
Greenacres | 2902 Jog Rd. (10th Ave. N.) | 561-966-1288 | www.saigontokyorestaurant.com
"Large portions" of "great" Vietnamese cuisine plus sushi and other Japanese dishes at "inexpensive" rates make this Greenacres pit stop one of "the bargains of the county"; otherwise, there's not much to say about the dependable service and small, no-frills space.

Sailfish Marina *Seafood* | 17 | 22 | 17 | $32 |
Palm Beach Shores | Sailfish Marina Resort | 98 Lake Dr. (¼ mi. south of Blue Heron Blvd.) | 561-842-8449 | www.sailfishmarina.com
Views are the "main pleasure" of this PB Shores seafood "institution" (circa 1952), and there's certainly a lot to look at: from "fishing boats

coming in and out" of the marina to "sunsets" over the Intracoastal; the "simple" fish dishes are "decent" and priced right, and the "airy", tropical space is "kid-friendly" but also boasts a "boisterous" bar.

Saito's Japanese Steakhouse *Japanese/Steak*
19 | 16 | 18 | $35

West Palm Beach | CityPlace | 700 S. Rosemary Ave. (Okeechobee Blvd.) | 561-296-8881
Palm Beach Gardens | Midtown Plaza | 4675 PGA Blvd. (Garden Square Blvd.) | 561-202-6888
Boynton Beach | 8316 Jog Rd. (bet. Gateway & Le Chalet Blvds.) | 561-369-1788
Wellington | 10240 W. Forest Hill Blvd. (Rte. 441) | 561-296-8888
www.saitosteakhouse.com

It's "showtime!" at these outlets of a Japanese steakhouse chainlet that "bring in the crowds" for "entertaining" hibachi cooking and "serviceable" sushi; "kids" love the slicing, dicing pyrotechnics, and their adult minders dig the "reasonable" tabs.

Sapori *Italian*
▽ 28 | 20 | 25 | $56

Boca Raton | Royal Palm Pl. | 301 Via de Palmas (S. Federal Hwy.) | 561-367-9779

"True artist" Marco Pindo is in the kitchen of this Royal Palm Place sleeper creating "exquisite" Italian masterpieces of "outstanding" fish and fresh pasta dishes; other times he's out front working his "charm"; there's really only room for improvement in the "expensive" wine prices (but you can BYO) and decor that "could be softened" ("turn down the lighting").

Sara's Kitchen *American*
- | - | - | I

Palm Beach Gardens | City Ctr. | 2000 PGA Blvd. (U.S. 1) | 561-540-2822 | www.saraskitchenllc.com

"Pancakes extraordinaire" and other solid breakfast and lunch items beckon fans to this American cafe tucked inside a Palm Beach Gardens office building; the "helpful" staffers "make you feel like one of the family" and they don't even charge you much for the privilege.

NEW Scuola Vecchia Pizza e Vino Ⓜ *Pizza*
- | - | - | M

Delray Beach | 522 E. Atlantic Ave. (NE 6th Ave) | 561-865-5923 | www.scuolavecchiapizzeria.com

Early fans rave about the "genuine" Neapolitan pies topped with "über-fresh" ingredients at this pizza parlor that recently rolled into Downtown Delray; it's not exactly cheap, but an "eager-to-please" staff keeps diners happy in the bright, modern space that's dressed with Italian marble and arty tilework.

Ⓩ Seasons 52 *American*
23 | 24 | 23 | $42

Palm Beach Gardens | 11611 Ellison Wilson Rd. (PGA Blvd.) | 561-625-5852
Boca Raton | 2300 NW Executive Center Dr. (Glades Rd.) | 561-998-9952
www.seasons52.com
See review in Ft. Lauderdale/Broward County Directory.

FOOD	DECOR	SERVICE	COST

Sláinte Irish Pub ◑ *Pub Food* | 17 | 16 | 17 | $26 |

Boynton Beach | Renaissance Commons | 1500 Gateway Blvd.
(N. Congress Ave.) | 561-742-4190 | www.slaintepubs.com

This midpriced pub in Boynton Beach serves solid Gaelic grub amid "sparse" surroundings; but some feel it's "more appropriate for the bar crowd than for dining" with its TVs "tuned to every sporting event on earth" and noise level that can border on "deafening."

Sloan's Ice Cream *Ice Cream* | 22 | 21 | 18 | $10 |

West Palm Beach | 112 S. Clematis St. (Narcissus Ave.) | 561-833-3335
West Palm Beach | CityPlace | 700 S. Rosemary Ave. (Okeechobee Blvd.) | 561-833-4303
Palm Beach Gardens | Downtown at the Gdns. |
11701 Lake Victoria Gardens Ave. (PGA Blvd.) | 561-627-4301
Boca Raton | Mizner Park | 329 Plaza Real (N. Federal Hwy.) | 561-338-9887
www.sloansonline.com

This "wonderful, old-fashioned ice-cream parlor chain" is "immensely popular" with "kids and adults" thanks to its "delicious", "deluxe" scoops, ranked Palm Beach's No. 1 Bang for the Buck (it's "expensive for the ice cream" but worth it); the "fairy-tale" settings are full of "fun" extras: "candy treats", "gag gifts" and "the coolest bathrooms anywhere."

NEW Smokehouse Grille & Wingery *BBQ* | – | – | – | M |

Boca Raton | 9908 W. Yamato Rd. (State Rd. 7) | 561-852-7474 | www.smokehousegw.com

Barbecue-starved Bocaites beat a path to this new 'cue contender with a ruggedly handsome interior (corrugated metal, rough-hewn wood) and a huge custom smoker out back; Memphis-style ribs and brisket are dry rubbed with secret 'Magic Dust', and there's a variety of sauces available as well as wings, sausages, rotisserie chicken and more; P.S. the happy hour (11 AM–7 PM daily) has "excellent beer specials."

Snappers *Seafood* | 18 | 15 | 17 | $33 |

Boynton Beach | Oakwood Sq. | 398 N. Congress Ave. (Old Boynton Rd.) | 561-375-8600 | www.snappers.com

"Everybody raves" about the "cedar-plank halibut" at this Boynton Beach seafooder, but otherwise its "simple" fish dishes are mostly notable for being "large" and a "good value"; some complain of "sporadic" service and an "institutional" feel in the dining areas, but that doesn't deter the hordes that keep it "crowded."

NEW SoLita Delray *Italian* | 21 | 22 | 20 | $49 |

Delray Beach | 25 NE Second Avenue (Atlantic Ave.) | 561-899-0888 | www.solitaitalian.com

See review in Ft. Lauderdale/Broward County Directory.

Spoto's Oyster Bar *Seafood* | 22 | 19 | 21 | $44 |

Palm Beach Gardens | 4560 PGA Blvd. (Military Trail) | 561-776-9448 | www.spotosoysterbar.com

"Incredibly tasty" bivalves – "fresh from the Cape" and elsewhere – are the "best bet" at John Spoto's "pricey" but shucking "good" seafooder in Palm Beach Gardens; the "young" staff always "delivers, no matter how busy" the "bustling", "casual" space gets, though conversationalists may want to "eat outside where it's quieter"; P.S. a small bar area with TVs and occasional live jazz can soak up the overflow.

Station House *Seufood/Steak* | 22 | 12 | 19 | $47 |

Lantana | 233 W. Lantana Rd. (N. Federal Hwy.) | 561-547-9487

Station Grille *Seafood/Steak*

Lantana | 200 W. Lantana Rd. (N. Federal Hwy.) | 561-547-6022
www.stationrestaurants.com

Lobsters "big enough to ride" are expertly cooked in "every variation possible" for a "fair price" at this "surf 'n' turf" duo in Lantana (with a newer Deerfield outpost); some say the "tired" decor could use "spiffing", but the staff is reasonably "efficient" and early-bird specials are a worthwhile "bargain."

Stir Crazy *Asian* | 19 | 17 | 18 | $25 |

Boca Raton | Boca Raton Town Ctr. | 6000 Glades Rd. (bet. Butts Rd. & St. Andrews Blvd.) | 561-338-7500 | www.stircrazy.com
See review in Ft. Lauderdale/Broward County Directory.

Stresa *Italian* | 19 | 14 | 18 | $39 |

West Palm Beach | 2710 Okeechobee Blvd. (bet. Congress Ave. & Palm Beach Lakes Blvd.) | 561-615-0200

Perhaps it's "not exciting", but this "old standby" in West Palm Beach is "always busy" thanks to its "hearty" red-sauce standards that are "well prepared and well priced"; the "homey" digs could use some "redecorating", but "loyal patrons" appreciate the "experienced" staff that "knows every inch of the place", "well-worn" or not.

Sundy House Ⓜ *American* | 22 | 27 | 22 | $54 |

Delray Beach | Sundy House | 106 S. Swinton Ave. (Atlantic Ave.) | 561-272-5678 | www.sundyhouse.com

Lovebirds flock to the "gorgeous" garden filled with "lush", "exotic" foliage – truly one of the "prettiest" settings in the county – on the grounds of this "charming" old Delray Beach manse turned boutique inn; the New American menu is "well executed" and the service is solid, but for a "special occasion" the setting alone is worth the "splurge"; P.S. Sundy brunch is quite "an event."

Sushi Jo's *Japanese* | 23 | 15 | 18 | $38 |

Manalapan | Ritz-Carlton Palm Beach | 100 S. Ocean Blvd. (E. Ocean Ave.) | 561-533-6000
West Palm Beach | 319 Belvedere Rd. (S. Dixie Hwy.) | 561-868-7893
Palm Beach Gardens | PGA Commons | 5080 PGA Blvd. (Hickory Dr.) | 561-691-9811
Boynton Beach | Ocean Plaza | 640 E. Ocean Ave. (SE 6th Ct.) | 561-737-0606

Thai Jo *Thai*

West Palm Beach | 700 S. Rosemary Ave. (Okeechobee Blvd.) | 561-832-3545
www.sushijo.com

"Fresh, fresh, fresh" fish "nicely presented" in "innovative" rolls stars at this chain of sushi specialists that also feature a supporting cast of simple Japanese apps and salads; the staff is "sometimes a little slow", but the "modern" spaces, "interesting" sake selections and moderate prices pull in a "young crowd"; P.S. the unrated Thai Jo is a newer Thai spin-off.

Sushi Simon *Japanese* ▽ 23 | 16 | 20 | $37

Boynton Beach | 1614 S. Federal Hwy. (off E. Woolbright Rd.) | 561-731-1819

Simon says "come" to this Boynton Beach storefront sushi joint for "creative" rolls with "silly" names made from the "freshest" fish; once you make peace with the idiosyncrasies of the menu – no hot food except by special request, and "beware of specials with no prices" listed – the "sweet" staff will "make you feel at home."

Tabica Grill *American* 21 | 17 | 21 | $36

Jupiter | The Jupiter Reserve Plaza | 901 W. Indiantown Rd. (Pennock Ln.) | 561-747-0108 | www.tabicagrill.net

The name of this "perennial" Jupiter multitasker is an apt portmanteau of the words 'tavern', 'bistro' and 'cafe' – it boasts a "great bar" and offers "home-cooked" American, plus lighter wraps and sandwiches by day; the "reasonable" tabs and "pleasant" staff remain "low-profile" thanks to the strip-mall digs, and that's just the way "neighborhood" folks like it.

Table 42 *Italian* 21 | 18 | 20 | $40

Boca Raton | Royal Palm Pl. | 399 SE Mizner Blvd. (S. Federal Hwy.) | 561-826-2625 | www.grrestaurant.com

This "hip" Italian from Gary Rack "belongs more in Miami or NYC" than Boca Raton, what with its "updated" "red-sauce" menu, mod look and "fun", young crowd that hangs on the patio; although it's "on the expensive side" for what it is, there are deals to be had – like the "can't-be-missed" $5 burger night on Wednesdays.

Ta-boo *American/Continental* 23 | 22 | 22 | $52

Palm Beach | 221 Worth Ave. (bet. Hibiscus Ave. & S. County Rd.) | 561-835-3500 | www.taboorestaurant.com

"Quintessentially Palm Beach", this Worth Avenue "tradition" (since 1941) is "always a destination" for everyone from "ladies [who] lunch" to the "famed and infamous" turning heads at dinner to the "barflies" who descend "late" when it morphs into a "pickup bar"; there's a "cordial" staff and a "fairly priced" Continental–New American menu that "never disappoints", "so wear your pink shirt and lime-green pants" and go.

Talay Thai *Thai* 24 | 19 | 20 | $39

Palm Beach Gardens | 7100 Fairway Dr. (PGA Blvd) | 561-691-5662 | www.talayonpga.net

Talay-ho! cry those on the hunt for "excellent", fiery Thai fare, because chef Charlie Soo is a "marvel" at this "family-owned" Siamese he runs with hostess 'Mama Soo' at Palm Beach Gardens' PGA National complex; an "attractive" series of stepped spaces graced by soft lighting further justifies prices some find a little "high" for the genre.

	FOOD	DECOR	SERVICE	COST

Taso's Greek Taverna *Greek* ▽ 19 | 12 | 16 | $26
Delray Beach | 14802 S. Military Trail (Atlantic Ave.) | 561-637-7671 | www.tasosgreektaverna.com

The antithesis of the nightclublike tavernas in the area, this "small", "bare-bones" spot in Delray Beach serves humble "home-cooked" Hellenic eats; prices are a downright "bargain", however some feel that service glitches can detract.

Taverna Kyma *Greek* 20 | 16 | 18 | $35
Boca Raton | 6298 N. Federal Hwy. (Forsyth St.) | 561-994-2828 | www.tavernakyma.com

On weekends, a "cranked-up sound system" and cries of "*opa!*" echo in this cavernous Hellenic honky-tonk in Boca while a belly dancer distracts from somewhat "inconsistent" service; midweek and out on the patio it's more "quiet", allowing diners to focus on the "flavorful" midpriced Greek dishes coming out of the open kitchen.

Taverna Opa *Greek* 19 | 16 | 18 | $36
West Palm Beach | CityPlace | 700 S. Rosemary Ave. (Okeechobee Blvd.) | 561-820-0002 | www.tavernaoparestaurant.com

See review in Ft. Lauderdale/Broward County Directory.

Temple Orange *Italian/Mediterranean* ▽ 24 | 23 | 25 | $63
Manalapan | Ritz-Carlton Palm Beach | 100 S. Ocean Blvd. (E. Ocean Ave.) | 561-533-6000 | www.templeorangepalmbeach.com

Set in Manalapan's "elegant" Ritz-Carlton, this upscale entry offers Italian-Med bites either in a "minimalist" dining room with floor-to-ceiling ocean views or out on the patio where diners can enjoy the sea "breeze" first hand; either way, admirers find it "truly amazing", although representatives of the lower tax brackets just wish prices would "come down to earth."

Tempura House *Chinese/Japanese* ▽ 18 | 16 | 16 | $35
Boca Raton | 9858 Clint Moore Rd. (Rte. 441) | 561-883-6088

The midpriced menu at this Boca Asian covers a lot of ground in both China and Japan (including "huge" sushi rolls, pepper steak and, yes, tempura), but what "kids love" is the "fun show" at the hibachi tables; the wood-lined space is modest and service doesn't always measure up, but it's usually "busy" nonetheless.

Thaikyo Asian Cuisine *Japanese/Thai* ▽ 19 | 17 | 21 | $39
Manalapan | Plaza Del Mar | 201 S. Ocean Blvd. (E. Ocean Ave.) | 561-588-6777 | www.thaikyo.com

When Manalapan locals "just can't face cooking" they head to this "little" mango-hued joint for "basic" sushi along with other Japanese and Thai standards; tabs are low, service is "welcoming" and there's "live music on the weekends" too.

NEW 3800 Ocean *American/Seafood* ▽ 23 | 25 | 22 | $53
Riviera Beach | Marriott Singer Island | 3800 N. Ocean Dr. (Bimini Ln.) | 561-340-1795 | www.marriott.com

Utilizing "whatever's fresh" (including "local" catch), chef Dean James Max brings the same brand of "inventive" Americana he showcases at Ft. Lauderdale's 3030 Ocean to this "expensive" new-comer in the Marriott in Riviera Beach; the renovated Solu space now sports an open kitchen and chef's table as well as expanded portals to the "fabulous" ocean view; P.S. the space becomes the more casual Ocean Grille for breakfast and lunch.

☑ 32 East *American*   25 | 21 | 23 | $55

Delray Beach | 32 E. Atlantic Ave. (bet. 1st & Swinton Aves.) | 561-276-7868 | www.32east.com

Chef Nick Morfogen "continues to surprise and impress" with his "nightly changing" dinner menu featuring "fresh, local ingredients" at this New American "favorite" in Delray Beach; service is "above par", and though tabs are "on the pricey side", it draws a "young, energetic" crowd that turns the inside into a "festive" "zoo" – those who prefer not to "scream" can sit outside and watch "*tout* Delray" stroll by on "fashionable" Atlantic Avenue.

This Is It Café *American/Diner*   - | - | - | I

West Palm Beach | Northwood Vill. | 444 24th St. (N. Dixie Hwy.) | 561-655-3301

A sibling of Royal Café in Jupiter, this "old-style diner" is a "real find" in Northwood Village, slinging homey American comfort food; "fast" service, moderate bills and a nautically themed setting complete the picture.

III Forks *Steak*   20 | 23 | 21 | $62

Palm Beach Gardens | Midtown Plaza | 4645 PGA Blvd. (Military Trail) | 561-630-3660 | www.iiiforks.com

Opinions are split on these Hallandale and Palm Beach Gardens surf 'n' turf siblings imported from Texas; pros praise the "melt-in-your-mouth" cuts, "more-than-competent" service and "elegant" mahogany-trimmed setting, while critics call it "overpriced" and claim the steaks "seem to have gone south" (the Food score is down three points this year).

Tin Muffin Café ☒✍ *American*   23 | 18 | 23 | $20

Boca Raton | 364 E. Palmetto Park Rd. (bet. SE 3rd & 4th Aves.) | 561-392-9446

"Lovely" "for a ladies' lunch", this "charming", "little" bakery cafe in Boca serves up "homemade" American daytime fare like soups and sandwiches (11 AM–4 PM); "wonderful muffins" and "friendly" service are rewards for putting up with "tight seating" and a cash-only policy.

Too Bizaare *Eclectic*   19 | 20 | 18 | $38

Jupiter | 287 E. Indiantown Rd. (Intracoastal Pointe Dr.) | 561-745-6262 | www.toobizaare.com

The "funky" thrift-shop decor "borders on weird" at this Eclectic hangout in Jupiter where patrons lounge on "comfy" couches while sipping wines and tucking into "interesting" small plates and sushi; if some surveyors find the execution only "adequate", at least the tabs are low, the setting is a great "conversation piece" and it's "always an experience."

	FOOD	DECOR	SERVICE	COST

TooJay's Original Gourmet Deli *Deli*
| 18 | 12 | 17 | $23 |

Lake Worth | 419 Lake Ave. (S. M St.) | 561-582-8684
Palm Beach | Royal Poinciana Plaza | 313 Royal Poinciana Way (Cocoanut Row) | 561-659-7232
Palm Beach Gardens | Downtown at the Gdns. |
11701 Lake Victoria Gardens Ave. (PGA Blvd.) | 561-622-8131
Jupiter | The Bluffs | 4050 U.S. 1 (Marcinski Rd.) | 561-627-5555
Boca Raton | Glades Plaza | 2200 Glades Rd. (NW Executive Center Dr.) | 561-392-4181
Boca Raton | Regency Court Plaza | 3013 Yamato Rd. (Jog Rd.) | 561-997-9911
Boca Raton | Polo Shoppes | 5030 Champion Blvd. (N. Military Trail) | 561-241-5903
Boynton Beach | Boynton Beach Mall | 801 N. Congress Ave. (bet. Boynton Beach & Gateway Blvds.) | 561-740-7420
Vero Beach | Treasure Coast Plaza | 555 21st St. (6th Ave.) | 772-569-6070
Wellington | Wellington Green Mall | 10300 W. Forest Hill Blvd. (Rte. 441) | 561-784-9055
www.toojays.com
Additional locations throughout the Palm Beach County area
"It ain't Katz's", but this "dependable" "NY-style" deli chain is nonetheless "jammed with snowbirds" seeking "huge, jaw-unhinging sandwiches", black-and-white cookies and other "comfort food at comfortable prices"; some say it "used to be better", and note "rundown" "dinerlike" digs and service that "varies wildly" ("quick" vs. "just threw food at us").

Top of the Point 🏢Ⓜ *American*
| - | - | - | E |

West Palm Beach | Phillips Point Office Bldg. | 777 S. Flagler Dr. (Okeechobee Blvd.) | 561-832-2424 | www.phillipspointclub.com
Set atop Phillips Point in Downtown West Palm Beach, this romantic entry owned by The Breakers treats guests to stellar panoramic views and creative American cuisine at lofty prices; look for dishes like scallops with corn chowder and bacon crisps matched with wines from the resort's award-winning list served in a huge beige-and-brown window-wrapped room; P.S. breakfast and lunch is for members only.

Tramonti *Italian*
| 25 | 20 | 20 | $57 |

Delray Beach | 119 E. Atlantic Ave. (bet. SE 1st & 2nd Aves.) | 561-272-1944 | www.tramontidelray.com
"Crowded with a capital 'C'" and "noisy with a capital 'N'", this Delray Italian – a spin-off of Angelo's of Mulberry Street in NYC – packs them in for "superb" red-sauce fare that "rivals the old country"; it's "expensive", and service gets mixed marks ("top-notch" vs. "haughty"), but it's a great "place to celebrate" or to "see and be seen", especially on the patio.

Trattoria Romana *Italian*
| 26 | 21 | 22 | $63 |

Boca Raton | 499 E. Palmetto Park Rd. (NE 5th Ave.) | 561-393-6715 | www.trattoriaromanabocaraton.com
A real "class act", this Boca Italian puts out "terrific" "old-fashioned" fare (with a "don't-miss" antipasto bar) that keeps it perpetually

"crowded"; a recent renovation added a "much-needed" bar pouring cocktails and wine that "makes waits a lot more enjoyable", although some still take issue with "expensive" prices and service that seems to "favor regulars."

Triple Eight Lounge at the Falcon House 🖼 Ⓜ *American*

— | — | — | M

Delray Beach | 116 NE Sixth Ave. (bet. SW 1st & 2nd Sts.) | 561-243-9499 | www.facebook.com/Falconhouse

"Tapas are the thing" at this sexily dressed but modestly priced contemporary American resto-lounge from Karl Alterman housed in a circa-1925 cottage in Delray; prices are moderate, and there's "always a fun crowd" warming the stools and slurping "creative cocktails" at both the inside and outside bars.

Truluck's *Seafood*

24 | 24 | 24 | $61

Boca Raton | Mizner Park | 351 Plaza Real (bet. NE 3rd & 5th Sts.) | 561-391-0755 | www.trulucks.com

The "excellent" seafood at this "upscale" surf 'n' turf mini-chain is literally just "off the boat" (it has "its own fleet") but "don't expect stressed species on the menu" given its committment to sustainable aquaculture; "knowledgeable" service, "powerfully good" drinks and "lively" bars with live piano music make the "expensive" tabs more palatable.

Tryst *American*

— | — | — | M

Delray Beach | 4 E. Atlantic Ave. (N. Swinton Ave.) | 561-921-0201 | www.trystdelray.com

Kick back with the locals at this casual spot on the Avenue in Delray, a sibling of nearby 32 East, that pairs reasonably priced creative American small and large plates with a long list of craft brews and domestic vinos (available in half bottles); the small publike space, treated with brick walls, dark woods and low pendant lighting, gives off an unpretentious, convivial feel.

Two Georges Waterfront Grille *Seafood*

15 | 17 | 17 | $29

Boynton Beach | 728 Casa Loma Blvd. (SE 6th St.) | 561-736-2717 | www.twogeorgesrestaurant.com

Talk about "easygoing", even the random "friendly pelican" is part of the "bar scene" at this Boynton Beach "mainstay" where the drinks and "fabulous" views of the "boats going by" trump the midpriced but "just ok" seafood and "decent" service; with the recent acquisition and rebranding of the old Cove restaurant further down the Intracoastal in Deerfield Beach, now there really are two Georges.

264 the Grill *American*

17 | 18 | 20 | $44

Palm Beach | 264 S. County Rd. (Royal Palm Way) | 561-833-6444 | www.264thegrill.com

This "old-fashioned" gathering spot near Worth Avenue serving "basic" American "comfort food" plus Continental staples is "not as upscale as other Palm Beach spots", but it's also less expensive; "seniors" appreciate the "comfy" atmosphere, "friendly" vibe and "good-value" early-bird special, which also makes it a "convenient pre-show" stop; P.S. there's live jazz Wednesday and Sunday nights.

NEW Umi FishBar & Grill *Asian/Seafood*   ▽ 26 | 23 | 22 | $46
Palm Beach Gardens | Harborside Plaza | 2401 PGA Blvd. (Prosperity Farms Rd.) | 561-472-7900 | www.umifishbar.com

A "showstopper" from Carmine Giardini (Carmine's Coal Fired Pizza, CG Burgers), this upscale Palm Beach Gardens entry serves "creative" Asian fusion small and large plates plus "amazing" sushi and char-grilled Japanese robata items in a "striking", nightclubby space; a "loud" soundtrack fuels the "hot" bar scene – both inside and out on the deck overlooking the marina and waterway.

Uncle Joe's Chinese *Chinese*   20 | 10 | 18 | $24
Palm Beach Gardens | 436 / Northlake Blvd. (Military Trail) | 561-/99-9883 | www.unclejoeschinesefood.com

They do a "staggering" take-out business at this low-key "neighborhood" eatery in Palm Beach Gardens, a "solid choice" for "tasty" "Chinese-American" standards; "value" pricing and "quick" service complete the package.

Uncle Julio's *Tex-Mex*   18 | 19 | 19 | $32
Boca Raton | Mizner Park | 449 Plaza Real (bet. NE 3rd & 5th Sts.) | 561-300-3530 | www.unclejulios.com

"Displaced Texans" clomp into this Dallas-based chain link in Mizner Park for "big portions" of Tex-Mex eats at attractive prices; the jaded call the eats "ordinary", but the frozen drinks, a "spacious", "bustling" setting and a staff that "aims to please" are hits with many.

Uncle Tai's *Chinese*   23 | 21 | 21 | $44
Boca Raton | Boca Ctr. | 5250 Town Center Circle (S. Military Trail) | 561-368-8806 | www.uncle-tais.com

There are "no fortune cookies" at this "sophisticated" "gourmet Chinese" institution in Boca Raton, just "delicious", "upscale" cuisine that's "pricier than most", but "worth it"; "waiters in tuxes" wend their way through a "quiet and elegant" space that's very "relaxing", so it's "not the place for noisy kids."

Vagabondi 🚫Ⓜ *Italian*   24 | 18 | 24 | $52
West Palm Beach | 319 Belvedere Plaza | 319 Belvedere Rd. (S. Dixie Hwy.) | 561-249-2281 | www.vagabondirestaurant.com

"Word has gotten out" about this "terrific" "tiny" Northern Italian nook in West Palm Beach and its "well-thought-out" ingredients-driven menu on which "briny-fresh" fish is a standout; some advice: bring money because "pricing is high", bring a GPS or you might drive "right by" the "hard-to-find" strip mall and, lastly, reserve one of the 10 tables "well in advance."

Verdea Ⓜ *American*   - | - | - | E
Palm Beach Gardens | Embassy Suites | 4350 PGA Blvd. (N. Military Trail) | 561-691-3130 | www.verdearestaurant.com

It's a hunt to find this Palm Beach Gardens newcomer, but diners who ultimately arrive at the Embassy Suites Hotel are rewarded with an American menu that prominently features farm-to-fork vegetables, locally caught fish and sustainable meats in smart combinations; it's quite pricey, but the sophisticated modern dining room is dripping with class in the earth-toned drapes, banquettes, leather chairs and wood floors; P.S. the adjacent retail wine shop offers wines from its list.

Vic & Angelo's *Italian*
21 | 21 | 20 | $43

Palm Beach Gardens | PGA Commons | 4520 PGA Blvd. (Military Trail) | 561-630-9899
Delray Beach | 290 E. Atlantic Ave. (bet. 2nd & 3rd Aves.) | 561-278-9570
www.vicandangelos.com

"Lively", "noisy" and red-sauced all over, these "happening" Italian "mob scenes" serve classic dishes in "watch-out" portions plus "creative" pizzas; they're "great for large groups", in spite of "pricey" tabs and variable service ("attitude" vs. "attentive"); P.S. "hold onto your seat when the train comes rolling by" Delray's Atlantic Avenue link.

Village Tavern *American*
19 | 19 | 19 | $31

Boynton Beach | Renaissance Commons | 1880 N. Congress Ave. (Gateway Blvd.) | 561-853-0280 | www.villagetavern.com
See review in Ft. Lauderdale/Broward County Directory.

Villagio *Italian*
21 | 21 | 20 | $35

Boca Raton | Mizner Park | 344 Plaza Real (bet. NE 3rd & 5th Sts.) | 561-447-2257
See review in Miami/Dade County Directory.

Vivo Partenza *Italian*
∇ 23 | 25 | 21 | $54

Boca Raton | 1450 N. Federal Hwy. (Glades Rd.) | 561-750-2120 | www.vivobocaraton.com

"Glamorous" white furnishings, sheer curtains and loungey couches evoke "South Beach" in Boca (with "prices to match") at this "sophisticated" Italian from Tony Bova serving "inspired" regional favorites; add in a lovely patio and a vibrant bar with a "fun happy hour", and it's "definitely a place to impress."

Yard House ◐ *American*
19 | 19 | 19 | $31

Palm Beach Gardens | Downtown at the Gdns. | 11701 Lake Victoria Gardens Ave. (PGA Blvd.) | 561-691-6901 | www.yardhouse.com

A "gargantuan" suds selection (over 100 beers on tap) and "giant TVs" galore attract "mobs" of "lively, young" things on "game night" to this "booming" sports bar chain; an "encyclopedic" American menu delivered by a "fast" crew provides a solid food base for its "killer happy hour."

Ziree Thai & Sushi *Thai*
∇ 24 | 20 | 25 | $31

Delray Beach | 401 W. Atlantic Ave. (bet. NW 4th & 5th Aves.) | 561-276-6549 | www.zireethai.com

"Zireeously": trust pad Thai–loving surveyors and "make a beeline" to this "gem" in Delray Beach for "consistently great curry" and other "flavorful" favorites (even "decent quality" sushi); the bright atmosphere and service "with a smile" "make each meal a delight", and "inexpensive" tabs guarantee that the "wallet is happy too."

Zuccarelli's Italian Kitchen *Italian*

20 | 16 | 20 | $35

West Palm Beach | The Emporium Shoppes | 4595 Okeechobee Blvd. (N. Military Trail) | 561-686-7739 | www.zuccarellis.com

"Large portions" of "down-home" Southern Italian fare "just like mama used to make" feed the whole family at this "casual" "local" in West Palm Beach with "popular" prices; "neighborhood" folk appreciate the expanded outdoor seating options at its "new" digs across the street from its longtime location, even if they're "not as homey."

NAPLES
RESTAURANT
DIRECTORY

NAPLES

Absinthe *Mediterranean/Seafood* | 21 | 24 | 19 | $43 |

Naples | Collection at Vanderbilt | 2355 Vanderbilt Beach Rd. (Airport Pulling Rd.) | 239-254-0050 | www.absinthenaples.com

Diners "keep an eye out for the beautiful people" at this "swank" Naples Mediterranean at the Collection at Vanderbilt, where a "sophisticated", "ultramodern" setting gains "ambiance" from "vintage movies shown on the wall" and an "outdoor patio"; though "service is uneven", the seafood-centric menu of small and large plates offers lots of options "at an excellent price" and evenings bring "a large bar scene."

NEW Agave Southwestern Grill ● *Southwestern* | - | - | - | M |

Naples | 2380 Vanderbilt Beach Rd. (County Rd. 31) | 239-598-3473 | www.agavenaples.com

Brainchild of the husband-wife team behind Angelina's Ristorante in Bonita Springs, this zesty newcomer brings to Naples a midpriced, sizzling Southwestern menu with Mexican, Spanish and Native American influences; the spacious, sophisticated Southwestern setting sports a log-ceiling, an exhibition kitchen, wood-burning grill and a bar boasting one of the area's largest tequila collections (over 200), plus two outdoor seating areas.

Alexander's ⌧Ⓜ *American/European* | 22 | 20 | 23 | $40 |

Naples | 4077 Tamiami Trail N. (bet. Cypress Woods Dr. & Shady West Ln.) | 239-262-4999 | www.alexandersnaples.com

Known by locals as a "hidden secret", this Naples "favorite" offers "solid" New American–European fare delivered with "polished", "accommodating" service in a "clubby atmosphere"; the "inside is somewhat cramped" say a few, but a "lovely outdoor patio" and "wonderful early-bird specials" up the appeal; P.S. closed seasonally from June to late September.

Angelina's Ristorante *Italian* | 25 | 24 | 23 | $54 |

Bonita Springs | 24041 S. Tamiami Trail (Pelican Colony Blvd.) | 239-390-3187 | www.angelinasofbonitasprings.com

"Outrageously delicious" Italian fare is ferried by "efficient" servers at this "upscale, classy gem" in Bonita Springs; the "extraordinary surroundings" include "darkish woods", a "signature" wine tower (where a "wonderful selection" of bottles is stored), a "covered patio" and "intimate booths" whose curtains make them "great for that first date" – just remember to "bring your black card" because it's "pricey."

Arturo's *Italian*   22 | 21 | 23 | $41

Marco Island | 844 Bald Eagle Dr. (Collier Blvd.) | 239-642-0550 | www.arturosmarcoisland.com

"Old-time favorites" like a stuffed pork chop that's "a plate of heaven" keep fans coming to this "longtime favorite" Italian in a colonnaded Tuscanesque setting on Marco Island; a reasonably priced "wine list that complements the menu" and "outdoor seating" help make for a "perfect Southwest Florida night out", while the bar is "the locals' place to meet and greet" and the staff "ensures you have a great time."

AZN Azian Cuizine *Asian*   21 | 22 | 20 | $36

Naples | Mercato | 9118 Strada Pl. (Mercato Dr.) | 239-593-8818 | www.aznrestaurant.com

A "new favorite" on the Naples "scene", this "funky, fun, hip" spot "right in the middle of the Mercato" offers moderately priced "noodle dishes and Asian twists on steaks and seafood" plus "inventive" choices from the sushi bar; service is "friendly" and decor "Zen-like", though the atmosphere "can get busy and very loud" when filled with diners having a "fun night out."

Baleen *American/Seafood*   23 | 26 | 22 | $56

Naples | LaPlaya Beach & Golf Resort | 9891 Gulf Shore Dr. (Vanderbilt Beach Rd.) | 239-598-5707 | www.laplayaresort.com

"Everyone deserves to be spoiled at least once" at this "Gulf-side favorite" in Naples' LaPlaya Beach & Golf Resort where a "dimly lit" "beautiful setting" "opens up to magnificent views" of the sand, sea and sunset; regulars cite "well-prepared" American seafood and "knowledgeable service" but caution that this "bliss on the beach" doesn't come cheap.

Bamboo Café *French*   21 | 18 | 20 | $43

Naples | 755 12th Ave. S. (8th St.) | 239-643-6177 | www.bamboocafefrenchhomecooking.com

"Near City Dock" "in historic Downtown Naples", this French bistro "gem" offers a "change of pace" with its "great mussels" and escargots plus "interesting Moroccan tagines for more curious palates"; though some say the setting is "not much on atmosphere", the owners are "lovely" and tabs don't break the bank.

Bar Louie ◐ *American*   17 | 17 | 17 | $26

Ft. Myers | Gulf Coast Town Ctr. | 10035 Gulf Center Dr. (Alico Rd.) | 239-432-0389 | www.barlouieamerica.com

See review in Palm Beach Directory.

Bay House *Southern*   22 | 23 | 22 | $49

Naples | 799 Walkerbilt Rd. (Tamiami Trail N.) | 239-591-3837 | www.bayhousenaples.com

"The calming view" looking out on the Cocohatchee River at this Naples "local find" prompts regulars to "enjoy drinks outdoors" before heading in to the "romantic main dining room" for a "new take on Southern cooking" that's "pricey" but complemented by an "outstanding wine list and friendly service" plus a "beautiful fireplace" in winter; P.S. a recent renovation (and expansion of its bar) is not reflected in the Decor score.

Bha Bha Persian Bistro Ⓜ *Iranian/Persian*   24 | 20 | 23 | $40

Naples | 847 Vanderbilt Beach Rd. (Vanderbilt Dr.) | 239-594-5557 | www.bhabhapersianbistro.com

"Intensely flavored" Persian fare whisks surveyors "a world away" from the "storefront" setting of this "rare treat in Naples" that "always satisfies" with midpriced dishes such as "great lamb" and "sauces that are worthy of extra pieces of pita"; the modern decor with Mideastern touches is "pleasant" and "service is friendly and attentive", while Saturday night "belly dancing" adds extra ambiance.

Bistro 41 *American*   24 | 21 | 22 | $38

Ft. Myers | Bell Tower Shops | 13499 S. Cleveland Ave. (Daniels Pkwy.) | 239-466-4141 | www.bistro41.com

This "favorite" at Ft. Myers' Bell Tower Shops is a "sure hit for lunch or dinner" with its "consistent" American fare and wine selection ferried by servers who are "always friendly and attentive"; the "smart", "stylish" setting offers "comfortable" "indoor and outdoor seating", and the "$41 per couple" special that includes wine "can't be beat."

Bleu Provence *French*   27 | 24 | 26 | $57

Naples | 1234 Eighth St. S. (12th Ave.) | 239-261-8239 | www.bleuprovencenaples.com

"*C'est très bon!*" crow enthusiasts of this Naples "labor of love" that "enchants" with "consistent" French fare spanning "many of the traditional bistro dishes"; "from the moment you walk in, you're welcomed and delighted" by the "exceptional" staff and "handsome" Provençal decor, and while it's "pricey", there's "a fantastic early-bird special"; P.S. "in nice weather", try for the "wonderful" garden.

Blue Heron *Continental*   ▽ 27 | 21 | 25 | $73

Naples | 387 Capri Blvd. (County Rd. 952) | 239-394-6248 | www.the-blue-heron.com

Despite its Naples address, this "charming Old Florida–style" "waterside" Continental is located on the Isles of Capri near Marco Island, a setting that surveyors find "perfect for romantic occasions" with "picturesque views" as a backdrop for "all-inclusive meals" of "appetizer, soup, salad, main course and dessert" (you can also stop by just for drinks and apps); the quarters are "small" and the service is "excellent" plus "you can still wear shorts", so "what more can you ask?"; P.S. closed seasonally August through late September.

Blue Pointe Oyster Bar & Seafood Grill *Seafood/Steak*   24 | 20 | 23 | $33

Ft. Myers | Bell Tower Shops | 13499 S. Cleveland Ave. (Daniels Pkwy.) | 888-456-3463 | www.bluepointerestaurant.com

"Excellent" "oysters and other fresh seafood" are the big draws, though "it's hard not to fill up on the homemade bread served warm" at this Ft. Myers seafooder that's "lost in the back of a shopping center"; boosting the "good value" are improved Food and Service scores, plus "terrific outdoor dining for lunch or dinner."

Blue Water Bistro *Seafood*   23 | 23 | 22 | $44

Estero | Coconut Point Mall | 23151 Village Shops Way (Tamiami Trail) | 239-949-2583 | www.bluewaterbistro.net

"Mix and match wildly varied (flown in fresh daily) fish, sauces and sides" to pair with "generous" cocktails and "fairly priced" wines at this seafooder in Estero's Coconut Point Mall where the ocean-themed decor is "fabulous" and service is "friendly"; those who find the room too "loud" can "sit outside to enjoy the weather and the people-watching."

Blu Sushi *Japanese*   24 | 24 | 22 | $35

Ft. Myers | Gulf Coast Town Ctr. | 10045 Gulf Center Dr. (Ben Hill Griffin Pkwy.) | 239-334-2583
Ft. Myers | 13451 McGregor Blvd. (Cypress Lake Dr.) | 239-489-1500
www.blusushi.com

"Appearances mean everything and that includes the food" at this "happening" Japanese Ft. Myers duo that draws a "young and rowdy crowd" for "spendy" sushi and "great cocktails"; servers are "friendly" and the settings are "chicly decorated" but can get "loud and clubby" – "especially later" in the evening.

⊠ Bonefish Grill *Seafood*   22 | 19 | 21 | $36

Naples | 1500 5th Ave. S. (Davis Blvd.) | 239-417-1212
Bonita Springs | 26381 S. Tamiami Trail (Bonita Bay Blvd.) | 239-390-9208
Ft. Myers | 14261 S. Tamiami Trail (Hyde Park Dr.) | 239-489-1240
www.bonefishgrill.com
See review in Ft. Lauderdale/Broward County Directory.

NEW Bratta's Piano Bar &   - | - | - | M
Ristorante *American/Italian*

Ft. Myers | 12984 S. Cleveland Ave. (bet. Kenwood Ln. & 7 Lakes Blvd.) | 239-204-2020 | www.brattasristorante.com

This stylish, clubby piano bar recently debuted with a flourish in Ft. Myers, offering a midpriced Italian and American menu of ribstickers that ably dispatch hunger (sweet tooths simply must try the 'Grand Finale', a mini chocolate piano filled with fresh berries and espresso mousse); other draws are the nightly live music, exceptional happy-hour deals and the Sunday brunch buffet.

BrickTop's *American*   22 | 21 | 23 | $37

Naples | Waterside Shops | 5555 Tamiami Trail N. (West Blvd.) | 239-596-9112 | www.bricktops.com

Located at Naples' Waterside Shops, this American chain link with a "friendly staff and ambiance" in a "casual" modern setting offers a "moderately priced" "varied menu" plus additional seating "outside or in the bar"; it "hops at happy hour", and in season, better "be prepared for a long wait."

Brio Tuscan Grille *Italian*
23 | 23 | 23 | $38

Naples | Waterside Shops | 5505 Tamiami Trail N. (Pine Ridge Rd.) |
239-593-5319 | www.brioitalian.com

"Always crowded" thanks to its location at the "upscale Waterside
Shops" near the Naples Philharmonic Center, this "popular" outpost
of an Italian chain turns out fare that "won't disappoint" in a "comfortable" Tuscan setting tended by "upbeat servers"; adding to the
appeal is "wonderful" outdoor seating "near the bar" where patrons
say some of the "most beautiful" locals hang.

Bubble Room *American*
19 | 25 | 22 | $37

Captiva Island | 15001 Captiva Dr. (Andy Rosse Ln.) | 239-472-5558 |
www.bubbleroomrestaurant.com

"Eating takes a backseat to gawking at the artwork", "collectibles from
every era" and year-round "Christmas decorations" at this midpriced "retro-kitsch" "institution" on Captiva Island that "brings out
the kid in everyone" with its "patch-emblazoned" staffers "dressed
as scouts" who "cheerfully serve" "solid" American fare and "over-
the-top" cakes; P.S. "if you're looking for a quiet place, this is not it!"

Café & Bar Lurcat *American*
26 | 24 | 24 | $51

Naples | 494 Fifth Ave. S. (5th St.) | 239-213-3357 | www.cafelurcat.com
Whether you go for the "vibrant" "bar-and-tapas scene downstairs", the "upstairs fine dining", a seat outside at street level or the
"magical" balcony, you're in for a "hip" time at this "lovely" "see-
and-be-seen place for Naples' beautiful people"; as for the "pricey"
New American fare, it's "enticing", "unique", "well prepared" and
conveyed via a "friendly, helpful" staff; P.S. "don't miss" the warm
cinnamon donuts for dessert.

Campiello Ristorante *Italian*
25 | 25 | 24 | $50

Naples | 1177 Third St. S. (Broad Ave.) | 239-435-1166 |
www.campiello.damico.com

Voted the area's Most Popular eatery, this "always crowded" "Naples
landmark" offers an "outstanding" Italian menu with "something for
everyone", e.g. "inspired wood-fired pizzas, original pastas, distinctive appetizers and delicious wines", in a "noisy" dining room with
an "open kitchen", a "swinging bar" and on "the most happening patio in town"; "service can be rushed at times", but it's mostly "spectacular", and though it's "expensive", if you want to "ogle" the
"chichi set", this is the place.

Cantina Laredo *Mexican*
20 | 20 | 19 | $33

Ft. Myers | 5200 Big Pine Way (Cleveland Ave.) | 239-415-4424 |
www.cantinalaredo.com
See review in Palm Beach Directory.

☑ Capital Grille *Steak*
26 | 25 | 26 | $65

Naples | Mercato | 9005 Mercato Dr. (Tamiami Trail) | 239-254-0640 |
www.thecapitalgrille.com

Respondents say this "consistent" Naples link in the "highbrow" national steakhouse chain "gets it right every time", with "outstanding"

chops and sides and a "great" wine list (oenophiles suggest you "splurge on one of the big reds") presented by "courteous" servers who "know how to make an evening special"; true, you might have to "take out a second mortgage", but most feel "it's worth every dollar."

Charlie Chiang's *Chinese*   24 | 21 | 21 | $35
Naples | 12200 Tamiami Trail N. (Shores Ave.) | 239-593-6688 | www.charliechiangs.com
"Outstanding high-end Chinese" dishes including "some interesting (not your usual fare) choices" at moderate prices make for "excellent quality and value" at this Naples outpost of a mini-chain say fans who also praise the "efficient" service and "beautiful location on the water"; P.S. reservations, "particularly in season", can help avoid "long waits."

☑ Cheesecake Factory *American*   23 | 21 | 22 | $30
Naples | Coastland Ctr. Mall | 2090 Tamiami Trail N. (Golden Gate Pkwy.) | 239-435-1580 | www.thecheesecakefactory.com
"If you leave here hungry, it's your own fault" opine patrons of this Naples national chain link, because not only is there "a lot of variety" on its "dependable" American menu, but the portions are "gigantic" – indeed, you'll probably have "enough for leftovers", especially if you "leave room" for the "sublime" cheesecake; "reasonable prices", "nice ambiance" and "speedy", "observant" staffers complete the picture.

Chip's Sanibel Steakhouse *Seafood/Steak*   23 | 23 | 24 | $45
Sanibel | 1473 Periwinkle Way (Main St.) | 239-472-5700 | www.thesanibelsteakhouse.com
"Great steaks" and "tasty fish dishes" are served in a "refined and quiet" setting at this Sanibel stalwart that fans assure is "a better option than most of the chains"; though some find it a bit "pricey", "you really get a feel of South Florida", and it's also "a good bet" for a "romantic" dinner.

Chops City Grill *Seafood/Steak*   25 | 23 | 24 | $54
Naples | 837 Fifth Ave. S. (bet. 8th & 9th Sts.) | 239-262-4677
Bonita Springs | Brooks Grand Plaza | 8200 Health Center Blvd. (bet. Coconut Rd. & US 41) | 239-992-4677
www.chopscitygrill.com
A "handsome, upscale crowd" creates a "sophisticated buzz" at this "fashionable" Bonita Springs Naples duo, serving "beautifully plated", "delish" steaks, seafood and some sushi too; although it's "too noisy" for some, most just revel in the "fast-paced" atmosphere, which comes complete with "dynamite drinks", a "huge wine-by-the-glass selection", "sharp service" and "high prices."

Cloyde's Steak & Lobster House *Seafood/Steak*   22 | 21 | 21 | $49
Naples | Vill. on Venetian Bay | 4050 Gulf Shore Blvd. N. (Park Shore Dr.) | 239-261-0622 | www.cloydes.com
With its "view of Venetian Bay", this Naples staple is "always a pleasure", offering a "combination of steak and seafood" (including live Maine lobster) at "reasonable prices" in a traditional steakhouse

setting; "happy-hour bargains" are also an attraction, as is the "great burger" "available in the bar."

Côte d'Azur Ⓜ *French*   27 | 22 | 26 | $61

Naples | 11224 Tamiami Trail N. (bet. Immokalee & Walkerbilt Rds.) | 239-597-8867 | www.cotedazurrestaurant.com

It's "just a storefront in a strip mall", but once inside this "intimate" French bistro, you'll find Provençal fare so "skillfully prepared, artfully presented" and *magnifique* tasting, it earns Naples' No. 1 Food score; a "superb" staff and setting that, while "not fancy", is "cute" enough, with a blue-and-white "outdoor-cafe" look plus a real patio, are part of the "simply outstanding" package, which is matched by "special-occasion" pricing.

Cru Restaurant ◑ *American*   24 | 21 | 21 | $47

Ft. Myers | Bell Tower Shops | 13499 S. Cleveland Ave. (Daniels Pkwy.) | 239-466-3663 | www.eatcru.com

"Surprisingly sophisticated despite its mall location", this Ft. Myers New American under chef-owner Harold Balink proffers "wonderfully creative" small and large plates with global touches; though some find it "pricey", regulars give kudos to the service and wine list plus a happy hour that is "rocking every day", making it a "place to be seen."

Doc Ford   22 | 22 | 21 | $28
Fort Myers Beach *Floribbean/Seafood*

Ft. Myers Beach | 708 Fishermans Wharf (Old San Carlos Blvd.) | 239-765-9660 | www.docfords.com

Doc Ford's Sanibel Rum Bar & Grille *Floribbean/Seafood*

Sanibel | 975 Rabbit Rd. (Sanibel-Captiva Rd.) | 239-472-8311 | www.docfordssanibel.com

This Floribbean duo works "if you like rum", are "a fan of the books" (the 'Doc Ford' series by Randy Wayne White) or crave "reasonably priced" seafood that's "kicked up a notch" with "Caribbean and South American flavors"; service varies, but the Sanibel location has over two dozen TVs for sports fans, while Ft. Myers Beach offers "live music and a beautiful location" with a "view of the shrimp boats on Estero Bay."

Dock at Crayton Cove *Seafood*   20 | 20 | 21 | $33

Naples | 845 12th Ave. S. (8th St.) | 239-263-9940 | www.dockcraytoncove.com

"Great for an outdoor lunch with a pitcher of margaritas overlooking the docks", this "Naples institution" is "Old Florida at its best", with a "covered but still open-air" setting that makes "you feel like you're on an island in the tropics"; it's also "great for kids" since the "casual" seafood menu is a "good value" and service is "friendly."

Escargot 41 *French*   26 | 22 | 25 | $63

Naples | Park Shore Shopping Ctr. | 4339 Tamiami Trail N. (Morningside Dr.) | 239-793-5000 | www.escargot41.com

"A hidden gem in the corner of a strip mall", this Naples bistro does "excellent" renditions of "classic French" fare, with a "delicious" "variety" of the namesake gastropods ("a full page" of the menu is "devoted just to them"), in a "quaint, quiet", "romantic setting" overseen by "friendly" owners; regulars advise "book way in advance during the season", "save room" for a soufflé and be prepared for an "expensive" check (it's "worth it").

⨕ Five Guys *Burgers*
20 | 10 | 16 | $13

NEW **Naples** | Marquesa Plaza | 13020 Livingston Rd. (Pine Ridge Rd.) | 239-261-5624

Naples | Gateway Shoppes | 13585 Tamiami Trail (Country Rd. 888) | 239-566-1200

Naples | Goodlette Corners | 1410 Pine Ridge Rd. (Goodlette-Frank Rd.) | 239-261-5603

NEW **Estero** | 23050 Via Villagio Pkwy. (Tamiami Trail) | 239-948-7106

Ft. Myers | Village Shoppes at Health Pk. | 16230 Summerlin Rd. (Bass Rd.) | 239-267-2813

Ft. Myers | The Forum | 3268 Forum Blvd. (Dynasty Rd.) | 239-936-4169
www.fiveguys.com

See review in Miami/Dade County Directory.

Fleming's Prime Steakhouse & Wine Bar *Steak*
25 | 23 | 24 | $57

Naples | 8985 Tamiami Trail N. (Vanderbilt Beach Rd.) | 239-598-2424 | www.flemingssteakhouse.com

See review in Miami/Dade County Directory.

Grill, The *Steak*
26 | 26 | 28 | $73

Naples | Ritz-Carlton Naples | 280 Vanderbilt Beach Rd. (Bay Colony Dr.) | 239-598-6644 | www.ritzcarlton.com

Everything about this Naples "paean to fine dining" is "so very Ritz", from the "remarkable" steaks and "vast wine list" to the "superb service" (voted Naples' best) and "luxurious" "clublike setting" (which takes the top spot for Decor); so even if it's pricey, it's tough to beat for an "elegant" meal.

NEW Grimaldi's Pizza *Pizza*
– | – | – | M

Ft. Myers | Bell Tower Plaza | 13499 S. Cleveland Ave. (Daniels Pkwy.) | 239-432-9767 | www.grimaldispizzeria.com

See review in Palm Beach Directory.

Grouper & Chips *Seafood*
24 | 12 | 22 | $22

Naples | 338 Ninth St. N. (3rd Ave.) | 239-643-4577 | www.grouperandchips.net

Expect "zero ambiance" at this "tiny" "Naples institution" that's "all about the food" and "a must-stop for anyone serious about fresh grouper"; a "real bargain" with an "easygoing" staff, it's "popular with tourists and locals alike" for its "locally caught" "beer-battered" fish, fries and "fantastic" "seafood platters."

Handsome Harry's Third Street Bistro *American*
21 | 22 | 22 | $49

Naples | 1205 Third St. S. (12th Ave.) | 239-434-6400 | www.handsomeharrys.com

A "younger crowd" hits this "loungelike" "hot spot" in Naples where the "pricey" American fare has "flair", "but the real attraction is the bar scene" with music some nights prompting "dancing under the stars" as "white lights" "twinkle in the trees"; midday diners say it's "always crowded for lunch" at the "trendy and friendly" "sidewalk cafe."

HB's on the Gulf *American/Seafood*   19 | 23 | 21 | $40

Naples | Naples Beach Hotel & Golf Club | 851 Gulf Shore Blvd. N. (8th Ave.) | 239-435-4347 | www.naplesbeachhotel.com

"People can't get enough" of the "fantastic sunsets" at this American seafooder at the Naples Beach Hotel where patrons suggest ordering "finger food and cocktails" "on the patio" as "the perfect way to watch the evening begin"; while some say the "spectacular setting" "overrides" the "dependable" fare, fans laud the staff (its Service rating has improved), and recommend it for a "fabulous lunch" or "romantic dinner."

I.M. Tapas *Spanish*   ∇ 25 | 19 | 23 | $47

Naples | 965 Fourth Ave. N. (bet. 9th & 10th Sts.) | 239-403-8272 | www.imtapas.com

"Hidden away on a small side street", this Naples "treasure" "wows" with Spanish tapas "lovingly and proudly prepared" with "top-notch ingredients" and "a creative touch"; the simple, intimate setting is a "good place to hang, talk and share", abetted by "great" Iberian wines and "excellent service."

Jolly Cricket *British*   20 | 21 | 21 | $34

Naples | 720 Fifth Ave. S. (8th St.) | 239-304-9460 | www.thejollycricket.com

It is indeed "jolly" at this Naples spot offering a "soothing ambiance along prestigious Fifth Avenue" via a British Colonial setting deemed "almost too nice for a gastropub" and a "varied menu" with global touches; "quick", "efficient" service and "reasonably priced" tabs are further draws, as is Sunday brunch; P.S. check the website for summer hours.

Kelly's Fish House Dining Room *Seafood*   21 | 17 | 21 | $40

Naples | 1302 Fifth Ave. S. (Goodlette-Frank Rd.) | 239-774-0494 | www.kellysfishhousediningroom.com

Fans of "simply cooked" seafood fill the seats of this Naples "last of the old-time fish houses" where a "location on the water" sets the stage for "fried fish done right" and specialties like "fresh-off-the-boat" stone crabs; the "friendly" staffers are "real pros", while "reasonable prices" and decor featuring the "requisite nets, flying fish and bumpers on the walls" complete the picture; P.S. closed during September.

Le Lafayette *French*   ∇ 25 | 24 | 23 | $61

Naples | 375 13th Ave. (3rd St.) | 239-403-7861 | www.lelafayette.com

Feel "transported to the South of France" at this "charming", "comfortable" venue in Naples, where the "beautiful" patio is the place to be for "excellently prepared" *plats* plus "great wines and desserts"; "but is it worth the price?" – *oui* say fans, "every cent", especially for the "fabulous Sunday brunch."

	FOOD	DECOR	SERVICE	COST

Mad Hatter *American*
▽ 26 | 23 | 25 | $47

Sanibel | 6467 Sanibel-Captiva Rd. (Mangrove Ln.) | 239-472-0033 |
www.madhatterrestaurant.com

An "innovative" "gourmet menu" draws enthusiasts to this "old
beach cottage" in Sanibel that "aspires to present serious American
fare" and succeeds with its "wonderful selection of fresh fish [and]
steaks" as well as "outstanding appetizers and desserts", plus service
to match; since you can "watch the sunset" while you dine, roman-
tics consider it "well worth the price."

Marek's Collier
▽ 24 | 20 | 22 | $47
House 🅂🅜 *Continental/Seafood*

Marco Island | 1121 Bald Eagle Dr. (Collier Blvd.) | 239-642-9948 |
www.mareksrestaurant.com

"Knowing the history of the building" – the circa-1882 home of
Captain Bill Collier – makes it even "more enjoyable" to dine on
chef/co-owner Peter Marek's "superb", "high-end" Continental cuisine say devotees of this "renowned" Marco Island seafooder; those
who find the experience in the "main room" "a bit stuffy" can head
to the "bistro next door" for a less-expensive and "more modern
menu" in a "smart-casual setting"; P.S. closed seasonally August
through mid-October.

McCormick & Schmick's *Seafood*
20 | 20 | 21 | $46

Naples | Mercato | 9114 Strada Pl. (Vanderbilt Beach Rd.) |
239-591-2299 | www.mccormickandschmicks.com
See review in Palm Beach Directory.

Melting Pot *Fondue*
19 | 18 | 20 | $42

Ft. Myers | 13251 McGregor Blvd. (College Pkwy.) | 239-481-1717 |
www.meltingpot.com
See review in Miami/Dade County Directory.

MiraMare Ristorante *Italian*
21 | 26 | 21 | $48

Naples | Vill. on Venetian Bay | 4236 Gulf Shore Blvd. N. (Park Shore Dr.) |
239-430-6273 | www.miramarenaples.com

With its "exquisite" location, this Venetian Bay Italian offers the
"best ambiance in Naples" contend patrons promising that when
"sitting out on the deck", "you'll think you're in Venice", "absent the
gondolas"; the "pricey" Italian fare "doesn't quite match" up to the
setting and you can "expect to wait" during season, but the staff will
"make you happy you came."

Mucky Duck 🅂 *Pub Food*
19 | 20 | 21 | $28

Captiva Island | 11546 Andy Rosse Ln. SW (Captiva Dr.) | 239-472-3434 |
www.muckyduck.com

"The fantastic view of the sunset from the beach just steps away" is
the big draw at this Captiva Island pub long "famous" as "a fun
beach bar" with a "playful" yet "attentive" staff and "reasonably
priced" eats including "reliable" burgers and "fried food"; sit "outdoors" or at a "window seat" inside, and "make sure to text your
friends at home so they can see you on the webcam."

M Waterfront Grille *Continental*
23 | 24 | 23 | $55

Naples | Vill. on Venetian Bay | 4300 Gulf Shore Blvd. N. (Park Shore Dr.) | 239-263-4421 | www.mwaterfrontgrille.com

Its "beautiful waterfront location" is just part of the appeal of this Continental in North Naples' Venetian Village shopping center where "competent and solicitous" service matches the "delightful" cuisine from a "creative" chef; "a knowledgeable wine manager" offering "very good recommendations" completes the package that's "not inexpensive but worth it."

Naples Tomato *American/Italian*
23 | 21 | 22 | $42

Naples | 14700 Tamiami Trail N. (Old 41) | 239-598-9800 | www.naplestomato.com

For "great antipasti" (including a mozzarella bar), "delicious" "homemade pasta", "excellent lasagna" and "terrific specials" that "always tempt", all at "good prices", this "busy", "casual" Naples American-Italian is "a wise and reliable choice"; indeed, most folks find "everything exemplary" here, including the "knowledgeable", "attentive" service and especially the "amazing" wine program, featuring a "huge" variety and enomatic dispensers.

Old Captiva House *Floribbean/Seafood*
∇ 22 | 18 | 23 | $43

Captiva Island | 'Tween Waters Inn | 15951 Captiva Dr. (Raige Ct.) | 239-472-5161

"Just across the street" from the beach, this Captiva Island stalwart situated in the 'Tween Waters Inn suits special occasions with its Old Florida ambiance and "nicely presented" "excellent, creative" Floribbean cuisine featuring "fresh local fish"; live piano and views from the Sunset Room add to the appeal.

Outback Steakhouse *Steak*
18 | 15 | 19 | $31

Naples | 4910 Tamiami Trail N. (Castello Dr.) | 239-434-7100
Bonita Springs | 27230 Bay Landing Dr. (W. Terry St.) | 239-948-3575
NEW **Ft. Myers** | Gulf Coast Town Ctr. | 10045 Gulf Center Dr. (Royal Queen Blvd.) | 239-433-0097
www.outback.com

See review in Miami/Dade County Directory.

Pazzo! Cucina Italiana *Italian*
24 | 21 | 23 | $46

Naples | 853 Fifth Ave. S. (9th St.) | 239-434-8494 | www.pazzoitaliancafe.com

Part of the Chops City Grill family of restaurants, this "upbeat" Naples "standby" serves "moderately priced", "consistent" and "delicious upscale Italian" fare in a "chic setting" complete with sidewalk seating that offers "the best of people-watching"; the staff is "patient, attentive and always has a smile" and it's convenient for "a walk to the beach after dinner", just be sure to make "a reservation during season."

P.F. Chang's China Bistro *Chinese*
24 | 23 | 24 | $32

Naples | Granada Shoppes | 10840 Tamiami Trail N. (Immokalee Rd.) | 239-596-2174

(continued)

P.F. Chang's China Bistro

Ft. Myers | Gulf Coast Town Ctr. | 10081 Gulf Center Dr.
(Royal Queen Blvd.) | 239-590-9197
www.pfchangs.com

"Living up to its reputation", this "whimsical, exotic" chain duo's "yummy" "fusion of Chinese and American tastes" makes it a "step above your everyday Asian cuisine" ("love those lettuce wraps!"); there's "sometimes a lengthy wait for a table" and usually lots of "noise", but "well-paced, attentive" service and relatively "low prices" compensate.

Pincher's Crab Shack *Seafood*   20 | 18 | 21 | $28

Naples | Tin City | 1200 Fifth Ave S. (12th St.) | 239-434-6616
Bonita Springs | Bonita Crossing Plaza | 28580 Bonita Crossings Blvd.
(Lake Shore Dr.) | 239-948-1313
NEW **Ft. Myers** | Gulf Coast Town Ctr. | 10029 Gulf Center Dr.
(Alico Rd.) | 239-415-4040
Ft. Myers | McGregor Point | 15271 McGregor Blvd. (Iona Rd.) |
239-415-4009
Ft. Myers Beach | 18100 San Carlos Blvd. (Siesta Dr.) |
239-415-8973
Ft. Myers Beach | 6890 Estero Blvd. (Lenell Rd.) | 239-463-2909
www.pincherscrabshack.com

"Famous for stone crab legs", this "rustic/casual" Southwest Florida chain is "packed" to the gills in season with fans of the specialty and other "reliable" fare at "reasonable prices" including oysters and "mostly fried" seafood; the "laid-back" digs can get "a little noisy", but the staff is "always right on top of things."

Piola *Pizza*   22 | 17 | 19 | $26

Naples | Mercato | 9118 Strada Pl. (Vanderbilt Beach Rd.) |
239-592-5056 | www.piola.it
See review in Miami/Dade County Directory.

Prawnbroker *Seafood*   25 | 19 | 24 | $38

Ft. Myers | 13451-16 McGregor Blvd. (Cypress Lake Dr.) |
239-489-2226

Timbers Restaurant & Fish Market *Seafood*

Sanibel | 703 Tarpon Bay Rd. (Sanibel-Captiva Rd.) | 239-395-2722
www.prawnbroker.com

"Busy and big", these seafood chain links in Ft. Myers and Sanibel are among "the best" for "fresh fish with simple and honest preparations" such as the house specialty "crunchy grouper" in "portions that are more than enough"; "moderate prices" and "friendly service" further explain why regulars advise that you "must make reservations in winter."

Ridgway Bar & Grill *American/Continental*   23 | 22 | 23 | $45

Naples | 1300 Third St. S. (13th Ave.) | 239-262-5500 |
www.ridgwaybarandgrill.com

Chef/co-owner Tony Ridgway's Old Naples "favorite" is "simply lovely", offering a "well-executed menu" of New American–

Continental dishes and "quite a good wine list" plus service that's "excellent without being fawning"; while wallet-watchers flinch at the "big prices", the setting is "relaxed" indoors and out, with "a pleasant dinner made even better by the piano player" some nights.

Riverwalk *American/Seafood*   20 | 20 | 21 | $35

Naples | Tin City | 1200 Fifth Ave. S. (12th St.) | 239-263-2734 | www.riverwalktincity.com

Some say "it's all about the view over the water and boats" at this Naples American at Tin City, while others "always enjoy" the "great Florida seafood nicely prepared" and served in "good portions" by a "hustling" staff; the fare is "fairly priced", though the impatient caution that "no reservations" means long "waits in high times."

Roy's *Hawaiian*   26 | 24 | 25 | $52

Naples | 475 Bayfront Pl. (Goodlette-Frank Rd.) | 239-261-1416
Bonita Springs | Promenade in Bonita Springs | 26831 S. Bay Dr. (S. Tamiami Trail) | 239-498-7697
www.roysrestaurant.com

"You can't go wrong" at these outposts of Roy Yamaguchi's chain in Naples and Bonita Springs that get kudos for their "creative" Hawaiian fusion cuisine – including "incredible fish" – and "bustling, vibrant" dining rooms; service is "outstanding" all around and, yes, it's "expensive, but you get what you pay for", even more so if you go for the seasonal prix fixe "value."

Ruth's Chris Steak House *Steak*   26 | 24 | 25 | $65

Estero | Coconut Point Mall | 23151 Village Shops Way (Tamiami Trail) | 239-948-8888 | www.ruthschris.com

What some deem "the standard for an outstanding steak experience", this Estero chain outpost offers its "huge" portions of "sizzling", buttery beef in an "elegant" setting with "attentive service"; "expensive" pricing means it's the kind of place you go "for a celebratory meal", but for everyday noshing, i.e. "more reasonable" tabs, "try the happy-hour bar menu."

Sale e Pepe *Italian*   24 | 26 | 25 | $75

Marco Island | Marco Beach Ocean Resort | 480 S. Collier Blvd. (Spruce Ave.) | 239-393-1600 | www.sale-e-pepe.com

"Once you've found it, you will want to return often" to this "elegant", "spectacular spot" at Marco Beach Ocean Resort, where "courteous, helpful" staffers proffer "outstanding" Italian cuisine and an "extensive wine list" that suits "every budget" (the fare is across-the-board pricey); many find the "heavily" decorated interior "beautiful", but most prefer the "large patio" for a "fabulous seafront lunch" or a "sunset" dinner.

Sandy Butler *American*   ▽ 25 | 20 | 24 | $40

Ft. Myers | 17650 San Carlos Blvd. (Broadway Ave.) | 239-482-6765 | www.sandybutler.com

"Browse the gourmet offerings at the store next door while waiting" to be seated at this Ft. Myers American with an "interesting concept" that also strives to "raise the bar on dining close to the beach" by offering "outstanding" seafood-centric dishes at prices that can be a "bargain"; a room that's "quiet and comfortable" and an "amazing staff" add to the appeal.

Sea Salt *Italian/Seafood*   23 | 23 | 22 | $63

Naples | 1186 Third St. S. (12th Ave.) | 239-434-7258 | www.seasaltnaples.com

"Hands-on" chef-owner Fabrizio Aielli presides over this Naples "hot spot", incorporating "unusual ingredients" in "pricey" Italian creations that include "incredibly fresh seafood and pasta" dishes complemented by "an amazing wine list"; surveyors say "service varies wildly", but the "stylish" setting offers three seating options: a formal room, chef's table and more casual "outdoor" tables for "people-watching."

Shula's Steak House *Steak*   23 | 21 | 22 | $65

Naples | Hilton Naples & Towers | 5111 Tamiami Trail N. (Seagate Dr.) | 239-430-4999 | www.donshula.com
See review in Miami/Dade County Directory.

Snook Inn *American/Seafood*   20 | 17 | 20 | $29

Marco Island | 1215 Bald Eagle Dr. (Palm St.) | 239-394-3313 | www.snookinn.com

A "great old-time fish house" featuring "views of the water with the odd dolphin and manatee passing by", this "laid-back" Marco Island fixture is "favored by the locals" (some "come by boat") as "a great place to spend a lazy Sunday afternoon" "in flip-flops and shorts" dining on "fresh" American seafood; service that's "consistently efficient" and nightly "music in the outside bar" are extra draws.

St. George & The Dragon 🅂 🅼 *Steak*   20 | 18 | 20 | $46

Naples | 936 Fifth Ave. S. (9th St.) | 239-262-6546

With decor that reminds some of "an old wooden ship" and others of "1965", this "quiet and dimly lit" Naples "standby" serves up "consistent" steakhouse fare such as prime rib and "escargots in the shell" at prices that are "slightly less expensive" than the big chains; don't expect anything "fancy" – although a "jacket" is required in the main dining room in season.

Stir Crazy *Asian*   19 | 17 | 18 | $25

Estero | Coconut Pt. | 23106 Fashion Dr. (Sandy Ln.) | 239-498-6430 | www.stircrazy.com
See review in Ft. Lauderdale/Broward County Directory.

Stoney's Steakhouse *Steak*   23 | 22 | 24 | $61

Naples | 403 Bayfront Pl. (Goodlette-Frank Rd.) | 239-435-9353 | www.stoneyssteakhouse.com

Whether for "romance or family", it's "fine dining for everyone" at this big-"city-style steakhouse" in Naples where "surprisingly good", "reasonably priced" cuts of beef are the main attraction and portions are "big" ("so be sure to share"); there's a "nice local" crowd and live music in the piano bar Fridays and Saturdays; P.S. closes for September.

	FOOD	DECOR	SERVICE	COST

Strip House *Steak*
▽ 23 | 23 | 20 | $58

Naples | Naples Grande Beach Resort | 475 Seagate Dr. (West Blvd.) |
239-598-9600 | www.striphouse.com

"Bringing the Big Apple to Naples", this "dark, adult restaurant" doles
out "perfectly cooked steaks and great sides" in a "beautiful room" be-
decked with "red velvet drapes, flocked wallpaper" and "classic nude
pics"; all in all, it's quite a "surprise for a hotel-lobby restaurant", although the prices are as high as one would expect for the genre.

Sunshine Seafood Café *Seafood*
▽ 24 | 17 | 21 | $34

Captiva Island | 14900 Captiva Dr. (Laika Ln.) | 239-472-6200 |
www.captivaislandinn.com
Ft. Myers | 8750 Gladiolus Dr. (Winkler Rd.) | 239-489-2233 |
www.sunshineseafoodftmyers.com

"Unpretentious yet classy", this Southwest Florida duo specializes
in "reasonably priced" "fresh fish, delicious salads and desserts"
with an "attention to detail and quality" that its admirers say "truly
stands out"; the "little" Captiva Island setting is "cute" and "family"-
friendly, while the much larger Ft. Myers branch includes a lounge.

Table Apart, A 🖫Ⓜ *Eclectic*
25 | 16 | 25 | $40

Bonita Springs | 4295 Bonita Beach Rd. (bet. Valley & Vanderbilt Drs.) |
239-221-8540 | www.atableapart.com

There's "nothing fancy but the food" at this "neat little" "hidden gem
of Bonita Springs" known for its Eclectic "Hawaiian-French" "fusion
menu with excellent sauces and always-fresh meats and fish";
"pleasant service", a "comfortable", casual room and moderate
prices seal the deal; P.S. it's "not open off season" and you "must
make a reservation" in season.

Tommy Bahama's
Restaurant & Bar *Seafood*
21 | 22 | 21 | $42

Naples | 1220 Third St. S. (12th Ave.) | 239-643-6889 |
www.tommybahama.com

Fans of Tommy Bahama's "island-style" clothes "love" this "festive"
"indoor/outdoor" eatery where a "young crowd" comes to "hang
with the beautiful people of Naples" over "creative", "albeit pricey",
"tropical"-inspired seafood dishes and "wonderful drinks" – "the more
exotic" "the better"; "a casual atmosphere", "live music" and "servers
who make you feel welcome" further explain why it "gets crowded."

Truluck's *Seafood*
26 | 24 | 26 | $67

Naples | 698 Fourth Ave. S. (7th St.) | 239-530-3131 |
www.trulucks.com

Devotees say they're "truly lucky" to have this Naples chain link specializing in seafood that "couldn't be fresher" (it "has its own
fishery") – particularly "best-in-town" stone crabs ("as many as you
can devour" on Monday nights in season) – despite the fact that the
"deep menu" is "not for the faint of wallet"; "incomparable service"
and a "stylish" setting are two more reasons it's so "popular", so be
sure to "make a reservation well in advance" or try to sidle up to the
bar for the "great happy hour", when "all drinks are half-off."

	FOOD	DECOR	SERVICE	COST

USS Nemo *Seafood*
27 | 19 | 23 | $49

Naples | 3745 Tamiami Trail N. (Frank Whiteman Blvd.) | 239-261-6366 | www.ussnemorestaurant.com

"Locals" "would go 20,000 leagues" for the "to-die-for miso-glazed sea bass" and other "sublime" seafood with "exotic" Pacific Rim "flair", complemented by "delightful" "wine, beer and sake", at this "big hit" in Naples; "don't expect much sizzle" in the "nondescript strip-center" location or "undersea" decor theme ("they want you to feel like you're eating in the cramped quarters of a submarine", and it's "noisy" too), but do count on "friendly service" from the "knowledgeable" staff and "charming owners"; P.S. "make reservations or be prepared to wait."

Veranda, The Ⓢed *Southern*
26 | 26 | 26 | $46

Ft. Myers | 2122 Second St. (Broadway) | 239-332-2065 | www.verandarestaurant.com

"A wonderfully old-fashioned treat", this Ft. Myers "tradition" for "leisurely" "special occasions" boasts a "plantationlike" feel thanks to its "quaint", "elegant" setting in two early-1900s homes with a "beautiful" dining garden and what may be "the most romantic piano bar in the world"; what's more, "everything is scrumptious" on the "gourmet" Southern menu, "impeccable service" comes from a "professional staff" and, best of all, it's only "a bit pricey."

Vergina *Italian*
19 | 22 | 20 | $48

Naples | 700 Fifth Ave. S. (bet. 6th & 8th Sts.) | 239-659 7008 | www.verginarestaurant.com

Fans say this Naples local "favorite on Fifth" has "staying power" thanks to its "unusual pasta specials" and other "pricey" Italian fare coupled with "very good" service in a "pretty" setting; doubters who claim it "could be better" "skip the food and go for drinks at the beautiful bar" before they "dance the night away" to "live" music.

Wylds Café *American*
▽ 26 | 16 | 23 | $43

Bonita Springs | 4271 Bonita Beach Rd. (bet. Valley & Vanderbilt Drs.) | 239-947-0408 | www.wyldscafe.com

It's "a little out of the way" (some say "in the middle of nowhere") and "worth the drive" to this Bonita Springs "undiscovered gem" aver fans of its "consistently excellent" "New American" fare made with "high-quality" ingredients; the setting is nothing fancy, but the staff is "great" and it's "one of the best values around"; P.S. closes for the summer and reopens in October.

Yabba Island Grill *Caribbean/Seafood*
20 | 22 | 22 | $38

Naples | 711 Fifth Ave. S. (8th St.) | 239-262-5787 | www.yabbaislandgrill.com

"Delicious, colorful and fun" sums up the appeal of this "upscale-casual" Naples "inside/outside" Caribbean seafooder offering "fantastic" jerk chicken and other "interesting" "island fare" plus a "huge selection of rum" that makes for "great tropical cocktails"; service also "keeps everyone happy", and the party vibe kicks up with a late-night DJ Friday and Saturday.

INDEXES

All restaurants are in Miami/Dade County unless otherwise noted
(B=Broward County; K=Key West; N=Naples; P=Palm Beach County).

Latest openings, menus, photos and more free at ZAGAT.com   247

Cuisines

Includes names, locations and Food ratings.

AMERICAN

Absinthe	**Boca/P**	18
Alexander's	**Naples/N**	22
Ambry German	**Ft. Laud/B**	21
Aruba Beach	**Laud-by-Sea/B**	17
Atrio	**Brickell**	22
Baleen	**Naples/N**	23
Bar Louie	**multi.**	17
☑ Barton G.	**SoBe**	22
Bentley's	**Islamorada/K**	23
Big City Tav.	**Ft. Laud/B**	19
Big Pink	**SoBe**	20
Bimini Boatyard	**Ft. Laud/B**	17
Bin 595	**Plantation/B**	22
Bistro 41	**Ft. Myers/N**	24
☑ Bistro Mezz.	**Ft. Laud/B**	26
Bizcaya	**Coco Grove**	24
NEW Blade/Vida	**Miami Bch**	-
NEW Bratta's	**Ft. Myers/N**	-
Brewzzi	**multi.**	17
BrickTop's	**Naples/N**	22
Bubble Room	**Captiva Is/N**	19
Burger & Beer	**multi.**	23
By Word/Mouth	**Oakland Pk/B**	25
Café & Bar Lurcat	**Naples/N**	26
Café at Books & Books	**multi.**	21
☑ Café Chardonnay	**Palm Bch Gdns/P**	25
NEW Café Jamm	**Ft. Laud/B**	-
NEW Cafe L'Attico	**Miami Bch**	-
☑ Cafe Marquesa	**Key W./K**	28
☑ Cafe Maxx	**Pompano Bch/B**	27
Caffe Luna Rosa	**Delray Bch/P**	20
Camille's	**Key W./K**	22
☑ Canyon	**Ft. Laud/B**	27
NEW Carillon	**Miami Bch**	-
Casablanca	**Ft. Laud/B**	21
Charley's Crab	**Palm Bch/P**	20
Chart House	**Coco Grove**	20
☑ Cheesecake	**multi.**	20
☑ Cheesecake	**Naples/N**	23
CheeseMe	**Loc Varies**	-
City Diner	**W. Palm/P**	20
NEW City Hall	**Wynwood**	-
Clarke's	**SoBe**	22
Coconuts	**Ft. Laud/B**	23
NEW Crumb/Parchment	**Design Dist**	-
Cru Restaurant	**Ft. Myers/N**	24
Dada	**Delray Bch/P**	20
Dave's Last	**Lake Worth/P**	17
NEW Deck 84	**Delray Bch/P**	19
NEW DIG	**Delray Bch/P**	-
Dune Deck	**Lantana/P**	20
East City Grill	**Weston/B**	19
11 Maple St.	**Jensen Bch/P**	27
11th St. Diner	**SoBe**	20
NEW English Tap	**Boca/P**	-
Entre Nous	**No. Palm Bch/P**	23
E.R. Bradley	**W. Palm/P**	16
Essensia	**Miami Bch**	21
NEW 1500 Degrees	**Miami Bch**	24
Flagler Grill	**Stuart/P**	24
Flanigan's	**Coco Grove**	19
Floridian	**Ft. Laud/B**	18
Forge	**Miami Bch**	24
Front Porch	**SoBe**	21
Gables Diner	**Coral Gables**	17
GastroPod	**Loc Varies**	-
Gibraltar	**Coco Grove**	20
Gold Coast	**Coral Spgs/B**	21
Gordon Biersch	**Brickell**	18
NEW Green Table	**Coral Gables**	-
Grille/Congress	**Boca/P**	19
Grill on the Alley	**Aventura**	22
Handsome Harry's	**Naples/N**	21
Harry/Natives	**Hobe Sound/P**	19
HB's/Gulf	**Naples/N**	19
☑ Henry's	**Delray Bch/P**	21
Hi-Life	**Ft. Laud/B**	25
Hillstone	**Coral Gables**	-
☑ Houston's	**multi.**	23
Hurricane Café	**Juno Bch/P**	20
Ironwood	**Palm Bch Gdns/P**	18
Jade	**W. Palm/P**	23
J. Alexander	**multi.**	20
Jaxson's	**Dania Bch/B**	21
Jimmy Buffett's	**Key W./K**	13

Jimmy's Bistro	**Delray Bch/P**	26
Mark's	**multi.**	19
NEW John G's	**Manalapan/P**	–
JohnMartin's	**Coral Gables**	17
NEW Joint B&G	**Pinecrest**	–
Kaiyo Grill	**Islamorada/K**	–
NEW Kane Steakhouse	**SoBe**	–
Kelly's Carib.	**Key W./K**	21
Leopard Lounge	**Palm Bch/P**	18
Le Tub	**H'wood/B**	21
Living Room	**Boynton Bch/P**	15
NEW Local Craft	**Coral Gables**	–
Lola's	**H'wood/B**	24
☑ Louie's	**Key W./K**	26
Lou's Beer	**Miami Bch**	21
Lucille's	**Weston/B**	22
Mad Hatter	**Sanibel/N**	26
Magnum	**UES**	23
Marker 88	**Islamorada/K**	21
☑ NEW Market 17	**Ft. Laud/B**	26
Mason Jar	**Ft. Laud/B**	–
☑ Max's	**Boca/P**	22
NEW Max's Harvest	**Delray Bch/P**	–
Meat Market	**SoBe**	25
Michael R.	**Palm Bch/P**	18
☑ Michaels	**Key W./K**	26
☑ Michael's	**Design Dist**	27
☑ Michy's	**UES**	27
NEW Mr. Collins	**Bal Harbour**	–
Mondo's	**No. Palm Bch/P**	18
☑ Morada Bay	**Islamorada/K**	22
Morgans	**multi.**	24
NEW Ms. Cheezious	**Loc Varies**	–
Mucky Duck	**Captiva Is/N**	19
Naples Tomato	**Naples/N**	23
Nick & Johnnie's	**Palm Bch/P**	16
915 Bistro	**Key W./K**	25
Oceans 234	**Deerfield Bch/B**	19
Office	**Delray Bch/P**	20
Old Calypso	**Delray Bch/P**	19
101 Ocean	**Laud-by-Sea/B**	21
Original Pancake House	**multi**	20
☑ Palm Beach Grill	**Palm Bch/P**	25
Panorama	**Coco Grove**	–
Pelican Café	**Lake Pk/P**	21
Pelican Rest.	**Lake Worth/P**	–

Pelican RestCafé	**SoBe**	21
Pier Top	**Ft. Laud/B**	26
Pilar	**Aventura**	23
NEW Piñon Grill	**Boca/P**	22
☑ Pisces	**Key W./K**	27
NEW Pl8 Kitchen	**Ft. Laud/B**	–
Prelude/Barton G.	**Downtown**	22
Racks Downtown	**Boca/P**	21
Red Light	**UES**	23
Rhythm Café	**W. Palm/P**	24
Ridgway	**Naples/N**	23
Riverwalk	**Naples/N**	20
Rock Fish	**Kendall**	24
NEW Roxy	**No. Miami**	–
NEW Royal	**SoBe**	–
Royal Café	**Jupiter/P**	20
NEW Russell's	**Palm Bch Gdns/P**	23
S&S	**Downtown**	23
Sandy Butler	**Ft. Myers/N**	25
Sarabeth's	**Key W./K**	24
Sara's	**Palm Bch Gdns/P**	–
Scotty's	**Coco Grove**	14
☑ Seasons 52	**multi.**	23
Shor American	**Key W./K**	–
660/Angler's	**SoBe**	23
Sloppy Joe's	**Key W./K**	13
NEW Slow Food	**Loc Varies**	–
Snook Inn	**Marco Is/N**	20
Soyka	**UES**	20
Square One	**Key W./K**	21
NEW Star Bistro	**Cooper City/B**	–
Station Grille/Hse.	**multi.**	22
STK Miami	**Miami Bch**	22
Sundy House	**Delray Bch/P**	22
Sunfish	**Ft. Laud/B**	24
NEW Sustain	**Downtown**	21
NEW Symcha's	**SoBe**	25
Tabica Grill	**Jupiter/P**	21
Ta-boo	**Palm Bch/P**	23
NEW 3800 Ocean	**Riviera Bch/P**	23
☑ 3030 Ocean	**Ft. Laud/B**	20
☑ 32 East	**Delray Bch/P**	25
This Is It Café	**W. Palm/P**	–
Tin Muffin Café	**Boca/P**	23
Titanic Brewery	**Coral Gables**	17
Top of the Point	**W. Palm/P**	–
NEW Trio/Bay	**No. Bay Vill**	–

Triple Eight | **Delray Bch/P**	–
Tryst | **Delray Bch/P**	–
NEW Tudor House | **SoBe**	–
Two Chefs | **So. Miami**	23
Two Friends | **Key W./K**	18
264 the Grill | **Palm Bch/P**	17
NEW Verdea | **Palm Bch Gdns/P**	–
Village Grille | **Laud-by-Sea/B**	20
Village Tav. | **multi.**	19
Whisk Gourmet | **So. Miami**	25
White Lion | **Homestead**	18
Wish | **SoBe**	25
Wylds Café | **Bonita Springs**	26
NEW Wynwood | **Wynwood**	17
Yard Hse. | **multi.**	19
YOLO | **Ft. Laud/B**	21

ARGENTINEAN

Argentango | **H'wood/B**	18
Graziano's | **multi.**	25
Las Vacas | **Miami Bch**	24
Novecento | **multi.**	19
Zuperpollo | **Coral Way**	18

ASIAN

Aizia | **Hallandale/B**	19
Asia de Cuba | **SoBe**	22
AZN Azian Cuizine | **Naples/N**	21
Café Sambal | **Brickell**	22
Z Café Sharaku | **Ft. Laud/B**	28
China Grill | **multi.**	22
NEW Gigi | **Wynwood**	24
Lan | **So. Miami**	23
NEW Miso Hungry | **Loc Varies**	–
Mr. Yum | **Little Havana**	–
Origin Asian | **multi.**	21
NEW Pubbelly | **Miami Bch**	24
NEW Pubbelly Sushi | **Miami Bch**	–
NEW Saia | **Ft. Laud/B**	–
Z Setai | **SoBe**	23
Stir Crazy | **multi.**	19
NEW Umi | **Palm Bch Gdns/P**	26
Wild E. Asian | **Ft. Laud/B**	17
Yuga | **Coral Gables**	26

AUSTRIAN

Fin & Claw | **Lighthse Pt/B**	20
Fritz & Franz | **Coral Gables**	17

BAKERIES

Croissants | **Key W./K**	24
NEW Crumb/Parchment | **Design Dist**	–
Icebox Café | **SoBe**	22
NEW On the Menu | **Davie/B**	18
Paul | **multi.**	20

BARBECUE

Bulldog Barbecue | **No. Miami**	18
Mississippi | **multi.**	22
Park Ave. BBQ | **multi.**	21
Pit Bar-B-Q | **West Dade**	21
Rock n Roll Ribs | **Coral Spgs/B**	24
Shorty's | **multi.**	22
NEW Smokehouse | **Boca/P**	–
Tom Jenkins' | **Ft. Laud/B**	25
Turtle Kraals | **Key W./K**	18

BRAZILIAN

Braza Leña | **multi.**	24
Brazaviva | **multi.**	20
Chima Brazilian | **Ft. Laud/B**	25
Fogo de Chão | **SoBe**	23
Gol! | **Delray Bch/P**	16
Grimpa | **Brickell**	25
SushiSamba | **SoBe**	23

BRITISH

Blue Anchor | **Delray Bch/P**	17
NEW English Tap | **Boca/P**	–
Jolly Cricket | **Naples/N**	20
Kingshead Pub | **Sunrise/B**	21

BURGERS

Brass Ring Pub | **multi.**	24
Bulldog Barbecue | **No. Miami**	18
Burger & Beer | **multi.**	23
CG Burgers | **multi.**	19
NEW Chuck Burger | **Palm Bch Gdns/P**	–
8 Oz. Burger | **SoBe**	20
Filling Station | **Downtown**	17
Z Five Guys | **multi.**	20
NEW 5 Napkin Burger | **SoBe**	–
NEW Flip Burger | **No. Miami**	25
NEW Gourmet Burger | **Jupiter/P**	–
Grease Burger | **W. Palm/P**	20

Hamburger Heaven | **Palm Bch/P** 21
NEW Harry Burger | **Aventura** 22
Jimmy Buffett's | **Key W./K** 13
Latin Burger | **Loc Varies** -
Le Tub | **H'wood/B** 21
OneBurger | **Coral Gables** 22
Relish | **W. Palm/P** 21
Scotty's | **Coco Grove** 14
Shake Shack | **SoBe** 22

CAJUN

Shuck N Dive | **Ft. Laud/B** 19

CALIFORNIAN

Lime Fresh Mex. | **multi.** 19

CARIBBEAN

Aruba Beach | **Laud-by-Sea/B** 17
Bagatelle | **Key W./K** 21
Café Solé | **Key W./K** 24
Calypso | **Pompano Bch/B** 24
Kelly's Carib. | **Key W./K** 21
Z Louie's | **Key W./K** 26
Martin's | **Key W./K** 22
Z Morada Bay | **Islamorada/K** 22
Mo's | **Key W./K** 23
Z Ortanique | **Coral Gables** 26
Sugar Reef | **H'wood/B** 24
Yabba Island | **Naples/N** 20

CHEESE SPECIALISTS

Cheese Course | **multi.** 25

CHEESESTEAKS

Big Al's Steaks | **multi.** 19

CHILEAN

Viva Chile | **Davie/B** -

CHINESE

(* dim sum specialist)
Charlie Chiang's | **Naples/N** 24
NEW China Beach* | **W. Palm/P** -
China Dumpling* | **Boynton Bch/P** 20
China Pavillion* |
  Pembroke Pines/B -
Chow Down Grill | **multi.** -
Christina Wan's | **Ft. Laud/B** 21
Christine Lee's | **Hallandale/B** 22
NEW Dim Ssäm à Gogo* |
  Loc Varies -

Z Hakkasan* | **Miami Bch** 26
Helen Huang's | **H'wood/B** -
Indian Chillies |
  Pembroke Pines/B -
Kon Chau* | **Westchester** 24
Z Mai-Kai | **Ft. Laud/B** 16
NEW Miss Yip* | **Downtown** 16
NEW Mr. Chef's* | **Aventura** 24
Mr. Chow | **SoBe** 22
New Chinatown | **So. Miami** 20
P.F. Chang's | **multi.** 20
P.F. Chang's | **multi.** 24
NEW Philippe Chow | **Boca/P** -
Z Rainbow Palace | **Ft. Laud/B** 26
Z Silver Pond | **Laud Lks/B** 25
Tempura Hse. | **Boca/P** 18
NEW 3 Chefs | **Downtown** -
Z Toa Toa* | **Sunrise/B** 26
Tony Chan's | **Downtown** 23
Tropical Chinese* | **Westchester** 26
Uncle Joe's | **Palm Bch Gdns/P** 20
Uncle Tai's | **Boca/P** 23

COFFEE SHOPS/ DINERS

Big Pink | **SoBe** 20
Camille's | **Key W./K** 22
City Diner | **W. Palm/P** 20
11th St. Diner | **SoBe** 20
Floridian | **Ft. Laud/B** 18
Gables Diner | **Coral Gables** 17
Howley's | **W. Palm/P** 18
Jumbo's | **Liberty City** -
News Cafe | **SoBe** 18
Original Pancake House | **multi.** 20
Royal Café | **Jupiter/P** 20
S&S | **Downtown** 23
This Is It Café | **W. Palm/P** -

CONTINENTAL

Bistro | **Jupiter/P** 21
Blue Heron | **Naples/N** 27
Brooks | **Deerfield Bch/B** 21
Cafe Cellini | **Palm Bch/P** 24
Z Café L'Europe | **Palm Bch/P** 27
Kathy's | **Boca/P** 25
Marek's | **Marco Is/N** 24
M Waterfront | **Naples/N** 23

CUISINES

Ridgway	**Naples/N**	23
Runyon's	**Coral Spgs/B**	22
Ta-boo	**Palm Bch/P**	23
Tatiana	**Hallandale/B**	-
264 the Grill	**Palm Bch/P**	17
Z Villa/Barton G.	**SoBe**	24

CRAB SPECIALISTS

Billy's Stone	**H'wood/B**	23
Captain Jim	**No. Miami**	23
Gulfstream Bistro	**W. Palm/P**	18
Z Joe's Stone	**SoBe**	27
Kelly's Fish	**Naples/N**	21
Pincher's Crab	**multi.**	20
Riggins	**Lantana/P**	20
Rustic Inn	**Ft. Laud/B**	22
Rusty Anchor	**Stock Island/K**	21
Truluck's	**multi.**	24
Truluck's	**Naples/N**	26

CREOLE

Old Calypso	**Delray Bch/P**	19
Shuck N Dive	**Ft. Laud/B**	19

CUBAN

Asia de Cuba	**SoBe**	22
Bahamas Fish	**W. Miami**	20
Bongos Cuban	**multi.**	16
Casa Larios	**multi.**	19
Casa Paco	**So. Miami**	21
Cuban Cafe	**multi.**	19
David's	**SoBe**	19
NEW De Rodriguez	**SoBe**	21
Don Ramon	**multi.**	19
El Mago/Fritas	**Little Havana**	-
El Meson	**Key W./K**	18
El Siboney	**Key W./K**	25
Z Enriqueta's	**Wynwood**	24
Havana	**W. Palm/P**	21
Havana Harry's	**multi.**	19
Havana's	**Cooper City/B**	-
Islas Canarias	**multi.**	22
La Casita	**Coral Gables**	23
La Casona	**W. Sunset**	-
Lario's/Beach	**SoBe**	20
Las Culebrinas	**multi.**	21
Las Vegas	**multi.**	21
Little Havana	**multi.**	22

Mario's Catalina	**Ft. Laud/B**	-
Molina's	**Hialeah**	25
Padrino's	**multi.**	21
Puerto Sagua	**SoBe**	23
Sergio's	**multi.**	20
Z Versailles	**Little Havana**	21

DELIS

Ben's Kosher	**Boca/P**	20
Deli Lane	**multi.**	17
Flakowitz	**multi.**	18
Kevin's	**Palm Bch Gdns/P**	-
Z LaSpada's	**multi.**	25
Old Heidelberg	**Ft. Laud/B**	21
TooJay's	**multi.**	18

ECLECTIC

Adriana	**Surfside**	25
Aura	**SoBe**	19
Balans	**multi.**	19
Barracuda Grill	**Marathon/K**	21
Barú Urbano	**Brickell**	15
Berries	**Coco Grove**	20
Bizaare Cafe	**Lake Worth/P**	19
Blackfin Bistro	**Key W./K**	22
NEW Buccan	**Palm Bch/P**	25
Buena Vista	**UES**	24
Z Cafe Maxx	**Pompano Bch/B**	27
Cheese Course	**multi.**	25
Cottage	**Lake Worth/P**	20
Dada	**Delray Bch/P**	20
Democratic/Beer	**Downtown**	-
NEW Dining Rm.	**SoBe**	-
NEW Dirty Martini	**Palm Bch Gdns/P**	-
Dolores/Lolita	**Brickell**	19
Dynamo	**SoBe**	-
NEW Eden	**SoBe**	21
Elle's	**Miramar/B**	21
NEW 5 Napkin Burger	**SoBe**	-
GastroPod	**Loc Varies**	-
Globe Cafe	**Coral Gables**	17
Grand Café	**Key W./K**	22
Grand Lux	**multi.**	19
Grateful Palate	**Ft. Laud/B**	24
NEW Haven Gastro	**SoBe**	-
Hog Snappers	**Tequesta/P**	26
Icebox Café	**SoBe**	22

Vote at ZAGAT.com

CUISINES

Il Mercato | **Hallandale/B** 26

Jimmy Johnson's | **Key Largo/K** 18

Jimmy'z Kitchen | **multi.** 25

Leopard Lounge | **Palm Bch/P** 18

NEW LuLu | **Coco Grove** 16

Mango's Tropical | **SoBe** 13

NEW Market 17 | **Ft. Laud/B** 26

Maya Tapas | **SoBe** 17

NEW M Bar | **Ft. Laud/B** -

NEW Michele's | **Ft. Laud/B** -

Mustard Seed | **Plantation/B** 25

NEW Nemesis | **Downtown** -

Nexxt Cafe | **SoBe** 18

Nikki | **SoBe** 16

Off the Grille | **multi.** 26

NEW Pangea | **Wellington/P** -

NEW Peacock | **Coco Grove** -

Pelican Landing | **Ft. Laud/B** 21

Pierre's | **Islamorada/K** 27

NEW Pincho Factory | **Westchester** -

NEW Pl8 Kitchen | **Ft. Laud/B** -

Santiago's | **Key W./K** 27

NEW Soirée at Vice | **SoBe** -

Sugarcane | **Downtown** 25

Table Apart | **Bonita Springs** 25

Tantra | **SoBe** 21

Tasters | **Tavernier/K** -

Too Bizaare | **Jupiter/P** 19

Town Kit. | **So. Miami** 19

Upper Deck | **Key W./K** 25

Van Dyke Cafe | **SoBe** 16

W Wine | **Design Dist** 16

NEW Wynwood | **Wynwood** 17

EUROPEAN

Alexander's | **Naples/N** 22

Angelique | **Coral Gables** 18

Azul | **Brickell** 27

Cheese Course | **multi.** 25

NEW LuLu | **Coco Grove** 16

Martin's | **Key W./K** 22

Vienna Café | **Davie/B** 24

FLORIBBEAN

Blue Heaven | **Key W./K** 25

Doc Ford's | **multi.** 22

Flagler Grill | **Stuart/P** 24

Guanabanas | **Jupiter/P** 18

Johnny V | **Ft. Laud/B** 24

Latitudes | **H'wood/B** 18

Old Captiva Hse. | **Captiva Is/N** 22

NEW Route 9 | **Coral Gables** 20

FONDUE

Melting Pot | **multi.** 19

FRENCH

Bleu Provence | **Naples/N** 27

Buena Vista | **UES** 24

Café Boulud | **Palm Bch/P** 26

Café des Artistes | **Jupiter/P** 23

Café Pastis | **So. Miami** 23

Café Solé | **Key W./K** 24

Chanticleer | **Islamorada/K** -

Chez Jean-Pierre | **Palm Bch/P** 28

Côte d'Azur | **Naples/N** 27

NEW DB Bistro Moderne | **Downtown** 26

Din. Rm./Little Palm | **Little Torch Key/K** 28

Escargot 41 | **Naples/N** 26

Green/Cafe | **Coco Grove** 19

La Riviera | **Airport** -

La Sandwicherie | **multi.** 25

Le Bistro | **Lighthse Pt/B** 22

Le Croisic | **Key Biscayne** 22

Le Lafayette | **Naples/N** 25

Maison Carlos | **W. Palm/P** 26

Michy's | **UES** 27

NEW On the Menu | **Davie/B** 18

Palme d'Or | **Coral Gables** 28

NEW Paris/Town | **Palm Bch Gdns/P** -

Pascal's | **Coral Gables** 27

Paul | **multi.** 20

Sage | **multi.** 22

Saint Tropez | **Ft. Laud/B** 22

Uvas | **UES** 19

FRENCH (BISTRO)

A la Folie Café | **SoBe** 21

Bamboo Café | **Naples/N** 21

Banana Cafe | **Key W./K** 23

Café La Bonne | **Ft. Laud/B** 22

Croissants | **Key W./K** 24

George's/Grove | **Coco Grove** 22

George's/Sunset | **So. Miami** 20

Gourmet Diner | **No. Miami Bch** 18

La Creperie | **Lauderhill/B** 24

La Goulue | **Bal Harbour** 21

Le Bouchon/Grove | **Coco Grove** 24

Le Provençal | **Coral Gables** 22

NEW LouLou | **Miami Riv** —

Otentic | **SoBe** —

Petit Rouge | **No. Miami** 26

Pistache | **W. Palm/P** 23

Provence | **SoBe** 24

GASTROPUB

Gratify | Amer. | **W. Palm/P** —

NEW Joint B&G | Amer. | —
Pinecrest

Jolly Cricket | British | 20
Naples/N

NEW Local Craft | Amer. | —
Coral Gables

Lou's Beer | Amer. | **Miami Bch** 21

NEW Pubbelly | Asian | 24
Miami Bch

Tryst | Amer. | **Delray Bch/P** —

GERMAN

Ambry German | **Ft. Laud/B** 21

Checkers/Munchen | 22
Pompano Bch/B

Fritz & Franz | **multi.** 17

Old Heidelberg | **Ft. Laud/B** 21

Royal Bavarian | **UES** 21

GREEK

Andros | **Lake Worth/P** 21

NEW Egg & Dart | **Design Dist** —

🛭 Greek Islands | **Ft. Laud/B** 25

Mandolin | **Design Dist** 25

Mazza | **Pembroke Pines/B** —

My Big Fat Greek | **Dania Bch/B** 20

Mykonos | **Coral Way** 20

Taso's Greek | **Delray Bch/P** 19

Taverna Kyma | **Boca/P** 20

Taverna Opa | **multi.** 19

Trata | **Ft. Laud/B** —

HAITIAN

Tap Tap | **SoBe** 22

HAWAII REGIONAL

Roy's | **multi.** 26

HEALTH FOOD

(See also Vegetarian)

🛭 Canyon Ranch | **Miami Bch** 19

Green Gourmet | **Delray Bch/P** —

HOT DOGS

Dogma Grill | **UES** 20

ICE CREAM PARLORS

Jaxson's | **Dania Bch/B** 21

Sloan's | **multi.** 22

INDIAN

Bombay Darbar | **Coco Grove** 23

NEW Copper Chimney | 25
Sunny Is Bch

Guru | **SoBe** 22

House of India | **Coral Gables** 19

Imlee | **Pinecrest** 25

India Hse. | **Plantation/B** 21

Indian Chillies | **Pembroke Pines/B** —

NEW Indus | **W. Palm/P** —

Madras | **Pompano Bch/B** 22

Mint Leaf | **multi.** 21

Udipi | **Sunrise/B** 23

Woodlands | **Lauderhill/B** 26

INDONESIAN

Bali Café | **Downtown** 25

NEW Dapur | **Ft. Laud/B** —

Indomania | **Miami Bch** 25

IRISH

Clarke's | **SoBe** 22

NEW Fadó Irish Pub | **Brickell** 17

Finnegan's | **Key W./K** 19

JohnMartin's | **Coral Gables** 17

Maguires Hill 16 | **Ft. Laud/B** 16

Mickey Byrne's | **H'wood/B** —

Paddy Mac's | **Palm Bch Gdns/P** 19

Sláinte Irish | **Boynton Bch/P** 17

ISRAELI

Pita Hut | **Miami Bch** 20

ITALIAN

(N=Northern; S=Southern)

Abbondanza | **Key W./K** 20

Acquolina | **multi.** 22

Anacapri | **multi.** 22

Angelina's | **Bonita Springs** 25

🛭 Anthony's Runway | 24
Ft. Laud/B

CUISINES

Noodles Panini | **Ft. Laud/B**	23
Oggi Caffe | **No. Bay Vill**	25
Osteria del Teatro | N | **SoBe**	26
NEW Ovenella | **Boca/P**	-
Papichi | **Pinecrest**	20
Paradiso | **Lake Worth/P**	25
Pazzo! | **Naples/N**	24
Pelican Café | **Lake Pk/P**	21
Pelican RestCafé | **SoBe**	21
Peppy's | N | **Coral Gables**	21
Perricone's | **Brickell**	22
Portobello | N | **Jupiter/P**	23
Primavera | N | **Oakland Pk/B**	20
Prime Italian | **SoBe**	24
Quattro | N | **SoBe**	20
Racks Italian | **No. Miami Bch**	20
Randazzo's | **Coral Gables**	20
Renato's | **Palm Bch/P**	24
Renzo's | S | **Boca/P**	22
Revales | **UES**	-
Romeo's Cafe | N | **Coral Way**	26
Rosalia's | **Aventura**	17
Rosinella | **multi.**	20
Sale e Pepe | **Marco Is/N**	24
Salute! | **Key W./K**	22
Sapori | **Boca/P**	28
Sardinia | **Miami Bch**	26
Scarpetta | **Miami Bch**	25
NEW Scuola Vecchia | S | **Delray Bch/P**	-
Sea Salt | **Naples/N**	23
Serafina | S | **Ft. Laud/B**	23
Z Sette Bello | **Ft. Laud/B**	26
SoLita | **multi.**	21
Soya & Pomodoro | **Downtown**	23
NEW Spartico | **Coco Grove**	-
Spiga | N | **SoBe**	24
Stresa | N | **W. Palm/P**	19
Table 42 | **Boca/P**	21
NEW Tagliatelle Miaml | **SoBe**	-
Tarantella | **Weston/B**	21
Temple Orange | **Manalapan/P**	24
Timo | **Sunny Is Bch**	25
Timpano | **Ft. Laud/B**	23
Tiramesu | **SoBe**	21
Tommy's Italian | **Davie/B**	23
Tramonti | **Delray Bch/P**	25
Trattoria Bella | **Margate/B**	-

Tratt. Luna | **Pinecrest**	24
Tratt. Romana | **Boca/P**	26
Tratt. Sole | **So. Miami**	20
Tuscan Grill | N | **Ft. Laud/B**	20
Tutto Pasta | **Brickell**	22
Vagabondi | **W. Palm/P**	24
Z Valentino's | **Ft. Laud/B**	27
Vergina | **Naples/N**	19
Via Luna | **Ft. Laud/B**	21
Vic & Angelo's | **multi.**	21
Vigneto's | **multi.**	21
Villagio | **multi.**	21
Vivo Partenza | **Boca/P**	23
Zuccarelli's | S | **W. Palm/P**	20

JAMAICAN

Irie Isle | **No. Miami Bch**	-

JAPANESE

(* sushi specialist)

Ambrosia* | **Key W./K**	26
Asia Bay* | **multi.**	25
Asian Fin | **Palm Bch Gdns/P**	25
Bali Café* | **Downtown**	25
NEW Blade/Vida* | **Miami Bch**	-
Bluefin Sushi* | **multi.**	25
NEW Blue Ginger* | **Pembroke Pines/B**	-
Blue Sea* | **SoBe**	24
Blu Sushi* | **Ft. Myers/N**	24
Bond St.* | **SoBe**	25
Christine Lee's* | **Hallandale/B**	22
Coco Asian Bistro* | **Ft. Laud/B**	24
Doraku* | **SoBe**	23
Echo | **Palm Bch/P**	24
Eddie Hills* | **Hallandale/B**	23
Fuji Hana* | **multi.**	22
Galanga* | **Wilton Manors/B**	23
Hiro Japanese* | **No. Miami Bch**	21
Z Hiro's Yakko-San* | **No. Miami Bch**	27
Ichiban* | **Davie/B**	19
Kaiyo Grill* | **Islamorada/K**	-
Kampai | **multi.**	22
Kiko | **Plantation/B**	26
Z Lemongrass* | **Ft. Laud/B**	22
Maiko* | **SoBe**	-
NEW Makoto | **Bal Harbour**	25
Marumi Sushi | **Plantation/B**	-

Ɀ Matsuri* | **So. Miami** 27

Moon Thai* | **multi.** 23

Ɀ Naoe* | **Sunny Is Bch** 29

Ɀ Nobu Miami* | **SoBe** 27

Ɀ Oishi Thai* | **No. Miami** 26

NEW Pubbelly Sushi* | **Miami Bch** –

Ra Sushi* | **multi.** 19

Red Koi Truck* | **Loc Varies** –

Red Koi* | **Coral Gables** 25

Saigon Tokyo* | **Greenacres/P** 22

Saito's | **multi.** 19

Sakura* | **Coral Gables** 24

Sawa* | **Coral Gables** 21

Shibui* | **Kendall** 24

Siam Palace* | **So. Miami** 23

NEW Soi Asian* | **Downtown** –

Sushi Hse.* | **No. Miami Bch** 22

Sushi Maki* | **multi.** 21

Su Shin Izakaya* | **Coral Gables** 23

Su Shin Thai* | **Lauderhill/B** 22

Sushi Rock* | **SoBe** 21

SushiSamba* | **SoBe** 23

Sushi Siam/Rock* | **multi.** 22

Sushi Simon* | **Boynton Bch/P** 23

Sushi/Thai Jo's* | **multi.** 23

Tempura Hse. | **Boca/P** 18

Thai Cuisine* | **Key W./K** –

Thai Hse. II* | **No. Miami Bch** 24

Thai Island* | **Key W./K** –

Thaikyo Asian | **Manalapan/P** 19

NEW Tokyo Blue | **Ft. Laud/B** 20

Tokyo Sushi* | **Ft. Laud/B** 23

Toni's Sushi* | **SoBe** 25

NEW 2B Asian* | **Little Havana** 25

Ɀ Zuma* | **Downtown** 28

JEWISH

Ben's Kosher | **Boca/P** 20

KOREAN

(* barbecue specialist)

Myung Ga* | **Weston/B** 29

Sakaya Kitchen | **Downtown** 22

KOSHER/ KOSHER-STYLE

Ben's Kosher | **Boca/P** 20

Café Emunah | **Ft. Laud/B** 25

Pita Hut | **Miami Bch** 20

LEBANESE

Khoury's | **So. Miami** 21

Marhaba Med. | **So. Miami** 25

Mazza | **Pembroke Pines/B** –

MEDITERRANEAN

Absinthe | **Naples/N** 21

Alladin | **Palm Bch Gdns/P** 18

AltaMare | **SoBe** 24

Andros | **Lake Worth/P** 21

Azur | **Key W./K** 25

Bizcaya | **Coco Grove** 24

Casablanca | **Ft. Laud/B** 21

City Cellar | **W. Palm/P** 20

NEW Egg & Dart | **Design Dist** –

Eos | **Brickell** 21

George's/Grove | **Coco Grove** 22

George's/Sunset | **So. Miami** 20

Green/Cafe | **Coco Grove** 19

H2O | **Ft. Laud/B** 18

Ilios | **Ft. Laud/B** –

Joseph's Wine | **Delray Bch/P** 23

Ɀ La Brochette | **Cooper City/B** 28

La Cigale | **Delray Bch/P** 24

La Riviera | **Airport** –

Lido | **SoBe** 22

Maroosh | **Coral Gables** 25

Michelle Bernstein/Omphoy | **Palm Bch/P** 24

Mondo's | **No. Palm Bch/P** 18

915 Bistro | **Key W./K** 25

Oasis | **Miami Bch** 21

Pasha's | **multi.** 19

NEW Pied à Terre | **SoBe** –

Pita Grille | **No. Palm Bch/P** 23

Por Fin | **Coral Gables** 23

NEW Route 9 | **Coral Gables** 20

Sawa | **Coral Gables** 21

660/Angler's | **SoBe** 23

NEW Star Bistro | **Cooper City/B** –

Tapas & Tintos | **multi.** 20

Temple Orange | **Manalapan/P** 24

Timo | **Sunny Is Bch** 25

Uvas | **UES** 19

Vita by Baoli | **SoBe** –

NEW Wine Depot | **SoBe** 20

CUISINES

MEXICAN

Bad Boy Burrito	**Key W./K**	24
Cabo Flats	**Palm Bch Gdns/P**	16
Caliente Kitchen	**Delray Bch/P**	22
Cantina Laredo	**multi.**	20
Casa Maya	**Deerfield Bch/B**	24
Chéen Huaye	**No. Miami**	25
Chico's Cantina	**Key W./K**	–
NEW Cinco Cantina	**Coral Gables**	–
NEW Dos Caminos	**Ft. Laud/B**	19
Z Eduardo/San Angel	**Ft. Laud/B**	27
El Rancho	**multi.**	19
El Toro	**Homestead**	23
NEW Jefe's	**Loc Varies**	–
Latin Burger	**Loc Varies**	–
Lime Fresh Mex.	**multi.**	19
Mercadito	**Downtown**	21
NEW Nacho Mamas	**Loc Varies**	–
NEW Pancho Villa	**No. Miami**	–
Paquito's	**No. Miami Bch**	22
Rocco's Tacos	**multi.**	20
Rosa Mexicano	**Brickell**	22
Salsa Fiesta	**Wynwood**	–
Talavera	**Coral Gables**	24
T-Mex	**Ft. Laud/B**	17

MIDDLE EASTERN

Daily Bread	**Pinecrest**	24
Ferdo's Grill	**Ft. Laud/B**	20
Kabobji	**multi.**	22
Leila	**W. Palm/P**	22
Maroosh	**Coral Gables**	25
Orig. Daily	**Coco Grove**	26
Pasha's	**multi.**	19
Pita Grille	**No. Palm Bch/P**	23
Sawa	**Coral Gables**	21

NEW ENGLAND

Kelly's Landing	**Ft. Laud/B**	21
Legal Sea Foods	**Boca/P**	21
Linda Bean's	**Delray Bch/P**	17
Whale Raw	**Parkland/B**	17

NEW WORLD

Z Ortanique	**Coral Gables**	26

NICARAGUAN

El Novillo	**multi.**	22
Guayacan	**Little Havana**	21
Los Ranchos	**multi.**	21

NUEVO LATINO

Z Cabana	**multi.**	22
NEW De Rodriguez	**SoBe**	21
Mesazul	**Doral**	–
Yuca	**SoBe**	20

PACIFIC RIM

USS Nemo	**Naples/N**	27

PAN-LATIN

NEW Bernie's L.A.	**SoBe**	26
NEW Cevichery	**SoBe**	–
Z Din. Rm./Little Palm	**Little Torch Key/K**	28
Hot Tin Roof	**Key W./K**	25
Jaguar	**Coco Grove**	22
Michelle Bernstein/Omphoy	**Palm Bch/P**	24
Z OLA	**SoBe**	27
Olivos	**Doral**	26

PERSIAN

Bha Bha	**Naples/N**	24
Kuluck	**Tamarac/B**	–
Pasha Hse.	**Plantation/B**	20
Rice Hse.	**multi.**	22

PERUVIAN

Adriana	**Surfside**	25
Ceviche 105	**Downtown**	25
NEW Cevichery	**SoBe**	–
NEW Cholo's	**No. Miami Bch**	–
El Chalán	**multi.**	23
El Gran Inka	**multi.**	21
Z Francesco	**Coral Gables**	26
Giovanni's	**Pembroke Pines/B**	–
La Cofradia	**Coral Gables**	25
La Rosa Nautica	**Boca/P**	–
Z Nobu Miami	**SoBe**	27
Panorama	**Coco Grove**	–
Salmon	**Little Havana**	25
Saxsay	**Sunrise/B**	–
SushiSamba	**SoBe**	23
Tumi	**Margate/B**	20

PIZZA

Andiamo! Pizza | **UES**	25
☑ Anthony's Pizza | **multi.**	22
Archie's Pizza | **Key Biscayne**	21
Big Cheese | **So. Miami**	21
Blú la Pizzeria | **So. Miami**	21
Bugatti Pasta | **Coral Gables**	23
NEW Cafe L'Attico | **Miami Bch**	-
Carmine's | **Jupiter/P**	19
Cucina Dell' Arte | **Palm Bch/P**	21
D'Angelo | **Oakland Pk/B**	25
El Tamarindo | **Hallandale/B**	22
NEW Forno 52 | **Palmetto Bay**	-
☑ Frankie's Pizza | **Westchester**	26
Fratelli | **SoBe**	22
Grimaldi's | **multi.**	-
NEW Harry's Pizzeria | **Design Dist**	-
Hot Pie | **W. Palm/P**	26
Mario The Baker | **multi.**	20
Mellow Mushroom | **Delray Bch/P**	21
Mike's | **Kendall**	-
NEW Naked Pizza | **SoBe**	18
NEW Ovenella | **Boca/P**	-
Piola | **multi.**	22
Pizza Girls | **W. Palm/P**	20
Pizza Rustica | **multi.**	19
Pizzeria Oceano | **Lantana/P**	-
Renzo's | **Boca/P**	22
Rosinella | **multi.**	20
NEW Scuola Vecchia | **Delray Bch/P**	-
NEW Spartico | **Coco Grove**	-
Spris | **multi.**	22
Tutto Pizza | **Brickell**	24
Vic & Angelo's | **multi.**	21

PUB FOOD

Bar Louie | **multi.**	17
Blue Anchor | **Delray Bch/P**	17
Brass Ring Pub | **multi.**	24
Clarke's | **SoBe**	22
Dave's Last | **Lake Worth/P**	13
NEW English Tap | **Boca/P**	-
NEW Fadó Irish Pub | **Brickell**	17
Finnegan's | **Key W./K**	19
NEW Harrison's | **W. Miami**	-

JohnMartin's | **Coral Gables**	17
Kingshead Pub | **Sunrise/B**	21
Maguires Hill 16 | **Ft. Laud/B**	10
Michael R. | **Palm Bch/P**	18
Mickey Byrne's | **H'wood/B**	-
Mucky Duck | **Captiva Is/N**	19
Paddy Mac's | **Palm Bch Gdns/P**	19
NEW Roxy | **No. Miami**	-
Sláinte Irish | **Boynton Bch/P**	17
Titanic Brewery | **Coral Gables**	17

PUERTO RICAN

Old San Juan | **W. Miami**	22

RUSSIAN

Tatiana | **Hallandale/B**	-

SALVADORAN

El Tamarindo | **multi.**	22

SANDWICHES

(See also Delis)

Big Al's Steaks | **multi.**	19
Cheese Course | **multi.**	25
CheeseMe | **Loc Varies**	-
Deli Lane | **multi.**	17
☑ Enriqueta's | **Wynwood**	24
Jimmy'z Kitchen | **multi.**	25
La Sandwicherie | **multi.**	25
☑ LaSpada's | **multi.**	25
NEW Ms. Cheezious | **Loc Varies**	-
NEW 100 Montaditos | **Downtown**	-
Paul | **multi.**	20
Perricone's | **Brickell**	22
Russo's Subs | **multi.**	-
NEW Slow Food | **Loc Varies**	-
TooJay's | **multi.**	18

SEAFOOD

☑ A&B Lobster | **Key W./K**	23
Absinthe | **Naples/N**	21
Adriana | **Surfside**	25
A Fish/Avalon | **SoBe**	23
Alabama Jacks | **Key Largo/K**	20
AltaMare | **SoBe**	24
Area 31 | **Downtown**	22
Aruba Beach | **Laud-by-Sea/B**	17
Bagatelle | **Key W./K**	21

Bahamas Fish | **W. Miami**	20
Baleen | **Naples/N**	23
Banana Boat | **Boynton Bch/P**	15
Bentley's | **Islamorada/K**	23
Billy's Stone | **H'wood/B**	23
Bimini Twist | **W. Palm/P**	21
🆕 Blue Door Fish | **SoBe**	23
☑ Blue Moon Fish | **multi.**	24
Blue Pointe | **Ft. Myers/N**	24
Bluepoint Grill | **H'wood/B**	18
Blue Water Bistro | **Estero/N**	23
☑ Bonefish Grill | **multi.**	22
B.O.'s Fish | **Key W./K**	24
Café Emunah | **Ft. Laud/B**	25
Calypso | **Pompano Bch/B**	24
Calypso's/Grille | **Key Largo/K**	23
Cap's | **Lighthse Pt/B**	17
Captain Charlie | **Juno Bch/P**	27
Captain Jim | **No. Miami**	23
Captain's Tav. | **Pinecrest**	23
Casablanca | **Ft. Laud/B**	21
🆕 Catch Grill | **Biscayne**	–
Charley's Crab | **Palm Bch/P**	20
Chart House | **Ft. Laud/B**	20
Chip's | **Sanibel/N**	23
Chops City Grill | **multi.**	25
☑ Chops Lobster | **Boca/P**	26
City Oyster | **Delray Bch/P**	22
Cloyde's | **Naples/N**	22
Coconuts | **Ft. Laud/B**	23
Commodore | **Key W./K**	23
Conch Republic | **Key W./K**	17
Conchy Joe's | **Jensen Bch/P**	19
Cool'A Fishbar | **Palm Bch Gdns/P**	22
Council Oak | **H'wood/B**	24
Disco Fish | **W. Miami**	19
Doc Ford's | **multi.**	22
Dock/Crayton | **Naples/N**	20
Dockside Sea | **Lake Pk/P**	19
Duffy's Steak | **Key W./K**	18
☑ 15th St. Fish | **Ft. Laud/B**	19
Fin & Claw | **Lighthse Pt/B**	20
☑ Four Seasons | **Palm Bch/P**	25
☑ Francesco | **Coral Gables**	26
Garcia's | **Miami Riv**	23
🆕 GG's | **H'wood/B**	20
Gold Coast | **Coral Spgs/B**	21
Green Turtle Inn | **Islamorada/K**	22
Grille 66 | **Ft. Laud/B**	24
Grillfish | **SoBe**	20
Grouper & Chips | **Naples/N**	24
Guanabanas | **Jupiter/P**	18
Gulfstream Bistro | **W. Palm/P**	18
Half Shell | **Key W./K**	23
HB's/Gulf | **Naples/N**	19
Hog Snappers | **Tequesta/P**	26
Ireland's | **Weston/B**	26
Island Grill | **Islamorada/K**	24
JB's | **Deerfield Bch/B**	18
Jetty's | **Jupiter/P**	22
☑ Joe's Stone | **SoBe**	27
☑ Kee Grill | **multi.**	24
Kelly's Fish | **Naples/N**	21
Kelly's Landing | **Ft. Laud/B**	21
Keys Fisheries | **Marathon/K**	26
☑ La Dorada | **Coral Gables**	26
La Rosa Nautica | **Boca/P**	–
Lazy Loggerhead | **Jupiter/P**	24
Legal Sea Foods | **Boca/P**	21
Linda Bean's | **Delray Bch/P**	17
Little Moir's | **Jupiter/P**	26
Mangoes | **Key W./K**	18
Marek's | **Marco Is/N**	24
Marker 88 | **Islamorada/K**	21
Michelle Bernstein/Omphoy | **Palm Bch/P**	24
McCormick/Schmick | **multi.**	20
Monty's | **multi.**	17
North Ocean | **Ft. Laud/B**	–
Oceanaire | **Brickell**	24
Oceans 234 | **Deerfield Bch/B**	19
Old Calypso | **Delray Bch/P**	19
Old Captiva Hse. | **Captiva Is/N**	22
Old Florida | **Wilton Manors/B**	19
Papa Hughie's | **Lighthse Pt/B**	24
Pelican Landing | **Ft. Laud/B**	21
Pepe's | **Key W./K**	24
Pilar | **Aventura**	23
Pilot House | **Key Largo/K**	19
Pincher's Crab | **multi.**	20
☑ Pisces | **Key W./K**	27
Player's Club | **Wellington/P**	17
Prime Catch | **Boynton Bch/P**	21
☑ Prime One | **SoBe**	27
Quinn's | **SoBe**	25

Red Fish Grill | **Coral Gables** 22
Red Light | **UES** 23
NEW Rickenbacker |
  Key Biscayne 20
Riggins | **Lantana/P** 20
River House | **Palm Bch Gdns/P** 22
River Oyster Bar | **Miami Riv** 25
Riverwalk | **Naples/N** 20
Rock Fish | **Kendall** 24
Roy's | **multi.** 26
NEW Russell's |
  Palm Bch Gdns/P 23
Rustic Inn | **Ft. Laud/B** 22
Rusty Anchor | **Stock Island/K** 21
Sailfish Marina |
  Palm Bch Shores/P 17
Salute! | **Key W./K** 22
Schooner Wharf | **Key W./K** 14
NEW Sea | **Laud-by-Sea/B** -
Sea Salt | **Naples/N** 23
Z Seven Fish | **Key W./K** 27
Shor American | **Key W./K** -
Snappers | **Boynton Bch/P** 18
Snapper's Waterfront |
  Key Largo/K 20
Snook Inn | **Marco Is/N** 20
Southport Raw | **Ft. Laud/B** 20
Spoto's | **Palm Bch Gdns/P** 22
Station Grille/Hse. | **multi.** 22
Sunfish | **Ft. Laud/B** 24
Sunshine Seafood | **multi.** 24
NEW Tagliatelle Miami | **SoBe** -
Tarpon Bend | **multi.** 20
NEW 3800 Ocean |
  Riviera Bch/P 23
Z 3030 Ocean | **Ft. Laud/B** 26
III Forks | **multi.** 20
Timpano | **Ft. Laud/B** 23
Tommy Bahama's | **Naples/N** 21
Truluck's | **multi.** 24
Truluck's | **Naples/N** 26
Turtle Kraals | **Key W./K** 18
Two Georges | **multi.** 15
NEW Umi | **Palm Bch Gdns/P** 26
USS Nemo | **Naples/N** 27
Via Luna | **Ft. Laud/B** 21
Whale Raw | **Parkland/B** 17
Whale's Rib | **Deerfield Bch/B** 20

Yabba Island | **Naples/N** 20
Ziggie | **Islamorada/K** 25

SMALL PLATES

(See also Spanish tapas specialist)
Bin No. 18 | Italian |
  Downtown 23
Bizaare Cafe | Eclectic |
  Lake Worth/P 19
NEW Buccan | Eclectic |
  Palm Bch/P 25
Caffe Da Vinci | Italian |
  Bay Harbor Is 17
Cottage | Eclectic |
  Lake Worth/P 20
D'Angelo | Italian |
  Oakland Pk/B 25
NEW Dapur | Asian | **Ft. Laud/B** -
11 Maple St. | Amer. |
  Jensen Bch/P 27
Elle's | Eclectic | **Miramar/B** 21
NEW Gigi | Asian | **Wynwood** 24
Gratify | Amer. | **W. Palm/P** -
NEW Haven Gastro | Eclectic |
  SoBe -
Z Hiro's Yakko-San | Japanese |
  No. Miami Bch 27
Hot Tin Roof | Pan-Latin |
  Key W./K 25
Leila | Mideast. | **W. Palm/P** 22
NEW LuLu | Eclectic |
  Coco Grove 16
NEW M Bar | Eclectic |
  Ft. Laud/B -
Z Michael's | Amer. |
  Design Dist 27
Z Palme d'Or | French |
  Coral Gables 28
NEW Pl8 Kitchen |
  Amer./Eclectic | **Ft. Laud/B** -
NEW Pubbelly | Asian |
  Miami Bch 24
River Oyster Bar | Seafood |
  Miami Riv 25
Santiago's | Eclectic | **Key W./K** 27
Sugarcane | Eclectic |
  Downtown 25
Too Bizaare | Eclectic |
  Jupiter/P 19
NEW Trio/Bay | Amer. |
  No. Bay Vill -

CUISINES

☑ Upper Deck	Eclectic	Key W./K	25
NEW Wine Depot	Med.	SoBe	20

SOUL FOOD

NEW Daddy's Soul	SoBe	-
Mahogany Grille	Miami Gdns	-

SOUTHERN

Bay House	Naples/N	22
Jumbo's	Liberty City	-
Veranda	Ft. Myers/N	26
Whisk Gourmet	So. Miami	25
NEW Yardbird	SoBe	-

SOUTHWESTERN

NEW Agave	Naples/N	-
☑ Canyon	Ft. Laud/B	27
Lost & Found	Design Dist	17

SPANISH

(* tapas specialist)

NEW Andalus*	Design Dist	20
Cafe Seville*	Ft. Laud/B	25
Casa Juancho	Little Havana	24
Casa Paco*	So. Miami	21
Disco Fish	W. Miami	19
El Carajo*	Coral Way	22
Ilios*	Ft. Laud/B	-
I.M. Tapas*	Naples/N	25
NEW Jamon Jamon*	Miami Riv	-
La Barraca*	H'wood/B	20
☑ La Dorada	Coral Gables	26
Las Culebrinas	multi.	21
NEW Lizarran*	Coral Gables	-
Mario's Catalina	Ft. Laud/B	-
NEW 100 Montaditos	Downtown	-
Por Fin	Coral Gables	23
Spanish Gdns.*	Islamorada/K	-
☑ Sra. Martinez*	Design Dist	25
Tapas & Tintos*	multi.	20
Triple Eight*	Delray Bch/P	-
Xixón Cafe*	Coral Way	23

STEAKHOUSES

☑ Abe/Louie's	Boca/P	26
Ambry German	Ft. Laud/B	21
Bimini Twist	W. Palm/P	21
☑ BLT Steak	SoBe	25
Blue Pointe	Ft. Myers/N	24
Bourbon Steak	Aventura	25
Braza Leña	Islamorada/K	24
Brazaviva	Doral	20
☑ Capital Grille	multi.	26
Chima Brazilian	Ft. Laud/B	25
Chip's	Sanibel/N	23
Chops City Grill	multi.	25
☑ Chops Lobster	Boca/P	26
Christy's	Coral Gables	24
Cloyde's	Naples/N	22
Commodore	Key W./K	23
Council Oak	H'wood/B	24
Cut 432	Delray Bch/P	25
Duffy's Steak	Key W./K	18
El Novillo	multi.	22
NEW 1500 Degrees	Miami Bch	24
5300 Chop House	Doral	24
Flagler Steak	Palm Bch/P	26
Fleming's Prime	multi.	25
Fogo de Chão	SoBe	23
Gotham Steak	Miami Bch	23
Graziano's	multi.	25
Grill	Naples/N	26
Grille 66	Ft. Laud/B	24
Grimpa	Brickell	25
Hollywood Prime	H'wood/B	24
Ireland's	Weston/B	26
JB's	Deerfield Bch/B	18
NEW Kane Steakhouse	SoBe	-
☑ Kee Grill	multi.	24
Las Vacas	Miami Bch	24
Los Ranchos	multi.	21
Meat Market	SoBe	25
Mesazul	Doral	-
Miami's Chophse.	Downtown	19
Morton's	multi.	25
☑ NY Prime	Boca/P	25
North Ocean	Ft. Laud/B	-
Okeechobee	W. Palm/P	23
Outback	multi.	18
☑ Palm	Bay Harbor Is	28
Palm Beach Steak	Palm Bch/P	21
Pepe's	Key W./K	24
Player's Club	Wellington/P	17
Prime Italian	SoBe	24
☑ Prime One	SoBe	27

Prime Steakhouse | Key W./K `23`
NEW Rail Las Olas | Ft. Laud./D `24`
🅩 Red Steak | SoBe `27`
River House | Palm Bch Gdns/P `22`
Ruth's Chris | multi. `26`
Ruth's Chris | Estero/N `26`
Saito's | multi. `19`
Shula's | multi. `23`
Smith/Wollensky | SoBe `23`
Station Grille/Hse. | multi. `22`
🅩 Steak 954 | Ft. Laud/B `24`
St. George/Dragon | Naples/N `20`
STK Miami | Miami Bch `22`
Stoney's Steak | Naples/N `23`
Strip House | Naples/N `23`
III Forks | multi. `20`
Timpano | Ft. Laud/B `23`
Ziggie | Islamorada/K `25`

TEX-MEX

Taco Rico | multi. `22`
T-Mex | SoBe `17`
Uncle Julio's | Boca/P `18`

THAI

Asia Bay | multi. `25`
Bangkok Bangkok | Coral Gables `19`
Bangkok Bangkok | Kendall `23`
Bluefin Sushi | multi. `25`
Eddie Hills | Hallandale/B `23`
Fuji Hana | multi. `22`
Galanga | Wilton Manors/B `23`
Justine Thai | Margate/B `22`
Kampai | multi. `22`
Kiko | Plantation/B `26`
🅩 Lemongrass | multi. `22`
Moon Thai | multi. `23`
🅩 Oishi Thai | No. Miami `26`
Panya Thai | No. Miami Bch `25`
Red Koi Truck | Loc Varies `-`
Red Koi | Coral Gables `25`
Safire | Lake Worth/P `26`
Siam Cuisine | Wilton Manors/B `19`
Siam Palace | So. Miami `23`
NEW Soi Asian | Downtown `-`

Sukhothai | Ft. Laud/B `24`
Sushi Maki | multi. `21`
Su Shin Thai | Lauderhill/B `21`
Sushi Siam Rock | multi. `21`
Sushi/Thai 305 | multi. `23`
Talay Thai | Palm Bch Gdns/P `24`
Tamarind | Miami Bch `24`
Thai Cuisine | Key W./K `-`
Thai Hse. II | No. Miami Bch `24`
Thai Hse. S. | SoBe `19`
Thai Island | Key W./K `-`
Thaikyo Asian | Manalapan/P `19`
🅩 Thai Spice | Ft. Laud/B `26`
NEW 2B Asian | Little Havana `25`
Ziree Thai | Delray Bch/P `24`

TURKISH

A La Turca | H'wood/B `23`
Hakan | SoBe `20`
Mandolin | Design Dist `25`

URUGUAYAN

Zuperpollo | Coral Way `18`

VEGETARIAN

(* vegan)
Café | Key W./K `26`
Darbster* | Lake Worth/P `-`
Helen Huang's | H'wood/B `-`
Here/Sun | No. Miami `17`
Julio's | No. Miami Bch `-`
Sublime | Ft. Laud/B `21`
Udipi | Sunrise/D `23`
Woodlands | Lauderhill/B `26`

VIETNAMESE

Basilic Viet. | Laud-by-Sea/B `22`
Cay Da | Boca/P `21`
Hy-Vong | Little Havana `26`
La Tre | Boca/P `22`
🅩 Lemongrass | multi. `22`
Little Saigon | No. Miami Bch `19`
Miss Saigon | multi. `23`
Pho 78 | multi. `23`
Saigon Cuisine | Margate/B `24`
Saigon Tokyo | Greenacres/P `22`
NEW 3 Chefs | Downtown `-`

Locations

Includes names, cuisines and Food ratings.

Miami/Dade County

BISCAYNE/ DOWNTOWN
(Including Brickell Area and Miami River)

Area 31 | *Seafood*	22
Atrio | *Amer.*	22
Z Azul | *Euro.*	27
Balans | *Eclectic*	19
Bali Café | *Indonesian*	25
Barú Urbano | *Eclectic*	15
Bin No. 18 | *Italian*	23
Bongos Cuban | *Cuban*	16
Burger & Beer | *Burgers*	23
Café Sambal | *Asian*	22
Z Capital Grille | *Steak*	26
NEW Catch Grill | *Seafood*	-
Ceviche 105 | *Peruvian*	25
Cheese Course | *Eclectic*	25
NEW Crazy About You | *Eclectic*	21
NEW Damn Good Burger | *Burgers*	-
NEW DB Bistro Moderne | *French*	26
Deli Lane | *Deli*	17
Democratic/Beer | *Eclectic*	-
Dolores/Lolita | *Eclectic*	19
El Gran Inka | *Peruvian*	21
Eos | *Med.*	21
NEW Fadó Irish Pub | *Pub*	17
Filling Station | *Burgers*	17
Garcia's | *Seafood*	23
Gordon Biersch | *Amer.*	18
Graziano's | *Argent./Steak*	25
Grimpa | *Brazilian/Steak*	25
Z Il Gabbiano | *Italian*	27
NEW Jamon Jamon | *Spanish*	-
La Loggia | *Italian*	21
La Sandwicherie | *French/Sandwiches*	25
NEW La Scalina | *Italian*	-
Lime Fresh Mex. | *Cal./Mex.*	19
Los Ranchos | *Nicaraguan/Steak*	21
NEW LouLou | *French*	-

Mario The Baker | *Italian/Pizza*	20
Mercadito | *Mex.*	21
Miami's Chophse. | *Steak*	19
Mint Leaf | *Indian*	21
NEW Miss Yip | *Chinese*	16
Morton's | *Steak*	25
NEW Nemesis | *Eclectic*	-
Novecento | *Argent.*	19
Oceanaire | *Seafood*	24
NEW 100 Montaditos | *Sandwiches/Spanish*	-
Pasha's | *Med.*	19
Perricone's | *Italian*	22
P.F. Chang's | *Chinese*	20
Piola | *Pizza*	22
Pizza Rustica | *Pizza*	19
Prelude/Barton G. | *Amer.*	22
Rice Hse. | *Persian*	22
River Oyster Bar | *Seafood*	25
Rosa Mexicano | *Mex.*	22
Rosinella | *Italian*	20
Sakaya Kitchen | *Korean*	22
Sake Room | *Japanese*	-
S&S | *Diner*	23
NEW Soi Asian | *Japanese/Thai*	-
Soya & Pomodoro | *Italian*	23
Sugarcane | *Eclectic*	25
Sushi Maki | *Japanese*	21
Sushi Siam/Rock | *Japanese/Thai*	22
NEW Sustain | *Amer.*	21
NEW 3 Chefs | *Chinese*	-
Tony Chan's | *Chinese*	23
Truluck's | *Seafood/Steak*	24
Tutto Pasta | *Italian*	22
Tutto Pizza | *Pizza*	24
Z Zuma | *Japanese*	28

CORAL GABLES

Anacapri | *Italian*	22
Angelique | *Euro.*	18
Bangkok Bangkok | *Thai*	19
Bugatti Pasta | *Italian*	23
Café at Books & Books | *Amer.*	21
Caffe Abbracci | *Italian*	25

Caffe Vialetto	*Italian*	25
Christy's	*Steak*	24
NEW Cinco Cantina	*Mex.*	-
Z Five Guys	*Burgers*	20
Fleming's Prime	*Steak*	25
Fontana	*Italian*	26
Z Francesco	*Peruvian*	26
Fritz & Franz	*German*	17
Gables Diner	*Diner*	17
Globe Cafe	*Eclectic*	17
Graziano's	*Argent./Steak*	25
NEW Green Table	*Amer./Veg.*	-
Havana Harry's	*Cuban*	19
Hillstone	*Amer.*	-
House of India	*Indian*	19
Il Grissino	*Italian*	22
JohnMartin's	*Amer./Irish*	17
La Casita	*Cuban*	23
La Cofradia	*Peruvian*	25
Z La Dorada	*Seafood/Spanish*	26
La Palma	*Italian*	21
Le Provençal	*French*	22
NEW Lizarran	*Spanish*	-
NEW Local Craft	*Amer.*	-
Mario The Baker	*Italian/Pizza*	20
Maroosh	*Med./Mideast.*	25
Mint Leaf	*Indian*	21
Miss Saigon	*Viet.*	23
Moon Thai	*Japanese/Thai*	23
Morton's	*Steak*	25
OneBurger	*Burgers*	22
Z Ortanique	*Carib./New World*	26
Z Palme d'Or	*French*	28
Z Pascal's	*French*	27
Pasha's	*Med.*	19
Peppy's	*Italian*	21
Por Fin	*Med./Spanish*	23
Randazzo's	*Italian*	20
Red Fish Grill	*Seafood*	22
Red Koi	*Japanese/Thai*	25
NEW Route 9	*Floribbean/Med.*	20
Ruth's Chris	*Steak*	25
Sakura	*Japanese*	24
Sawa	*Med./Mideast*	21
Z Seasons 52	*Amer.*	23
Spris	*Pizza*	22
Sushi Maki	*Japanese*	21

Su Shin Izakaya	*Japanese*	23
Taco Rico	*Tex-Mex*	22
Talavera	*Mex.*	24
Tarpon Bend	*Seafood*	20
Titanic Brewery	*Amer.*	17
Villagio	*Italian*	21
Yard Hse.	*Amer.*	19
Yuga	*Asian*	26

CORAL WAY/ LITTLE HAVANA

Casa Juancho	*Spanish*	24
El Carajo	*Spanish*	22
El Mago/Fritas	*Cuban*	-
Guayacan	*Nicaraguan*	21
Hy-Vong	*Viet.*	26
Islas Canarias	*Cuban*	22
Mr. Yum	*Asian*	-
Mykonos	*Greek*	20
Romeo's Cafe	*Italian*	26
Salmon	*Peruvian*	25
Sergio's	*Cuban*	20
NEW 2B Asian	*Asian*	25
Z Versailles	*Cuban*	21
Xixón Cafe	*Spanish*	23
Zuperpollo	*S Amer.*	18

DESIGN DISTRICT/ UPPER EAST SIDE

NEW Andalus	*SW*	20
Andiamo! Pizza	*Pizza*	25
Balans	*Eclectic*	19
Buena Vista	*Eclectic/French*	24
NEW Crumb/Parchment	*American*	-
Dogma Grill	*Hot Dogs*	20
NEW Egg & Dart	*Greek/Med.*	-
Fratelli Lyon	*Italian*	22
NEW Harry's Pizzeria	*Pizza*	-
Lost & Found	*SW*	17
Magnum	*Amer.*	23
Maitardi	*Italian*	21
Mandolin	*Greek*	25
Z Michael's	*Amer.*	27
Z Michy's	*Amer./French*	27
Pasha's	*Med.*	19
Red Light	*Amer.*	23
Revales	*Italian*	-
Royal Bavarian	*German*	21

LOCATIONS

Soyka | *Amer.* 20

Z Sra. Martinez | *Spanish* 25

Uvas | *French/Mediterranean* 19

W Wine | *Eclectic/Wine Bar* 16

KEY BISCAYNE

Archie's Pizza | *Pizza* 21

Cioppino | *Italian* 23

El Gran Inka | *Peruvian* 21

Le Croisic | *French* 22

Novecento | *Argent.* 19

Origin Asian | *Asian* 21

NEW Rickenbacker | *Seafood* 20

Sushi Siam/Rock | 22
  Japanese/Thai

MIAMI BEACH

(Including Bal Harbour,
Bay Harbor Island, Little Haiti,
Sunny Isles Beach, Surfside and
Wynwood; see also South Beach)

Adriana | *Peruvian/Seafood* 25

Asia Bay | *Japanese/Thai* 25

NEW Blade/Vida | -
  Amer./Japanese

Burger & Beer | *Burgers* 23

Cafe Avanti | *Italian* 25

NEW Cafe L'Attico | -
  Amer./Italian

Café Prima | *Italian* 23

Café Ragazzi | *Italian* 23

Caffe Da Vinci | *Italian* 17

Z Canyon Ranch | *Health* 19

NEW Carillon | *Amer.* -

Carpaccio | *Italian* 23

NEW Cecconi's | *Italian* 22

CG Burgers | *Burgers* 19

Chow Down Grill | *Chinese* -

NEW City Hall | *Amer.* -

NEW Copper Chimney | *Indian* 25

El Rancho | *Mex.* 19

Z Enriqueta's | 24
  Cuban/Sandwiches

Essensia | *Amer.* 21

NEW 1500 Degrees | 24
  Amer./Steak

Z Five Guys | *Burgers* 20

Forge | *Amer.* 24

George's Rest. | *Italian* 23

NEW Gigi | *Asian* 24

Gotham Steak | *Steak* 23

Z Hakkasan | *Chinese* 26

Il Mulino NY | *Italian* 24

Indomania | *Indonesian* 25

Jimmy'z Kitchen | 25
  Eclectic/Sandwiches

Joey's Italian | *Italian* 24

Jumbo's | *Diner* -

Kabobji | *Mideast.* 22

La Goulue | *French* 21

Las Vacas | *Argent./Steak* 24

Las Vegas | *Cuban* 21

Lime Fresh Mex. | *Cal./Mex.* 19

Lou's Beer | *Amer.* 21

NEW Makoto | *Japanese* 25

Mario The Baker | *Italian/Pizza* 20

NEW Mr. Collins | *Amer.* -

Morgans | *Amer.* 24

Morton's | *Steak* 25

Z Naoe | *Japanese* 29

Oasis | *Med.* 21

Oggi Caffe | *Italian* 25

Z Palm | *Steak* 28

Pita Hut | *Israeli* 20

NEW Pubbelly | *Asian* 24

NEW Pubbelly Sushi | *Asian* -

Salsa Fiesta | *Mex.* -

Sardinia | *Italian* 26

Scarpetta | *Italian* 25

Shula's | *Steak* 23

STK Miami | *Amer./Steak* 22

Tamarind | *Thai* 24

Tapas & Tintos | *Med./Spanish* 20

Timo | *Italian/Med.* 25

NEW Trio/Bay | *Amer.* -

NEW Wynwood | *Eclectic* 17

NORTH DADE

(Including Aventura, Miami
Gardens, North Miami and
North Miami Beach)

Z Anthony's Pizza | *Pizza* 22

Bella Luna | *Italian* 23

Bourbon Steak | *Steak* 25

Bulldog Barbecue | *BBQ* 18

Captain Jim | *Seafood* 23

Chéen Huaye | *Mex.* 25

Z Cheesecake | *Amer.* 20

NEW Cholo's | *Peruvian* -

El Gran Inka	*Peruvian*	21
NEW Flip Burger	*Burgers*	25
Fuji Hana	*Japanese/Thai*	22
Gourmet Diner	*French*	18
Grand Lux	*Eclectic*	19
Grill on the Alley	*Amer.*	22
NEW Heavy Burger	*Burgers*	22
Here/Sun	*Veg.*	17
Hiro Japanese	*Japanese*	21
Z Hiro's Yakko-San	*Japanese*	27
Z Houston's	*Amer.*	23
Irie Isle	*Jamaican*	–
Julio's	*Veg.*	–
Kabobji	*Mideast.*	22
Kampai	*Japanese/Thai*	22
Lime Fresh Mex.	*Cal./Mex.*	19
Little Havana	*Cuban*	22
Little Saigon	*Viet.*	19
Mahogany Grille	*Soul Food*	–
Mario The Baker	*Italian/Pizza*	20
Melting Pot	*Fondue*	19
Morton's	*Steak*	25
NEW Mr. Chef's	*Chinese*	24
Z Oishi Thai	*Japanese/Thai*	26
Original Pancake House	*Amer.*	20
Outback	*Steak*	18
NEW Pancho Villa	*Mex.*	–
Panya Thai	*Thai*	25
Paquito's	*Mex.*	22
Pasha's	*Med.*	19
Paul	*Bakery/Sandwiches*	20
Petit Rouge	*French*	26
P.F. Chang's	*Chinese*	20
Pilar	*Amer./Seafood*	23
Racks Italian	*Italian*	20
Rice Hse.	*Persian*	22
Rosalia's	*Italian*	17
NEW Roxy	*Pub*	–
Sushi Hse.	*Asian/Japanese*	22
Sushi Siam/Rock	*Japanese/Thai*	22
Thai Hse. II	*Thai*	24

SOUTH BEACH

A Fish/Avalon	*Seafood*	23
A la Folie Café	*French*	21
AltaMare	*Med./Seafood*	24
Asia de Cuba	*Asian/Cuban*	22

Aura	*Eclectic*	19
Balans	*Eclectic*	19
Z Barton G.	*Amer.*	22
NEW Bernie's L.A.	*Pan-Latin*	26
Big Pink	*Diner*	20
Z BLT Steak	*Steak*	25
NEW Blue Door Fish	*Seafood*	23
Blue Sea	*Japanese*	24
Bond St.	*Japanese*	25
Bongos Cuban	*Cuban*	16
Café at Books & Books	*Amer.*	21
Caffé Milano	*Italian*	17
Z Casa Tua	*Italian*	24
NEW Cevichery	*Pan-Latin/Peruvian*	–
China Grill	*Asian*	22
Chow Down Grill	*Chinese*	–
Clarke's	*Amer./Irish*	22
NEW Daddy's Soul	*Soul Food*	–
Da Leo Trattoria	*Italian*	18
David's	*Cuban*	19
NEW De Rodriguez	*Cuban/Nuevo Latino*	21
NEW Dining Rm.	*Eclectic*	–
Doraku	*Japanese*	23
Dynamo	*Eclectic*	–
NEW Eden	*Eclectic*	21
8 Oz. Burger	*Burgers*	20
El Chalán	*Peruvian*	23
11th St. Diner	*Diner*	20
El Rancho	*Mex.*	19
Escopazzo	*Italian*	25
Z Five Guys	*Burgers*	20
NEW 5 Napkin Burger	*Burgers*	–
Fogo de Chão	*Brazilian/Steak*	23
Fratelli	*Italian*	22
Front Porch	*Amer.*	21
Grazie Italian	*Italian*	25
Grillfish	*Seafood*	20
Guru	*Indian*	22
Hakan	*Turkish*	20
NEW Haven Gastro	*Eclectic*	–
Hosteria Romana	*Italian*	21
Icebox Café	*Bakery/Eclectic*	22
Jimmy'z Kitchen	*Eclectic/Sandwiches*	25
Z Joe's Stone	*Seafood*	27
NEW Kane Steakhouse	*Steak*	–

LOCATIONS

La Locanda	*Italian*	24
Lario's/Beach	*Cuban*	20
La Sandwicherie	*French/Sandwiches*	25
Lido	*Med.*	22
Lime Fresh Mex.	*Cal./Mex.*	19
Macaluso's	*Italian*	25
Maiko	*Japanese*	-
Mango's Tropical	*Eclectic*	13
Maya Tapas	*Eclectic*	17
Meat Market	*Steak*	25
Miss Saigon	*Viet.*	23
Monty's	*Seafood*	17
Mr. Chow	*Chinese*	22
NEW Naked Pizza	*Pizza*	18
News Cafe	*Diner*	18
Nexxt Cafe	*Eclectic*	18
Nikki	*Eclectic*	16
Z Nobu Miami	*Japanese*	27
Z OLA	*Pan-Latin*	27
Osteria del Teatro	*Italian*	26
Otentic	*French*	-
Pasha's	*Med.*	19
Paul	*Bakery/Sandwiches*	20
Pelican RestCafé	*Amer./Italian*	21
NEW Pied à Terre	*Med.*	-
Piola	*Pizza*	22
Pizza Rustica	*Pizza*	19
Prime Italian	*Italian/Steak*	24
Z Prime One	*Seafood/Steak*	27
Provence	*French*	24
Puerto Sagua	*Cuban*	23
Quattro	*Italian*	20
Quinn's	*Seafood*	25
Z Red Steak	*Steak*	27
Rice Hse.	*Persian*	22
Rosa Mexicano	*Mex.*	22
Rosinella	*Italian*	20
NEW Royal	*Amer.*	-
Z Setai	*Asian*	23
Shake Shack	*Burgers*	22
660/Angler's	*Amer./Med.*	23
Smith/Wollensky	*Steak*	23
NEW Soirée at Vice	*Eclectic*	-
Spiga	*Italian*	24
Spris	*Pizza*	22
Sushi Rock	*Japanese*	21
SushiSamba	*Japanese/S Amer.*	23

Sushi Siam/Rock	*Japanese/Thai*	22
NEW Symcha's	*Amer.*	25
Taco Rico	*Tex-Mex*	22
NEW Tagliatelle Miami	*Italian/Seafood*	-
Tantra	*Eclectic*	21
Tapas & Tintos	*Med./Spanish*	20
Tap Tap	*Haitian*	22
Thai Hse. S.	*Thai*	19
Tiramesu	*Italian*	21
T-Mex	*Tex-Mex*	17
Toni's Sushi	*Japanese*	25
NEW Tudor House	*Amer.*	-
Van Dyke Cafe	*Eclectic*	16
Vic & Angelo's	*Italian*	21
Z Villa/Barton G.	*Continental*	24
Vita by Baoli	*Med.*	-
NEW Wine Depot	*Med./Wine Bar*	20
Wish	*Amer.*	25
NEW Yardbird	*Southern*	-
Yuca	*Nuevo Latino*	20

SOUTH DADE

(Including Coconut Grove, Cutler Ridge, Dadeland, Homestead, Kendall, Palmetto Bay, Pinecrest, South Miami and West Sunset)

Anacapri	*Italian*	22
Z Anthony's Pizza	*Pizza*	22
Bangkok Bangkok	*Thai*	23
Berries	*Eclectic*	20
Big Cheese	*Pizza*	21
Bizcaya	*Amer./Med.*	24
Blú la Pizzeria	*Pizza*	21
Bombay Darbar	*Indian*	23
Z Bonefish Grill	*Seafood*	22
Café Pastis	*French*	23
Caffe Portofino	*Italian*	24
Calamari	*Italian*	18
Captain's Tav.	*Seafood*	23
Casa Larios	*Cuban*	19
Casa Paco	*Cuban/Spanish*	21
CG Burgers	*Burgers*	19
Chart House	*Amer./Seafood*	20
Z Cheesecake	*Amer.*	20
Chef Adrianne's	*Eclectic*	25
Daily Bread	*Mideast.*	24

Deli Lane | *Deli*	17
El Rancho | *Mex.*	19
El Toro | *Mex.*	23
Z Five Guys | *Burgers*	20
Flanigan's | *Amer.*	19
NEW Forno 52 | *Pizza*	-
Fuji Hana | *Japanese/Thai*	22
George's/Grove | *French/Med.*	22
George's/Sunset | *French/Med.*	20
Gibraltar | *Amer.*	20
Green/Cafe | *French/Med.*	19
Havana Harry's | *Cuban*	19
Imlee | *Indian*	25
Jaguar | *Pan-Latin*	22
NEW Joint B&G | *Amer.*	-
Kampai | *Japanese/Thai*	22
Khoury's | *Lebanese*	21
La Casona | *Cuban*	-
Lan | *Asian*	23
Las Culebrinas | *Cuban/Spanish*	21
Le Bouchon/Grove | *French*	24
Lime Fresh Mex. | *Cal./Mex.*	19
Los Ranchos | *Nicaraguan/Steak*	21
NEW LuLu | *Eclectic*	16
Marhaba Med. | *Lebanese*	25
Z Matsuri | *Japanese*	27
Melting Pot | *Fondue*	19
Mike's | *Pizza*	-
Miss Saigon | *Viet.*	23
Monty's | *Seafood*	17
Moon Thai | *Japanese/Thai*	23
New Chinatown | *Chinese*	20
Off the Grille | *Eclectic*	26
Orig. Daily | *Mideast.*	26
Original Pancake House | *Amer.*	20
Origin Asian | *Asian*	21
Outback | *Steak*	18
NEW Oye Cuban Grill | *Cuban*	20
Panorama | *Amer./Peruvian*	-
Papichi | *Italian*	20
NEW Peacock | *Eclectic*	-
P.F. Chang's | *Chinese*	20
Pizza Rustica | *Pizza*	19
Ra Sushi | *Japanese*	19
Rice Hse. | *Persian*	22
Rock Fish | *Amer.*	24
Scotty's | *Amer.*	14

Sergio's | *Cuban*	20
Shibui | *Japanese*	24
Shorty's | *BBQ*	22
Siam Palace | *Thai*	23
NEW Spartico | *Italian/Pizza*	-
Sushi Maki | *Japanese*	21
Sushi Siam/Rock |	22
Japanese/Thai	
Taco Rico | *Tex-Mex*	22
Town Kit. | *Eclectic*	19
Tratt. Luna | *Italian*	24
Tratt. Sole | *Italian*	20
Two Chefs | *Amer.*	23
Villagio | *Italian*	21
Whisk Gourmet | *Amer.*	25
White Lion | *Amer.*	18

WEST DADE

(Including the Airport, Doral,
Hialeah, Miami Lakes, Westchester
and West Miami)

Anacapri | *Italian*	22
Z Anthony's Pizza | *Pizza*	22
Bahamas Fish | *Cuban/Seafood*	20
Basilico | *Italian*	26
Z Bonefish Grill | *Seafood*	22
Brazaviva	20
Casa Larios | *Cuban*	19
Disco Fish | *Seafood/Spanish*	19
El Chalán | *Peruvian*	23
El Novillo | *Nicaraguan/Steak*	22
5300 Chop House | *Steak*	24
Z Frankie's Pizza | *Pizza*	26
Graziano's | *Argent./Steak*	25
NEW Harrison's | *Pub*	-
Islas Canarias | *Cuban*	22
Kon Chau | *Chinese*	24
La Riviera | *French/Med.*	-
Las Culebrinas | *Cuban/Spanish*	21
Los Ranchos | *Nicaraguan/Steak*	21
Mario The Baker | *Italian/Pizza*	20
Mesazul | *Nuevo Latino/Steak*	-
Molina's | *Cuban*	25
Off the Grille | *Eclectic*	26
Old San Juan | *Puerto Rican*	22
Olivos | *Pan-Latin*	26
Original Pancake House | *Amer.*	20
Outback | *Steak*	18
P.F. Chang's | *Chinese*	20

NEW Pincho Factory | *Eclectic* —
Pit Bar-B-Q | *BBQ* 21
Pizza Rustica | *Pizza* 19
Rice Hse. | *Persian* 22
Sergio's | *Cuban* 20
Shorty's | *BBQ* 22
Shula's | *Steak* 23
Taverna Opa | *Greek* 19
Tropical Chinese | *Chinese* 26

Keys

KEY WEST

Z A&B Lobster | *Seafood* 23
Abbondanza | *Italian* 20
Ambrosia | *Japanese* 26
Antonia's | *Italian* 27
Azur | *Med.* 25
Bad Boy Burrito | *Mexican* 24
Bagatelle | *Carib./Seafood* 21
Banana Cafe | *French* 23
Blackfin Bistro | *Eclectic* 22
Z Blue Heaven | *Floribbean* 25
B.O.'s Fish | *Seafood* 24
Braza Leña | *Brazilian* 24
Café | *Veg.* 26
Z Cafe Marquesa | *Amer.* 28
Café Solé | *Carib./French* 24
Camille's | *Amer.* 22
Chico's Cantina | *Mex.* —
Commodore | *Seafood/Steak* 23
Conch Republic | *Seafood* 17
Croissants | *Bakery/French* 24
Duffy's Steak | *Seafood/Steak* 18
El Meson | *Cuban* 18
El Siboney | *Cuban* 25
Finnegan's | *Pub* 19
Grand Café | *Eclectic* 22
Half Shell | *Seafood* 23
Hot Tin Roof | *Pan-Latin* 25
Jimmy Buffett's | *Amer.* 13
Kelly's Carib. | *Amer./Carib.* 21
La Trattoria | *Italian* 22
Z Louie's | *Amer./Carib.* 26
Mangia Mangia | *Italian* 20
Mangoes | *Seafood* 18
Martin's | *Euro.* 22
Z Michaels | *Amer.* 26

Mo's | *Caribbean* 23
915 Bistro | *Amer./Med.* 25
Outback | *Steak* 18
Pepe's | *Seafood/Steak* 24
Z Pisces | *Amer./Seafood* 27
Prime Steakhouse | *Steak* 25
Salute! | *Italian/Seafood* 22
Santiago's | *Eclectic* 27
Sarabeth's | *Amer.* 24
Schooner Wharf | *Seafood* 14
Z Seven Fish | *Seafood* 27
Shor American | *Seafood* —
Sloppy Joe's | *Amer.* 13
Square One | *Amer.* 21
Strip House | *Steak* 24
Thai Cuisine | *Thai* —
Thai Island | *Thai* —
Turtle Kraals | *BBQ/Seafood* 18
Two Friends | *Amer.* 18
Z Upper Deck | 25
  Eclectic/Wine Bar

OTHER KEYS

(Including Islamorada, Key Largo,
Little Torch Key and Marathon)
Alabama Jacks | *Seafood* 20
Barracuda Grill | *Eclectic* 21
Bentley's | *Seafood* 23
Braza Leña | *Brazilian* 24
Calypso's/Grille | *Seafood* 23
Chanticleer | *French* —
DiGiorgio's | *Italian* —
Z Din. Rm./Little Palm | 28
  French/Pan-Latin
Green Turtle Inn | *Seafood* 22
Island Grill | *Seafood* 24
Jimmy Johnson's | *Eclectic* 18
Kaiyo Grill | *Amer./Asian* —
Keys Fisheries | *Seafood* 26
Marker 88 | *Seafood* 21
Z Morada Bay | 22
  Amer./Caribbean
Z Pierre's | *Eclectic* 27
Pilot House | *Seafood* 19
Rusty Anchor | *Seafood* 21
Snapper's Waterfront | *Seafood* 20
Spanish Gdns. | *Spanish* —
Tasters | *Eclectic* —
Ziggie | *Seafood/Steak* 25

Ft. Lauderdale/ Broward County

FT. LAUDERDALE

Ambry German | *Amer./German* 21
☑ Anthony's Pizza | *Pizza* 22
☑ Anthony's Runway | *Italian* 24
Asia Bay | *Japanese/Thai* 25
Big City Tav. | *Amer.* 19
Bimini Boatyard | *Amer.* 17
☑ Bistro Mezz. | *Amer./Italian* 26
☑ Bonefish Grill | *Seafood* 22
Bongusto! | *Italian* 24
Café Emunah | *Kosher/Seafood* 25
NEW Café Jamm | *Amer.* -
Café La Bonne | *French* 22
☑ Cafe/Martorano | *Italian* 24
Cafe Seville | *Spanish* 25
☑ Café Sharaku | *Asian* 28
☑ Cafe Vico | *Italian* 25
Caffé Europa | *Italian* 23
☑ Canyon | *SW* 27
☑ Capital Grille | *Steak* 26
Casablanca | *Amer./Med.* 21
☑ Casa D'Angelo | *Italian* 27
Chart House | *Seafood* 20
☑ Cheesecake | *Amer.* 20
Chima Brazilian | *Brazilian/Steak* 25
China Grill | *Asian* 22
Christina Wan's | *Chinese* 21
Coco Asian Bistro | *Asian* 24
Coconuts | *Amer./Seafood* 23
Da Campo | *Italian* 23
NEW Dapur | *Asian* -
NEW Dos Caminos | *Mex.* 19
☑ Eduardo/San Angel | *Mex.* 27
El Tamarindo | *Salvadoran* 22
Ferdo's Grill | *Mideast.* 20
☑ 15th St. Fish | *Seafood* 19
☑ Five Guys | *Burgers* 20
Floridian | *Diner* 18
Fritz & Franz | *German* 17
Grateful Palate | *Eclectic* 24
☑ Greek Islands | *Greek* 25
Grille 66 | *Seafood/Steak* 24
Hi-Life | *Amer.* 25
H2O | *Italian/Med.* 18

Ilios | *Med./Spanish* -
☑ Il Mulino | *Italian* 22
J. Alexander | *Amer.* 20
J. Mark's | *Amer.* 19
☑ Johnny V | *Floribbean* 24
Kelly's Landing | *New Eng./Seafood* 21
☑ Kitchenetta | *Italian* 27
NEW La Dolce Vita | *Italian* -
☑ LaSpada's | *Deli/Sandwiches* 25
Las Vegas | *Cuban* 21
☑ Lemongrass | *Asian* 22
Maguires Hill 16 | *Pub* 16
☑ Mai-Kai | *Chinese* 16
Mario's Catalina | *Cuban/Spanish* -
☑ NEW Market 17 | *Amer./Eclectic* 26
Mason Jar | *Amer.* -
NEW M Bar | *Eclectic* -
Melting Pot | *Fondue* 19
NEW Michele's | *Eclectic* -
Morton's | *Steak* 25
Noodles Panini | *Italian* 23
North Ocean | *Seafood/Steak* -
Old Heidelberg | *German* 21
Original Pancake House | *Amer.* 20
Outback | *Steak* 18
Pelican Landing | *Eclectic* 21
P.F. Chang's | *Chinese* 20
Pier Top | *Amer.* 26
Pizza Rustica | *Pizza* 19
NEW Pl8 Kitchen | *Amer./Eclectic* -
☑ Rainbow Palace | *Chinese* 26
NEW Rare Las Olas | *Steak* 21
Rocco's Tacos | *Mex.* 20
Rustic Inn | *Seafood* 22
Ruth's Chris | *Steak* 25
☑ Sage | *French* 22
NEW Saia | *SE Asian* -
Saint Tropez | *French* 22
☑ Seasons 52 | *Amer.* 23
Serafina | *Italian* 23
☑ Sette Bello | *Italian* 26
Shuck N Dive | *Burgers* 19
Shula's | *Steak* 23
SoLita | *Italian* 21
Southport Raw | *Seafood* 20

⊠ Steak 954 | *Steak*	24
Sublime | *Vegan/Veg.*	21
Sukhothai | *Thai*	24
Sunfish | *Amer./Seafood*	24
Tarpon Bend | *Seafood*	20
⊠ Thai Spice | *Thai*	26
⊠ 3030 Ocean | *Amer./Seafood*	26
Timpano | *Italian/Steak*	23
T-Mex | *Tex-Mex*	17
NEW Tokyo Blue | *Asian*	20
Tokyo Sushi | *Japanese*	23
Tom Jenkins' | *BBQ*	25
Trata | *Greek*	-
Truluck's | *Seafood*	24
Tuscan Grill | *Italian*	20
⊠ Valentino's | *Italian*	27
Via Luna | *Italian*	21
Wild E. Asian | *Asian*	17
YOLO | *Amer.*	21

GREATER FT. LAUDERDALE

(Including Lauderdale-by-the-Sea, Oakland Park and Wilton Manors)

Aruba Beach | *Amer./Carib.*	17
Basilic Viet. | *Viet.*	22
⊠ Blue Moon Fish | *Seafood*	24
By Word/Mouth | *Amer.*	25
D'Angelo | *Italian/Pizza*	25
Galanga | *Japanese/Thai*	23
⊠ LaSpada's | *Deli/Sandwiches*	25
Old Florida | *Seafood*	19
101 Ocean | *Amer.*	21
Primavera | *Italian*	20
NEW Sea | *Seafood*	-
Siam Cuisine | *Thai*	19
Village Grille | *Amer.*	20

NORTHEAST BROWARD COUNTY

(Including Deerfield Beach, Lighthouse Point and Pompano Beach)

⊠ Anthony's Pizza | *Pizza*	22
Brooks | *Continental*	21
⊠ Cafe Maxx | *Amer./Eclectic*	27
Calypso | *Carib./Seafood*	24
Cap's | *Seafood*	17
Casa Maya | *Mex.*	24

Checkers/Munchen | *German*	22
Fin & Claw | *Austrian/Seafood*	20
Gianni's | *Italian*	24
⊠ Houston's | *Amer.*	23
JB's | *Seafood/Steak*	18
J. Mark's | *Amer.*	19
La Veranda | *Italian*	24
Le Bistro | *French*	22
Little Havana | *Cuban*	22
Madras | *Indian*	22
Oceans 234 | *Seafood*	19
Papa Hughie's | *Seafood*	24
Shorty's | *BBQ*	22
Station Grille/Hse. | *Seafood/Steak*	22
Two Georges | *Seafood*	15
Whale's Rib | *Seafood*	20

NORTHWEST BROWARD COUNTY

(Including Coconut Creek, Coral Springs, Margate, Parkland and Tamarac)

⊠ Anthony's Pizza | *Pizza*	22
Big Al's Steaks | *Cheesesteaks*	19
Bluefin Sushi | *Japanese/Thai*	25
⊠ Blue Moon Fish | *Seafood*	24
⊠ Bonefish Grill | *Seafood*	22
CG Burgers | *Burgers*	19
Cheese Course | *Eclectic*	25
⊠ Five Guys | *Burgers*	20
Gold Coast | *Amer.*	21
Jasmine Thai | *Thai*	22
Kuluck | *Persian*	-
⊠ LaSpada's | *Deli/Sandwiches*	25
Lime Fresh Mex. | *Cal./Mex.*	19
Melting Pot | *Fondue*	19
Moon Thai | *Japanese/Thai*	23
Original Pancake House | *Amer.*	20
Outback | *Steak*	18
Rock n Roll Ribs | *BBQ*	24
Runyon's | *Continental*	22
Saigon Cuisine | *Viet.*	24
Saito's | *Japanese/Steak*	19
TooJay's | *Deli*	18
Trattoria Bella | *Italian*	-
Tumi | *Peruvian*	20
Whale Raw | *New Eng.*	17

SOUTHEAST BROWARD COUNTY

(Including Dania Beach, Hallandale and Hollywood)

Acquolina	*Italian*	22
Aizia	*Asian*	19
A La Turca	*Turkish*	23
Argentango	*Argent.*	18
Billy's Stone	*Seafood*	23
Bluepoint Grill	*Seafood*	18
Bongos Cuban	*Cuban*	16
Brio Tuscan	*Italian*	21
☑ Cafe/Martorano	*Italian*	24
Cantina Laredo	*Mex.*	20
Cheese Course	*Eclectic*	25
Christine Lee's	*Chinese*	22
Council Oak	*Steak*	24
Eddie Hills	*Japanese/Thai*	23
El Tamarindo	*Pizza/Salvadoran*	22
Fulvio's 1900	*Italian*	22
NEW GG's	*Seafood*	20
Helen Huang's	*Chinese/Veg.*	-
Hollywood Prime	*Steak*	24
☑ Il Mercato	*Eclectic*	26
Jaxson's	*Ice Cream*	21
La Barraca	*Spanish*	20
Las Vegas	*Cuban*	21
Latitudes	*Floribbean*	18
Le Tub	*Burgers*	21
Lola's	*Amer.*	24
Mama Mia	*Italian*	20
Mickey Byrne's	*Pub*	-
My Big Fat Greek	*Greek*	20
Padrino's	*Cuban*	21
Piola	*Pizza*	22
Pizza Rustica	*Pizza*	19
☑ Sage	*French*	22
Sugar Reef	*Carib.*	24
Tatiana	*Continental/Russian*	-
Taverna Opa	*Greek*	19
III Forks	*Steak*	20
Yard Hse.	*Amer.*	19

SOUTHWEST BROWARD COUNTY

(Including Cooper City, Miramar and Pembroke Pines)

☑ Anthony's Pizza	*Pizza*	22
NEW Blue Ginger	*Japanese*	-

Brio Tuscan	*Italian*	21
Capriccio	*Italian*	23
☑ Cheesecake	*American*	20
China Pavillion	*Chinese*	-
Elle's	*Eclectic*	21
Giovanni's	*Italian/Peruvian*	-
Havana's	*Cuban*	-
Indian Chillies	*Chinese/Indian*	-
☑ La Brochette	*Med.*	28
Las Vegas	*Cuban*	21
Lime Fresh Mex.	*Cal./Mex.*	19
Mazza	*Greek/Lebanese*	-
Melting Pot	*Fondue*	19
Outback	*Steak*	18
Pho 78	*Viet.*	23
Ra Sushi	*Japanese*	19
Salsa Fiesta	*Mex.*	-
NEW Star Bistro	*Amer./Med.*	-
Stir Crazy	*Asian*	19
Village Tav.	*Amer.*	19

WEST BROWARD COUNTY

(Including Davie and Weston)

Acquolina	*Italian*	22
☑ Anthony's Pizza	*Pizza*	22
Bistro 555	*Italian*	24
☑ Bonefish Grill	*Seafood*	22
Cheese Course	*Eclectic*	25
East City Grill	*Amer.*	19
Ichiban	*Japanese*	19
Il Toscano	*Italian*	20
Ireland's	*Seafood/Steak*	26
☑ LaSpada's	*Deli/Sandwiches*	25
Lucille's	*Amer.*	22
Mario The Baker	*Italian/Pizza*	20
Moon Thai	*Japanese/Thai*	23
Myung Ga	*Korean*	29
NEW On the Menu	*French*	18
Original Pancake House	*Amer.*	20
Shorty's	*BBQ*	22
Tarantella	*Italian*	21
Tommy's Italian	*Italian*	23
Vienna Café	*Euro.*	24
Vigneto's	*Italian*	21
Viva Chile	*Chilean*	-

LOCATIONS

WEST CENTRAL BROWARD COUNTY

(Including Lauderdale Lakes, Lauderhill, Plantation and Sunrise)

Z Anthony's Pizza	*Pizza*	22
Bin 595	*Amer.*	22
Z Bonefish Grill	*Seafood*	22
Brazaviva	*Brazilian*	20
Z Cheesecake	*Amer.*	20
Grand Lux	*Eclectic*	19
India Hse.	*Indian*	21
J. Alexander	*Amer.*	20
Kiko	*Japanese/Thai*	26
Kingshead Pub	*Pub*	21
La Creperie	*French*	24
Las Vegas	*Cuban*	21
Mario The Baker	*Italian/Pizza*	20
Marumi Sushi	*Japanese*	-
Mustard Seed	*Eclectic*	25
Original Pancake House	*Amer.*	20
Outback	*Steak*	18
Padrino's	*Cuban*	21
Pasha Hse.	*Persian*	20
Paul	*Bakery/Sandwiches*	20
P.F. Chang's	*Chinese*	20
Pho 78	*Viet.*	23
Saxsay	*Peruvian*	-
Z Silver Pond	*Chinese*	25
Su Shin Thai	*Japanese/Thai*	22
Z Toa Toa	*Chinese*	26
TooJay's	*Deli*	18
Udipi	*Indian/Veg.*	23
Vigneto's	*Italian*	21
Villagio	*Italian*	21
Woodlands	*Indian/Veg.*	26

Palm Beach/Palm Beach County & Environs

CENTRAL PALM BEACH COUNTY

(Including Greenacres, Lake Worth, Lantana and Palm Beach)

Andros	*Greek/Med.*	21
Bice	*Italian*	22
Bimini Twist	*Seafood/Steak*	21
Bizaare Cafe	*Eclectic*	19
NEW Blind Monk	*Wine Bar*	18
Z Bonefish Grill	*Seafood*	22

Brewzzi	*Amer./Italian*	17
NEW Buccan	*Eclectic*	25
Z Cabana	*Nuevo Latino*	22
Z Café Boulud	*French*	26
Cafe Cellini	*Continental*	24
Café Centro	*Italian*	19
Z Café L'Europe	*Continental*	27
Cafe Sapori	*Italian*	24
Charley's Crab	*Seafood*	20
Z Cheesecake	*Amer.*	20
Z Chez Jean-Pierre	*French*	28
NEW China Beach	*Chinese*	-
City Cellar	*Med.*	20
City Diner	*Amer.*	20
Cottage	*Eclectic*	20
Couco Pazzo	*Italian*	22
Cucina Dell' Arte	*Italian*	21
Darbster	*Vegan*	-
Dave's Last	*Pub*	17
Don Ramon	*Cuban*	19
Dune Deck	*Amer.*	20
Echo	*Asian*	24
E.R. Bradley	*Amer.*	16
Fiorentina	*Italian*	19
Flagler Steak	*Steak*	26
Z Four Seasons	*Seafood*	25
Gratify	*Amer.*	-
Grease Burger	*Burgers*	20
Gulfstream Bistro	*Seafood*	18
Hamburger Heaven	*Burgers*	21
Havana	*Cuban*	21
Hot Pie	*Pizza*	26
Howley's	*Diner*	18
Il Bellagio	*Italian*	20
NEW Indus	*Indian*	-
Jade	*Amer.*	23
NEW John G's	*Amer.*	-
Leila	*Mideast.*	22
Leopard Lounge	*Amer./Eclectic*	18
NEW Luigi's	*Italian*	-
Maison Carlos	*French/Italian*	26
Z Marcello	*Italian*	28
Michelle Bernstein/Omphoy	*Med.*	24
McCormick/Schmick	*Seafood*	20
Michael R.	*Amer.*	18
Mississippi	*BBQ*	22
Morton's	*Steak*	25

Nick & Johnnie's | *Amer.*	16
Okeechobee | *Steak*	23
Outback | *Steak*	18
🅱 Palm Beach Grill | *Amer.*	25
Palm Beach Steak | *Steak*	21
Paradiso | *Italian*	25
Park Ave. BBQ | *BBQ*	21
Pelican Rest. | *Amer.*	-
P.F. Chang's | *Chinese*	20
Pistache | *French*	23
Pizza Girls | *Pizza*	20
Pizzeria Oceano | *Pizza*	-
Relish | *Burgers*	21
Renato's | *Italian*	24
Rhythm Café | *Amer.*	24
Riggins | *Seafood*	20
Rocco's Tacos | *Mex.*	20
Russo's Subs | *Sandwiches*	-
Ruth's Chris | *Steak*	25
Safire | *Asian*	26
Saigon Tokyo | *Japanese/Viet.*	22
Saito's | *Japanese/Steak*	19
Sloan's | *Ice Cream*	22
Station Grille/Hse. | *Seafood/Steak*	22
Stresa | *Italian*	19
Sushi/Thai Jo's | *Japanese/Thai*	23
Ta-boo | *Amer./Continental*	23
Taverna Opa | *Greek*	19
Temple Orange | *Italian/Mediterranean*	24
Thaikyo Asian | *Japanese/Thai*	19
This Is It Café | *Amer./Diner*	-
TooJay's | *Deli*	18
Top of the Point | *Amer.*	-
264 the Grill | *Amer.*	17
Vagabondi | *Italian*	24
Zuccarelli's | *Italian*	20

MARTIN COUNTY

(Including Jensen Beach and Stuart)

🅱 Anthony's Pizza | *Pizza*	22
🅱 Bonefish Grill | *Seafood*	22
Conchy Joe's | *Seafood*	19
11 Maple St. | *Amer.*	27
Flagler Grill | *Floribbean*	24
Outback | *Steak*	18
Park Ave. BBQ | *BBQ*	21

NORTH CENTRAL PALM BEACH COUNTY

(Including Lake Park, N. Palm Beach, Palm Beach Gardens, Palm Beach Shores and Riviera Beach)

Alladin | *Med.*	18
🅱 Anthony's Pizza | *Pizza*	22
Asian Fin | *Asian*	25
Big Al's Steaks | *Cheesesteaks*	19
🅱 Bonefish Grill | *Seafood*	22
Brass Ring Pub | *Pub*	24
Brio Tuscan | *Italian*	21
Cabo Flats | *Mex.*	16
🅱 Café Chardonnay | *Amer.*	25
Cantina Laredo | *Mex.*	20
🅱 Capital Grille | *Steak*	26
CG Burgers | *Burgers*	19
🅱 Cheesecake | *Amer.*	20
NEW Chuck Burger | *Burgers*	-
Cool'A Fishbar | *Seafood*	22
NEW Dirty Martini | *Eclectic*	-
Dockside Sea | *Seafood*	19
Entre Nous | *Amer.*	23
Figs | *Italian*	21
🅱 Five Guys | *Burgers*	20
Grimaldi's | *Pizza*	-
Ironwood | *Amer.*	18
J. Alexander | *Amer.*	20
Kevin's | *Deli*	-
Limoncello | *Italian*	20
Melting Pot | *Fondue*	19
Mondo's | *Amer./Med.*	18
Original Pancake House | *Amer.*	20
Outback | *Steak*	18
Paddy Mac's | *Pub*	19
NEW Paris/Town | *French*	-
Park Ave. BBQ | *BBQ*	21
Pelican Café | *Amer./Italian*	21
Pita Grille | *Med./Mideast.*	23
Ra Sushi | *Japanese*	19
River House | *Seafood/Steak*	22
NEW Russell's | *Seafood*	23
Russo's Subs | *Sandwiches*	-
Ruth's Chris | *Steak*	25
Sailfish Marina | *Seafood*	17
Saito's | *Japanese/Steak*	19
Sara's | *Amer.*	-
🅱 Seasons 52 | *Amer.*	23

LOCATIONS

Sloan's | *Ice Cream* 22
Spoto's | *Seafood* 22
Sushi/Thai Jo's | *Japanese/Thai* 23
Talay Thai | *Thai* 24
🆕 3800 Ocean | 23
   Amer./Seafood
III Forks | *Steak* 20
TooJay's | *Deli* 18
🆕 Umi | *Asian/Seafood* 26
Uncle Joe's | *Chinese* 20
🆕 Verdea | *Amer.* -
Vic & Angelo's | *Italian* 21
Yard Hse. | *Amer.* 19

NORTH PALM BEACH COUNTY

(Including Hobe Sound, Juno Beach, Jupiter and Tequesta)

Bistro | *Continental* 21
Buonasera | *Italian* 24
Café des Artistes | *French* 23
Captain Charlie | *Seafood* 27
Carmine's | *Italian/Pizza* 19
CG Burgers | *Burgers* 19
Evo | *Italian* -
🆕 Gourmet Burger | *Burgers* -
Guanabanas | *Floribbean* 18
Harry/Natives | *Amer.* 19
Hog Snappers | *Eclectic/Seafood* 26
Hurricane Café | *Amer.* 20
Jetty's | *Seafood* 22
🔁 Kee Grill | *Seafood/Steak* 24
Lazy Loggerhead | *Seafood* 24
Little Moir's | *Seafood* 26
Outback | *Steak* 18
Park Ave. BBQ | *BBQ* 21
Portobello | *Italian* 23
Royal Café | *Diner* 20
Tabica Grill | *Amer.* 21
Too Bizaare | *Eclectic* 19
TooJay's | *Deli* 18

SOUTH PALM BEACH COUNTY

(Including Boca Raton, Boynton Beach and Delray Beach)

🔁 Abe/Louie's | *Steak* 26
Absinthe | *Amer.* 18
🔁 Anthony's Pizza | *Pizza* 22
Arturo's | *Italian* 24

Banana Boat | *Seafood* 15
Bar Louie | *Amer.* 17
Ben's Kosher | *Deli/Jewish* 20
Big Al's Steaks | *Cheesesteaks* 19
Blue Anchor | *Pub* 17
Bluefin Sushi | *Japanese/Thai* 25
🔁 Bonefish Grill | *Seafood* 22
Brewzzi | *Amer./Italian* 17
🔁 Cabana | *Nuevo Latino* 22
Caffe Luna Rosa | *Italian* 20
Caliente Kitchen | *Mex.* 22
🔁 Capital Grille | *Steak* 26
Capri Rist. | *Italian* 23
Caruso's | *Italian* 24
🔁 Casa D'Angelo | *Italian* 27
Cay Da | *Viet.* 21
🔁 Cheesecake | *Amer.* 20
Cheese Course | *Eclectic* 25
China Dumpling | *Chinese* 20
🔁 Chops Lobster | 26
   Seafood/Steak
City Oyster | *Seafood* 22
Cuban Cafe | *Cuban* 19
Cut 432 | *Steak* 25
Dada | *Amer./Eclectic* 20
🆕 Deck 84 | *Amer* 19
🆕 DIG | *Amer.* -
🆕 English Tap | *Pub* -
🔁 Five Guys | *Burgers* 20
Flakowitz | *Deli* 18
Gol! | *Brazilian* 16
Grand Lux | *Eclectic* 19
Green Gourmet | *Health* -
Grille/Congress | *Amer.* 19
🔁 Henry's | *Amer.* 21
🔁 Houston's | *Amer.* 23
Il Girasole | *Italian* 25
J. Alexander | *Amer.* 20
Jimmy's Bistro | *Amer./Italian* 26
Josephine's | *Italian* 20
Joseph's Wine | *Med.* 23
Kathy's | *Continental* 25
🔁 Kee Grill | *Seafood/Steak* 24
La Cigale | *Med.* 24
La Luna | *Italian* 17
La Rosa Nautica | -
   Peruvian/Seafood
🔁 LaSpada's | *Deli/Sandwiches* 25

         Vote at ZAGAT.com

La Tre	*Viet.*	22
La Villetta	*Italian*	22
Legal Sea Foods	*Seafood*	21
Z Lemongrass	*Asian*	22
Linda Bean's	*Seafood*	17
Living Room	*Amer.*	15
Z Max's	*Amer.*	22
NEW Max's Harvest	*Amer.*	-
Mellow Mushroom	*Pizza*	21
Melting Pot	*Fondue*	19
Mississippi	*BBQ*	22
Morton's	*Steak*	25
Z NY Prime	*Steak*	25
Office	*Amer.*	20
Old Calypso	*Amer./Creole*	19
Original Pancake House	*Amer.*	20
Outback	*Steak*	18
NEW Ovenella	*Italian/Pizza*	-
Padrino's	*Cuban*	21
Park Ave. BBQ	*BBQ*	21
P.F. Chang's	*Chinese*	20
NEW Philippe Chow	*Chinese*	-
NEW Piñon Grill	*Amer.*	22
Pizza Rustica	*Pizza*	19
Prime Catch	*Seafood*	21
Racks Downtown	*Amer.*	21
Renzo's	*Italian*	22
Rocco's Tacos	*Mex.*	20
Ruth's Chris	*Steak*	25
Saito's	*Japanese/Steak*	19
Sapori	*Italian*	28
NEW Scuola Vecchia	*Pizza*	-
Z Seasons 52	*Amer.*	23
Sláinte Irish	*Pub*	17
Sloan's	*Ice Cream*	22
NEW Smokehouse	*BBQ*	-
Snappers	*Seafood*	18
SoLita	*Italian*	21
Stir Crazy	*Asian*	19
Sundy House	*Amer.*	22
Sushi Simon	*Japanese*	23
Sushi/Thai Jo's	*Japanese/Thai*	23
Table 42	*Italian*	21
Taso's Greek	*Greek*	19
Taverna Kyma	*Greek*	20
Tempura Hse.	*Chinese/Japanese*	18
Z 32 East	*Amer.*	25

Tin Muffin Café	*Amer.*	23
TooJay's	*Deli*	18
Tramonti	*Italian*	25
Tratt. Romana	*Italian*	26
Triple Eight	*Amer.*	-
Truluck's	*Seafood*	24
Tryst	*Amer.*	-
Two Georges	*Seafood*	15
Uncle Julio's	*Tex-Mex*	18
Uncle Tai's	*Chinese*	23
Vic & Angelo's	*Italian*	21
Village Tav.	*Amer.*	19
Villagio	*Italian*	21
Vivo Partenza	*Italian*	23
Ziree Thai	*Thai*	24

ST. LUCIE COUNTY

Park Ave. BBQ	*BBQ*	21
TooJay's	*Deli*	18

WESTERN PALM BEACH COUNTY

(Including Royal Palm Beach and Wellington)

Z Anthony's Pizza	*Pizza*	22
Brass Ring Pub	*Pub*	24
Don Ramon	*Cuban*	19
Z Five Guys	*Burgers*	20
Original Pancake House	*Amer.*	20
Outback	*Steak*	18
NEW Pangea	*Asian*	-
Park Ave. BBQ	*BBQ*	21
Player's Club	*Seafood/Steak*	17
Saito's	*Japanese/Steak*	19
TooJay's	*Deli*	18

Naples

CITY OF NAPLES

Absinthe	*Med./Seafood*	21
NEW Agave	*SW*	-
Alexander's	*Amer./Euro.*	22
AZN Azian Cuizine	*Asian*	21
Baleen	*Amer./Seafood*	23
Bamboo Café	*French*	21
Bay House	*Southern*	22
Bha Bha	*Iranian/Persian*	24
Bleu Provence	*French*	27
Blue Heron	*Continental*	27
Z Bonefish Grill	*Seafood*	22

LOCATIONS

BrickTop's	*Amer.*	22
Brio Tuscan	*Italian*	23
Café & Bar Lurcat	*Amer.*	26
Campiello	*Italian*	25
☑ Capital Grille	*Steak*	26
Charlie Chiang's	*Chinese*	24
☑ Cheesecake	*Amer.*	23
Chops City Grill	*Seafood/Steak*	25
Cloyde's	*Seafood/Steak*	22
Côte d'Azur	*French*	27
Dock/Crayton	*Seafood*	20
Escargot 41	*French*	26
☑ Five Guys	*Burgers*	20
Fleming's Prime	*Steak*	25
Grill	*Steak*	26
Grouper & Chips	*Seafood*	24
Handsome Harry's	*Amer.*	21
HB's/Gulf	*Amer./Seafood*	19
I.M. Tapas	*Spanish*	25
Jolly Cricket	*British*	20
Kelly's Fish	*Seafood*	21
Le Lafayette	*French*	25
McCormick/Schmick	*Seafood*	20
MiraMare	*Italian*	21
M Waterfront	*Continental*	23
Naples Tomato	*Amer./Italian*	23
Outback	*Steak*	18
Pazzo!	*Italian*	24
P.F. Chang's	*Chinese*	24
Pincher's Crab	*Seafood*	20
Piola	*Pizza*	22
Ridgway	*Amer./Continental*	23
Riverwalk	*Amer./Seafood*	20
Roy's	*Hawaiian*	26
Sea Salt	*Italian/Seafood*	23
Shula's	*Steak*	23
St. George/Dragon	*Steak*	20
Stoney's Steak	*Steak*	23
Strip House	*Steak*	23
Tommy Bahama's	*Seafood*	21
Truluck's	*Seafood*	26
USS Nemo	*Seafood*	27
Vergina	*Italian*	19
Yabba Island	*Caribbean/Seafood*	20

COLLIER COUNTY

(See also City of Naples)

Arturo's	*Italian*	22
Marek's	*Continental/Seafood*	24
Sale e Pepe	*Italian*	24
Snook Inn	*Amer./Seafood*	20

LEE COUNTY

(Including Bonita Springs, Captiva Island, Estero, Ft. Myers, Ft. Myers Beach and Sanibel)

Angelina's	*Italian*	25
Bar Louie	*Amer.*	17
Bistro 41	*Amer.*	24
Blue Pointe	*Seafood/Steak*	24
Blue Water Bistro	*Seafood*	23
Blu Sushi	*Japanese*	24
☑ Bonefish Grill	*Seafood*	22
NEW Bratta's	*Amer./Italian*	-
Bubble Room	*Amer.*	19
Cantina Laredo	*Mex.*	20
Chip's	*Seafood/Steak*	23
Chops City Grill	*Seafood/Steak*	25
Cru Restaurant	*Amer.*	24
Doc Ford's	*Floribbean/Seafood*	22
☑ Five Guys	*Burgers*	20
Grimaldi's	*Pizza*	-
Mad Hatter	*Amer.*	26
Melting Pot	*Fondue*	19
Mucky Duck	*Pub*	19
Old Captiva Hse.	*Floribbean/Seafood*	22
Outback	*Steak*	18
P.F. Chang's	*Chinese*	24
Pincher's Crab	*Seafood*	20
Prawnbroker/Timbers	*Seafood*	25
Roy's	*Hawaiian*	26
Ruth's Chris	*Steak*	26
Sandy Butler	*Amer.*	25
Stir Crazy	*Asian*	19
Sunshine Seafood	*Seafood*	24
Table Apart	*Eclectic*	25
Veranda	*Southern*	26
Wylds Café	*Amer.*	26

Special Features

Listings cover the best in each category and include names, locations and
Food ratings. Multi-location restaurants' features may vary by branch.

BOAT DOCKING FACILITIES

Alabama Jacks | **Key Largo/K**	20
Banana Boat | **Boynton Bch/P**	15
Blue Heron | **Naples/N**	27
⚡ Blue Moon Fish | **Laud-by-Sea/B**	24
Calypso's/Grille | **Key Largo/K**	23
Cloyde's | **Naples/N**	22
Commodore | **Key W./K**	23
Conchy Joe's | **Jensen Bch/P**	19
Da Campo | **Ft. Laud/B**	23
NEW Deck 84 | **Delray Bch/P**	19
⚡ Din. Rm./Little Palm | **Little Torch Key/K**	28
Doc Ford's | **Ft. Myers Bch/N**	22
Dock/Crayton | **Naples/N**	20
⚡ 15th St. Fish | **Ft. Laud/B**	19
Garcia's | **Miami Riv**	23
NEW GG's | **H'wood/B**	20
Grille 66 | **Ft. Laud/B**	24
Guanabanas | **Jupiter/P**	18
Half Shell | **Key W./K**	23
⚡ Houston's | **Pompano Bch/B**	23
Island Grill | **Islamorada/K**	24
Jetty's | **Jupiter/P**	22
Jimmy Johnson's | **Key Largo/K**	18
Keys Fisheries | **Marathon/K**	26
Lido | **SoBe**	22
Marker 88 | **Islamorada/K**	21
Monty's | **multi.**	17
⚡ Morada Bay | **Islamorada/K**	22
Old Calypso | **Delray Bch/P**	19
Old Captiva Hse. | **Captiva Is/N**	22
Pelican Landing | **Ft. Laud/B**	21
⚡ Pierre's | **Islamorada/K**	27
Prime Catch | **Boynton Bch/P**	21
Racks Italian | **No. Miami Bch**	20
Red Fish Grill | **Coral Gables**	22
NEW Rickenbacker | **Key Biscayne**	20
River House | **Palm Bch Gdns/P**	22
Riverwalk | **Naples/N**	20
Roy's | **Naples/N**	26
Rustic Inn | **Ft. Laud/B**	22
Sailfish Marina | **Palm Bch Shores/P**	17
Schooner Wharf | **Key W./K**	14
⚡ Seasons 52 | **Palm Bch Gdns/P**	23
Snapper's Waterfront | **Key Largo/K**	20
Snook Inn | **Marco Is/N**	20
Southport Raw | **Ft. Laud/B**	20
Tony Chan's | **Downtown**	23
Turtle Kraals | **Key W./K**	18
Two Georges | **multi.**	15
Wild E. Asian | **Ft. Laud/B**	17
⚡ Zuma | **Downtown**	28

BREAKFAST

(See also Hotel Dining)

A la Folie Café | **SoBe**	21
Bagatelle | **Key W./K**	21
Balans | **SoBe**	19
Banana Cafe | **Key W./K**	23
NEW Bernie's L.A. | **SoBe**	26
Berries | **Coco Grove**	20
Big Pink | **SoBe**	20
⚡ Blue Heaven | **Key W./K**	25
Café at Books & Books | **multi.**	21
Café La Bonne | **Ft. Laud/B**	22
Caffe Luna Rosa | **Delray Bch/P**	20
Camille's | **Key W./K**	22
NEW Cecconi's | **Miami Bch**	22
City Diner | **W. Palm/P**	20
Croissants | **Key W./K**	24
NEW Crumb/Parchment | **Design Dist**	-
David's | **SoBe**	19
Deli Lane | **multi.**	17
Dune Deck | **Lantana/P**	20
11th St. Diner | **SoBe**	20
Floridian | **Ft. Laud/B**	18
Green/Cafe | **Coco Grove**	19
Guanabanas | **Jupiter/P**	18
Hamburger Heaven | **Palm Bch/P**	21

Howley's | **W. Palm/P**	_18_
Hurricane Café | **Juno Bch/P**	_20_
Islas Canarias | **Little Havana**	_22_
NEW John G's | **Manalapan/P**	_-_
La Casona | **W. Sunset**	_-_
Lazy Loggerhead | **Jupiter/P**	_24_
Mustard Seed | **Plantation/B**	_25_
News Cafe | **SoBe**	_18_
Nexxt Cafe | **SoBe**	_18_
NEW On the Menu | **Davie/B**	_18_
Original Pancake House | **multi.**	_20_
Pepe's | **Key W./K**	_24_
Puerto Sagua | **SoBe**	_23_
Royal Café | **Jupiter/P**	_20_
S&S | **Downtown**	_23_
Sarabeth's | **Key W./K**	_24_
Sergio's | **multi.**	_20_
660/Angler's | **SoBe**	_23_
Square One | **Key W./K**	_21_
Sugar Reef | **H'wood/B**	_24_
This Is It Café | **W. Palm/P**	_-_
TooJay's | **multi.**	_18_
Van Dyke Cafe | **SoBe**	_16_
Z Versailles | **Little Havana**	_21_

BRUNCH

Z Abe/Louie's | **Boca/P**	_26_
Aruba Beach | **Laud-by-Sea/B**	_17_
Balans | **SoBe**	_19_
Bizcaya | **Coco Grove**	_24_
Z Blue Heaven | **Key W./K**	_25_
Z Blue Moon Fish | **multi.**	_24_
Z Café Boulud | **Palm Bch/P**	_26_
Café Solé | **Key W./K**	_24_
Caffe Luna Rosa | **Delray Bch/P**	_20_
Camille's | **Key W./K**	_22_
NEW Cecconi's | **Miami Bch**	_22_
Charley's Crab | **Palm Bch/P**	_20_
Chart House | **Ft. Laud/B**	_20_
NEW City Hall | **Wynwood**	_-_
NEW Deck 84 | **Delray Bch/P**	_19_
Deli Lane | **multi.**	_17_
Democratic/Beer | **Downtown**	_-_
11th St. Diner | **SoBe**	_20_
E.R. Bradley | **W. Palm/P**	_16_
Icebox Café | **SoBe**	_22_
La Palma | **Coral Gables**	_21_
Z Louie's | **Key W./K**	_26_

Martin's | **Key W./K**	_22_
Nexxt Cafe | **SoBe**	_18_
Nikki | **SoBe**	_16_
Perricone's | **Brickell**	_22_
NEW Piñon Grill | **Boca/P**	_22_
NEW Royal | **SoBe**	_-_
Z Sage | **Ft. Laud/B**	_22_
Sailfish Marina | **Palm Bch Shores/P**	_17_
Sarabeth's | **Key W./K**	_24_
Sergio's | **multi.**	_20_
660/Angler's | **SoBe**	_23_
Soyka | **UES**	_20_
Z Steak 954 | **Ft. Laud/B**	_24_
Sugar Reef | **H'wood/B**	_24_
Sundy House | **Delray Bch/P**	_22_
Ta-boo | **Palm Bch/P**	_23_
NEW Tudor House | **SoBe**	_-_
YOLO | **Ft. Laud/B**	_21_

BUFFET

(Check availability)

Aruba Beach | **Laud-by-Sea/B**	_17_
Bin 595 | **Plantation/B**	_22_
Bizcaya | **Coco Grove**	_24_
Z Blue Moon Fish | **Laud-by-Sea/B**	_24_
Braza Leña | **multi.**	_24_
Brazaviva | **Sunrise/B**	_20_
Cioppino | **Key Biscayne**	_23_
NEW Copper Chimney | **Sunny Is Bch**	_25_
Z Din. Rm./Little Palm | **Little Torch Key/K**	_28_
E.R. Bradley | **W. Palm/P**	_16_
Essensia | **Miami Bch**	_21_
Fontana | **Coral Gables**	_26_
Gol! | **Delray Bch/P**	_16_
House of India | **Coral Gables**	_19_
Imlee | **Pinecrest**	_25_
India Hse. | **Plantation/B**	_21_
Indian Chillics | **Pembroke Pines/B**	_-_
NEW Indus | **W. Palm/P**	_-_
Kuluck | **Tamarac/B**	_-_
La Palma | **Coral Gables**	_21_
Le Lafayette | **Naples/N**	_25_
Madras | **Pompano Bch/B**	_22_
Maya Tapas | **SoBe**	_17_

Mesazul | **Doral**   -

Z Morada Bay | **Islamorada/K**   22

Old San Juan | **W. Miami**   22

Olivos | **Doral**   26

Paddy Mac's | 19
  Palm Bch Gdns/P

Padrino's | **multi.**   21

Pasha Hse. | **Plantation/B**   20

Perricone's | **Brickell**   22

Sea Salt | **Naples/N**   23

Sundy House | **Delray Bch/P**   22

NEW Tokyo Blue | **Ft. Laud/B**   20

Trattoria Bella | **Margate/B**   -

Udipi | **Sunrise/B**   23

Uvas | **UES**   19

Woodlands | **Lauderhill/B**   26

BUSINESS DINING

Z Abe/Louie's | **Boca/P**   26

Aizia | **Hallandale/B**   19

Ambry German | **Ft. Laud/B**   21

Arturo's | **Boca/P**   24

Asian Fin | **Palm Bch Gdns/P**   25

Bice | **Palm Bch/P**   22

Bizcaya | **Coco Grove**   24

Bluepoint Grill | **H'wood/B**   18

Z Bonefish Grill | **Plantation/B**   22

Bourbon Steak | **Aventura**   25

Brio Tuscan | **multi.**   21

Z Café Boulud | **Palm Bch/P**   26

Z Café Chardonnay | 25
  Palm Bch Gdns/P

NEW Café Jamm | **Ft. Laud/B**   -

Z Café L'Europe | **Palm Bch/P**   27

Z Cafe/Martorano | **H'wood/B**   24

Z Cafe Maxx | **Pompano Bch/B**   27

Café Sambal | **Brickell**   22

Cafe Sapori | **W. Palm/P**   24

Cafe Seville | **Ft. Laud/B**   25

Caffe Abbracci | **Coral Gables**   25

Caffé Milano | **SoBe**   17

Z Capital Grille | **multi.**   26

Caruso's | **Boca/P**   24

Z Casa D'Angelo | **Ft. Laud/B**   27

NEW Catch Grill | **Biscayne**   -

NEW Cecconi's | **Miami Bch**   22

Chima Brazilian | **Ft. Laud/B**   25

Z Chops Lobster | **Boca/P**   26

Christy's | **Coral Gables**   24

Cioppino | **Key Biscayne**   23

Cloyde's | **Naples/N**   22

Côte d'Azur | **Naples/N**   27

Council Oak | **H'wood/B**   24

Cut 432 | **Delray Bch/P**   25

Da Campo | **Ft. Laud/B**   23

Dolores/Lolita | **Brickell**   19

Don Ramon | **W. Palm/P**   19

East City Grill | **Weston/B**   19

Echo | **Palm Bch/P**   24

NEW Eden | **SoBe**   21

Z Eduardo/San Angel | 27
  Ft. Laud/B

Elle's | **Miramar/B**   21

El Novillo | **Miami Lks**   22

Evo | **Tequesta/P**   -

NEW 1500 Degrees | 24
  Miami Bch

Z 15th St. Fish | **Ft. Laud/B**   19

Flagler Steak | **Palm Bch/P**   26

Fontana | **Coral Gables**   26

Gibraltar | **Coco Grove**   20

Gold Coast | **Coral Spgs/B**   21

Grateful Palate | **Ft. Laud/B**   24

Graziano's | **Westchester**   25

Grille 66 | **Ft. Laud/B**   24

Grill on the Alley | **Aventura**   22

Havana Harry's | **Coral Gables**   19

Z Il Gabbiano | **Downtown**   27

I.M. Tapas | **Naples/N**   25

Ireland's | **Weston/B**   26

Ironwood | **Palm Bch Gdns/P**   18

Jaguar | **Coco Grove**   22

J. Alexander | **Palm Bch Gdns/P**   20

Z Joe's Stone | **SoBe**   27

Z Johnny V | **Ft. Laud/B**   24

Kathy's | **Boca/P**   25

La Cigale | **Delray Bch/P**   24

Z La Dorada | **Coral Gables**   26

La Riviera | **Airport**   -

Leila | **W. Palm/P**   22

Little Havana | **No. Miami**   22

Z Louie's | **Key W./K**   26

Z Mai-Kai | **Ft. Laud/B**   16

Maison Carlos | **W. Palm/P**   26

NEW Makoto | **Bal Harbour**   25

Z NEW Market 17 | **Ft. Laud/B**   26

SPECIAL FEATURES

NEW Max's Harvest | Delray Bch/P	-
NEW M Bar | Ft. Laud/B	-
Michelle Bernstein/Omphoy | Palm Bch/P	24
Mesazul | Doral	-
MiraMare | Naples/N	21
Morton's | multi.	25
M Waterfront | Naples/N	23
Z NY Prime | Boca/P	25
Oceanaire | Brickell	24
Office | Delray Bch/P	20
Z Oishi Thai | No. Miami	26
Okeechobee | W. Palm/P	23
Olivos | Doral	26
Z Ortanique | Coral Gables	26
Osteria del Teatro | SoBe	26
Z Palm | Bay Harbor Is	28
Z Palm Beach Grill | Palm Bch/P	25
Z Palme d'Or | Coral Gables	28
Panorama | Coco Grove	-
Paradiso | Lake Worth/P	25
Z Pascal's | Coral Gables	27
Pelican Café | Lake Pk/P	21
Perricone's | Brickell	22
P.F. Chang's | No. Miami Bch	20
NEW Pied à Terre | SoBe	-
Z Pierre's | Islamorada/K	27
NEW Piñon Grill | Boca/P	22
Pistache | W. Palm/P	23
Prime Catch | Boynton Bch/P	21
Z Prime One | SoBe	27
Prime Steakhouse | Key W./K	25
Provence | SoBe	24
Z Rainbow Palace | Ft. Laud/B	26
NEW Rare Las Olas | Ft. Laud/B	21
Rosinella | Brickell	20
NEW Route 9 | Coral Gables	20
NEW Royal | SoBe	-
Roy's | multi.	26
NEW Russell's | Palm Bch Gdns/P	23
Ruth's Chris | multi.	25
NEW Saia | Ft. Laud/B	-
Sakura | Coral Gables	24
Scarpetta | Miami Bch	25
Sea Salt | Naples/N	23

Z Seasons 52 | multi.	23
Shibui | Kendall	24
Shula's | multi.	23
Smith/Wollensky | SoBe	23
Spoto's | Palm Bch Gdns/P	22
STK Miami | Miami Bch	22
Strip House | Key W./K	24
Sunfish | Ft. Laud/B	24
NEW Sustain | Downtown	21
NEW Symcha's | SoBe	25
Table 42 | Boca/P	21
Ta-boo | Palm Bch/P	23
Temple Orange | Manalapan/P	24
NEW 3800 Ocean | Riviera Bch/P	23
Z 3030 Ocean | Ft. Laud/B	26
Z 32 East | Delray Bch/P	25
III Forks | multi.	20
Timpano | Ft. Laud/B	23
Tony Chan's | Downtown	23
Top of the Point | W. Palm/P	-
Tratt. Sole | So. Miami	20
Truluck's | multi.	24
NEW Umi | Palm Bch Gdns/P	26
Via Luna | Ft. Laud/B	21
Villagio | multi.	21
Wild E. Asian | Ft. Laud/B	17
Yuca | SoBe	20

CELEBRITY CHEFS

Tim Andriola	
Timo | Sunny Is Bch	25
Michelle Bernstein	
NEW Crumb/Parchment | Design Dist	-
Michelle Bernstein/Omphoy | Palm Bch/P	24
Z Michy's | UES	27
Z Sra. Martinez | Design Dist	25
Daniel Boulud	
Z Café Boulud | Palm Bch/P	26
NEW DB Bistro Moderne | Downtown	26
Adrianne Calvo	
Chef Adrianne's | Kendall	25

Scott Conant
  Scarpetta | **Miami Bch**   25

Clay Conley
  NEW Buccan | **Palm Bch/P**   25

Paula DaSilva
  NEW 1500 Degrees | 24
  Miami Bch

Jamie DeRosa
  NEW Tudor House | **SoBe**   –

Micah Edelstein
  NEW Nemesis | **Downtown**   –

Angelo Elia
  Z Casa D'Angelo | **multi.**   27
  D'Angelo | **Oakland Pk/B**   25

Todd English
  Da Campo | **Ft. Laud/B**   23
  NEW English Tap | **Boca/P**   –
  Figs | **Palm Bch Gdns/P**   21

Marcello Fiorentino
  Z Marcello | **W. Palm/P**   28

Cindy Hutson
  Z Ortanique | **Coral Gables**   26

Dewey LoSasso
  Forge | **Miami Bch**   24

Steve Martorano
  Z Cafe/Martorano | **multi.**   24

Nobu Matsuhisa
  Z Nobu Miami | **SoBe**   27

Bernie Matz
  NEW Bernie's L.A. | **SoBe**   26

Dean James Max
  NEW 3800 Ocean | 23
  Riviera Bch/P
  Z 3030 Ocean | **Ft. Laud/B**   26

Nick Morfogen
  Z 32 East | **Delray Bch/P**   25

Makoto Okuwa
  NEW Makoto | **Bal Harbour**   25

Pascal Oudin
  Z Pascal's | **Coral Gables**   27

Mike Perrin
  11 Maple St. | **Jensen Bch/P**   27

Alfred Portale
  Gotham Steak | **Miami Bch**   23

Eduardo Pria
  Z Eduardo/San Angel | 27
  Ft. Laud/B

Douglas Rodriguez
  NEW De Rodriguez | **SoBe**   21
  Z OLA | **SoBe**   27

Philippe Ruiz
  Z Palme d'Or | **Coral Gables**   28

Oliver Saucy
  Z Cafe Maxx | 27
  Pompano Bch/B

Michael Schwartz
  NEW Harry's Pizzeria | –
  Design Dist
  Z Michael's | **Design Dist**   27

Claude Troisgros
  NEW Blue Door Fish | **SoBe**   23

Johnny Vinczencz
  Z Johnny V | **Ft. Laud/B**   24

Geoffrey Zakarian
  NEW Tudor House | **SoBe**   –

CHILD-FRIENDLY

(Alternatives to the usual fast-food
places; * children's menu available)

Abbondanza	**Key W./K**	20
Andiamo! Pizza	**UES**	25
Antonia's	**Key W./K**	27
Archie's Pizza*	**Key Biscayne**	21
Bagatelle*	**Key W./K**	21
Bahamas Fish*	**W. Miami**	20
Balans	**SoBe**	19
Banana Cafe	**Key W./K**	23
Bangkok Bangkok	**Coral Gables**	19
Bangkok Bangkok	**Kendall**	23
Barracuda Grill*	**Marathon/K**	21
Bella Luna	**Aventura**	23
NEW Bernie's L.A.	**SoBe**	26
Berries	**Coco Grove**	20
Big Cheese*	**So. Miami**	21
Big Pink*	**SoBe**	20
Bizcaya*	**Coco Grove**	24
Z Blue Heaven*	**Key W./K**	25
Z Bonefish Grill*	**Kendall**	22
Bongos Cuban*	**Downtown**	16
Bongusto!	**Ft. Laud/B**	24
B.O.'s Fish	**Key W./K**	24
Café at Books & Books	**SoBe**	21
Café Sambal*	**Brickell**	22
Calypso's/Grille*	**Key Largo/K**	23
Camille's*	**Key W./K**	22
Captain's Tav.*	**Pinecrest**	23

SPECIAL FEATURES

Carpaccio | **Bal Harbour**	23
Casa Paco* | **So. Miami**	21
Cay Da | **Boca/P**	21
CG Burgers* | **multi.**	19
Charley's Crab* | **Palm Bch/P**	20
☑ Cheesecake | **multi.**	20
Chico's Cantina* | **Key W./K**	–
Christina Wan's | **Ft. Laud/B**	21
NEW Chuck Burger | **Palm Bch Gdns/P**	–
Conch Republic* | **Key W./K**	17
Conchy Joe's* | **Jensen Bch/P**	19
Croissants | **Key W./K**	24
NEW Crumb/Parchment | **Design Dist**	–
Daily Bread | **Pinecrest**	24
Da Leo Trattoria | **SoBe**	18
David's* | **SoBe**	19
Deli Lane* | **multi.**	17
Dogma Grill | **UES**	20
Duffy's Steak* | **Key W./K**	18
Dune Deck* | **Lantana/P**	20
East City Grill* | **Weston/B**	19
El Chalán* | **multi.**	23
11th St. Diner | **SoBe**	20
El Meson* | **Key W./K**	18
El Novillo* | **multi.**	22
El Rancho* | **SoBe**	19
Ferdo's Grill* | **Ft. Laud/B**	20
Finnegan's* | **Key W./K**	19
☑ Five Guys* | **multi.**	20
Floridian | **Ft. Laud/B**	18
Front Porch | **SoBe**	21
Fuji Hana | **Aventura**	22
Gables Diner* | **Coral Gables**	17
Garcia's | **Miami Riv**	23
Gourmet Diner* | **No. Miami Bch**	18
Grand Café* | **Key W./K**	22
Grazie Italian | **SoBe**	25
☑ Greek Islands | **Ft. Laud/B**	25
Green/Cafe* | **Coco Grove**	19
Guanabanas | **Jupiter/P**	18
Guayacan* | **Little Havana**	21
Half Shell* | **Key W./K**	23
Hamburger Heaven | **Palm Bch/P**	21
Harry/Natives* | **Hobe Sound/P**	19
NEW Harry's Pizzeria | **Design Dist**	–
Havana* | **W. Palm/P**	21
Havana Harry's | **Coral Gables**	19
Helen Huang's | **H'wood/B**	–
Here/Sun* | **No. Miami**	17
Hiro Japanese | **No. Miami Bch**	21
☑ Hiro's Yakko-San | **No. Miami Bch**	27
Hosteria Romana | **SoBe**	21
House of India | **Coral Gables**	19
Howley's* | **W. Palm/P**	18
Icebox Café | **SoBe**	22
Ichiban* | **Davie/B**	19
☑ Il Mulino* | **Ft. Laud/B**	22
Il Toscano | **Weston/B**	20
Islas Canarias | **multi.**	22
Jaguar | **Coco Grove**	22
Jasmine Thai | **Margate/B**	22
Jaxson's* | **Dania Bch/B**	21
JB's* | **Deerfield Bch/B**	18
Jetty's* | **Jupiter/P**	22
Kaiyo Grill* | **Islamorada/K**	–
Kampai* | **multi.**	22
Kelly's Carib.* | **Key W./K**	21
Khoury's | **So. Miami**	21
La Casita* | **Coral Gables**	23
La Casona* | **W. Sunset**	–
☑ La Dorada* | **Coral Gables**	26
Lan | **So. Miami**	23
La Palma | **Coral Gables**	21
La Sandwicherie | **SoBe**	25
Las Culebrinas* | **multi.**	21
☑ LaSpada's | **multi.**	25
Las Vegas* | **multi.**	21
La Trattoria | **Key W./K**	22
Lazy Loggerhead | **Jupiter/P**	24
Le Bistro | **Lighthse Pt/B**	22
Le Bouchon/Grove | **Coco Grove**	24
Le Provençal | **Coral Gables**	22
Little Havana* | **multi.**	22
Los Ranchos* | **multi.**	21
Madras* | **Pompano Bch/B**	22
☑ Mai-Kai* | **Ft. Laud/B**	16
Mangoes* | **Key W./K**	18
Marhaba Med. | **So. Miami**	25
Mario The Baker* | **multi.**	20
Maroosh | **Coral Gables**	25
Martin's | **Key W./K**	22
Mellow Mushroom | **Delray Bch/P**	21

Z Michaels* | **Key W./K**	26
Miss Saigon | **multi.**	23
Z Morada Bay* | **Islamorada/K**	22
Mo's | **Key W./K**	23
Mykonos | **Coral Way**	20
New Chinatown | **So. Miami**	20
News Cafe | **SoBe**	18
Oceans 234* | **Deerfield Bch/B**	19
Oggi Caffe* | **No. Bay Vill**	25
Old Florida* | **Wilton Manors/B**	19
Outback* | **multi.**	18
Paddy Mac's* | **Palm Bch Gdns/P**	19
Padrino's* | **multi.**	21
Papa Hughie's* | **Lighthse Pt/B**	24
Papichi | **Pinecrest**	20
Park Ave. BBQ* | **multi.**	21
Pasha Hse. | **Plantation/B**	20
Pasha's | **multi.**	19
Pelican RestCafé | **SoBe**	21
Pepe's* | **Key W./K**	24
Peppy's | **Coral Gables**	21
NEW Pincho Factory | **Westchester**	-
Piola | **SoBe**	22
Pit Bar-B-Q* | **West Dade**	21
Pizza Girls | **W. Palm/P**	20
Pizza Rustica | **multi.**	19
Puerto Sagua | **SoBe**	23
Randazzo's | **Coral Gables**	20
NEW Rickenbacker | **Key Biscayne**	20
Riggins* | **Lantana/P**	20
Rosalia's | **Aventura**	17
Rosinella | **multi.**	20
Royal Café | **Jupiter/P**	20
Rustic Inn* | **Ft. Laud/B**	22
Rusty Anchor | **Stock Island/K**	21
Sailfish Marina* | **Palm Bch Shores/P**	17
Sergio's* | **multi.**	20
Shibui* | **Kendall**	24
Shor American* | **Key W./K**	-
Shorty's* | **multi.**	22
Shula's* | **multi.**	23
Siam Cuisine | **Wilton Manors/B**	19
Siam Palace | **So. Miami**	23
Sloan's | **multi.**	22

NEW Smokehouse* | **Boca/P**	-
Soyka* | **UES**	20
Spiga | **SoBe**	24
Spris* | **multi.**	22
Sukhothai | **Ft. Laud/B**	24
Su Shin Izakaya | **Coral Gables**	23
Su Shin Thai | **Lauderhill/B**	22
Sushi Rock | **SoBe**	21
Sushi Siam/Rock | **multi.**	22
Taco Rico* | **Coral Gables**	22
Tamarind | **Miami Bch**	24
Tap Tap | **SoBe**	22
Tarantella* | **Weston/B**	21
Thai Cuisine* | **Key W./K**	-
Thai Hse. S. | **SoBe**	19
This Is It Café | **W. Palm/P**	-
Tiramesu | **SoBe**	21
Titanic Brewery* | **Coral Gables**	17
T-Mex | **SoBe**	17
Tokyo Sushi | **Ft. Laud/B**	23
Tom Jenkins' | **Ft. Laud/B**	25
Toni's Sushi | **SoBe**	25
Tony Chan's | **Downtown**	23
TooJay's* | **multi.**	18
Tratt. Luna | **Pinecrest**	24
Tropical Chinese | **Westchester**	26
Tumi* | **Margate/B**	20
Turtle Kraals* | **Key W./K**	18
Tutto Pasta | **Brickell**	22
Tutto Pizza | **Brickell**	24
Two Chefs | **So. Miami**	23
Two Friends* | **Key W./K**	18
Uvas | **UES**	19
Van Dyke Cafe | **SoBe**	16
Z Versailles* | **Little Havana**	21
Whale's Rib* | **Deerfield Bch/B**	20

DANCING

Aruba Beach | **Laud-by-Sea/B**	17
Banana Boat | **Boynton Bch/P**	15
Bongos Cuban | **multi.**	16
NEW Bratta's | **Ft. Myers/N**	-
Z Cafe/Martorano | **H'wood/B**	24
Cucina Dell' Arte | **Palm Bch/P**	21
NEW Dirty Martini | **Palm Bch Gdns/P**	-
Dolores/Lolita | **Brickell**	19
El Meson | **Key W./K**	18

SPECIAL FEATURES

E.R. Bradley	W. Palm/P	16	Z Cafe Maxx	Pompano Bch/B	27
Handsome Harry's	Naples/N	21	Café Ragazzi	Surfside	23
JB's	Deerfield Bch/B	18	Captain's Tav.	Pinecrest	23
Jimmy Buffett's	Key W./K	13	Chart House	Coco Grove	20
Kuluck	Tamarac/B	-	Z Cheesecake	multi.	20
Lario's/Beach	SoBe	20	Cioppino	Key Biscayne	23
Leopard Lounge	Palm Bch/P	18	City Diner	W. Palm/P	20
Mango's Tropical	SoBe	13	Conch Republic	Key W./K	17
Monty's	multi.	17	Croissants	Key W./K	24
My Big Fat Greek	Dania Bch/B	20	NEW Crumb/Parchment	Design Dist	-
Nikki	SoBe	16		
Old Calypso	Delray Bch/P	19	Daily Bread	Pinecrest	24
Pelican Landing	Ft. Laud/B	21	Escopazzo	SoBe	25
Z Pierre's	Islamorada/K	27	Fin & Claw	Lighthse Pt/B	20
NEW Rare Las Olas	Ft. Laud/B	21	Fontana	Coral Gables	26
Red Koi	Coral Gables	25	Z Four Seasons	Palm Bch/P	25
Sloppy Joe's	Key W./K	13	Gourmet Diner	No. Miami Bch	18
NEW Soirée at Vice	SoBe	-	Graziano's	Westchester	25
SoLita	multi.	21	Hi-Life	Ft. Laud/B	25
Stoney's Steak	Naples/N	23	Hillstone	Coral Gables	-
Tantra	SoBe	21	Hot Tin Roof	Key W./K	25
Tapas & Tintos	multi.	20	Z Houston's	No. Miami Bch	23
Tarpon Bend	Ft. Laud/B	20	Icebox Café	SoBe	22
Tatiana	Hallandale/B	-	Jaguar	Coco Grove	22
Taverna Opa	multi.	19	Jaxson's	Dania Bch/B	21
Timpano	Ft. Laud/B	23	Lan	So. Miami	23
NEW Tokyo Blue	Ft. Laud/B	20	Z NEW Market 17	Ft. Laud/B	26
Trattoria Bella	Margate/B	-	Z Michaels	Key W./K	26
NEW Trio/Bay	No. Bay Vill	-	Morton's	multi.	25
Van Dyke Cafe	SoBe	16	Old Calypso	Delray Bch/P	19
Vergina	Naples/N	19	NEW On the Menu	Davie/B	18
Village Grille	Laud-by-Sea/B	20	Z Ortanique	Coral Gables	26
Vita by Baoli	SoBe	-	Z Palme d'Or	Coral Gables	28
Vivo Partenza	Boca/P	23	Paul	multi.	20
Yabba Island	Naples/N	20	Pepe's	Key W./K	24
Yuca	SoBe	20	Portobello	Jupiter/P	23
			Z Prime One	SoBe	27
			Royal Bavarian	UES	21

DESSERT SPECIALISTS

A la Folie Café	SoBe	21	Ruth's Chris	Coral Gables	25
Z Azul	Brickell	27	Z Seasons 52	Coral Gables	23
Z Barton G.	SoBe	22	Z Seven Fish	Key W./K	27
Big Pink	SoBe	20	Sloan's	multi.	22
Billy's Stone	H'wood/B	23	Smith/Wollensky	SoBe	23
Z Blue Heaven	Key W./K	25	Soyka	UES	20
By Word/Mouth	Oakland Pk/B	25	NEW Star Bistro	Cooper City/B	-
Z Café Boulud	Palm Bch/P	26	SushiSamba	SoBe	23
Z Café L'Europe	Palm Bch/P	27	Temple Orange	Manalapan/P	24
			Z 32 East	Delray Bch/P	25

Timo | **Sunny Is Bch** — 25

TooJay's | **multi.** — 18

NEW 2B Asian | **Little Havana** — 25

Wish | **SoBe** — 25

Z Zuma | **Downtown** — 28

DINING ALONE

(Other than hotels and places with counter service)

A la Folie Café | **SoBe** — 21

Alladin | **Palm Bch Gdns/P** — 18

Andros | **Lake Worth/P** — 21

Angelique | **Coral Gables** — 18

Z Anthony's Pizza | **Plantation/B** — 22

Asian Fin | **Palm Bch Gdns/P** — 25

Balans | **SoBe** — 19

Bella Luna | **Aventura** — 23

NEW Bernie's L.A. | **SoBe** — 26

Big Al's Steaks | **Delray Bch/P** — 19

Big Pink | **SoBe** — 20

Bizaare Cafe | **Lake Worth/P** — 19

Blue Water Bistro | **Estero/N** — 23

Brass Ring Pub | **multi.** — 24

Bubble Room | **Captiva Is/N** — 19

Z Cabana | **W. Palm/P** — 22

Cabo Flats | **Palm Bch Gdns/P** — 16

Café at Books & Books | **multi.** — 21

Cafe Cellini | **Palm Bch/P** — 24

Z Café Chardonnay | **Palm Bch Gdns/P** — 25

Café des Artistes | **Jupiter/P** — 23

Café Emunah | **Ft. Laud/B** — 25

Caliente Kitchen | **Delray Bch/P** — 22

Carmine's | **Jupiter/P** — 19

CG Burgers | **Jupiter/P** — 19

Cheese Course | **Weston/B** — 25

City Diner | **W. Palm/P** — 20

Coconuts | **Ft. Laud/B** — 23

Cool'A Fishbar | **Palm Bch Gdns/P** — 22

Croissants | **Key W./K** — 24

NEW Crumb/Parchment | **Design Dist** — –

Cuban Cafe | **Boca/P** — 19

Dada | **Delray Bch/P** — 20

Darbster | **Lake Worth/P** — –

NEW Deck 84 | **Delray Bch/P** — 19

Doc Ford's | **Sanibel/N** — 22

Dockside Sea | **Lake Pk/P** — 19

Dogma Grill | **UES** — 20

Don Ramon | **W. Palm/P** — 19

Dune Deck | **Lantana/P** — 20

Echo | **Palm Bch/P** — 24

11th St. Diner | **SoBe** — 20

El Tamarindo | **Ft. Laud/B** — 22

NEW Fadó Irish Pub | **Brickell** — 17

Z 15th St. Fish | **Ft. Laud/B** — 19

Filling Station | **Downtown** — 17

Fin & Claw | **Lighthse Pt/B** — 20

Z Five Guys | **Palm Bch Gdns/P** — 20

NEW Flip Burger | **No. Miami** — 25

Garcia's | **Miami Riv** — 23

NEW Gourmet Burger | **Jupiter/P** — –

Gourmet Diner | **No. Miami Bch** — 18

Grateful Palate | **Ft. Laud/B** — 24

Gratify | **W. Palm/P** — –

Green/Cafe | **Coco Grove** — 19

Green Gourmet | **Delray Bch/P** — –

Grillfish | **SoBe** — 20

Grouper & Chips | **Naples/N** — 24

NEW Heavy Burger | **Aventura** — 22

Here/Sun | **No. Miami** — 17

Hillstone | **Coral Gables** — –

Z Hiro's Yakko-San | **No. Miami Bch** — 27

Z Houston's | **No. Miami Bch** — 23

Howley's | **W. Palm/P** — 18

Icebox Café | **SoBe** — 22

NEW Indus | **W. Palm/P** — –

Jaguar | **Coco Grove** — 22

Jaxson's | **Dania Bch/B** — 21

Jimmy's Bistro | **Delray Bch/P** — 26

Z Joe's Stone | **SoBe** — 27

Kathy's | **Boca/P** — 25

Kelly's Carib. | **Key W./K** — 21

Kevin's | **Palm Bch Gdns/P** — –

Lan | **So. Miami** — 23

Z LaSpada's | **multi.** — 25

Las Vegas | **Miami Bch** — 21

Le Croisic | **Key Biscayne** — 22

Le Tub | **H'wood/B** — 21

Lime Fresh Mex. | **multi.** — 19

Linda Bean's | **Delray Bch/P** — 17

Little Havana | **No. Miami** — 22

Living Room | **Boynton Bch/P** — 15

NEW Luigi's | **W. Palm/P** — –

Maiko | **SoBe**	-
NEW Makoto | **Bal Harbour**	25
Mangoes | **Key W./K**	18
Marker 88 | **Islamorada/K**	21
Z Michy's | **UES**	27
Monty's | **multi.**	17
Morton's | **Brickell**	25
Mykonos | **Coral Way**	20
Naples Tomato | **Naples/N**	23
News Cafe | **SoBe**	18
Office | **Delray Bch/P**	20
Off the Grille | **Kendall**	26
Okeechobee | **W. Palm/P**	23
OneBurger | **Coral Gables**	22
NEW 100 Montaditos | **Downtown**	-
NEW On the Menu | **Davie/B**	18
Otentic | **SoBe**	-
Outback | **Delray Bch/P**	18
Paddy Mac's | **Palm Bch Gdns/P**	19
Z Palm Beach Grill | **Palm Bch/P**	25
Paquito's | **No. Miami Bch**	22
Park Ave. BBQ | **Boca/P**	21
Paul | **multi.**	20
Pelican Café | **Lake Pk/P**	21
Pelican Rest. | **Lake Worth/P**	-
P.F. Chang's | **multi.**	20
Pita Grille | **No. Palm Bch/P**	23
Pizza Rustica | **multi.**	19
Pizzeria Oceano | **Lantana/P**	-
Z Rainbow Palace | **Ft. Laud/B**	26
Relish | **W. Palm/P**	21
Rhythm Café | **W. Palm/P**	24
Riggins | **Lantana/P**	20
River Oyster Bar | **Miami Riv**	25
Royal Café | **Jupiter/P**	20
NEW Russell's | **Palm Bch Gdns/P**	23
Sakura | **Coral Gables**	24
S&S | **Downtown**	23
Sara's | **Palm Bch Gdns/P**	-
NEW Scuola Vecchia | **Delray Bch/P**	-
Z Seasons 52 | **Ft. Laud/B**	23
Shula's | **Miami Lks**	23
Smith/Wollensky | **SoBe**	23
NEW Soi Asian | **Downtown**	-

Southport Raw | **Ft. Laud/B**	20
Station Grille/Hse. | **Lantana/P**	22
Sunfish | **Ft. Laud/B**	24
Tamarind | **Miami Bch**	24
Taverna Kyma | **Boca/P**	20
Tempura Hse. | **Boca/P**	18
This Is It Café | **W. Palm/P**	-
Titanic Brewery | **Coral Gables**	17
Tommy's Italian | **Davie/B**	23
Toni's Sushi | **SoBe**	25
Too Bizaare | **Jupiter/P**	19
TooJay's | **multi.**	18
Two Georges | **Boynton Bch/P**	15
Uncle Joe's | **Palm Bch Gdns/P**	20
Uvas | **UES**	19
Villagio | **Coral Gables**	21
NEW Wynwood | **Wynwood**	17
Yard Hse. | **Hallandale/B**	19
Zuccarelli's | **W. Palm/P**	20

EARLY-BIRD MENUS

Ambry German | **Ft. Laud/B**	21
Bimini Twist | **W. Palm/P**	21
Bistro | **Jupiter/P**	21
Bleu Provence | **Naples/N**	27
Café Emunah | **Ft. Laud/B**	25
Café Prima | **Miami Bch**	23
Capri Rist. | **Boca/P**	23
Captain Charlie | **Juno Bch/P**	27
Charley's Crab | **Palm Bch/P**	20
Christina Wan's | **Ft. Laud/B**	21
Dockside Sea | **Lake Pk/P**	19
Don Ramon | **W. Palm/P**	19
Entre Nous | **No. Palm Bch/P**	23
NEW GG's | **H'wood/B**	20
Handsome Harry's | **Naples/N**	21
Helen Huang's | **H'wood/B**	-
Here/Sun | **No. Miami**	17
Hurricane Café | **Juno Bch/P**	20
Jetty's | **Jupiter/P**	22
Z Kee Grill | **multi.**	24
La Luna | **Boca/P**	17
Le Lafayette | **Naples/N**	25
Z Mai-Kai | **Ft. Laud/B**	16
Mama Mia | **H'wood/B**	20
Z Max's | **Boca/P**	22
MiraMare | **Naples/N**	21
Mondo's | **No. Palm Bch/P**	18

Okeechobee | W. Palm/P — 23
Old Calypso | Delray Bch/P — 19
Old Florida | Wilton Manors/B — 19
Osteria del Teatro | SoBe — 26
Palm Beach Steak | Palm Bch/P — 21
NEW Philippe Chow | Boca/P — -
Pita Grille | No. Palm Bch/P — 23
Quattro | SoBe — 20
Riggins | Lantana/P — 20
Tabica Grill | Jupiter/P — 21
Taverna Kyma | Boca/P — 20
Taverna Opa | W. Palm/P — 19
Tiramesu | SoBe — 21
Tramonti | Delray Bch/P — 25
Trattoria Bella | Margate/B — -
Tumi | Margate/B — 20
264 the Grill | Palm Bch/P — 17
Uncle Tai's | Boca/P — 23
Vergina | Naples/N — 19

ENTERTAINMENT

(Call for days and times of performances)

A Fish/Avalon | varies | SoBe — 23
Aruba Beach | live music | Laud-by-Sea/B — 17
Bistro 41 | live music | Ft. Myers/N — 24
Blue Anchor | live music | Delray Bch/P — 17
Z Blue Heaven | solo guitarist | Key W./K — 25
Bongos Cuban | DJ/salsa | Downtown — 16
NEW Bratta's | piano, singers, etc. | Ft. Myers/N — -
Cafe Avanti | piano | Miami Bch — 25
Casa Juancho | Spanish | Little Havana — 24
NEW Dirty Martini | bands | Palm Bch Gdns/P — -
El Meson | salsa | Key W./K — 18
Finnegan's | Irish/live music | Key W./K — 19
Fritz & Franz | live music | Coral Gables — 17
Globe Cafe | jazz | Coral Gables — 17
Gordon Biersch | live music | Brickell — 18
Guanabanas | live music | Jupiter/P — 18

NEW Haven Gastro | DJ | SoBe — -
JB's | live music | Deerfield Bch/B — 18
Jimmy Buffett's | live music | Key W./K — 13
JohnMartin's | varies | Coral Gables — 17
La Barraca | flamenco | H'wood/B — 20
Z La Dorada | live music | Coral Gables — 26
Lario's/Beach | DJ | SoBe — 20
Leila | belly dancers | W. Palm/P — 22
Living Room | live music | Boynton Bch/P — 15
Magnum | piano | UES — 23
Z Mai-Kai | Polynesian show | Ft. Laud/B — 16
Mango's Tropical | live music | SoBe — 13
Marhaba Med. | belly dancers | So. Miami — 25
NEW Michele's | live music | Ft. Laud/B — -
Monty's | live music | multi. — 17
Nikki | DJ | SoBe — 16
Paddy Mac's | live music | Palm Bch Gdns/P — 19
Perricone's | jazz | Brickell — 22
NEW Russell's | piano | Palm Bch Gdns/P — 23
Sloppy Joe's | rock | Key W./K — 13
Spoto's | jazz | Palm Bch Gdns/P — 22
Square One | piano | Key W./K — 21
NEW Soirée at Vice | DJ | SoBe — -
SushiSamba | DJ | SoBe — 23
Tantra | DJ/drummer | SoBe — 21
Tap Tap | Haitian band | SoBe — 22
Tatiana | cabaret/dancers | Hallandale/B — -
Taverna Opa | varies | H'wood/B — 19
Titanic Brewery | karaoke/ live music | Coral Gables — 17
NEW Tokyo Blue | DJ/live music | Ft. Laud/B — 20
Van Dyke Cafe | live music | SoBe — 16
Village Grille | live music | Laud-by-Sea/B — 20

SPECIAL FEATURES

Vita by Baoli | DJ | **SoBe**	–
Yuca | salsa | **SoBe**	20
Zuperpollo | international music | **Coral Way**	18

FOOD TRUCKS

CheeseMe | **Loc Varies**	–
NEW Dim Ssäm à Gogo | **Loc Varies**	–
GastroPod | **Loc Varies**	–
NEW Jefe's | **Loc Varies**	–
Latin Burger | **Loc Varies**	–
NEW Miso Hungry | **Loc Varies**	–
NEW Ms. Cheezious | **Loc Varies**	–
NEW Nacho Mamas | **Loc Varies**	–
Red Koi Truck | **Loc Varies**	–
NEW Slow Food | **Loc Varies**	–

GREEN/LOCAL/ ORGANIC

Berries | **Coco Grove**	20
Bourbon Steak | **Aventura**	25
Café | **Key W./K**	26
Café Emunah | **Ft. Laud/B**	25
Z Cafe Maxx | **Pompano Bch/B**	27
Calypso's/Grille | **Key Largo/K**	23
Z Canyon Ranch | **Miami Bch**	19
Darbster | **Lake Worth/P**	–
NEW DIG | **Delray Bch/P**	–
11 Maple St. | **Jensen Bch/P**	27
Escopazzo | **SoBe**	25
Fontana | **Coral Gables**	26
Z Four Seasons | **Palm Bch/P**	25
Fratelli Lyon | **Design Dist**	22
Graziano's | **Westchester**	25
NEW Green Table | **Coral Gables**	–
Here/Sun | **No. Miami**	17
Julio's | **No. Miami Bch**	–
NEW Local Craft | **Coral Gables**	–
Z NEW Market 17 | **Ft. Laud/B**	26
NEW Max's Harvest | **Delray Bch/P**	–
Meat Market | **SoBe**	25
Z Nobu Miami | **SoBe**	27
Oceanaire | **Brickell**	24
Palm Beach Steak | **Palm Bch/P**	21
Z Palme d'Or | **Coral Gables**	28

Paradiso | **Lake Worth/P**	25
NEW Slow Food | **Loc Varies**	–
Sublime | **Ft. Laud/B**	21
NEW Sustain | **Downtown**	21
Z 32 East | **Delray Bch/P**	25
NEW Verdea | **Palm Bch Gdns/P**	–

HISTORIC PLACES

(Year opened; * building)

1863 | 915 Bistro* | **Key W./K**	25
1877 | El Meson* | **Key W./K**	18
1882 | Marek's* | **Marco Is/N**	24
1884 | Bagatelle* | **Key W./K**	21
1890 | Turtle Kraals* | **Key W./K**	18
1892 | Pisces* | **Key W./K**	27
1902 | Sundy House* | **Delray Bch/P**	22
1905 | 11 Maple St.* | **Jensen Bch/P**	27
1909 | Pepe's | **Key W./K**	24
1910 | Louie's* | **Key W./K**	26
1912 | Veranda* | **Ft. Myers/N**	26
1913 | Joe's Stone | **SoBe**	27
1917 | Sloppy Joe's* | **Key W./K**	13
1920 | Café* | **Key W./K**	26
1920 | Café Solé* | **Key W./K**	24
1920 | Michaels* | **Key W./K**	26
1920 | Old Captiva Hse.* | **Captiva Is/N**	22
1920 | Tap Tap* | **SoBe**	22
1920 | Uvas* | **UES**	19
1922 | Soya & Pomodoro* | **Downtown**	23
1923 | Dolores/Lolita* | **Brickell**	19
1924 | Dada* | **Delray Bch/P**	20
1924 | La Palma* | **Coral Gables**	21
1924 | Van Dyke Cafe* | **SoBe**	16
1925 | Triple Eight* | **Delray Bch/P**	–
1926 | Palme d'Or* | **Coral Gables**	28
1926 | Sra. Martinez* | **Design Dist**	25
1927 | Casablanca* | **Ft. Laud/B**	21
1928 | Cap's* | **Lighthse Pt/B**	17
1929 | Pelican Café* | **Lake Pk/P**	21
1930 | Mandolin* | **Design Dist**	25
1930 | Morgans* | **Wynwood**	24

1930 | Villa/Barton G.* | SoBe	24
1930 | Ziggie* | Islamorada/K	25
1933 | Gol!* | Delray Bch/P	16
1934 | Mangia Mangia* | Key W./K	20
1935 | Relish* | W. Palm/P	21
1937 | Floridian* | Ft. Laud/B	18
1938 | S&S | Downtown	23
1940 | Cafe Avanti* | Miami Bch	25
1941 | Pied à Terre* | SoBe	-
1941 | Ta-boo | Palm Bch/P	23
1945 | Hamburger Heaven | Palm Bch/P	21
1947 | Alabama Jacks | Key Largo/K	20
1947 | Green Turtle Inn | Islamorada/K	22
1947 | HB's/Gulf* | Naples/N	19
1947 | Okeechobee | W. Palm/P	23
1948 | 11th St. Diner* | SoBe	20
1948 | Russo's Subs | W. Palm/P	-
1950 | Blú la Pizzeria* | So. Miami	21
1950 | Howley's | W. Palm/P	18
1950 | Pilot House | Key Largo/K	19
1951 | Shorty's | So. Miami	22
1952 | Harry/Natives | Hobe Sound/P	19
1952 | Kelly's Fish* | Naples/N	21
1952 | Sailfish Marina | Palm Bch Shores/P	17
1955 | Frankie's Pizza | Westchester	26
1955 | Jumbo's | Liberty City	-
1955 | Rustic Inn | Ft. Laud/B	22
1955 | Two Georges | Boynton Bch/P	15
1956 | 1500 Degrees* | Miami Bch	24
1956 | Jaxson's | Dania Bch/B	21
1956 | Mai-Kai | Ft. Laud/B	16
1956 | Red Light* | UES	23
1957 | Pelican Landing* | Ft. Laud/B	21
1960 | Ambry German | Ft. Laud/B	21
1962 | Puerto Sagua | SoBe	23

HOLIDAY MEALS

(Special prix fixe meals offered at major holidays)

Adriana | Surfside	25
A la Folie Café | SoBe	21
Antonia's | Key W./K	27
Z Azul | Brickell	27
Bentley's | Islamorada/K	23
Brooks | Deerfield Bch/B	21
Bugatti Pasta | Coral Gables	23
Capriccio | Pembroke Pines/B	23
Casa Juancho | Little Havana	24
Cioppino | Key Biscayne	23
Escopazzo | SoBe	25
Fontana | Coral Gables	26
Gables Diner | Coral Gables	17
Z La Dorada | Coral Gables	26
La Palma | Coral Gables	21
Lario's/Beach | SoBe	20
La Riviera | Airport	-
Las Vacas | Miami Bch	24
Legal Sea Foods | Boca/P	21
Z NEW Market 17 | Ft. Laud/B	26
Z Michael's | Design Dist	27
Z Michy's | UES	27
Mr. Chow | SoBe	22
Olivos | Doral	26
Z Ortanique | Coral Gables	26
Z Palme d'Or | Coral Gables	28
Z Pascal's | Coral Gables	27
Ruth's Chris | Coral Gables	25
Sardinia | Miami Bch	26
Scarpetta | Miami Bch	25
Z Setai | SoBe	23
SushiSamba | SoBe	23
Tap Tap | SoBe	22
NEW 3800 Ocean | Riviera Bch/P	23
Timo | Sunny Is Bch	25
TooJay's | multi.	18
Wish | SoBe	25

HOTEL DINING

Acqualina Hotel	
Il Mulino NY | Sunny Is Bch	24
Alexander Hotel	
Shula's | Miami Bch	23
Avalon	
A Fish/Avalon | SoBe	23

SPECIAL FEATURES

Betsy Hotel
  Z BLT Steak | **SoBe**   25

Biltmore Hotel
  Fontana | **Coral Gables**   26
  Z Palme d'Or | **Coral Gables**   28

Blue, The
  5300 Chop House | **Doral**   24

Blu, Motel
  Red Light | **UES**   23

Boca Raton Marriott
  Absinthe | **Boca/P**   18

B Ocean Fort Lauderdale
  NEW Saia | **Ft. Laud/B**   -

Brazilian Court Hotel
  Z Café Boulud | **Palm Bch/P** 26

Breakers, The
  Flagler Steak | **Palm Bch/P**   26

Cadet Hotel
  NEW Pied à Terre | **SoBe**   -

Canyon Ranch Hotel & Spa
  Z Canyon Ranch | 19
    Miami Bch
  NEW Carillon | **Miami Bch**   -

Casa Tua
  Z Casa Tua | **SoBe**   24

Chesterfield Hotel
  Leopard Lounge | **Palm Bch/P**   18

Conrad Miami Hotel
  Atrio | **Brickell**   22

Crown at Miami Beach
  Morton's | **Miami Bch**   25

Delano Hotel
  NEW Blue Door Fish | **SoBe**   23
  Blue Sea | **SoBe**   24

Doral Golf Resort & Spa
  Mesazul | **Doral**   -

Dream South Beach
  NEW Tudor House | **SoBe**   -

Eden Roc Renaissance
  NEW 1500 Degrees | 24
    Miami Bch

Embassy Suites
  NEW Verdea | -
    Palm Bch Gdns/P

Epic Hotel
  Area 31 | **Downtown**   22
  Z Zuma | **Downtown**   28

Fontainebleau Miami Beach
  NEW Blade/Vida | -
    Miami Bch
  Gotham Steak | **Miami Bch**   23
  Z Hakkasan | **Miami Bch**   26
  Scarpetta | **Miami Bch**   25

Four Seasons Hotel
  Pasha's | **Brickell**   19

Four Seasons Resort
  Z Four Seasons | 25
    Palm Bch/P

Gansevoort South Beach Hotel
  STK Miami | **Miami Bch**   22

Grand Doubletree Hotel
  Tony Chan's | **Downtown**   23

Grove Isle Hotel & Spa
  Gibraltar | **Coco Grove**   20

Harbor Beach Marriott Resort
  Z 3030 Ocean | **Ft. Laud/B**   26

Hilton Bentley Miami/SoBe
  NEW De Rodriguez | **SoBe**   21
  Prime Italian | **SoBe**   24

Hilton Ft. Lauderdale Beach
  Ilios | **Ft. Laud/B**   -

Hilton Ft. Lauderdale Marina
  China Grill | **Ft. Laud/B**   22

Hilton Naples & Towers
  Shula's | **Naples/N**   23

Hollywood Beach Marriott
  Latitudes | **H'wood/B**   18

Hotel, The
  Wish | **SoBe**   25

Hyatt Key West Resort
  Shor American | **Key W./K**   -

Hyatt Regency Bonaventure
  Ireland's | **Weston/B**   26

Hyatt Regency Pier 66
  Grille 66 | **Ft. Laud/B**   24
  Pelican Landing | **Ft. Laud/B**   21
  Pier Top | **Ft. Laud/B**   26

Il Lugano Hotel
  Da Campo | **Ft. Laud/B**   23

JW Marriott Marquis Miami
  NEW DB Bistro Moderne | 26
    Downtown

LaPlaya Beach & Golf Resort
  Baleen | **Naples/N**   23

SPECIAL FEATURES

Townhouse Hotel
  Bond St. | **SoBe** 25

Turnberry Isle Hotel & Resort
  Bourbon Steak | **Aventura** 25

'Tween Waters Inn
  Old Captiva Hse. |
  Captiva Is/N 22

Viceroy Hotel
  Eos | **Brickell** 21

Westin Beach Resort
  Shula's | **Ft. Laud/B** 23

Westin Diplomat Resort
  Hollywood Prime | **H'wood/B** 24

W Ft. Lauderdale
  🅩 Steak 954 | **Ft. Laud/B** 24

W South Beach
  Mr. Chow | **SoBe** 22

Z Ocean Hotel
  Front Porch | **SoBe** 21

LATE DINING

(Weekday closing hour)

NEW Agave | 12 AM | **Naples/N** –
A la Folie Café | 12 AM | **SoBe** 21
Aura | 12 AM | **SoBe** 19
Balans | varies | **multi.** 19
Bar Louie | varies | **multi.** 17
Big Al's Steaks | varies |
  Delray Bch/P 19
Big City Tav. | 12 AM |
  Ft. Laud/B 19
Big Pink | 12 AM | **SoBe** 20
Bizaare Cafe | 12 AM |
  Lake Worth/P 19
NEW Blind Monk | 12 AM |
  W. Palm/P 18
Blue Anchor | 12 AM |
  Delray Bch/P 17
Bluepoint Grill | varies |
  H'wood/B 18
Blue Sea | 12 AM | **SoBe** 24
Brass Ring Pub | 1 AM | **multi.** 24
Buena Vista | 12 AM | **UES** 24
Burger & Beer | 1 AM | **multi.** 23
Cabo Flats | varies |
  Palm Bch Gdns/P 16
NEW Cafe L'Attico | 12 AM |
  Miami Bch –
Café Prima | 12 AM | **Miami Bch** 23
Café Ragazzi | 12 AM | **Surfside** 23

Caffe Abbracci | varies |
  Coral Gables 25
Caffé Milano | 12 AM | **SoBe** 17
🅩 Cheesecake | varies |
  Coco Grove 20
China Grill | 12 AM | **SoBe** 22
Chow Down Grill | 4 AM | **SoBe** –
Christine Lee's | 12 AM |
  Hallandale/B 22
Clarke's | 12 AM | **SoBe** 22
NEW Copper Chimney |
  12 AM | **Sunny Is Bch** 25
Cottage | 1:30 AM |
  Lake Worth/P 20
NEW Crazy About You | varies |
  Brickell 21
Cucina Dell' Arte | 3 AM |
  Palm Bch/P 21
Cut 432 | varies | **Delray Bch/P** 25
Dada | 1:30 AM | **Delray Bch/P** 20
NEW Daddy's Soul | varies |
  SoBe –
Dave's Last | 1 AM |
  Lake Worth/P 17
David's | 24 hrs. | **SoBe** 19
Democratic/Beer | 5 AM |
  Downtown –
NEW Dining Rm. | 12 AM |
  SoBe –
NEW Dirty Martini | 2 AM |
  Palm Bch Gdns/P –
Dolores/Lolita | 12 AM |
  Brickell 19
NEW Eden | 12 AM | **SoBe** 21
8 Oz. Burger | 12 AM | **SoBe** 20
11th St. Diner | 12 AM | **SoBe** 20
NEW English Tap | varies |
  Boca/P –
E.R. Bradley | 3 AM | **W. Palm/P** 16
Escopazzo | 12 AM | **SoBe** 25
NEW Fadó Irish Pub | 12 AM |
  Brickell 17
Finnegan's | 2 AM | **Key W./K** 19
NEW 5 Napkin Burger | varies |
  SoBe –
Flanigan's | 4 AM | **Coco Grove** 19
Floridian | 24 hrs. | **Ft. Laud/B** 18
Fratelli | 12 AM | **SoBe** 22
George's Rest. | 12 AM |
  Miami Bch 23

Restaurant	Hours	Location	Rating
NEW Gigi	varies	**Wynwood**	24
Globe Cafe	1 AM	**Coral Gables**	17
Gordon Biersch	12 AM	**Brickell**	18
Grease Burger	12 AM	**W. Palm/P**	20
Hakan	12 AM	**SoBe**	20
Havana	24 hrs.	**W. Palm/P**	21
NEW Haven Gastro	12:30 AM	**SoBe**	–
Hiro Japanese	3:30 AM	**No. Miami Bch**	21
Z Hiro's Yakko-San	3:30 AM	**No. Miami Bch**	27
Hosteria Romana	12 AM	**SoBe**	21
Howley's	2 AM	**W. Palm/P**	18
NEW Joint B&G	3 AM	**Pinecrest**	–
Jumbo's	24 hrs.	**Liberty City**	–
NEW Kane Steakhouse	varies	**SoBe**	–
Kingshead Pub	varies	**Sunrise/B**	21
La Locanda	12 AM	**SoBe**	24
La Palma	12 AM	**Coral Gables**	21
La Sandwicherie	varies	**multi.**	25
Las Vacas	12 AM	**Miami Bch**	24
Le Tub	3:30 AM	**H'wood/B**	21
Little Saigon	1 AM	**No. Miami Bch**	19
Lost & Found	3 AM	**Design Dist**	17
Lou's Beer	2 AM	**Miami Bch**	21
NEW LuLu	varies	**Coco Grove**	16
Mama Mia	12 AM	**H'wood/B**	20
Mango's Tropical	4 AM	**SoBe**	13
Marumi Sushi	1:30 AM	**Plantation/B**	–
Maya Tapas	12 AM	**SoBe**	17
Meat Market	12 AM	**SoBe**	25
Mercadito	12 AM	**Downtown**	21
NEW Naked Pizza	varies	**SoBe**	18
News Cafe	24 hrs.	**SoBe**	18
Novecento	12 AM	**Brickell**	19
101 Ocean	1 AM	**Laud-by-Sea/B**	21
Pasha's	varies	**SoBe**	19
Pelican RestCafé	1 AM	**SoBe**	21
NEW Pincho Factory	varies	**Westchester**	–
Piola	varies	**multi.**	22
Pizza Rustica	varies	**multi.**	19
NEW Pl8 Kitchen	varies	**Ft. Laud/B**	–
Prime Italian	12 AM	**SoBe**	24
Z Prime One	12 AM	**SoBe**	27
NEW Pubbelly	12 AM	**Miami Bch**	24
NEW Pubbelly Sushi	varies	**Miami Bch**	–
Puerto Sagua	2 AM	**SoBe**	23
Renzo's	12 AM	**Boca/P**	22
Rocco's Tacos	varies	**Ft. Laud/B**	20
Rosa Mexicano	varies	**SoBe**	22
Rosinella	12 AM	**SoBe**	20
NEW Roxy	varies	**No. Miami**	–
Sardinia	12 AM	**Miami Bch**	26
Sawa	12 AM	**Coral Gables**	21
Sergio's	12 AM	**multi.**	20
Sláinte Irish	1 AM	**Boynton Bch/P**	17
Smith/Wollensky	2 AM	**SoBe**	23
NEW Soirée at Vice	2 AM	**SoBe**	–
Southport Raw	varies	**Ft. Laud/B**	20
Spris	1 AM	**SoBe**	22
STK Miami	varies	**Miami Bch**	22
Sugarcane	varies	**Downtown**	25
Sushi Hse.	3 AM	**No. Miami Bch**	22
Sushi Rock	12 AM	**SoBe**	21
SushiSamba	12 AM	**SoBe**	23
Tantra	12 AM	**SoBe**	21
Tapas & Tintos	1 AM	**multi.**	20
Tatiana	2 AM	**Hallandale/B**	–
Taverna Opa	varies	**H'wood/B**	19
Thai Hse. S.	12 AM	**SoBe**	19
Tiramesu	12 AM	**SoBe**	21
T-Mex	varies	**multi.**	17
NEW Tokyo Blue	12 AM	**Ft. Laud/B**	20
Toni's Sushi	12 AM	**SoBe**	25
Two Friends	1 AM	**Key W./K**	18

SPECIAL FEATURES

Van Dyke Cafe | 2 AM | **SoBe**	16
☑ Versailles | 1 AM | **Little Havana**	21
Vita by Baoli | 2 AM | **SoBe**	-
Yard Hse. | varies | **multi.**	19
Zuperpollo | 12 AM | **Coral Way**	18

MICROBREWERIES

Brewzzi | **multi.**	17
Gordon Biersch | **Brickell**	18
Kelly's Carib. | **Key W./K**	21
Titanic Brewery | **Coral Gables**	17

NEWCOMERS

Agave | **Naples/N**	-
Andalus | **Design Dist**	20
Bernie's L.A. | **SoBe**	26
Blade/Vida | **Miami Bch**	-
Blind Monk | **W. Palm/P**	18
Blue Door Fish | **SoBe**	23
Blue Ginger | **Pembroke Pines/B**	-
Bratta's | **Ft. Myers/N**	-
Buccan | **Palm Bch/P**	25
Café Jamm | **Ft. Laud/B**	-
Cafe L'Attico | **Miami Bch**	-
Carillon | **Miami Bch**	-
Catch Grill | **Biscayne**	-
Cecconi's | **Miami Bch**	22
Cevichery | **SoBe**	-
China Beach | **W. Palm/P**	-
Cholo's | **No. Miami Bch**	-
Chuck Burger | **Palm Bch Gdns/P**	-
Cinco Cantina | **Coral Gables**	-
City Hall | **Wynwood**	-
Copper Chimney | **Sunny Is Bch**	25
Crazy About You | **Brickell**	21
Crumb/Parchment | **Design Dist**	-
Daddy's Soul | **SoBe**	-
Damn Good Burger | **Downtown**	-
Dapur | **Ft. Laud/B**	-
DB Bistro Moderne | **Downtown**	26
Deck 84 | **Delray Bch/P**	19
De Rodriguez | **SoBe**	21
DIG | **Delray Bch/P**	-
Dim Ssäm à Gogo | **Loc Varies**	-
Dining Rm. | **SoBe**	-
Dirty Martini | **Palm Bch Gdns/P**	-

Dos Caminos | **Ft. Laud/B**	19
Eden | **SoBe**	21
Egg & Dart | **Design Dist**	-
English Tap | **Boca/P**	-
Fadó Irish Pub | **Brickell**	17
1500 Degrees | **Miami Bch**	24
5 Napkin Burger | **SoBe**	-
Flip Burger | **No. Miami**	25
Forno 52 | **Palmetto Bay**	-
GG's | **H'wood/B**	20
Gigi | **Wynwood**	24
Gourmet Burger | **Jupiter/P**	-
Green Table | **Coral Gables**	-
Grimaldi's | **Palm Bch Gdns/P**	-
Harrison's | **W. Miami**	-
Harry's Pizzeria | **Design Dist**	-
Haven Gastro | **SoBe**	-
Heavy Burger | **Aventura**	22
Indus | **W. Palm/P**	-
Jamon Jamon | **Miami Riv**	-
Jefe's | **Loc Varies**	-
John G's | **Manalapan/P**	-
Joint B&G | **Pinecrest**	-
Kane Steakhouse | **SoBe**	-
La Dolce Vita | **Ft. Laud/B**	-
La Scalina | **Downtown**	-
Lizarran | **Coral Gables**	-
Local Craft | **Coral Gables**	-
LouLou | **Miami Riv**	-
Luigi's | **W. Palm/P**	-
LuLu | **Coco Grove**	16
Makoto | **Bal Harbour**	25
☑ Market 17 | **Ft. Laud/B**	26
Max's Harvest | **Delray Bch/P**	-
M Bar | **Ft. Laud/B**	-
Michele's | **Ft. Laud/B**	-
Miso Hungry | **Loc Varies**	-
Miss Yip | **Downtown**	16
Mr. Collins | **Bal Harbour**	-
Mr. Chef's | **Aventura**	24
Ms. Cheezious | **Loc Varies**	-
Nacho Mamas | **Loc Varies**	-
Naked Pizza | **SoBe**	18
Nemesis | **Downtown**	-
100 Montaditos | **Downtown**	-
On the Menu | **Davie/B**	18
Ovenella | **Boca/P**	-

Oye Cuban Grill | **Pinecrest**	20
Pancho Villa | **No. Miami**	-
Pangea | **Wellington/P**	-
Paris/Town | **Palm Bch Gdns/P**	-
Peacock | **Coco Grove**	-
Philippe Chow | **Boca/P**	-
Pied à Terre | **SoBe**	-
Pincho Factory | **Westchester**	-
Piñon Grill | **Boca/P**	22
Pl8 Kitchen | **Ft. Laud/B**	-
Pubbelly | **Miami Bch**	24
Pubbelly Sushi | **Miami Bch**	-
Rare Las Olas | **Ft. Laud/B**	21
Rickenbacker | **Key Biscayne**	20
Route 9 | **Coral Gables**	20
Roxy | **No. Miami**	-
Royal | **SoBe**	-
Russell's | **Palm Bch Gdns/P**	23
Saia | **Ft. Laud/B**	-
Scuola Vecchia | **Delray Bch/P**	-
Sea | **Laud-by-Sea/B**	-
Slow Food | **Loc Varies**	-
Smokehouse | **Boca/P**	-
Soi Asian | **Downtown**	-
Soirée at Vice | **SoBe**	-
Spartico | **Coco Grove**	-
Star Bistro | **Cooper City/B**	-
Sustain | **Downtown**	21
Symcha's | **SoBe**	25
Tagliatelle Miami | **SoBe**	-
3800 Ocean | **Riviera Bch/P**	23
3 Chefs | **Downtown**	-
Tokyo Blue | **Ft. Laud/B**	20
Trio/Bay | **No. Bay Vill**	-
Tudor House | **SoBe**	-
2B Asian | **Little Havana**	25
Umi | **Palm Bch Gdns/P**	26
Verdea | **Palm Bch Gdns/P**	-
Wine Depot | **SoBe**	20
Wynwood | **Wynwood**	17
Yardbird | **SoBe**	-

OFFBEAT

Abbondanza | **Key W./K**	20
Alladin | **Palm Bch Gdns/P**	18
Andiamo! Pizza | **UES**	25
Andros | **Lake Worth/P**	21
Bahamas Fish | **W. Miami**	20

Bali Café | **Downtown**	25
Banana Cafe | **Key W./K**	23
☑ Barton G. | **SoBe**	22
Barú Urbano | **Brickell**	15
Bentley's | **Islamorada/K**	23
Berries | **Coco Grove**	20
Bizaare Cafe | **Lake Worth/P**	19
NEW Blind Monk | **W. Palm/P**	18
☑ Blue Heaven | **Key W./K**	25
B.O.'s Fish | **Key W./K**	24
Bubble Room | **Captiva Is/N**	19
By Word/Mouth | **Oakland Pk/B**	25
Café Emunah | **Ft. Laud/B**	25
☑ Cafe/Marturano | **multi.**	24
Café Pastis | **So. Miami**	23
Caliente Kitchen | **Delray Bch/P**	22
Calypso | **Pompano Bch/B**	24
Calypso's/Grille | **Key Largo/K**	23
Cap's | **Lighthse Pt/B**	17
NEW Cecconi's | **Miami Bch**	22
Ceviche 105 | **Downtown**	25
NEW Cevichery | **SoBe**	-
Cheese Course | **Weston/B**	25
Cool'A Fishbar | **Palm Bch Gdns/P**	22
NEW Crazy About You | **Brickell**	21
NEW Crumb/Parchment | **Design Dist**	-
Dada | **Delray Bch/P**	20
Darbster | **Lake Worth/P**	-
David's | **SoBe**	19
Democratic/Beer | **Downtown**	-
Doc Ford's | **Sanibel/N**	22
El Carajo | **Coral Way**	22
11th St. Diner | **SoBe**	20
NEW Fadó Irish Pub | **Brickell**	17
Ferdo's Grill | **Ft. Laud/B**	20
Gables Diner | **Coral Gables**	17
Garcia's | **Miami Riv**	23
George's/Grove | **Coco Grove**	22
George's/Sunset | **So. Miami**	20
NEW Gigi | **Wynwood**	24
Gol! | **Delray Bch/P**	16
Gourmet Diner | **No. Miami Bch**	18
Green Gourmet | **Delray Bch/P**	-
Half Shell | **Key W./K**	23
NEW Heavy Burger | **Aventura**	22
Howley's | **W. Palm/P**	18
Hy-Vong | **Little Havana**	26

SPECIAL FEATURES

Jaxson's | **Dania Bch/B** 21
Jimmy's Bistro | **Delray Bch/P** 26
Jimmy'z Kitchen | **multi.** 25
Jumbo's | **Liberty City** -
Z La Brochette | **Cooper City/B** 28
Lario's/Beach | **SoBe** 20
Le Tub | **H'wood/B** 21
Little Saigon | **No. Miami Bch** 19
Living Room | **Boynton Bch/P** 15
NEW Local Craft | **Coral Gables** -
Lou's Beer | **Miami Bch** 21
NEW LuLu | **Coco Grove** 16
Z Mai-Kai | **Ft. Laud/B** 16
Maitardi | **Design Dist** 21
Mango's Tropical | **SoBe** 13
Mario's Catalina | **Ft. Laud/B** -
Melting Pot | **multi.** 19
Miss Saigon | **Coral Gables** 23
Monty's | **Coco Grove** 17
Mo's | **Key W./K** 23
Mustard Seed | **Plantation/B** 25
Nikki | **SoBe** 16
Pepe's | **Key W./K** 24
Pilot House | **Key Largo/K** 19
NEW Pincho Factory | **Westchester** -
Pizzeria Oceano | **Lantana/P** -
NEW Pubbelly | **Miami Bch** 24
Puerto Sagua | **SoBe** 23
Rhythm Café | **W. Palm/P** 24
Rock n Roll Ribs | **Coral Spgs/B** 24
Romeo's Cafe | **Coral Way** 26
Rusty Anchor | **Stock Island/K** 21
Salute! | **Key W./K** 22
S&S | **Downtown** 23
Sawa | **Coral Gables** 21
Scotty's | **Coco Grove** 14
Z Seven Fish | **Key W./K** 27
Shorty's | **multi.** 22
Shuck N Dive | **Ft. Laud/B** 19
Sloppy Joe's | **Key W./K** 13
NEW Soi Asian | **Downtown** -
NEW Soirée at Vice | **SoBe** -
Tantra | **SoBe** 21
Tap Tap | **SoBe** 22
Taverna Opa | **multi.** 19
Titanic Brewery | **Coral Gables** 17
T-Mex | **SoBe** 17

Triple Eight | **Delray Bch/P** -
Turtle Kraals | **Key W./K** 18
Tuscan Grill | **Ft. Laud/B** 20
NEW 2B Asian | **Little Havana** 25
Two Friends | **Key W./K** 18
Two Georges | **Deerfield Bch/B** 15
Z Versailles | **Little Havana** 21
Villagio | **Coral Gables** 21
White Lion | **Homestead** 18
NEW Wynwood | **Wynwood** 17
Zuperpollo | **Coral Way** 18

OUTDOOR DINING

(G=garden; P=patio; S=sidewalk;
T=terrace;)
Z A&B Lobster | P, T | 23
  Key W./K
Acquolina | P | **Weston/B** 22
A Fish/Avalon | S, T | **SoBe** 23
NEW Agave | P | **Naples/N** -
A la Folie Café | G, T | **SoBe** 21
AltaMare | S | **SoBe** 24
Andiamo! Pizza | P | **UES** 25
Aruba Beach | P | 17
  Laud-by-Sea/B
Asia Bay | T | **Ft. Laud/B** 25
Bagatelle | G, T | **Key W./K** 21
Balans | S, T | **SoBe** 19
Banana Boat | P | **Boynton Bch/P** 15
Banana Cafe | P | **Key W./K** 23
Barracuda Grill | P | 21
  Marathon/K
Z Barton G. | G | **SoBe** 22
Berries | G | **Coco Grove** 20
Bice | P | **Palm Bch/P** 22
Bimini Boatyard | P | **Ft. Laud/B** 17
Bizaare Cafe | T | **Lake Worth/P** 19
Bizcaya | T | **Coco Grove** 24
Z Blue Heaven | G, P | 25
  Key W./K
Z Blue Moon Fish | T | 24
  Laud-by-Sea/B
Bongos Cuban | T | **Downtown** 16
Brewzzi | P | **multi.** 17
Buonasera | P | **Jupiter/P** 24
Z Cabana | S | **Delray Bch/P** 22
Café at Books & Books | G, S | 21
  multi.
Z Café Boulud | G, T | 26
  Palm Bch/P

Mangoes | G, P | **Key W./K** — 18

Mango's Tropical | P | **SoBe** — 13

Maroosh | T | **Coral Gables** — 25

Martin's | G | **Key W./K** — 22

Z Max's | P | **Boca/P** — 22

NEW Max's Harvest | S, T | — −
Delray Bch/P

Maya Tapas | P, S | **SoBe** — 17

Z Michaels | G | **Key W./K** — 26

Monty's | P | **multi.** — 17

Z Morada Bay | P | **Islamorada/K** — 22

News Cafe | G, P, S | **SoBe** — 18

Nexxt Cafe | P, S | **SoBe** — 18

Nikki | G | **SoBe** — 16

915 Bistro | P | **Key W./K** — 25

North Ocean | P | **Ft. Laud/B** — −

Oceans 234 | P | **Deerfield Bch/B** — 19

Office | P | **Delray Bch/P** — 20

Paddy Mac's | P | — 19
Palm Bch Gdns/P

Paradiso | S | **Lake Worth/P** — 25

Pasha's | P | **multi.** — 19

NEW Peacock | G, T | — −
Coco Grove

Pelican Landing | P | **Ft. Laud/B** — 21

Pepe's | P | **Key W./K** — 24

Perricone's | G, T | **Brickell** — 22

P.F. Chang's | P | **multi.** — 20

Z Pisces | P | **Key W./K** — 27

Pizza Girls | S | **W. Palm/P** — 20

Player's Club | P | **Wellington/P** — 17

Portobello | T | **Jupiter/P** — 23

Prime Catch | P | **Boynton Bch/P** — 21

Red Fish Grill | P | **Coral Gables** — 22

Renato's | T | **Palm Bch/P** — 24

NEW Rickenbacker | T | — 20
Key Biscayne

River Oyster Bar | S | **Miami Riv** — 25

Rustic Inn | P | **Ft. Laud/B** — 22

Safire | S | **Lake Worth/P** — 26

Sailfish Marina | P | — 17
Palm Bch Shores/P

Salute! | P | **Key W./K** — 22

Sapori | P, T | **Boca/P** — 28

Scotty's | P | **Coco Grove** — 14

Serafina | P | **Ft. Laud/B** — 23

Z Setai | P | **SoBe** — 23

Shula's | P | **Ft. Laud/B** — 23

Smith/Wollensky | P | **SoBe** — 23

Spoto's | P | **Palm Bch Gdns/P** — 22

Spris | S | **multi.** — 22

Square One | T | **Key W./K** — 21

Z Steak 954 | T | **Ft. Laud/B** — 24

Sugar Reef | S | **H'wood/B** — 24

Sundy House | G, P, T | — 22
Delray Bch/P

Sushi Rock | P | **SoBe** — 21

SushiSamba | S | **SoBe** — 23

Sushi Siam/Rock | P, S | **multi.** — 22

Sushi/Thai Jo's | S | **W. Palm/P** — 23

NEW Symcha's | P | **SoBe** — 25

Tabica Grill | S | **Jupiter/P** — 21

Tap Tap | P | **SoBe** — 22

Thaikyo Asian | P, T | — 19
Manalapan/P

Z Thai Spice | G, P | **Ft. Laud/B** — 26

Z 32 East | P, S | **Delray Bch/P** — 25

Tin Muffin Café | S | **Boca/P** — 23

Tiramesu | G, P, S | **SoBe** — 21

NEW Tokyo Blue | P | **Ft. Laud/B** — 20

Tramonti | P, S | **Delray Bch/P** — 25

Tratt. Sole | S | **So. Miami** — 20

NEW Trio/Bay | P | **No. Bay Vill** — −

Triple Eight | P | **Delray Bch/P** — −

Turtle Kraals | G, P, T | — 18
Key W./K

Two Friends | P | **Key W./K** — 18

Uncle Tai's | P | **Boca/P** — 23

Uvas | T | **UES** — 19

Van Dyke Cafe | S, T | **SoBe** — 16

Via Luna | T | **Ft. Laud/B** — 21

Vic & Angelo's | P | **multi.** — 21

Vita by Baoli | G, T | **SoBe** — −

White Lion | G, P | **Homestead** — 18

Wild E. Asian | T | **Ft. Laud/B** — 17

NEW Wine Depot | P, T | **SoBe** — 20

WIsh | G, T | **SoBe** — 25

YOLO | P, S | **Ft. Laud/B** — 21

Yuca | S | **SoBe** — 20

PEOPLE-WATCHING

Z A&B Lobster | **Key W./K** — 23

Absinthe | **Boca/P** — 18

Absinthe | **Naples/N** — 21

A Fish/Avalon | **SoBe** — 23

Angelique | **Coral Gables** — 18

Z Anthony's Runway | **Ft. Laud/B** 24

Aruba Beach | **Laud-by-Sea/B** 17

Asia Bay | **Ft. Laud/B** 25

Asia de Cuba | **SoBe** 22

Aura | **SoBe** 19

Bahamas Fish | **W. Miami** 20

Balans | **SoBe** 19

Z Barton G. | **SoBe** 22

Bice | **Palm Bch/P** 22

Big City Tav. | **Ft. Laud/B** 19

Bimini Boatyard | **Ft. Laud/B** 17

Z Bistro Mezz. | **Ft. Laud/B** 26

NEW Blade/Vida | **Miami Bch** –

NEW Blind Monk | **W. Palm/P** 18

NEW Blue Door Fish | **SoBe** 23

NEW Blue Ginger | **Pembroke Pines/B** –

Z Blue Heaven | **Key W./K** 25

Blue Sea | **SoBe** 24

Brio Tuscan | **Hallandale/B** 21

NEW Buccan | **Palm Bch/P** 25

Cabo Flats | **Palm Bch Gdns/P** 16

Café & Bar Lurcat | **Naples/N** 26

Café at Books & Books | **multi.** 21

Café Centro | **W. Palm/P** 19

Z Café L'Europe | **Palm Bch/P** 27

Z Cafe/Martorano | **multi.** 24

Caffé Europa | **Ft. Laud/B** 23

Caffé Milano | **SoBe** 17

Caliente Kitchen | **Delray Bch/P** 22

Campiello | **Naples/N** 25

Cantina Laredo | **Hallandale/B** 20

Carpaccio | **Bal Harbour** 23

Z Casa Tua | **SoBe** 24

NEW Cecconi's | **Miami Bch** 22

NEW Cevichery | **SoBe** –

Chart House | **Coco Grove** 20

Cheese Course | **Weston/B** 25

China Grill | **multi.** 22

Chops City Grill | **multi.** 25

Z Chops Lobster | **Boca/P** 26

Christine Lee's | **Hallandale/B** 22

City Cellar | **W. Palm/P** 20

City Diner | **W. Palm/P** 20

Coconuts | **Ft. Laud/B** 23

Commodore | **Key W./K** 23

Council Oak | **H'wood/B** 24

NEW Crazy About You | **Brickell** 21

NEW Crumb/Parchment | **Design Dist** –

Cucina Dell' Arte | **Palm Bch/P** 21

Da Campo | **Ft. Laud/B** 23

Da Leo Trattoria | **SoBe** 18

D'Angelo | **Oakland Pk/B** 25

Dave's Last | **Lake Worth/P** 17

NEW Deck 84 | **Delray Bch/P** 19

Democratic/Beer | **Downtown** –

NEW De Rodriguez | **SoBe** 21

Doraku | **SoBe** 23

Echo | **Palm Bch/P** 24

NEW English Tap | **Boca/P** –

E.R. Bradley | **W. Palm/P** 16

NEW Fadó Irish Pub | **Brickell** 17

NEW 1500 Degrees | **Miami Bch** 24

Floridian | **Ft. Laud/B** 18

Forge | **Miami Bch** 24

Fratelli Lyon | **Design Dist** 22

Front Porch | **SoBe** 21

Garcia's | **Miami Riv** 23

Globe Cafe | **Coral Gables** 17

Gotham Steak | **Miami Bch** 23

Grateful Palate | **Ft. Laud/B** 24

Gratify | **W. Palm/P** –

Green/Cafe | **Coco Grove** 19

Grimaldi's | **Palm Bch Gdns/P** –

Guanabanas | **Jupiter/P** 18

Half Shell | **Key W./K** 23

Havana Harry's | **Coral Gables** 19

Hosteria Romana | **SoBe** 21

H2O | **Ft. Laud/B** 18

Ilios | **Ft. Laud/B** –

I.M. Tapas | **Naples/N** 25

JB's | **Deerfield Bch/B** 18

Jimmy'z Kitchen | **SoBe** 25

Z Joe's Stone | **SoBe** 27

Z Johnny V | **Ft. Laud/B** 24

Joseph's Wine | **Delray Bch/P** 23

Kathy's | **Boca/P** 25

Lario's/Beach | **SoBe** 20

Las Vacas | **Miami Bch** 24

Latitudes | **H'wood/B** 18

La Trattoria | **Key W./K** 22

Le Bouchon/Grove | **Coco Grove** 24

Le Croisic	**Key Biscayne**	22	Scarpetta	**Miami Bch**	25
Leopard Lounge	**Palm Bch/P**	18	Sea Salt	**Naples/N**	23
Le Tub	**H'wood/B**	21	Shula's	**Miami Lks**	23
Living Room	**Boynton Bch/P**	15	Sloppy Joe's	**Key W./K**	13
NEW LuLu	**Coco Grove**	16	**NEW** Soirée at Vice	**SoBe**	-
NEW Makoto	**Bal Harbour**	25	SoLita	**Ft. Laud/B**	21
Mangoes	**Key W./K**	18	Soyka	**UES**	20
Mango's Tropical	**SoBe**	13	Spris	**SoBe**	22
Z Max's	**Boca/P**	22	**Z** Sra. Martinez	**Design Dist**	25
NEW Max's Harvest	**Delray Bch/P**	-	Sushi Rock	**SoBe**	21
Maya Tapas	**SoBe**	17	SushiSamba	**SoBe**	23
NEW M Bar	**Ft. Laud/B**	-	Sushi Siam/Rock	**SoBe**	22
Michelle Bernstein/Omphoy	**Palm Bch/P**	24	**NEW** Sustain	**Downtown**	21
			NEW Symcha's	**SoBe**	25
Meat Market	**SoBe**	25	Table 42	**Boca/P**	21
MiraMare	**Naples/N**	21	Ta-boo	**Palm Bch/P**	23
NEW Miss Yip	**Downtown**	16	Tamarind	**Miami Bch**	24
Monty's	**Coco Grove**	17	Tantra	**SoBe**	21
Morton's	**multi.**	25	Tatiana	**Hallandale/B**	-
News Cafe	**SoBe**	18	Taverna Opa	**multi.**	19
Z NY Prime	**Boca/P**	25	**Z** 32 East	**Delray Bch/P**	25
Nexxt Cafe	**SoBe**	18	III Forks	**multi.**	20
Nikki	**SoBe**	16	Tiramesu	**SoBe**	21
Z Nobu Miami	**SoBe**	27	**NEW** Tokyo Blue	**Ft. Laud/B**	20
Office	**Delray Bch/P**	20	Toni's Sushi	**SoBe**	25
101 Ocean	**Laud-by-Sea/B**	21	Tramonti	**Delray Bch/P**	25
Z Palm	**Bay Harbor Is**	28	**NEW** Trio/Bay	**No. Bay Vill**	-
Z Palm Beach Grill	**Palm Bch/P**	25	Triple Eight	**Delray Bch/P**	-
Palm Beach Steak	**Palm Bch/P**	21	Two Georges	**multi.**	15
Z Palme d'Or	**Coral Gables**	28	**NEW** Umi	**Palm Bch Gdns/P**	26
NEW Paris/Town	**Palm Bch Gdns/P**	-	Van Dyke Cafe	**SoBe**	16
			Z Versailles	**Little Havana**	21
Perricone's	**Brickell**	22	Via Luna	**Ft. Laud/B**	21
NEW Piñon Grill	**Boca/P**	22	Vic & Angelo's	**Palm Bch Gdns/P**	21
Pistache	**W. Palm/P**	23			
Player's Club	**Wellington/P**	17	Village Grille	**Laud-by-Sea/B**	20
Z Prime One	**SoBe**	27	Villagio	**multi.**	21
NEW Pubbelly	**Miami Bch**	24	Vita by Baoli	**SoBe**	-
Racks Downtown	**Boca/P**	21	Vivo Partenza	**Boca/P**	23
NEW Rare Las Olas	**Ft. Laud/B**	21	Wish	**SoBe**	25
Relish	**W. Palm/P**	21	**NEW** Wynwood	**Wynwood**	17
Rosa Mexicano	**SoBe**	22	**NEW** Yardbird	**SoBe**	-
Rosinella	**SoBe**	20	Yuca	**SoBe**	20
NEW Royal	**SoBe**	-	**Z** Zuma	**Downtown**	28
NEW Saia	**Ft. Laud/B**	-			
S&S	**Downtown**	23	**POWER SCENES**		
Sardinia	**Miami Bch**	26	**Z** Abe/Louie's	**Boca/P**	26
			Antonia's	**Key W./K**	27

Asia de Cuba | **SoBe**	22		🆕 100 Montaditos |	–
🅩 Azul | **Brickell**	27		**Downtown**	
Big City Tav. | **Ft. Laud/B**	19		🅩 Ortanique | **Coral Gables**	26
🅩 Bistro Mezz. | **Ft. Laud/B**	26		🅩 Palm | **Bay Harbor Is**	28
🆕 Blue Door Fish | **SoBe**	23		🅩 Palme d'Or | **Coral Gables**	28
🅩 Cafe/Martorano | **H'wood/B**	24		Panorama | **Coco Grove**	–
Caffe Abbracci | **Coral Gables**	25		🅩 Pascal's | **Coral Gables**	27
Caffe Da Vinci | **Bay Harbor Is**	17		Perricone's | **Brickell**	22
🅩 Capital Grille | **multi.**	26		Pilot House | **Key Largo/K**	19
Carpaccio | **Bal Harbour**	23		Player's Club | **Wellington/P**	17
🅩 Casa D'Angelo | **Ft. Laud/B**	27		🅩 Prime One | **SoBe**	27
Casa Juancho | **Little Havana**	24		Quattro | **SoBe**	20
🅩 Casa Tua | **SoBe**	24		Racks Downtown | **Boca/P**	21
Chima Brazilian | **Ft. Laud/B**	25		🆕 Rare Las Olas | **Ft. Laud/B**	21
China Grill | **Ft. Laud/B**	22		🆕 Royal | **SoBe**	–
🅩 Chops Lobster | **Boca/P**	26		Ruth's Chris | **Coral Gables**	25
Christine Lee's | **Hallandale/B**	22		Sardinia | **Miami Bch**	26
Cioppino | **Key Biscayne**	23		Scarpetta | **Miami Bch**	25
D'Angelo | **Oakland Pk/B**	25		Sea Salt | **Naples/N**	23
Echo | **Palm Bch/P**	24		🅩 Seven Fish | **Key W./K**	27
🆕 1500 Degrees |	24		Shibui | **Kendall**	24
Miami Bch			Shula's | **multi.**	23
Flagler Steak | **Palm Bch/P**	26		Smith/Wollensky | **SoBe**	23
Forge | **Miami Bch**	24		SoLita | **Delray Bch/P**	21
🅩 Four Seasons | **Palm Bch/P**	25		🅩 Sra. Martinez | **Design Dist**	25
Fratelli Lyon | **Design Dist**	22		STK Miami | **Miami Bch**	22
Gibraltar | **Coco Grove**	20		Ta-boo | **Palm Bch/P**	23
Gordon Biersch | **Brickell**	18		Tantra | **SoBe**	21
Grateful Palate | **Ft. Laud/B**	24		🅩 32 East | **Delray Bch/P**	25
Graziano's | **Westchester**	25		Toni's Sushi | **SoBe**	25
Havana Harry's | **Coral Gables**	19		Truluck's | **Ft. Laud/B**	24
Ireland's | **Weston/B**	26		🅩 Versailles | **Little Havana**	21
🅩 Joe's Stone | **SoBe**	27		Via Luna | **Ft. Laud/B**	21
🅩 Johnny V | **Ft. Laud/B**	24		Vivo Partenza | **Boca/P**	23
La Palma | **Coral Gables**	21			
La Riviera | **Airport**	–		**PRIVATE ROOMS**	
Le Croisic | **Key Biscayne**	22		(Restaurants charge less at off times; call for capacity)	
Le Provençal | **Coral Gables**	22		Absinthe | **Boca/P**	18
🆕 Makoto | **Bal Harbour**	25		🆕 Agave | **Naples/N**	–
🅩🆕 Market 17 | **Ft. Laud/B**	26		Antonia's | **Key W./K**	27
MiraMare | **Naples/N**	21		Bice | **Palm Bch/P**	22
Morton's | **multi.**	25		Bimini Boatyard | **Ft. Laud/B**	17
🅩 NY Prime | **Boca/P**	25		Bin 595 | **Plantation/B**	22
🅩 Nobu Miami | **SoBe**	27		Bizcaya | **Coco Grove**	24
Oceanaire | **Brickell**	24		🅩 Blue Moon Fish |	24
Office | **Delray Bch/P**	20		**Coral Spgs/B**	
Oggi Caffe | **No. Bay Vill**	25		Bourbon Steak | **Aventura**	25
			Brooks | **Deerfield Bch/B**	21

☑ Cabana	**Delray Bch/P**	22
☑ Café Boulud	**Palm Bch/P**	26
☑ Café L'Europe	**Palm Bch/P**	27
☑ Cafe Maxx	**Pompano Bch/B**	27
☑ Capital Grille	**multi.**	26
NEW Catch Grill	**Biscayne**	–
Charley's Crab	**Palm Bch/P**	20
☑ Chez Jean-Pierre	**Palm Bch/P**	28
Dada	**Delray Bch/P**	20
East City Grill	**Weston/B**	19
Echo	**Palm Bch/P**	24
El Novillo	**Miami Lks**	22
NEW English Tap	**Boca/P**	–
Escopazzo	**SoBe**	25
NEW 1500 Degrees	**Miami Bch**	24
☑ Four Seasons	**Palm Bch/P**	25
Globe Cafe	**Coral Gables**	17
Gold Coast	**Coral Spgs/B**	21
Graziano's	**multi.**	25
Hollywood Prime	**H'wood/B**	24
Il Bellagio	**W. Palm/P**	20
Kathy's	**Boca/P**	25
Kelly's Carib.	**Key W./K**	21
La Casona	**W. Sunset**	–
La Creperie	**Lauderhill/B**	24
☑ La Dorada	**Coral Gables**	26
La Palma	**Coral Gables**	21
La Riviera	**Airport**	–
Leopard Lounge	**Palm Bch/P**	18
Little Havana	**No. Miami**	22
☑ Mai-Kai	**Ft. Laud/B**	16
Mangoes	**Key W./K**	18
Martin's	**Key W./K**	22
Melting Pot	**multi.**	19
Mesazul	**Doral**	–
☑ Michaels	**Key W./K**	26
NEW Michele's	**Ft. Laud/B**	–
Morton's	**multi.**	25
915 Bistro	**Key W./K**	25
Oceanaire	**Brickell**	24
☑ Ortanique	**Coral Gables**	26
Paddy Mac's	**Palm Bch Gdns/P**	19
☑ Palme d'Or	**Coral Gables**	28
Paradiso	**Lake Worth/P**	25
NEW Philippe Chow	**Boca/P**	–
Pier Top	**Ft. Laud/B**	26
☑ Pisces	**Key W./K**	27

☑ Prime One	**SoBe**	27
☑ Rainbow Palace	**Ft. Laud/B**	26
Renato's	**Palm Bch/P**	24
River House	**Palm Bch Gdns/P**	22
Rustic Inn	**Ft. Laud/B**	22
Ruth's Chris	**Ft. Laud/B**	25
☑ Sage	**H'wood/B**	22
Smith/Wollensky	**SoBe**	23
Stresa	**W. Palm/P**	19
Sublime	**Ft. Laud/B**	21
Tap Tap	**SoBe**	22
☑ 3030 Ocean	**Ft. Laud/B**	26
☑ 32 East	**Delray Bch/P**	25
Timpano	**Ft. Laud/B**	23
NEW Trio/Bay	**No. Bay Vill**	–
Truluck's	**multi.**	24
NEW Tudor House	**SoBe**	–
Two Chefs	**So. Miami**	23
Uncle Tai's	**Boca/P**	23
NEW Verdea	**Palm Bch Gdns/P**	–
Yuca	**SoBe**	20

PRIX FIXE MENUS

(Call for prices and times)

Brooks	**Deerfield Bch/B**	21
☑ Café Boulud	**Palm Bch/P**	26
☑ Din. Rm./Little Palm	**Little Torch Key/K**	28
☑ Kee Grill	**multi.**	24
☑ La Dorada	**Coral Gables**	26
Le Bistro	**Lighthse Pt/B**	22
Maroosh	**Coral Gables**	25
Melting Pot	**multi.**	19
☑ Naoe	**Sunny Is Bch**	29
☑ Nobu Miami	**SoBe**	27
NEW Philippe Chow	**Boca/P**	–
Renato's	**Palm Bch/P**	24
Romeo's Cafe	**Coral Way**	26
SushiSamba	**SoBe**	23
264 the Grill	**Palm Bch/P**	17

QUICK BITES

Absinthe	**Naples/N**	21
Angelique	**Coral Gables**	18
☑ Anthony's Pizza	**multi.**	22
Basilic Viet.	**Laud-by-Sea/B**	22
Berries	**Coco Grove**	20
Big Cheese	**So. Miami**	21

🆕 Blue Ginger | Pembroke Pines/B	–
Brass Ring Pub | Royal Palm Bch/P	24
Brewzzi | multi.	17
Bugatti Pasta | Coral Gables	23
Cabo Flats | Palm Bch Gdns/P	16
Café Centro | W. Palm/P	19
Café des Artistes | Jupiter/P	23
Café Emunah | Ft. Laud/B	25
Caffé Europa | Ft. Laud/B	23
Caliente Kitchen | Delray Bch/P	22
Camille's | Key W./K	22
Carmine's | Jupiter/P	19
CG Burgers | Jupiter/P	19
Cheese Course | multi.	25
Cottage | Lake Worth/P	20
Cuban Cafe | Boca/P	19
Daily Bread | Pinecrest	24
David's | SoBe	19
Deli Lane | multi.	17
🆕 DIG | Delray Bch/P	–
Doc Ford's | Ft. Myers Bch/N	22
Dockside Sea | Lake Pk/P	19
Dogma Grill | UES	20
11th St. Diner | SoBe	20
El Siboney | Key W./K	25
El Toro | Homestead	23
🆕 English Tap | Boca/P	–
Eos | Brickell	21
E.R. Bradley's | W. Palm/P	16
Finnegan's | Key W./K	19
🔁 Five Guys | Palm Bch Gdns/P	20
Floridian | Ft. Laud/B	18
Front Porch | SoBe	21
Gordon Biersch | Brickell	18
Gratify | W. Palm/P	–
Green/Cafe | Coco Grove	19
Grimaldi's | Palm Bch Gdns/P	–
Grouper & Chips | Naples/N	24
Guanabanas | Jupiter/P	18
Hamburger Heaven | Palm Bch/P	21
🆕 Harry's Pizzeria | Design Dist	–
Havana | W. Palm/P	21
Havana Harry's | Coral Gables	19
Hot Pie | W. Palm/P	26
Icebox Café | SoBe	22
Il Grissino | Coral Gables	22
Joey's Italian | Wynwood	24
Kevin's | Palm Bch Gdns/P	–
La Casita | Coral Gables	23
La Casona | W. Sunset	–
Lan | So. Miami	23
La Sandwicherie | SoBe	25
🔁 LaSpada's | multi.	25
Las Vegas | Miami Bch	21
Latitudes | H'wood/B	18
Le Tub | H'wood/B	21
Lime Fresh Mex. | SoBe	19
Maiko | SoBe	–
Marumi Sushi | Plantation/B	–
Mason Jar | Ft. Laud/B	–
🔁 Michael's | Design Dist	27
Miss Saigon | SoBe	23
Molina's | Hialeah	25
Mykonos | Coral Way	20
Myung Ga | Weston/B	29
News Cafe | SoBe	18
North Ocean | Ft. Laud/B	–
Office | Delray Bch/P	20
OneBurger | Coral Gables	22
Orig. Daily | Coco Grove	26
Otentic | SoBe	–
🆕 Ovenella | Boca/P	–
Paquito's | No. Miami Bch	22
🆕 Paris/Town | Palm Bch Gdns/P	–
Park Ave. BBQ | multi.	21
Pasha's | multi.	19
Paul | multi.	20
Pelican Landing | Ft. Laud/B	21
P.F. Chang's | multi.	20
Pho 78 | Pembroke Pines/B	23
Piola | SoBe	22
Pistache | W. Palm/P	23
Pit Bar-B-Q | West Dade	21
Pizza Girls | W. Palm/P	20
Pizza Rustica | multi.	19
Puerto Sagua | SoBe	23
Racks Downtown | Boca/P	21
Ra Sushi | Palm Bch Gdns/P	19
Relish | W. Palm/P	21
Rice Hse. | SoBe	22
Royal Café | Jupiter/P	20

SPECIAL FEATURES

Saigon Cuisine | **Margate/B**	24
Sakaya Kitchen | **Downtown**	22
Sara's | **Palm Bch Gdns/P**	–
Saxsay | **Sunrise/B**	–
Sergio's | **multi.**	20
Shake Shack | **SoBe**	22
Shorty's | **multi.**	22
🆕 Smokehouse | **Boca/P**	–
Southport Raw | **Ft. Laud/B**	20
Spris | **multi.**	22
Sushi Siam/Rock | **SoBe**	22
Sushi/Thai Jo's | **W. Palm/P**	23
Table 42 | **Boca/P**	21
Taco Rico | **Coral Gables**	22
Taverna Kyma | **Boca/P**	20
Taverna Opa | **W. Palm/P**	19
Tempura Hse. | **Boca/P**	18
This Is It Café | **W. Palm/P**	–
T-Mex | **SoBe**	17
Tokyo Sushi | **Ft. Laud/B**	23
Tom Jenkins' | **Ft. Laud/B**	25
TooJay's | **multi.**	18
Tutto Pasta | **Brickell**	22
Tutto Pizza | **Brickell**	24
🅉 Versailles | **Little Havana**	21
Village Grille | **Laud-by-Sea/B**	20
Wild E. Asian | **Ft. Laud/B**	17
Zuperpollo | **Coral Way**	18

QUIET CONVERSATION

AltaMare | **SoBe**	24
Ambry German | **Ft. Laud/B**	21
Antonia's | **Key W./K**	27
Arturo's | **Boca/P**	24
Bagatelle | **Key W./K**	21
Balans | **SoBe**	19
Bali Café | **Downtown**	25
Bangkok Bangkok | **Coral Gables**	19
Bangkok Bangkok | **Kendall**	23
Barracuda Grill | **Marathon/K**	21
Bistro 555 | **Davie/B**	24
Bizaare Cafe | **Lake Worth/P**	19
🅉 BLT Steak | **SoBe**	25
🆕 Blue Door Fish | **SoBe**	23
🆕 Blue Ginger | **Pembroke Pines/B**	–
🅉 Bonefish Grill | **Plantation/B**	22

Brazaviva | **Sunrise/B**	20
Cafe Avanti | **Miami Bch**	25
Cafe Cellini | **Palm Bch/P**	24
🅉 Café Chardonnay | **Palm Bch Gdns/P**	25
Café Emunah | **Ft. Laud/B**	25
🆕 Café Jamm | **Ft. Laud/B**	–
🅉 Cafe Marquesa | **Key W./K**	28
Café Sambal | **Brickell**	22
Cafe Sapori | **W. Palm/P**	24
Cafe Seville | **Ft. Laud/B**	25
🅉 Café Sharaku | **Ft. Laud/B**	28
Caffe Da Vinci | **Bay Harbor Is**	17
Caffe Vialetto | **Coral Gables**	25
🅉 Canyon Ranch | **Miami Bch**	19
🅉 Capital Grille | **Palm Bch Gdns/P**	26
Capri Rist. | **Boca/P**	23
🆕 Carillon | **Miami Bch**	–
Caruso's | **Boca/P**	24
Casa Maya | **Deerfield Bch/B**	24
🆕 Catch Grill | **Biscayne**	–
Chef Adrianne's | **Kendall**	25
🅉 Chez Jean-Pierre | **Palm Bch/P**	28
Cloyde's | **Naples/N**	22
Côte d'Azur | **Naples/N**	27
Da Campo | **Ft. Laud/B**	23
🆕 DIG | **Delray Bch/P**	–
DiGiorgio's | **Key Largo/K**	–
🆕 Dining Rm. | **SoBe**	–
🅉 Eduardo/San Angel | **Ft. Laud/B**	27
Elle's | **Miramar/B**	21
El Tamarindo | **Ft. Laud/B**	22
Entre Nous | **No. Palm Bch/P**	23
Escopazzo | **SoBe**	25
Evo | **Tequesta/P**	–
🅉 15th St. Fish | **Ft. Laud/B**	19
Fin & Claw | **Lighthse Pt/B**	20
🅉 Francesco | **Coral Gables**	26
George's Rest. | **Miami Bch**	23
Giovanni's | **Pembroke Pines/B**	–
Gold Coast | **Coral Spgs/B**	21
Green/Cafe | **Coco Grove**	19
🆕 Green Table | **Coral Gables**	–
Grillfish | **SoBe**	20
Grill on the Alley | **Aventura**	22

Restaurant	Rating
Gulfstream Bistro | **W. Palm/P**	18
Guru | **SoBe**	22
NEW Harry's Pizzeria | **Design Dist**	–
Hi-Life | **Ft. Laud/B**	25
Hy-Vong | **Little Havana**	26
Icebox Café | **SoBe**	22
Ichiban | **Davie/B**	19
Ilios | **Ft. Laud/B**	–
Z Il Mercato | **Hallandale/B**	26
Il Toscano | **Weston/B**	20
India Hse. | **Plantation/B**	21
Indian Chillies | **Pembroke Pines/B**	–
Indomania | **Miami Bch**	25
Jimmy's Bistro | **Delray Bch/P**	26
Joey's Italian | **Wynwood**	24
Kelly's Carib. | **Key W./K**	21
La Cigale | **Delray Bch/P**	24
NEW La Dolce Vita | **Ft. Laud/B**	–
Z La Dorada | **Coral Gables**	26
La Riviera | **Airport**	–
Las Vegas | **multi.**	21
Latitudes | **H'wood/B**	18
La Tre | **Boca/P**	22
Le Bistro | **Lighthse Pt/B**	22
Z Lemongrass | **Ft. Laud/B**	22
Leopard Lounge | **Palm Bch/P**	18
Lola's | **H'wood/B**	24
Maiko | **SoBe**	–
Maison Carlos | **W. Palm/P**	26
NEW Makoto | **Bal Harbour**	25
Mario's Catalina | **Ft. Laud/B**	–
Z NEW Market 17 | **Ft. Laud/B**	26
Martin's | **Key W./K**	22
Marumi Sushi | **Plantation/B**	–
Mason Jar | **Ft. Laud/B**	–
Michelle Bernstein/Omphoy | **Palm Bch/P**	24
Mesazul | **Doral**	–
NEW Mr. Chef's | **Aventura**	24
Mustard Seed | **Plantation/B**	25
North Ocean | **Ft. Laud/B**	–
Oceans 234 | **Deerfield Bch/B**	19
Z Oishi Thai | **No. Miami**	26
NEW On the Menu | **Davie/B**	18
Z Palm Beach Grill | **Palm Bch/P**	25
Palm Beach Steak | **Palm Bch/P**	21
Z Palme d'Or | **Coral Gables**	28
Panorama | **Coco Grove**	–
Z Pascal's | **Coral Gables**	27
Pelican Café | **Lake Pk/P**	21
Peppy's | **Coral Gables**	21
NEW Pied à Terre | **SoBe**	–
Pier Top | **Ft. Laud/B**	26
NEW Piñon Grill | **Boca/P**	22
Portobello | **Jupiter/P**	23
Prime Steakhouse | **Key W./K**	25
Provence | **SoBe**	24
Z Rainbow Palace | **Ft. Laud/B**	26
Renato's | **Palm Bch/P**	24
Romeo's Cafe | **Coral Way**	26
NEW Route 9 | **Coral Gables**	20
Ruth's Chris | **Coral Gables**	25
Safire | **Lake Worth/P**	26
Z Sage | **Ft. Laud/B**	22
NEW Saia | **Ft. Laud/B**	–
Saigon Cuisine | **Margate/B**	24
Saxsay | **Sunrise/B**	–
NEW Sea | **Laud-by-Sea/B**	–
Z Seasons 52 | **multi.**	23
Serafina | **Ft. Laud/B**	23
Z Seven Fish | **Key W./K**	27
660/Angler's | **SoBe**	23
NEW Star Bistro | **Cooper City/B**	–
Stresa | **W. Palm/P**	19
Strip House | **Key W./K**	24
Sukhothai | **Ft. Laud/B**	24
Sundy House | **Delray Bch/P**	22
Sunfish | **Ft. Laud/B**	24
NEW Sustain | **Downtown**	21
NEW Symcha's | **SoBe**	25
NEW Tagliatelle Miami | **SoBe**	–
Talay Thai | **Palm Bch Gdns/P**	24
Tarpon Bend | **Coral Gables**	20
Temple Orange | **Manalapan/P**	24
Thai Hse. S. | **SoBe**	19
NEW 3800 Ocean | **Riviera Bch/P**	23
III Forks | **Hallandale/B**	20
Z Toa Toa | **Sunrise/B**	26
Tommy's Italian | **Davie/B**	23
Toni's Sushi | **SoBe**	25
Top of the Point | **W. Palm/P**	–
Trata | **Ft. Laud/B**	–
Tratt. Luna | **Pinecrest**	24

SPECIAL FEATURES

Truluck's | **Ft. Laud/B**	24
Two Chefs | **So. Miami**	23
264 the Grill | **Palm Bch/P**	17
Udipi | **Sunrise/B**	23
Vagabondi | **W. Palm/P**	24
☑ Valentino's | **Ft. Laud/B**	27
Via Luna | **Ft. Laud/B**	21
☑ Villa/Barton G. | **SoBe**	24
Village Grille | **Laud-by-Sea/B**	20
Villagio | **Sunrise/B**	21
Viva Chile | **Davie/B**	-
Wild E. Asian | **Ft. Laud/B**	17

RAW BARS

☑ Azul | **Brickell**	27
Bay House | **Naples/N**	22
Bentley's | **Islamorada/K**	23
☑ Blue Moon Fish | **multi.**	24
Blue Pointe | **Ft. Myers/N**	24
Bluepoint Grill | **H'wood/B**	18
Charley's Crab | **Palm Bch/P**	20
City Oyster | **Delray Bch/P**	22
Conch Republic | **Key W./K**	17
Conchy Joe's | **Jensen Bch/P**	19
Council Oak | **H'wood/B**	24
Dave's Last | **Lake Worth/P**	17
NEW De Rodriguez | **SoBe**	21
Dock/Crayton | **Naples/N**	20
Gotham Steak | **Miami Bch**	23
Half Shell | **Key W./K**	23
Keys Fisheries | **Marathon/K**	26
McCormick/Schmick | **Naples/N**	20
Meat Market | **SoBe**	25
Mercadito | **Downtown**	21
Mesazul | **Doral**	-
Monty's | **multi.**	17
Oceanaire | **Brickell**	24
Old Florida | **Wilton Manors/B**	19
Pepe's | **Key W./K**	24
Prime Catch | **Boynton Bch/P**	21
Prime Italian | **SoBe**	24
Quinn's | **SoBe**	25
Racks Downtown | **Boca/P**	21
Red Koi | **Coral Gables**	25
Red Light | **UES**	23
River Oyster Bar | **Miami Riv**	25
NEW Royal | **SoBe**	-

☑ Sage | **H'wood/B**	22
Sailfish Marina | **Palm Bch Shores/P**	17
Schooner Wharf | **Key W./K**	14
NEW Soirée at Vice | **SoBe**	-
Southport Raw | **Ft. Laud/B**	20
Spoto's | **Palm Bch Gdns/P**	22
☑ Sra. Martinez | **Design Dist**	25
☑ Steak 954 | **Ft. Laud/B**	24
Sugarcane | **Downtown**	25
SushiSamba | **SoBe**	23
Tarpon Bend | **Coral Gables**	20
NEW 3800 Ocean | **Riviera Bch/P**	23
☑ 3030 Ocean | **Ft. Laud/B**	26
Prawnbroker/Timbers | **Sanibel/N**	25
NEW Umi | **Palm Bch Gdns/P**	26
Vita by Baoli | **SoBe**	-
Whale Raw | **Parkland/B**	17
Whale's Rib | **Deerfield Bch/B**	20

ROMANTIC PLACES

A la Folie Café | **SoBe**	21
AltaMare | **SoBe**	24
Angelique | **Coral Gables**	18
Antonia's | **Key W./K**	27
Arturo's | **Marco Is/N**	22
Arturo's | **Boca/P**	24
Asia Bay | **Ft. Laud/B**	25
Asia de Cuba | **SoBe**	22
Atrio | **Brickell**	22
☑ Azul | **Brickell**	27
Bagatelle | **Key W./K**	21
Baleen | **Naples/N**	23
Bice | **Palm Bch/P**	22
Blackfin Bistro | **Key W./K**	22
Bleu Provence | **Naples/N**	27
☑ BLT Steak | **SoBe**	25
NEW Blue Door Fish | **SoBe**	23
☑ Blue Moon Fish | **Laud-by-Sea/B**	24
Bond St. | **SoBe**	25
Bourbon Steak | **Aventura**	25
Brooks | **Deerfield Bch/B**	21
Buonasera | **Jupiter/P**	24
☑ Café Boulud | **Palm Bch/P**	26
☑ Café Chardonnay | **Palm Bch Gdns/P**	25

Café des Artistes | **Jupiter/P**	23
NEW Cafe L'Attico | **Miami Bch**	-
Z Café L'Europe | **Palm Bch/P**	27
Z Cafe Marquesa | **Key W./K**	28
Cafe Sapori | **W. Palm/P**	24
Cafe Seville | **Ft. Laud/B**	25
Z Café Sharaku | **Ft. Laud/B**	28
Caffé Europa | **Ft. Laud/B**	23
Caffe Vialetto | **Coral Gables**	25
Z Canyon Ranch | **Miami Bch**	19
Capri Rist. | **Boca/P**	23
NEW Carillon | **Miami Bch**	-
Caruso's | **Boca/P**	24
Casablanca | **Ft. Laud/B**	21
Z Casa D'Angelo | **multi.**	27
Z Casa Tua | **SoBe**	24
NEW Catch Grill | **Biscayne**	-
NEW Cecconi's | **Miami Bch**	22
Chart House | **Coco Grove**	20
Chef Adrianne's | **Kendall**	25
Z Chez Jean-Pierre | **Palm Bch/P**	28
Cioppino | **Key Biscayne**	23
Coco Asian Bistro | **Ft. Laud/B**	24
Côte d'Azur | **Naples/N**	27
Da Campo | **Ft. Laud/B**	23
NEW De Rodriguez | **SoBe**	21
NEW Dining Rm. | **SoBe**	-
Z Din. Rm./Little Palm | **Little Torch Key/K**	28
Dolores/Lolita | **Brickell**	19
Z Eduardo/San Angel | **Ft. Laud/B**	27
Elle's | **Miramar/B**	21
Entre Nous | **No. Palm Bch/P**	23
Escopazzo | **SoBe**	25
Z 15th St. Fish | **Ft. Laud/B**	19
Flagler Steak | **Palm Bch/P**	26
Fontana | **Coral Gables**	26
Z Four Seasons | **Palm Bch/P**	25
Z Francesco | **Coral Gables**	26
George's Rest. | **Miami Bch**	23
NEW GG's | **H'wood/B**	20
Gibraltar | **Coco Grove**	20
Grateful Palate | **Ft. Laud/B**	24
Grille 66 | **Ft. Laud/B**	24
Hi-Life | **Ft. Laud/B**	25
Hillstone | **Coral Gables**	-

Hot Tin Roof | **Key W./K**	25
Z Houston's | **No. Miami Bch**	23
Z Il Gabbiano | **Downtown**	27
Z Il Mercato | **Hallandale/B**	26
Z Johnny V | **Ft. Laud/B**	24
Kathy's | **Boca/P**	25
Kelly's Carib. | **Key W./K**	21
Z La Brochette | **Cooper City/B**	28
La Cigale | **Delray Bch/P**	24
NEW La Dolce Vita | **Ft. Laud/B**	-
La Palma | **Coral Gables**	21
La Riviera | **Airport**	-
Latitudes | **H'wood/B**	18
La Veranda | **Pompano Bch/B**	24
Leopard Lounge | **Palm Bch/P**	18
Le Provençal | **Coral Gables**	22
NEW Local Craft | **Coral Gables**	-
Z Louie's | **Key W./K**	26
NEW LouLou | **Miami Riv**	-
NEW LuLu | **Coco Grove**	16
Maison Carlos | **W. Palm/P**	26
Maitardi | **Design Dist**	21
NEW Makoto | **Bal Harbour**	25
Mandolin | **Design Dist**	25
Mario's Catalina | **Ft. Laud/B**	-
Marker 88 | **Islamorada/K**	21
Z NEW Market 17 | **Ft. Laud/B**	26
Martin's | **Key W./K**	22
Meat Market | **SoBe**	25
Melting Pot | **multi.**	19
Z Michaels | **Key W./K**	26
MiraMare | **Naples/N**	21
Z Morada Bay | **Islamorada/K**	22
Morgans | **Wynwood**	24
Morton's | **Brickell**	25
Z Naoe | **Sunny Is Bch**	29
915 Bistro | **Key W./K**	25
North Ocean | **Ft. Laud/B**	-
Oceans 234 | **Deerfield Bch/B**	19
Z OLA | **SoBe**	27
Z Palme d'Or | **Coral Gables**	28
Panorama | **Coco Grove**	-
Pelican Café | **Lake Pk/P**	21
Peppy's | **Coral Gables**	21
Perricone's | **Brickell**	22
NEW Pied à Terre | **SoBe**	-
Z Pierre's | **Islamorada/K**	27

SPECIAL FEATURES

NEW Piñon Grill | **Boca/P**	22
Portobello | **Jupiter/P**	23
Primavera | **Oakland Pk/B**	20
Prime Steakhouse | **Key W./K**	25
Z Rainbow Palace | **Ft. Laud/B**	26
Red Fish Grill | **Coral Gables**	22
Renato's | **Palm Bch/P**	24
Romeo's Cafe | **Coral Way**	26
NEW Royal | **SoBe**	-
Z Sage | **Ft. Laud/B**	22
NEW Saia | **Ft. Laud/B**	-
Saint Tropez | **Ft. Laud/B**	22
NEW Sea | **Laud-by-Sea/B**	-
Serafina | **Ft. Laud/B**	23
Z Setai | **SoBe**	23
Z Seven Fish | **Key W./K**	27
660/Angler's | **SoBe**	23
Smith/Wollensky | **SoBe**	23
Spiga | **SoBe**	24
Z Sra. Martinez | **Design Dist**	25
Strip House | **Key W./K**	24
Sugar Reef | **H'wood/B**	24
Sundy House | **Delray Bch/P**	22
NEW Sustain | **Downtown**	21
NEW Symcha's | **SoBe**	25
Ta-boo | **Palm Bch/P**	23
NEW Tagliatelle Miami | **SoBe**	-
Talay Thai | **Palm Bch Gdns/P**	24
Tantra | **SoBe**	21
Temple Orange | **Manalapan/P**	24
NEW 3800 Ocean | **Riviera Bch/P**	23
Z 3030 Ocean | **Ft. Laud/B**	26
III Forks | **Hallandale/B**	20
Toni's Sushi | **SoBe**	25
Top of the Point | **W. Palm/P**	-
Trata | **Ft. Laud/B**	-
Tratt. Luna | **Pinecrest**	24
Tratt. Romana | **Boca/P**	26
Tratt. Sole | **So. Miami**	20
Truluck's | **Ft. Laud/B**	24
Tuscan Grill | **Ft. Laud/B**	20
Z Valentino's | **Ft. Laud/B**	27
Veranda | **Ft. Myers/N**	26
Via Luna | **Ft. Laud/B**	21
Z Villa/Barton G. | **SoBe**	24
Villagio | **Sunrise/B**	21
Vita by Baoli | **SoBe**	-
Wild E. Asian | **Ft. Laud/B**	17
Wish | **SoBe**	25

SLEEPERS

(Good food, but little known)

Bad Boy Burrito | **Key W./K**	24
Bentley's | **Islamorada/K**	23
Bistro 555 | **Davie/B**	24
Bizcaya | **Coco Grove**	24
Blue Sea | **SoBe**	24
Bombay Darbar | **Coco Grove**	23
Bongusto! | **Ft. Laud/B**	24
Braza Leña | **multi.**	24
Café | **Key W./K**	26
Café Emunah | **Ft. Laud/B**	25
Caffe Portofino | **Pinecrest**	24
Calypso's/Grille | **Key Largo/K**	23
Capri Rist. | **Boca/P**	23
Chef Adrianne's | **Kendall**	25
Commodore | **Key W./K**	23
Flagler Grill | **Stuart/P**	24
Fontana | **Coral Gables**	26
George's Rest. | **Miami Bch**	23
Hog Snappers | **Tequesta/P**	26
Hot Pie | **W. Palm/P**	26
Hot Tin Roof | **Key W./K**	25
I.M. Tapas | **Naples/N**	25
Indomania | **Miami Bch**	25
Ireland's | **Weston/B**	26
Jade | **W. Palm/P**	23
Jimmy's Bistro | **Delray Bch/P**	26
Kiko | **Plantation/B**	26
La Creperie | **Lauderhill/B**	24
Magnum | **UES**	23
Maison Carlos | **W. Palm/P**	26
Marek's | **Marco Is/N**	24
Marhaba Med. | **So. Miami**	25
Molina's | **Hialeah**	25
Myung Ga | **Weston/B**	29
Off the Grille | **multi.**	26
Olivos | **Doral**	26
Orig. Daily | **Coco Grove**	26
Panya Thai | **No. Miami Bch**	25
Papa Hughie's | **Lighthse Pt/B**	24
Petit Rouge | **No. Miami**	26
Pho 78 | **multi.**	23
Pier Top | **Ft. Laud/B**	26
Pita Grille | **No. Palm Bch/P**	23

Provence | **SoBe**	24
Rock Fish | **Kendall**	24
Rock n Roll Ribs | **Coral Spgs**/B	24
Safire | **Lake Worth**/P	26
Saigon Cuisine | **Margate**/B	24
Sakura | **Coral Gables**	24
Salmon | **LIttle Havana**	25
S&S | **Downtown**	23
Sapori | **Boca**/P	28
Siam Palace | **So. Miami**	23
Soya & Pomodoro | **Downtown**	23
Strip House | **Key W.**/K	24
Strip House | **Naples**/N	23
Sushi Simon | **Boynton Bch**/P	23
Tamarind | **Miami Bch**	24
Temple Orange | **Manalapan**/P	24
Tokyo Sushi | **Ft. Laud**/B	23
Tommy's Italian | **Davie**/B	23
Tutto Pizza | **Brickell**	24
Udipi | **Sunrise**/B	23
Woodlands | **Lauderhill**/B	26
Ziggie | **Islamorada**/K	25
Ziree Thai | **Delray Bch**/P	24

SPECIAL OCCASIONS

☑ A&B Lobster | **Key W.**/K	23
☑ Abe/Louie's | **Boca**/P	26
Absinthe | **Boca**/P	18
Arturo's | **Boca**/P	24
Asia de Cuba | **SoBe**	22
Baleen | **Naples**/N	23
NEW Blue Door Fish | **SoBe**	23
☑ Blue Moon Fish | **Laud-by-Sea**/B	24
Brooks | **Deerfield Bch**/B	21
☑ Café Boulud | **Palm Bch**/P	26
☑ Café L'Europe | **Palm Bch**/P	27
☑ Cafe Marquesa | **Key W.**/K	28
☑ Cafe/Martorano | **multi.**	24
☑ Café Sharaku | **Ft. Laud**/B	28
☑ Casa D'Angelo | **Ft. Laud**/B	27
☑ Casa Tua | **SoBe**	24
Chef Adrianne's | **Kendall**	25
Chima Brazilian | **Ft. Laud**/B	25
China Grill | **Ft. Laud**/B	22
Cioppino | **Key Biscayne**	23
Cloyde's | **Naples**/N	22
Commodore | **Key W.**/K	23

Côte d'Azur | **Naples**/N	27
Da Campo | **Ft. Laud**/B	23
NEW Dining Rm. | **SoBe**	-
☑ Din. Rm./Little Palm | **Little Torch Key**/K	28
☑ Eduardo/San Angel | **Ft. Laud**/B	27
Elle's | **Miramar**/B	21
Escopazzo | **SoBe**	25
Evo | **Tequesta**/P	-
☑ 15th St. Fish | **Ft. Laud**/B	19
Fontana | **Coral Gables**	26
Fratelli Lyon | **Design Dist**	22
George's/Grove | **Coco Grove**	22
George's/Sunset | **So. Miami**	20
George's Rest. | **Miami Bch**	23
Gibraltar | **Coco Grove**	20
Grateful Palate | **Ft. Laud**/B	24
Grille 66 | **Ft. Laud**/B	24
Hot Tin Roof | **Key W.**/K	25
Ireland's | **Weston**/B	26
Ironwood | **Palm Bch Gdns**/P	18
☑ Johnny V | **Ft. Laud**/B	24
☑ La Brochette | **Cooper City**/B	28
La Cigale | **Delray Bch**/P	24
La Riviera | **Airport**	-
☑ Louie's | **Key W.**/K	26
NEW Makoto | **Bal Harbour**	25
☑ Marcello | **W. Palm**/P	28
Marker 88 | **Islamorada**/K	21
☑ NEW Market 17 | **Ft. Laud**/B	26
Martin's | **Key W.**/K	22
Melting Pot | **Palm Bch Gdns**/P	19
☑ Nobu Miami | **SoBe**	27
Oceanaire | **Brickell**	24
☑ Pierre's | **Islamorada**/K	27
Pier Top | **Ft. Laud**/B	26
Renato's | **Palm Bch**/P	24
River House | **Palm Bch Gdns**/P	22
Roy's | **multi.**	26
Ruth's Chris | **Ft. Laud**/B	25
Ruth's Chris | **Estero**/N	26
NEW Saia | **Ft. Laud**/B	-
Scarpetta | **Miami Bch**	25
Serafina | **Ft. Laud**/B	23
☑ Setai | **SoBe**	23
660/Angler's | **SoBe**	23
NEW Soirée at Vice | **SoBe**	-

Z Sra. Martinez | **Design Dist**	25
STK Miami | **Miami Bch**	22
Strip House | **Key W./K**	24
Sundy House | **Delray Bch/P**	22
NEW Sustain | **Downtown**	21
NEW Symcha's | **SoBe**	25
Tatiana | **Hallandale/B**	-
Taverna Opa | **Doral**	19
NEW 3800 Ocean | **Riviera Bch/P**	23
Z 3030 Ocean | **Ft. Laud/B**	26
III Forks | **multi.**	20
Top of the Point | **W. Palm/P**	-
NEW Trio/Bay | **No. Bay Vill**	-
Truluck's | **multi.**	24
Veranda | **Ft. Myers/N**	26
Via Luna | **Ft. Laud/B**	21
Z Villa/Barton G. | **SoBe**	24
Vivo Partenza | **Boca/P**	23
Whisk Gourmet | **So. Miami**	25
Wild E. Asian | **Ft. Laud/B**	17

TEEN APPEAL

Abbondanza | **Key W./K**	20
Anacapri | **Cutler Bay**	22
Z Anthony's Pizza | **multi.**	22
Archie's Pizza | **Key Biscayne**	21
Aruba Beach | **Laud-by-Sea/B**	17
NEW Bernie's L.A. | **SoBe**	26
Berries | **Coco Grove**	20
Big Pink | **SoBe**	20
Z Blue Heaven | **Key W./K**	25
Bubble Room | **Captiva Is/N**	19
NEW Cafe L'Attico | **Miami Bch**	-
Z Cheesecake | **multi.**	20
Coconuts | **Ft. Laud/B**	23
NEW Crumb/Parchment | **Design Dist**	-
Darbster | **Lake Worth/P**	-
Dave's Last | **Lake Worth/P**	17
11th St. Diner | **SoBe**	20
El Rancho | **Kendall**	19
Filling Station | **Downtown**	17
NEW Flip Burger | **No. Miami**	25
Floridian | **Ft. Laud/B**	18
NEW Forno 52 | **Palmetto Bay**	-
Z Frankie's Pizza | **Westchester**	26

Front Porch | **SoBe**	21
Hamburger Heaven | **Palm Bch/P**	21
NEW Harrison's | **W. Miami**	-
NEW Heavy Burger | **Aventura**	22
Z Hiro's Yakko-San | **No. Miami Bch**	27
Hot Pie | **W. Palm/P**	26
Z Il Mulino | **Ft. Laud/B**	22
Jaxson's | **Dania Bch/B**	21
NEW Joint B&G | **Pinecrest**	-
Kelly's Carib. | **Key W./K**	21
Kelly's Landing | **Ft. Laud/B**	21
La Casona | **W. Sunset**	-
La Sandwicherie | **SoBe**	25
Z LaSpada's | **multi.**	25
Lime Fresh Mex. | **Downtown**	19
Mangoes | **Key W./K**	18
Mario The Baker | **multi.**	20
Mellow Mushroom | **Delray Bch/P**	21
Melting Pot | **multi.**	19
NEW Naked Pizza | **SoBe**	18
News Cafe | **SoBe**	18
OneBurger | **Coral Gables**	22
NEW 100 Montaditos | **Downtown**	-
Outback | **multi.**	18
NEW Pancho Villa | **No. Miami**	-
Paquito's | **No. Miami Bch**	22
P.F. Chang's | **multi.**	20
NEW Pincho Factory | **Westchester**	-
Piola | **SoBe**	22
Pit Bar-B-Q | **West Dade**	21
Pizza Girls | **W. Palm/P**	20
Pizza Rustica | **multi.**	19
Randazzo's | **Coral Gables**	20
Rock n Roll Ribs | **Coral Spgs/B**	24
NEW Roxy | **No. Miami**	-
Salmon | **Little Havana**	25
Salsa Fiesta | **Wynwood**	-
Z Seasons 52 | **Coral Gables**	23
Shake Shack | **SoBe**	22
Sloan's | **multi.**	22
NEW Spartico | **Coco Grove**	-
Spris | **multi.**	22
Stir Crazy | **multi.**	19

Sushi Maki | **multi.**	21	
Taco Rico | **Coral Gables**	22	
Tamarind | **Miami Bch**	24	
Taverna Opa | **Doral**	19	
Vic & Angelo's | **Palm Bch Gdns/P**	21	
Zuccarelli's | **W. Palm/P**	20	

THEME RESTAURANTS

☑ Barton G. | **SoBe**	22
☑ Cafe/Martorano | **H'wood/B**	24
Cantina Laredo | **multi.**	20
Casa Maya | **Deerfield Bch/B**	24
Checkers/Munchen | **Pompano Bch/B**	22
Chima Brazilian | **Ft. Laud/B**	25
Democratic/Beer | **Downtown**	–
Doc Ford's | **Ft. Myers Bch/N**	22
NEW Dos Caminos | **Ft. Laud/B**	19
El Meson | **Key W./K**	18
Guanabanas | **Jupiter/P**	18
Jaxson's | **Dania Bch/B**	21
Jimmy Buffett's | **Key W./K**	13
Kingshead Pub | **Sunrise/B**	21
Kuluck | **Tamarac/B**	–
La Tre | **Boca/P**	22
Maguires Hill 16 | **Ft. Laud/B**	16
☑ Mai-Kai | **Ft. Laud/B**	16
Melting Pot | **multi.**	19
My Big Fat Greek | **Dania Bch/B**	20
Old Heidelberg | **Ft. Laud/B**	21
Outback | **multi.**	18
Paddy Mac's | **Palm Bch Gdns/P**	19
Ra Sushi | **Palm Bch Gdns/P**	19
Rock n Roll Ribs | **Coral Spgs/B**	24
Shuck N Dive | **Ft. Laud/B**	19
Shula's | **Ft. Laud/B**	23
Sloppy Joe's | **Key W./K**	13
Sublime | **Ft. Laud/B**	21
Tatiana | **Hallandale/B**	–
Taverna Opa | **multi.**	19
NEW Tokyo Blue | **Ft. Laud/B**	20

TRENDY

Absinthe | **Boca/P**	18
Absinthe | **Naples/N**	21
Asia de Cuba | **SoBe**	22
☑ Azul | **Brickell**	27

Balans | **SoBe**	19
☑ Barton G. | **SoBe**	22
Big City Tav. | **Ft. Laud/B**	19
Big Pink | **SoBe**	20
☑ Bistro Mezz. | **Ft. Laud/B**	26
NEW Blade/Vida | **Miami Bch**	–
NEW Blind Monk | **W. Palm/P**	18
NEW Blue Ginger | **Pembroke Pines/B**	–
☑ Blue Heaven | **Key W./K**	25
Blue Sea | **SoBe**	24
Blu Sushi | **Ft. Myers/N**	24
Bond St. | **SoBe**	25
Brio Tuscan | **multi.**	21
NEW Buccan | **Palm Bch/P**	25
☑ Cabana | **Delray Bch/P**	22
Café & Bar Lurcat | **Naples/N**	26
NEW Café Jamm | **Ft. Laud/B**	–
☑ Cafe/Martorano | **multi.**	24
Caffe Abbracci | **Coral Gables**	25
Caliente Kitchen | **Delray Bch/P**	22
Campiello | **Naples/N**	25
Cantina Laredo | **Hallandale/B**	20
☑ Canyon | **Ft. Laud/B**	27
☑ Capital Grille | **Ft. Laud/B**	26
Carpaccio | **Bal Harbour**	23
☑ Casa Tua | **SoBe**	24
NEW Catch Grill | **Biscayne**	–
NEW Cecconi's | **Miami Bch**	22
Ceviche 105 | **Downtown**	25
Chima Brazilian | **Ft. Laud/B**	25
China Grill | **multi.**	22
☑ Chops Lobster | **Boca/P**	26
Cottage | **Lake Worth/P**	20
NEW Crazy About You | **Brickell**	21
Dada | **Delray Bch/P**	20
D'Angelo | **Oakland Pk/B**	25
NEW Dapur | **Ft. Laud/B**	–
Darbster | **Lake Worth/P**	–
Doc Ford's | **Ft. Myers Bch/N**	22
Echo | **Palm Bch/P**	24
E.R. Bradley | **W. Palm/P**	16
NEW Fadó Irish Pub | **Brickell**	17
NEW 1500 Degrees | **Miami Bch**	24
Forge | **Miami Bch**	24
Fratelli Lyon | **Design Dist**	22
NEW Gigi | **Wynwood**	24

Restaurant	Location	Rating
Globe Cafe	Coral Gables	17
Grand Lux	multi.	19
Grateful Palate	Ft. Laud/B	24
Gratify	W. Palm/P	-
NEW Green Table	Coral Gables	-
NEW Heavy Burger	Aventura	22
Hi-Life	Ft. Laud/B	25
Hillstone	Coral Gables	-
Z Houston's	Pompano Bch/B	23
I.M. Tapas	Naples/N	25
Jade	W. Palm/P	23
JB's	Deerfield Bch/B	18
Jimmy'z Kitchen	multi.	25
Joey's Italian	Wynwood	24
Z Johnny V	Ft. Laud/B	24
Joseph's Wine	Delray Bch/P	23
Kaiyo Grill	Islamorada/K	-
NEW La Dolce Vita	Ft. Laud/B	-
Lario's/Beach	SoBe	20
Latitudes	H'wood/B	18
Leila	W. Palm/P	22
Leopard Lounge	Palm Bch/P	18
Lime Fresh Mex.	SoBe	19
Little Moir's	Jupiter/P	26
NEW Local Craft	Coral Gables	-
Lola's	H'wood/B	24
Mangoes	Key W./K	18
Mango's Tropical	SoBe	13
Z NEW Market 17	Ft. Laud/B	26
NEW Max's Harvest	Delray Bch/P	-
NEW M Bar	Ft. Laud/B	-
Michelle Bernstein/Omphoy	Palm Bch/P	24
Meat Market	SoBe	25
Mercadito	Downtown	21
MiraMare	Naples/N	21
NEW Miss Yip	Downtown	16
NEW Naked Pizza	SoBe	18
Nikki	SoBe	16
Office	Delray Bch/P	20
Oggi Caffe	No. Bay Vill	25
Z Ortanique	Coral Gables	26
NEW Pubbelly	Miami Bch	24
NEW Pubbelly Sushi	Miami Bch	-
Racks Downtown	Boca/P	21
Ra Sushi	Palm Bch Gdns/P	19
Red Koi	Coral Gables	25
Relish	W. Palm/P	21
Rocco's Tacos	Ft. Laud/B	20
Rosa Mexicano	SoBe	22
NEW Route 9	Coral Gables	20
NEW Roxy	No. Miami	-
Safire	Lake Worth/P	26
NEW Saia	Ft. Laud/B	-
Sake Room	Downtown	-
Sardinia	Miami Bch	26
Sawa	Coral Gables	21
Scarpetta	Miami Bch	25
Z Seasons 52	Ft. Laud/B	23
Z Setai	SoBe	23
Z Seven Fish	Key W./K	27
Shake Shack	SoBe	22
NEW Soi Asian	Downtown	-
NEW Soirée at Vice	SoBe	-
SoLita	multi.	21
Soyka	UES	20
NEW Spartico	Coco Grove	-
Spoto's	Palm Bch Gdns/P	22
Z Sra. Martinez	Design Dist	25
Sugarcane	Downtown	25
Sushi Rock	SoBe	21
Sushi/Thai Jo's	W. Palm/P	23
NEW Sustain	Downtown	21
NEW Symcha's	SoBe	25
Table 42	Boca/P	21
Ta-boo	Palm Bch/P	23
Tantra	SoBe	21
Taverna Opa	multi.	19
Z 32 East	Delray Bch/P	25
NEW Tokyo Blue	Ft. Laud/B	20
Toni's Sushi	SoBe	25
Tratt. Romana	Boca/P	26
NEW Trio/Bay	No. Bay Vill	-
Triple Eight	Delray Bch/P	-
Truluck's	Ft. Laud/B	24
Turtle Kraals	Key W./K	18
Van Dyke Cafe	SoBe	16
Villagio	multi.	21
Vita by Baoli	SoBe	-
Whisk Gourmet	So. Miami	25
Wild E. Asian	Ft. Laud/B	17
NEW Wine Depot	SoBe	20

NEW Wynwood | **Wynwood**	17
YOLO | **Ft. Laud/B**	21
Z Zuma | **Downtown**	28

VIEWS

Z A&B Lobster | **Key W./K**	23
Acquolina | **Weston/B**	22
Aizia | **Hallandale/B**	19
Aruba Beach | **Laud-by-Sea/B**	17
Asia Bay | **Ft. Laud/B**	25
Atrio | **Brickell**	22
Z Azul | **Brickell**	27
Bagatelle | **Key W./K**	21
Balans | **Brickell**	19
Baleen | **Naples/N**	23
Banana Boat | **Boynton Bch/P**	15
Bay House | **Naples/N**	22
Billy's Stone | **H'wood/B**	23
Bimini Boatyard | **Ft. Laud/B**	17
Blue Heron | **Naples/N**	27
Z Blue Moon Fish | **Laud-by-Sea/B**	24
Café & Bar Lurcat | **Naples/N**	26
Z Café Boulud | **Palm Bch/P**	26
Café des Artistes | **Jupiter/P**	23
Café Sambal | **Brickell**	22
Caffe Luna Rosa | **Delray Bch/P**	20
Calypso's/Grille | **Key Largo/K**	23
NEW Catch Grill | **Biscayne**	-
Charley's Crab | **Palm Bch/P**	20
Chart House | **Coco Grove**	20
China Grill | **Ft. Laud/B**	22
Christine Lee's | **Hallandale/B**	22
Cioppino | **Key Biscayne**	23
Cloyde's | **Naples/N**	22
Coconuts | **Ft. Laud/B**	23
Commodore | **Key W./K**	23
Conch Republic | **Key W./K**	17
Conchy Joe's | **Jensen Bch/P**	19
Da Campo | **Ft. Laud/B**	23
NEW Deck 84 | **Delray Bch/P**	19
NEW De Rodriguez | **SoBe**	21
Z Din. Rm./Little Palm | **Little Torch Key/K**	28
NEW Dirty Martini | **Palm Bch Gdns/P**	-
Doc Ford's | **Ft. Myers Bch/N**	22
Dock/Crayton | **Naples/N**	20

Dockside Sea | **Lake Pk/P**	19
Dune Deck | **Lantana/P**	20
Eos | **Brickell**	21
E.R. Bradley | **W. Palm/P**	16
Z 15th St. Fish | **Ft. Laud/B**	19
Flagler Steak | **Palm Bch/P**	26
Z Four Seasons | **Palm Bch/P**	25
Garcia's | **Miami Riv**	23
NEW GG's | **H'wood/B**	20
Gibraltar | **Coco Grove**	20
Grille 66 | **Ft. Laud/B**	24
Guanabanas | **Jupiter/P**	18
Half Shell | **Key W./K**	23
HB's/Gulf | **Naples/N**	19
Hot Tin Roof | **Key W./K**	25
Z Houston's | **No. Miami Bch**	23
H2O | **Ft. Laud/B**	18
Il Bellagio | **W. Palm/P**	20
Z Il Gabbiano | **Downtown**	27
Ilios | **Ft. Laud/B**	-
Il Mulino NY | **Sunny Is Bch**	24
Island Grill | **Islamorada/K**	24
JB's | **Deerfield Bch/B**	18
Jetty's | **Jupiter/P**	22
Jimmy Johnson's | **Key Largo/K**	18
Kevin's | **Palm Bch Gdns/P**	-
Keys Fisheries | **Marathon/K**	26
Lario's/Beach | **SoBe**	20
NEW La Scalina | **Downtown**	-
Latitudes | **H'wood/B**	18
Lazy Loggerhead | **Jupiter/P**	24
Le Tub | **H'wood/B**	21
Lido | **SoBe**	22
Los Ranchos | **Biscayne**	21
Z Louie's | **Key W./K**	26
Lucille's | **Weston/B**	22
Mad Hatter | **Sanibel/N**	26
Marker 88 | **Islamorada/K**	21
Z Max's | **Boca/P**	22
Michelle Bernstein/Omphoy | **Palm Bch/P**	24
Meat Market | **SoBe**	25
Mesazul | **Doral**	-
NEW Mr. Collins | **Bal Harbour**	-
Monty's | **multi.**	17
Z Morada Bay | **Islamorada/K**	22
Morton's | **Miami Bch**	25
M Waterfront | **Naples/N**	23

My Big Fat Greek | **Dania Bch/B** 20
Z NY Prime | **Boca/P** 25
Nikki | **SoBe** 16
North Ocean | **Ft. Laud/B** -
Oceans 234 | **Deerfield Bch/B** 19
Old Calypso | **Delray Bch/P** 19
Panorama | **Coco Grove** -
NEW Paris/Town | -
  Palm Bch Gdns/P
Pelican Café | **Lake Pk/P** 21
Pelican Landing | **Ft. Laud/B** 21
Pelican RestCafé | **SoBe** 21
Z Pierre's | **Islamorada/K** 27
Pier Top | **Ft. Laud/B** 26
Pincher's Crab | **multi.** 20
Pistache | **W. Palm/P** 23
Prime Catch | **Boynton Bch/P** 21
Prime Steakhouse | **Key W./K** 25
Quinn's | **SoBe** 25
Racks Italian | **No. Miami Bch** 20
Red Fish Grill | **Coral Gables** 22
Red Light | **UES** 23
NEW Rickenbacker | 20
  Key Biscayne
River House | **Palm Bch Gdns/P** 22
Riverwalk | **Naples/N** 20
NEW Royal | **SoBe** -
Roy's | **Naples/N** 26
NEW Saia | **Ft. Laud/B** -
Sailfish Marina | 17
  Palm Bch Shores/P
Schooner Wharf | **Key W./K** 14
Scotty's | **Coco Grove** 14
Z Seasons 52 | 23
  Palm Bch Gdns/P
Serafina | **Ft. Laud/B** 23
Shor American | **Key W./K** -
Shula's | **multi.** 23
Smith/Wollensky | **SoBe** 23
Snapper's Waterfront | 20
  Key Largo/K
Snook Inn | **Marco Is/N** 20
Z Sra. Martinez | **Design Dist** 25
Z Steak 954 | **Ft. Laud/B** 24
Strip House | **Key W./K** 24
Sugar Reef | **H'wood/B** 24
Sundy House | **Delray Bch/P** 22
Taverna Opa | **H'wood/B** 19

Temple Orange | **Manalapan/P** 24
Thai Island | **Key W./K** -
NEW 3800 Ocean | 23
  Riviera Bch/P
Z 3030 Ocean | **Ft. Laud/B** 26
NEW Tokyo Blue | **Ft. Laud/B** 20
Tony Chan's | **Downtown** 23
NEW Trio/Bay | **No. Bay Vill** -
Turtle Kraals | **Key W./K** 18
Tuscan Grill | **Ft. Laud/B** 20
Two Georges | **multi.** 15
NEW Umi | **Palm Bch Gdns/P** 26
Z Upper Deck | **Key W./K** 25
Van Dyke Cafe | **SoBe** 16
Veranda | **Ft. Myers/N** 26
Via Luna | **Ft. Laud/B** 21
Whale Raw | **Parkland/B** 17
Wild E. Asian | **Ft. Laud/B** 17
Wish | **SoBe** 25
NEW Wynwood | **Wynwood** 17
Yuca | **SoBe** 20
Z Zuma | **Downtown** 28

VISITORS ON EXPENSE ACCOUNT

Z Abe/Louie's | **Boca/P** 26
Absinthe | **Boca/P** 18
Arturo's | **Boca/P** 24
Asia de Cuba | **SoBe** 22
Z Azul | **Brickell** 27
Baleen | **Naples/N** 23
Bice | **Palm Bch/P** 22
Bleu Provence | **Naples/N** 27
NEW Blue Door Fish | **SoBe** 23
Bourbon Steak | **Aventura** 25
Brazaviva | **Sunrise/B** 20
Z Café Boulud | **Palm Bch/P** 26
Z Café Chardonnay | 25
  Palm Bch Gdns/P
Z Café L'Europe | **Palm Bch/P** 27
Z Cafe Marquesa | **Key W./K** 28
Z Cafe/Martorano | **multi.** 24
Z Cafe Maxx | **Pompano Bch/B** 27
Cafe Sapori | **W. Palm/P** 24
Caffe Abbracci | **Coral Gables** 25
Caffé Milano | **SoBe** 17
Z Capital Grille | **multi.** 26
Carpaccio | **Bal Harbour** 23

☑ Casa D'Angelo | Ft. Laud/B	27
☑ Casa Tua | SoBe	24
☑ Chez Jean-Pierre | Palm Bch/P	28
Chima Brazilian | Ft. Laud/B	25
China Grill | multi.	22
☑ Chops Lobster | Boca/P	26
Christine Lee's | Hallandale/B	22
Christy's | Coral Gables	24
Cioppino | Key Biscayne	23
Cloyde's | Naples/N	22
Côte d'Azur | Naples/N	27
Council Oak | H'wood/B	24
Cut 432 | Delray Bch/P	25
Da Campo | Ft. Laud/B	23
Echo | Palm Bch/P	24
☑ Eduardo/San Angel | Ft. Laud/B	27
Escargot 41 | Naples/N	26
Escopazzo | SoBe	25
NEW 1500 Degrees | Miami Bch	24
Flagler Grill | Stuart/P	24
Fontana | Coral Gables	26
☑ Four Seasons | Palm Bch/P	25
Gibraltar | Coco Grove	20
Gotham Steak | Miami Bch	23
Grateful Palate | Ft. Laud/B	24
Grille 66 | Ft. Laud/B	24
Hollywood Prime | H'wood/B	24
☑ Il Gabbiano | Downtown	27
Ireland's | Weston/B	26
Ironwood | Palm Bch Gdns/P	18
☑ Joe's Stone | SoBe	27
Joey's Italian | Wynwood	24
☑ Johnny V | Ft. Laud/B	24
Kathy's | Boca/P	25
La Cigale | Delray Bch/P	24
Leopard Lounge | Palm Bch/P	18
Le Provençal | Coral Gables	22
☑ Louie's | Key W./K	26
☑ Mai-Kai | Ft. Laud/B	16
MiraMare | Naples/N	21
Monty's | Coco Grove	17
Morton's | multi.	25
☑ NY Prime | Boca/P	25
☑ Nobu Miami | SoBe	27
Oceanaire | Brickell	24
☑ Ortanique | Coral Gables	26

Osteria del Teatro | SoBe	26
☑ Palm | Bay Harbor Is	28
☑ Palme d'Or | Coral Gables	28
Panorama | Coco Grove	-
☑ Pascal's | Coral Gables	27
NEW Pied à Terre | SoBe	-
☑ Pierre's | Islamorada/K	27
Pier Top | Ft. Laud/B	26
☑ Prime One | SoBe	27
Prime Steakhouse | Key W./K	25
NEW Rare Las Olas | Ft. Laud/B	21
Roy's | multi.	26
Ruth's Chris | multi.	25
Ruth's Chris | Estero/N	26
Scarpetta | Miami Bch	25
Sea Salt | Naples/N	23
☑ Setai | SoBe	23
Shula's | multi.	23
Smith/Wollensky | SoBe	23
SoLita | Ft. Laud/B	21
Square One | Key W./K	21
STK Miami | Miami Bch	22
Strip House | Key W./K	24
Strip House | Naples/N	23
SushiSamba | SoBe	23
Ta-boo | Palm Bch/P	23
NEW 3800 Ocean | Riviera Bch/P	23
☑ 3030 Ocean | Ft. Laud/B	26
☑ 32 East | Delray Bch/P	25
III Forks | multi.	20
Timpano | Ft. Laud/B	23
Tony Chan's | Downtown	23
Top of the Point | W. Palm/P	-
Truluck's | multi.	24
Truluck's | Naples/N	26
Via Luna | Ft. Laud/B	21
☑ Villa/Barton G. | SoBe	24
☑ Zuma | Downtown	28

WATERSIDE

Acquolina | Weston/B	22
Aizia | Hallandale/B	19
Alabama Jacks | Key Largo/K	20
Area 31 | Downtown	22
Aruba Beach | Laud-by-Sea/B	17
Asia Bay | Ft. Laud/B	25
☑ Azul | Brickell	27

Baleen	**Naples/N**	23
Banana Boat	**Boynton Bch/P**	15
Bay House	**Naples/N**	22
Billy's Stone	**H'wood/B**	23
Bimini Boatyard	**Ft. Laud/B**	17
Blue Heron	**Naples/N**	27
☑ Blue Moon Fish	**Laud-by-Sea/B**	24
Bluepoint Grill	**H'wood/B**	18
Café des Artistes	**Jupiter/P**	23
Café Sambal	**Brickell**	22
Caffe Luna Rosa	**Delray Bch/P**	20
Calypso's/Grille	**Key Largo/K**	23
Cap's	**Lighthse Pt/B**	17
NEW Catch Grill	**Biscayne**	–
Charley's Crab	**Palm Bch/P**	20
Chart House	**Coco Grove**	20
China Grill	**Ft. Laud/B**	22
Chops City Grill	**Bonita Springs**	25
Coconuts	**Ft. Laud/B**	23
Commodore	**Key W./K**	23
Conch Republic	**Key W./K**	17
Conchy Joe's	**Jensen Bch/P**	19
Da Campo	**Ft. Laud/B**	23
NEW De Rodriguez	**SoBe**	21
☑ Din. Rm./Little Palm	**Little Torch Key/K**	28
NEW Dirty Martini	**Palm Bch Gdns/P**	–
Doc Ford's	**Ft. Myers Bch/N**	22
Dock/Crayton	**Naples/N**	20
Dockside Sea	**Lake Pk/P**	19
Dune Deck	**Lantana/P**	20
East City Grill	**Weston/B**	19
E.R. Bradley	**W. Palm/P**	16
☑ 15th St. Fish	**Ft. Laud/B**	19
Flagler Steak	**Palm Bch/P**	26
Garcia's	**Miami Riv**	23
NEW GG's	**H'wood/B**	20
Gibraltar	**Coco Grove**	20
Grille 66	**Ft. Laud/B**	24
Guanabanas	**Jupiter/P**	18
Half Shell	**Key W./K**	23
Hot Tin Roof	**Key W./K**	25
☑ Houston's	**Pompano Bch/B**	23
H2O	**Ft. Laud/B**	18
Ilios	**Ft. Laud/B**	–
Il Mulino NY	**Sunny Is Bch**	24

Il Toscano	**Weston/B**	20
Island Grill	**Islamorada/K**	24
JB's	**Deerfield Bch/B**	18
Jetty's	**Jupiter/P**	22
Kevin's	**Palm Bch Gdns/P**	–
Keys Fisheries	**Marathon/K**	26
NEW La Scalina	**Downtown**	–
Latitudes	**H'wood/B**	18
Lazy Loggerhead	**Jupiter/P**	24
Le Tub	**H'wood/B**	21
Lido	**SoBe**	22
Los Ranchos	**Biscayne**	21
☑ Louie's	**Key W./K**	26
Lou's Beer	**Miami Bch**	21
Lucille's	**Weston/B**	22
Marker 88	**Islamorada/K**	21
MiraMare	**Naples/N**	21
NEW Mr. Collins	**Bal Harbour**	–
Monty's	**multi.**	17
☑ Morada Bay	**Islamorada/K**	22
Morton's	**Miami Bch**	25
Mr. Chow	**SoBe**	22
M Waterfront	**Naples/N**	23
My Big Fat Greek	**Dania Bch/B**	20
☑ NY Prime	**Boca/P**	25
Nikki	**SoBe**	16
North Ocean	**Ft. Laud/B**	–
Oceans 234	**Deerfield Bch/B**	19
Old Calypso	**Delray Bch/P**	19
Pelican Landing	**Ft. Laud/B**	21
☑ Pierre's	**Islamorada/K**	27
Pincher's Crab	**multi.**	20
Pistache	**W. Palm/P**	23
Prime Catch	**Boynton Bch/P**	21
Prime Steakhouse	**Key W./K**	25
Racks Italian	**No. Miami Bch**	20
Red Fish Grill	**Coral Gables**	22
Red Light	**UES**	23
River House	**Palm Bch Gdns/P**	22
Riverwalk	**Naples/N**	20
NEW Royal	**SoBe**	–
Roy's	**Naples/N**	26
Rustic Inn	**Ft. Laud/B**	22
Sailfish Marina	**Palm Bch Shores/P**	17
Salute!	**Key W./K**	22
Schooner Wharf	**Key W./K**	14
Scotty's	**Coco Grove**	14

ⓩ Seasons 52	Palm Bch Gdns/P	23
Serafina	Ft. Laud/B	23
Shor American	Key W./K	–
Shula's	multi.	23
Smith/Wollensky	SoBe	23
Snapper's Waterfront	Key Largo/K	20
Snook Inn	Marco Is/N	20
Southport Raw	Ft. Laud/B	20
ⓩ Steak 954	Ft. Laud/B	24
Strip House	Key W./K	24
Sublime	Ft. Laud/B	21
Sugar Reef	H'wood/B	24
Sundy House	Delray Bch/P	22
ⓩ 3030 Ocean	Ft. Laud/B	26
Tony Chan's	Downtown	23
NEW Trio/Bay	No. Bay Vill	–
Turtle Kraals	Key W./K	18
Two Georges	multi.	15
ⓩ Upper Deck	Key W./K	25
Via Luna	Ft. Laud/B	21
ⓩ Villa/Barton G.	SoBe	24
Village Grille	Laud-by-Sea/B	20
Whale Raw	Parkland/B	17
Wild E. Asian	Ft. Laud/B	17
ⓩ Zuma	Downtown	28

WINNING WINE LISTS

Absinthe	Boca/P	18
AltaMare	SoBe	24
Anacapri	Pinecrest	22
Angelique	Coral Gables	18
ⓩ Azul	Brickell	27
Bleu Provence	Naples/N	27
NEW Blue Door Fish	SoBe	23
ⓩ Blue Heaven	Key W./K	25
Blú la Pizzeria	So. Miami	21
Brio Tuscan	Pembroke Pines/B	21
Bugatti Pasta	Coral Gables	23
ⓩ Café Boulud	Palm Bch/P	26
ⓩ Café Chardonnay	Palm Bch Gdns/P	25
ⓩ Café L'Europe	Palm Bch/P	27
ⓩ Cafe Marquesa	Key W./K	28
ⓩ Cafe Maxx	Pompano Bch/B	27
Café Sambal	Brickell	22
Cafe Sapori	W. Palm/P	24

Cafe Seville	Ft. Laud/B	25
Caffe Abbracci	Coral Gables	25
Caffe Da Vinci	Bay Harbor Is	17
Caffé Milano	SoBe	17
ⓩ Canyon Ranch	Miami Bch	19
Captain Charlie	Juno Bch/P	27
Captain's Tav.	Pinecrest	23
Carpaccio	Bal Harbour	23
ⓩ Casa D'Angelo	Boca/P	27
Casa Juancho	Little Havana	24
Chops City Grill	multi.	25
Cioppino	Key Biscayne	23
City Cellar	W. Palm/P	20
Da Campo	Ft. Laud/B	23
D'Angelo	Oakland Pk/B	25
ⓩ Din. Rm./Little Palm	Little Torch Key/K	28
Doraku	SoBe	23
East City Grill	Weston/B	19
NEW Eden	SoBe	21
El Carajo	Coral Way	22
11 Maple St.	Jensen Bch/P	27
Elle's	Miramar/B	21
Escopazzo	SoBe	25
Flagler Grill	Stuart/P	24
Fontana	Coral Gables	26
ⓩ Four Seasons	Palm Bch/P	25
Fratelli Lyon	Design Dist	22
Fulvio's 1900	H'wood/B	22
Globe Cafe	Coral Gables	17
Gold Coast	Coral Spgs/B	21
Gourmet Diner	No. Miami Bch	18
Grateful Palate	Ft. Laud/B	24
Graziano's	Westchester	25
Grazie Italian	SoBe	25
Grille 66	Ft. Laud/B	24
ⓩ Henry's	Delray Bch/P	21
Hot Tin Roof	Key W./K	25
ⓩ Il Mercato	Hallandale/B	26
Ireland's	Weston/B	26
NEW Jamon Jamon	Miami Riv	–
ⓩ Joe's Stone	SoBe	27
Joey's Italian	Wynwood	24
ⓩ Johnny V	Ft. Laud/B	24
Kelly's Carib.	Key W./K	21
ⓩ Kitchenetta	Ft. Laud/B	27
La Riviera	Airport	–
La Trattoria	Key W./K	22

SPECIAL FEATURES

Le Bistro	**Lighthse Pt/B**	22
Lola's	**H'wood/B**	24
Z Louie's	**Key W./K**	26
NEW LouLou	**Miami Riv**	–
Mangia Mangia	**Key W./K**	20
Z Marcello	**W. Palm/P**	28
Marker 88	**Islamorada/K**	21
Z NEW Market 17	**Ft. Laud/B**	26
Melting Pot	**Boca/P**	19
Z Michaels	**Key W./K**	26
Z Michael's	**Design Dist**	27
Z Michy's	**UES**	27
Z Morada Bay	**Islamorada/K**	22
Morton's	**multi.**	25
Z NY Prime	**Boca/P**	25
915 Bistro	**Key W./K**	25
Oceanaire	**Brickell**	24
Olivos	**Doral**	26
Z Ortanique	**Coral Gables**	26
Z Palm	**Bay Harbor Is**	28
Z Palme d'Or	**Coral Gables**	28
Z Pascal's	**Coral Gables**	27
Z Pierre's	**Islamorada/K**	27
Z Prime One	**SoBe**	27
Prime Steakhouse	**Key W./K**	25
Quattro	**SoBe**	20
NEW Rare Las Olas	**Ft. Laud/B**	21
Z Red Steak	**SoBe**	27
Roy's	**multi.**	26
Salute!	**Key W./K**	22
Sardinia	**Miami Bch**	26
Scarpetta	**Miami Bch**	25
Z Setai	**SoBe**	23
Shula's	**multi.**	23
Smith/Wollensky	**SoBe**	23
Snappers	**Boynton Bch/P**	18
Square One	**Key W./K**	21
STK Miami	**Miami Bch**	22
Strip House	**Key W./K**	24
NEW Sustain	**Downtown**	21
Z 3030 Ocean	**Ft. Laud/B**	26
Z 32 East	**Delray Bch/P**	25
III Forks	**Hallandale/B**	20
Timo	**Sunny Is Bch**	25
Top of the Point	**W. Palm/P**	–
Truluck's	**Ft. Laud/B**	24
Via Luna	**Ft. Laud/B**	21
Vienna Café	**Davie/B**	24
Z Villa/Barton G.	**SoBe**	24
W Wine	**Design Dist**	16

ALPHABETICAL
PAGE INDEX

All restaurants are in Miami/Dade County unless otherwise noted
(B=Broward County; K=Key West; N=Naples; P=Palm Beach County)

Latest openings, menus, photos and more – free at ZAGAT.com   321

ALPHA INDEX

ALPHA INDEX

ALPHA INDEX

ALPHA INDEX

Wine Vintage Chart

This chart is based on a 30-point scale. The ratings (by U. of South Carolina law professor **Howard Stravitz**) reflect vintage quality and the wine's readiness to drink. A dash means the wine is past its peak or too young to rate. Loire ratings are for dry whites.

Whites	95	96	97	98	99	00	01	02	03	04	05	06	07	08	09	10
France:																
Alsace	24	23	23	25	23	25	26	22	21	22	23	21	26	26	23	26
Burgundy	27	26	22	21	24	24	23	27	23	26	26	25	26	25	25	-
Loire Valley	-	-	-	-	-	-	-	25	20	22	27	23	24	24	24	25
Champagne	26	27	24	25	25	25	21	26	21	-	-	-	-	-	-	-
Sauternes	21	23	25	23	24	24	29	24	26	21	26	25	27	24	27	-
California:																
Chardonnay	-	-	-	-	22	21	24	25	22	26	29	24	27	23	27	-
Sauvignon Blanc	-	-	-	-	-	-	-	-	-	25	24	27	25	24	25	-
Austria:																
Grüner V./Riesl.	22	-	25	22	26	22	23	25	25	24	23	26	25	24	25	-
Germany:	22	26	22	25	24	-	29	25	26	27	28	26	26	26	26	-

Reds	95	96	97	98	99	00	01	02	03	04	05	06	07	08	09
France:															
Bordeaux	25	25	24	25	24	29	26	24	26	25	28	24	24	25	27
Burgundy	26	27	25	24	27	22	23	25	25	23	28	24	24	25	27
Rhône	26	22	23	27	26	27	26	-	26	25	27	25	26	23	27
Beaujolais	-	-	-	-	-	-	-	-	-	27	25	24	23	28	25
California:															
Cab./Merlot	27	24	28	23	25	-	27	26	25	24	26	24	27	26	25
Pinot Noir	-	-	-	-	-	-	26	25	24	25	26	24	27	24	26
Zinfandel	-	-	-	-	-	-	25	24	26	24	23	21	26	23	25
Oregon:															
Pinot Noir	-	-	-	-	-	-	-	26	24	25	24	25	24	27	24
Italy:															
Tuscany	25	24	29	24	27	24	27	-	24	27	25	26	25	24	-
Piedmont	21	27	26	25	26	28	27	-	24	27	26	26	27	26	-
Spain:															
Rioja	26	24	25	22	25	24	28	-	23	27	26	24	24	25	26
Ribera del Duero/Priorat	25	26	24	25	25	24	27	-	24	27	26	24	25	27	-
Australia:															
Shiraz/Cab.	23	25	24	26	24	24	26	26	25	25	26	21	23	26	24
Chile:	-	-	-	-	24	22	25	23	24	24	27	25	24	26	24
Argentina:															
Malbec	-	-	-	-	-	-	-	-	25	26	27	26	26	25	-